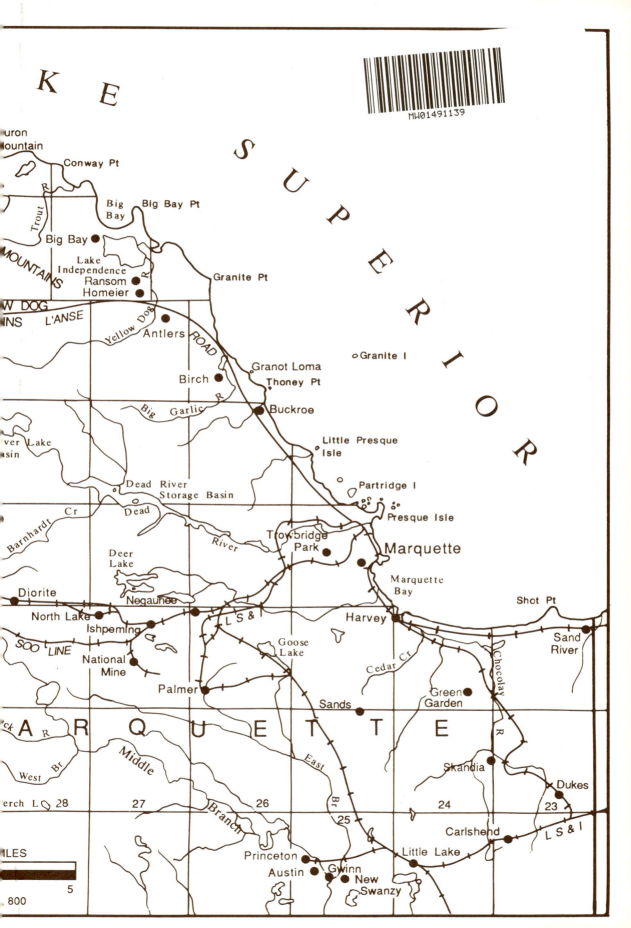

Superior Heartland

A Backwoods History

Volume 1 – Books One and Two

C. Fred Rydholm

Winter Cabin

Books

Superior Heartland

A Backwoods History

Superior Heartland: A Backwoods History was originally
published privately by C. Fred Rydholm. This edition published by
Winter Cabin Books & Services, 393 West Crescent St., Marquette, MI
49855, by arrangement with the author.

Graphic Design Consultant: Judy M. Johnson

Editors: Liz Chaffee – Tom Dixon

Printed by Edwards Brothers, Inc.,
2500 South State Street, Ann Arbor, MI 48106

Stories from Superior Heartland is available on compact-disk
as retold by the author from TopWater Productions
393 West Crescent Street, Marquette, MI 49855
(906-226-9849); www.superiorheartland.com

Library of Congress Catalog Number 89-90710
ISBN 0-9744679-0-1   Set Vols. I & II

Author's Note: I have never read a book on the history of the Upper Peninsula that I haven't discovered an error either in the facts presented or in the spelling or printing. These books will be no different, except due to the sheer size of the work, the number of errors will be magnified.

I appreciate having these errors pointed out to me so that they could be corrected, should there be another printing.

These books are dedicated to my family, my friends, students of history and anyone with a love for Michigan's Upper Peninsula, but especially to the people connected with and responsible for Huron Mountain Club, now in its centennial year, without whom much of this story could never have happened.

— Summer, 1989

Table of Contents

Volume One

Book One
The North End of the Bentley Trail

Table of Contents

iii

Table of Contents

Preface

Henry Ford, one of the protagonists of Fred Rydholm's fascinating and comprehensive history of Michigan's Upper Peninsula, once observed that "History is more or less bunk."

"We want to live in the present," he asserted, "and the only history that is worth a tinker's dam is the history we make today."

This might seem like a surprising statement from one who spent millions collecting memorabilia from early America for a museum in Dearborn, Michigan. But Ford's contempt for academic history, with its diplomatic shenanigans, wars, abstract economics, cultural rises and falls, reflects a feeling that history has little direct significance in people's perception of everyday life.

Nevertheless, historians have always told stories. Reaching for human memories is particularly important for historians of localities and communities, since the history they write about was most likely made by people with no particular motivation to leave a written account for posterity.

During the past few decades, professional historians have begun to appreciate the importance of local history. Grassroots social movements of our own time have made historians aware that the experience of ordinary people is as vital to historical understanding as is knowledge of government policy. To understand Lincoln, you have to know what it was like to experience slavery. To understand the reforms of Roosevelt, you need to know what it was like to be out of work. The personal experiences of laborers, lumbermen, strikers, poor people, ethnic minorities, war resistors, women and families help make the actions of political leadership intelligible. Now that serious interest in local history has arisen, professional historians have begun to develop new approaches, as the recent scholarly outpouring of oral histories should demonstrate.

Fred Rydholm's book is a vivid collective memory of an area of Michigan's Upper Peninsula. While modestly subtitled "A Backwoods History," it covers a period that saw intensive development of these backwoods through logging and mining, the coming of the internal combustion engine, the rise and decline of the "gilded age" as reflected in accounts of "wilderness" camps and clubs. The effects of two world wars and a depression are seen in the lives and stories of those who lived through them. Industrialists Henry Ford and Cyrus McCormick, whose mass-produced machines so profoundly altered American life, are direct participants. The interwoven stories, anecdotes, facts and speculations reach as far back as the ancient bronze age.

Descendants of the actors in this drama will feel the emotional enrichment of learning about a past which has so plainly and directly affected their own lives and which is unique to this type of historical inquiry. Despite his disparaging remarks about "history", Henry Ford himself might have felt a similar quickening of spirit as he assembled his collection of buildings, tools, carriages, music boxes, Cigar Store Indians and other paraphernalia at Dearborn, a museum whose entrance bears the inscription, "The farther you look back, the farther you can see ahead."

— Richard Bentley

Foreward

At nightfall, the wind came up and the distant lightning closed in as Fred's old Dodge truck cleared the woods and clattered out onto the Yellow Dog Plains. Fred had asked Bob Schreiber and me up to his Halfway Cabin for two nights: we jumped at the chance!

The creaking jackpines and the hissing scrub brush were a fit setting for the legendary Windego as we made a water stop at the small creek that was the headwaters of the Salmon Trout River. Then, in a few minutes, we pulled into what was left of the camp that marked the halfway point on the two–day trek from the shore of Superior to White Deer Lake.

The rain was just starting as we brought our gear into the small tar paper shack that had been the old guide's cabin. At each flash and clap Bob and I could see that we were on the edge of a small lake and that the hulk of the main cabin loomed next door – its roof long since down.

Taking no chances as to what might lurk on the floor on such a night, Bob and I took to the top bunk – head to foot in our bags; Fred was on the bottom so that he could defend us from whatever..... With a small fire in the box stove, it was just right for the Windego and other stories, and we were not disappointed.

The morning dawned bright and clear... with six inches of water in the cabin. Fred's tail was wet. In our undershorts we waded barefoot out of the mucky cabin and stood by the shore of the lake we were in. He turned and with a sweeping gesture that included the rising sun, chirping birds, keening cicadas, croaking frogs, and rustling birch trees said, "You know, there is a type of insect in this lake that I've never seen or heard of anywhere else; they come when they are called!" With that he shouted, "HEY!", and in an instant the water's surface was black with bugs that disappeared almost as fast. Bob and I kept those bugs hopping while Fred started one of his great breakfasts.

In the years that followed, I returned to "The Plains" several times, once doing the 20–odd–mile trek through the swamps with Fred and Indian

Tom (Wastaken). I learned of the mysteries of the Finnish sauna – with ladies and other former strangers. Finally, about 30 years after the first visit, my wife, Cynthia, and I spent the weekend up there with Fred and June and other boyhood chums and spouses. We learned of his great project; he had been writing for years of the lore and the families of the U.P. Several others had started to do the typing, but shied away when they saw the scope of the editing job that lay ahead.

I had a brand new computer and knew of a former student at school who was a very fine editor. Thus, did Liz Chaffee and I sign on for this six–year voyage. She did the editing and typing and I the assembly, final revisions, and printouts.

Perhaps nothing can better express how rewarding this journey has been than Fred's own words which end his most recent letter (of instructions):

"Thought for the day:

All accomplishments start with an urge.
The urge is blind without knowledge.
The knowledge is vain without work.
But work is empty without love."

Thomas H. Dixon
Berkshire School
Sheffield, Mass.
December, 1988

I t was the summer of 1942. The war (World War II) was under way in the Pacific but I was all signed up to go to Albion College so I decided to get as much education as I could before I had to go. I was eighteen years old.

At this particular moment I was walking a trail I knew well with "Indian Jim" Dakota. No one knew the country around the Cedar Creek in the Huron Mountains better than Jim and I was trying to learn everything I could from him.

Jim was a river guard for the Huron Mountain Club and his job was to keep poachers off the river. Even the word "poacher" was held in very low esteem and contempt in my mind. I was spending two weeks with Jim, helping him patrol for poachers, repair bridges, replace rotting hewn logs in the trail and put up "no trespassing" signs at key points.

We were headed upstream, maybe a mile by trail above the camp, when I noticed this big hemlock all blazed up. I'd seen that tree several times before and had wondered about it. It wasn't a witness tree, I knew that it had to have something to do with the trail. I'd ask Jim.

Well, it wasn't as easy as all that; you just didn't ask Jim anything right out, when you're walking in the woods. In the first place we were walking very quietly. When we wanted each other to notice something we pointed at it. As we approached the tree with the blazes I did this. Jim acknowledged by smiling silently and by a slight nod of his head. At the time, Jim was some distance behind me and was literally sneaking alongside the trail. He was old, close to 70, and his gait was leisurely but marked with purpose. He was aware of every spot he placed his foot. He left no trail. With the light stick he carried, Jim would scratch out sandy spots in the trail so a good print would be left by any man or animal who happened to pass that way. When he came to a fork in the trail Jim would place an innocent twig or stalk of grass across each fork and on our return trip he would read his signs and know exactly who went where.

He always seemed to be thinking and planning ahead as he walked along and had silent ways of letting me know when he didn't like my behavior. There were times when he'd make a suggestion or tell stories that implied how I should act. I always tried to cooperate, and Jim liked me for trying, but I had a tendency to be noisy, talkative and in a hurry. In past years I had made many trips to his campsite and, when within a hundred yards or so of his tent, I used to holler or give a loud shout to get his attention and warn him that I was coming, but I had gotten over that kind of behavior around Jim. It was easier to howl like a wolf, yip like a coyote or hoot like an owl. That pleased him; it sounded more in keeping with the surroundings and wasn't so harsh or startling. He always knew who it was.

We had several hiding places along the river; Jim called them resting places. They were secluded spots where we could sit and talk unobserved. Actually, we hadn't seen a soul in the week or so that I had been there, but there was always the chance, and Jim wanted to know first. One of these hiding places, my favorite, was coming up soon. When we reached it, I'd ask Jim about the blazes.

Jim and I arrived at the pool cautiously, looked up and down the stream, and watched the woods for a few moments for an odd color, a quick movement or some telltale sign. Jim sniffed the air. Everything was as it should be, and we could proceed to the hiding place.

The creek at this point came rushing down over a short falls into a round, deep, clear pool. Beside the pool was a rather high conical mound of earth blanketed with pine needles, and on top of it was an enormous white pine tree, easily four and a half or five feet in diameter. From our view, the tree looked magnificent and healthy as it climbed skyward with a slight lean over the pool and a little upstream.

We circled the mound of earth upward, and, coming on the far side, there was a split in the tree's bark at the bottom, wide enough for a narrow doorway to the interior. Jim carefully worked himself inside with me right behind him. Inside the whole trunk was hollow, I don't know how high up. We sat side by side on a soft mound of slightly damp rotted wood, not too tight a fit. Our visibility was very limited but we could rest, listen and talk quietly, our voices muffled to an outsider by the tree and rushing water.

After a few chuckles and a little kidding, which always took place, I asked Jim what all those old blazes on that big hemlock were for.

"That's where the old Bentley Trail took off south," replied Jim.

I was familiar with the name "Bentley," they had a cabin at the club and a boy my age named Cyrus. He was a good fisherman and very friendly, and it seemed to me that I'd heard of the Bentley Trail before or had seen it written on a map, but now I was curious; I didn't know anything about it.

"Where does it go?" I asked, "Maybe we can follow it?"

Jim smiled and got a far away look in his eyes.

"It goes all the way to White Deer Lake," he said, "but that trail hasn't been used in years. This one is the "old" Bentley; there's a "new" one east of here that comes out of Canyon Lake. They're both abandoned and grown over now."

"I'll bet we could follow them, Jim, or at least you could, couldn't you?" I said rather excitedly.

"I guess so," answered Jim, still in his far far off mood, "but it would take a couple of days."

"A couple of days!," I gasped, "How long are those trails anyway?"

"They're about 25 miles, I guess," said Jim, "they go all the way from the club to McCormick's camp at White Deer Lake. McCormick and Bentley were partners years ago. They had a big lodge on White Deer Lake and were members of the club. Bentley built two trails across here — the new one was really something; hewn—log walks, bridges, a halfway house; you walk on part of the old trail when you come from Mountain Lake over Burnt Mountain to the Cedar Creek camp. Part of the trail up the Cedar Creek is the old Bentley; where there's two trails, one following the river and the other back in the woods following a straighter route, that's the old Bentley. They used to call that Bentley Point down there on Mountain Lake where the Burnt Mountain trail starts." My curiosity was aroused. Who was McCormick? When were those trails built, and why two of them? Every answer I got made the whole thing more fascinating.

That night, in our tent, all the sensations of the previous nights were gone. I couldn't feel the hard boards I was sleeping on. (I slept on the floor). I didn't feel the cold I had felt the night before or, for that matter, the heat when Jim had fired up the stove. I didn't hear the whip—poor—will, or the rush of the river, or the drumming of the "patridge" as Jim called it. My mind was wandering out on the trail, down the lakes. The word "abandoned" seemed to grip me. It seemed so mysterious. Were the trails still discernible? When did Bentley and McCormick die? Why hadn't other people used the trails? I had worked for the club for two years, why hadn't someone told me about the trails?

Jim didn't seem to know the answers or at least enough of them or in the detail I was searching for.

That fall (October 1942) I joined the Navy, but was told to stay in school and wait for my call.

In September I attended Albion College as a freshman and the next summer (1943) I started to pursue the history of the Bentley Trail that so intrigued me. I was called to active duty on July 1st of that year but returned to follow through on my project in the summer of 1946.

From 1948 through 1950 I taught school in Republic. My research had lead me to the Bentley Halfway cabin, which I was able to purchase in 1949. In 1950 and 1951 I became a year—round counselor at Clear Lake Camp near Battle Creek, Michigan.

In a Michigan History class at Western Michigan University in 1950 under Dr. Charles Starring, we were asked to do some research on a piece of Michigan history. Having gathered information on the Bentley Trail, I used it as the subject of my 65—page history term paper.

Starring was fascinated. He had never heard of the Bentley Trail, and, as hard as he looked, he could find no reference to it. In fact, he didn't know there was such country as I described left in Michigan. He thought some of my claims to be so far out that he made a special trip that summer to visit me at Huron Mountain Club.

Upon leaving, he was ecstatic. His parting advice was, by all means elaborate on your story, get pictures, talk to people, find the history of this whole area. There is no written history of this area or the trail and very little of the region is recorded. You've got a good start — but it's just a start. You raise more questions than you answer. Just get it down, just for the record — before it's all lost.

I've started that history four times since then, each time going a little further with it and adding more detail.

The first was with the daughter of an old friend of mine, Mrs. Eleanor "Pert" O'Neal of Negaunee. The daughter, Mary Germaine O'Neal was going to be a "ghost" writer. I considered myself a poor writer and a poor speller, but I could put things on tape. I gathered my multitudinous notes and got started, but we soon bogged down in detail. It didn't work, in fact it hardly got off the ground. This was about 1955 or 56.

The second try was around 1962 to 64 with another lady. She was a free lance writer and wrote a lot of short stories and newspaper articles. I gave her many of my notes and papers as well as tapes for her to start with. I never saw them again.

The third try, about 1972, was with an English teacher, Mrs. Susan Black, in the school where I was teaching in Marquette. She became interested in my original try, the one I had done for Dr. Starring; she could see I wasn't much of a writer but had more material than many who have written several books.

Mrs. Black tried many ideas, tapes, outlines etc. She finally decided that there was no other way to get it down but for me to sit down and write it. She would reorganize it, correct it and type it, but I had to write it. I disliked writing, was a terrible typist and my thoughts ran ahead of my pen. I was always too busy, and short on time but with her encouragement I was able to get some of it on paper.

For two or three years up to 1975, we wrote in the winter months and gathered loose ends during the rest of the year. We established a goal to be finished during the 1976 National bicentennial year, but several things began to happen that made our goal virtually impossible. The Bentley Trail history began to spill over into the history of Huron Mountain Club, White Deer Lake, several individuals and almost to the history of the county. The scope of the project became far more than Mrs. Black or anyone else had anticipated. She became involved in graduate studies beyond her second masters degree and lost interest. She eventually went on to get a doctorate and became an assistant superintendent of the Marquette Public Schools. However, I have always been grateful for the impetus which Susan Black gave these writings.

In 1976 I built a garage with a second floor in it. It was designed by my friend, Leigh St. John, in about two minutes after I had spent weeks with a complicated four gable design. I finished off an upstairs room where I could finally put in one place all my books, pictures, notes and previous attempts. There I made another valiant try over the next three years. I enlisted numerous volunteer typists.

One portion which became Book III came into shape in 1978 and a second piece (Book II) was ready for it's final rewrite. I had by then decided to separate what I had written into these two books and also realized there would have to be two more to tell the whole story.

By 1979, volunteers had typed a final copy of Book III, but it wasn't what I wanted, it wasn't good. Some material was changed, some put in different order. I hired a typist, rewrote 30 pages at a time and it was finished in 1981.

It was in 1979, when I was making one of several visits to the wife of Ted Tonkin who had been the manager of White Deer Lake Camp for 38 years, that I met, for the first time, their daughter and son—in—law, the Cooley's, from Durango, Colorado. Of course, "Peanuts" and I had much in common and her husband had graduated from Albion College.

Mrs. Cooley ("Peanuts") became interested in my project, especially the White Deer Lake part, with which she was so closely attached during her early life. After some correspondence with Kay Cooley over the next six months she offered to type the White Deer Lake portion, Book II. We carried on the same method, I would rewrite thirty pages at a time and send them to her. When I got them back, I would send her another thirty.

Chris Edgar, grandson of Harry Hansen of Big Bay was a special friend of mine. He and his two brothers had worked with us at Huron Mountain. Chris' uncle, mother, aunt, wife and sister—in—law had all worked there. He met his wife at Huron Mountain.

Linda, Chris' wife was also the daughter and grand—daughter of old friends and neighbors of my family for ages. Chris was especially interested in the Huron Mountain, Big Bay and Marquette portion of the book.

Chris is now a lawyer in Grand Rapids. He offered me a typist, one who had just retired from his office. This prospect fell through, but while he was making other arrangements, I discovered that another friend of mine, Jon Clark, also a lawyer to whom I had given large portions of Book I to read, had typed what I had given him and had made several copies of it.

Between 1979 and 1982 I laboriously dug out a huge basement under our house at Lakewood, shovelful after tedious shovelful, breathing in the dust of decades past. Warm in winter from a woodstove, I was able to work more conveniently than in the garage where in winter you could only regulate the temperature at too hot or too cold. I continued writing at one or the other of the two desks I set up in the new basement.

It was through Jon Clark that Tom Dixon of Sheffield, Massachusetts heard about my book. I had known Tom since he was a very young boy at Huron Mountain Club. He was always a special friend. Tom had great interest in the area and great organizational abilities. He could see what great difficulties I was having getting my books together.

Tom Dixon told me that I should have the whole thing put on a word processor. I had never heard of one even though at that time they were being used across the country. Tom said he would take care of the whole thing if I wanted him to. I should start by sending him the part III which I had done, he would have a former student of his, Liz Chaffee, whom he highly recommended, put it on a word processor, correct and edit it and get it into final form. This was in 1983, it would still be a long and laborious process.

By 1984, part III was done and I had received almost all of part II from Mrs. Cooley in Durango which was then sent to Liz Chaffee in Sheffield.

Tom and Cindy Dixon were taking a sabbatical leave from Berkshire School in 1985 and 86. He wanted to see the book wrapped up by the time they left, but things were moving very slowly and it was impossible. Liz was just then completing part I, II and III were done.

During this period the Dixons took their leave. They went on an extensive tour 'round the world trip, with several stops in England, a dozen cities in the Soviet Union and a dozen more in China, before ending up in

Hongkong and then returning via Hawaii. Tom also made a thorough study of computer systems during this sabbatical year both here and in other countries.

By the time of his return in the fall of 1986, part I, II and III of "Superior Heartland" were complete and Liz was diligently working on part IV. I was gaining great hopes that the book would finally by published sometime during the sesquicentennial year of the State of Michigan. (1987)

As I look back over the years that I have worked on my project, I am amazed at how much more interest there is in regional history now than there was a few decades ago. Several historical museums and the Maritime Museum have sprung up in the county, a dozen books have been written and my Marquette County History class, for which I had trouble getting eight people to attend in 1968, is full every session today.

Of the many books written in recent years, all are quite limited in their scope. I hope my book will provide an overall picture of the region that includes these others. It should provide an overall time frame for other more detailed books on local history. In former years, I've noticed local people confusing Father Baraga with Father Marquette or portraying them as contemporaries. This is no longer a common error.

I have a large collection of photographs that have been in the family for years. To these I have added many more obtained from friends and families of people I have written about. I obtained more from the tremendous collections at the Marquette County Historical Society and at Huron Mountain Club. Photographers such as Fred Cleary, Kim Hatch, Steve Paull and Lawrence Beltrame have contributed some of their pictures and some of their skills and a lot of work was done professionally by Ike Wood, himself the author of a recent publication on local history, "One Hundred Years of Hard Labor." It is a history of Marquette prison.

But the greatest help as far as historical photos is concerned, a literal bonanza that came our way in recent years, was the generosity and cooperation of John Mark "Jack" Deo. Jack was more than a photographer, he was a young man with a dream. He wanted to collect the history of the Upper Peninsula in pictures. He turned out to be a man with the right idea at the right time.

Jack was born in Henry Ford hospital in Detroit in 1953. My book was well under way at that time. He grew up in the shadow of history in one of the Ford houses at the Dearborn Museum and attended school in Dearborn. He became interested in the historic aspects of Dearborn Village. He had a friend and neighbor who was a tin typist and his mother was an antique collector.

xv

Jack was graduated from Edsel Ford High School and was the photographer for the school newspaper there. He attended Henry Ford Community College for two years and then came to Northern Michigan University in 1973.

After his marriage to Cindy Gill of Dearborn, Jack and his bride moved to Marquette permanently and opened a unique photographic studio above Doncker's Candy Store next to the Delft Theater. He had purchased Mr. Childs old wooden studio camera, which he set up and provided century old clothing and furniture to take old fashioned pictures. Besides this he began a collection of old cameras and photographic equipment and early pictures of the area that soon expanded to the Copper Country, Alger County and over the rest of the Upper Peninsula. In a few years time, the Deo's had built up one of the finest private collections of historical photos in and of the Upper Peninsula.

By providing Jack with some old photos he has given me some special consideration to get photographic work done for these writings besides providing special photographs from his collection. I am deeply indebted to him for this.

Then, of course, much material was acquired through the Marquette County Historical Society, an organization I have been affiliated with for probably fifty years, forty of those years as a dues paying member and nearly thirty years as a member of it's Board of Directors. In this connection I must give special thanks to Mrs. Helen L. Paul, her sister Mrs. Abby Roberts, Mr. Kenyon Boyer, Ernest Rankin, and more recently Mr. Frank Paul, Mrs. Marcy Houlmont, Rachel Crary, Mrs. Frances Porter and the other researchers at the Society. They have all given of their time and talents.

I have received wonderful cooperation from Jack Martin, George Johnson and from my friends who are or have been employees, members or guests at Huron Mountain Club, most of whom are mentioned in the text.

Richard Bentley, Bill Manierre, Mrs. Hibbs, Mrs. Dunbough, Cameron Waterman (Jr. and Sr.), Tom Evinrude, Richard Hendrickson, Mrs. Woolley, Mr. and Mrs. Jere DuCharme, Mr. and Mrs. Cam Farwell, Christ Andersen, the Sises, George Baker, Ken Nowell, Mrs. Lu McCampbell and many others gave freely of their information.

There were other helpers and volunteers from time to time. Typists, Carolyn Cooper, Jon Clark, Kent Bourland and more recently Mary Allie's and Malinda Stamp's work on a computer. Then the many who worked at camp and on the trail and those who helped organize trips: Bob Hanson, Skip Schneider, Mr. and Mrs. Seth Johnson, Mr. and Mrs. Russel Dees, Carolyn Cooper, Phil Paul, Paul Kotila and many others and still more who gave advice and encouragement, Jim Carter, Clyde Steele, Ike Wood, Willard Cohodas, Alf Jentoft, Marvin Hanson, Jon Clark, Dan Sise, Burton Boyum, Wilbur Treloar, Bob Clark, and those who read or listened, Jack Wiseman, Donald McDonnell, Dick Bentley, Jon Clark, Phil Paul, Joe Dunham, Arnold Mulzar, Bill and Peter Gray and many, many of my students.

To these and many other families and institutions such as the McCormick Estate Offices, Smithsonian Institution, Peter White Library, Huron Mountain Club, George Johnson, Mr. and Mrs. Pete Temple, Milton "Mink" Thompkins, Mrs. Kenny Goldsworthy, Mr. and Mrs. Bud Wentzel, Camp Soso Alumni Association, the Vargo's at Bay Cliff Health Camp I owe a debt of gratitude.

And there have been others whom I should thank, just too many to mention them all, but such is the story of the massing of the following information.

It just so happens now, that the completion of these books will coincide with the Centennial Celebration of Huron Mountain Club.

C. Fred Rydholm

Book One

The North End of the Bentley Trail

Discovering

The secret streams that flow beneath the cliffs of colored stone,
The forests thick and healthy with birch and pine and oak,
Surrounded by the greatest lakes this World has ever known,
The black bear's awesome presence as he roams the hills and fields,
The call of the timberwolf, the loon's lonesome trill,
The eagle soaring high above, the trout lies deep and still,
These are what I treasure, the only way I measure
The feeling that I have for this fine land.
There is so much to discover when you're a long time lover
Of Northern Michigan

with permission of and written by
Mark Mitchell, Marquette, Michigan

On the south shore of Lake Superior is an area about 75 miles from East to West, and 40 miles from North to South. This area was bypassed by development, but blessed with an abundance of all that modern man is now working to preserve or restore. It has what every state in the Union had and, for the most part, lost, sometime in the rush to inhabit the land. There are untouched lakes, trout streams, waterfalls and a miniature mountain range. In many parts of the country what Man has built has been crowded and permanent; here, the structures are few, simple, and temporary. In many places across our land, settlers have devastated huge areas for their structures, but here the buildings are gently placed among the trees.

In the late 1960's and early 70's, we suddenly realized that in many places we had overdeveloped, overused, overpopulated, and overpolluted. It was time to backtrack or go under. But this area, small as it is, had been spared. There are many reasons why; some are obvious, like the hard winters, but some are obscure. The fact remains, though, that through at least the first two centuries of our nation's history, the area of which we speak has remained relatively unspoiled.

Much has been written on the history of Lake Superior. We must review some of this, as it pertains to our subject. The rest may be new, as much of it has never been written or told.

At the north end of the Bentley Trail lies Lake Superior and the most prominent and well–defined mountains of the Huron Group. Also nestled among the mountains is a cluster of 12 or 14 beautiful clear lakes (there are a few bodies of water that may better be called ponds or marshes), all but one of which drain into Lake Superior by way of the short, picturesque Pine River. The final mile or so of this river parallels the shore of the great lake before merging into it. The Bentley family cabin, built by Cyrus Bentley and owned by the next two or three generations of his family, is perched on the sand point at the mouth of the river. The area surrounding this spot, stretching a hundred miles in every direction, has a rich and intriguing history which fades into the distant past.

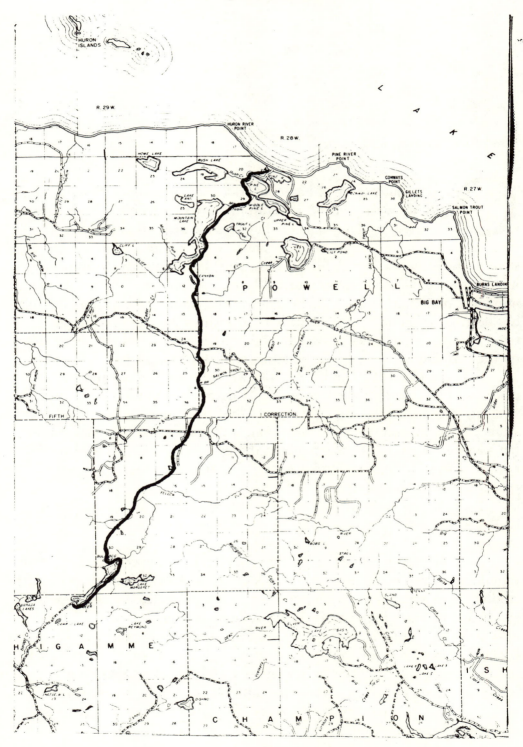

North parts of Baraga and Marquette counties, showing general route of the Bentley Trail.

Book One

A Little Geology

The rock formations of the Huron Mountains may be divided into three groups, the oldest of which are the Keewatin. These are said to be upwards of 3.5 billion years old, and are found in a relatively small area. In the Huron Mountains, this Keewatin schist appears as bluish–colored crystalline igneous rock, often having streaks of quartzite in it. There are some outcroppings of it around the Burnt Mountain area near Cedar Creek and Cliff Stream. It is also found just under the pink granite on the knobs east of Big Bay.

The Laurentian rocks, younger than the Keewatin but still very old, are the granites. These are the most conspicuous of the high rock formations and, according to Dr. John Hughes of Northern Michigan University, the Laurentian granite is about 2.6 billion years old. They appear as white–to–slightly–pink granite found on all the high rock knobs. These knobs are the highest places where the Laurentian granite formations appear south of Canada and, being precambrian, would be some of the oldest mountains in the world. According to Dorr and Eschman, they may be the remains of the Penokean Range of mountains which covered the north central United States at one time. The formations pass under Lake Superior and reappear on the Canadian shore, suggesting a severe depressing action or folding of the rock where the lake is. Canada has a great deal of this particular formation.

The third group, the Huronian, are much younger than the Keewatin schist or the Laurentian granites. These take the form of slates and some graphite. Nearly all of Arvon Township in Baraga County, west of the Huron Mountains, is slate. Over a century ago, there were five or six slate quarries in that township. Drillings done by the State of Michigan in 1977 on the Yellowdog Plains, near the source of the Salmon Trout River, turned up huge masses of slate at depths of 400 feet. Hamblin and Homer have concluded that Keweenauson conglomerates, deposited by streams flowing into the basin, probably came from the general area of the Huron Mountains, again suggesting that they must have been much higher at one time.

Along the Lake Superior shore is the Lake Superior, or Cambrian, sandstone. This is the Jacobsville sandstone of the lower and middle Cambrian age but, again according to Dr. Hughes, its deposition may have come in late precambrian times. The sandstone lay along the base of the mountains. It was highly prized as a building material up to the beginning of the 20th Century, and was quarried at Jacobsville on the Keweenaw Peninsula, Gillette's Landing on Salmon Trout Bay, Thoney Point, several

3

places in Marquette, Laughing Whitefish Point in Alger County just east of the Laughing Whitefish River, and at Deerton. This type of sandstone is also found west of the Keweenaw Peninsula. There it is known as Bayfield sandstone, and was quarried in and around the Apostle Islands.

While the aforementioned formations are found in the Huron Mountain district, the Marquette City region has some interesting ones of its own. Dorr and Eschman tell us the greenish rocks found so commonly in Marquette are the Kitchi and Mona formations. They are some of the oldest rock formations in the Upper Peninsula. The Mona formations include the pillow structures which formed when molten lava flowed out under water. They are found west of the viaduct on U.S. 41 and 28. Then, further west, are the younger Huronian iron formations of the Marquette Range. The north central U. P. is truly a geological paradise.

Although the Ice Age lasted several million years, it occurred in very recent times as compared with the age of the rock formations which have been mentioned. It was a time when several glacial ice sheets invaded the region, altering it drastically with each invasion.

There were four long advances of these glaciers. Their slow movement south was caused by the tremendous force of miles–thick ice to the north, and it is believed that the glaciers above the current location of the Great Lakes may have been up to two miles thick. The weight of the glaciers and other deposits is believed to have caused the depressions where the lakes are now.

The last of these ice sheets, lasting about fifty thousand years, started retreating and advancing as the earth warmed. The retreating gradually outdid the advancing, until about ten thousand years ago, the ice sheet finally retreated altogether from the north part of Marquette County. In many areas it left behind gravel beds called glacial moraines. One of these moraines, now called the Yellowdog Plains, lies up against the hills of the McCormick Tract to the south. In many places the glacial retreat also deposited hundreds of huge glacial boulders and millions of smaller ones as well as well–defined glacial gouges and scratches. The huge glacial boulders are especially noticeable on the north side of Huron Mountain along Rush Lake and throughout the McCormick Tract. The Rush Lake area also has a series of vertical walls up to 40 feet high and 100 yards long. These must have been formed as the earth there was buckling and sinking, as there is the unusual phenomenon of Huron Mountain being the highest point along the shore and right beside it Rush Lake, the deepest lake in the Upper Peninsula. Some of the best glacial scratches are found on the westernmost Huron Island, partially under the former lighthouse crew's living quarters.

Glacial scratches found on top of the westernmost Huron Islands.

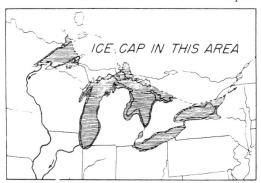

Figure 1. Lake Algonquin. Younger than 6500 B.C. but older than 3000 B.C.; probably from about 5500 B.C. to 4500 B.C.

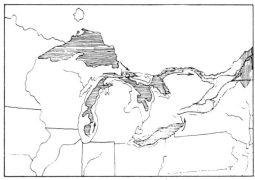

Figure 3. Lakes Chippewa and Stanley. Older than 1700 B.C.; probably 3500 B.C. to 2000 B.C.

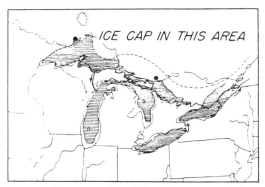

Figure 2. Transition from Lake Algonquin to Lakes Chippewa and Stanley. 3000 B.C. or older, but considerably younger than 6500 B.C.; probably 4500 B.C. to 3500 B.C.

Figure 4. Nipissing Great Lakes. 1700 B.C.–1500 B.C. and probably somewhat later, but earlier than 650 B.C., the date of the post-Nipissing Algoma state; probably 2000 B.C. to 1000 B.C.

The lakes in the Huron Mountains are glacial, and many former beaches are visible in nearly every sandy beach area along Lake Superior in Marquette County.

As the waters of the receding glacier settled into the various depressions at its base, their levels varied greatly over a long period of time. These lake levels varied from over 1,200 feet above sea level at the highest to about 565 feet at the lowest.

We must remember that these figures are measured from the present sea level. Because a great deal of the earth's water was frozen in the glacier prior to eight or nine thousand years ago, the ocean waters may have been as much as 180 feet below the present sea level. Recent explorations by Jacques Cousteau found stalactites and stalagmites in ocean caves 165 feet under water.

Jack Hough tells us in his Geology of the Great Lakes that about 12,000 years ago a lake known as Glacial Lake Keweenaw stood at these high levels. Bordered by the glacier on the north, it flowed south into the Mississippi. At that time, Lakes Michigan and Huron were one known as Lake Kirkfield, which had an elevation of about 565 feet above sea level.

After a short intervening ice advance, Glacial Lake Duluth was formed about 11,000 years ago. Its level was somewhat below 1,200 feet, but it still flowed south through the St. Croix outlet to the Mississippi. Lakes Michigan and Huron rose to 605 feet and formed Lake Algonquin. About 10,000 years ago, Lake Duluth changed its outlet as the ice receded, so that it flowed east toward the St. Lawrence. Meanwhile, Lake Algonquin became glacial Lake Chippewa (now Michigan) and Stanley (now Huron). About 4,500 years ago these three lakes merged to form one, Lake Nipissing, which stood at 605 feet above sea level and 1,000 years later became Lake Algoma at 595 feet. The present level of Lake Superior is approximately 602 feet, with Lakes Huron and Michigan at about 580 feet. These levels have been relatively constant for the last 1,000 to 1,500 years.

During the years of the receding of the glacial lakes, there must have been an isolated group of islands, or at least a remote peninsula, where many generations of animal life evolved. Their isolation from the rest of the species caused subtle differences.

To be specific, we find some animals isolated in the region of the Huron Mountains. The blue–tailed skink, a small striped lizard with a blue tail, is quite common from Sugar Loaf Mountain to the Big Huron River and south five or six miles, but it is not found anywhere else for 350 or 400 miles in any direction. The common milk snake appears in a small range of the Huron Mountains, and then nowhere else for 200 or 300 miles. The

Blandings Turtle is another isolated in this area and not found for many miles around, and the ones here run somewhat larger than their counterparts found elsewhere. One turtle, measured by Mr. Richard A. Rice Jr. of Huron Mountain, was found to be somewhat larger than that listed as the "world's largest." The coyotes of the Upper Peninsula are a larger subspecies of the coyote found elsewhere. They are often called "brush wolves" to distinguish them from timber wolves and prairie coyote. A tiger beetle found along Lake Superior shores in Marquette County, also found in Emmet County on the tip of Lower Michigan is thought to be an altogether separate species. The predominantly westerly winds would have carried it east, not from Emmet to Marquette. In Howe Lake there is a snail (of which there are no known living specimens) found nowhere else in the world; a fish, Huronicus – a subspecies of Lake Trout in Rush Lake – is also unique in the world. The same is the case for a kind of herring in Ives Lake; the list goes on.

Early Man

It was about the time that Lake Keweenaw was being formed, 12,000 years ago, that the first man must have appeared on what is now Michigan's Upper Peninsula as he roamed along the edge of the glacier.

The oldest evidence we find of these prehistoric inhabitants was found on the shores of Lake Duluth by a Mr. Eugene J. Dietz of Iron River, Wisconsin. The following is quoted in part from a letter written to me on October 12, 1974:

> I have lived in northern Wisconsin off and on since 1929. Served as county agent in Iron County (Wisconsin) from June 1929 to 1939, during which time I became interested in the geology of Northern Wisconsin. I then moved to Madison, having a small farm there, and because so much evidence of Indian occupation appeared on my farm, I became interested in archeology, joined in the local society of archaeology, and became acquainted with several professors at the University in that field.
>
> Came back to northern Wisconsin about 1951, doing some farming. Have continued my interest in geology and archaeology.
>
> Knowing that glacial Lake Duluth was the last of the preglacial lakes in this area, and wondering whether Man may have lived near this lake, in 1955 I made a search on a roadway that skirted the old lake shore. I was lucky in finding a few tiny bits of chipping debris,

indicating that Man had once stopped and made stone tools. Subsequently I tried many digs near where I had found evidence, but could never find anything more.

In 1973, I made a thorough dig, the details of which I shall not go into here, and I eventually found an ancient domicile site. I found the dwelling site to be a circle eleven feet in diameter, with a fireplace in the center. I garnered tools and chipping flakes within this dwelling site. There was also evidence of a grave within the domicile circle.

The generally accepted age of Glacial Lake Duluth is 11,000 years. It is obvious that there were people living in Northern Wisconsin during the tundra–taiga period of glacial time who were not the same origin as the fluted pointmakers who were living in southern Wisconsin and southern Michigan in the same time frame.

In the "Accent North and T. V. Tab" of the Duluth Sunday News Tribune, June 23, 1974, there appeared a two–page story of Mr. Dietz's findings. The article states that the shoreline of Lake Duluth was 575 feet above Lake Superior, which is why the campsite is so far inland. Dietz explains that the men of this era used spears and lances, rather than bows and arrows, to bring down game. In addition to the initial point on the spear head (made of wood or bone), sharp flakes of chert were inserted.

Besides chips and spearheads, Dietz turned up a burin (a tool used to cut slots in wood, bone, or antler, to insert the chert blades), fireplace rocks, two knives fashioned from sharp stones, scrapers, a planing tool, and bits of human bone and tooth. The plane is like none other ever found in Wisconsin. The artifacts are very similar to European finds from the late Paleolithic era.

These prehistoric men who roamed this ancient shore were probably summer dwellers, hunters of caribou and waterfowl, and were probably a few thousand years ahead of the next group known to have come here – the "Copperdiggers."

Where could these men have come from? Charles Amsden, formerly of the Southwest Museum in Highland Park, Los Angeles, explains the accepted theory:

Up on the northwest tip of Alaska there is a 50–mile shallow strait separating it from the eastern tip of Siberia. In summer, you'd probably find Eskimo paddling back and forth in their skin boats, while in winter, the strait (Bering Strait) is often choked with ice, which you could scramble over dryshod. In very ancient times, it was easier still because the land stood above the water level. This is the road by which many plants and animals got from the old world to the new. So we shouldn't think of two hemispheres as separated by vast oceans, but rather as joined firmly together beneath that little strip of ocean called the Bering Strait, with plants and animals and man going back and forth since long ages past. Yes, men, too; they follow the animals, just as the Indians followed the buffalo herds up and down the Great Plains.

Many discoveries have been made to bear out the theory that Man evolved in Africa. There are no signs of their having developed here, but their progress can be carefully followed from Africa up into Asia and Europe. Amsden goes on:

> There are only three great races or physical divisions of humanity in the whole world today, as everyone agrees. They are Caucasian, Negroid and Mongoloid, or white, black and brown.

While the blacks stayed in Africa, the whites migrated north into Europe in small bands and fought each other for centuries, becoming very aggressive. But it was the brown race, the nomads in the very early days, who populated the earth. They first moved into Asia, then spread out to the Atlantic via Finland and Lapland, and east across the Bering Strait into North America, Central America, and South America. He is the Eskimo, the Indian, the Inca, the Aztec and the Toltec. He traveled west again by the sea to the islands of the Pacific, and is the Polynesian. Amsden again:

> If the American Indian came from Asia across the Bering Strait he should be one of that group. Surely enough, he is. He has in some degree every outstanding characteristic of that race. I'll mention only a few that we can all appreciate: complexion, shape of face, slanting eyes, color and texture of hair. Most convincing of all is a curious peculiarity of the upper front teeth. In 85% of the Mongoloids these teeth have incurved edges, shaping them like a shovel. The Indians have them too.

We can roughly measure time in reference to the great climatic cycle known as the "Ice Age." There are coal deposits within the Arctic Circle, which means that the arctic regions once had a climate warm enough to grow the plants that formed coal. There are several theories as to how this came about, such as the changing of the earth's axis and "continental drift." The Continental Drift theory was first proposed by a German in the early 1920's, but is just now gaining acceptance.

At any rate, the coal is there and the arctic region was warm for a long period of time. At the other extreme of climate are the glacial deposits which prove that our Great Lakes region once lay under a sheet of ice up to two miles thick. Four times, a great climatic change caused the formation of ice sheets over northern Europe and North America. Three times in between these cold spells were warm spells, when plant and animal life changed radically. The Ice Age took a million years, with the climate deteriorating for a million years before that in a sort of building–up stage.

Local Discoveries about the Ice Age

We now have some definite dates for the recession of the last glacial ice from the Upper Peninsula. In 1975, when the Cleveland Cliffs Iron Company was building a tailings basin for the Tilden Mine east of Goose Lake in the Sand Plains south of Marquette, the tractor driver noticed that he was clipping off tree stumps as he pushed what appeared to be undisturbed sand.

The work was temporarily halted, and Dr. James W. Merry and Dr. John D. Hughes were summoned to study the site. Over the next two years (1976–77) Dr. Merry, a botanist, determined that the trees were black spruce; Dr. Hughes, a geographer and earth scientist, determined that the trees had been covered by sands rushing down the rivers of the glaciers. A small lake in the area, Gribbons Lake, gave the area its name, Gribbons Basin. Radioactive carbon dating of the wood in the buried trees produced an average age of 9,980 years. Similar finds of old wood in mines and diggings in other parts of the Upper Peninsula have pretty well established the period of the last recession of the glaciers and the approximate time of the formation of the present land forms and general shoreline.

Quimby, of the Chicago Museum of Natural History, states that the lands of the Huron Mountain region were buried by glacial ice until about 7,000 B.C. or slightly later.

Proof that ancient Man lived in America before the recession of the last glacier is easy to find in many places. Besides Dietz's find along Lake Duluth, a human skull, not of the most modern type, was found under ten feet of glacial silt in Minnesota, near the southern edge of the last glacial wave. At several places in the Great Plains region, flint implements were found among bones of a species of buffalo that lived during the Ice Age. One of these finds was of eighteen such implements and thirty or forty bison, all of which lay buried under thirteen feet of a peculiar kind of soil called loess, which was blowing around the country when the glaciers were not so far away. In other cases, similar implements lay among the bones of a mammoth, an elephant now extinct. In Nevada, the remains of a campfire were found in Gypsum Cave, below a solid layer of the dung of another extinct animal that flourished in the late Ice Age, the ground sloth known as Nothrotherium. A cave in New Mexico yielded a flint implement and the bones of a musk ox, an animal built for a much colder climate then that of New Mexico today.

From the mud layers laid down by the melting and freezing of the last glacier, it was determined many years ago that the earliest man in America came 20 or 30 thousand years ago. More recent findings have located a group of pygmies similar to some found in Malaysia and neighboring territories that go back to 40,000 B.C. In 1980 George Carter estimated that a conservative date for Man's entry into America may be as early as 100,000 years ago. They would have been of a Neanderthal type. After reading that date, I spoke with Dr. Carter in San Diego, California and he mentioned a 200,000 year date. I later wrote to Dr. Carter, asking for some particulars. The return letter, dated April 14, 1983:

Dear Mr. Rydholm,

The 200,000 year date is for the Calico site in the Mojave desert. It is a closed system uranium date done by James Bischoff at the U.S.G.S. lab at Menlo Park in California and corroborated by Ku at U.S.C. There is also a 100,000 year desert varnish date for the surface of the site – Oberlander, Geography, U.C. Berkeley. The 250,000 year date is for the Hueyatlaco site in Mexico, near Mexico City. It is a composite of dates, but is less secure as to stratigraphy.

It looks more and more likely that Man originated in East Africa, but all we can say with great certainty is that it was somewhere in the warm belt that stretches from Southeast Asia across India into Africa. It now appears that Man moved into Europe a bit earlier than 800,000. He was living in northern Greece by 1,000,000.

All dates are changing astonishingly at the moment, so one must keep one's fingers crossed until this surge of new and vastly older dates settles down.

Sincerely yours,
George I. Carter

As of 1987, Dr. Carter was at the Southern Methodist University; he is now Professor Emeritus.

And so we find that early Man had been moving throughout the western hemisphere for at least a quarter of a million years. This changes the picture considerably from what was previously believed. However, since the glacier covered the north Marquette County area until such recent times, we could not have any evidence of people being here until the retreat of the last glacier. Now we find that Man followed the edge of the retreating ice sheet and came to the land that is now Upper Michigan, at the edge of Glacial Lake Duluth, about 11,850 years ago. These people have been named Paleo–Indians – Indians of the stone age.

As the glacial lake receded, ancient Man, scouring the shoreline, noticed a striking thing about the Lake Superior region – millions of tons of pure, native copper were here. The land was very barren and anyone wandering over its surface, and especially along its shores, could not have missed the exposed pure copper. It was of two types: the native, mass or trapped copper embedded in the rock which had to be dug for, and the glacial or "float" copper that had been freed by the glacier and lay in chunks of all sizes in its free state. Many pieces were small enough to be picked up and carried away.

Copper in the Upper Peninsula

Now, copper was also the first metal discovered by man in Europe. It is the only metal in the world found in its free state in large quantities, and is said to have first been discovered on the Isle of Cyprus about 6,000 B.C. to 8,000 B.C. Copper utensils found in Egypt were believed to be more than 5,000 years old. In the time of the Romans, the island of Cyprus was famous for the production of copper or Cyprian brass, hence the name cuprum, from which the word copper is derived. Ancient man dug copper in a small area in Yugoslavia, on the Sinai Peninsula, and in the ancient mines in Asia Minor. Some ancient copper was also mined in Cornwall, England, but there mainly as late as the 18th Century.

If we consider that the ice left the Keweenaw Peninsula about 9,000 years ago, then it could have been as early as 7,000 B.C. that copper was discovered in America.

The civilizations of Europe, Asia and North Africa moved through the late stone age, the copper age, and the bronze age to the iron age. Some time after the discovery of copper there around 7,000 years ago, they began improving the properties of copper by amalgamating it with zinc and tin to form bronze and brass, thus moving into the bronze age about 3,000 B.C. The bronze age lasted until about 1,000 B.C.

The systematic digging of copper in the Copper Country on the Keweenaw Peninsula and Isle Royale began sometime around 3,000 B.C.; this lasted at least 2,000 years. Several theories were put forth as to who these ancient copper diggers were.

Many scientists felt that there had to have been some organized trade route taking copper away from here, as there was far too much copper removed from the area to have been used only by the local Indians. Besides, very little of this local copper has been found among any of the Indian tribes in the U.S. Small amounts of it have been found throughout the United States from coast to coast in the forms of spearheads, arrowheads, trinkets, deathmasks, and religious objects. It has been found in Central and South America even as far south as Chile, but never in any amount that would indicate the end of a trade route according to the amount of copper removed. This left only Europe and the Mediterranean World that were the great smelters and users of copper during the Copper and Bronze Ages, which coincided exactly with the period when the copper was removed from the Upper Peninsula. But no one would dare suggest that people came from Europe or Asia this early in history just to get copper.

The whole question of ancient copper diggers came into focus in 1848 near the village of Rockford on the Keweenaw Peninsula. A miner named William Knapp was looking for a place to spend the night in the woods out of the weather. He noticed a small cave at the base of a bluff. As he was clearing the place out, he pulled out some roundish rocks that had a peculiar groove around them. Curious, he dug further until he came to some chunks of native copper in the rock.

Knapp deduced that prehistoric people must have mined there. He discovered many similar pits in the surrounding woods. All of them had copper, and all of them had the round, grooved rocks, which turned out to be hammer–stones. It was obvious to him that intelligent people had done a tremendous amount of exploring and mining in the area. His discovery made prospecting quite easy. All a prospector had to do was look for old pits, where there were always hammers and copper. Stone hammers were found by the wagonload, and one pit contained a chunk of freed copper weighing 16 tons. It was ten feet long, three feet wide, and two feet thick, and had been raised up on a crib of logs. It looked as though an intelligent, experienced engineer with only manpower and primitive tools had directed the work.

13

It didn't take an expert to conclude that these were experienced miners who dug here. In fact, a 26–year–old Indian agent, J. Logan Chipman, viewing the Copper Country for the first time in 1853, wrote:

The changes which have marked the influx of white population have been so like the witchery of a fairy tale, that, instead of abating they have increased the wonder of the world. Nothing has contributed so much to this result as the discovery of the vast works of the ancient miners. Scattered over an extent of hundreds of miles, evincing a degree of skill that seems to require utensils of a more effective nature than have yet been discovered, and of a magnitude which, upon the hypothesis that their authors had no other means of excavation, must have required the labor of a population as redundant as those of the states of antiquity, they will ever remain an impenetrable secret to science.

In 1862, a publication of the Smithsonian Institution related the results of an expedition to the Keweenaw Peninsula that was conducted by Charles Whittlesey.

A summation of the expedition's conclusions are as follows:

1–An ancient people of whom history gives no account extracted copper from the veins of Lake Superior.

2–They did it in a crude way by means of fire, by the use of copper wedges or gads, and by stone mauls.

3–They penetrated the earth but a short distance, their deepest workings being equal to those of the old copper and tin mines of Cornwall wrought before the conquest of Britain by the Romans.

4–They sought chiefly for small masses or lumps, since they did not have tools for cutting large masses.

5–There is no evidence of cultivation of the soil nor of mounds, homes, roads or canals: however, they had darts, spears and daggers of copper.

6–They were numerous, industrious and persevering, and the work must have been the equivalent of 10,000 men working for over 1,000 years.

7–All work ceased by A.D. 1,200.

Charles Whittlesey did much archeological work in the 1850's and 1860's in the central Upper Peninsula. He lived for a period of 15 years or

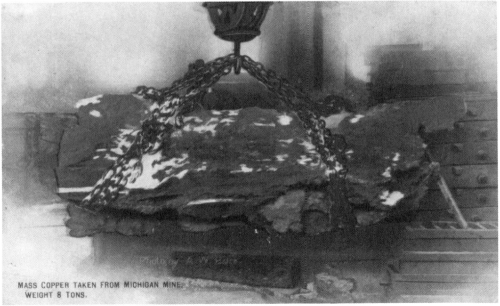

Top: This 5,000–+ pound piece of copper was found raised on cribbing in one of the ancient mines near McCargo's Cove on Isle Royale.
Bottom: A 16,000 pound piece of mass copper removed from the Michigan Mine.

Anglers locate 5,950-pound slab of nearly pure copper

WHITE PINE, Mich. (AP) — Copper Range Co. is preparing to display at its White Pine mine a 5,950-pound slab of nearly pure native copper discovered by two local anglers.

The slab was discovered Sept. 26 and transported Monday to the mine, where it will be displayed but not processed, said Bob Seasor, director of geology at Copper Range.

The slab, 82 inches long, 64 inches wide and about six feet thick, will be appraised later. At current spot prices for copper, the specimen — more than 99 percent pure — is worth more than $6,000.

Bill and Erick Yrjana found the slab while fishing near a ravine on western Upper Peninsula land whose mineral rights are owned by Copper Range, Seasor said. The men were paid $500 for directing company officials to the find.

Michigan's Upper Peninsula is one of the few areas in the world where native copper, termed float copper by geologists, is found. The largest such specimen, on display in downtown Calumet, weighs more than 9,000 pounds.

Another piece, weighing about 3,750 pounds and named the Ontonagon boulder, is on display at the Smithsonian Institution in Washington, D.C. Jesuit missionaries discov-ered that specimen in the early 1660s about 14 miles upstream from Lake Superior on the Ontonagon River.

Glaciers probably carried the Ontonagon boulder and the Yrjanas' find to their respective resting places about 10,000 years ago, Seasor said.

Top: Piece of copper presently on display in Calumet, Michigan (author in photo).
Bottom: Clipping from 1987 Mining Journal

more on Presque Isle, where he had a farm on a hill near the location of Kawbawgam's grave. This, of course, was a lighthouse reserve belonging to the U.S. Government at the time.

Some of the most detailed and thought–provoking ideas about the copper diggers have come from the observations and writings of Octave J. Du Temple and Professor Roy W. Drier, formerly of Michigan Tech University in Houghton, Michigan. At this writing Du Temple is still living; Drier died about ten years ago.

Octave Du Temple writes:

> Copper was known to the Egyptians approximately 9,000 years ago. We do not know all the sources for the amounts of Egyptian copper nor the method of refining it. There is no evidence that links Egyptian copper with the Lake Superior region but of course this possibility must be considered. It is estimated that 500 million pounds to perhaps more than a billion pounds of copper were mined prehistorically in the Lake Superior area and it is still a mystery as to where it went.
>
> Charcoal samples from two pits on Isle Royale proved to be 3,500 to 4,000 years old. There are an estimated 5,000 of these pits around Lake Superior, most of them on the Keweenaw Peninsula. Archeologists are finding that civilizations are older and that people roamed the earth much more widely than used to be believed. It now seems entirely possible that a copper trade existed several thousand years ago between America, Europe, Asia, and South America.

Du Temple goes on to theorize on the amount of copper that has been removed from the Lake Superior region:

> If one assumes that an average pit is 20 feet in diameter and 30 feet deep, then it appears that something like 1,000 to 1,200 tons of ore were removed per pit. If the ore averaged 5% or 100 lbs. per ton, then approximately 100,000 pounds of copper were removed per pit. If 5,000 pits existed, as earlier estimates indicated, and all pits are copper–bearing, then 100,000 pounds per pit means 500 million pounds of copper were mined in prehistoric times – all of it without anything more than fire, stone hammers, and man power. If the ore sampled 15%, and if more than 5,000 pits existed, then over 1.5 billion pounds of copper were mined. In 20 years (1929 to 1949) Calumet and Hecla mined 509 million pounds of copper, using practically all electric power.

17

At present (1988) Octave Du Temple is the Executive Secretary of the American Nuclear Society

It has been pointed out that it would have been easy to locate much of the copper since some float copper would be lying right on the surface, but Du Temple says that these people, nevertheless, had to be excellent prospectors. Every mine that has been opened in the Lake Superior area is known to have been worked in prehistoric times. One can only imagine how long it took these prehistoric people to locate these ore beds and to work them by the crude methods they used. The scale of the operation would indicate a strongly metallurgically oriented culture.

Du Temple goes on:

> In spite of the time and effort (perhaps as many as 10,000 men working for 1,000 years) it is believed that they were free men and not slaves. Apparently these prehistoric people carried their dead back with them, which would probably not be the case if slaves were employed.

Another person well–versed on the ancient copper diggers is Professor Roy Ward Drier. He studied them for many years and was chosen to head up the expedition funded by Mr. Joseph Gannon of Marquette in 1953. Professor Drier writes for "Inside Michigan" July 1953, Vol.3 #7:

> As historic mining spread throughout the present Copper Country it was found that these ancient explorers had mined on every productive vein in the region. As some of these veins did not outcrop at the surface but were discovered only upon excavation, it is seen that these prehistoric peoples possessed a gift or an ability which present day man would find very valuable.
>
> Fifty miles northwest across storm–tossed Lake Superior is located Isle Royale, 50 miles long, 8 miles across, and reaching an elevation of 500 ft. Lake Superior lies in a huge syncline or basin and some of the same geological formations outcrop on the island as on the Peninsula but dipping in the south instead of north. The lay of the formations caused the early white miners to wonder about the possibility of copper being found on the island. When the first miners explored the island in the late 1840's they found that these prehistoric people had been there before them and had mined on all the worthwhile lodes on the island. They found pits (mines) of 0 to 30 feet in diameter and as deep as 60 feet. For reasons of

inaccessibility, short season, ruggedness of topography, the problem of food supply, and poorness of lodes, Isle Royale was not prospected by prehistoric man as intensively as the mainland and as a result many of the pits are as the prehistoric miners left them, except for the natural filling in due to vegetation and decay.

The McCargo Cove region, on the north shore of the island, abounds in these ancient pits; in fact an engineer who was working at the Minong Mine, situated on one of the pits there, estimated from the extent of the ancient workings in that region of a very few square miles, and the mining methods of the ancients, that they represented the efforts of ten thousand men working for a thousand years, just in that one region of Isle Royale. In the Rockland region (on the mainland) the pits form an almost continuous line 30 miles long; in fact the copper bearing region, extending 100 miles from Keweenaw Point to the Porcupine Mountains, was all mined by these prehistoric miners.

The Ancients' mining methods naturally were very primitive. They consisted of heating the face of the formation with fire and then throwing water on the heated surface. This caused the rock to crack and spall and they then worked on the spalled rock and vein with stone hammers and copper wedges, chisels and gouges. By this method they sank "shafts" as deep as 50 feet in solid rock and excavated trenches 100 feet wide. Some trenches on Isle Royale were provided with auxiliary drains, while in some more nearly shaft–like pits were found the remains of wooden and leathern receptacles for removing water and possibly broken ore from the pit. Early investigations concluded that from a million to a million and a half pounds of copper were recovered.

In several of the pits, masses as large as 6,000 pounds were found raised up on crib–work. It is difficult to imagine what these miners expected to do with these enormous masses of metal once they did get them on the surface because they had no means of separating or removing any but knobs or pieces of copper projecting out from the main body of the mass. At the location of the Minong Mine, on the island, it is said a mass of about 5,000 pounds was found elevated on crib–work, though in general the Island miners seemed to be of an earlier or less advanced type.

The most important tool of these miners was the hammer–stone, or maul. These mauls are usually egg–shaped boulders varying in weight up to over 40 pounds, and of a variety found on the shores of Lake

Superior or in the glacial drift of the region. With the exception of a few locations in Keweenaw County, all of the mauls found on the peninsula have a circumferential groove, which undoubtedly used to enable the mauls to be attached to handles by means of thongs, withes or crotches. Some of the larger mauls are found with two grooves. It is thought that these larger hammer–stones were attached to bent–over saplings and used as stamps. None or very few of the stone mauls found on Isle Royale have grooves. Certainly the grooved hammer–stones are evidence of a later stage of civilization or at least a reversal of the average slope of the civilization curve. Only one copper maul was ever recorded found and that near Ontonagon. In general the character of the Island diggings is older and more interesting.

Samuel Knapp is said to have removed ten wagonloads of mauls from one location near Rockland and walled up a well with them. The mauls in the McCargo Cove region were estimated at a thousand tons. Very few undamaged mauls have been found. Most of them show the signs of hard usage, both ends of the grooved mauls being chipped and broken, while the ungrooved variety have only one end chipped, indicating their having been held in the hand while being used.

Some of the pits were only half worked and some of the old mining operations were found with tools left in them, just as though the miner had quit for the day, and planned to return.

Indian legends make no mention of these mining operations which were of a magnificence and magnitude worthy of being included in the history of any race. The legends do mention that a white race was driven out far back in Indian history. The fact that Indian legends indicate that pieces of copper were revered as Manitous or gods would seem to prove that they were not the people who mined and used copper industrially.

The above quotation can also be found in a book written by Drier and Du Temple, published privately in 1961 and 1965, entitled <u>Prehistoric Copper Mining in the Lake Superior Region</u>.

Closer to Home

Some other scientists who have studied the copper diggers are George I. Quimby and Albert C. Spaulding of the University of Michigan. They searched museums for copper artifacts and discovered that many had been recovered from the Keweenaw waterway. These artifacts included knives, chisels, spearpoints, arrowheads, and less common tools and weapons such as adzes and spuds. There were even some needles, both with and without eyes, as well as some small ceremonial pieces. The fact that so many artifacts were found near the ship canal would make it seem that there was a great deal of travel in the area.

Indeed, everything seems to bear out the theory that these people did much traveling by water. Finds of hammer–stones and stone hammers other than at mining pits have almost all been along the Lake Superior shore.

In Marquette county a good hammer–stone came through the mudsucker being used to dredge a marshy area southeast of Squaw Beach, the site of the Harbor of Refuge in Big Bay in the late 1960's. Kelly Temple of Big Bay, who was working on the mudsucker, saved the stone because of the unnatural–looking ring around it. The stone was recognized as a hammer–stone by another Big Bay resident, Norman Boulden. This stone was to have become the property of the Marquette County Historical Society, as this was the wish of Mr. Boulden. However, before it ever got to the Society collection it was "borrowed" by a collector of such items to use in an illustrated talk he was going to give. The man moved out of the area, and the hammer–stone went with him.

The Society does have two other hammer–stones that were turned up in Marquette County, both in the vicinity of Presque Isle.

Then there are the relatively unknown copper workings just north of Harvey, and south of the Marquette Prison on what is known as the Megassey Bluff. There were 30 or 40 ancient copper pits in this area.

Clyde Steele tells the story of a visit to Alec Mead, shortly before Alec died in St. Mary's Hospital at 93 years of age, in 1957. Clyde, who had worked with Alec years before, had gone to see him. He wanted to tell Alec that he had found the copper diggings which Alec had told him about when they were surveying in the early 1930's. Alec was very feeble and quite deaf at the time. When Clyde mentioned the copper mines, Alec perked up and asked if he had found any hammer–stones around there. Clyde said he hadn't. Alec went on to tell about when, as a boy, he worked with his dad in one of these mines. It was about 20 feet deep and had a drift running off to the east. He said there were hundreds of broken hammer–stones around there but they had only found one unbroken one. Alec's father had this one on his desk as a paperweight for over 30 years. Despite this report and several others like it, hammer–stones actually found in Marquette County are extremely rare. At the time, in the early 1880's, there was no realization of the age or extent of the copper diggings. Alec said that all those pits were opened up by the "Indians."

There were also workings on Michipicoten Island on Lake Superior's north shore and a few minor diggings on the Canadian mainland.

Clyde Steele was born in Marquette, July 5, 1908. His father, Robert Steele, was the first white child born in Marquette after the fire of 1868. Robert's father, Andrew Steele, drove a mule team on the plank road and also drove the first locomotive brought to Marquette, The Sebastopol, in 1855. Clyde himself has always been interested in the history of Marquette, and since his father lived to be 94 years old and always had a clear mind, Clyde has become a great source of stories of old Marquette.

The best place to search for copper artifacts in Marquette County is just upstream from the mouth of the Carp River. This was listed on the earliest maps as a wintering spot and agricultural location for Indians for ages. One Jesuit writing told of several acres of dome–type wigwams with smoke rising from the center of each at this spot. There have been at least three copper axes, all of about the same shape and size (about six inches long) all found in that vicinity. Countless other artifacts have been turned up there over the years. Unfortunately this area has undergone numerous man–made changes over the past half–century but it still remains one of the best possibilities for a find. Many arrowheads and spearheads have also been found along the beaches of Marquette County, the main areas being Compeau's Creek, Presque Isle, and the beach along M–28 east.

In 1984, a local writer, historian, and archeologist, Jim Paquette of Negaunee, unearthed several ancient copper sites on the north shore of Negaunee's Teal Lake, and he has written a paper on the settlement mentioned by Whittlesey in 1854.

Paquette wrote:

It was in the year of 1856 that the well–noted scholar and observer, Charles Whittlesey, wrote his detailed account of the discovery and identification of the ancient Indian copper mining operations in the Lake Superior district. Published in 1863 in Volume 13 of the Smithsonian Contributions to Knowledge, Whittlesey's report is considered today to be the best record and description of the early discoveries of prehistoric 'Indian diggings' and related artifacts here in Michigan's Upper Peninsula.

Jim Paquette goes on to tell how he stumbled onto Whittlesey's account of numerous copper Indian artifacts found by workmen employed by

John Burt while making a dam across the Carp River near Marquette. He detailed the discovery, described some of the artifacts, and went on to tell of another discovery.

> Near the mouth of the Carp River there are remains of cabins, placed in a row like houses in a village. This is shown by a line of heaps of stone and clay, like the remains of chimneys, and connected with them a slight ridge of clay, resembling the low embankments around a log building after the timber has decayed. They may have been formed of clay which was used to daub the chinks. A forest of ancient growth covered these ruins. Although I know of no historical evidence illustrating the point, I should hesitate to give them greater antiquity than the early French adventurers. It is about 200 years since the Jesuits established themselves on Lake Superior. Traders may have preceded them by thirty years and constructed cabins at places not mentioned by the Jesuits.

In the same paper, Paquette mentions reading of the discovery of a large buried cache of fur trader trading items at the site of the Marquette prison when workmen were digging near the Carp River during construction of the prison in 1887.

It seems strange that artifacts should still turn up readily at Presque Isle when it has been carefully worked over by visitors for well over a century, but still they come up with some astounding finds. A case in point took place in the summer of 1982, when Steve Lindberg of Marquette found a copper arrowhead in the rocks near the breakwater at the Island by chance – just leaned over and picked it up. The next day he returned to search there and found another in nearly the same place.

These arrowheads and spearheads do not necessarily represent the copper that was dug in ancient times. Everyone seems to have known that the copper was here. The Sauk and the Fox Indians of Wisconsin were known to have made summer visits into the Upper Peninsula looking for small pieces of float copper. Indeed, it was traded in small amounts for centuries. Literally hundreds of tribes throughout Canada, the U.S., Mexico, and Central and South America were found to have small amounts of copper, all of it coming from Michigan's Upper Peninsula. But this could not have been the destination of the extensive and well–organized copper mining that went on three to five thousand years ago.

Three theories have been expounded as to who the copper diggers were, in addition to the one that they were the local Indians. One theory is

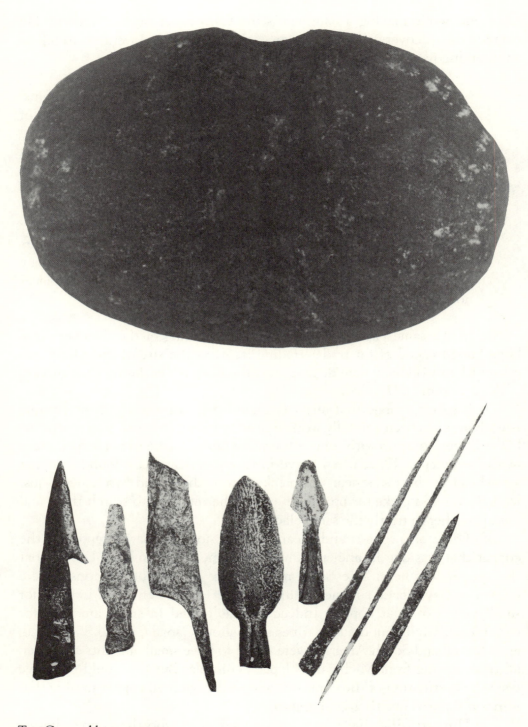

Top: Grooved hammerstone.
Bottom: Some of the various types of copper artifacts that have been found at various sites.

Top: Bronze artifacts from China from tomb of Qin Shi Huangdi.
Courtesy Dr. James R. Acocks.
Bottom: Joseph Gannon (c. 1900). Mr. Gannon was born in Dubuque, Iowa, but his family moved to Fort Dodge in 1880. He attended the schools of Fort Dodge through two years of high school when he moved to Chicago in 1892. In Chicago, Mr. Gannon worked for a wholesale grocery (Sprague, Warner & Co.) and joined the Illinois Naval Militia. He also became quite an athlete during this period (1892–98), taking part in many city track and cross–country meets.
In 1898, Gannon joined the Navy and took part in the Battle of Santiago in the Spanish–American War. In his later years, at the suggestion of Admiral Lahey, he wrote a book about his views of the battle to settle some historical conflicts. The book, "The U. S. S. Oregon and the Battle of Santiago," was published by Comet Press of New York in 1958.
In 1899, Joseph Gannon was transferred to northern Michigan as a salesman for Sprague Warner, and in 1909 organized the Gannon Grocery Co. This he sold to the Carpenter Cook Co. of Menominee in 1950.
Besides being a leader in establishing the commission form of government in Marquette in 1912 and a charter commissioner, Mr. Gannon was the main impetus and chairman of the committee that brought K. I. Sawyer Air Force Base to Marquette County in the 1950's.
From 1903 to 1918, Joe Gannon made five trips with George Shiras III into Canada to photograph wild animals.

that an ancient trade route took the copper west across the Bering Strait. Indeed Michigan copper may have turned up in China a few hundred years B.C.

Dr. James R. Acocks of Marquette was traveling in China and ran across the tomb of Qin Shi Huangdi, the Emperor from 221 to 210 B.C. He was the first Emperor to unite all China. The tomb itself is about a mile square, discovered in 1974 and partially excavated. Among the relics were spear points and metal points for poles made of bronze. This bronze contains minute amounts of gold and silver. As far as it is known, the only place in the world where gold and silver are found in the copper is Michigan's Upper Peninsula. The Craig Mine and the Daniels Mine at Birch, in Marquette County, were opened as copper and silver mines, but it was found that they assayed higher in gold than either of the other metals.

To identify Lake Superior copper, one merely has to test for silver. There is no other copper found alloyed with silver that was mined in ancient times. All Lake Superior copper has two percent or more of silver in it. Nuggets of copper with almost pure silver as a part of them are not uncommon in the Copper Country. Pieces of copper and silver have been nicknamed "half–breeds" in that part of the country, and are a coveted find for rockhounds and mineral collectors. Up to 1982, gold* and silver were removed from the copper taken in the Upper Peninsula, with two percent silver left in the finished product. In 1983 a new process was introduced at the White Pine copper operation in Ontonagon County to take all the silver and other metals out of Lake Superior copper.

A theory set forth by Mr. Joseph Cuthbert Gannon (1876–1965) of Marquette was that the copper people were sea–mammal hunters, an ancient people who lived in the Arctic region and circled the North Pole. Mr. Gannon spent much time and money studying the copper people. In the early 1950's he financed an expedition to Isle Royale which was headed by Professor Ray Drier, to help solve the puzzle. Besides several places in Europe and Asia, some places in Africa that were never worked, and similar tiny amounts in Arizona, Mr. Gannon found three other places in the world where pure copper is found. One is an island off the coast of Russia, near the Aleutians. The other two are in the extreme north of Canada. None were worked in ancient times, and all are insignificant lodes as compared with the Lake Superior region.

Gannon's conclusion about the identity of the copper diggers did, to a certain extent, tie in nicely with some discoveries by Dr. Louis Giddings, Jr., made while he was on a U.S. Navy–sponsored expedition to gather climatic data in Northern Alaska and Canada. His findings support the theory that

* There is no gold in Western U. P. copper.

there was a prehistoric culture circling the top of the globe between 1,000 and 10,000 years ago. If so, these people could have been the traders who took copper to the old world from the new.

A third theory, which came from a study made by Michigan Tech University in Houghton, suggests that the copper was taken south via the Mississippi drainage route, probably to South America. The lack of continuity in Indian folklore could be explained by this theory. As the ice front retreated northward, relieving a large load on the earth's crust, the crust heaved up again. The outlet to the Mississippi rose higher and higher. Eventually, the lake spilled out to the St. Lawrence River. Thus any people who were accustomed to paddling up the Mississippi to mine copper in Lake Superior would find less and less water in the river each summer, until the creek dried up and access was cut off completely. Then there would be no more copper mining. However, at the same time, there would be a new route open into Lake Superior from the east, and a different people could come in with no knowledge of the ancient miners. This is the only theory of the three that does not acknowledge the copper getting to Europe. Furthermore, while copper was found among the ancient civilizations of South America, the amounts could have come from the local (Columbia) mines.

Early Indians

It is not known exactly what Indian tribes first lived in the Lake Superior country but, since the Indians of earlier times were even more nomadic than in later years, there could have been many. Scientists have called Indians who lived in the Great Lakes region from 500 B.C. to 100 B.C. and made pottery and burial mounds "Early Woodland Indians." The Middle Woodland Indians were here from 100 B.C. to 800 A.D., and the Late Woodland culture ranged between 800 A.D. and 1,600 A.D. It is possible that some of the Late Woodland people were at least a little agricultural, because some of the later Chippewa were able to raise some corn in favorable years in certain places on the south shore of Lake Superior.

The history of the Ojibwe people tells us that they came from "the shores of the great salt water toward the rising sun." Their home had been on the Atlantic Ocean, around the mouth of the St. Lawrence River and down the east coast. It is to these people that we attribute the development of the birchbark canoe, and over the years they followed the great waterways westward in these canoes. The Ojibwe were a large and powerful people at the time, and when they encountered the Lakota and Dakota (both a part of the Sioux today) in the western lakes region, they forced them further westward to the Great Plains.

Because of the severe climate – long winters with little food – the Ojibwe spread themselves very thin over a large area. The only place they could collect in larger numbers was where food was plentiful, such as around the Apostle Islands near the west end of Lake Superior and at the rapids of the Sault Ste. Marie, where fish were plentiful. Some went beyond the Great Lakes northwest into Manitoba and Saskatchewan. These became the Plains Ojibwe; the Northern Ojibwe moved north of Lake Superior and, pushing the Cree ever further northward, covered all of southern Ontario. The Southeastern Ojibwe lived to the north of Lakes Erie and Ontario and on the shores of Lake Huron, including most of lower Michigan. It was the Central Ojibwe who peopled Northern Minnesota, Wisconsin, and all of the Upper Peninsula of Michigan.

All of this great and once–powerful tribe are known as the "people of the woods" or the "Woods Indians." They had many skills that made them particularly adapted to the woods and waters. They had developed ingenious traps, snares and fishing techniques. They are said to be the originators of the toboggan, the classic "Michigan style" snowshoe, but their mainstay was the birchbark canoe. It was by this craft that they made their way by water thousands of miles inland. The craft can still be made from readily available forest resources with the simplest of tools if one possesses the skills and, except for its fragility, the design hasn't been improved on to this day.

Historic Indians

These Indians who the white men found living in the Great Lakes region represent the "Three Fires" – Ottawa, Chippewa, and Potowatami. They call themselves and all Indians the Anishnabe (First People). At first they were the "Otchipwe" as written by Bishop Frederick Baraga. The French pronounced it "Ojibway" and the English called it "Chippewa." The two names are used today and sometimes the Central Ojibwe are called the Chippewa, but they are all the same people. They make up the nucleus of the Algonquin Nation. This huge nation was made up of many tribes and, though some have drifted far from the main groups, they can still be recognized by their language origin. Besides the Ottawa, Chippewa, and Potowatami there are the Fox, the Sac, the Sauk, Menominee, Pocumtue, Narragoset, Munsee, Massachuset, Massauaketon, Pennocook, Penobscot, Mohican, Delaware, Shawnee, Miami (or Omaumeg), Kickapoo, Sutia,

Cheyenne and Arapaho, Salteaux, Ok–ewein, and, yes, the Sanguinay (whom the whites called the Beaver), as well as many others.

The Algonquin tribes occupied the region around the Great Lakes and practically all of the drainage area into these waters. North of them were the Cree (also of Algonquin origin), west of them were the Sioux, south of them were a group of tribes collectively called the Illinois, and east of them were the Iroquois, made up of such tribes as the Seneca, Cayuga, Oneida, Mohawk, Onandagas, and, after 1712, Tuscaroras – a league known as the Six Nations. For hundreds of years, the greatest enemies of the Algonquin People were the Iroquois and the Sioux. The warring, if any, was all east and west, seldom if ever north and south. This was the picture when the first white men paddled their way to the great "Inland Seas" in the 16th and 17th Centuries.

It has been well established that the first European to see Lake Superior was Etienne Brule; however, until recently there was much speculation that the Norsemen were in this region sometime around 1365 A.D.

The Norsemen

Four or five finds around Lake Superior led people to believe that the Norsemen must have been here. The theory was based on the fact that the Norsemen did colonize the northeast coast of North America, Greenland, and Iceland.

Actually, several countries claim to be the first to have set foot on these shores. There is a Welsh legend of a priest who sailed off for a few years to a far–off land, and the Welsh claim he must have been in America. The Irish say that Irish monks visited America many times in skin boats and set up lonely monasteries there long before the Norsemen (see The Brendan Voyage by Tim Severin).

The Finns claimed to have settled in Rhode Island, and have much research to back up this claim.

The finding of the "Kensington Stone" in Kensington, Minnesota in 1898 was most convincing. According to a book written by Hjalmer R. Holand, and published by Twaye Publishers, of New York in 1956, a group of Vikings were trying to circumnavigate "Vinlandia Insula" – the island of Vinland – in the year 1362. They traveled northwest to Hudson Bay and south to James Bay. Realizing that there was still a huge land mass to the west, the party took to the rivers which brought them to the divide flowing toward the Great Lakes, specifically Lake Superior and the Mississippi. At a campsite near the present Kensington, Minnesota, they were attacked by Indians and half their number were killed. They left the message on the stone at that time.

Holand's translation of the stone is as follows:

(We are) 8 Goths (Swedes) and 22 Norwegians on exploration journey from Vinland round about the west. We had camped by (a lake with) 2 skerries one day's journey north from this stone. We were (out) and fished one day. After we came home (we) found ten of our men red with blood and dead. A.V.M. (Ave Virgo Maria) save (us) from evil. (We) have ten men by the sea to look after ships 14 days journey from this island. (In the) year (of our Lord) 1362.

Holand traces the remains of the group via mooring stones, fire–steels, and other various Norse implements to the Mississippi River where he theorizes the party was lost.

The main finds in the Lake Superior region which have led many to believe the Norsemen reached that body of water were the "Republic Axe" in the Michigamme River near Republic, Michigan; the "Beardmore Armor," a sword, battle–axe and part of a shield found in a cave just east of Lake Nipigon on the north shore of Lake Superior; and the "Norse Altar," now called the "Mystery Stone," on top of Huron Mountain.

A very reliable historian from Marquette, Dr. Richard Sonderegger, made quite a thorough study of the Kensington Stone and found it absolutely, without a doubt, not authentic. He is backed on this opinion by many other historians. However, at Kensington there is a huge replica of the stone and it is easy to be convinced by the excitement of the local believers. They have erected an 18–foot statue of a Viking, believed to be the largest in the world.

The find near Beardmore, Ontario was made by James Dodd in the 1920's. It proved to be authentically Norwegian, and was purchased by the Royal Ontario Museum of Archeology in Toronto. There were many twists and turns to this story also, but the matter was settled when Dodd died and his son came forward and said he was with his father when the articles were planted. They had apparently been taken out of Norway by a collector and, in order to have license, he pretended they had been found.

The Republic axe was picked out of the Michigamme River near the beginning of the twentieth century by a prospector when he stooped down to drink. Again everything about the find seemed reliable. It found its way to the Marquette County Historical Society, and Mrs. Helen L. Paul sent it to

Upper left: Kensington Runestone
Upper right: Top – Sam Mackey axe – owned by Walter Mackey. Bottom – Republic axe – owned by the Marquette County Historical Society – photo by Jack Deo.
Bottom: Ruins of Norse Building (c. 1,000 A. D. – At present this is the only authenticated Norse settlement in North America. – L'Anse aux Meadows.

New York for identification in the 1930's. It was identified as a Norse battle–axe. The new highway through Republic was named the Leif Erickson Highway, which it still is, and everyone was convinced that the Vikings had been here.

In 1937, the axe had come back to the Marquette Historical Society and a group of people were crowded around it as it lay on a table when Sam Mackey, a Finnish carpenter who had been doing a lot of work around the museum for Mrs. Paul, pushed his way through to see what all the excitement was about. When he saw it was the axe, he said he had one just like it at home. The next day he came in with his axe, and it was indeed almost identical. Sam explained that these axes were made in Finland around 1760 and were not a weapon at all, but were used to flatten or hew round logs of a cabin already erected. Since that time, at least five of these axes have turned up in the central Upper Peninsula. The highway is still called the Leif Erickson Highway, but the axe is most certainly a case of mistaken identity.

With the crumbling of one story after another, the possibility of the "Mystery Stone" on the top of Huron Mountain having anything to do with the Vikings seems ridiculous, and the overwhelming opinion of authorities today is that the Vikings did not get far from the east coast. *See page 850.2.

The story most Americans know about the Vikings is that Eric the Red was a violent, antisocial Viking leader who was banished from Norway. The group were Norsemen but became "Vikings," which is the Norse word for "pirates." A Norse saga tells us that Eric and his father had to move to a Norse colony in Iceland in 980 A.D. because of some killings, and it was here that Leif Erickson, the famous Viking leader, was born.

Eric got into trouble there also, and had to leave Iceland. He and his followers sailed off for three years, and when he returned he told wondrous tales of a far–off land he called Greenland, later admitting he had chosen the name to appeal to people so they would go there. Some followed him back to Greenland's harsh shore and made a living there, but Leif went on to explore further west, setting up quarters in what is now Newfoundland. The one site that could be "Vinland the Good" where Leif built some large houses, was identified in the 1950's by Helge Ingstad, an archeologist. It was at L'Anse aux Meadows, near Epoves Bay on the northeast coast of Newfoundland. Three groups of turf structures unearthed there were carbon–dated to the Viking period, and some artifacts found that match other Norse objects.

Ditlev Thyssen, a Norse scholar from Denmark, tells us that the old Norse sagas give most of the story. He reported it in the Epigraphic Society Occasional Publications, Vol. 11, Part 2, 1983; quoted here in part:

The Norwegians made trade with Greenland a royal monopoly. The Greenlanders had probably not expected this. They had, of course, wanted to do their own trading.

A Norwegian trader would not risk his men, cargo – and for all in the world, not his ship – to go to Greenland to trade.

The sailing to Greenland alone would take six to eight weeks, and most of the things offered in Greenland could be had from northern Norway or Russia, which was closer.

In 1267 the Eskimos appeared on the northwestern coast of Greenland. The winters were getting more and more severe in the beginning of the 14th century. The people of Greenland gave up their Christian faith and turned toward the west.

In 1347 a ship came from Greenland storm–driven to Iceland with 17 men on board. They had been to Marlland (America).

Toward 1350 the colonies began to decline. Communication between the two settlements on Greenland was never frequent. An expedition was launched from the Eastern Settlement to contact the Western Settlement and drive away their enemies, the Skraelings (Indians). Arriving there they found nobody – only a good many sheep running wild. There was no sign of battle.

The Icelandic Annals from 1379 inform us that 'The Skraelings made a raid on the Greenlanders, killing 18 men and carrying off two boys as slaves.'

The last mention of Greenland dates from 1410. 'In the year of our Lord 1408,' they write, 'we were present in Hvalsey Church and witnessed a wedding.'

In the 15th Century German and English pirates made repeated raids on Iceland. They might have extended their activities to Greenland. Niels Egede, a son of a missionary sent by the Danish government, grew up in Greenland and relates a story told to him in the early 18th Century by a shaman living in the ruins of the Eastern Settlement. The story recounted how Eskimos and Norse had been living uneasily – until some sinister strangers arrived.

Three small ships sailed in from the southwest to plunder, and some of the Norse were killed. The next year a whole fleet arrived and fought with them, plundering and killing. The year after, the dreadful pirates came back again. The Eskimos saw them and fled up the fiord, taking some of the Norse women and children along. When they returned in the autumn they saw no people, but everything had been carried away, and the houses and farms were burned down.

The only trace of the settlement that a visitor to southwest Greenland found in 1540 was a dead man lying face down on the ground. He was wearing a hood and clothes made of coarse woolens and sealskin. Beside him lay a knife, badly bent and almost worn away. Was this the last trace of this Western Viking? No – the rank and file went to America to get timber. Some settled down and some went on great expeditions. They did not leave many traces, for their tools and iron weapons were hard to come by. But they left runic writings and mooring holes cut in rocks. The runes were mostly just a date carved in a rock. There are not many, and they are found far apart. The oldest runic writing yet found in America is from Massachusetts. It consists of runes from both the old 24–rune alphabet and runes from the 16–rune alphabet from the Viking Age. In Massachusetts we have a runic inscription indicating Nov. 24, 1009. An amulet in Maine is dated 1010. The next runic inscription known was carved two years later in 1012 in what is now Oklahoma. Two more runic dates were carved in eastern Oklahoma, one in 1017 not too far from the first one which is close to the present town called Heavener. There are runic inscriptions in Rhode Island. Erik Gnupson from Iceland was responsible for the original Vinland map from 1122. Seven dated runic puzzles by Henricus, the name Gnupson later took, which are spread along a 300–mile long shoreline, proves that the Vinland he speaks of was centered in what later became New England.

Thyssen also mentions finds around Kensington and Beardmore, finding some anthracite coal in the Viking settlements of Greenland that probably came from Rhode Island, where a pit is exposed near the coast, and many other possible finds that show the Greenlanders went back and forth to America. The Europeans still had heard relatively little about America, so for all intents and purposes it did not exist for them.

Columbus changed all this when he attempted to go east by sailing west in 1492. When he reported that he had found the island off the coast of India, the first thought of the seafaring nations of Europe was to find a new water route to the fabulous wealth of China, since their old route had been closed by the hostile Turks. There is one thing, however, that ties the Columbus voyages to the Lake Superior region, and that is the fact that the first "Indians" (Columbus thought he had reached India) he encountered were noted to have been wearing copper beads and trinkets. With what is known now, we can assume that this was Lake Superior copper.

Book One

John Cabot

John Cabot, who had the same idea as Columbus, sailed on behalf of King Henry VII of England just five years later. He was the first European to explore the northeast coast of North America since the Viking period, and he didn't know they had been there. To Cabot this was unexplored territory, and he was expecting to find China.

Like many others from the Mediterranean, Cabot – who was born Giovanni Caboto in Genoa, Italy – was attracted to the challenging Atlantic. He moved to Bristol, England's leading port, and changed his name to John Cabot.

Little is known of this brave sailor, as only the crudest of maps and a portion of his journal have been preserved, but it is a matter of record that Cabot was given an impressive send–off in 1497, as England too wanted prizes in this new business of exploration.

With his sons and a crew of 18 men he sailed in one little ship, the Matthew. To avoid encroaching on Spanish claims and risking war, Cabot's plan was to take the northerly route to Asia. He did not know this was the route of the Vikings. After seven cold weeks of sailing, land was sighted and soon Cabot was ashore, claiming this land for England. According to a paper written by S. L. Smith in 1915 (page 153 – <u>Prehistoric Copper Mining in the Lake Superior Region</u> – Drier and Du Temple) Cabot encountered natives with copper ornaments.

No one knows where Cabot first landed in North America, but it has been conjectured that the land he claimed for the English King may have been Labrador or Newfoundland. When he returned to Bristol he was given an enthusiastic welcome, but his only discovery of wealth was fishing grounds where fish could be caught by the basket. He told of plans he had made to return to his landing place; from there he would sail westward, hugging the coast, until he came to Japan ("Chipongu") which, the English assumed, was the source of spices and gems.

On a crude map, Cabot named various points of land and islands, Cape Discovery, Island of St. John, St. George's Cape, the Trinity Islands, and English Cape. These may be, according to some authorities, the present Cape North, St. Paul Island, Cape Ray, St. Pierre and Miguelon, and Cape Race, all in the area of Cabot Strait.

With the talk of riches and commerce, English merchants financed his second voyage the following year (1498). On this trip there were five ships and 200 men. One ship was damaged in a storm off the Irish coast and had to return. The other four sailed the northern route to Greenland. There

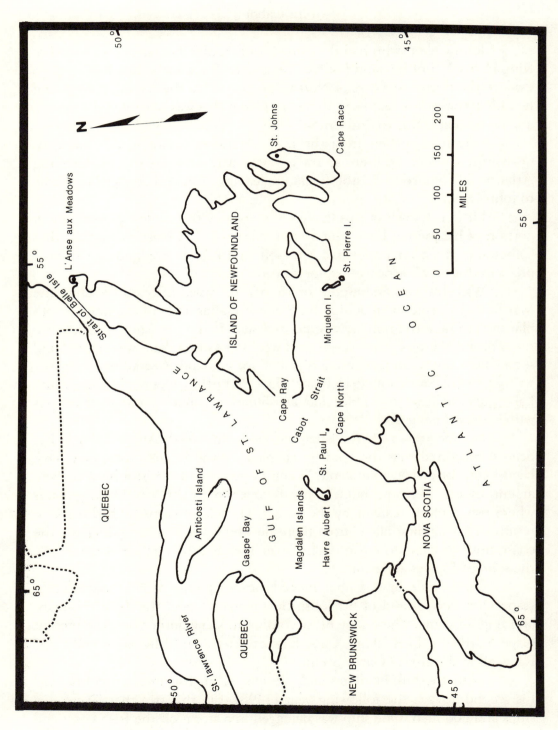

By Cartography Lab N. M. U.

was some mutiny caused by fear and uncertainty, and when they met ice obstruction they were forced to turn south.

Cabot completely missed the one inlet that could have led him into the interior of the North American continent, the St. Lawrence, but he did record the hook of land that is the Cape Cod Peninsula. There were no dramatic results from John Cabot's explorations in the north.

Excluded from the New World by Spain's warnings, England turned instead to European wars to test her growing strength and confidence, and Cabot was long dead before she could give her attention to settling his discovery.

Jacques Cartier

In 1534, Jacques Cartier was commissioned by the French king Francis I to find a passage around or through the North American continent to the Orient. With two ships and 61 men, Cartier reached Newfoundland and entered the Strait of Belle Isle. Following the south side of the Strait, he was led down almost the whole west coast of Newfoundland. Off St. George's Bay a storm drove the ships out into the Gulf. He mistook Magdalen and Prince Edward Islands for the main shore of the south side of this great gulf. Following the coast of the present New Brunswick northward, he was greatly disappointed to discover that Chaleur Bay was not a strait. Cartier went ashore in Gaspe Harbor, where he remained for ten days.

It was here in Gaspe Harbor in 1534 that an event took place that would eventually lead the French into Lake Superior, but it is little noted as such by historians. For the first time the French explorers met and befriended a group of Wyndot Indians. They made an attempt to communicate with them. These Wyndots were a tribe of the Iroquois nation who inhabited the northeast coastal region of America, having moved there from the south into the ancient home of the Ojibwe. The Wyndot tribe inhabited the area around Quebec.

The peculiar hair style of the Iroquois men – a stripe of hair in the middle of the head and clean–shaven on both sides – reminded the French of the wild boar found in France which had a high ridge down his back with hair that stood up when it was angry. The boar was called in French a "huron" and, not knowing what to call these Indians, they gave them the name "Hurons."

When leaving Gaspe Harbor and having only very limited communications with the Hurons, Cartier carried off two of them in hopes of being able to communicate better with them. By treating them kindly, he hoped they would serve as guides to a route inland.

They did lead Cartier to a passage between the island of Anticosti and the Quebec shore, where he noted the great waterway coming from the west and south. He decided to return to France before fall and come back the following year to explore the strait and what lay beyond it. Heading eastward along the Quebec shore, Cartier soon regained the Strait of Belle Isle and, recrossing the Atlantic, reached St. Malo on September 5th, 1534.

On May 19, 1535, Cartier set sail again from St. Malo, this time with three vessels. Passing through the strait of Belle Isle, he anchored on August 9th in Pillage Bay, opposite Anticosti, which he named the "Bay of St. Lawrence," a name which spread to the gulf and the river.

Still using the two Hurons as guides – and after a full year together their communication had become quite accurate – the ships proceeded through the passage north of Anticosti and anchored on September 1st at the mouth of the Saguenay, which the two Indians informed Cartier was the name of a kingdom "rich and wealthy in precious stones." Since the Saguenay flowed from the west, this was just the general direction they were pointing which they called the region of the Saguenay. They could have been referring to ingots of copper or pieces of float copper, as this is the only substance of value known to come from the west.

On reaching the island of Orleans, they pointed to the location of a Huron village on the opposite shore and called it "Canada," the Huron word for "village." Not seeing the village, the French took the word to mean the whole mainland, which it has been called ever since.

Leaving his two larger vessels in the mouth of the St. Charles River which enters the St. Lawrence, Cartier set off westward with the bark and the longboats. The bark grounded in St. Peter Lake, but the longboats were rowed as far as the Huron–Iroquois village of Hochelaga, where Montreal now stands, on October 2, 1535. Further progress was stopped by the Lachine rapids, and Cartier remained there with the Hurons that winter.

When Cartier was moving up the St. Lawrence in 1535, the Indians again pointed out the region of the Saguenay, a very vague one, stretching away without any fixed limits to the north and to the west, which they said was inhabited, and from that land came some red copper which they called "caignetdaze." The French called it "Cyure rouge." In the spring of 1536, Cartier set out in the bark and longboats toward his vessels and crew, which had wintered at the mouth of the St. Johns. In order to give Francis I authentic information of this mythical northern Mexico, Cartier again seized some Hurons. This time he took a Huron chief and eleven of the head men of the village to take back to France.

On his return trip down the river, Cartier saw "a great knife" made of this "red copper" in possession of some Montagnais (an Iroquois tribe). They presented it to their chief, who was returning to France with Cartier.

When the party reached the St. Charles, they found that 25 of their men had died of scurvy during the winter. Cartier sought further information about the kingdom of the Saguenay, which he was informed could be reached more easily by following the route laid out by the Algonquin, up the Ottawa River. On his return trip to France with the 12 elders of the Huron village, Cartier passed south of Anticosti and entered the Atlantic Ocean through Cabot Strait, reaching St. Malo on July 16th of 1536.

Five years passed while Cartier studied the limited knowledge of the captured Hurons as to riches, routes, and inhabitants of the far–off region of the Saguenay. In 1541 he set sail again with five vessels. They set up living quarters at Cape Rouge, nine miles above present Quebec. The Seigneur de Roberval, who was to sail at a later date, had been chosen to command this post, but when he did not arrive, Cartier made another examination of the rapids of Lachine, before sending men up the Ottawa River. The trip was far more difficult than they had anticipated, with some 45 portages of the heavy longboats. It was too much for the men, and they did not get to the great inland sea the Hurons spoke of (Lake Huron); the "precious stones" they had been told about proved worthless and they found no copper.

Roberval did set sail in April of 1542, but on reaching the mouth of the St. John's he met Cartier on his way back to France, very disappointed. Cartier never returned to America again, and while Roberval remained that winter of 1542, Cartier's report caused the French authorities to lose interest. Roberval was recalled in 1543. French exploration and interest in the interior and a route to the western ocean died for the remainder of that century, but later several attempts were made to colonize the region around the mouth of the St. Lawrence, as the French wished to take advantage of the friendliness of the Hurons living there. Language barriers had, for the most part, been overcome, and the Indians seemed eager to trade furs for white men's goods.

Other Expeditions

By 1550, only the polar regions of the world had not been explored in the eager search for a trade route to Asia. The Spanish and Portuguese had claimed Central and South America, and the Dutch and English further north. Since the French had claims around the mouth of the St. Lawrence, the English reasoned that there must be a way around the north part of the continent, as there was around the south end. Martin Frobisher, John Davis, William Baffin and Henry Hudson all braved the frozen Arctic in attempts to find a northwest passage that England could control, but all routes were blocked by ice. Hudson also had claims on behalf of the Dutch, who had hired him. Hudson lost his life when his crew mutinied in the bay that bears his name, and set him adrift with his 14–year–old son and a few faithful men, a cruel and certain death for a great explorer.

Samuel de Champlain

Samuel de Champlain came to Canada in 1603 as a geographer on the third expedition to attempt to start a colony there. He ascended the St. Lawrence as far as Montreal, following a written description made by Cartier almost 70 years before. From the Indians near the present Montreal area he learned of the waterways to Lake Huron, Niagara Falls, the Detroit River, and the copper of Lake Superior; he also learned of the shorter route of the A–da–wa (Ottawa), the traders, up the Ottawa River and the Mattawa to Lake Nipissing and down the French River to Lake Huron. He learned much more than Cartier had ever known – but this was knowledge accumulated over many years. The description of the copper region was very vague, but this and the hint of these great waterways and unbelievable inland seas beyond led to speculation that this might finally be the long–sought route to the western ocean.

After failing in an attempt to establish a colony in Nova Scotia, Champlain returned to the St. Lawrence in 1608 and established Quebec, the first permanent French colony in America. In all, Champlain made ten voyages from France to the St. Lawrence and back; he died in Canada on December 25th, 1635.

Brule

In his early days, Champlain had begun a policy of sending promising young men back to the homelands of visiting Indians that arrived in ever–increasing numbers from the great inland seas to trade their furs at the French colony. Etienne Brule was the first of these "Coureurs de Bois" – runners or messengers of the woods – and as a teen–ager he accompanied an Algonquin chief homeward in 1610. In the ensuing years he traveled up the

Champlain Map – reputed to be the oldest of the Great Lakes Region (1632). By permission of Clements Library – University of Michigan, Ann Arbor, Michigan.

Great Lakes ahead of any other white man. His job was to learn the geography of the country and the language of the people so that French exploration and colonization would be made easier in the years to come.

From Brule's Discoveries and Explorations by Consul Willshire Butterfield:

Etienne Brule was essentially a woodsman; his fondness for savage life was remarkable. But he wrote nothing; and his verbal recitals, as they were taken down from his own lips, and recorded by Champlain, Sagard, and Le Caron, are not calculated to awaken, at once, the thought that they border on the marvelous. However, as we contemplate more and more his courage and perseverance among the Indian nations which he visited and with some of which he lived several years, our curiosity gives way to admiration and astonishment.

A French historian named Gabriel Sagard gives us the best account of Brule and another bold coureur de bois, who seems to have only one name, Grenolle (sometimes written Grenoll, Greneau, and Grenoble) who was with Brule on the first penetration by white men into Lake Superior. All accounts of Grenolle, if there were any, are lost, but Brule, who is credited with being the first white man to set eyes on Lake Superior, told Sagard the story himself in 1626, three years after he made the trip. Brule was vague and undescriptive, so at best we have only the roughest of records of the journey.

When one reads the original translation of Sagard, it can be seen that we must depend more on Sagard than Brule for accuracy and detail. Sagard makes statement such as: "It is probable they took the north route" and "it is conjectured" that such and such happened.

From the tale he heard from Brule, Sagard relates that they traveled the northern shore of Lake Superior to its westernmost end, the present location of Duluth, and then returned via the same route, stopping at Isle Royale where they observed Indians working a copper mine – the only such reference to this in historic time, incidentally.

It is difficult to think that an intrepid explorer like Etienne Brule – who paddled these waters ahead of every other white man, covering the three westernmost lakes and all the way to Hudson Bay, who openly associated with tribes hostile to each other, who returned to the wilderness even after having been tortured by the Indians (he was eventually killed and eaten by the Hurons) – would have left out the south shore of this largest of lakes, having already explored its north shore, but we must remember that he was traveling with the Algonquins and was not the leader of the group. Whatever

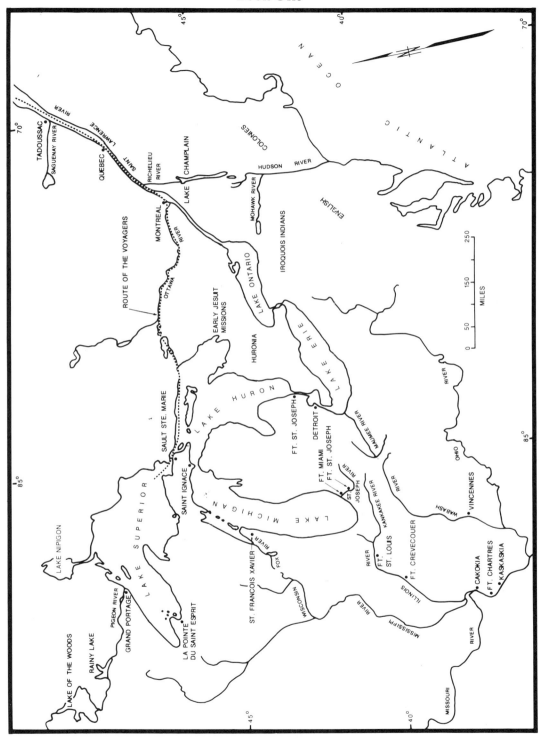

By Cartography Lab N. M. U.

the reasons, although he spent nearly 20 years in the area, it is the accepted fact among historians that Brule did not travel the south shore of Lake Superior.

However, if we dare to assume from the scattered bits of knowledge of the voyages of Brule and Grenoble that at some time they did travel the south shore of Lake Superior, then they would have been the first Europeans in historic times to pass along the shores of present Marquette County and camp within its borders. While this is a distinct probability, history will never record it as such, for we have but one record. The Indians working the copper mines on Isle Royale as reported by Brule were, according to Sagard, either Beavers or Ouimisaga. Of the Indians Brule met in the Grand Lac country were the "People of the Falls" (Soo Rapids), called "Sauteurs" by the French. All of these tribes were Algonquins, ancestors of the Ottawa–Otchipwe, generally known today as the Ottawa, Chippewa, and Potowatami, who at that time had only recently driven the Sioux westward.

For some time after Brule's first report, Governor Samuel de Champlain had gotten other vague reports of the great inland sea to the south of Lake Superior that led him to believe that Asia was on its western shore. In 1634 he outfitted another famous coureur de bois, Jean Nicolet, with a beautiful Chinese–style silken robe and sent him off to meet the great Khan.

Following the Ottawa–French river route, as usual, to Lake Huron, Nicolet and a group of Indians passed through the Strait of Mackinac and, proceeding along the south shore of the present Upper Peninsula in Lake Michigan (then the Lake of the Illinois), made their way to its western shore. Somewhere in the vicinity of Green Bay, or possibly a little further south, Nicolet went ashore dressed in his fine silks and carrying two pistols which he fired into the air. The story goes that the Indians who met him and witnessed this spectacle were much impressed and in great awe, doing what they could to treat him with respect, but Nicolet found neither silks, spices, nor Chinese. His report to Champlain did a great deal toward clearing up the geography of the midwest. For the first time Champlain had an idea of the unbelievable size of the American continent, and he realized that these truly were huge inland lakes in the center of a vast continent. It took a lifetime for Samuel de Champlain to learn this fact, for he died the following year.

While this is the traditional and accepted story, it may be a complete misinterpretation.

In the December 1966 issue of the Michigan History Magazine (vol. L, No. 4), Harry Dever of Cedarville published an article stating that Nicolet's landing on the west shore of Lake Michigan is a myth.

Dever gives some very logical and convincing arguments, some of which are as follows:

The propounder of the Nicolet myth was John Gilmary Shea, who used as his source the 'Jesuit Relations'. Later writers have overestimated the carefulness of Shea's analysis and have paid too much attention to Shea and his followers and not enough to the Relations.

One can easily see how Shea was misled. There are four points in the Relations that seem to substantiate his theory:

First: The name of the tribe that Nicolet went to visit was the Ouinipigou. Shea plausibly concluded that the tribe was the Wisconsin Winnebago.

Second: According to the Relations, all the tribes between Huronia and Nicolet's destination spoke Algonquin, except the Ouinipigou. This seemed to indicate that the Ouinipigou were Winnebago, for the Winnebago spoke Siouan dialect, not Algonquin.

Third: The Ouinipigou were said to be three hundred leagues west of Huronia. This could reasonably be Green Bay.

Fourth: Nicolet names tribes near the Ouinipigou that were found over a third of a century later in the neighborhood of Green Bay.

This was the basis of Shea's case. Nevertheless, there are three points that refute it, and neither Shea nor any of his successors has given these the attention they deserve.

First: Father Vemont indicated that the Ouinipigou gave Nicolet a nickname: "Manitou Ininiou," (Wonderful Man), which is Algonquin not Siouan. Shea's theory appeared three years before the publication of Hiawatha, after which everyone learned a little tortured Chippewa. It isn't likely that Shea, who was not an Algonquin scholar, knew that "manitou" was an Algonquin word. So Shea may not have known, but most of his more modern successors must have known that manitou is Algonquin. Yet they naively repeated the impossible tale (author: as I have) that this was a name bestowed on Nicolet by a Siouan tribe.

Second: Father LeJeune's Relation plainly shows that Nicolet found the Ouinipigou up the eastern shore of Lake Superior. After naming the many tribes that Nicolet found north of Huronia, at the foot of Georgian Bay and near the Sault, Father LeJeune continued:

Beyond this rapid we find the little lake [Whitefish Bay], upon the

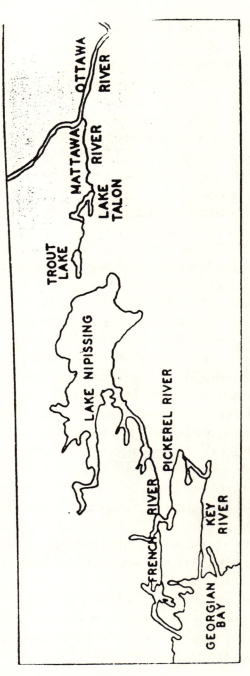

THE VOYAGEURS' HIGHWAY INTO THE UPPER GREAT LAKES AREA

Voyageurs highway to Lake Superior.

shores of which, to the North, are the Roquai. To the North of these are the Montoue....Passing this smaller lake, we enter the second fresh water sea [Lake Superior], upon the shores of which are the Marouimine; and still farther, upon the same banks, dwell the Ouinipigou.

How could anyone reasonably interpret that as a voyage across the northern part of Lake Huron, through the Straits of Mackinac, and across Lake Michigan and Green Bay? There is no question that Nicolet went as far as the Sault. "Beyond this rapid" (Sault) can only refer to the direction of Lake Superior.

Third: Father LeJeune's Relation states that Nicolet said that, if he had continued his journey up a big river for three days, he would have reached the sea. Now this, obviously does not apply to the Fox River in Wisconsin, nor does it seem to apply to the Montrell in Ontario. The explanation is that the French of that time, not nearly so familiar with the native languages as historians would have us believe, misunderstood the meaning of Ouinipigou. They thought it meant "salt water," hence: "the sea," whereas the term actually meant "nasty water," but they also called some other places by this name, such as Green Bay, Lake Winnipeg and Wenebegon Lake (Sudbury County, Ontario). The last might reasonably be reached after a three day's journey up the Montreal River by portage to the Cow River. One map of Nicolet's time shows a small Lac des Puants up a river east of the Sault, which must be the Mississagi and its continuation, the Wenebegon River. ("Puant" is French for "stinking" or "foul smelling.")

Why, then, did Nicolet say the Ouinipigou did not speak Algonquin? In Nicolet's time, Algonquin did not refer to the large family of languages that are today included in the term, Algonquin. At that time, the French used it only for the language now called Ojibwe (Chippewa), as contrasted with the Cree dialect, which they called Montagnais. Therefore, Nicolet's Ouinipigou spoke Cree, not what he called Algonquin, though that is its present classification.

Furthermore, Nicolet mentioned no difficulty in communicating with the Ouinipigou, and he correctly translated the nickname they gave him. No Frenchman at that time had reported any contact with Siouan speakers. Moreover, the nickname showed that their language differed slightly from Ojibwe. The Ojibwe would have called him "Manitou Inini," not "Manitou Ininiou," which is probably the correct version of the Ouinipigou nickname. Of course, Winnebago is not the Wisconsin Winnebago's name for their tribe. (It was Hochenagra, Otchargo, etc.). The Winnebagos were probably called "nasty waters" by the Algonquins because they lived on Green Bay. Father Marquette was also misled by the meaning of Ouinipigou, because he looked all over Green Bay for salt springs and found none, but he said he found plenty of nasty water.

Father Vemont also mentions that Nicolet concluded a major peace agreement with the Ouinipigou. He probably did. But he certainly could not conclude a major agreement with a tribe whose language he could not understand (Winnebago, i.e. Siouan). Yet he would have no trouble communicating with the Algonquin Ouinipigou.

Because Nicolet went north to Lake Superior, rather than west to Lake Michigan, historians must carefully reassess many of the shaky premises of early 17th Century historiography. This necessitates a reinterpretation of the tribal wars, fur trade, and exploration of that period.

The Hurons Go West

The early contacts and friendships with the French by the Hurons and the resulting trade goods that they were able to obtain caused great jealousy between the Hurons and the other neighboring Iroquois tribes. These tribes had nothing that the Hurons wanted to trade for the coveted kettles, iron axes, knives and other various white man's goods. Soon raids on the Hurons began to occur, which eventually became vicious and escalated into a full scale war.

Battle after bloody battle had occurred among the Iroquois until the Hurons were finally driven up the water route of the Algonquins, the Ottawa River, to Lake Nipissing, and down the French River to what soon became known as the lake of the Hurons. They settled in small villages around this great lake, south to the shores on either side of the Detroit River, and to the north shore of Lake Erie. To the French this whole area became known as "Huronia." Several Jesuits, as well as the coureurs de bois, lived in and around Huronia with the Hurons. The long friendship between the French and the Hurons had drawn many French westward.

Two of these Jesuits, Father Isaac Jacques and Father Charles Raymboult, who had been living with the Hurons on Lake Huron, were the first Jesuits to reach the rapids of the Soo. In 1641 they too saw the Saulteurs that Brule had reported fishing the rapids. They named the spot Sault Sainte Marie (the rapids of St. Mary) and the river St. Mary's River.

The Hurons in Lake Superior

The first activity of actual historic record along the shores of the Marquette County area occurred in 1650. In the first half of the 17th Century the Huron Indians had come into greater and greater disfavor with the other tribes of the Iroquois Nation, due primarily to their relationship with the French. The English had colonized the east coast of the present United States and had befriended the more southern Iroquois tribes. Since the English and the French were at odds with one another, the whole Iroquois Nation had sided with the English against a tribe of their own people, the Hurons.

After a series of raids on Huronia by the Iroquois war parties coming out of the east, the Hurons were ever farther dispersed. In the course of time these raids had brought the Iroquois all the way from the St. Lawrence River country to the Mississippi River, the Lake Michigan region and in the north, to the eastern end of Lake Superior. The Hurons had been split into many small bands that fled in all directions.

It was one of these small groups that, in 1650, made its way along the southern shore of Lake Superior. In the present Marquette and Baraga County region, this small bedraggled band of Hurons encountered the friendly woodland Ojibwe. Even though the Hurons were Iroquois and natural enemies of the Ojibwe, they were granted asylum by the large group of Ojibwe in the Keweenaw Bay area. However, the Hurons were not allowed to stay at Keweenaw Bay. They were told they could have their encampment in the bay beyond the point to the east, now known as Huron Bay, and that their berry patch would be at the mouths of the next two rivers to the east. The westernmost of these rivers later became known as the Huron Woman's River, and today is known as the Big Huron River. The smaller river to the east is today known as the Little Huron River, and the name carried over to the group of islands three and a half miles offshore, the Huron Islands. Even further to the east, they were given another berry patch which would ripen a week or two ahead of the other two and would have excellent berries even in a bad year because it was on the top of a mountain, Huron Mountain.

Today the name which came from that small band of frightened, fleeing Indians is given to the whole group of granite knobs in the region, the

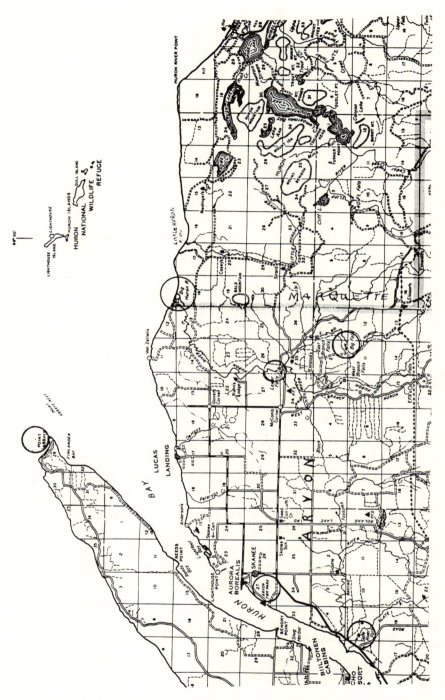

Huron influence in Lake Superior – Huron Bay, Huron Islands, Big Huron River, Little Huron River, Huron River Point, Huron Mountain, Huron Mountain Club, all in the Huron Mountains.

Huron Mountains. This name is sometimes used to refer to the whole tip of the Laurentian shield that is exposed in Marquette and Baraga Counties, all the way from Lake Superior to Highway U.S. 41 and beyond. It is to this small band of Hurons, mostly women and children, who lived on these shores for not more than 20 years over three centuries ago, that these places owe their names.

Observations of Helen L. Paul

From the research of the late Mrs. Helen Longyear Paul, we find some interesting facts and insights about the Ojibwe and Huron Indians. She writes of the name "Tah–qua–men–non," which on the Jesuit map of 1671 we find written "Ou–ta–koua–men–on." Now "Men–on," or as it is often written, "Minong," always referred to a berry field, from the Ojibwe word "Min" (berry) and "ong" (an ending denoting place). We know that the Indian word for Isle Royale was "Minong," which has been translated to mean not only a berry place but a reserved berry place, a place that belonged by tribal right to some special group. "Ou–ta–kua" is a usual Jesuit method of spelling the word we now call "Ottawa." Consequently, the name "outakuamenon" as given on the 1671 map, meant the reserved berry patch of the Ottawa Indians.

This gives us insight into the old Indian name for the Dead River in Marquette. It is written on several early maps and is also mentioned in some of the first geological and government reports. As spelled, the name is "Ne–ka–men–on." These reports were made by Englishmen. Had they been written by Frenchmen, the word would have been spelled with a "qu" instead of a "k" and then it would have been obvious that the first two syllables referred to the Noquet tribe, whose winter quarters were on Bay de Noc, or "Bay de Noquet" near Escanaba, but who moved in June 45 miles north to the blueberry fields of the Dead River, which they regarded as their special reserved blueberry crop.

Reading articles on the household lives of the Ojibwe Indians, we find that they moved at least four times a year following the seasons and the food supply. Winter quarters were established where one could spear fish through the ice. In the spring, the whole tribe made a trek to a sugar–maple grove, which was regarded as inviolable property of that particular tribe, although it might number no more than 20 to 40 people. When the maple sugar season was over the tribe migrated again to the summer location where the squaws could get berries and raise corn, beans, and squash, and where the

Helen Longyear Paul (c. 1931) Courtesy of Phillip Paul (son).

medicine men could grow a little tobacco. In the fall, the tribe moved to a good hunting ground.

It is necessary to understand this method of life, and the fact that food gatherers needed about 200 square miles of territory per person to avoid starvation in the harsh land of Upper Michigan. The Indian tribes of this region were very small. Father Marquette, who passed by these shores in the summers of 1669 through 1671, speaks of the Noquet Indians as occupying the land along the south shore of Lake Superior to the east of Keweenaw Point, and estimated the total number of the tribe to be less that 150 souls. It must have been this band of Noquet, who summered along the shore north of Marquette and wintered at Bay de Noc near Escanaba, that took in the fleeing Hurons in the summer of 1650.

The Noquets had several reasons for coming to what is now Marquette for the summer. Not only were there big fine blueberry patches on the plains near the mouths of the rivers, but there was also the sheltered valley of the Carp River. This was one of the very few locations along the whole south shore where one could raise corn. The old survey map of 1846 shows a small square of "Indian Gardens" located in a bend of the Carp River below the protecting cliffs of Mount Mesnard. These gardens must have been very old because, as mentioned before, many of the copper artifacts found during the white occupation came from this vicinity, and we know that as far back as records go, Carp River was one of the very few places on Superior's south shore where Indian families could live the year around.

In some other observations of Mrs. Paul, we find that the old survey maps and records mention an Indian trail from the mouth of the Little Huron River leading southeasterly toward Huron Mountain, which became a broad, beaten path like a portage when it neared the shore of Mountain Lake at the foot of Huron Mountain on the southwest side. Moreover, in this part of the country this is the only trail leading inland from Lake Superior. This very short, broad trail from the mouth of the Little Huron to the base of Huron Mountain, just a few miles long, is of particular interest. Why should there be such a well–used trail to this spot?

First, the trail would go to Anne Lake (formerly called Portage Lake) and then with just a short portage on to Mountain Lake, the largest in the area. Second, there are the blueberries on Huron Mountain. Third, this became a possible explanation for the "mystery stone." While the Algonquins made nothing with stone in the whole area, the Iroquois, Mrs. Paul suggests, might have. She referred to this stone as an "Indian altar." Then there is still another phenomenon right there at the end of the trail – the only cactus bed in the whole Upper Peninsula.

This is Mrs. Paul's explanation:

> The southern cliffs of Mt. Huron offer the only suitable location for cactus growth to be found anywhere in the region, as most of the other ridges near the Huron River are covered with a heavy growth of timber. This cactus is Opuntia Fragilis, which grows wild in the Dells of Wisconsin and is found nowhere else in Michigan. The area it covers is extremely small to be a wild type, as only a few acres are inhabited by this plant.

Helen Paul felt that it must have been planted there for a reason by someone who knew well the habits of the plant. Even today it is a source of great surprise to anyone who encounters the cactus as it grows profusely on the southern slope of the mountain. Many have returned to Huron Mountain Club after an outing complaining of having accidentally sat in a clump of this cactus, to everyone's amusement.

Helen Paul:

> But why should the Indians have made this strongly marked trail leading to the cactus patch? The answer is found in Hoffman's Indian Researches where he states that cactus spines mixed with the decayed liver of animals was used to anoint the tips of arrows when the Indians went on the warpath, because when shot into a wound they produced a festering sore that would not heal. This little cactus plantation is therefore probably the reason why the mountain also, as well as the river, is named for the disinherited tribe of Hurons. In the histories we find them fighting valorously at the side of their allies, the Ojibwe, so that one is not surprised to find that the only remains they have left behind are of a warlike character.

Not everyone agrees with Helen Paul on this explanation for the cactus on Huron Mountain. There are, however, several untimbered, rocky slopes in the region, similar to Mt. Huron, where no cactus is found, and the actual plot where this cactus is found is less than one acre. Still, some believe it to be a wild species. There is another place in Michigan where wild cactus grows: St. Joseph's County in the extreme southwest corner of southern Michigan. However, this grows in the grass and is a different species altogether.

Book One

The Defeat of the Iroquois

We have spoken of the Iroquois raids that sent the small band of Hurons into the far reaches of Lake Superior in 1650. As a result of these raids into the lower peninsula of Michigan and southern Ontario, these areas were almost completely depopulated. The lower Michigan tribes were driven west. The Potowatami, Sauk, Fox, Massauaketon and others developed new homes in the lands west of Lake Michigan, the ancient home of the Winnebago.

While there was much concern among the French, especially the traders and Jesuits, the Europeans at Quebec and Montreal did not learn the fate of the Huron exiles for several years, as communication was entirely cut off.

In 1653 a great Iroquois war party penetrated the Wisconsin Country. Part of this invading force headed northwest into Lake Superior. The word had traveled far ahead of them, and a counterforce had gathered from the scant population of Ottawa, Chippewa and Hurons living along the south shore of Lake Superior, and was moving east to meet them.

As they approached the east end of the lake the allies became more and more cautious, hiding behind the various points and sending scouts ahead to take advantage of the element of surprise. However, when they met the Iroquois just west of the Soo, even this advantage was not enough to defeat the larger Iroquois war party that had come so many miles determined to wipe out the last Huron. The vanquished defenders fled northeast in the growing darkness to regroup on the Canadian shore, while the victorious Iroquois returned to camp on the nearby point where the ambush had occurred. During the night, the defenders came back and wiped out the whole Iroquois party. This was the "Battle of Iroquois Point." The point where the battle was fought, near Pendill Bay west of Sault Ste. Marie, is called Iroquois Point to this day.

It had been some years since the fur–traders' canoes from the upper lakes had dared run the gauntlet of the hostile Iroquois to get to Montreal, but the news of the Battle of Iroquois Point spread rapidly through the land. With the Iroquois menace gone, it was just a short time before a great fleet of Lake Superior trading canoes set out for Montreal and Quebec, laden with furs. The colonists there welcomed them with open arms. They had never seen so many furs, and were very curious as to where they had come from.

The First Voyageurs

Two Frenchmen made arrangements to return with the trading canoes to discover for themselves the source of such huge amounts of furs. They became the first two Europeans of actual historic record to travel the south shore of Lake Superior, the first two modern Europeans to set foot in what is now Marquette County. These men were Medart Chavart, Sieur de Groseillier, and Pierre Esprit, Sieur de Radisson. They were brothers–in–law, as Medart Groseillier had married the widowed sister of Pierre Radisson.

In 1654 Des Groseillier made his first voyage with the returning Indian canoes into the Great Lakes region. This was nearly a half century after the founding of Quebec. It is well established now that Pierre Radisson, who would have been only 13 or 14 years old at the time, did not accompany the older Groseillier on this first trip, which lasted two years. It is also pretty well established that Groseillier did not go into Lake Superior on this voyage.

Three years later, however, Groseillier and Radisson returned to the Great Lakes country. This time in 1659 they traveled together with Chippewa Indians and for the first time described "Gitchee Gumee," as the Indians called Lake Superior, to the Europeans. The idea of such huge amounts of fresh water in the middle of a continent was entirely new to learned people of the time. As we now know, there is no other spot on earth like it; Lake Superior has the greatest surface area of any lake in the world, and one fifth of the world's fresh water is in the Great Lakes.

Apparently at least one other unknown coureur de bois reached "the upper lake" (lac superieur) but left no good account of what he saw. Sometime before 1658 he must have navigated a part of it, for he left a beautifully colored map in the Paris Archives, with a brief account of what he saw and what the Indians told him about the rest of the lake.

In a written description done some ten years after the trip was made, Radisson told of coming to the rapids which separated Lake Huron from Lake Superior:

This rapids was formerly the residence of the Indians who were with us (Chippewa). We made great cheer with the fish that they call 'Assickmack' which means 'whitefish.' The bear, the beaver, and the moose showed themselves often, but to their cost. Indeed, it was to us like a terrestrial paradise after such long fasting, and such great labors, to find ourselves able to choose our own diet and to rest when we had a mind to...But the season was far spent and we had to use diligence and leave that desirable place...The weather was agreeable when we began to navigate upon the great extent of water so calm and the air so clear. We crossed in a pretty broad place (Whitefish Bay?) and came to an island most delightful for the diversity of its fruits (Grand Island?)...At ten o'clock the same night we gained the firm land, six leagues away. Here we found a small river. I was so curious that I inquired its name. They called it 'pauabickkomefibs,' which means copper. I was taken to a place which was not 200 paces in the woods, where many pieces of copper were uncovered.

Since these writings were done ten years after the trip, it is evident that these events are out of order, and the aforementioned places could have been anywhere along the south shore. It is possible that the copper they uncovered was from a trader's cache. If he was correct, the river would be near Grand Marais.

...from this place we went along the shore, which is most delightful and wondrous, for its nature that made it so pleasant to the eye, the spirit, and the belly. As we went along, we saw banks of sand so high that one of our Indians went up for curiosity. Up there he looked no bigger than a crow. That place is very dangerous when there is a storm, for there is no landing place...After that we came to a remarkable place. It is a bank of rocks that the Indians make sacrifices to. They call it 'Nanitoucksinagoit' which means 'likeness of the devil.' There come here many kinds of birds which make their nests here, including the gulls, which are a white sea bird of the bigness of a pigeon...It's like a great portal (Portal Rock) by reason of the beating of the waves. The lower part of the opening is as big as a tower and grows bigger in going up. There are in that place caves very deep caused by the same violence...The coast of rocks is five or six leagues in length and there is scarcely a place to put a boat in in safety from the waves.

Some days afterwards we arrived at a very beautiful point of land (Pointe Abbaye) where there are three beautiful islands (the Huron Islands). From this place we discovered a bay very deep (Keweenaw Bay) where a river empties itself with a noise, because of the quantity and depth of the water...We found some pools made by beaver (they are in the portage waterway). We must break them in order to pass. The sluice being broken, what a wonderful thing to see the industry of that animal, which had drowned more than twenty leagues of ground and cut all the trees...drowning good soil with dead water,

Three early photos of Pictured Rocks – Is it any wonder that people down through the ages stood in awe of these unique formations produced by the elements?

wherein moss two feet thick grows, and when you think to go safe and dry, if you take not great care, you sink down to...the middle of your body...Having passed that place, we made a portage through the land for two leagues. The way was well beaten because of the (Indian) comers and goers, who by making that passage shorten their trip by eight days around the point which goes very far out into that great lake...In the end of that point there is an island, as I am told, all of copper. This I have not seen. They say that from the island of copper, which is a league in the lake, when they want to cross the lakes in fair weather, beginning from sunrise to sunset, they come to a great island (Isle Royale) from where they come the next morning to firm land. So by reasoning that the Indians accomplish twenty leagues per day (60 miles) that lake should be six score and ten leagues wide.

Such was the first description of the south shore of Lake Superior, written over 300 years ago. There were about a dozen canoes in the party which went as far as Chequamegon Bay, where they built a fort in 1659. Radisson says there is a channel where "We took all kinds of fish, sturgeons of a vast size, and pike seven feet long." He also tells us that the geese were curious and came up to him, and could easily be killed.

They remained the following winter and returned in 1660 to Quebec. While in the Lake Superior country he says they also killed moose, stags, buffalo (he called them wild cows), caribou, fallow does and bucks, and cougars. "Afterwards, however, a very heavy snowfall caused near starvation." Apparently Groseillier and Radisson returned by the northern route. The Groseillier–River has moved up and down the north shore on different maps. Today it is called the Gooseberry River, as "Groseillier" is the French word for gooseberry.

Groseillier had returned from his first voyage with valuable furs. Realizing the potential of the fur trade, he made preparations for the second trip with Radisson, but at the last minute they were unable to be sanctioned by the French government.

After much delay they decided to go anyway, without the sanctions. When they returned from this second voyage with many more furs and much valuable information on the Lake Superior country, they were fined for undertaking the journey without authorization. They appealed without success, so Groseillier and Radisson took their proposal to King Charles II of England. With his authority, the two were instrumental in founding the great Hudson's Bay Company in 1660, thus starting the greatest fur company of all time and today one of the oldest North American corporations.

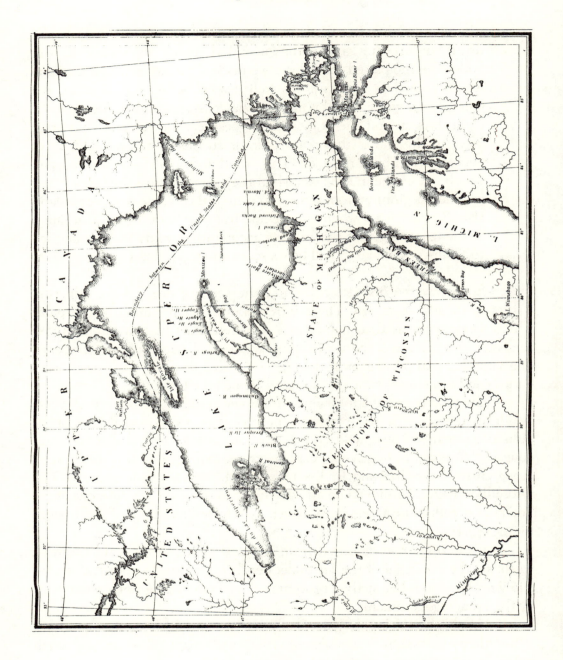

Lake Superior 1845

The next two decades saw the erratic Radisson alternating in the service of France and England in Hudson Bay, Canada, and the Caribbean. In 1687 he became an English subject and spent the rest of his life in London. He died in 1710.

The Coming of the Jesuits

It was on the first voyage that Groseillier learned that there was indeed a band of Hurons living on Lake Superior. When the Jesuits were informed of this, some of them were eager to find the Hurons. The Jesuits were well known to this band when they were in their previous home in the Georgian Bay area of Lake Huron. Now for the first time there was reason to send missionaries to Lake Superior.

When the Indian canoes of the first voyage turned homeward, they carried with them two Jesuits bound for Lake Superior. Neither reached the Grand Lac; one was killed by a straggling Iroquois war party, and the other died alone after being abandoned by the fleeing Ottawa.

The return of the second voyage of Groseillier and Radisson to the Lake Superior country in 1660 consisted of 60 canoes heavily laden with furs. Again two Jesuits were chosen to return with them. After one was for some reason unable to go, Father Rene Menard, a frail, aging priest of 56, was left to be the first Jesuit to enter Lake Superior. He would be the third European to travel the shore of Marquette County.

Menard left Montreal in 1660 and arrived at Keweenaw Bay in mid–October. He had expected to find his friends, the Hurons, somewhere in the Huron Bay area, but was told at Keweenaw Bay that they had all moved west to Chequamegon Bay.

His journey had been a perilous one, and he wrote:

> of many dangers from the lakes, which were very stormy; from the torrents and waterfalls, fearful to behold, which we were forced to cross in a frail shell; from hunger, which was our almost constant companion; and from the Iroquois, who made war upon us.

Being reluctant to go on this late in the season, Father Menard remained with a band of Indians at Keweenaw Bay near L'Anse in the winter of 1660–61. In March he was put out of his hut for rebuking the chief of the tribe for a display of savage behavior. As luck would have it, the weather was unusually mild that spring of 1661, and the priest was able to survive in a shelter of balsam boughs. He was rescued by fur traders who took him to Chequamegon.

There, to his great disappointment, Menard learned from the Ottawas that the Hurons had moved southeast. In May of that year a lone Huron came to Chequamegon with a message that his people were starving to death. Immediately Father Menard started out with the Indian as his guide, in hopes of baptizing as many of them as he could before they were overtaken by death. On some unknown portage he was separated from his companion, and was never seen again.

Recent scholars have attempted to trace his route. The Hurons were somewhere north of Green Bay, and Menard had traveled east to the Ontonagon River. Ascending that river for many miles, he and his guide had made several portages into smaller rivers flowing south. It was in the vicinity of Lac Veux Dessart, it is now believed, that he was carrying goods around a portage while his companion took the canoe through the rapids. Menard apparently lost his way.

In retrospect we can say that Rene Menard was an extremely devout man, and certainly one his Jesuit brothers could look on with great pride. He had spent many years with the Hurons in Ontario and had followed them to the western reaches of Lake Superior, thus being the first person to bring the gospel west of Sault Ste. Marie. Appropriately, a street and a high hill in south Marquette bear his name. Mount Mesnard (the modern spelling), just south of the present Shiras Hills subdivision, is the highest elevation in the city and had a surge tank erected on it in 1912, used in connection with the small hydroelectric plant on the Carp River. It was taken out of service in 1980. In 1962, a tourist attraction and lookout area was built on Mount Mesnard by Don Pearce of Marquette, just north of the surge tank. The name of the tourist attraction is Mount Marquette, and this has caused some confusion, but the rock knob on the hill is still Mount Mesnard. Mount Marquette only operated for six or seven years. In the early 1980's the Kaufman Ski Hill was built on the north slope of Mount Mesnard, which further added to the confusion.

Father Claude Allouez

Four years after the death of Rene Menard, the next "blackrobe," as these Jesuits were affectionately called, made his way to Lake Superior with a

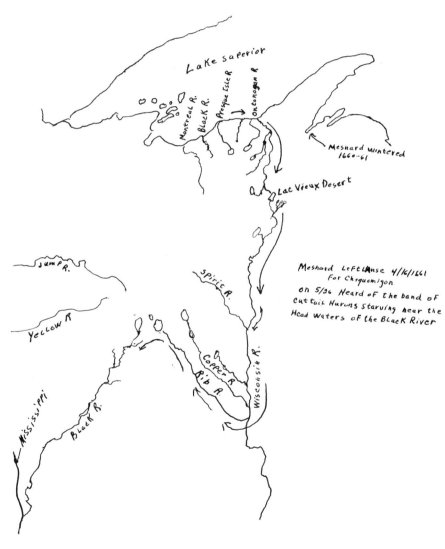

Speculated route of Rene Menard (not drawn to scale).

returning band of Ottawa fur–trading canoes. In Quebec it seemed as though Chequamegon at the Apostle Islands was a place where many Indians of the various tribes congregated, and it was decided to establish a mission there.

A strong young priest of 28 was chosen, Father Claude Allouez. He was destined to do great works among the Ottawa–Chippewa and the Hurons at Chequamegon and Green Bay over the ensuing years. In 1665, Allouez made the treacherous journey up the Ottawa River to Lake Huron and along the south shore of Lake Superior, and established a mission at Chequamegon which he named La Pointe du Saint Esprit, after the long sand spit that extended out into the bay. The name "La Pointe" is still used there to denote a small village on the nearest island to Bayfield, Wisconsin, and is the oldest name in Wisconsin conferred by a white man.

We must remember that only the land of Upper Michigan was known to the Europeans at that time, and no white man had visited the lower peninsula because of the hostility of the Iroquois toward the French. The Iroquois lived around Lakes Erie and Ontario, and this prevented any trade in that area. The only route open to explorers was the route the friendly Hurons had shown them.

A year or so after the mission at La Pointe was established, Allouez realized that many of the Hurons were near Green Bay. He asked for, and was granted, permission to establish another mission in that area. On the Fox River, where De Pere, Wisconsin is now, Father Allouez started the Mission of St. Francis Xavier. Allouez remained in the Great Lakes region for many years, and has been honored with the naming of a county in Wisconsin and a small community near the southern border of Keweenaw County.

Father Marquette

It was soon realized that Sault Ste. Marie was a focal point of all the travelers to the Lake Superior region and the great northwest, even more important than La Pointe. In 1668, Father Jacques Marquette was sent to Sault Ste. Marie to start a mission there. The following year he was joined by his superior, Father Claude Dablon.

The founding of the mission at the Soo by Father Marquette makes that city the oldest in the Midwest, and Marquette a special person in the realm of Michigan history. However, his greatest works were yet to come. With Allouez having gone to Green Bay, Marquette was asked in 1669 to go check on things in La Pointe.

Book One

In a letter written at Chequamegon Bay about this first trip along the south shore of Lake Superior (then called Lac du Tracy) in 1669, Marquette wrote:

> ...on my arrival here, after months' navigation of snow and through ice, which closed my way and kept me in constant peril of life.

Marquette arrived at La Pointe in September of 1669. It took him over a month of traveling to get there, so it is safe to assume that he made much of his trip in August. In the "Book of Huron Mountain," William R. Folsom writes of this freakish summer blizzard that:

> There seem to have been great climatic changes taking place in the Huron Mountain Region in the three intervening centuries.

Others report it as just unseasonable weather or an unusual year.

Up to this time we have seen only five or six white men pass these Marquette County shores, in the half century or more that the "Grand Lac" was known to Europeans. These, however, are only the ones of record. There were hundreds of Indians who paddled these shores, and now there were fur traders in ever increasing numbers – at first Indians bringing their winter "take" to Montreal and Quebec, and then the French voyageurs. Otter, marten, and mink, but mainly beaver were the furs brought to trade in Quebec and Montreal for a surprising assortment of goods, few of which the Indians had ever seen before. They especially liked the iron kettles, axes, knives, and other iron products. Cloth from England, beads from Italy, brandy from France, and guns and gunpowder. At first these were luxuries, but as time went on they became necessities. The Indians were slowly building up a trade that would soon be taken over by the white fur traders, then the fur companies and the voyageurs.

Lake Superior, called "Gitchee Gumee" (big water) by the Indians, was called the "Grand Lac" (big lake) or "Lac Superieur" (upper lake) by the French. It was called "Lake Tracy" by Allouez and Marquette in 1666–71 and "Lake Conde" by 1685. Marquette's map calls Lake Superior "Lac Superieur ou de Tracy" – the upper lake of Tracy. Tracy was the Marquis de Alexandre de Prouville Tracy, commander of military forces in New France after 1671.

As late as 1819 the name "Lake Algoma" was used, but the Indian "Gitchee Gumee" and the French "Superieur" seem to have prevailed through the centuries.

65

It was on this great Lake Superior that one name became more famous than all the rest: Pere Jacques Marquette. Actually Father Marquette originally was to be sent to the land of the Illinois Indians. It was for this mission that he studied their language for two years in Quebec. He had arrived from France as a young priest of 28 in 1666. In two years he had learned several dialects of the Illinois Indians, as well as dialects of the Ottawa–Chippewa and Huron. He seemed to have an ear for the difficult Indian dialects, and was said to have known six or seven of them. In contrast, his superior, Father Dablon, could not speak any.

The Jesuit Fathers of Quebec had one job for Marquette to complete before going to the land of the Illinois: to start the mission at Sault Ste. Marie.

Being at the Soo with Father Dablon in 1669 when Allouez had gone to Green Bay and left La Pointe without a priest, it was logical that Marquette was asked to spend the winter there before heading to his appointed task among the Illinois.

This trip to La Pointe, his first on Lake Superior, was the one made under such adverse conditions, battered by cold winds and snow. The lake was said to be full of ice chunks that constantly tore at their fragile canoes, and they were always soaking wet. Often a fire could not be started, and they were forced to huddle under their canoe or what protection they could find until conditions were such that they could continue their western journey.

Marquette at Marquette

Father Marquette's second trip on Lake Superior, returning from La Pointe to the Soo, was made in April of 1670. This trip was with a flotilla of Indian trading canoes. The weather was warm, and the trip relatively pleasant. Legend has it that one of the campsites commonly used by these Indians was what is now Lighthouse Point, just north of Marquette's lower harbor. There were good campsites which were commonly used about 30 or 40 miles apart on the south shore of Lake Superior. Traveling west from Grand Marais along the Pictured Rocks, one came to another one of the famous campsites in and around Munising Bay, the most used being on Grand Island. Covering the next 40 or 50 miles, which was a good day's paddle into the wind, brought them to another famous camping spot at Lighthouse Point. In Munising, protection could be found on all sides, and likewise at Lighthouse Point; because of the lay of the beaches there, shelter could be found from nearly any wind. Since the winds are usually westerly or

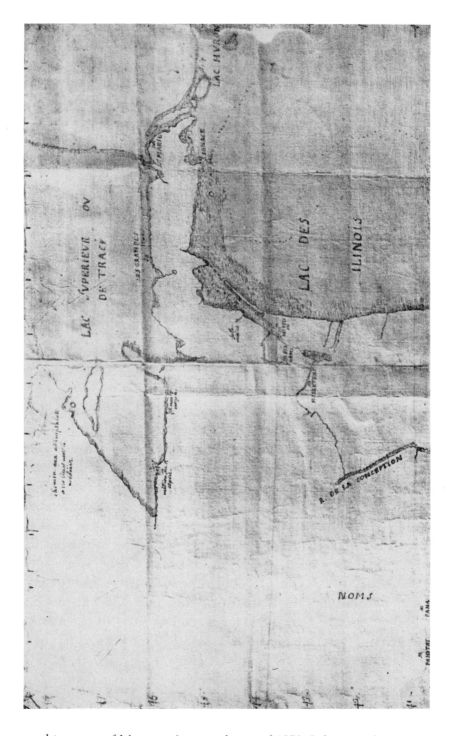

A copy–machine copy of Marquette's original map of 1872. It has now been moved to the Archives de la Compagnee de Jesus, Province du Canada–francais, Saint Jerome, P. Quebec.

northwesterly, the beach which faces southeast, with rocks on each end (now in front of the Coast Guard Station) was the most frequently used. At this time the beach was broad, and a thick forest would have hung over it from a rather abrupt hill behind. Local Indians told Peter White that this became Father Marquette's favorite stopover site.

Father Marquette assumed that he would be sent to the Illinois country after he reached the mission at the Soo, and did not expect to return to Chequamegon Bay. However, due to an impending war with the Sioux Indians to the west of La Pointe, some of the Ottawa–Chippewa came east to Sault Ste. Marie. Some came for refuge, but others were seeking help in the form of arms or allies. A Sioux chieftain had been killed by a band of young Chippewa braves, and revenge was inevitable.

Marquette decided that he had to return to La Pointe that same fall and spend the winter convincing as many as possible to return with him to the eastern end of the lake the following spring. It is very likely that, on this third trip along Superior's south shore in the fall of 1670 and on his fourth and last trip in the spring of 1671, Marquette made notes of shoreline features for the map he made of the south shore of the Lake. The map itself was drawn at the Mission of St. Francis Xavier near Green Bay after he returned from his famous exploration of the Mississippi with Louis Joliet in 1673. This map is presently in the archives of the College Sainte Marie in Montreal. It is too accurate to have been drawn completely from memory.

Indian legends also tell us that Marquette said a Mass at Lighthouse Point; there is no other record of it but as with all the legends, it was known by all the Indians who frequented Lake Superior. To bear out the legend, Marquette's map only shows one prominent river on the whole north crest of the Upper Peninsula and another small one in Whitefish Bay near the Soo. The one river shown starts in an inland lake and flows into what has to be the huge bay between Lighthouse Point and Shot Point, sometimes called Iron Bay or Marquette Bay. This would be the Carp River and the lake could only be Teal Lake. Today the Carp River runs into and out of Deer Lake, north of Ishpeming, and that is the main source of the river. Deer Lake has been dammed up to form a huge basin. Formerly the river also ran out of Teal Lake, but since the water of Teal Lake is being used by the city of Negaunee, very little flows into the Carp at the present time. It would seem that if Marquette made a point of putting one inland lake, the river coming from it, and a special bay on his map, that he had a special interest and familiarity with this particular area, either from his own experience or from having talked at length with Indians who lived there. The accuracy of the map and the Indian legend support each other. It seems very likely that Marquette said a Mass at Lighthouse Point.

There is also no record of when this Mass was said, but it was evidently in the spring of 1671, when he was making his fourth and final trip along the south shore.

Marquette Again at Marquette

The circumstances of this particular journey are unprecedented. Marquette spent the winter of 1670–71 traveling from family to family throughout the Chequamegon Bay area, convincing his flock that they should return with him to a place to be chosen by Father Dablon. The word had traveled far and wide that the migration would take place in the spring of 1671.

It is said that Indian freighters could travel 40 to 60 miles or more in a day depending on winds and weather, but this trip, in 1671, was a migration of four or five hundred people in nearly 200 various–sized canoes. The trip was made very slowly, probably covering as little as ten or 12 miles on some days; it would be difficult to average more than 20 miles a day under the circumstances. Broad, flat open forest land or pleasant sandy beaches would be their choice for campsites. In Marquette County the protection of Lighthouse Point was the best. The mouth of the Huron Woman's River, Cliff River (Pine River today) Beach, Conway Beach, Squaw Beach, Middle Island, Little Presque Isle or around Presque Isle all were good, and they could have used any of them.

What a regatta this must have been! Scores of various sized and shaped canoes with families, old and young people, dogs, babies in their tickinaggons and all their worldly possessions. Certainly this was the occasion that the Mass was said at Lighthouse Point. Chances are that many Indians living along the shore attended the Mass. Such a spectacle would linger in the legends of a people for hundreds of years. Indirectly this was the legend that gave the city of Marquette its name and coincidentally was exactly 200 years before Marquette's incorporation as a city in 1871.

The Carp River area and the river itself seems to have had a very great significance to the Indians, and played an important role in the lives of the Indians and the early white settlers. Besides the short trail from the Little Huron River to the base of Huron Mountain, there were several other well–used trails. There was one main trail which followed the shoreline of Lake Superior. At present Au Train there was a trail leading south to Bay de

Noc, and from L'Anse at the head of Keweenaw Bay was another trail heading south to Lac View Dessart. Then there was a heavily traveled trail along the Carp River at present Marquette. It went from Lake Superior to Teal Lake, where it split into two parallel trails to Lake Michigamme, from which was a canoe route to Lake Michigan via the Michigamme River and the Menominee River. Somewhere a half–day trip up the Carp are supposed to be some pictographs mentioned by Henry Schoolcraft. It was the site of the first settlement in Marquette County, and near its mouth was an age–old Indian dwelling site. It was used as a route to the early iron deposits, and is the grave site of Chief Marjegeesick. The Carp River is worthy of being the only river on Marquette's map; except perhaps the Ontonagon, there is no other of such importance.

Marquette at St. Ignace

Father Claude Dablon had chosen Mackinac Island as the new home of the migrating Ottawa–Chippewa and Huron Indians, who had returned to La Pointe after the Mission was started there. Dablon spent the winter of 1670–71 on the island, and established the Mission of St. Ignatius. When Marquette and his Indians arrived there in 1671 they remained on the island only a short time, then decided for reasons of food supply and possible attack that it would be to their advantage to be on the mainland. Marquette chose a spot on the nearby mainland and set up the mission there. This is the site of the city of St. Ignace today. Marquette had known this mission from its beginnings, and it became his pride. It is named for the patron saint of the Jesuit Order. Today, St. Ignace is considered the second oldest city in Michigan, and both of the first two are credited with having been started by Father Jacques Marquette.

This completes the story of Father Marquette on Lake Superior, and it leaves no doubt as to why his name should be so well remembered here, but even at this point he had not yet accomplished his greatest works.

Marquette had sent word to France of a huge south–flowing river far to the west of Lake Superior. King Louis XIV was taking great interest in the new world, and that year (1671) Jean Talon had sent St. Lusson to put on a great ceremony at Sault Ste. Marie before a host of Indians who had gathered there for the occasion. St. Lusson proclaimed all the land surrounding the Great Lakes to be New France. Talon, who was the Intendent or Governor of New France and still eager to find a route to the western sea, commissioned Louis Joliet, a coureur de bois from Quebec, to explore the great river and find out which ocean it entered.

70

Book One

Marquette on the Mississippi

On December 8, 1672, Joliet arrived at St. Ignace with authorization from Father Dablon for Father Marquette to accompany him. It was customary in those days to send a priest along on such expeditions, and since Marquette was well–known among the Indians and could speak with most they would be encountering, he was a good choice. He also had a personal interest in knowing about the great river.

The first leg of the journey was to see Father Allouez at the Fox River. The Indians from there took them as far as the headwaters of the Wisconsin River, near what is now Portage, Wisconsin. Descending the Wisconsin, they reached the Mississippi. It was during this trip down the Wisconsin that Marquette first became ill with what is now believed to be typhoid fever. Marquette was extremely ill during the rest of the journey.

When they reached the Illinois country they found many tracks on the riverbank. Following a well–beaten path, the party came to a village of Illinois Indians. These Indians were amazed that Marquette could speak with them in their own tongue, and grew very fond of him. They asked him to remain among them.

Marquette explained the mission of the expedition, and told the Illinois that he would return to them when he and Joliet had determined the destination of the Mississippi.

Unlike the northern tribes, the various tribes of the Illinois had one great chief who ruled over all the people. They were cultured, peaceful, and highly agricultural. The expedition was taken to their chief, who gave Marquette a highly decorated calumet (peace pipe) in hopes of giving them a safe journey among the hostile tribes further south.

Marquette used the calumet to good advantage when they reached the fork of the Arkansas River. They were informed by the Indians there that the Mississippi entered the Gulf of Mexico and that the Spanish were there. The expedition turned north again and traveled up the Illinois and Kankakee Rivers. With the aid of the friendly Kankakee Indians, they portaged into the Chicago River. Again the Indians begged Marquette to remain, but he was so sick – at this point having to be carried – that he told them he must return to Green Bay and remain with Father Allouez for the winter. He promised to return when he had regained his strength.

Marquette and Joliet descended the Chicago River and camped at its mouth. They then traveled up the west coast of Lake Michigan to Green Bay, where Marquette remained the winter of 1673–74 with Father Allouez. It was at this time that Marquette drew his map of the south shore of Lake Superior that shows the detail of Marquette Bay, the Carp River, and Teal Lake.

Louis Joliet headed back to Montreal with the report on the exploration of the Mississippi, but right at the end of his long journey, with a full view of Montreal before him, his canoe capsized in the Lachine Rapids, his voyageurs were all drowned, and his journal lost forever. Louis escaped with his life, but it was the journal of Jacques Marquette which then became the official document of the expedition. It was sent to Quebec some time after his death, and had to be released by the church before it could be sent to France.

Joliet did no more exploring for France. He was given a large piece of the Island of Anticosti in the St. Lawrence, where he lived out his life.

Marquette, desperately ill, fulfilled his promise to return to the land of the Illinois late in the summer of 1674. The Indians built a log cabin for him on the bank of the south branch of the Chicago River, and took care of him there during the winter of 1675. He had done his greatest works that fall and had covered a great deal of ground as a sick man. He and his party left the cabin on March 30, 1675, to go back to the Illinois Indians. He was so weak and sick at this time that he was actually carried from place to place, but even in this condition he preached, baptized and carried out a tremendous amount of priestly duties.

Realizing that he did not have long to live, Father Marquette asked if he could be taken to his mission in St. Ignace, where he could die among his own people. He considered St. Ignace his mission and his home. The torturous journey up the windswept east coast of Lake Michigan ended when Marquette said he was too weak to go on. He thought if he could rest a few days he could possibly muster enough strength to continue the voyage on to St. Ignace. His companions found a secluded spot near a backwater at the mouth of a river, where they made a shelter in which the dying priest could rest.

Jacques Marquette died on May 18, 1675, just 14 days before his 38th birthday. He was buried at the mouth of the Pere Marquette River in Ludington. Today this spot is marked by an iron cross.

A few years after his death, Marquette's remains were taken to St. Ignace by a group of Ottawa from his own mission there. His bones, washed and placed in a carefully made birchbark casket, were buried beneath a church on June 9th, 1677. The casket was buried as close as possible to the altar, resting Indian–fashion on wooden supports. In 1706 the village was burned by the French to keep it out of the hands of the British, and the burning floor of the church, together with pieces of timber from above, fell on the tomb and burned the top and sides of the casket. Two years later the mission was renewed and a new church built in "Old Mackinac."

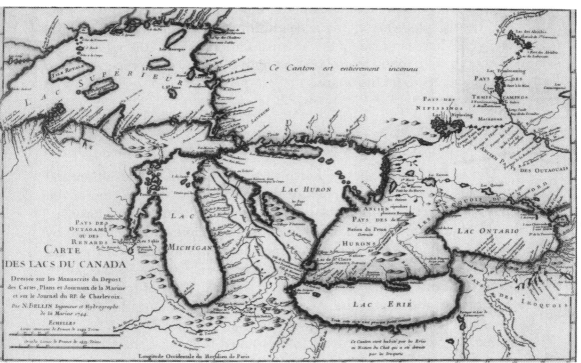

Top: The grave of Pere Marquette, Marquette Park, St. Ignace. Picture taken about 1908.
Bottom: Highly respected cartographer N. Bellin's map of the upper lakes, even as late as 1744, showed the "phantom islands" or islands that did not exist on Lake Superior.
By permission of Clements Library, University of Michigan, Ann Arbor, Michigan.

Marquette Park at St. Ignace

By the 200th anniversary of the death of Pere Marquette, the ground where the first church once stood had fallen into the hands of Mr. David Murray. He was asked if a search might be made on the property, but he would not give permission. Then he was approached by the chief pastor of the diocese, Bishop Mrak, who dug the first spadeful of dirt opening the ground when Mr. Murray gave in. A long trench was dug and soon pieces of timber, hewn planks and joists were uncovered, both burned and rotted. Finally, remains of the birchbark casket were recovered, and 30 or 40 pieces of bone were found. These were gathered by Father Edward Jacker, Pastor of St. Ignace from 1873 to 1878. He later became well–known in Marquette when he was appointed the first administrator of the diocese there.

Again the bones were washed; at this time some were sent to Marquette University in Milwaukee, but most were replaced where they had been found. In 1882 the present monument was erected over the grave, and the area was named Marquette Park. This, however, did not end the digging. In 1973, nearly 300 years after his death, an archeological team from the University of Michigan made a dig at this location. Again, the ashes of the burned church were found, corroborating both the story and proper location for modern scientists and historians.

New France

The upper lakes region – north of the Great Lakes and all around Lake Superior – was first mentioned to the Europeans as the "region of the Saguenay" and later a more defined area around Lake Huron as "Huronia." During the time so far reviewed, this land, though unofficially controlled by the French, was under no governmental jurisdiction. Michigan was the land of the Algonquin, the land of the "Three Fires" – Chippewa in the north, Ottawa in the center, and Potowatami in the south. West of Lake Superior were the Sioux, and south and east of Lakes Erie and Ontario were the Iroquois.

But by 1670, intendant Jean Talon wanted to expand the territory of King Louis XIV of France. He felt something must be done soon, as the Hudson's Bay Company would soon be sending agents down to Lake Superior. He sent Nicolas Perrot, an explorer familiar with native languages, to assemble all the northern tribes at the rapids of the Soo the following spring.

To represent the King, Talon sent Francis Dumont, Sieur de St. Lusson. And so on June 14, 1671, amid great ceremony attended by crowds of Indians and four Jesuit missionaries, St. Lusson proclaimed all the lands in the Great Lakes region as "New France." He did not know how much territory he had claimed for the King, nor where its boundaries were, but we can be sure that it included all of the present Upper Peninsula of Michigan. This was the same year that Father Marquette established his mission at St. Ignace, which soon became one of New France's most important western outposts and lasted for many years.

However, a year later in 1672, even before Marquette and Joliet left on their famous expedition to the Mississippi, a new governor for New France had arrived: Louis de Buade, Count Frontenac. In time Frontenac became New France's greatest governor, serving until 1682 and then again from 1689 to 1698. Between 1689 and 1763, Britain and France were engaged in four wars on both sides of the Atlantic. In America they were called King William's War (1689–1697), Queen Anne's War (1702–1713), King George's War (1744–1748), and the French and Indian War (1754–1761). In Europe the wars had different names and dates. No battles of any of these wars were fought in Michigan, although many men from Michigan, both Indian and European, went to far–off places to do battle on the side of France.

The Voyage of the Griffin

In 1679 La Salle built the "Griffin" above Niagara Falls. The idea was to have a ship that would take the place of many fur–trading canoes. Though it never got into Lake Superior, it did skirt the south shore of the Upper Peninsula in Lake Michigan, and should be mentioned here because it was the first sailing ship on the Great Lakes.

Launched on her maiden voyage in June of the same year, she made her way to Green Bay through Lakes Erie, St. Clair, Huron and Michigan (then known as Lake of the Illinois). In late September she was loaded with furs and headed back, but was lost in a storm, presumably somewhere in the Georgian Bay of Lake Huron. She was never seen or heard of again. The voyage of the Griffin proved the superiority of the Ojibwe canoes for carrying on the fur trade, and it was over a century before they were challenged again for that purpose.

THE CORRECT RIG OF THE GRIFFIN.

Top: The Griffin
Bottom: Voyageurs shooting a rapids in a North canoe. The original of this painting, by artist Frances Hopkins, is in the Public Archives of Canada in Ottawa. Courtesy of Jerry Smith.

La Salle, who was not on the Griffin when it went down, waited in vain for her to return to Lake Michigan. He later went down the Mississippi by canoe and claimed that region all the way to New Orleans for France.

The Era of the Voyageurs

The fur trade had begun to increase in the late 1600's and now, due to demands for furs in Europe, the trading routes had increased in size, going north and west out of Lake Superior all the way to the region of the Great Slave Lake and beyond.

This was the era of the "Voyageurs," probably the most colorful period in Lake Superior's long history. In 1763 Britain took over the land of the upper lakes region from France, including all of the Upper Peninsula. By then the fur trade was just reaching its peak, and the French voyageurs continued to flourish under British rule and even later, when the Americans took over in 1783.

Grace Les Nute, probably the greatest authority on Lake Superior history, describes these hardy people in her book Lake Superior:

> The Northwest Company had in its employ several thousand voyageurs, or canoemen, besides the guides, interpreters and clerks. The voyageurs have the distinction of being one of the few classes of men in American and Canadian history who have been unique on this continent, not only in their origin as a class, but also in their manner of life, customs, language and dress. They came from the Canadian–French settlements along the lower St. Lawrence, where the traditions of voyaging into the Indian country had been handed down from father to son for several generations. It was considered a proper social step in those communities for a young man to go into the pays d'en haut, the upper country, on trading expeditions in the employ of some bourgeois. To take this step one made an engagement with an agent of the trading company, which specified the wages and other terms of the contract. In May an expedition would be sent out from Montreal – several canoes organized into a "brigade." The vessels of this flotilla were birch bark canoes, but not of the simple Indian style. They were about forty feet long and had to be carried on the portages by several men, where an Indian canoe could be carried by one man.

The voyageurs had their final fling in Montreal, said their emotional farewells, assembled at the pier of the Northwest Company above the Lachine Rapids clad in their plumes and best regalia, heard their last Mass at St. Anne's, and pushed off to the strains of one of their paddling songs. They were renowned for these songs. The Irish poet, Thomas Moore, heard them singing on a trip, and was so impressed that he wrote a famous poem in imitation of one of their best–loved songs. The words of the first stanza are:

Faintly as tolls the evening chime
Our voices keep tune and our paddles keep time
Soon as the woods on shore look dim,
We'll sing at St. Anne's our parting hymn,
Row brothers, row, the stream runs fast
The rapids are near, and the daylight's past.

Their route led them up the Ottawa River, through Lake Nipissing, down the French River into Georgian Bay, across the top of the Huron, up the St. Mary's, around the falls at the Soo, into Lake Superior. If they were going to points along the south shore they of course took the southern route to La Pointe. Most, however, were bound north and west; these took the great arc of the lake on the north shore.

The Voyageurs were renowned for their strength, docility and cheery dispositions. They were almost invariably courteous. They were proud of their race, their origins, their language and their metier. The highest praise a voyageur could give to anyone was "That is a voyageur." Ten to fifteen of them manned a Montreal canoe: six to ten a north canoe. Their packs, whether of trade goods or furs, almost invariably weighed ninety pounds. Two of the packs was the usual burden for a voyageur in making a portage. Some boasted of carrying many more, however.

Upon arrival at their destination, it was with flag flying proudly from the stern of the canoe, the bouts (end paddlers) standing in great state in the high, pointed ends of the craft, twelve or so red–bladed paddles puncturing the water of Lake Superior in unison to the tune of a lively song, and every voyageur clad in his best array. The descendants of these proud people are found throughout the Lake Superior towns and villages, but the hundreds of songs and the music they went to are, for the most part, lost.

So these were the voyageurs, the canoemen who plied the waters of Lake Superior on their way to the pays d'en haut from the time of Marquette to the middle of the 19th Century. In the last few decades (since 1960) there have been attempts to locate and revive some of their songs before they are all lost.

As the fur trade reached further into the northwest, there developed two groups of voyageurs – the "Nor'westers" and the "Pork–eaters." The Nor'westers lived in the Canadian wilderness, gathering furs from the Indians of that region. Each spring they would make the long, treacherous journey over the sometimes still ice–clogged rivers to the rendezvous at Grande Portage. The Grande Portage was nine miles long from Grande Portage Bay on Lake Superior to Fort Charlotte (named after the wife of King George III of England) on the Pigeon River. This portage bypasses a 20–mile series of falls at the mouth of the Pigeon River.

The Pork–eaters were called this because their food on the 2,500–mile trip from Montreal to Grande Portage, consisted of corn that had been soaked in lye to get the shell off, and pork fat. This was mixed ahead of time and carried on the trip. About a quart a day would supply one voyageur with enough energy for his strenuous work. The Nor'westers' ration was pemmican, a mixture of powdered buffalo meat and grease. The buffalo meat was dried and pounded with heavy sticks to a powder, then mixed with the fat.

During the French period on Lake Superior, Indians from the Upper Peninsula rallied to the call of their French rulers again and again at Mackinac to defend New France. The French were successful in turning most of the Lake Superior tribes against the English. These allies of New France poured out of the woods of Michigan, Wisconsin and Minnesota, journeying even as far as Montreal and Niagara to participate in French assaults on the extended British frontier.

In 1731, La Verendrye, (known as the pioneer explorer of the prairies) with members of his family, passed through Lake Superior. A year later he established Fort St. Pierre on Rainey Lake. This post, and others after it, lasted nearly through the 19th Century. The voyageurs did much passing back and forth to all these posts of the Upper Lakes to keep them supplied with men and materials. Each little garrison in the west, especially La Pointe, faithfully supplied its quota of men to fight the battle of France against General Braddock, Robert Rogers and George Washington. Nearly all of them took the south shore route, traveling along the Marquette County shore and camping at the favorite campsites each night on their way through Lake Superior.

In 1763, and after the decisive battle between Generals Wolfe and Montcalm had been fought on the Plains of Abraham at Quebec September 13, 1759, the British took over the land and the fur trade in the Great Lakes.

One of the first British fur traders to arrive at the Straits of Mackinac was 24–year–old Alexander Henry, disguised as a Frenchman for his safety. Within a few weeks he found himself embroiled in an Indian uprising that resulted in the capture of Fort Michelimackinac. The uprising later became known as "Pontiac's Conspiracy."

For almost a century the British had been working to gain the favor of the Indians. They had sold the Indians liquor when the French hesitated, had paid more for pelts, and had given the Indians gifts. Following the French and Indian War and after the English had taken over, all favors stopped.

Sir Jeffrey Amherst, commander of the British forces in America, decreed that the giving of presents must stop, that the Indians get only goods for their furs, and that the sale of liquor to the Indians be cut drastically. To add to these changes, with independent traders breaking up the French hold on the fur trading, an epidemic of cheating began. British soldiers were scornful of the Indians, and taunted them for their gullibility.

Early in May, Chief Pontiac besieged Fort Detroit and on June 2nd, 1763, the attack took place at Fort Michelimackinac. During an apparently friendly game of baggatway honoring King George's birthday, some 400 Indians had assembled outside the palisade walls of the fort. The gates were open, and the playing ball was purposefully tossed over the stockade wall into the Fort. As the young warriors swept into the fort, Indian women who had been watching the games handed them weapons that they had concealed under their clothes and blankets.

The Indians did not harm the French, but slaughtered 21 British and captured another 20, some of whom were later tortured and killed, and a few eaten. Because young Alexander Henry had previously been adopted by Chief Wawatam, the chief spoke on his behalf at the council fire, and his life was spared.

Pontiac had formed a great plan to have Indians simultaneously attack the forts at St. Joseph, Green Bay, Fort Pitt, Niagara and Sandusky. The conspiracy was generally considered unsuccessful because Pontiac was unable to take Detroit.

Soon the British were reviving the French transportation system by river, lake and portage to the interior. The peak of the fur trade was reached about the time of the American revolution. In 1774 a total of 60 huge canoe loads of furs were moved over the Grand Portage into Lake Superior from Canada alone, and furs were still coming into the small trading posts along the south shore of Lake Superior, such as those at La Pointe, Grand Island, and Grand Marais and, possibly, one at the mouth of the Carp at Marquette, although at this late date it would have been abandoned. The Montreal traders had built a strong, growing concern which neither the Hudson's Bay Company nor the American colonists could break into. However, the free–wheeling competition had its harmful effects.

Alexander Henry, visiting Grand Portage in 1775, said that the traders:

> were in a state of extreme hostility, each pursuing his own interests in such a manner as might most injure his neighbor.

To protect themselves, they began to form partnerships and companies. The Northwest Company emerged as the most profitable of these partnerships.

During the English regime (1763–1783) both Alexander Henry and Jonathan Carver wrote descriptions of Lake Superior, but neither mentions any of the shoreline of Marquette or Baraga Counties.

With his partner, Cadotte, Alexander Henry spent the winter of 1765 at the head of Lake Superior. From his travels along the peninsular waterways he reported silver on the Iron River and considerable virgin copper at Michipicoten. In 1770, Alexander Henry and Alexander Baxter formed the first mining company to exploit the silver and copper of the region.

Henry built a barge and a 40–ton sloop, the first ever to sail on Lake Superior. The purpose of this combination was to haul copper from a mining venture in Ontonagon in 1771 and 1772. After establishing a camp and laying out the work, Henry returned to the Sault for the winter. The next spring, his schooner was loaded with supplies and dispatched to the mouth of the Ontonagon where, much to the surprise of those in charge, they found the entire party awaiting their arrival. The miners had dug a shaft horizontally into a clay bluff during the winter, and when the frost left the ground it all caved in. This was the end of this venture.

Alexander Henry on Lake Superior

Henry was the first to describe large chunks of copper in the sand on the banks of the Ontonagon River. He also mentions the "Ontonagon Boulder," a huge piece of copper found on a sand bar weighing upwards of three thousand pounds, and shown to him by Indians. While the Ontonagon venture failed, he did mine some copper later on Michipicoten Island, some of which was said to have reached England.

Alexander Henry was one of the most colorful traders in the upper lakes region. He led an extremely exciting and almost charmed life. At 21, as a soldier in the King's army, he nearly died when his boat was swamped in the Lachine Rapids; about a year later, as a fur trader, he took refuge from a blizzard in an Indian camp and was attacked by an angry Indian. He escaped by fleeing down the ice–filled St. Lawrence in a leaky canoe. Later his French Fur Trader disguise was discovered at Fort Michelimackinac, and 60 Chippewas in war paint marched to the cabin where he was hiding in a garret. They searched to no avail, but later he was turned over to the Indians by the French family who had hidden him. An Indian named Wenniway held a knife to his throat, then apparently for no reason dropped the knife and walked away. An hour later another brave came for Henry and took him outside. The brave had Henry strip so that his clothes wouldn't be bloodstained when the brave wore them after Henry was murdered, but Henry was spared this time also. There were other trying moments, including the time of near–starvation while wintering with Indians in the woods of Upper Michigan.

Alexander Henry must have camped often along the shores of Marquette and Baraga Counties, but there is no record of where or when. There is, however, a powder horn at the Marquette County Historical Museum with the name John Gould and a date of Dec. 12, 1776. It is apparent that he camped at what is now the foot of Baraga Avenue some time after that date. It was found about 75 years later, by Amos R. Harlow.

This was during the days leading up to, and during, the American Revolution. Fur trading in the northwest ran a brisk, uninterrupted course throughout the Revolution, with Detroit and Niagara handling almost a fourth of the pelts exported from Canada during that period.

The United States Takes Over the North Country

It was in 1783, at the Treaty of Paris, that Benjamin Franklin drew the border between Canada and the United States. Legend has it that he drew the line from the West into Lake Superior, dipped his quill, then, knowing of the copper on Isle Royale, drew the line north of that island to put it within the U.S. border, even though the island is only 15 miles from the Canadian shore and 45 miles from the American shore.

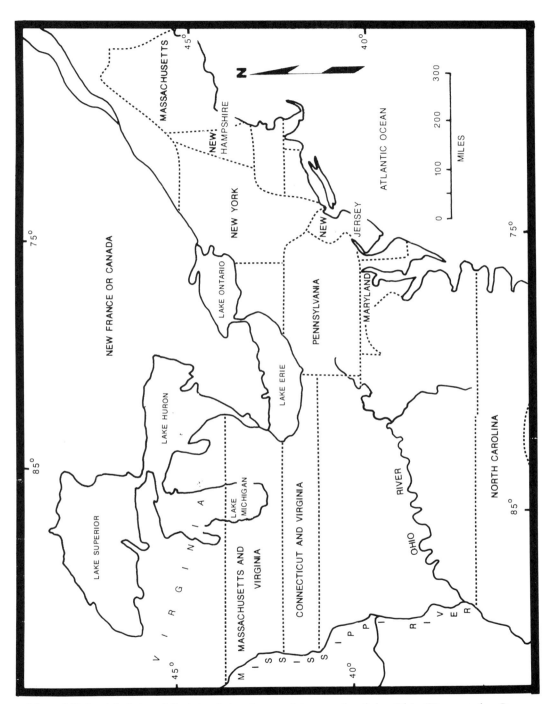

Map of Colonial claims. Virginia claimed everything north of the Ohio River to the Great Lakes. Map produced at cartography lab of N.M.U.

Superior Heartland

Long after the Treaty of Paris had been settled and signed, British garrisons were maintained in Detroit and Mackinac because the U.S. had not fulfilled certain terms of the Treaty. In fact, Britain went on planning for lands she had legally given up in the treaty as if she never intended to relinquish them. By Act of Parliament in 1791 they divided the land into upper and lower Canada, with Michigan in Upper Canada.

Before the Revolutionary War, the vast stretch of country northwest of the Ohio River – later divided into the states of Ohio, Indiana, Illinois, Michigan and Wisconsin – was a part of the British province of Quebec. As a result of Wolfe's victory on the Plains of Abraham, Great Britain acquired it from France in the treaty of 1763. Like the French, the British ministry intended to keep the region as an enormous hunting ground for the benefit of the Indians and fur traders.

Some of the American colonies were claiming parts of this land in strips all the way to the Pacific Ocean. At the same time, both Pennsylvania and Virginia claimed the whole area. Pennsylvania's claim was only on paper, but Virginia's claim was backed up by the daring campaign of George Rogers Clark and his Virginia Riflemen, who took over the forts at Kaskaskia and Cahokia, and defeated and captured the British General Hamilton at Vincennes, on behalf of Virginia. They renamed that place Patrick Henry after the then–governor of Virginia. After the Revolution, Hamilton was made Lieutenant Governor of Quebec by the British (1785) and died as Governor of Domenica in 1796. George Rogers Clark was an older brother of William Clark, who with Meriwether Lewis led the Lewis and Clark expedition to the Pacific in 1804–1806. The U.S. had bought that land from France in the Louisiana Purchase of 1803.

Clark's victory, achieved with almost no outside help, was vital in extending Virginia's sphere of influence. In a series of brilliant moves, Clark captured the southern key points of the Great Northwest, and held them by military force and his strong personal influence until the negotiation of the Treaty of 1783.

The English peace commissioners at first had no intention of giving up the northwest, as they claimed it was a part of Canada. But throughout the negotiations, Jay (later to become the first Chief Justice of the Supreme Court and Governor of New York) and Franklin persisted in demanding the country which Clark had won and was still holding.

Lord Shelbourne was the English negotiator who finally yielded. He defended his position by maintaining in Parliament that after all, the fur trade of the Northwest (which was all the English wanted of that vast area) was not worth fighting for. Nevertheless, Jay and Franklin could have found no footing for their contention, had Clark not been in actual possession of the country. It was a prime factor in the final results of the treaty.

So, while the British still held Detroit and Mackinac, Upper Michigan and the Great Northwest technically became a part of the United States of America, and also of the State of Virginia, at least until the Ordinance of 1785 officially put it in the Northwest Territory.

Settling the Land

There was no stemming the tide of settlers who began moving across the Alleghenies into the new territory, and so provisions to deal with them were made in the Ordinance of 1787. This was the famous Northwest Ordinance which provided for a government for the Northwest Territory. The area was huge, from the Ohio River to the international boundary, and of course including all of Michigan when the British would give it up.

The Ordinance of 1785 had already stated that the land would be surveyed and sold to the highest bidder. It provided for fair treatment of the Indians, in that no land could be sold until a treaty with them had been signed. At first, one section (640 acres) was the smallest amount of land that could be sold, and the minimum price was one dollar per acre. Later, this was reduced to 80 acres. There were to be 36 sections in each township, and the 16th section of each township was to be reserved for the support of schools.

The ordinance also provided for the transition into statehood in three steps. At first, the territory would be governed by a governor, a secretary and three judges, all appointed by the President.

When the territory had 5,000 free male inhabitants it could elect a legislative council who, in turn, could elect a delegate to the Congress. The delegate could speak on behalf of the territory, but was not permitted to vote. When a part of the territory contained 60,000 free inhabitants, it could draw up a constitution and apply for statehood. The Northwest Territory could become no less than three and no more than five states.

The Northwest Ordinance, which governed the Northwest Territory including all of Michigan, provided for a great deal of freedom. It was passed in New York City by the Congress of Confederation at the same time that the Constitutional Convention was meeting in Philadelphia to draw up the Constitution of the United States. There were, however, six articles in the Ordinance of 1787 which contained freedoms not provided in the U.S. Constitution. Four of these had to be added later as amendments. The articles granted freedom of religion, trial by jury, prohibition of slavery, provided that schools should forever be encouraged, and urged considerate treatment of Indians. The first four were not provided for in the original Constitution of the United States.

Before the ordinance could be put in force, there were many skirmishes between the Americans and the British in the years between 1780 and 1795. None of them took place in Upper Michigan. It wasn't until September 1st of 1796, thirteen years after the Treaty of Paris and nine years after the Northwest Ordinance was passed, that British Lieutenant Andrew Foster and his men finally withdrew from Fort Mackinac, and Major Henry Burbeck and 110 American soldiers took over. For the first time, Michigan was a full–fledged, undisputed part of the United States.

John Johnston

During these years (1790–1800) things in the Upper Peninsula went on as usual and little if any effects of these distant arguments between nations were felt by the inhabitants. There was an early settler of the Sault Ste. Marie area, having arrived there in 1792, who became famous in Upper Peninsula history and was a great help to the Americans. He was an Irish fur trader named John Johnston. Probably because he married the youngest daughter of a great Indian chief of the Chequamegon Bay region, Waub–o–jeeg, he became one of the most influential traders of the upper lakes. For years their home was the center of hospitality at this important crossroad. Johnston's wife, O–sha–gus–co–day–way–qua (Woman of the Green Prairie), who was later given the Christian name "Susan," was respected by Indians and Europeans alike, and had a great influence on both. She was a striking woman with marked intelligence, and brought rich heritage of Ojibwe ways to their eight children. They all spoke English and Ojibwe flawlessly.

While John Johnston spent much time traversing Lake Superior from end to end, he made two trips along the shoreline of the entire lake, one in 1792 and the other in 1807, and wrote descriptions of it in great detail. He was one of the earliest to describe Presque Isle in Marquette City. Of it he wrote:

> The peninsula...projects northeast and is curious from being one half freestone (sandstone) and the other half basalt (granite).

This would be a striking feature to a keen observer traveling toward the west. There are no granite formations on the south shore until you reach the Chocolay River ("Chocolate River" on the old maps) and then to have huge cliffs of both granite and sandstone together side by side would seem quite unusual. Further on, he states about the "black rocks" on the northwest end of the island:

> The Indians find in the fissures of this last a black substance not unlike limestone,which, when pounded they put a small bag of it and boil with any stuff they wish to dye black; the color, however, is not bright, though lasting; the same quantity will serve many times without any apparent diminution of strength.

Historian Grace Nute feels that this, then:

> may be the the source of the black dyes so much used by the Chippewa and other Algonquin tribes in making their moccasins and other pieces of apparel black, and, of course, thus the source of the name 'Blackfoot Indians'.

Johnston was always conscious of mineral and metal, and spent much time at the Riviere du Morts (the Dead River in Marquette) exploring for copper. He also stated:

> It is to be remarked that the metallic rocks of the peninsula (Presque Isle) are the only ones in the whole circuit of the lake which have neither trees, shrubs nor vegetation of any kind growing on them, though many others, not nearly so high and equally devoid of soil, are almost covered with stunted pines. This the mineralists may account for as they please, but I found on them what was more acceptable than any vegetable: a quantity of seagull eggs which were as large as those of turkeys and which when fried in a pan with some pork, made an excellent supper, with a dish of aromatic tea.

Evidently the "metallic rocks" he refers to are again the famous "black rocks" on the northwest tip of the island between Sunset Point and the cove. It has long been believed that these rocks are some of the oldest in the world, but we now know that the mona and kitchi schists commonly found in and around Marquette are older. These are intrusive rocks and must be contemporary with the greenstones and granites. Older rock is found further west in the Mississippi River Valley of Minnesota. They are thought to be nearly four billion years old.

Johnston proceeded west a short distance, rounding a certain headland, and found a sandy bay and a small river of clear water. This, he wrote, is "Potter's Bay." It can only mean that he followed the shoreline of Middle Bay along what is known as "First Beach." While there is scarcely much of a "headland" there now, there must have been one two centuries ago. The "Potter's Bay" he speaks of would be a bay between First Beach and Middle Island Point, and the "small clear creek going into it" today is Compeau's Creek.

Of the bay and the river, Johnston says:

> In the bed of the river, I found a part of one of the earthen pots used by the Indians before they had the use of copper and tin kettles. It is the only specimen of the kind that I ever saw, and a ruder attempt at pottery, I believe, was never seen.

Grace Nute comments that it is no wonder archaeologists struggle largely in vain to find shards of early pottery around Lake Superior, if Johnston as early as 1792 could find but one specimen.

While very little pottery has been found until recently, in 1950 a huge Indian mound was unearthed in Keweenaw Bay by members of the Lake Superior Archaeological Society. There have also been a few isolated graves along the sandy beaches east of Marquette that were uncovered by erosion, and Richard Saari of Marquette discovered quite a collection of pieces of ancient pottery. In this find was a copper arrowhead and a copper spear–point about five inches long. Further down the shore in the same area a grave was exposed about 1954 by wave action. The body was apparently that of a female with a club foot, estimated to be between 30 and 40 years old. The body had been wrapped in moss and rolled up in birch bark for burial. The remains are at the Marquette County Historical Society.

Johnston continues his description on up the shore of Lake Superior to the northwest (1792 and 1807):

> Off Potter's Head (Middle Island Point) about four leagues out (12 miles) in a northerly direction, lies a small island, apparently round and pretty high (Granite Island or Granite Rock), which when looked at from the shore in a calm, clear evening fills the mind with a pleasing melancholy and a desire for a quiet sequestration, where every worldly care and every mean passion should be lulled to rest, and the heart left at full liberty to examine itself, develop each

complicated fold, wash out each stain with a repentant tear, and finally become worthy of holding converse with nature, approach the celestial Portals and, though at an infinite distance, be permitted a glimpse of its Almighty Sovereign...our Father and God.

When I made my first voyage in the lake, which is now fifteen years ago, I tarried opposite Contemplation Island, as I call it (near Stewart's Cove) for four days; and I recollect having filled ten or twelve pages of my journal with reflections, remarks and some practical effusions, the results of so much spare time.

One of the first references to the shoreline between Big Bay and L'Anse is in Johnston's following passage:

> On doubling the point (Point Abbaye) you enter the Bay of Kewaynan (Keweenaw Bay) which is four leagues broad at the entrance, and continues for nearly the same breadth for three leagues, and narrows gradually to the end, which is a circular basin of about a league.

Kewaynan means "the way made straight by means of a portage."

But when he had described the bay, the portage, and the Indian village on the cliffs above Portage Lake, he remembered some years earlier an evening in May of 1803 and made his first reference to the Huron Mountains:

> The mountains from behind the Huron River bend back towards the south as if to make way for two bays, and then wheeling around to the north for the tongue of land called by the French L'Anse and the Indians 'Keewaynan,' here the Indians have a summer village and cultivate some maize.

The trips John Johnston made were usually in an open boat with hired oarsmen. The boats were rowed, probably by as many as eight men, rather than paddled like a canoe. He speaks of camping at the mouth of the Huron River in May of 1803 and of having his watch stop twice in the same place – the middle of Keweenaw Bay – several years apart. He had to send the watch to Montreal for repairs – "picking it up a year later." Johnston attributed the incident to "some powerful magnetic influence." And, as do all the other early visitors to Lake Superior, he mentions that the Indians "have found pieces of virgin copper of the purest kind."

Top: The John Johnston house at Sault Ste Marie (c. 1900).
Bottom: The Astor Tower at Astoria, Oregon. Known as the Astor Column, this monument to the fur trade was built by the heirs of John Jacob Astor and the Great Northern Railway to commemorate the founding of Astoria. The spiral of pictures depicts the history of the fur trade. The column stands 725 feet above sea level overlooking the Columbia River.

It was on one of his early fur–trading trips to Chequamegon that John Johnston met O–sha–gus–co–day–way–qua, the daughter of Chief Waub–o–jeeg, who was highly respected among the Lake Superior tribes, and lived in the La Pointe area. He was immediately attracted to her, and asked the chief for his daughter's hand in marriage.

The chief answered that he had been cheated by the French and the English alike and that he did not trust any white man. Johnston explained that he was neither French nor English, he was Irish, and that he always tried to be an honorable man. Waub–o–jeeg told him to go away for one full year. At the end of that time, if he was still interested, he should return and ask again. Johnston left and returned again a year later, and married O–sha–gus–co–day–way–qua.

More on the Fur Trade

During these years when the Upper Peninsula was a part of the Northwest Territory, the main activity was the business of the various fur companies. The companies each had their small trading posts spotted along the shores of the lake, many of which have left no record. They were usually on points or bays, or sometimes at the mouths of rivers. Many of these bays, points and rivers still retain the French names that were given them by the fur traders and voyageurs. Some have been Anglicized. Along the central Upper Peninsula shore is Grand Marais (Big Marsh), Grand Isle (Grand Island), Au Train, Riviere des Morts (Dead River), Presque Isle, St. John River, Yellowdog River, Pointe Abbaye, L'Anse, and there must have been something at the mouth of the Carp in Marquette.

During the British period the fur traders were Scots, British, Irish, and Colonials. They too had trading posts, often at the same places where the French posts had been. Some posts lasted only a year or two, some were just meeting places where a fur buyer would stay a few weeks, and some were old–time posts with cabins and a small stockade, like L'Anse, Grand Island, and Grand Marais.

In 1808, John Jacob Astor came from New York and started the famous American Fur Company, with headquarters on Mackinac Island where the Northwest Company had already been established for years. Astor bought the English traders' Southwest Company, and his American Fur Company became one of the largest business enterprises of its day.

When the English first took over in 1763, the fur trade had stopped almost completely for a few years, and the French posts had fallen into ruins or been burned by the Indians. The portages of the pays d'en haut became choked with windfalls and brush. Alexander Henry had been the first of a growing number of daring Englishmen to pass through Lake Superior to open the trade routes for the English. Many traders were plundered; some were killed and scalped. But the lure of the 400 percent profit kept them coming, and soon the fur trade was re–established.

Jonathan Carver, who had also written about Lake Superior, was an American in search of a northwest passage on behalf of Major Robert Rogers, the famous organizer of Rogers' Rangers. Carver traveled as far as Grande Portage and back.

Peter Pond, another American and a controversial one who had killed a few people in his day, brought the fur trade to the far reaches of the northwest when he crossed the great Methye Portage and built a fort 30 miles south of Lake Athabasca. From there he pushed on up the Peace River. He intended to present his map to the Empress of Russia. The Russians were establishing themselves on the west coast of Alaska.

By 1799, Alexander Henry the younger, actually a nephew of the original Alexander Henry, had come to Lake Superior and traveled it to the pays d'en haut where he spent many years as a Nor'wester. He rubbed elbows with the great traders and explorers – Alexander McKenzie, Martin Frobisher, and Simon Fraser, all famous names on today's maps. McKenzie was the first European to reach the Pacific by land north of Mexico.

Henry the younger drowned in the Columbia River on May 21, 1814, having followed the fur trading routes all the way to the Pacific Ocean. He had been staying in the fort built by Lewis and Clark in 1805. These fur traders who led the way across the Canadian mountain wilderness, settling in the Washington and Oregon region in the early 19th Century, were the deciding influence to have it become a part of the United States in a treaty with Britain in 1846. The fur traders had a great influence on nearly all the treaties between Britain and the United States.

An interesting book, The Savage Country, by Walter O'Meara, tells the story of Alexander Henry, the younger's life in the pays d'en haut, and details the fur trade of that period. (1960 – Houghton Mifflin Co., Boston)

The War of 1812

In the early years of the 19th Century, the British and Americans were still arguing about boundaries. These dissensions, and others, culminated in the War of 1812, which had little or no effect on Lake

Superior or the Upper Peninsula. It should be noted, however, that the Indians who had sided with the French against the English were now allies of the English against the Americans.

The British on St. Joseph's Island were the first in this region to learn about the outbreak of hostilities. No Americans here were aware that the war was taking place. Under cover of darkness the British landed a force of men on the north end of Mackinac Island on July 17th, 1812. The next morning the American commander of Fort Mackinac, Lt. Porter Hanks, learned that the United States and England were at war and at the same time discovered a large force of the enemy perched on the hill above them behind the fort. He surrendered.

Two years later, in 1814, an American naval force arrived expecting to retake the fort, but their guns could not reach it from their ships. They landed but were repulsed by the English and Indians who were hidden in the woods. The Americans lost 64 men, including their second–in–command, Major Andrew Holmes. The English held the fort until after the peace treaty. As a result of the War of 1812, Congress passed an act in 1816 under which foreigners were prohibited from trading in American territory. This act, directed at the British, drove the Hudson's Bay Company north and left the valuable fur trade along the south shore of Lake Superior wholly to the Northwest and American Fur Companies. The former company went out of business in 1825 and the latter continued until 1836.

While fur trading on a smaller scale continued for many years, the end of the great fur companies brought an end to the great 200–year era of the voyageurs on Lake Superior. After 1800, there had been a slow transition from canoes to open, two–masted Mackinac boats. These were double–ended, light and fast, and could be rowed, paddled, or sailed. There were also a few larger private or company–owned sailing vessels on Lake Superior.

Spanish Influence?

Strange as it may seem. there are some names that suggest Spanish influence just east of Sault Ste. Marie on the north shore of Lake Huron. There are two cities, "Spanish" and "Espanola" and the Spanish River at that location. In trying to get the answer to this riddle, many possibilities were discovered by the people of Spanish.

Encyclopedia Canadiana, the only encyclopedia to mention Spanish River, states that it is in the Sudbury and Algoma Districts of Ontario, rises in Biskatasi Lake and flows south for 153 miles through heavily wooded country, emptying into the North Channel of Lake Huron about 30 miles east of the town of Blind River. The river was so called by H. W. Bayfield, the admiralty surveyor, in 1819–22 because Spanish Indians had at one time lived in the area. The town was named after the river.

The Sault Daily Star of Tuesday, May 7, 1957, states: "This community is believed to have been named for the first navigator of the stream, a Spaniard, who stopped here."

There is a report that the name came from all the Mexicans that worked on the Canadian Pacific Railroad, but the name came before the railroad.

The Canadian Board of Geographic Names attributes the name, "Spanish," to stories which must have been hammered out over the moccasin telegraph that a mythical Mexican settled in the upper reaches of the river.

In 1815 it is known that the name "Spanish" appeared on Bouchette's maps of navigable lakes and streams along the North Shore and Georgian Bay. This states that it was named in contra–distinction to the French River, which emptied into the Bay southeast of the Spanish River outlet.

While it seems that the origins of the Spanish names has been lost in antiquity, there are several reports that seem to have credence beyond the others. These tell of an Indian chief and family who have lived in the upper reaches of the Spanish River for hundreds of years. The name of the descendants of this family today is "Espaniel" and members of this family live in Biscotassing and in Estaire.

Espaniel may have been closer to Espanol in the Indian tongue and some intellect of the past who spoke Spanish could have easily decided to give the English meaning to the river. The town was started when the railroad came through in 1872 and a boxcar was set up for a store which supplied the needs of a few families in the area. We would be hard pressed to find anything concerning the real Spaniards in this region of the French trade route. It is quite certain that there were no Spanish Indians there, but just a family named Espaniel.

Dividing the Northwest Territory

When Ohio became a state in 1803, the Upper Peninsula became, just for a few years, a part of the Indiana Territory. This territory included the present states, all having Indian names, of Michigan (Great Water), Indiana

(Indian Land), Wisconsin (Wild, Rushing River), and Minnesota (Cloudy Water).

In 1805, the Michigan Territory was formed. At that time only the eastern tip of the Upper Peninsula, including St. Ignace and Sault Ste. Marie, were in it, while the remainder was still a part of the Indiana Territory. President Jefferson appointed William Hull to be the first governor of the Michigan Territory, with August Brevoort Woodward as chief justice and Frederick Bates as senior associate judge.

In 1818, Illinois became a state. By act of Congress, the Michigan Territory was extended to include part of Minnesota, all of Wisconsin and the rest of the Upper Peninsula. Lewis Cass was appointed governor of this vast Michigan Territory, and at once he proposed a government expedition to look over this huge region he was responsible for.

Lewis Cass

The expedition, provided for by act of Congress in 1818, wasn't actually undertaken until 1820. Its purposes were to get better acquainted with the various Indian tribes and to gain their confidence, to arrange for treaties, and to investigate reported mineral deposits along Lake Superior's south shore. They also wished to make an accurate map of the shoreline with some place names for references.

Accompanying Cass on the expedition as mineralogist was Henry R. Schoolcraft, who later married a daughter of John Johnston, the Irish fur trader. After the expedition was completed, Cass appointed Schoolcraft to the post of Indian Agent at the Soo. Others accompanying Cass on the expedition were Charles C. Trowbridge; Captain David B. Douglass, a professor at West Point, as map maker; and James Duane Doty as journalist.

All told, the expedition consisted of 40 men traveling in three large birch bark canoes, thirty–five feet long and six feet wide, each capable of a cargo of four tons. The canoes had been specially constructed for the Cass Expedition.

Leaving Detroit amid much fanfare on May 24, 1820, they took just over two weeks to reach Mackinac Island, where they remained a week gathering additional supplies.

Next, they headed for Sault Ste. Marie to meet with some Chippewa chiefs. From Fort Mackinac they picked up two more canoes and 22 soldiers provided by the commandant of the garrison for the Governor's protection. This brought the expedition to the full complement of 40. The second day out of Fort Mackinac, the flotilla passed the ruins of the British fort on St. Joseph's Island, which the American troops had burned in 1814 at the end of the 1812 War.

At the Soo, they met the family of John Johnston. Johnston himself was not home but his wife Susan was – she was the most influential person in the area – and she and her son George were very hospitable. They brought the party to a camping spot near a Chippewa village of some two or three hundred men, women and children. George Johnston introduced Cass to the chiefs.

Governor Cass asked the Indian leaders for a piece of land on which to construct a fort that would secure the border between the United States and Canada. This made the Indians very solemn, as they had fought beside the British in the War of 1812 and were still loyal to their former allies.

After a day of discussing the question among themselves, one of the chiefs, named Sassaba, who had been nicknamed "The Count," appeared in a full British officer's uniform and spoke angrily to the governor. He thrust his spear into the ground, kicked aside the presents which had been presented to him, and stalked from the tent, followed by the others. Later, Captain Douglass saw Sassaba raise a British flag in front of his lodge. He notified Cass, who ordered his soldiers to arms.

Taking his interpreter with him, Cass marched into the Indian village, through a group which had assembled. He tore down the flag and trampled it underfoot. Through his interpreter he told the Indians that this was American soil and only the American flag could fly here. If the British flag was raised again, the Indians would be destroyed. Cass' audacity caught the Indians so off guard that none made a move to stop him as he carried the British flag back to his tent.

The Indians held a council of war that went on into the night. Hostility rose, but when it seemed as though a battle could not be averted, the wife of John Johnston, O–shaw–gus–ko–day–way–qua, daughter of the great Waub–o–jeeg, came to the council fire. She told the chiefs not to take sides in the rivalries of white nations. To do so would only bring suffering and vengeance upon their own people. She said that they should negotiate a treaty that would benefit the Indians and that everyone could live with.

This could have been a serious incident, as Cass' party was greatly outnumbered, but the Indians had great respect for Susan Johnston and they listened to her and agreed. They drew up and signed a treaty that ceded a tract of land on which Fort Brady was built two years later. In the treaty, as in most of the treaties of the Lakes Indians, it was specified among other things that they be allowed to fish the rapids forever.

Book One

On June 18, 1820, the expedition moved west along the south shore of Lake Superior. They were greatly impressed with the cliffs and rock formations of the Pictured Rocks, which stretch for miles along the shore east of Grand Island in Munising Bay. Schoolcraft was amazed by the:

> variety in coloured form of these rocks...the surprising groups of overhanging precipices, towering walls, caverns, waterfalls, and prostrate ruins, which are here mingled in most wonderful disorder.

The Indians thought of these rocks as the dwelling place of Manitous, and always left gifts of tobacco.

The party camped on Grand Island and later ate at the mouth of the Chocolay River.

On June 22nd the Cass party erected on Presque Isle the first American flag ever to fly over Lake Superior. The cove on the north end is not mentioned; however, they did land on the north end of the peninsula and, as the cove is the only good landing spot, it may be assumed that they landed there. In that event, the flag was placed in the vicinity of Sunset Point.

Trowbridge, whose journal of the trip was published in 1942, writes, "The country near Presque Isle is very mountainous and presents a handsome prospect."

The explorers continued west along the coastline, with Schoolcraft noting the Huron Mountains and commenting on the evidence left at different Indian campsites along the way, especially at the mouth of the "Huron Woman's River, where there were cedar bark sheds, wigwam frames, rattles, etc." They also referred to the "Huron Woman's Islands," suggesting that women made up most of the band of Huron refugees that made this spot their home nearly two centuries earlier.

The journalist made much of the treacherous paddle across the "grand traverse" from Point Abbaye across Keweenaw Bay to the entrance of the Portage River. It must have been a little choppy during their crossing.

Governor Cass wanted to see the great copper boulder described by Alexander Henry. They reached the Ontonagon River on June 27th and started upstream by canoe and on foot to find this curiosity. The journey became so strenuous for the Governor that he decided not to go on, but the others located the boulder on a sandbar by the stream. They found it was not pure copper as they had been led to believe, but rather rock with a great amount of copper interspersed.

Lewis Cass 1782–1866. Courtesy of Allen Ledyard (Descendent)

Cass had asked the party to bring some of it to him, and they tried ever so hard to do so. They built a fire around the boulder to get the copper hot, then threw cold water on it. Pieces of rock broke loose, but no copper. They tried to move it and were successful for about three feet. In the end, they were unable to bring any of it back to the Governor.

The expedition had met with very few Indians along the way, but at La Pointe they encountered many. It is possible that they had gathered there for some special reason and would soon disperse to other locations along the lake.

Trowbridge described many of their dances, specifically the war dance, pipe dance, buffalo dance, bear dance, and others. Much has been written about the depravity of early Indians, but Trowbridge remarks that the party's:

> attentions were attracted and our affections excited toward a young chief, whose conduct clearly demonstrated to us that greatness of mind, suavity of manner and filial affection are not altogether confined to the civilized world.

At the western end of the lake, Cass ascended the St. Louis River to the American Fur Company's fort on Sandy Lake. Here, chiefs of the local band of Chippewas addressed the Governor as "Father," declared their loyalty to the United States, and complained about the depredations of the Sioux. Cass promised to make peace between the two nations.

The Cass party descended the Mississippi to the Wisconsin then, via that river and the Fox, went into Lake Michigan (reversing the route taken by Marquette and Joliet). Following the west shore of Lake Michigan southward, they circled the southern end of the lake and then went by river to Niles. They traveled overland from Niles back to Detroit on foot.

Lewis Cass became a great statesman. Born in Exeter, New Hampshire in 1782, he was a lawyer and member of the Ohio bar and became a brigadier general during the War of 1812. Cass was Governor of the Michigan Territory for 18 years. From 1831 to 1836 he was Secretary of War and later an ambassador to Paris. From 1845 to 1857 he sat in the United States Senate and in 1848 he ran for the presidency of the United States as a democrat. He was defeated by Zachary Taylor. Lewis Cass died in Detroit in 1866.

There was a second Army expedition on Lake Superior in 1823, but it is relatively unimportant as far as the Upper Peninsula is concerned, as it followed the north shore route.

The Schoolcraft Expedition

As stated before, Henry R. Schoolcraft married the daughter of John and Susan Johnston and in 1822 became the Indian Agent at the Soo. He held this position until 1841, during which time he studied in depth the life of the Ojibwe people and wrote a six–volume work on them. These works were eagerly read by both Americans and Europeans of the time, and provided the inspiration for the poem "Song of Hiawatha" by Henry Wadsworth Longfellow. "Hiawatha" is a story of the Ojibwe legends, life, and traditions. In the story, Hiawatha was born on the shore along the central part of Lake Superior. The poem became a classic, parts of which are still memorized by schoolchildren in every English–speaking country on earth.

Schoolcraft spent the whole summer of 1831 along the south central shore of Lake Superior, from Munising to L'Anse, studying the local Indian bands. This was the same summer that a now–famous young chief Marje Gesick, whom local people think of as the chief of the Negaunee band, was camped at the mouth of the Pine River where Huron Mountain Club is now located. This was their summer campground, their all–important blueberry field. This group had been coming to this spot for many summers. It was most likely the evidence of these people that the Cass Expedition had found there 11 years before. Their fall hunting ground was the area around Teal Lake where the city of Negaunee now stands. In the winter they moved to an ice–fishing location and did their trapping, and in the spring their home was on the shore near Buckroe, where they fished the Garlic River and made maple sugar back in the hardwood toward Echo Lake. At Buckroe they would hail the American Fur Company ship on its first spring run and sell their winter's take of furs, sometimes purchasing some supplies off the ship. By May they were on their way up along the shore to their summer campground at Pine River, where they would remain through August or even September if the berry season lasted that long.

It was here at their summer camp that summer of 1831 that Charlotte, the daughter of Marje Gesick, was born. The same Charlotte became the wife of Kawbawgam and is buried beside him on Presque Isle.

It was also in 1831 that Bishop Frederic Baraga first came to Detroit as a young priest. He was assigned to the diocese of Detroit which, at that time, included the entire Michigan Territory. It was not until 1835 that Baraga reached Lake Superior. Like "Huron" and "Marquette," his name would eventually adorn many places of the central Upper Peninsula.

Schoolcraft became very interested in the land's geology, its people, and its history that summer of 1831, and wanted more time and help with his

Michigan Counties 1803

The area to the east of Knox County was
still under the military control of the
British at this time.

Michigan Counties 1790

Wayne County as set off by Governor William
Henry Harrison in 1803. The Territory of
Michigan came into existence in 1805.

Superior Heartland

Indiana Territory

Illinois Territory

Michigan Territory

Michigan Counties 1818

BROWN

MICHILIMACKINAC

MACOMB

WAYNE

MONROE

Brown County, as set off and organized, was to lie
to the south of the headwaters of the rivers that
flow into Lake Superior.

work. He proposed a third expedition for this study. That year he had heard from the Indians that the lake the Cass party had claimed as being the beginning of the Mississippi River, which they named "Cass Lake," was not correct. The Cass Party, the Indians said, had not explored far enough. While Schoolcraft had several purposes for the study, he gave as one goal of the journey the discovery of the true source of the Mississippi.

Traveling, as usual, in three large birchbark canoes, the Schoolcraft Expedition left Sault Ste. Marie on June 7, 1832. Following the south shore of Lake Superior to the west, they named and described places along the way. The botanist, geologist, physician and surgeon on this trip was young Dr. Douglas Houghton, another man who was to become well–known among the inhabitants of the central Upper Peninsula. Houghton later had a great influence in the development of the area, and his younger brother, Jacob, is credited with the founding of the Village of Michigamme in 1872.

By now Schoolcraft was well known and respected by the Indians, and he stopped and talked with as many of them as he was able to along the way. The party named the prominence on the edge of the lake just north of Marquette "Mount Schoolcraft," but the name didn't take. It is the one called "Sugar Loaf" today.

Schoolcraft examined the mouths of some of the rivers they passed, and ascended the Ontonogon to show the group the "Ontonogon Boulder," as it had come to be called, that large piece of float copper which by 1832 had become a very much–talked–about curiosity among the people who traveled the Lake Superior country. Schoolcraft wrote of it:

> The quantity of the boulder may have been diminished since its first discovery, and the marks of chisels and axes upon it, with the broken tools lying around, prove that portions have been cut off and carried away.

The expedition reached Fond du Lac, present location of Duluth, and then went on to discover and name Lake Itasca as the source of the Mississippi River. They returned to the Soo via the same south shore route.

Pioneer Sailing Masters

Over the next few years, there appeared on the lake several ship's captains who were to become well–known in the lake history. One of them was Captain Calvin Ripley, who owned and operated a small sailing vessel out of the Soo. She was called the FUR TRADER, named after the FUR

TRADER belonging to the Northwest Company that was wrecked at the Soo in 1812. Ripley's FUR TRADER was for hire for nearly any purpose. When not under hire, the FUR TRADER made its way along the south shore, buying furs from the Indians and selling them, in turn, to the fur companies when the price was right.

There were no depth charts in the 1830s, and only inaccurate maps. Sailors in the large, clumsy sailing vessels had poor control maneuvering close to shore along rocky coasts. They had to constantly take soundings and watch for rocks. Whenever they saw rocks protruding above the surface, they assumed there were others nearby, just out of sight. For this reason they avoided what is now Marquette's lower harbor. Just a hundred yards or so out from a sand beach stood a small group of imposing–looking rocks, protruding 20 or 30 feet out of the water.

Some time in the 1830s, Captain Ripley found himself just off the mouth of the Carp River in a bad northeast storm. He had nowhere else to go. Taking advantage of the wind, he cautiously made his way toward the dangerous looking rocks, always keeping his distance and hoping to get behind them. To his surprise he found there was deep water all around the rocks, and he could bring the FUR TRADER right in alongside them and conveniently tie up, much as he would to a wharf. Over the next decade or so this became a regular stop for Captain Ripley and his ship, and Indians met him there with furs. It also became a place of refuge in bad weather, and the rocks acquired the name of Ripley's Rocks. It seems, however, that the rest of the harbor still had a reputation of being shallow, full of submerged rocks, and treacherous. For years, only the FUR TRADER dared venture close to shore at this point.

Three other captains who dared the dangers of this powerful and enchanted lake were brothers, the Stanards.

There were originally four brothers, only three of whom became captains. They were sons of Asa and Sarah Stanard of Hudson, New York. Charles C. Stanard (1804–1854) was the oldest and probably the most famous of the four, at least on Lake Superior. The second oldest was Walter W. Stanard (1808–1891), who did not become a captain. Next was Captain Benjamin A. Stanard (1810–1890) who also became famous as a naturalist, and the youngest, Captain John J. Stanard (1812–1881)

Discovery of Stannard Rock

A fur–trading vessel, the JOHN JACOB ASTOR, was built and launched above the Soo rapids on July 30th, 1835. The American Fur

Company, which built the ship, had employed Captain Charles Stanard to take her on her maiden voyage from the Soo to Copper Harbor at the tip of the Keweenaw Peninsula. On August 26th, Stanard, who was heading toward the open sea to avoid being blown ashore by a terrific storm, spotted what at first appeared to be an overturned boat. He cautiously edged the Astor close enough to see that it was a huge rock submerged in 6 to 12 feet of water, and maybe more than a half–mile long. The tremendous waves dashed over it, exposing the rock two to four feet above the water. From that time on the Stanards sounded in any unknown water, regardless of how far they were from land, as Superior was thought to be as shallow as Michigan and Huron.

It turned out that this was an extreme exception. The rock was named in honor of its discoverer, Captain Charles C. Stanard. From 1835 to 1878 the U.S. Government spent vast sums of money installing markers, buoys, beacons and bells on or near the rock to insure the safety of mariners. All proved inadequate because they could not withstand the constant battering of the waves nor the force of the moving ice.

In 1878, Congress appropriated $305,000 for the construction of a permanent lighthouse operating 24 hours a day. Captain John A. Bailey, a famous government engineer, was in charge of building the cement and steel lighthouse. A cribbing was constructed in Huron Bay and floated to the site, where the cement was poured. It is 43 miles northwest of Marquette and about 25 miles northeast of Huron Mountain Club. The glow from the light can be seen from the beach on some nights, and almost any time from the tops of Ives and Fortress Mountains or "Old Baldy" along the old Big Bay Road. It is said to be the most isolated lighthouse in the world, but since about 1958, when a man died in an accident at the rock, it has been unmanned, and operates automatically. The light stands 102 feet above the water, and on a clear night can be seen for a great distance.

In his Centennial History of Arvon Township, Marvin Hanson tells of a little village of some thirty government workers established at Sand Point and nicknamed "Stannardville." We should note that the Stanards all spelled their name with one "n," while today all references to the Light have two.

The work project at Stannardville was to design and build a crib and beacon to be hauled to and erected upon Stannard Reef, 30 miles out in Lake Superior.

Hanson writes:

> The government crew commenced work in June of 1877. The structure of granite was cut and assembled at Sand Point and

dismantled and set up on the Reef. Severe storms kept wrecking the crib attached to the reef; thus 5 years were required to complete Stannard Rock Beacon. Stannardville was then abandoned. The circular base on which the beacon was modeled is still visible at Sand Point.

Many Skanee men were employed on the project. Skanee farmers supplied the village with farm produce. Sam Shears stayed on to tend the Sand Point Beacon light. Sam also engaged in commercial fishing.

First Thought of Iron

While it had been known for centuries that there was copper in the Upper Peninsula, no one realized the amount of iron that could be found. It had been mentioned only as a distant possibility. One of the first reported specimens came as early as 1830 to a fur trader named Peter Barbeau from the Soo. He gave specimens of high grade iron ore to a Professor Charles T. Jackson, a mineralogist who was in the area because of his interest in copper. The specimens had come from the Carp River area. Jackson made tests and declared that there was high–grade iron somewhere in the region. Jackson questioned Barbeau as to where the specimens had come from, but Barbeau only knew that he had gotten them from Indians near the Carp River when he was buying furs along the lakes some years earlier. Jackson told many prospectors to be on the lookout for iron as well as copper.

Struggling for Statehood

It was also during these years (1834–1837) that Michigan was struggling to become a state. No other state had such problems. The trouble started back in 1817 when a surveyor named William Harris surveyed a line called for by the Ohio Constitution. The Harris line put Toledo (then a Michigan city) in Ohio.

Governor Cass protested to the federal government, and President James Monroe ordered a new survey in accord with the act which established the Michigan Territory. If Harris had been ordered to run the line as stated in the Ordinance of 1787, they could have avoided all the trouble. Even though a mistake had been made, the Ohio Legislature hastily ratified the Harris

Line as the northern border of their state, since it gave them more land and access to another port on Lake Erie.

A year earlier, a bill authorizing Michigan to frame a constitution was introduced on January 15, 1816, and became a law on April 13th. The provision about the line designated in the Ordinance of 1787 had been altered to read the 42nd degree of latitude. In the Senate it was altered to read "an east–west line drawn through a point ten miles north of the southern extreme of Lake Michigan."

It was in this form that the bill was finally enacted. The 10–mile extension deprived Michigan of such present–day cities as Michigan City, South Bend, and Elkhart. The 42–degree line would have omitted the present–day Berrien, Cass, St. Joseph, and Branch Counties, including the cities of Niles, Dowagiac, Sturgis and Coldwater. As late as December of 1833, Indiana was seeking to obtain the St. Joseph River as the boundary of the state.

There was much protest, and the Secretary of the Treasury ordered that the Ohio boundary be re–marked in compliance with the Act of 1812. John Fulton did the work, but very inaccurately. He finished the line in 1818. It turned out to be five miles south of the Harris Line at the Indiana boundary, and eight miles south at the Lake Erie end. The tract in between, some 468 square miles, has been known ever since as the "Toledo Strip," and it was this strip that became the area of controversy.

A territorial election held in 1832 proved overwhelmingly that Michigan wanted to become a state but, because of the boundary dispute, nothing could be done. It was brought up again in 1834, but Ohio again saw to it that the issue was put off.

By this time, Lewis Cass had resigned after 18 years as governor of the Michigan Territory. He had turned this leadership over to 19–year–old Steven T. Mason, the aggressive "Boy Governor."

In 1834 Mason, then 22, took some revolutionary steps. He urged that Michigan take a census to establish her requisite population and frame a constitution, establish a state government, elect senators and representatives, and demand admission to the Union.

The Ordinance of 1787 guaranteed admission to the Union upon attainment of 60,000 inhabitants. Indiana had been admitted by a special enabling act with only 35,000. The census of 1835 proved that Michigan had over 85,000 inhabitants. And so, even though it was a revolutionary procedure, the voters approved the plan by a great majority. Elections were held, a constitution was drawn up, and Michigan proceeded to become a

Indian Cessions

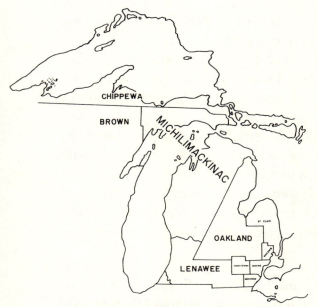

Michigan Counties 1828

Lenawee County was organized in 1826 and the lands
gained under the treaty of Chicago were attached.
(Revised Laws, 1827: 591). In 1829 the territory
gained under the treaty of Carey Mission was attached.
(Terr. Laws, II: 709)

Counties in 1828 and Indian Secessions.

108

state in 1835. However, it was an illegal state since it had not been admitted by the federal government.

President Andrew Jackson dismissed Acting Governor Steven T. Mason and appointed Secretary John S. Horner to replace him. When Horner arrived in Michigan he was jeered and ignored. Mason took it upon himself to convene a territorial legislature in Green Bay, but nothing could legally be done there because of the absence of the legal Governor Horner.

Michigan was fighting a losing argument. The established states of Ohio and Indiana would surely win out over a territory. But the issue became so heated that both Ohio and Michigan summoned their militia to arms, led by their two respective governors. In 1835, Ohio extended her boundaries to the Harris Line. Michigan responded with heavy penalties for any infringement on her territory. Governor Mason had his militia assembled in Toledo while Governor Lucas had his men in Perrysburg, just a short distance away. Both were ready to fight. President Jackson sent peace commissioners to the scene, and there was no battle. It has been said that a mule was shot, and a soldier shot himself in the leg. These were the only casualties of the Toledo War.

From that time on, the rest of the debates were in Washington, and we know how it all came out. Indiana retained her existing boundary and Ohio got Toledo, her boundary being the Harris Line running to the north cape of Maumee Bay on Lake Erie. Michigan was given the Upper Peninsula, although they had not asked for it. In fact, at a special convention held in Ann Arbor to vote on the proposal on September 26, 1836, they voted not to accept it.

In retrospect, it looked as though all they had to do was accept the Upper Peninsula and Michigan could become a state. A few leaders called a second "Convention of Assent" also at Ann Arbor on December 14, 1836.

Some nasty things were said at both of these conventions about this land above the Straits, and there were many assembled there who truly believed it was such a wasteland that only Indians would ever live there. The session was heated and loud, but when the vote was finally taken the Upper Peninsula was accepted. And so on January 26, 1837, Michigan became the 26th state, and the Upper Peninsula was a part of it.

Central U.P.'s First Settler

While Michigan had been an illegal state in 1836, the Treaty of Washington was signed. In it, the Indians ceded to the federal government all the rest of the land not under a treaty in the lower peninsula of Michigan, plus all the land east of the Chocolay and Escanaba Rivers in the Upper Peninsula. Governor Cass had laid the groundwork for this treaty ahead of time, as he had been eager to clear title to the land to make room for settlers.

Thus, by the time Michigan became a state, all of its lands were open to mineral exploration and settlement except those west of the Chocolay and Escanaba Rivers. Ironically, all the great deposits of copper and iron were in the portion yet unceded.

One of the first settlers to take advantage of the treaty of 1836 was Abraham Williams.

As a young man in his 20's, Williams had come to Sault Ste. Marie on a fishing trip. He was originally from Vermont, but had a wish to move west. The Soo was a rough frontier settlement in those days, and while he wanted to move there because of the excellent fishing on Lake Superior, he later chose Decatur, Illinois as a better place to raise a family.

While at the Soo, an Indian chief named Omenominee from Grand Island befriended Williams and invited him to come and live on his island. The chief told him he was welcome to use some buildings that had been abandoned in 1834 by the American Fur Company. Several years later, after a trip to see the area, Williams moved to Grand Island in Munising Bay.

In 1840, he left Decatur for Lake Superior. Traveling in an ox–drawn covered wagon to Chicago, also a small frontier town at the time, he and his family boarded the sailing vessel BLACK HAWK, a ship said to have been used in the Black Hawk War five or six years earlier, and sailed to Sault Ste. Marie. Here they chartered the MARY ELIZABETH, which, after being calmed many days, finally brought Abraham Williams and his family to Grand Island, landing there on July 30, 1840.

The Fur Company had left four log houses when they closed the Grand Island Post, and Williams moved into one of them. Mr. and Mrs. Williams raised 12 children on Grand Island, and their descendants were still on the island over a century later. The sixth, seventh, and eighth generations of the Williams family still reside at Powell's Point, Munising, and Marquette today.

Abraham Williams was the first white settler on the south central shore of Lake Superior. He built several strong log cabins and continued to be a close friend of Chief Omenominee and his band of Grand Island Indians for the rest of his life. For at least the next ten years, no canoes, mackinaw boats, or small sailing vessels went along Superior's south shore without stopping at Grand Island.

In 1840 another war broke out between the Chippewas and the

Abraham Williams.

Sioux, and Williams and his family witnessed the comings and goings of the Indians in their fearful war–paint, as did Father Baraga, who had been at La Pointe since 1836. Indian life changed rapidly with the coming of the white settlers, but the Williamses would always be grateful for the many kindnesses of the Indians.

After Michigan became a state in 1837, steps were taken to open up the Upper Peninsula. Dr. Douglas Houghton, who had been on the Schoolcraft Expedition in 1832 as a young man, was now appointed Geologist for the State of Michigan in 1837. He had accompanied Schoolcraft to Ontonogon to see the Ontonagon Boulder. Houghton had managed to get a piece off it, and also had found a loose piece or two in the area which he carried back with him. Pure, native copper was always a curiosity. He had found traces of copper in many places.

The Penny Journal of 1840

There was a Charles W. Penny, who was born in Putnam County, New York, in 1812 and had moved to Detroit. In 1840 he was invited to accompany Douglas Houghton on an expedition to Lake Superior. Penny kept a journal, which was passed down in his family. A grandson of Charles Penny, Gregory Harrier of Berkeley, California, sent it to John Voelker to read and Voelker saw to it that the Marquette Historical Society obtained the journal, which was edited by well–known local historians, James R. Carter and Ernest H. Rankin, who had it published under the name of "North to Lake Superior" in 1970 on behalf of the Society.

This trip in 1840 was really the climax of Houghton's survey of the mineral deposits of Central Upper Michigan. Most of the expedition returned to Detroit by August, but Houghton remained to further explore the south shore and the Keweenaw Peninsula, as well as the area between the Ontonagon and Montreal Rivers; the latter was, at the time, in disputed claims by the states of Michigan and Wisconsin.

Penny's Journal covers the period from May 21, 1840, when they left Detroit, to July 31, when they returned.

Portions of the journal describing the central south shore of Lake Superior are quoted here. They are approaching the Chocolay River from the east on Monday, June 15th. Penny remarks that, while the nights are cold, the days are as warm as southern climes.

The red sandstone still shows itself, but is somewhat changed. It is much harder and is mixed with feldspar, mica, and quartz. We camped on the east side of the Chocolate River, (author: just East of my present home, as the mouth was then about a mile to the east) having traveled following the windings of the coast – about 30 miles. This is the largest stream we have passed since leaving Whitefish Point and is the boundary between the United States and the Indianlands– the country west of this not having been ceded by the Indians. Since we landed, I have caught a trout, eaten my supper and written my journal, and I am now ready for blanket.

Tuesday, June 16th

We are now in a region where the geologists begin to work. We have parted company with the sandstone, and got among hills as high and as rocky as those of New England. About two miles from Chocolate River we ascended a hill (author: most likely Sauk Lookout, where the rock cut near the south city limits is today) and spent all the forenoon examining it. It is composed of primary rock; not granite, but the next thing to it. At the base of the rock is found talc–slate, horn–blende and several other minerals. The top of the rock is composed almost entirely of white quartz, and is elevated near three hundred feet above the lake. The upper surface of the rock is worn, as if immense weights had been drawn over it. It is almost as hard as flint and, consequently, retains perfectly all these creases, hollows and scratches. The line of these scratches is from N.E. by E. to S.W. by S. It is supposed that vast bodies of earth and transition rock were once swept over these heights and deposited in various places.

In the afternoon, we traveled two miles farther and fixed our city at the mouth of "La Rivere des Morts" or Dead River– so called because its banks have long been a place of burial for the Indians.

The party has mistaken the Carp River for the Dead River, just as the Cass party had done 20 years earlier. In that case, they called the Dead the "Presque Isle River" and the Carp "The Dead River." This has confused some historians into believing the Cass party planted the flag on Little Presque Isle. Luckily, the Houghton party were corrected by Captain Johnson coming from L'Anse. Perry's Journal resumes:

Here we had great sport catching trout. We took fifty in little over an hour, some of them very large, being about 14 inches long and weighing, as near as I could judge, a pound and a half. They were all meat, and I might almost say ready cooked, for our men clean and cook them before they are fairly dead. I have sat down and eaten one of them, well cooked, that fifteen minutes before was swimming free in the river.

Wednesday, June 17th

We have had another rainy day. The storms have seemed to be accompanied by more thunder than in any portion of the state. The Doctor (Houghton) says it is a thundering country. We have been confined to our tents for the greater part of the day; but caught some trout and killed a duck. We have also seen some red deer, but, as they were never known to be in these parts before, we are not provided with a rifle or ball to shoot them. Heretofore, the caribou, or reindeer, have been the only kind seen in so high a latitude. Our men today completed the net which Dr. Houghton ordered made to catch whitefish and Mackinaw trout! It is a set–net and is in the water tonight for the first time. If it answers our expectations, we shall laugh and grow fat, and have some pork besides; long to breed a famine. We went up this river this afternoon in our smallest boat and found it very rapid – as swift in many places as the Sault Ste Mary. When the current was too strong for us, the men would jump into the water and haul us up. They are admirable water dogs.

Thursday, June 18th

A delightful morning – pure air and bright sun; and what added materially to our enjoyment, we found two noble whitefish and a trout in our net. What a feast did we make of our breakfast and dinner. Stayed in camp all the forenoon – busied in reading and writing and assisting the Doctor with his minerals. In the afternoon we embarked, after a stay of two days, and proceeded almost to Presque Isle, where we went on shore and encamped for the night. Capt. Johnson soon after arrived and encamped at the same place, on his way from Le Ance (L'Anse) to the Sault Ste Mary's. We were mistaken in calling the river where we were yesterday the Des Morts. This is the true Des Morts; and the other is not laid down on either of our maps. The two rivers are nearly equal in size and not to exceed five miles miles apart. I wrote three letters to send by Capt Johnson.

Between these two rivers is Granite Point (now called Lighthouse Point) jutting out into the lake a quarter of a mile, composed of high ledges of a species of granite in which horn–blende takes the place of mica.

Friday, June 19th.

Our encampment has not changed today. In the forenoon the geological corps went to Presque Isle and remained until 2 o'clock examining the different strata of rock. The examination is not yet completed; but they found, in what is called the lower sandstone, lead,iron and sulphate of copper and brought off many very good specimens. They also found asbestos, These minerals seem to be strongly mixed together. In a piece of rock three inches square, the iron pyrites seem to be diffused through the mass, while the other minerals appear in small, detached quantities. There is considerable portion of copper through the vein, but not enough to warrant any experiment of mining. The vein containing these minerals occurs at the junction of the red sandstone and trap rocks, about a mile north of the River Des Morts. The Doctor brought away 150 pieces of rock. In the afternoon we ascended the river a mile and a half, when we came to a rapid that stopped our boat. The river leaps along over a ledge of granite or gneiss rock, and falls about 20 feet in a quarter of a mile.

The water over some portion of the rock was shallow so that we could walk through it. On these rocks we found quantities of carp or suckers, and we immediately soused in and began to catch them with our hands. It was grand sport. The water roared and foamed around us and the inequalities of the rock rendered a foothold rather uncertain. But we cared little for wetting. The suckers would gather in the deepest holes in the rock, and we stationed ourselves around to prevent their escape. In a short time we had caught thirty–five of the largest kind. But they are so much inferior to our whitefish and trout that we can not think of eating them. The country on the river, as far as we went, is worthless, being alternate sandridge and marsh. Farther back among the hills, it looks much better. There is an abundance of sugar maple in the valleys and a farmer could live there very well. We killed two ducks and returned. Then came the packing of minerals, which is no small job, as each piece had to be dried, labeled and wrapped in a piece of paper. The Doctor has already put up 6 1/2 barrels of them.

Saturday, June 20th

This morning early the whole party went upon Presque Isle. The extreme eastern point of the island bears east from the mouth of River

Douglas Houghton (1840s) Courtesy Michigan Tech University

Des Morts one mile.... (author: We will omit here a description of the island in geological terms.)

In the afternoon we embarked, and proceeded to the west side of Granite Point, where we encamped at the mouth of a small stream (Harlow's Creek today), the name of which we have not yet learned. It empties into the lake about five miles N.W. of the river– Des Morts. Granite Point (Little Presque Isle) is a knob of granite about thirty feet high connected with the land by red sandstone. It is almost an island as the strip of sandstone is not over four rods in width. On our way we landed and ascended one of the highest knobs of granite we have seen. (This is Sugar Loaf, 1,077 feet above sea level, 475 feet above Lake Superior. It was known as Tatosh to the Indians, but at this point had been named Schoolcraft Mountain.) It is very steep and we had some difficulty in getting to the top. But the view we obtained well repaid our labor. Some five or six islands lie scattered in the lake before us, while far in the distance appeared the dim outlines of Grand Islands and Pictured Rocks. In the west rose a succession of granite knobs, one above the other as far as the eye could extend. These peaks are sharp and but scantily covered with scrubs of evergreen. They lie in something like regular ranges, which bear from North by West to South by East. The knob we were on measured four hundred and fifty feet in height.

Sunday, June 21st

We have had a day of rest – a sabbath in the wilderness. A clear sky, bright sun and brisk north–west wind rendered it pleasant as heart could wish; and yet we were not content without our fire. Noone has strayed away from camp, for a walk in the wild woods has ceased to be a novelty. We need the Bible I dare say much more than we would have done had we been in Detroit. Shakespeare was duly honored, as he is everyday when we travel. When on the water someone of the party usually reads his plays to the others. But our time was not wholly occupied in reading. Each had a little writing to do, a little overhauling of trunks, a few rips and rents to sew up; and for myself I had a small washing to attend to. Some of my clothing had been long in mourning 'in dust and ashes' for the washtub; and so I tied them together and anchored them on a rock amid the dashing waves. They were kept in constant motion and by the middle of the afternoon were quite clean. I stretched my fish line from tree to tree and hung my clothes up. Thus the waves washed and the wind dried them. But who will do the ironing? Ah! There's the rub. I shall have to put them between my blankets and lie on them.

Monday, June 22nd

Dr. Houghton and his assistants spent the morning in taking some instrumental observations of the sun and moon; and in examining the rocks in the neighborhood. They are similar to those we passed on Saturday, and curious only in their geologic character. Before noon we embarked, keeping along the coast, with a gentle favorable breeze. We stopped at the Garlic River, an inconsiderable stream, and took dinner; after which we continued our course to the mouth of Pine River, passing St. John's River (Yellow Dog) without stopping, and encamped about sunset. We have advanced today about 20 miles. The coast shows the red sandstone most of the way with an occasional knob of granite. The trap rock has not been seen since we left the Garlic River. The country as far as we could see back from the lake is covered with sharp hills (Huron Mountains), which are composed almost entirely of granite. Opposite our encampment are three or four Indian lodges. The old chief (possibly Marje Gesick) came over and, after eating some supper and receiving some tobacco, sat and smoked the pipe of peace with us till near eleven o'clock. He ate very sparingly of what was set before him for supper – putting most of the hardbread and pork into a corner of his blanket for his children. So it seems an Indian is not destitute of parental feeling, notwithstanding the number of his wives. (author: One of those children could have been his daughter, Charlotte, who later married Kawbawgam; she would have been nine years old, as she was born at this location in 1831.)

The rugged and bold outlines of Point Keeweenaw stretching away into the lake are plainly seen from this place– distant about 30 miles. They do not appear more than 10 or 15 miles away, and their appearance is similar enough. One moment you can see them – the next they are melted into thin air, and presently you begin to see their tops hanging in the air, like the baseless fabric of vision. I never saw such an instance of the refraction of light.

Tuesday, June 23rd.

There is nothing to invite the attention of a geologist in the neighborhood of Pine River, consequently, after a short excursion, the Doctor returned, having killed a porcupine, which we had served up at supper. The flavor of the meat is not unpleasant, but there was something about it that reminded me of very young veal and that I should do nothing in its favor. We went over to the Indian lodges; and I am more and more convinced that Indians, in their natural state are not the miserable beings which they become when brought into immediate contact with the whites. The girls were all dressed in red frocks, and the boys, with the exception of a few that had taken off their clothes, were dressed much more decently than the poor people in cities.

In the forenoon we moved on as far as the Huron River, against a stiff head wind. This is a longer stream than most we have passed and might be classed with the Two Hearted or Chocolate for size. It is eight miles west of Pine River.

Penny also mentions an Indian burial ground there at the Huron and three graves of white people "covered over with pine logs over which is erected a cross." One bears the date: Aug 1822, one 1833, "and the other was illegible."

The Famous Ontonagon Boulder

Now, as official State Geologist, Houghton was eager to explore the rest of the Upper Peninsula, and this is just what he did over the next few years. While his report, published in 1841, warned that there were no quick riches on the shores of Lake Superior, it also gave news of extensive copper deposits on the Keweenaw Peninsula. The news spread quickly to the eastern seaboard and the rest of the nation, and there was much curiosity concerning the unique Ontonagon Boulder.

One of the first coppermen to reach Lake Superior was a Mr. Julius Eldred, a hardware merchant from Detroit. He had first heard about the boulder from a member of the Cass expedition and had given it much thought over the years. He proceeded straight to the Ontonagon River. He believed that this huge piece of copper was so unique that it would indeed be a valuable attraction in the city. It was already famous, having been described by Alexander Henry, Lewis Cass, Henry Schoolcraft and Douglas Houghton. The boulder is actually 50 inches long, 40 inches wide, 18 inches thick, and weighs about 3,500 pounds.

Believing that the boulder belonged to the Indians, Eldred sought out a Chippewa chief in the Ontonagon area and paid him $150. After studying the boulder and its location that summer of 1841, he returned to Detroit to devise a method of moving it the next year. Upon his return in the summer of 1842, all his attempts to move the boulder proved futile, and he was forced to return to Detroit without it.

In those years, miners and prospectors were working illegally until the Treaty of La Pointe was signed in 1842, ceding the rest of the Upper Peninsula to the U.S. Government.

The land had not yet been surveyed, but temporary mineral claims were being issued until a survey could be completed. A Colonel Hammond had taken out a permit to mine on the land where the boulder lay, shortly after the treaty was signed. He sent James K. Paul and a party of miners to the site.

Back in Detroit, during the winter of 1842–1843, Eldred built a sturdy, flat cart just large enough for the boulder to rest on and constructed some sections of strap railroad track. These were mounted on ties so they could be moved in two sections, one ahead of the other.

In the summer of 1843, he again returned to Ontonagon with a crew of 20 men, his cart, tracks and much rope, pulleys and other paraphernalia to accomplish his task. He had also obtained a permit to mine that section of land from General Walter Cunningham. When he arrived at the site, he found Jim Paul and his miners guarding the boulder. Hammond's claim had been issued directly from the Secretary of War. Eldred had no recourse but to purchase the boulder again, this time for $1,365.

Using greased skids and block and tackle, they slowly skidded the boulder up a 50–foot cliff and placed it on the waiting cart. This operation took his 20–man crew a full week.

For over four miles, over hills and through valleys, hindered by thick underbrush and swarms of mosquitoes, they inched the cart along the sections of track, moving the sections of rail from the rear to the front every 16 feet. It was a slow and laborious process, but at last the huge copper specimen was placed on a raft in the main river and floated down to Lake Superior.

By the time the boulder was ready to be loaded aboard a ship, the government agent had received orders from the Secretary of War to seize it. He did seize it, at first, but after listening to Eldred's story and realizing Eldred had taken every legal precaution and had the papers to prove it, and seeing the expense and trouble he had gone through, he decided that Eldred was the rightful owner. The agent let him load the boulder and take it to Detroit. There, Eldred put the natural phenomenon on public display in a tent on Jefferson Avenue, for a fee of 25 cents per person.

Meanwhile, in Washington, there was a growing feeling that the copper specimen should be in Washington. An Englishman named Smithson had donated a sum of money for a National Museum. He had actually left it to a nephew with the stipulation that the residue of the estate go to the United States Government for this purpose. The nephew died, and plans were in the works to build the museum at this time. The Ontonagon Boulder seemed to be just the kind of exhibit that should be in such a museum, a one–of–a–kind, natural phenomenon that was historically famous and should belong to all the people, that should be preserved and placed where all the people might view it at the nation's capital.

And so again the order came from Washington – the U.S. District Attorney this time – that the boulder be confiscated. Over Eldred's protests, it was taken by soldiers and placed on the revenue cutter ERIE which took it through Lake Erie, the Erie Canal, and on to New York City. Eldred followed it every mile of the way. After much debate which lasted some three years or more, with a great deal of publicity the first session of the 28th Congress passed an act on January 26, 1847, authorizing the Secretary of War to make a settlement. Eldred and his sons were granted $5,664.98.

The boulder was temporarily placed in the yard of the Quartermaster's Bureau of the War Department, where it remained for eight years. In 1855, for some reason, it was moved to the Patent Office and finally in 1858 found its home in the U. S. National Museum.

During the 1960's there was an uproar to the effect that the Ontonagon Boulder had lost its identity. People at the Museum didn't know what you were talking about when you asked to see it. Accusations were made that the exhibit was gathering dust somewhere and was lost to history, and there was talk of returning it to Michigan.

In 1971, the boulder was moved to the National Museum of Natural History's "Our Restless Earth" display in the Physical Geology Hall. This seemed to satisfy everyone, and the famous Ontonagon Boulder rests there today.

In 1987, the people of Michigan were celebrating three historical events: the Bicentennial of the Constitution of the United States, the Bicentennial of the Northwest Ordinance, and the Sesquicentennial (150 years) of the State of Michigan.

As a part of these celebrations, after a 144–year absence, the Ontonagon Boulder was returned to Ontonagon, Michigan to be featured in the Annual Labor Day Parade. In beautiful weather huge crowds watched the famous 3,708–pound chunk of float copper carried down the street on a raised platform on the back of a truck. From there it went on display at the

Top: Fort Wilkins.
Bottom: Ontonagon Boulder with girl. Compliments of Harold Banks Jr., Museum Specialist, Division of Petroleum, Smithsonian Institution.

122

A. E. Seaman Mineralogical Museum at Michigan Tech University in Houghton, where it remained for a month before being returned to Washington, D.C.

Upper Peninsula Mineral Rush

Through 1843 and 1844 the Ontonagon Boulder received nationwide publicity, and the eyes of the whole country were on that remote wasteland in the far north, Michigan's Upper Peninsula. With this great surge of publicity, prospectors, capitalists and adventurers turned their thoughts westward and northward and a small migration started toward the Copper Country. The land had still not been surveyed, so no claims could be bought outright, but they could be leased for three years. The mineral leases were tracts of nine square miles, and six pounds of every hundred pounds of copper had to be paid to the government. Later in 1847 when the survey had been completed, the sale of mineral lands in quarter sections (160 acres) was allowed.

Between 1843 and 1846, the first great mining rush in the U.S. took place in the Copper Country of Michigan's Upper Peninsula. Hundreds of permits were issued and many companies were formed. Most of the speculators were from the east, especially New York and Boston.

The inevitable happened. Many of the new settlers were disillusioned, as everything was very expensive or unavailable. Supplies were slow to arrive, or never arrived at all. The copper, even when found, was difficult to get out of the rock. The winters were longer and more severe than they had dreamed. Even in the summer, life was complicated by poor maps, no roads, endless swamps and mosquitoes. Even under these conditions, ever–enthusiastic reports from some of the operations encouraged still more eastern investors.

In 1844, Dr. Charles T. Jackson, the geologist, was hired by a group of Boston financiers to operate the Lake Superior Copper Company. It and its successors operated at a loss before going bankrupt in 1849, but Jackson became well known on the Peninsula and did much to further the copper industry and later the iron industry.

Fort Wilkins

Another company formed by men from Pittsburgh and Boston in 1844, was more fortunate. Near Eagle River, high on the Keweenaw

Peninsula, they opened a vein which led to a mass of native copper. Later, along with other copper masses, they found silver. The Pittsburgh and Boston Company paid the district's first dividend in 1848.

Except for a few minor, isolated incidents, there were no problems with the Indians when the first whites came to settle in the Upper Peninsula. Most of the Indians felt that they had been treated fairly and did not blame individuals if they weren't, and they were often helpful to the endeavors of the outsiders. However, with such an influx of miners to the Keweenaw Peninsula, many made it known in Washington that they felt a little uneasy about the Indians, no matter how peaceful they seemed. They felt that the Government should provide some protection.

In answer to these demands, in 1844 the U. S. built Fort Wilkins on the shores of Lake Fanny Hooe at the tip of the Keweenaw Peninsula, near Copper Harbor. The fort was named after the then Secretary of War. Legend has it that the lake was named after the fort commander's daughter, Fanny, after she disappeared and her bonnet was found floating in the lake. Actually, the lake was named for a different Fanny, one who, in the fort's first year of operation, visited her brother-in-law, Dan Ruggles, a lieutenant stationed there.

Except possibly for the psychological well–being of some miners, Fort Wilkins proved to be a worthless expenditure, as the Indians continued to be friendly. The fort was in a bad location as well. It would have taken days to get help to uprisings that could have taken place in hours, and there was little or no communication. Besides, it was an extremely lonely and desolate post for the men to spend the winter. When the Mexican War broke out in 1846, the garrison, except for a skeleton caretaking force, was ordered away. The fort was finally evacuated in 1870 and the land purchased by Houghton and Keweenaw Counties. Later it was deeded to the State of Michigan.

William Austin Burt and the Discovery of Iron

When Michigan had become the 26th state in 1837, one of the first jobs that young, energetic Dr. Douglas Houghton performed as State Geologist was to convince the Federal Government that the geological survey should be accompanied by a federal land subdivision survey. Houghton was to do the geological survey, and the man chosen to do the land survey was William Austin Burt.

Burt was born in Petersham, Massachusetts, and moved to western New York where he married Phoebe Cole on the 4th of July in 1813; they were both 19. The couple had two sons before William took an exploring trip to the midwest by canoe and on foot. In 1820 he returned to Michigan as a surveyor.

Top: William Austin Burt.
Bottom: Burt's Solar Compass – courtesy of John Burt with special permission from the Smithsonian Institution.

Four of William Austin Burt's sons. Top left, Austin (3rd son) 1818–1894, Top right, John (1st son) 1814–1886, Lower left, Wells (4th son) 1820–1887, Lower right, William (5th son) 1825–1898. Courtesy of John Burt (descendent)

Eventually, William Austin Burt was considered to be one of the most conscientious and capable land surveyors in the country. In 1835, Burt invented the solar compass to be more exact in his survey work; the magnetic compass, even though easy to use, was subject to local deviation. Burt had established himself as a notable inventor in 1829 when he obtained a patent for a printing machine which was a forerunner of the modern typewriter.

His machine had little effect on the business world until a breakthrough nearly a half century later, in 1873, by Christopher Sholes. As the typewriter evolved, positions for women were found in business and another plank in the equal rights doctrine was laid. By World War II the typewriter was considered essential business equipment, but Burt's original invention was almost forgotten.

In 1851 Burt received a prize for his solar compass at the first World's Fair in London, and in 1856 he obtained a patent for an equatorial sextant for navigation at sea.

Early in 1840, Burt received instructions to begin the survey which would eventually take him to Upper Michigan. On August 25th, 1840, he carried the survey across the Straits of Mackinac and established the north end of Michigan's principal meridian at the end of Meridian Street in Sault Ste Marie.

During the next several summers, Burt – assisted by his sons John and Austin, Mr. Richard Taylor and Michael Doner (both Indians), and Jacob Houghton, a much younger brother of Douglas Houghton – continued the survey. Jacob Houghton opened an iron mine in Michigamme in 1872, and John and Austin Burt became very prominent in the annals of Upper Michigan history in later years. In 1843 Houghton devised a plan that would combine the linear and geographical survey.

It was on September 19, 1844 that Burt and his survey party discovered iron ore at the present location of Negaunee, near Teal Lake. On that trip from lower Michigan, they had made a flat–bottomed boat from lumber they obtained at a mill near the present city of Escanaba, the only mill on Lake Michigan west of St. Ignace. Poling their way up the Escanaba River as far as they were able and then by foot to the south boundary of Township 43N, where they began their survey. Heading North on the line between Ranges 24 and 25 West, the surveyors came out on Lake Superior. They must have had a glorious view from the top of the bluff North of Harvey (later known as Sauk Lookout) where the rock cut today marks the boundary between Sands and Chocolay Townships. The party arrived here on September 15, 1844, and Burt could see Presque Isle and all of Marquette Bay.

From the corner they surveyed West on the North line of the present Sands and Negaunee Townships, and on September 18th they set the post at the corner between Range 26 and 27 West, where they camped on the shore of Teal Lake (about where the Negaunee pumping station is today). This post, just South of the highway is now marked by a historical marker placed by the Marquette Historical Society in 1987.

The following day, September 19, 1844, when they were working in Township 47 north, Range 27 west, just south of Teal Lake, the compass needle began to fluctuate to such a degree that Burt told his men to spread out and see what they could find. Each returned with a sample of iron ore.

In his diary, Burt speaks of the line:

This line is very extraordinary on account of a great variation of the needle and the circumstance attending the survey of it. Commenced in the morning, the 19th of September, weather clear. The variation high and fluctuating in the first miles, Section 1. On Sections 12 and 13, variations of all kinds from south 87 degrees east, to north 87 degrees west. In some places the north end of the needle would tip to the bottom of the box, and would not settle anywhere. In other places it would have variations...in the distance of a few chains. Camped on a small stream on Section 13.

At the end of the field notes for the survey of the east boundary of Township 47 north Range 27 west, Burt wrote:

Two good solar compasses were used on the township line, and the variations of the needle determined by both. Spathic and hematite iron ore abound this line.

The story goes on to say that it rained on September 20th, and both the solar compass and the magnetic compass became useless. On Sept. 21st, it snowed three to six inches. This left the group in a terrible predicament, as they had eaten the last of their provisions. Earlier, they had cached provisions seven miles east–southeast, but now they did not dare trust the compass. Cutting a tree, the men captured and ate two porcupines that were in it. Finally the weather cleared and they proceeded by solar compass to their provisions.

This land where iron was discovered was the fall hunting ground of the band of Indians led by Chief Marje Gesick. In fact, one unsubstantiated report says that the survey party met Marje Gesick and his 13–year–old daughter Charlotte at an encampment on the east end of Teal Lake. At any rate, the Indians heard all the reports of iron and knew exactly where they were talking about when told of the discovery. The iron, without specific location, had also been reported by Douglas Houghton in 1841, but the final report of his survey was never published, and it is assumed it was lost when Houghton was drowned during an October storm in 1845, just off Eagle River. His 1841 report recognized the great mineral wealth of the region and reported it in the most guarded language. He was very conscious of the hazards of life and capital that its development might entail. While the report was devoted mainly to the copper potential of the Upper Peninsula, he mentioned iron as a good possibility, judging from the geologic formations he observed along the shore. Even without the final report, the knowledge of the discovery of iron ore was spread throughout the land by word of mouth. Burt sent specimens to Washington and a man named Vanalstine, living in Oakland county, claimed to have procured a piece of this ore from one of Burt's men, and had it tested in a blacksmith's forge in the late fall of 1844.

The Wreck of the ASTOR

We return now to September 19, 1844, the day Burt and his men discovered iron. At the very same time an incident was taking place which involved the sailing ship JOHN JACOB ASTOR, with Benjamin Stanard at the helm. At this time there were only a dozen ships on Lake Superior, besides the Astor: the MADELINE, a scow large enough to carry 300 barrels of fish; the schooner WILLIAM BREWSTER; the SISCOWIT; the ALGONQUIN; the CHIPPEWA; the FLORENCE; the SWALLOW; the UNCLE TOM; the FUR TRADER; the NAPOLEON; and the MERCHANT. The ASTOR was bringing supplies up to Copper Harbor mining camps, with plans to stop along the south shore on the return route to pick up furs. On September 19, 1844, the Astor with its 112–ton burden, was anchored off Copper Harbor in a terrific northwest gale. She broke anchor, and in a gallant effort Captain Ben Stanard tried to sail her into the protection of the harbor. Because of the storm she foundered on the rocks inside the point, despite efforts to help by the soldiers from Fort Wilkins. No lives were lost, and with Stanard's crew and the assistance of miners and soldiers most of the cargo was saved from the wreck. This was the end of the JOHN JACOB ASTOR.

This Lake is put down from the old map as represented by the person locating N.º 593 and by him called "Teal Lake

593 133

Michigan Counties 1852

Top: Talcott Harbor – It is the bay lying between Presque Isle and Middle Island Point. Also a small map of Teal Lake – apparently named by Philo Everet. From a Government Mineral Survey Map of 1845. Obtained by author from Dan Sise in exchange for a German WWI helmet.
Bottom: Six original U.P. Counties.

Marquette County Is Formed

Technically, the whole of the Upper Peninsula was Michilimackinac (and later Chippewa) County until 1843. At that time the Upper Peninsula was divided into six counties under an act of the state legislature passed March 9, 1843. The counties were drawn to facilitate the surveying. Marquette County was designated as that area bounded by the line between Range 23 and 24 West, the north line of T41N, the line between R37 and 38W, and the adjacent shoreline of Lake Superior. At the same time Marquette, Schoolcraft and Ontonagon Counties were attached to Chippewa County for judicial purposes.

In 1845, an amendment was passed which drew Marquette's northern boundary southward to the north line of Town 49N. This put all of present Powell Township into Houghton County. At the same time Marquette, Schoolcraft, and Ontonagon Counties were made part of the judicial circuit based in Houghton County, as a unit of representation in the legislature.

Marquette Township was first included in Carnes Township, created by legislative act on February 29, 1844. It included all the land in Marquette County. In 1845 Carnes Township was changed to MacLeod Township with no change in boundary. The name "Marquette Township" finally was established over this territory on February 15th, 1848, an area still including all of Marquette County.

Talcott Harbor

It was also in 1843 and 1844 that the War Department ordered a survey of mineral claims on the lands ceded to the United States by the Indians in the Treaty of La Pointe in 1842. These lands were between the Chocolate (Chocolay) River and Fond du Lac (Duluth).

In charge of the survey was General John Stockton, U.S. Agent. The survey party was organized under the direction of Lieutenant Colonel George Talcott; the actual work being carried out by A. B. Gray, assisted by John Seib.

In the Marquette area there were no less than 80 claims made by 1845. These were all recorded on Gray's map, including 32 claims in the Huron Mountains and four at the mouths of the Little and Big Huron Rivers. There were hundreds in the Copper Country.

Among several interesting aspects of Gray's map is that Teal Lake is shown far to the south of its now–known position. A note reads: "This lake is

Chief Marje Gesick and daughter Charlotte
Mrs. Rankin tells of being good friends with Chief Marje Gesick when he lived near the mouth of the Carp River and she was a little girl living below the bluff on Lake Street. He tapped on her window one night and brought her a fawn. He used to pull her pigtails when he came to visit.
Charlotte was born at the mouth of the Pine River in 1831.

The mysterious and controversial photo of nine Indian chiefs and a white man. A study of this photo is discussed in the March 2, 1967 issue of the Mining Journal by Ernest Rankin. The picture has been identified two different ways:

1 – Top right: Rev. J. H. Pitezel, Mon–go–sid (Loon's Foot) from L'Anse, Mon–Gose (Little Loon) Marquette, Matchi–Gizig (Bad Day), (usually spelled Marje–Gesick nowadays) of Marquette, Kawbawgam of Marquette, and As–Sin–Nins (Little Stones, or Pebbles) of L'Anse, and Mu–Kwa–Da (Man Who Creeps, Who Does Not Walk). Seated: Ma–dosh of Marquette, Kish–kit–a–wa–ge (Man with an Ear Cut Off) of Munising.

Or, from Benjamin Armstrong's book "Early Life Among the Indians," page 68, Left to right, standing, Rev. Benjamin Armstrong, Ah–moose (Little Bee) Lac Flambeau, Kish–ke–taw–wa (Cut–ear), Bad River, Ba–ques (He Sews) La Court O'Rielles, Ah–do–ga–zik (Last Day), Bad River, O–be–quot (Firm) Fond–du–Lac, Shing–quot–onse (Little Pine), and front row seated Ja–ge–gwa ya (Can't Tell) La Pointe, Na–gan–ab (He sits Ahead), Fond Du Lac, and O–Ma–Shin–a–Way (Messenger), Bad River.

The Methodist mission was established at L'Anse in 1834 and the Rev. Pitezel came there in 1844. The only known photo of Marje Gesick is from this picture.

Benjamin G. Armstrong came to St. Croix, Wisconsin in 1840. Armstrong went to Washington in a group of five in 1852 and ten in 1862.

For what it's worth, when the author first saw this picture in the 1950s, the first remark that was made was "The man seated on the left in the front row is Madosh" There were no names on the photo. The man was later identified as Madosh.

Author: at the time I knew August Madosh pictured here with his son David, August was full–blooded Chippewa, David is one–half. The resemblance of the man in the picture and August Madosh was so striking (when August was younger, that to me they seemed to be the same person. August died in 1987. He was a great grandson of Madosh.

put down from the old map as represented by the person locating (claim) No. 593 and by him called, 'Teal Lake'."

The bay at Munising is called, "Cass Bay" and Partridge Island is called, "Clara's Island." No doubt this name became attached to a small island north of Partridge with the "C" dropped as "Larus Island" today.

On the beautiful bay between Middle Island Point and Presque Isle, the party camped during the last week of September in 1844. They called their campsite, "Camp Gray" and the harbor, "Talcott Harbor." Because of the dangerous northern exposure, this beautiful harbor was never developed.

Chief Marje Gesick

Now there was a second step to the discovery of iron on Michigan's Upper Peninsula. Newspapers throughout the nation announced Burt's men returning with the reports that iron had been located and the specimens to prove it, but, since the whole area was such a remote wilderness, it took a great deal of time and planning to do something about it. So little or nothing was done to develop the iron industry for a year or so after the discovery.

Philo M. Everett of Jackson did some planning with friends. In June of 1845, a company was organized in Jackson, Michigan, for exploring the mineral regions along the south shore of Lake Superior. The articles of association were filed on July 23, 1845, and on the same day Philo Marshall Everett, the treasurer of the company, started for Sault Ste. Marie with three other men: S. T. Carr, Ed Rockwell, and a Mr. Monroe. The other company officers were President A. V. Berry and Secretary J. W. Kirtland.

From the Soo, Mr. Everett and his party went by Indian canoe toward the Carp River to locate the "mountain of iron" that was marked on Burt's government survey map.

At the Soo they had hired Louis Nolan, a half–breed Cree Indian, to guide them to the "iron mountain." He had managed the American Fur Company trading post at Grand Island for several years before it closed, and he knew well the Indian families of the Carp River area. Later to become Sheriff of the Soo, Nolan was a powerful giant of a man and an excellent woodsman. He claimed to know exactly where the iron could be found.

After landing south of Ripley's Rock near the mouth of the Carp River, the group made their way west, climbing all the while toward the iron hills. They explored the rugged hills and woods where Negaunee now stands, but were unable to find anything. It seemed to the Jackson men that Louis

Top: August and David Madosh – oldest and youngest of a large family (c. 1983).
Bottom: A rare photo of Kawbawgam (center). Courtesy of Jack Deo.

Top: Charlotte and papoos in a Tic-a-Na-gon.
Bottom: Mud-dway-osh (Sound of wind in feathers or Eagle flying by) George Madosh of Marquette 1989 – He is current president of the Native Americans of Marquette County, an inter–tribal group representing any people of Indian descent. George represents the oldest family in the Marquette area, descendents of the Noquet Band of Achipway who wintered at Bay de Noc and summered along the shore from the mouth of the Chocolay to the mouth of the Big Huron Rivers for hundreds of years.

136

Nolan was lost most of the time. Discouraged, they decided to return to Lake Superior and head for the Copper Country.

Near L'Anse, Everett's party encountered Chief Marje Gesick, whose summer wigwam in the past had been located at Pine River, but at that time he was living just east of the Carp River. His group was sometimes referred to as "The Teal Lake Band," since their fall hunting ground was the land south of Teal Lake.

After hearing Everett's story, the chief assured him he could show him the iron. Everett himself now had his mind set on investigating a story about another copper boulder near Lac Vieux Desert and decided to walk there from L'Anse to investigate the story, but he sent Carr and Ed Rockwell back with the Chief to locate the "iron mountain."

To become an Ojibwe Chief, one had to be born into it, appointed or elected. Usually, chiefs had either shown their leadership qualities as great warriors or via great wisdom in times of crisis. A few were appointed by the Federal Government, and some, on whom the Government had bestowed a medal, were simply considered to be a chief; such chiefs were not well accepted by the Indians.

A chief by birth, Marje Gesick was said to have about 40 braves in his band. During his life, he had three wives,– two at the same time throughout most of it. Most of his six children by his first wife, Margaret, died young. His second wife, Susan, bore Charlotte (who married Kawbawgam) and a son, Kennedy, who died young. There were no children by the third marriage.

Chief Marje Gesick was kind and accommodating. He was understanding, honorable, and very religious. He maintained prayer houses at different locations near their various campsites. He was also very superstitious about the magnetic qualities of the "mountain of iron," and would not approach it directly. It is claimed that he would circle the mountain and back toward it. But he did lead the party to the spot where, tradition has it, an overturned pine tree exposed a great quantity of iron ore beneath its roots.

This was established as the site of the Jackson Mine, the first iron mine in the Lake Superior region. Although the party came from Jackson, Michigan, some have said that this is not necessarily the reason for the naming of the mine. They say that the mine may have been named for Professor Charles T. Jackson, the geologist from Boston. Years earlier he had announced that there was iron in the region of the Carp River, and the Everett Party may have felt that they had located Jackson's iron. But the generally accepted story is that it was named for the city of Jackson.

The same summer (1845) Marje Gesick led Dr. J. Lang Cassels' exploring party to iron on an adjoining piece of property. Dr. Cassels, a

Top: The pine stump under which iron ore was exposed. Philo Everett was brought to this spot by Marje Gesick.
Lower left: Philo Everett
Lower right: Frederick Owens Clark who defended Charlotte in the famous trials – son-in-law of Amos R. Harlow. Courtesy of Alden Clark.

partner in the Dead River Silver and Copper Company of Cleveland, took out a permit from the War Department to start the Cleveland Iron Mining Company there. Marje Gesick said that all this land south of Teal Lake was his tribe's special fall hunting grounds. He did not object to the white men removing the iron ore, as he understood the Indians had given them that right by treaty, but he did want his people to still be able to hunt there. Few Indians understood that they had given up title to the land in the Treaty of La Pointe in 1842. They weren't able to imagine any man owning the land. Their main concern in most of the treaties was that they could retain the fishing and hunting rights which were their livelihood.

Philo Everett's group fully realized that they could not have found the iron without Marje Gesick's assistance. To show their appreciation, they gave the chief a note certifying him as part owner of the Jackson Mine. It reads as follows: (Note that they were still calling the Carp River the "Dead")

River du Mort
May 30, 1846

This may certify that in consideration of services rendered by Madjigijig, a Chippeway Indian, in hunting ores of Location No. 593 of the Jackson Mining Co. that he is entitled to twelve undivided one–hundredths part of the interest of said mining company in said location No.

A. V. Berry, Superintendent
J. W. Kirtland, Secretary

This paper, though never honored in his lifetime, became the old chief's most coveted possession. He kept it in a little birchbark box in his wigwam. Wherever he went, the box went. Even when he went fishing, he carried the little box in the bottom of his canoe. Marje Gesick died in relative poverty. He died in the boat of Jack La Pete (also named Francis Nolan and son of Louis Nolan). Jack went to pick him up when he was sick, and the old chief died between Middle Island Point and Presque Isle in about 1862. His grave is in a small Indian cemetery on a hill southeast of the two falls on the Carp River, near the Carp River Forge site. The exact spot is unknown today, as the wooden–work marking the graves has long since gone. Charlotte, his daughter and the wife of Kawbawgam, found the box containing the paper in her father's canoe after his death.

Kawbawgam and Charlotte had two or three children, all of whom died at birth or in infancy. A very good friend, Jeremy Compo (or Compeau) of Marquette, took the paper through two trials, the final one before the State Supreme Court in 1884, and a judgment was collected on Charlotte's behalf.

Frederick Owens Clark, Charlotte's attorney, wrote an article, part of which follows:

> Up to 1884 the Jackson Mining Co. had realized in dividends and surpluses about 9 millions of dollars from this iron hill. The property had passed from the control of the original group at an early date. It was so difficult to develop, and so difficult to bring to market, they lost the stock and the property passed into the hands of eastern capital until the Supreme Court of Michigan pronounced favorably upon the justice of the claim. Kawbawgam and his wife Charlotte were supported the rest of their lives largely by the proceeds of the judgment collected against the Jackson Iron Co. based on the paper Marje Gesick received from the predecessor company.

Despite the fact that there was a small judgment handled by Peter White, the case was actually lost by Kawbawgam.

Actually, the settlement with the Jackson Mining Company was supposed to be for $30,000; however, according to the descendants of the family, they settled for $9,500. The descendants were Fred and Charlotte Cadotte, who were adopted by Kawbawgam.

Fred Cadotte was a descendant of the Cadotte who was the partner of Alexander Henry and who was said to have been one of the first white traders living on Lake Superior. His daughter, Charlotte went by the name of Mary Tabeaux, whose great–granddaughter is today the second wife of H. M. "Mutt" Robinson of the Sugar Loaf location.

This story is the historical basis for the novel "Laughing Whitefish" by Robert Traver (pen name of John Voelker of Ishpeming).

Settlers in the Marquette Area

The first activity by whites within the present city limits of Marquette took place in 1845. A group of prospectors found silver and lead in the rocky cove near the north end of Presque Isle. On their way east to file a claim, raise capital, form a company and get supplies and equipment, they stopped at Grand Island and asked Abraham Williams to build two log cabins on the flat beachland between Presque Isle and the mouth of the Dead River. They would be about on the south parking lot of the Presque Isle Marina today. The group called themselves the New York and Lake Superior Mining Co.

Williams, an excellent carpenter, built the cabins in 1845 and the group returned in the fall of 1846, bringing with them a force of 15 men and two women. They labored in the area for about a year. Several other buildings were erected during that time besides the cabins Williams had built, including a barn, storehouse, and blacksmith shop. During the winter and spring of 1846, mules traveled every day from the camp to the mine, and their trail can still be discerned where they went over the bluff, climbing it just a few hundred feet east of the present deer pen, and then along the top of the bluff to the cove. Equipment was hauled in and lead and silver ore out. Three pits were dug with great difficulty, the first two being continually swamped by the wave action of Lake Superior. The third pit was upon a bluff to the east, a shaft ten feet square was sunk to about 40 feet.

The Huron Mountains Surveyed

There was much activity up and down the lake that summer of 1846, with the comings and goings of Indians, surveyors, Philo Everett's party and the New York and Lake Superior Mining Company group at Presque Isle, to say nothing of the greater influx of people on their way to Copper Country. To help take care of the traffic, the first steamer (called a "propeller") was the INDEPENDENCE, dragged around the portage at the Soo and put in Lake Superior in the winter of 1845–46; and in 1846 a second one, the JULIA PALMER. Most of these people, and even the steamers sometimes, would stop to visit Abraham Williams, who now had a thriving trading post going at Grand Island. Occasionally that summer, visitors stopped in to look over the Presque Isle mining operation, one of whom was an aspiring young journalist named Alfred P. Schwineford.

The schooner MERCHANT carried a group of surveyors up to Huron Mountain that summer of 1846. William Ives was hired by Bela Hubbard, the assistant of head surveyor William Burt, to survey the section lines inside the township Burt had laid out the year before from the Garlic River to the Big Huron River.

Ives had been William Austin Burt's head compassman in 1844 when they discovered iron ore at Negaunee. He had emigrated from Sheffield, Massachusetts to Detroit in 1840 and was already a surveyor when he arrived.

William Johnston sent Ives his commission in March of 1843 as deputy surveyor of Michigan on Burt's recommendation. He made three surveys for Douglas Houghton in 1845.

The township lines in the Huron Mountains had already been drawn when William Ives and his party left Detroit in May of 1846 to subdivide townships into sections, each one a mile square, for Bela Hubbard.

In 1845, Burt described the Huron Mountains as "rocky knobs rising to a height of 1,400 feet above a cluster of small lakes to the north, and feeding many streams."

When Ives wrote in 1846, "Run six miles during one day," it meant measuring these miles by chain and compass, straight uphill or down, across streams or lakes, according to the lines of survey. To measure lakes, Burt mounted his telescope on a raft. They both mentioned the "swarms of blood–thirsty flies and moschetoes."

The Huron Mountain Quadrangle of the Geological survey map shows Ives Lake, Mount Ives and Ives Hill. Today, Ives Hill is called "Lookout Mountain," the highest in the Huron group, all named for the man who first subdivided the township into sections.

A story persisted down through the years that William Ives broke his leg near Ives Lake and remained some months on its shores, recuperating, but there is no mention of this in his journal, and the story is probably just fiction.

The following is from his journal of that summer of 1846. The party left Detroit on May 12, 1846. It consisted of Ives, John M. Titus of Oil Creek, Pennsylvania; Jacob L. Brown of Flint; Sylvester H. Burgess of Redford; Ovid Pillet of Canada; and Henry M. Wheaton of Detroit. They traveled to Sault Ste. Marie on the steamship DETROIT and arrived at the Soo at dark on the 14th:

> Moved up to and camped at the head of the falls and portage on Sault Ste. Marie's River about noon. We found the provisions which was shipped from Detroit on the steamer BENJAMIN FRANKLIN, provisions to be shipped to Huron River, Lake Superior, at the upper storehouse of Mr. Brown. I engaged passage for all my party and shipment of all the provisions to Du Mort River (Dead River) and me to be landed at Huron River if weather will permit, on the schooner MERCHANT.

(The MERCHANT was a top–sail schooner of about 75 tons. She was hauled across the portage into Lake Superior in 1845 and was sailed by

Captain Brown. The Merchant was wrecked and sunk with all hands aboard off Grand Island in 1847.)

21st. Left Sault Ste. Marie half past 7 A.M. with about 60 passengers on board, most of them bound for the copper mines.

23rd. When thick fog cleared, we found ourselves about 20 miles NNE from Presque Isle. We then headed for the Huron Islands. Weather clear 2 P.M. with a thick fog along the coast and the hills showing themselves above. 5 P.M. landed at Huron River, on ground to be surveyed. Dr. Tirrell and two men with him. (apparently waiting for them) We found L. S. Scranton with a party of exploring men and Mr. Bull, agent of the Franklin Mining Co., also camped there.

24th. 7:30 A.M., I left for Presque Isle with Wharton and Pellet in our small boat to carry 3 1/2 barrels of provisions to the Jackson Mining Company and some of Dr. Tirrell's stuff. Some men belonging to the New York & Lake Superior Mining Co., Mr. Larned, agent, with a life boat, carried Dr. Tirrell and his men and two barrels of provisions for me to Garlic River.

2 P.M. we landed about 5 miles from Garlic River, in a squall of wind and rough sea. Towards night the lake calmed and we rowed and camped at Garlic River with Dr. Tirrell's men. He had gone to Presque Isle.

25th 7 A.M. Rowed and landed Dr. Tirrell's men at a small stream a little west of Granite Point. 10 A.M.–1 P.M. We landed on the NW corner of Presque Isle (the Cove) where the New York Mining Co. were mining and took dinner with Mr. Larned, agent. We returned and camped at Garlic River."

May 27th: I and Mr. Pellet went to a trap and granite point protruding from the sand rock on the west side of the bay (Big Bay). I killed a porcupine and had it cooked for supper. Camped same place.

This place is now called the "black rocks" west of Bay Cliff Health Camp at Big Bay.

Between the 29th of May and the 14th of June, the Ives party surveyed land from the Garlic River to Middle Island Point. From the 14th to the 23rd of June, they worked their way up to Iron River at Big Bay.

It is often said that Lake Independence was so named because the lake was shaped like the steamer INDEPENDENCE that brought them up the lake. However, the party actually came up the lake on the schooner

MERCHANT and further, the reason for the name of the lake is obvious in the next passage of Ives' record.

On Independence Day – July 4, 1846 – the notes read in part:

> Wet morning, lay in camp all day, wrote notes, made maps, and wrote general descriptions. Went swimming and trimmed a tall tamarack tree for a liberty pole. Camp same as last night. Sunshine and cloudy day.

They had reached the lake the day before on the 3rd and stayed there two nights, taking the 4th off from work. Erecting a "liberty pole" was a common practice to celebrate Independence Day. Ives did it again on July 4, 1847, when he was surveying Isle Royale. His notes in that instance read:

> Stayed at camp, had a spruce tree trimmed which was about 12 inches in diameter and 50 feet high for a liberty pole. We all gave cheers which made the woods ring. We had lemonade without spirits except nature's spirits which we all enjoyed.

On June 24 they camped on what would later be named Conway Lake, and on the 26th they camped at the mouth of the Pine River. "Brown cut his foot with an axe, which will probably lay him up for three or four weeks." This may be the basis of the story that Ives himself broke his leg. The men took Brown to the Big Huron River but Ives remained at Pine River alone for a few days. On the 28th, the men returned without Brown but:

> brot (sic) with them Charles Debinshire to fill Brown's place. We went up the river (Pine) and left the boat and run 3 miles and camped on a lake in Section 33 (Ives Lake)

> August 3rd – Run 6 miles, camp north side of a small lake in Section 34, T52N, R28 (Third Pine Lake). The men built a fire. It spread and came very near burning up the tent and blankets.

> August 4th – Run and meandered about 4 miles, camped about a mile from the mouth of Pine River in Section 21. Professor Mather was camped here with two Indians ("Professor Mather" was William P. Mather, professor of natural science, Ohio University). He was going to explore the locations of this district. He spent only one day's time in exploring.

August 8th – very thick fog until noon, brush wet, cleared off P.M. Meandered about 3 miles on Mountain Lake but could not go around on account of its roughness. We crossed from the west side over on part of one of Burt's old rafts.

August 10th – Clear – Run and meandered 5 miles, camped at the mouth of Pine River. Burgess, Wheaton and Derby went to Huron River P.M. after a bag of pork. They sailed up in about an hour.

August 11th – The men returned 10 A.M., took the boat up the (Pine) river, took packs for all of us, moved them over to Pine Lake, rafted down and camped on point in Section 28. (This is the point at the north side of the narrows between First and Second Pine Lakes) There we caught 4 pickerel (they were probably northern pike, but they have called pike "pickerel" in this lake until only recently) and two large bass which were first rate.

In all, Ives' group worked about two months in the Huron Mountain area, putting in the section lines. They camped on Mountain Lake, Ann Lake, Howe Lake, and Cliff Lake. Derby got lost and they had to search for him, finding him just at dark. Brown recovered at the base camp at the mouth of the Big Huron and returned to work.

On October 28th the party sailed and rowed from the Huron River to the Dead River, 46 miles' distance, where they stayed in the house of the New York miners with three other men.

Ovid Pillet stopped at the Du Mort River, saying that he should try to get employment in some of the mining companies for the winter. He took one boat back with 40 or 50 pounds of flour, one tin basin full of sugar, and the blanket and the match safe which is charged.

On their way back to the Soo at the end of September, the party camped about a mile from the Williams' on the mainland, but went to the trading post the next morning for supplies. Ives described the pictured rocks. At the Soo they boarded the steamer DETROIT and headed south.

When William Ives arrived in Detroit on November 12th, he learned for the first time of the deaths of his father and mother, who died four hours apart, and of the death of his sister Olive.

The Jackson Mine and Forge

Early in the spring of the following year (1847), Philo Everett returned from Jackson to the Carp River. The previous fall, he had hired many of the group from the defunct silver mine on Presque Isle and one or two from the Ives party to cut a road from the lake shore up to the mine. This road started just south of the present Gaines Rock and proceeded west up the present Jackson Street. Parts of the road can still be seen at the base of Burt's Peak, paralleling Mountain Street in the area of the Bothwell School, and there are still pilings of the deck near Gaines Rock.

Just below the two falls on the Carp River, Everett's group proceeded to build the first, albeit temporary, settlement of any size in Marquette County. The Barney family set up a forge and the company filed articles of incorporation on April 30th, 1848, under the directorship of Philo Everett, Abram M. Berry, William A. Ernst, Fairchild Farrand, and John Western. Abram V. Berry was the company's first president.

Three hundred pounds or so of iron ore were taken to the Branch County Iron Works in Jackson for testing, some 50 pounds of which are said to be in a private garden behind one of the older homes in that city to this day. It is the first iron ore ever removed commercially from the Lake Superior region.

The wagon road cut by Everett's men went from Lake Superior to the forge site below the two falls, and then on to their own square–mile claim in the iron hills, which they later called Jackson Mountain. Today this spot is just north of the extreme western end of Iron Street in Negaunee. The crew also constructed some log buildings at the forge site in 1847 and cut timber for the forge itself.

On July 7, 1847, the steamer INDEPENDENCE arrived with 24 men, two women, and equipment for the forge, By January of 1848, Carp River was reorganized as a village, and William B. McNair became the first postmaster in Marquette County. A yoke of oxen arrived on the Independence before winter, with Ariel N. Barney's son, Sam, to drive them. A dam was built and a water–powered sawmill put into operation.

It was on February 10, 1848, that the first Lake Superior iron bloom was made in the region. It was produced by Ariel N. Barney at the Carp River Forge.

In March the dam gave way. It was rebuilt and the forge was put into operation again by early summer. But before the new dam could gain a head of water strong enough to run the sawmill, a food shortage developed. The men whip–sawed enough lumber to make a boat and sailed it down to

Top: Ariel N. Barney.
Bottom: Carp River Forge site. The picture was taken nearly a half-century after the forge was abandoned, but the log dam across the Carp River can be seen clearly. Courtesy of the Iron Mining Museum, now located on the site.

Abraham Williams' Trading Post on Grand Island for supplies. In the same small boat, five men, including Ariel and Sam Barney, brought six or seven hundred pounds of bar–iron to the Soo in May. This iron was sent to Jackson and put on display there.

The Marquette Company

Meanwhile, Robert J. Graveraet had become interested in the iron country. He was half Indian, born on Mackinac Island in 1820 of a Chippewa mother and a Dutch father. Graveraet's father was Henry Graveraet (a name of numerous spellings), who came to Mackinac Island around 1800. His mother was Charlotte Livingston, an educated Chippewa woman with a Scottish father who for a time taught school in St. Ignace. There were 16 children in the Graveraet family.

Robert was well acquainted with the south shore of Lake Superior. Even as a boy of 14, he had been an interpreter on some of Henry Schoolcraft's many trips to the south shore in the 1830's. Now as a powerful man nearing 30, he had intimate knowledge of the iron deposits, and had a claim which he believed was located on or near the Cleveland and Superior Mountains.

With all the reports of money to be made in Michigan's Upper Peninsula, and requests for capital from prospectors and entrepreneurs, many eastern investors and speculators were traveling or sending representatives to the Copper Country to make investigations first–hand. One of these men was a wealthy woolen–goods manufacturer from Worcester, Massachusetts by the name of Waterman A. Fisher. Fisher employed an attorney, Dr. Edward Clark, to investigate copper in 1848.

En route to Lake Superior, Clark stopped at Mackinac Island, where he met Robert Graveraet, described as one who knew much about the mineral resources on Lake Superior's south shore. After much discussion about copper on the Keweenaw, Graveraet told Clark about his iron claim and suggested he stop at Carp River. He told Clark to look over the forge and then go on up to the Jackson Mine. Following Graveraet's suggestion, Clark visited the forge and was given an iron bloom nine inches long, which he took back to Worcester.

The bloom was then taken to a factory in Worcester for testing. It was heated and drawn into a wire which proved to be extremely high quality iron. Waterman Fisher was very impressed and sent for Robert Graveraet. After their meeting, Fisher decided to invest in iron rather than copper.

To protect his investment, Fisher asked for and received the services of Amos Rogers Harlow, also from Worcester. Harlow was a strong and reliable friend and a genius with machinery. He designed and made machinery for the Fisher woolen mills. In fact, Fisher announced that he would not go into the venture unless Harlow promised to be in charge of it. Harlow did consent, and he became the fourth member of the company, the man in charge of the Lake Superior operation.

At Graveraet's suggestion, they would call the new company the Marquette Iron Company, as its operation would be in Marquette County. They planned to build a forge and a company town somewhere along the shore near the point where Indian tradition said the great explorer priest, Father Marquette, had said a mass nearly 200 years earlier.

The company filed articles of incorporation on May 5th, 1849. It was capitalized at $150,000, most of which had been put up by Waterman Fisher. Harlow went to work purchasing a forge and a sawmill which he assembled in Worcester during the winter of 1849. As early in the spring as possible, these would be moved to Lake Superior.

Founding Father Amos Rogers Harlow

Amos Harlow was born on April 23, 1815, in a small town near Worcester. He came from a prominent colonial family that traces back to New England Pilgrims John Alden and Governor Bradford. At age 14 he went to work in Worcester for a company that developed and produced machinery used in woolen mills. By the time the iron company was formed, he had a son, George Harlow, and a small daughter, Ellen Josephine Harlow. The son had been born to Mr. Harlow's first wife, who had died. Harlow had then married Olive Bacon, to whom Ellen was born.

Early in the spring of 1849, Graveraet, who had been in Worcester, returned to Mackinac Island and hired ten men to go to the Carp River with him. These men would get the claim ready to mine and prepare a site for the equipment Mr. Harlow would bring. The youngest of these men was a rather slight 18–year–old boy named Peter White.

Peter White Comes to Marquette

Peter had been born in Rome, New York. The family moved to Green Bay, Wisconsin when he was nine. At 15 he left home and, with the lure of the copper country in his mind, he went to Mackinac Island in 1846. This was the jumping–off place to Lake Superior.

From a Biographical sketch by Biographical Publishing Company, Chicago, IL., 1908

He reached Sault Ste Marie just too late to secure passage on the steamer, MERCHANT, which ill fated vessel sank with all on board that very trip. Soon after, by securing employment on the BELA HUBBARD, which was then plying between Detroit and Sault Ste Marie, he was able to start in the direction of the goal of his desires. This unseaworthy vessel capsized off Thunder Bay Island, and, although no one was drowned, the crew was considerably buffeted by the waves before they were taken onboard the propeller, CHICAGO. It was when boarding this vessel that Peter had the misfortune to break his arm, and by the time the boy reached Detroit and was able to consult a surgeon, it was in such a state that the practitioner decided to amputate it immediately, and, but for the intervention of a visiting surgeon, Dr. Zina Pitcher, our distinguished subject would probably gone maimed through the rest of his life. Dr. Pitcher's skill soon reduced the swelling, put the member in splints and his strong left arm in after years has done its full share of the world's work.

Some years later, Dr. Pitcher died and was buried in an unmarked grave in Detroit. The Detroit papers started a subscription to erect a monument, and, of course, Peter White was one of the first to send a generous check. However, the entire amount needed was raised in one day, and Peter's letter did not arrive until long after the subscription was closed.

When Mr. White's eloquent letter was read by the responsible florist, he was so impressed that he offered to plant flowers on the grave for each succeeding year.

Peter worked for a year in Detroit at the store of Freeman Brothers on Jefferson Avenue and then left for Mackinac Island, where he attended school for a few years.

Samuel K. Haring was the collector of customs there, and Peter stayed with him. He had taken a liking to the boy and did what he could to help him. At age 16, Peter made a trip to the Soo, working on a government survey.

When Robert Graveraet appeared on the island in the spring of 1849 in search of men, Haring recommended Peter White to him and urged Peter to join the expedition.

The group boarded the little sidewheeler TECUMSEH for the journey to the Soo. The tiny ship had to buck the spring ice all the way and nearly sank once. It took ten days to get to the Soo. From there, they left for the future site of Marquette.

Peter White tells the story:

> We succeeded in crowding our large Mackinac barge up the rapids or falls, at Sault Ste. Marie, and embarking ourselves and provisions, set sail on Lake Superior for the Carp River iron region. After eight days of rowing, towing, poling and sailing, we landed on the spot immediately in front of where Mr. George Craig's dwelling house stands (on the shore south of Gaines' Rock). That was called Indian Town and was the landing place of the Jackson Company. We put up that night at the cedar house of Charlie Bawgam. It is true his rooms were not many, but he gave us plenty to eat, clean and well cooked. I remember that he had fresh venison, wild ducks and geese, fresh fish, good bread and butter, coffee and tea, and splendid potatoes.

Chief Kawbawgam ("Charlie Bawgam") was born at Sault Ste. Marie, one story says, in 1798. His gravestone on Presque Isle reads: 1799. This date comes from Peter White's eulogy at his burial, in which he said that the Chief had "lived in three centuries." Others have placed his birth date sometime between 1810 and 1815, while historian Mary C. Nertolis' story on him gives a date of 1819.

While taking testimony for the trial between Jeremy Campo and The Jackson Iron Company in 1882, the Chief himself said he was either 71 or 77 years old, which would place his birthdate between between 1805 and 1811. At any rate he was very old when he died in 1902.

His father was Charles Makadoaque, and his mother a Scottish–Indian named Charlotte Sare. Charlie married Charlotte at the Soo and came to the Carp River with Robert Graveraet in the spring of 1846. He built a log house north of the Carp River where he and Charlotte were living when Graveraet appeared with Peter White in 1849. Even at that time Charlotte would have been 18 years old and Kawbawgam somewhere between 40 and 50. He was the Chief of the small band living at Indian Town near Gaines Rock that summer.

Peter White continues his story:

> The next morning we started for the much talked about iron hills; each one had a pack strap and a blanket, and was directed to exercise his own discretion in putting into a pack what he thought he could

carry. I put up 40 pounds and marched bravely up the hills with it for a distance of two miles, by which time I was as good as used up. Graveraet came up, and taking my pack on top of his, a much heavier one, marched on with both, as if mine was only the addition of a feather, while I trudged on behind, and had hard work to keep up. Graveraet, seeing how fatigued I was, invited me to get on top of his load, saying he would carry me too, and he could have done it I believe; but I had too much pride to accept his offer.

We arrived at the little brook which runs by George Rublein's old brewery (this was later Father Pinton's farm, now Sisters of St. Paul) We made some tea and lunched, after which I took my pack and carried it without much difficulty. We stopped a few minutes at the Jackson Forge where we met Mr. Everett, Charles Johnston, Alexander McKerchie, A.N. Barney, N.E. Eddy, Nahun Keys and others. At the Cleveland Mine, then known as Moody's Location, we found Capt. Sam Moody and John H. Mann, who had spent the previous summer and winter there. I well remember how astonished I was the next morning when Capt. Moody asked me to go up with him to dig some potatoes for breakfast. He took a hoe and an old tin pail, and we ascended the high hill, now known as the Marquette Iron Company's Mountain, and on its pinnacle found half an acre partially cleared and planted to potatoes. He opened but one or two hills when his pail was filled with large perfectly sound potatoes, and then said: I may as well pull a few parsnips and carrots for dinner, to save coming up again, and sure enough he had them there in abundance. This was the month of May!...From this time 'til the 10th of July we kept possession of all the iron mountain then known west of the Jackson claim, employing our time fighting mosquitoes at night and the blackflies through the day; perhaps a small portion of it was given to denuding the iron hills of extraneous matter, preparing the way for the immense products that have since followed. On the 10th of July we came away from the mountains, bag and baggage, arriving at the lake shore, as we then termed it, before noon. Mr. Harlow had arrived with quite a number of mechanics, some goods, lots of money and, what was better than all, we got a glimpse of some female faces.

The Founding of Marquette

Mr. Harlow and his party, with a great deal of equipment, had come all the way from Worcester. In a letter to Waterman Fisher, Amos Harlow reported some of their experiences. His salutation was "to friend Fisher." Mr. Harlow explained that they had been unable to get on a steamer and had taken passage on the schooner ALGONQUIN. The ALGONQUIN was a 54–foot, 60–ton schooner that had been dragged over the portage at the Soo about ten years earlier. At the time there were two steamboats on the lake – the INDEPENDENCE and a side–wheeler, the JULIA PALMER – and six schooners.

Harlow goes on:

> One propeller (steamer) was broke down and one had left for Copper Harbor, 70 miles beyond us – so we looked around and got a schooner – after waiting until Tuesday to take up our stores from Detroit.

Mr. Harlow left his family, consisting of his wife Olive, three–year–old Ellen, and his mother–in–law Martha Bacon, at a private home in the Soo, but some other women in the group went on.

On July 5th, 1849 they reached the present Marquette on the schooner ALGONQUIN from the Soo. When the vessel had passed Laughing Whitefish Point, an east wind was blowing. Captain John McKay had previously decided that Iron Bay (now Marquette lower harbor) was no place for a schooner to be during an east wind. The prevailing opinion of the navigators was that Iron Bay was full of sunken rocks. Peter White thought they had therefore landed on the sand beach just north of Little Presque Isle, but apparently this was not the case.

In a letter to Fisher, written on July 8, 1849, Harlow gives the details as to where they spent that first night. At the Soo he had stopped in the land office and done some purchasing of land, sight unseen, from looking at a map.

> I found on going to the land office that the Jackson Co. had taken up no land at the harbor proper...Their land was where the road goes down to the lake, in fact they can't land half the time it is so exposed to the wind. But there is a capital place on the next section perfectly secure from the storm about a half mile from the Jackson road (This would be Marquette's present lower harbor).
>
> "But the best harbor is three miles from the Jackson road at the mouth of the Dead River. This river has any quantity of water power and you can go up with a schooner one mile to the first falls where there is a very good place to build. So confident was I and Clark that

we should go to the river that I bought two fractional sections for the benefit of the company, in my own name, thinking that no one (else) should get the mouth of this fine river...It lies both sides of the river...thus securing it at the mouth and cost me 56 dollars.

From the above passage, it is apparent that Harlow had induced Captain McKay to examine the mouth of the Dead and the ALGONQUIN lay in its backwaters for protection until they could return to Ripley's Rocks the next day in a favorable wind.

Harlow's letter continues:

Arriving at the Carp we found that the Jackson Co. had bought 2 or more lots (fractional forties or government lots) that they thought might have come in our way and we should want, to keep us out. But in this they are mistaken...they have not got which I want but their iron hill.

The Jackson Company, having arrived in the area two or three years ahead of the Harlow group, could have purchased any piece of land they wanted, but they did not foresee the possibility of a settlement on the lake shore. It took the astute eye of Amos R. Harlow to visualize, in the first hours after his arrival, a port city, a good harbor and the potential water power of the Dead River.

Peter White describes the landing of Harlow's party thus:

Despite an uncomfortable night on the sand (at the mouth of the Dead River) the group was enthusiastic the next day as they boarded the ship again to return to Ripley's Rocks, arriving there that afternoon. All were seized by the same thought and imagined they were about to found a great city.

Harlow's description of the same moment follows:

We unloaded our freight and rolled it up as steep a hill as Hinnicutt's Store (in Worcester) 160 barrels and put in the store house in as hot a sun as any in Massachusetts. (The store house was not a building, but a flat area beside a rock wall, a spot to store things.)

Then, as the story goes, Peter White cut the first tree, a small birch near the water's edge. They all joined in the clearing of a spot near what is now Lake Street and Baraga Avenue corner on the shore near Ripley's Rocks. They decided to call the future city "New Worcester" in honor of Mr. Harlow's hometown. As agent in charge of the operation, Mr. Harlow was the superintendent or village president. He had done nearly all of the planning, purchasing and hiring that had gone into the venture.

Peter White goes on with his story:

At one o'clock of that day, we commenced clearing the site of the present city of Marquette, though we called it Worcester in honor of Mr. Harlow's native city. We began chopping off the trees and the brush, at the point of rocks near the brick blacksmith shop, just south of the shore end of the Cleveland Ore Docks. (The rocks were near the present oil tanks by Spear's dock, which burned in 1979) We cut trees close to the ground and then threw them bodily over the bank onto the lake shore; then under the direction of Capt. Moody, we began the construction of a dock, which was to stand like the ancient pyramids, for future ages to wonder at and admire!....We did this by carrying these whole trees into the water and piling them in tiers crosswise, until the pile was even with the surface of the water. Then we wheeled sand and gravel upon it, and by the end of the second day, we had completed a structure which we looked upon with no little pride. Its eastward or outward end was solid rock, and all inside of that was solid dirt, brush and leaves. We could not see why it should not stand as firm and as long as the adjacent beach itself. A vessel was expected in a few days with a large lot of machinery and supplies, and we rejoiced in that fact that we had a dock upon which they could be landed. On the third day, we continued to improve it by corduroying the surface and by night of the third day it was, in our eyes, a thing of beauty to behold. Our chagrin may be imagined, when, on rising the next morning, we found that a gentle sea had come in during the night and wafted our dock to some unknown point. Not a trace of it remained; not even a poplar leaf was left to mark the spot. The sand of the beach was as clean and smooth as if it had never been disturbed by the hand of man. I wrote in the smooth sand with a stick: 'This is the spot where Capt. Moody built his dock.' The Captain trod upon the record, and said I would get my discharge at the end of the month, but he either forgot or forgave the affront. It was a long time before anyone had the hardihood to attempt the building of another dock...

...the propellers would come to anchor, sometimes as far as two miles from the shore, and the freight and passengers had to be landed

155

in small boats. Our large boilers, when they arrived, were plugged, thrown overboard, and floated ashore, and the machinery was landed with our mackinac boat or a skow which we had constructed. Cattle and horses were always pitched overboard and made to swim ashore...

...Under the leadership of James Kelly, the boss carpenter, who was from Boston, we improved our time, after six o'clock each evening, in erecting a log house for sleeping quarters for our particular party. When finished, we called it the Revere House, after a hotel of that name in Boston. This building stood on its original site as late as 1860...

...We continued clearing up the land south of Superior Street (present Baraga Avenue), preparing the ground for a forge, machine shop, sawmill and coal house.

Back on the 5th of July (1849) when Mr. Harlow was examining his purchase at the mouth of the Dead River, he had noticed two rather well–built log cabins near the bay on the south end of Presque Isle. Abraham Williams of Grand Island had built them in the shelter from the north and west winds for the defunct New York and Lake Superior Mining Co. Harlow, who had little time to build a cabin for himself, asked the men to check these out, as he would be returning to Boston to report to Waterman Fisher and order more supplies. The men dismantled the cabins and floated the logs to the Ripley Rock site, where they erected a cabin to temporarily house Mr. Harlow and his family until the sawmill became operative.

On his way back to Worcester, Mr. Harlow stopped at the government land office in the Soo, and on July 16, 1849, he purchased the 63 acre site of the present city of Marquette from the U.S. Government on behalf of the company. He also advertised for laborers from ports on Lake Michigan and Lake Huron.

In August, Captain Ripley arrived at his rocks in the FUR TRADER with a group of laborers, mostly Germans, with a few Irish and a few French. The Germans, all from Milwaukee, included August Machts, George Rublein, Francis Dolf, and the Atfield brothers.

Dr. Edward Clark, who was returning to the Marquette Forge site, came down with cholera and died at the Soo. Several others died on the vessel en route to New Worcester, and others were landed quite sick. As soon as the Indians at Indian Town just a short distance down the shore heard about the epidemic, they all fled within an hour to escape the disease, to them more fearful than smallpox.

156

Preparing for the First Winter

The goal of the entire community that year was to house themselves and get a forge set up and operating.

Peter White again:

> At this time, the first steam boiler ever set up in this country (Lake Superior) was ready to be filled with water and it had to be done the first time by hand. It was a locomotive boiler. A dollar and a half was offered for the job and I took it; working three days and a night or two, I succeeded in filling it. Steam was got up, and I was installed as engineer and fireman...
>
> ...That summer there were but few boats of any kind on the lake. The reliable mail, freight and passenger craft was the schooner FUR TRADER commanded by veteran Capt. Calvin Ripley, for whom the picturesque rock in Marquette Bay took its name.

There was a small cluster of log cabins near the harbor, then called Iron Bay. The focus was at the landing spot, Ripley's Rocks, and the village was later laid out from this point, with the main street running west. At first the street was called "Superior Street," but ten years after the death of Bishop Baraga it was officially changed to "Baraga Avenue" (1878).

Nearly every ship to arrive in the summer and fall of 1849 brought more people and equipment for mining, building, roadwork, smelting and timber cutting. With the untimely death of Dr. Edward Clark, the whole operation fell on the shoulders of Amos Harlow and Robert Graveraet. Graveraet's responsibilities were the mining and transportation of the ore, while Harlow was superintendent and later Village president and in charge of the company forge and sawmill. While the first sawmill was company–owned, Mr. Harlow soon set up a second one, privately owned, back in the woods, where the Holiday Inn is today.

During the five or six months of preparation prior to leaving Worcester, Amos Harlow had set up the machinery for a forge and the first sawmill. These would be transported piece–meal to Lake Superior during the summer.

Olive Harlow had problems with her teeth, and to alleviate that trouble she had them all pulled, as she knew this would be the best solution to facing life in the wilderness.

In November, Graveraet traveled to Mackinac Island for horses to haul the ore from the mines. The horses had been shipped there from

Chicago. Later mules were found to be better. On this trip he also ordered a supply of grain and other staples which would be necessary through the little town's first winter.

November slipped by, and still the supplies had not arrived. It was the general opinion that the community would go through great hardship without the supplies and the horses would surely have to be killed. The group of Germans became very concerned and guilty since they were the last large group to arrive. They felt that the settlement could survive without them, and made plans to return to Milwaukee on foot if winter set in before the ship arrived.

Well into December they lost all hope of seeing the supply ship. The Germans, except for George Rublein who still had hope of the ship's arrival, took what belongings they could carry and started walking the Indian Trail south along the lake to Au Train.

Within a few days, an Indian arrived from L'Anse with the news that the schooner SWALLOW was in L'Anse Bay loaded with the precious cargo meant for the new Worcester. It was unable to come into Iron Bay due to a bad storm and had run on to L'Anse and the protection of Keweenaw Bay. It had been there a week or more.

Two hardy volunteers decided to snowshoe to L'Anse to see what could be done about getting the supplies back to the village. They were Captain Sam Moody, who had arrived two years earlier in the employ of the Cleveland Company to guard the claim, and James Broadbent, a saltwater sailor; both men now worked for Graveraet. A messenger was sent to retrieve the Germans, who were almost to Au Train. They returned.

Moody and Broadbent set out north along the lake, carrying packs, snowshoes, and a gun. The Indians had made a trail all along the lake shore, but people walking from L'Anse to Marquette that summer took a great shortcut by traveling straight east out of L'Anse until they hit Lake Superior. This route brought them through the Yellowdog Plains, a broad, flat area covered for the most part with jackpine. This became the preferred route in later years. Heading west, people traveled from Marquette up along the lake shore to just north of Saux Head Lake, then headed northwesterly to the Yellowdog River. They would cross the Yellowdog and head straight west on the north side of the river. Keeping on the high ground north of the river and heading west would bring them out at L'Anse.

Moody and Broadbent must have followed this route, using snowshoes when they hit the deep snow away from the lake and in the high country of the Yellowdog Plains. It would have been a tough three–day hike early in the winter when the snow was soft.

When the pair reached L'Anse Bay, they found the SWALLOW stripped of its rigging and frozen solid in the ice.

At a dock on the Baraga side of the bay, they found the SISCOWIT, a 40–ton schooner about the same size as the SWALLOW and all rigged. It belonged to Captain Jim Bendry of L'Anse Bay, who had purchased it some years before from the American Fur Company. Captain Moody took charge, hiring many Indians to transfer the cargo from the SWALLOW to the SISCOWIT over the stern objections of Captain Bendry. Moody and Broadbent explained the desperate situation at the little town 80 miles down the lake. Just for good measure, they held off Bendry with a shotgun. All he could do was stand by and swear.

Captain James Bendry is considered to be the founder of the Village of Baraga. He was born in Wooten–Bassett, Wiltshire, England, on June 6, 1822. At the young age of 12 years Bendry left home and went aboard a merchant ship engaged in trade on the Mediterranean Sea. He shipped to America in 1838 and became part of the American merchant service sailing the Great Lakes out of Buffalo. He was shipwrecked while working on the brig, INDIANA.

In 1845 he found his way to Sault Ste. Marie and became a deck hand on the first steamer to ply the waters of Lake Superior; he made one trip to La Pointe and Eagle River that year. On that first trip of the INDEPENDENCE were C. C. Douglas, the Spencer Family, Albert Averill, Chief Mate Sam Moody, Chief Engineer Thomas Richie, and Captain Stanard, pilot. A man named Stafford was the cook.

Bendry remained with the steamer during the winter of 1846, and at the Soo that year married a Chippewa woman by whom he eventually had eleven children.

In 1848, Bendry purchased the schooner, SISCOWIT, and sailed it on Lake Superior. Late in the fall of 1849 in planning a lake trip he doubted he could get back before winter, so he had his wife and two young children accompany him on the voyage.

In a terrible storm off Keweenaw Point they were compelled to take refuge in L'Anse Bay. The next morning there was ice all around the ship, and they decided to remain there. With the help of Indians they constructed a dock and log cabin at what is now the Baraga side of L'Anse Bay.

With the SISCOWIT loaded, the Indians were sent for axes to chop a passage in the ice two or three miles long to get out to open water. The Indians pushed the SISCOWIT into thin, broken ice where they couldn't follow, and she was lost from sight in a snow squall. On Christmas day, the first to be celebrated in the tiny village, the SISCOWIT sailed into Iron Bay

159

MARQUETTE, 1849.

Top: New Worcester (Marquette) 1849. R. Acton photo. This is an artist's depiction and not accurate.
Bottom left: Amos R. Harlow.
Bottom right: Captain James Bendry. Courtesy of Mrs. St. Germain (descendent)

with the two men aboard. The tiny ship was listing badly and covered with ice a foot thick in places, and her sails were frozen stiff. They had come the whole distance from L'Anse in a heavy northwest gale and snowstorm. They had not seen land the entire distance.

There was much rejoicing when the SISCOWIT sailed into Ripley's Rock. The whole settlement turned out to help unload. The borrowed ship was in need of better protection than Iron Bay could provide for the winter, so they tried to get her into the blind slew east of the Chocolay River mouth. She missed the channel and they lost control of her in the breakers. The vessel was driven ashore and lay there at the mercy of the elements for the next 40 years, finally becoming buried in the sand as the shore eroded away from her. Every few years, when conditions are right, she can be observed to this day in about eight feet of water. Then she disappears again.

On April 20, 1978, my son, Frederick Kim Rydholm, rediscovered the SISCOWIT just out from the Robert Funk residence in Lakewood. Wave action under a bank of ice along the shore had exposed the full length of the hull in about five feet of water. Mr. Funk, the owner of the beach there, has the spot marked.

With money received for the SISCOWIT, Bendry purchased the land across L'Anse Bay upon which the village of L'Anse now stands.

Troubles

As stated, the Carp River Post Office was established on January 12, 1847, and William B. McNair was the first postmaster. Later, this job passed to Philo Everett. After the first few years of operation of the forge, the Carp River Post Office during the winter months was moved to Marquette, where there had been another post office established on September 14, 1849 with Amos R. Harlow as postmaster.

When the Carp River Forge ceased operations in 1851, the two post offices continued to remain in Marquette, then a village of less than 1,500 people. The headquarters of W. A. Bruce, the man in charge of the mails and the general mail contractor for the Upper Peninsula was in Green Bay, Wisconsin and Peter White's father was in his employ there.

When the Forge closed and Philo Everett resigned as postmaster, Bruce didn't know that Carp River had ceased to exist as a community and thought it was his duty to assign a new postmaster there. Knowing no other people, he assigned Peter White as the Postmaster of Carp River.

Top:. Harlow Farm – This was known as the Martha Bacon Farm or the Grandma Bacon Farm by the Harlow family. Martha Bacon, mother–in–law of Amos R. Harlow, is standing on the bridge over the dammed–up Whetstone Creek. Water–powered Harlow Sawmill is right, boarding house for mill workers left center, and barn, right center. With a close look, you can see cows in the pasture. This location is now a part of the Holiday Inn property in West Marquette. Courtesy of the Alden Clark family.
Bottom: Marquette in 1851. The big building is the Marquette Forge courtesy of the Marquette County Historical Society.

162

Peter White operated his post office out of the Marquette Iron Company Store, a convenient, widely patronized location, while Mr. Harlow's Marquette Post Office was in his home and only handled a small amount of family mail and some for the company. In Green Bay it looked like Carp River was a prospering and growing community and Marquette a dying village. As a result, mail going to Marquette was addressed to Carp River for several years until the the situation was straightened out in 1856.

During the winter there were only three or four mails. Mr. Harlow hired an Indian, Jimmeca, to go to L'Anse for mail at a cost of ten dollars a trip, the money being made up by subscription.

By this time, the troubled Jackson Company had suspended operations and the agent had left in the fall. The President of the company, "Czar" Jones, took over at that time, but all work at the mine and forge had ceased. Peter White said the men thought seriously of hanging and quartering Mr. Jones. He left early in the spring, and the Jackson Company was through.

The Cleveland Mine was opened near Ishpeming late in 1849, and in 1850 about five tons of ore was shipped to New Castle, Pennsylvania. It was made into blooms and bar iron with such success that it immediately attracted the attention of iron workers from Pennsylvania and Ohio to the new iron fields.

The Cleveland–Cliffs Iron Company of today has gone by this name since 1890, but the original company was incorporated in 1850 under the name of the Cleveland Iron Company, with M. L. Hewitt as its first president. The Cleveland iron Company was organized under a special charter granted by the legislature, previous to the adoption of the new constitution of 1850 which prohibited the legislature from granting special charters to corporations. In the spring of 1853, the company abandoned its special charter and organized under the general mining laws of the state as the Cleveland Iron Mining Company. The articles of association were signed by John Outhwaite, M. L. Hewitt, H. F. Brayton and E. M. Clark. The first ore taken from the Cleveland Company's property was hauled in wagons to the Jackson Forge.

By the spring of 1850, the Marquette Iron Company's forge was ready for making blooms. Many small shops and dwellings had sprung up and there was a small dock at which steamers could land.

By February of 1851, the first births of white children were recorded in the community. Joseph Bignall was the first boy, born February 12, 1851, and Kitty Everett the first girl. She was born on February 23rd.

Mail service in the early 1850's was so erratic that a mass meeting of Marquette residents was held on January 17, 1854 to see what could be done about it. It was decided that Peter White, who was Postmaster at Carp River (in Marquette), would travel to Green Bay to pick up the mail. He took along 1,000 letters to be posted. On his way to Green Bay, Peter encountered five double teams with huge loads of mail all bound for Lake Superior. The teams reached Marquette on January 21, 1854.

White went on to Green Bay where he telegraphed Senator Lewis Cass in Washington with the complaints concerning the poor mail service. Cass responded by sending a special agent of the Post Office Department, Henry Hart, to Green Bay to investigate the situation. While waiting for Hart, White busied himself by stuffing mail sacks with empty mail bags so that when Hart arrived he found 120 bags waiting to go to Lake Superior; actually, only thirty of them had mail in them. A new mail contract was let.

The Stanard Brothers

Some other little-known yet important events were taking place along the shores of the north part of Marquette County. We have heard the tale of Captain Charles Stanard and his discovery of Stannard Rock. Soon afterwards, Captain Benjamin A. Stanard made a hasty survey of the rock. This survey stood well for all navigators until a more exact one could be made by the government surveyor, Captain Meade.

Ben Stanard was the captain of the ASTOR when it was wrecked at Keweenaw Point in 1844, the first documented shipwreck on Lake Superior. She had been built at the Soo in 1835 by the American Fur Company, and had been under the command of both Charles and Ben Stanard. Ben was known best to his friends as a keen sportsman, great naturalist, and a pleasant social companion. When he was 15 years old, he enlisted as a cabin boy on the schooner RED JACKET. In 1828 he made Cleveland his home, but continued his life as a lake sailor, working himself upward until he became captain of the schooner JOHN QUINCY ADAMS. He sailed the lakes for 26 years continuously, commanding, besides the Adams, the DETROIT and the RAMSEY CROOKE. The latter was named after the president of the American Fur Company and was employed in the business of that corporation, running between Detroit and the Soo. Stanard retired from the lakes in 1853, and became Inspector of Hulls in Cleveland.

Ben Stanard belonged to natural history clubs like the Ark and Kirkland Society of Natural History. Both owe as much to him as to any other member. William Case was the originator of the Kirkland Society, and when it was in the formative period he depended especially upon Captain Ben Stanard to gather specimens and see that they were properly set up. The museum in the Case Building in Cleveland was extensive and beautiful, and many a nature lover was fortunate enough to be shown through by the Captain himself in his elderly years.

We have not heard much about the other Stanard brother who was a captain, but he was no less a noted figure on the Great Lakes. This was John Stanard. We read of him at the Soo when young Peter White arrived there for the first time as a boy of 16. He was a member of a boat crew under the direction of Captain Augustus Canfield. Canfield was in charge of the surveying work in the straits and St. Mary's River. On June 10th of that year, preparations were being made at the Soo to haul the schooner UNCLE TOM over the rapids. Preparatory to doing so, Captain Brown of the schooner SWALLOW, John G. Parker, Captain John Stanard, E. G. Seymour, Tom Richie, William Flynn, and Dr. Prouty got into a yawl and went over the rapids to sound the channel for the schooner. Captain Brown was in the stern steering the boat, Captain Stanard was in the bow piloting her down, and Parker was pulling the stroke oar. When the yawl got to the big fall, she filled with water forward, veered badly in the eddy, then capsized and floated down the river bottom–side–up. Opposite McKnight's Dock, Captain Brown and Mr. Parker clung to her bottom and were taken off by Captain Redmund Ryder. Shawano, an Indian chief, was out fishing in his canoe and saw Seymour go down. He paddled over to the spot and succeeded in pulling him up with his spear. Our source, "The Book of Peter White," says that all the rest were drowned, but actually Captain John Stanard was not. He went on to become one of the most respected seamen of the Great Lakes. Some said he was the greatest navigator of the early days on Lake Superior.

As master of the schooner SWALLOW, he ran for days in dense fog without land or bottom, and scarcely ever lost his direction. If he did, he would fire his gun and know by its echo if he was near land, and then determine by its vibrations the coast he was upon and how to shape his course. It was the same with his brothers. Long years of experience in sounding their way with the gun enabled them to judge the land with astonishing certainty, even when they could not see it. After being three days in a fog, without soundings or sight of land:

"All keep quiet," said Captain John, "til we ascertain if land is near and where we are: it ought to be pretty close...Fire!" The blaze opened the thick fog before the gun; the sound rolled over the water for a second, then crash! another...another...then the sound rumbled along to the eastward. "I thought so – the Huron Islands, did you hear it rattle among the mountains, and then roll along to the shore to the northeast? You don't hear it this way for there is no land, the bay makes away to the south...ready about" Then the short explanation was interrupted by a voice, "All ready, forward," and "Hard–a–lee," brought the SWALLOW into the wind. The sails shook for a moment, then she fell off, and we commenced "long and short legs" for Granite Point (today Little Presque Isle), where our iron pilot's loud hail brought forth a light from the miners, about 12 o'clock at night, which enabled us to beat through between the peninsula and two outer rocks into South Bay, under Granite Point." (from The Book of Huron Mountain")

John Stanard was also captain of one of the early steamers, the "Julia Palmer." She was launched on Lake Superior at the Soo in 1846 and he took her on her maiden voyage.

Also on John Stanard we find the following from the Lake Superior News and Mining Journal, published in Sault Ste. Marie by John R. Ingersoll on Saturday, May 31, 1849:

Lighthouse Keeper..."We are pleased to learn that our fellow townsman, Captain John Stanard, so favorably known by nearly all within the last few years, crossed the Father of Waters, has been appointed keeper of Detour Lighthouse at the mouth of the St. Mary's River. We know of no man in our state whose appointment would give more general satisfaction."

Captain John Stanard died in Cleveland, Ohio in 1881, and is buried there.

The Famous Huron Mountain Snail

It is the naturalist Ben, however, who figures more than the others in the history of Huron Mountain. The complete story is told in the Nautilus, Vol. XXI, No. 6, Oct. 1907. In a word, the article said that Captain Ben Stanard turned over an extremely rare snail to William Case in 1847. Two or three hundred specimens had been collected in an inland lake close to the south shore of Lake Superior, during one of Stanard's many excursions inland

166

Upper left: View of the Jackson Mine.
Upper right: Shaft and incline – Cleveland Iron Mine. Courtesy Mrs. Joe Gannon.
Lower left: Cleveland Mine. Courtesy Mrs. Joe Gannon.
Lower right: Huron Mountain Snail. (Helesoma Multivalvos Case). This snail is possibly extinct now, and this is the only known specimen in the U. P. It belongs to the author – a gift of Dr. Van de Schielle.(U. of M.) Photo by Jack Deo.

167

to study the flora and fauna of the region and to collect specimens for the museum.

The species Helesoma Multivolvis Case was described in 1847 by William Case, founder of Case Institute of Technology in Cleveland (now Case Western Reserve University). Case distributed a few of the specimens and deposited the balance of the collection in the Boston Society of Natural History. There are specimens in the British Museum, the American Museum of Natural History, and the Smithsonian Institution.

From that time until 1906 nothing further was known about the species, and no more ever turned up. There was much speculation as to where the snails came from, the final deduction being that they were from either Lake Fanny Hooe in Keweenaw County or Howe Lake in Marquette County, as Stanard had spent much time at both places waiting out storms.

The answer came in the summer of 1906: Dr. Charles A. Davis of Ann Arbor, Michigan, while in the field for the State Geological Survey, had the great good fortune to rediscover the genuine multivolvis on the north shore of Howe Lake in Marquette County. Nine specimens were obtained at this time. Comparisons were made, and there was no question as to the identity of the Howe Lake shells with Case's species. It is equally clear that multivolvis is a valid species, quite distinct from any other.

Bryant Walker, an early member of Huron Mountain Club who owned the property, made several searches there himself after conferring with Dr. Davis. Two visits there in July of 1907, each involving a careful search of the entire north shore, yielded only three specimens. It seems likely that the species lives in comparatively deep water during the summer and only comes toward shore for spawning purposes, if at all. Bryant Walker made his last visit to Howe Lake on August 3, 1907. On August 28th, his sister made another visit there and found seven more specimens, all genuine, but, unfortunately, all but one were broken, more or less.

Since that time no other specimens have ever been found anywhere, and the snail may be extinct. Perhaps without Ben Stanard's powers of observation and his acute knowledge of nature, it might have gone unknown. He has added his bit to the study of science and evolution, and to the history of this relatively unknown part of Marquette County.

King Strang's Warning

Another interesting point was brought up by "King Strang," the Mormon leader who settled on Beaver Island and became a member of the Michigan legislature just after Michigan became a state. It concerns the islands along the south shore of Lake Superior. He claims that when they drew up the act in 1843 to form six counties from Michilimackinac, it was so worded as to bound the new counties "along the margin of the lake" (Great Lakes), leaving the entire waters in Emmet and Cheboygan counties. No proposition was ever made to change this boundary. Manitoulin, the Hurons, Granite, Partridge, Grande and all the smaller off–shore islands like Larus, Garlic and Saukshead, were included in Emmet County by Act of 1840. The Act of 1843, dividing the Upper Peninsula into counties, does not extend to them, and they remain in Emmet, unless by remote implication the Constitution of 1850 has taken them out.

The Old Plank Road

From the date of the first settlements within the county, the construction of highways and railroads became a work of prime importance. Before the Upper Peninsula's railroads were built, plans were made for the construction of a system of plank roads. In 1850, by legislative enactment, provisions were made to found the Iron Bay and Carp River Road Company. John Western, Lewis Bascum, William A. Ernst, Amos Harlow, Frederick W. Kirtland, Philo Everett and Czar Jones were named commissioners of the company.

Provisions were made for the exact material for the plank road: "which shall be laid out at least two and not more than four rods wide (a rod is 5 1/2 yards, or 16 1/2 feet): and shall be so constructed as to have at least 16 feet width of good, smooth and permanent road, eight feet of which shall be made of plank not less than three inches thick." This was the simplest and cheapest solution available to keep heavy wagons from sinking into the mud and soft sand. The first road was about eight miles long from Lake Superior to Carp River and another four or five miles to the mines. The plank road served its purpose for oxen, mules and horses and wagons, but with the development of industry in the community it became essential to introduce better transportation facilities.

The first great development along these lines was the building of the first set of locks at the Soo.

The Soo Locks

Way back in 1798, the Northwest Fur Company took the first step to eliminate the rapids by making a small set of locks on the Canadian side to accommodate fur trading canoes. The lock was 38 feet long and 9 feet wide, with a lift of 9 feet and a draft of 2 1/2 feet. There was a tow path alongside the upper rapids to tow the canoes and bateaux through the rapids above the lock. It was the first lock ever built on the American continent. During the War of 1812, the lock was destroyed by U. S. troops, but today there is a model of the original lock near the Abitibi Paper Company Office under the bridge at the Canadian Soo.

In 1839 the State of Michigan tried to build a larger lock, but a dispute developed with the Federal Government over the plan. A contractor was at the site, but was forcibly stopped by Federal troops from Fort Brady. By 1852, with such great demands from mines on the Keweenaw and at Marquette, an agreement had been reached. Henry Ledyard, who had married the daughter of Lewis Cass, was placed in charge of drawing up and letting a contract to build a lock. The state would let the contract, but the Federal Government would grant 750,000 acres of land in Michigan to the builder at the completion of the project. Charles Harvey was in the right place at the right time.

Charles Thompson Harvey was born in Westchester, Connecticut on July 26, 1829. He was only 22 years old when he appeared at Sault Ste. Marie, in the employ of the Fairbanks Scales Company of New York. He was an experienced salesman even then, having previously been a cashier for S. D. Mills of New York. In 1853 he was sent to the Soo to install a set of scales for the portage railroad, which was a horse–drawn tram used to carry goods around the rapids. After discussing the matter with the Fairbanks Corning people in New York for financial backing, he went to Lansing where he was awarded the contract. His enthusiasm and salesmanship were factors in both cases.

The Saint Mary's Falls Ship Canal Company was formed on April 12th, 1853. Charles T. Harvey was in charge as Federal Agent for the company. Against tremendous odds Harvey met the challenge. He hired 1,600 men, which later reached 2,000. For them he had to build bunkhouses, mess–halls, and a hospital. He also started the first–known group insurance for the workmen. He had to purchase hundreds of horses and huge amounts of equipment and transport those necessities long distances by water to the Soo. There had to be horse barns, blacksmith shops, tool sheds and housing for feed, equipment and other supplies. They had to contend with 40–below–zero temperatures, a cholera epidemic, an outbreak of typhoid, and labor shortages. Harvey even invented and built a steam hammer on the spot for use in the construction. Despite the many adversities, the canal was completed within the specified time and the first vessel locked through on June 18th, 1855. It was the steamer ILLINOIS.

Top: Charles Thompson Harvey.
Bottom: Charles T. Harvey, home in Harvey (1985).

Upper left: Samuel Jones Tilden 1814–1886. He always looked like he smelled something bad.
Upper right: John Burt. Courtesy of John Burt (descendant).
Lower left: Old Collinsville furnace where the first pig iron in Lake Superior District was made. Courtesy of Bill Gray. (descendent of Lorenzo Harvey)
Lower right: King James Jesse Strang. From 1850 to 1856, Jesse Strang served as king of a dissident colony of Mormons on Beaver Island in upper Lake Michigan. His reign came to an abrupt end when he was murdered by two disenchanted followers in 1856.

The first year the locks were open, 1,449 tons of iron ore (all from the Port of Marquette) and 6,000,000 pounds of copper passed through. Five years later the iron tonnage had reached 114,000 tons, and the copper came to over 12,000,000. The Soo Canal was destined to become the most heavily used locks in the world, and carry more tonnage of minerals, grain, coal and cars than all of the next leading canals in the world. It was also the first of the 20 leading canals in the world to be built (with the possible exception of the Terneuzen–Ghent Canal, built in 1827 in Belgium and the Netherlands. This may or may not be considered one of the world's major canals).

With the canal completed in 1855, Harvey moved to Marquette. He had been there before the canal was built, and he believed the place for him to be was at the source of the iron industry. He stirred up a great controversy for choosing some of the finest timber and mineral lands in the state in payment for the canal. In fact, on the Keweenaw Peninsula, he chose the lands on which the Calumet and Hecla Mining Company built the most profitable mine in the world. By the turn of the next century it had paid out over $100,000,000 in dividends alone. He also had another feud running with Samuel J. Tilden of New York over lands that he had chosen. Tilden was President of the Iron Cliffs Mining Co., and Alexander Maitland was the local agent for that company. Tilden was a political and financial giant in New York. In 1874, he became Governor of that state and in 1876, as Democratic Candidate, he won the election for President of the United States by popular vote only to lose by one electoral vote to Rutherford B. Hayes of Ohio. Tilden Township and the Tilden Mine were named for Sam Tilden.

When Charles Harvey moved up the lake to the pleasant new community of Marquette, he was enthralled with it. He wrote to the Fairbanks–Corning people in June of 1855 that even though there was ice on the lake for 30 miles on his trip up, "The weather was delightful, warm and agreeable – I must say that I prefer this (Marquette) to any locality I have seen in all my travels."

Harvey first lived and boarded at the home of Mr. and Mrs. Philo Everett. In 1857 he built a home near the Chocolay River. He then went to New York State, where he married Sarah Van Epps and returned to Marquette with his new bride and his parents in 1858.

It was also in 1857 that C. T. Harvey organized the Pioneer Iron Co. and built a furnace in Negaunee. Harvey and Edward Hungerford went east and hired Stephen R. Gay and Lorenzo Harvey (no relative) from the Berkshire Iron Co. in West Stockbridge, Massachusetts. At the Collinsville Forge, which had been converted into a crude furnace, they forged the first

THE OLD HUDSON BAY CO.'S LOCK, AS RESTORED BY MR. FRANCIS H. CLERGUE.

Top: Fur Company Locks.
Bottom: Old State Locks (c. 1855).

pig iron to be made in a Lake Superior blast furnace. Collinsville was named after Edward K. Collins of New York, who became wealthy in the steamship business and came to Marquette in 1853 to build a forge and invest in iron mining. Up to this time, all iron in the region had been processed in forges or sent down the lakes as raw ore.

In 1859, Charles T. Harvey organized the Northern Iron Company and brought Lorenzo Harvey to Chocolay to build and manage a furnace there. This site was at the present mouth of the river (not where the Siscowit lay) and this new mouth was dredged and a dock built. The furnace was fueled by coal instead of charcoal. Charles Harvey and Joseph W. Edwards also built a sawmill on the opposite side of the river's mouth in 1860. Gay went on to the Copper Country, where there is a small town named for him there today.

The Chocolay Furnace ran until the coal supply was exhausted. Under considerable encouragement by the local farmers, who were clearing land, it was converted to using charcoal and a total of some 50 or more kilns were eventually built in the area. Harvey even experimented with several new types of charcoal kilns at Harvey.

The Chocolay Fire

In May of 1863, a terrible fire wiped out everything that had been built around Chocolay except the furnace itself. The sawmill and 18 other buildings were engulfed, leaving over 100 people homeless. Both Harvey's home and his office, as well as the home of his father, were lost. Charles Harvey was in New York at the time of the fire and, though shocked and saddened, he looked at the situation as an opportunity to start fresh. He drew up great plans for a new city.

His plan called for 16 blocks, parks, marinas, industrial areas, and a large harbor at the mouth of the river. He envisioned the town of Harvey as being a metropolis of the north, a sister city that would rival Marquette so that they could grow and prosper together. He built a beautiful second home on a bayou of the Chocolay River closest to Marquette. This he called his "Bayou House." It was two stories high, of board and baton construction, and quite elegant for its day. It was during this period of building that he convinced the Chicago and Northwestern Railroad to plan for a railroad into the Harvey Harbor. The plan went through, and a grade was built which can still be seen today (the Harvey Grade), but for several reasons the track was never laid.

Top: Lake Superior Mine. C. 1860's.
Bottom: Columbia.

Book One

The Marquette Strap Railway

The progress of the building of the Soo locks was being observed very carefully by the Marquette community. The watchers included John Burt who, as a surveyor, well knew the potential mineral wealth of the south shore.

He was appointed to a two–year term as the Canal's first superintendant by Michigan Governor Bingham. His main competition for the job was Vernon Brown, editor of the Lake Superior News at the Soo. Brown had been highly critical of Charles T. Harvey during the building of the canal. If the work was sloppy, it was because Harvey was racing to beat a May 19th deadline, after which the contract would be invalidated.

In preparation for the opening of the locks, efforts were made to upgrade the handling of iron ore at the port of Marquette. To improve the plank road, a strap railway was laid out on the roadbed – that is, a piece of strap iron was placed on wooden rails and small railroad–type wheels put on the ore carts. They were still hauled by mules like a tram. This increased the tonnage that the cart could carry, made it easier on the mules, and speeded up the haul somewhat, but they could still make only one trip per cart per day.

The strap railway went into operation on November 1, 1855, and had a hard life of about two years. It was not satisfactory. Cars would sometimes run away on the hills, killing the mules (the driver could jump free), and the iron strap was always coming loose or the wooden rail in some way needing repair.

Marquette's First Docks

In 1854, a year before the opening of the canal, the Cleveland Iron Mining Company hired Mr. Dan Merritt of Cleveland to construct a good substantial loading dock in Marquette Harbor. He arrived in Marquette on November 20, 1854, having hired a group of Frenchmen from the Soo to cut timber for the dock. Dan Merritt had built a merchandise dock at Eagle River the previous year. However, before the job had even got under way at Marquette, Mr. Merritt died of smallpox on December 20, 1854. He had contracted the disease from one of his employees.

On the 17th of February, 1855, Dan Merritt's son, D. H. Merritt, left Cleveland with James St. Clair, agent for the Cleveland Iron Mining Company. Traveling by way of Chicago, they met Mr. David Himrod, agent for the refinanced Jackson Company. The group arrived in Marquette on snowshoes on the 17th of March, 1855. The snow was four feet deep on the level.

Originally both companies were going to build one dock between them, but ultimately each built its own. The Jackson Company dock was constructed on the north side of the harbor parallel with the shore, and was completed in 1855. The dock started at the east end of Washington Street and went downhill by wooden trestle to eight feet above water level. The ore was delivered to the dock in wooden four–wheeled carts drawn by mules. The carts held about three tons of ore and made one trip per day. When the strap rail was added they carried about four tons. The cars were unloaded by men who shoveled the ore onto the dock. From there it was shoveled into wheelbarrows and wheeled up a gangplank to a waiting vessel. It took 20 to 30 men, working ten–hour days, some three to six days to load a ship of 200 to 300 tons. Three hundred tons was the largest ship in those days. On many ships the ore was dumped on the deck, but large loads were carried in the hold. The brig COLUMBIA carried the first load of Marquette iron ore through the locks.

It was also in 1855 that the Cleveland Iron Mining Company built their dock, but it had no trestle. The mule cars were run onto the level dock and the ore wheeled aboard the vessel, the same as at the Jackson Company dock.

The Upper Peninsula's First Railroad

That same year (1855), Heman B. Ely started to build the first railroad in the Upper Peninsula. It would carry ore from the Iron Mountain where Negaunee now stands to the docks at Marquette. The village had officially changed its name to "Marquette" in 1850 and the new railroad was to be called the "Iron Mountain Railroad." The Marquette Forge had burned in March of 1853, but the demand for iron was increasing and there were several other forges being built or in the planning stages.

Heman Ely was joined in the venture by his four brothers – Samuel P., George H., John J., and Harvey. John Burt, who had taken an important part in the building of the Soo Canal, also supported the railroad. The original survey had been done in 1852, but the clearing work didn't start until 1855. It was incorporated that year as the Marquette and Iron Mountain Railroad, with Mr. John Burt as President and Cornelius Donkersley as superintendent. The railroad was completed to the Lake Superior Mine, in what later became

Ishpeming, in 1857. Heman Ely did not see it completed, as he died suddenly in October of 1856.

The Iron Mountain Railroad grade crossed and recrossed the strap rail route several times, causing a great deal of controversy. Charles T. Harvey acted as mediator and the three mining companies settled their differences.

Before the Marquette Company's forge burned, it had been taken over by the newly organized Cleveland Iron Mining Co. This company was under the leadership of Dr. M. L. Hewitt of Marquette and John Outhwaite and Samuel L. Mather of Cleveland. Dr. Hewitt loved Marquette. He said that he "had visited many quarters of the globe, and every well–known health resort in the United States, and that, after thorough study of climatic, soil and water conditions, had found Marquette and vicinity to be the most healthful spot on the American continent." Dr. Hewitt's daughter later married Peter White.

Samuel L. Mather became President of the Cleveland Iron Mining Co. and recognized the benefit of merging their operations with the strongest companies on the Marquette Range. He began negotiations with Samuel J. Tilden, President of the Iron Cliffs Co. Just as Mather was about to complete the merger in 1880, he died, and his son William Guinn Mather became President of Cleveland Iron Co. In 1891, William Mather united the Cleveland Iron Mining Company with the Iron Cliffs Company and formed the Cleveland Cliffs Iron Company.

Alexander Maitland did not go with the same company. He became agent for the Republic Iron and Steel Co. and owned the Maitland mining properties, which were run by his son A. F. Maitland. Both concerns are now part of the Empire Mine.

Two docks were operating in Marquette Harbor before the railroad started hauling ore, and a third dock was finished just after the railroad was put into operation in 1857. Up to this time the Lake Superior, Cleveland and Jackson Companies were the organizations involved in shipping ore. They operated several years before other concerns got started in business, and these three were later referred to as "the three old companies." All three companies used the Iron Mountain Railroad, and by 1857 each had their own dock.

The World's First Pocket Dock

It was this third loading dock in Marquette, completed in 1857, that made history. It was built for the Lake Superior Mining Co., with three men holding much of the responsibility. One was Samuel P. Ely, a younger brother of Heman Ely who came to Marquette to build the first railroad. The second was John Burt, son of William Austin Burt and member of the survey party who discovered iron ore. John Burt had also brought the first newspaper to Marquette in 1855, when he moved the Lake Superior Journal from the Soo. He owned the Burt Block, a large building on south Front Street where he carried on his several businesses. The third gentleman was Lewis Henry Morgan of Rochester, New York. He was a cousin to the Ely brothers and, like them, he was interested in railroads and mineral properties. Lewis Morgan came to Marquette in 1856, and in 1863 he built the Morgan blast furnace near what later became Morgan Heights. Today, we can still see the subtle depressions that mark the rows of houses in the little company town of Morgan, near the crumbling remains of the furnace. This furnace was one of the few successful blast furnaces in the area and was in operation almost until the turn of the century. Morgan Creek also bears his name.

Lewis Morgan became internationally known in the scientific world for one more thing which should be mentioned here. He made one of the first thorough studies of the beaver which he encountered constantly during his mineral explorations, and wrote a remarkable treatise on the behavior of this animal which, later biologists have claimed, has never been improved on to this day.

Alfred Ekstrom was an iron moulder in Sweden. He came to Marquette in the early 1870's and worked, making pig iron at the Morgan Furnace. He was the grandfather of Hildegaard and Virginia Johnson of Marquette. Their mother was born at Morgan. The Johnson's are well-known in Marquette. Virginia Johnson was the Principal at the Vandenboom School, and Hildegaard Johnson has directed choirs at the Messiah Lutheran Church for 60 years.

These men, all locally famous in their own right, were the ones most responsible for the world's first pocket dock. Ely was agent for the Lake Superior Mining Co. and a director of the railroad.

One of the sailing captains had suggested that a dock be built high enough so that ore could slide down chutes into a vessel, thus eliminating the wheelbarrow loading crew. However, this idea presented a problem: what to do with the ore that used to be piled on the dock while waiting for a vessel? It was therefore decided to build the new dock twenty-five feet high and build storage pockets to hold the ore. Each pocket would have its own chute which, when lowered, could empty the ore from the pocket into the waiting ship. The result was the first pocket dock. This dock was built from the east end of Main Street into the bay and had 75 pockets. Today, what is left of this dock (now partly dismantled) is known as the "fishdock" in Marquette's lower harbor.

Upper left: William G. Mather.
Upper right: Captain Justus O. Wells, Master of the brig Columbia.
Middle: The first pocket docks.
Bottom: Ships at the First Pocket dock – Lower Harbor (1860s).

LIGHT HOUSE.

Top: While this picture was labeled the "Sabastopol," experts tell us it is not. It is, however, one of the early five or six engines similar to the Sabastopol. There is no known picture of the Sabastopol.
Bottom: Marquette Light (c. 1890).

The Upper Peninsula's First Locomotive

In September of 1857, the brig COLUMBIA returned to Iron Bay with a steam locomotive on her deck. It was the first locomotive to reach the Upper Peninsula and it had come all the way from Patterson, New Jersey. It weighed 25 tons and cost $11,000.

By this time, Peter White was the proprietor of the Cleveland Company's store. He was also the Postmaster, County Clerk and Marquette County's Registrar of Deeds. In addition, he was studying law, starting a collection of books that he would lend out, and, though still very young, was fast becoming one of the leading citizens of the community. Peter rowed out into the harbor to look over the locomotive. Someone had named it the "Sebastopol."

At the end of September, 1857, Peter White married Ellie S. Hewitt, the daughter of Dr. Morgan Hewitt.

When it came time to unload the Sebastopol, there was an angry mob of muleskinners on hand to prevent the unloading, but the captain of the COLUMBIA was not a man to back down easily. Taking note of their crude weapons and determined stance, he took the precaution to load a cap and ball gun, step out of the wheel house and level it at the crowd. He told them that his job was to deliver the locomotive on the dock at Marquette, and the first man who tried to stop him would be shot. The Sebastopol was unloaded without incident.

One of the muleskinners in the crowd was Andrew Steele, who later became the first driver of the locomotive. A second locomotive arrived a month later.

The First Ore Carrier

In 1855, George B. Russel of Detroit had the idea of building a ship especially to carry iron ore. He had established a shipyard in Hamtramck in 1854. The propeller B. L. WEBB was the first ship of its kind, and the first lake boat to have a beam of over 30 feet. Peter White wrote the first bill of lading of the first shipment of ore to leave the Northern Peninsula, a matter of seven barrels consigned to the B. L. WEBB by the Marquette Iron Company. But the consignment never was loaded onto the WEBB. On her first trip up to Marquette, loaded with grain and other supplies for the winter, she locked through into Lake Superior in November of 1856. Between the Soo and Marquette she burned to the waterline and sank, losing everything.

The first summer home, or what today may be called a grand camp, was built on the south shore of Teal Lake sometime in the 1850's by James Reynolds of Ohio, who came there each summer with many servants, boats and much equipment. George and Nancy Mall moved up from the Carp River Forge to act as winter caretakers there for a number of years.

Known locally as the "White House," there would probably be no record of it now if a local artist named Edwin Schrotki had not made two beautiful paintings of it. One of these paintings is in the Negaunee Historical Society and the other, shown here, is in the Marquette County Historical Society. The home burned in the early 1880's.

Schrotki did several other paintings in the area before leaving. Photo by Jack Deo.

Top: Jackson Company Dock – north side of the Bay – lower harbor.
Lower left: Jackson Company Dock at a later date.
Lower right: Wood ore carrier (1870s).

Again the little village was in the predicament of its first winter of 1849, as there was scarcely a ton of hay for the horses in all of Marquette. Fortunately, Mr. Tallman Whiting of the Soo realized the gravity of the situation and ordered a duplicate cargo sent up on the propeller GENERAL TAYLOR from Detroit. It was a dangerous undertaking, with no insurance offered this late in the year. He charged ridiculously high freight rates, but the trip was successful and the inhabitants of Marquette, Eagle Harbor and Ontonagon were glad to pay it.

The Marquette Light

While the locks were under construction in 1853, the first lighthouse was built on Lighthouse Point. This point is the focal point of the present City of Marquette, being a prominence on the lake shore about halfway between the northern and southern extremities of the city. The first structure was built in 1853 and then rebuilt in 1855. Thirteen years later the original structure was removed and a second, one–story lighthouse built. A second story was added to the building in 1906 to enlarge the living quarters, raising the light to 77 feet above the water level. This made it visible 10 to 15 miles away. It was changed from kerosene to electricity in 1927.

An interesting story was told about the lighthouse by Mr. Joe Gannon of Marquette. Mr. Gannon, who owned the Gannon Wholesale grocery, says he used to park by the waterworks to relax and unwind on his way home from work. One day he noticed a man looking intently at the lighthouse and making notes in a book. After striking up a conversation with the stranger, Gannon learned that he worked for the U.S. Government. The man said the lighthouse was once a replica of a friary at La Rabida, about four miles from the little seaport of Palos de la Frontera in Spain.

This, according to the stranger, was the place where Christopher Columbus stayed while visiting Queen Isabella. The man said that the original architect was familiar with the friary, and that Lighthouse Point reminded him so much of it that he designed the first lighthouse as an exact replica of it.

Christopher Columbus was in Portugal in 1484 making an effort to interest John II, King of Portugal, in furnishing him with ships, sailors and funds to make a voyage westward, seeking a new and easy contact with the Far East. The King referred the project to a junta, but in 1485 it was turned down. The same year Columbus' wife, Dona Felipa, died in Lisbon.

Saddened and discouraged but still firm in his desire to make the voyage, he decided to try his luck in Spain. He knew no one there except a sister of his late wife who was married to a Spaniard in Huelva, so Columbus set sail for that part of Spain with his five–year–old son, Diego.

As their ship rounded into Rio Tinto, he observed on a bluff overlooking the sea the buildings of the Franciscan friary, La Rabida. That suggested a solution to his problem of what to do with Diego, as it was well known that the good Brothers often gave shelter to the seafarers of that day. To the friars of La Rabida they brought tales of adventure with the known and unknown waters. In those days it was believed that beyond the Pillar of Hercules stretched the unknown sea with terrors that no man could face.

So, after landing at Palas instead of Huelva, Columbus walked with his little son four miles to the ancient Franciscan monastery, dedicated to Santa Maria de Rabida, knocked at the gate and asked the porter for a drink of water and some bread for the boy.

Fortunately, Antonio Marchena, a highly intelligent Franciscan who had studied astronomy, came to the gate and entered into conversation with Columbus. He invited both father and son to stay, accepted Diego as a pupil, and introduced Columbus to the Count of Medina Celi, a grandee of Spain and also a ship owner of Cadiz. The Count was instrumental in obtaining for Columbus an audience with King Ferdinand and Queen Isabella, who eventually furnished ships, men and supplies for his voyage in 1492.)

This story was told to me by Mr. Gannon, and several versions of it have been published in the Mining Journal from time to time. It has been a source of consternation to lighthouse historians, who say that there is no truth whatsoever to the story that the building was a replica of a friary. They say that if it was, there were 39 others just like it on the lakes. They point out that any small building with a tower at one end would look like a church, a friary or a lighthouse. Since we have no picture of the original, there is no way to make a judgment today. For some Marquette people, the story has become legend.

More on Charles T. Harvey

Charles T. Harvey was the organizer of the first charcoal iron furnace in the Peninsula, that of the Iron Cliffs Company, which built the Pioneer Furnace in Negaunee in 1857 with S. R. Gay and Lorenzo D. Harvey in charge. This furnace operated until 1893.

Harvey was also the founder of the Lake Superior Foundry Company in 1858. With four investors from Utica, New York – John Thorn, Isaac and Thomas Maynard, and Nathan E. Platt – they incorporated the foundry to build equipment for the local mines and railroads. The foundry was on the bay near the lower harbor. This business later became the Iron Bay Foundry in 1867 under the direction of D. H. Merritt and C. Y. Osborn, and in 1889 it was known as the Lake Shore Iron Works and, later, The Lake Shore Engine Works. This is now the Lake Shore Engineering Company.

Charles Harvey's interest in roads and railroads had few equals. He secured grants of 5,000,000 acres of land for Michigan railroads and participated in at least the planning and formation of several. With Samuel P. Ely he planned the Marquette–Stateline railroad, which never came to be but was supposed to connect with a railroad that ran from Fond du Lac, Wisconsin to Ontonagon. Harvey also had a survey made for the state road to Bay de Noc. It was in 1861 that the stage coach road was cut through the forest from Marquette to Masonville and Little Bay de Noc, and Harvey received the government contract to construct the road. After it was built, he organized and ran the first stagecoach line, carrying both passengers and mail in the fall of that year from Marquette to Green Bay. He purchased some land in the vicinity of what is now Carlshend as a stopover place or a place to change horses. While building the locks at the Soo, he proposed and built the first Presbyterian Church there. He became one of the leaders both personally and financially in building the Presbyterian Church at the corner of Blaker and Front Streets in Marquette in 1868. Harvey and Harlow were prime movers in forming the Presbyterian congregation in 1856. Their first services were held in the Harlow home and later in a mission house on Main Street, with the back of the building being across from the present Post Office. The church at Front and Blaker burned in 1933 and was rebuilt the following year.

In 1860, Harvey was involved with timber interests at Manistique and built the dam on the river there. Then he was off to New York City with an idea he had while at the Bayou House in Harvey. He hoped to alleviate the congestion of the city he had been reading about. His idea was an elevated railroad. In 1874 Harvey built a one–half mile trial elevated railroad on Greenwich Street and personally drove the first car along it. Governor R. E. Fenton of New York was one of the astonished but delighted passengers on the first commercial run.

Harvey became president of the company that built and expanded the New York "El," the first in the world. Journalists at the time said he was the first man to offer a practical solution to the problems of New York's crowded streets.

Top: Presbyterian church. It burned and was replaced in the early 1930's.
Bottom: Model of Harvey's first elevated train in the yard of his estate in New York. Courtesy Marquette County Historical Society.

Top: Charles T. Harvey in his first elevated track in New York City. Courtesy Marquette County Historical Society.
Bottom: The L'Anse Post Office, operated by the Bendry family, descendants of Captain Bendry. Courtesy of Mrs. St. Germain of Baraga.

Charles Harvey made a fortune in New York, and lost it there. About two years before his death in 1912, he told James Jopling in Marquette that he had lost his railroad and his fortune because he had quarreled with his friends in New York. His home in New York burned, but because of the heroic efforts of his domestic help, his wife and children were saved.

In 1863, during the great Chocolay fire, the Bayou House burned also, but was rebuilt the same year. At present (1985), the Charles T. Harvey home at 2461 US 41 South is owned by Carl Menze. Wide charred boards are exposed in the attic, and it is possible that this is the original house repaired, or they could have salvaged some of the lumber from the old house. In either case, it has to be one of the oldest frame houses in the county.

After returning to Marquette, Harvey continued with his river mouth project and rebuilt the Chocolay River Furnace at the expense of a half–million dollars. When the market for pig iron went to pieces, he gave up the furnace idea and it closed for good. The furnace and many of the 50 charcoal kilns nearby stood until well after the beginning of the 20th Century.

The little village of Harvey, while never becoming the rival to Marquette that Harvey had hoped, was never completely abandoned. Farmers, largely homesteaders on government lands, moved out of Marquette and spread over the nearby area in the 1870s and '80s. By 1885 there were well over 200 farmers in Chocolay Township with cleared farms. They sold hardwood timber in four–foot bolts to the hungry charcoal kilns at the Harvey Furnace and the pine to the sawmill there that was later taken over by George Sambrook. The pine was floated down the Chocolay River. They then raised hay, oats, extraordinarily large crops of fine potatoes, and strawberries that were every bit as good as those raised in much better growing regions of the nation.

In his later years, Charles Harvey moved away from Marquette for the winter months but kept his home here and returned each summer up until his death on March 14, 1912. He died alone and poor, in a hotel room in New York City within the sound of the elevated trains he invented. After his death, his wife spent some time at the Bayou House but died in Memphis, Tennessee in 1916. The Bayou House was sold to the D. S. Cowdens, who lived there for many years.

Charles T. Harvey was a planner, engineer and builder all his life. Besides being an important part of the planning and building of five railroads, the Soo Locks, and the New York "El," he was also involved with two sawmills and several blast furnaces in this country and Canada. In 1895–1899 he built the Hudson Bay, Ontario and Western Railroad north to

191

Hudson Bay. He was always a controversial figure in American history and many people have tried to discredit him. Part of the indignation toward Harvey stemmed from the fact that others had little control over what lands he chose, and that he had been paid more than people felt his services were worth. Author Stewart Halbrook called him the "lost man in American history." A Fairbanks–Morse official called him "the greatest engineer this country has ever produced."

Harvey was consulted extensively by Goethals, who engineered the Panama Canal. That canal, started by France in 1881 and completed by the U. S., opened in 1914, two years after Harvey died. At the Soo, no lock was ever named for him, though later locks, far easier to build, were named for the engineers who were responsible – General Poe, Godfred Weitzel and Charles Davis. They even saw fit to name one for General Douglas McArthur, who had no connection there. Harvey's first lock was called by his critics "Harvey's Ditch," and by his admirers "The Miracle Mile."

At any rate, Charles T. Harvey called Marquette his home wherever he was. At present, there is a new lock being planned at the Soo. It is to be the largest one yet, and will be constructed some time before 1990. Maybe this one will bear his name.

The First State Road

While Charles Harvey was responsible for the state road to Bay de Noc (Escanaba), it was not the first state road in the Marquette County area. Back in 1857 the railroad only went to the mines at Negaunee and Ishpeming, and the entire community was still isolated. With several blast furnaces starting up, three large mining operations and the town growing rapidly with prospectors, businessmen and sawmills, it was imperative that there be at least one good road linking it with the nearest community. It was unwise to depend entirely on ships for supplies and communications. The few harbors and the dangerous and undependable Lake Superior had too many tragedies. Many lives had been lost in attempts to run the storms.

In 1857, the community closest to Marquette was L'Anse. The Jackson Forge had been abandoned, but the mining camps near the Jackson Mine and the Cleveland and Superior Mines were beginning to grow, after work was begun at the Superior Mine. Other log buildings were erected in the area near Division Street (Ishpeming) adjoining the track of the Marquette, Houghton & Ontonagon Railroad. Even a few frame buildings

192

Top: The Cleveland Dock – lower harbor – 1870's – Note Ripley rock far right.
Bottom: Marquette's Lower Harbor (1870s)

were beginning to appear. Ishpeming dated back to 1854 when the Cleveland Iron Company began to work there in its first mine located at the "Sawmill Pit" and that year shipped 3,000 tons of ore. Before this, there had been several mining encampments in the area, as far back as 1848, but no thought of a community. Several homes on Johnson Street in Ishpeming allegedly are the originals from the days of D. L. Cassels Dead River Silver & Lead Mining Co., improved over the years with stucco, plaster and even basements. They are said to have been built of hewn logs in 1848 & '49, and are the oldest standing buildings in Marquette County.

With requests from both L'Anse and Marquette to state officials to have a road connecting these two very isolated villages, provisions were made in 1857 for such a road. Charles Johnson and Samuel Peck of Marquette, and Jacob B. Bennett of L'Anse, were in charge of construction. This was the first state road in Marquette County and the Upper Peninsula. Two years later, in 1859, Harvey's aforementioned Marquette to Bay de Noc road was authorized.

At the time L'Anse and Baraga, then collectively known as Keweenaw Bay, was home for a large number of Indian people living near both a Methodist and a Catholic mission, the former preceding the latter by some years. The two missions got along very well throughout their long existence and both provided schools and religious leadership for the Indian community.

The route of the Marquette–to–L'Anse Road (later called the Marquette Road) generally followed the old Indian route to L'Anse, that is, along the lake shore (though just a little inland in some places) to Saux Head Lake, where it bridged the outlet there, then up to and across the Yellowdog River, then straight west to L'Anse. A few pieces of this road still in use today are along parts of County Road 550, a piece a little way along the northeast side of the Yellowdog River and Bear Lake, and part of the Triple A Road on the Yellowdog Plains, from the top of the Camp 6 hill to the Andersen Homestead (today Stromquist's Camp). This piece of today's Triple A Road exactly follows the original route of the first state road in the Upper Peninsula. Earlier, there were military roads from St. Ignace to the Soo and from Green Bay to Fort Wilkins. From about 1858 to the mid–1870's, stagecoaches ran regularly between Marquette and L'Anse, and from 1860 to the mid–1870s they ran from Marquette to Bay de Noc in the summer months. When the railroads were completed to these places, the stagecoach runs became erratic and soon stopped.

Enlarging the Pocket Docks

The increase in demand for both pig iron and raw iron for the steel mills of the east made it necessary for more and larger docks to be built. Noting the success of the new operation on the Lake Superior Company's pocket dock, the Cleveland Company in 1858 erected a trestle with pockets on their old dock which had been built in 1855, but this new trestle was 30 feet above the water level. It still kept the same height from the mouth of the pocket as the Lake Superior Company's dock, thus allowing for five feet more of ore storage in each pocket. The new dock was also longer and contained 100 pockets. It went into the bay from Superior Street (now Baraga Avenue). With the completion of this dock, it was felt that the Port of Marquette could now handle all the ore that would be shipped for many years to come, and the little town had established itself as the greatest port on Lake Superior.

In 1861 the Civil War broke out and the demand for iron increased further. Vessels carrying 1,000 tons began to make their appearance on the lake. The railroad company constructed a new dock just north of the Cleveland Iron Company's dock. The new dock was 35 feet high, with correspondingly greater amounts of storage in the pockets. By the time this dock was completed in 1864 the railroad had seven engines, and a fleet of hopper cars that carried eight tons each had replaced the much smaller flat–bottomed cars.

Michigan sent far more than iron in support of the Union during the Civil War. When President Lincoln sent out the call for men, the Michigan Volunteers were the first to arrive in Washington. The President was quoted: "Thank God for Michigan." At the battle of Gettysburg, Michigan's "Iron Brigade" had the greatest casualties of any fighting unit and that battle proved to be the turning point of the war. Between men and iron, Michigan had a great influence in saving the Union.

More on Peter White's Activities

In 1857, besides his many other duties in the community, Peter White was elected the first State Representative from Marquette County. It was on September 29th of the same year that he married Ellen S. Hewitt, daughter of Dr. M. L. Hewitt, who was a founder of the Cleveland Mining Co.

Dr. Hewitt had come from New York State, studied medicine in Vermont, and moved to Cleveland in 1833. It was a small village of 2,500

Top: First National Bank. Corner of Spring and Front Streets. It was often referred to as Peter White's Bank.
Bottom: Marquette 1861. From an old, three–section print, gift of Leigh St. John. Restored by Jack Deo.

people at the time. It was Dr. Hewitt and some others who sent Professor J. L. Cassel to Lake Superior to look for mineral lands. Dr. Hewitt came to Marquette in 1853 and did not practice medicine after that. His other daughter married Samuel Mather.

Peter White had run for the legislature so he could be in Lansing with all the details of the steam railroad which they hoped would be built by the Elys. The property of the old Marquette Iron Co., which had been purchased by the Cleveland Company (64 acres in Marquette), was turned over to Peter to sell and he was soon in the real estate business as well.

When he showed up in Lansing for his first session of the legislature he caused a sensation. He had traveled from Marquette to Escanaba on snowshoes, then taken the stage to Fond du Lac, Wisconsin, and then walked the rest of the way to Lansing. It took him 15 days to get there. A great cheer rang out in the legislature as he took his seat, as his reputation had traveled ahead of him. From that time on, he was known as the Honorable Peter White. He was succeeded in 1863 by James Pendill.

Robert Graveraet, also elected in 1857, was the county's first State Senator. He was followed by Edwin B. Isham and then Peter White was elected the senator from this district for one two–year term.

Peter White also started a law office with Mr. M. H. Maynard, which was active for about ten years. Mr. Maynard continued on to become one of the oldest attorneys in the Upper Peninsula. He also held many of the offices that Peter White had. Peter also started an insurance company that is still in business today and, in fact is the oldest in Michigan. In 1864 he was a prime mover in the formation of the First National Bank. He had his own private bank before this, and ran both banks from the same office until he became president of the First National in 1869. Peter White remained its president for nearly 40 years until just a few years before his death, except for the year 1879–80 when C. H. Call served as president.

It seems as though these activities would be enough to keep many men busy, but in the case of Peter White there were more, many more than we can mention. He was also a member of the school board from its beginning in 1857, and held that office for over 50 years. Before the school board was formed, there was a Board of Inspectors. Amos R. Harlow, Robert Graveraet and Rev. Josiah More (who was also the local physician), were the prime movers for the schools back in 1849. The first Board of Inspectors was made up of Robert Graveraet and Philo Everett. Marquette's first school was in the home of Mrs. Harlow. The teachers were Mrs. Samuel Barney and Mrs. Dan Ball, and the four students were the Harlow and Bignall girls.

Edward Breitung

Many of the early settlers in Marquette started with little and were able to amass a fortune. One of the most successful of these was Edward Breitung, Sr. He was born in Germany in 1831, educated there, and then graduated as a mining engineer from the College of Mines in Meiningen. He traveled to America in 1849, learned English in Kalamazoo, and came to Marquette in 1855. He had been a clerk and a bookkeeper up until this time, but when he came to Marquette he got into the mercantile business. In his early years Ed Breitung was known for his thrift. He saved everything. He also did a lot of exploring and buying and selling of mineral lands.

In 1859, Mr. Breitung moved to Negaunee and took a job operating the Pioneer Furnace for Israel B. Case. He later became a partner in the operation and also opened a store in Negaunee. Through efficient handling of the furnace operation, Breitung was one of the few who made money. He invested his money in developing mineral lands on a small scale. With so many of the small mining operations throughout the Marquette Range failing (several hundred of them failed in the early years) Mr. Breitung was unable to find investors, so he had to proceed on his own. One of his first real successes was the Washington Mine, which he opened in 1864–65, and by 1870 he was opening the Negaunee hematite range.

Ed Breitung went to the Republic area in 1871 to investigate stories of some trappers who became lost because of problems with their compasses. He proceeded to open the Republic Mine, which soon became one of the largest and most profitable mines on the Marquette Range. A year later Jacob Houghton, a much younger brother of Douglas Houghton, opened the mines at Michigamme.

When the panic of 1873 hit the country, all the mines and furnaces closed down. There was no market for pig iron. Mr. Breitung bought all the pig iron that was available at a much reduced price. There were others, like Peter White, who did the same, but not to the extent that Ed Breitung did. Within a year or two he was the most prosperous man on the Marquette Range. He was elected to the State Legislature that year (1874) and held that office until 1877, when he ran successfully for State Senate. He became the mayor of Negaunee in 1880, an office he held for three terms, and then a member of the United States Congress from 1883 to 1885.

In 1873 Mr. Breitung began opening up the Menominee Range and in 1882 the Vermilion Range in Minnesota. He was considered one of the

Upper left: Sam Kaufman. Courtesy First National Bank.
Lower right: Juliet Graveraet Kaufman. Courtesy Marquette County Historical Society.

wealthiest and most powerful men in the region, and had built up the largest mining dynasty in the United States.

Sam Kaufman Marries Juliet Graveraet

Another prominent name in the annals of Marquette County history is that of Kaufman. The family goes back to Sam, who also arrived in Marquette in the very early days. Sam Kaufman was born in Bamberg, Bavaria, in 1837. He left Europe at the age of 13 and arrived in Ontonagon when he was 20, a peddler selling goods and clothing. A year later, in 1858, Sam came to Marquette and continued with his merchant's trade which was interrupted in 1861 when he was elected Sheriff of Marquette County. In August of that same year, he married Miss Juliet Graveraet, sister of Robert Graveraet.

Robert Graveraet's wife died in 1854. They were living in a nice home just south of where the Marquette Iron Company's forge used to be, beneath the bluff where the Chamber of Commerce building stands today. After the death of his wife, Graveraet's mother, father and two sisters came to live with him in Marquette. In 1860, both Robert's father and mother died within a few weeks of each other, leaving Robert and his two sisters alone in the large house.

Robert's parents were Henri G. Graveraet, born in Detroit in 1785, and Charlotte Livingston Graveraet, born in the same year in Canada. They both died in Marquette,– Henri on December 31, 1860 and Charlotte on January 17, 1861. Both are buried in Park Cemetery.

It was at this time that Juliet Ann (as the name was later written) the younger of the two Graveraet sisters, met and married Sam Kaufman. Sam was 24, Juliet 16.

Robert Graveraet himself died suddenly in 1861 as a result of violent bleeding from the stomach. There was some talk of foul play at the time since he was only 41 years old, but apparently it was a natural untimely death. He had been a prominent citizen in the community, and, when Sam Kaufman married Juliet, he became well–known immediately. They lived in Ishpeming for a short time. Sam was later a Justice of the Peace and Delegate to State Democratic Conventions. Though he continued to travel to Houghton and Ontonagon selling his wares, he also opened a clothing store in Marquette, first in partnership with Isaac Neuberger and later on his own. The Kaufmans had 11 children in the years that followed, and they had much to do with the growth and development, as well as the cultural settlement, of the city of Marquette.

Book One

The Wreck of the Jay Morse

Samuel Livingston Mather was the President of the Cleveland Iron Company, which was later the Cleveland–Cliffs Iron Company. He had been associated with the iron business since the 1840's. Mather had two sons, Sam Mather, Jr. and William G. Mather. Young Sam was around the iron mines of Negaunee and Ishpeming most of his adult life. He had two friends, Colonel James Pickands and Jay C. Morse, and the three of them decided to form a company and get into the iron business.

While acting as general agent for the Cleveland Iron Mining Company, Jay C. Morse had developed many business interests around the Marquette Range. He had been in Pickands' regiment during the Civil War. Pickands started a hardware store about 1866 on Lake Street at the foot of Superior Street (now Baraga Avenue). The sandstone building facing west is still there with the windows bricked in. Jay Morse sent Pickands all the business he could.

The Pickands' store and the Cleveland dock both miraculously escaped the fire in 1868.

The three men formed the company and ordered a new steamship to carry their iron. They named it the JAY MORSE. It was a powerful little ship, 79 feet long and 18 feet wide, and was to be used to tow ore barges and to bring schooners in and out of ports.

In June of 1867 the new JAY MORSE arrived in Marquette Harbor. Mr. Morse was very proud of the new ship, and invited all his friends to a party on board. They were going to take an evening ride around Presque Isle. There were 40 guests in all, including the Ely brothers, the Calls, the Maynards and, of course, Peter White.

The lake was so calm and the evening so beautiful that Captain Atkins decided to go on up the shore beyond Presque Isle and circle Partridge Island before returning to the lower harbor.

While just off Partridge Island on the land side, the ship came onto some hidden rocks. Without warning she lurched to a stop, throwing several people who were seated on the front railing into the water. Darius G. Maynard, a brother of M. H. Maynard, and law partner of Peter White was one of them. The others, two or three women, swam back to the sinking ship. Captain Atkins was injured in a fall as the ship struck the rocks. The ship slid backwards off the rocks and Joe Roleau, at the wheel when the accident happened, took the sinking ship toward the shallow water, where, in a billow of smoke and steam, she settled in about 14 feet of water not far from the rocky shore.

Roleau, on a makeshift raft of debris, searched for Maynard unsuccessfully and then went ashore. The rest of the survivors, many of them wet and cold, crowded onto the small portion of the bow deck that was still above the water and waited.

Joe Roleau became the hero of the whole tragic episode. He found his way through the woods to the Dead River, swam across it and headed for Marquette, in all a distance of about six miles. Arriving there in the wee hours of the morning, Roleau succeeded in locating Captain Bridges of the tug DUDLEY. It took some time for the Captain to find his engineer and build up a head of steam, but by dawn the DUDLEY was headed for the rescue.

Twelve hours after the MORSE sank, the DUDLEY came alongside it to take the shivering survivors back to Marquette. Mr. Maynard's body was never recovered.

The Morse was taken off the bottom a week later and, with a canvas patch over the hole in her hull, was towed to Saginaw where she underwent extensive repairs. She later returned to Marquette. After a short tour of duty at the Soo, she remained around Marquette for years under several different ownerships and was well–known to the inhabitants. Such was the tragic beginning of what was to become in 1883 the Pickands Mather Steamship Co.

The Death of Bishop Baraga

On January 19th, 1868, Bishop Baraga died in a building which is now on the corner of Mather and Fourth Streets in Marquette; (it has been moved a few blocks south to this spot). Baraga had been the first Bishop of the Marquette Catholic Diocese, which was moved here from the Soo in 1864. His successor was the Right Reverend Ignatius Mrak, who was consecrated February 7th, 1869.

The first cathedral, built in 1864, had its first service at midnight, a Christmas mass that year. This was before the building was entirely completed. This building was destroyed by fire on October 2nd, 1879.

Bishop Baraga was born to a respected Slavic family on June 29, 1797, in Austria. For five years he studied law, then theology, and was ordained a priest at age 26. He wrote one book in Austria which was greatly esteemed by its Slavic readers, and then came to the United States in 1830. After four months in Cincinnati as a missionary and student of English, Father Baraga proceeded to Arbre Croche (now Harbor Springs, Emmet County, Michigan) where he worked with the Ottawa Indians. Within three years he had mastered their language and published a prayer and hymn book for them. His flock included the Indians of the Beaver Islands in Lake Michigan and those settled in the Manistique area of the Upper Peninsula.

In July of 1837 Father Baraga traveled to La Pointe, the first missionary to be there since the departure of Jacques Marquette in 1671. He soon mastered the Otchipwe (Ojibwe–Chippewa) dialect of the Algonquin language and wrote a prayer book, hymn book, catechism and a biblical history book in that language. These books were printed while he was on a visit to Europe in 1853.

In 1843 Father Baraga was invited to Keweenaw Bay, where he founded his last and favorite mission of L'Anse Asinins (now the settlement which bears his name, Baraga). A Methodist Mission had already been established there a few years before, but the two missions cooperated and got along well.

The missions encouraged farming and built a log home for any family who would stay there. They did all they could to keep the Indians from their untiring thirst for alcohol, but were not always successful in their attempts.

It was here at the L'Anse mission that Father Baraga wrote his famous dictionary of the Otchipwe language, besides his large collection of religious and moral instructions for Indians. The dictionary was the first such ever written, and is in use even today.

With the opening of the Copper Country mines there was great demand for his pastoral services over Keweenaw, Houghton and Ontonagon Counties, and he regularly visited them for eight years. Everyone in the camps and rising villages looked forward to his visits, and many came to listen to his sincere but simple addresses, often repeated in two, three or four languages as the case required. He became the first pastor of many churches, and in 1853 was made the first Bishop of the region and took up residence in Sault Ste. Marie, then a central point for northern lower Michigan, the Upper Peninsula, and the parts of Wisconsin, Minnesota, and Canada that were near Lake Superior. In 1864, at his own request, he transferred to Marquette with the title of Bishop of Sault Ste. Marie and Marquette.

Bishop Baraga never fully recovered from the effects of rain and exposure on a boat journey four years previous to his death. In October of 1866, while at a Plenary Council meeting in Baltimore, he was stricken with apoplexy. Although he was able to travel home to Marquette, he gradually sank to his death in January of 1868. On the 30th he was buried in his cathedral. All shops and businesses were closed that day, and he was mourned by the whole population. By the time of his death he had given all his personal revenues to the needy.

In his years in the U.P., Baraga walked everywhere. He would not accept a ride in a buggy or wagon, if he were offered one. On trips from Marquette to the Soo and back, young men of the parish would walk part way with him and be met by others who lived in settlements along the way. He was a devout and humble man.

A Second Great Loss in 1868

Since before the outbreak of the Civil War, the village of Marquette had been enjoying a period of growth and prosperity. This all came to an abrupt halt on June 11, 1868, when a fire broke out in the yard of the Marquette, Houghton and Ontonogon Railroad, near the new dock at the foot of Main Street. Encouraged by a stiff breeze, it spread quickly to the dock and into the business section of the town. As the flames spread from building to building, people grabbed what they could carry and ran for safety. Peter White, who was at his bank in a corner of the Burt Building, had his employees gather all the money and bank records, put them into containers, and take them aboard a barge which was then moved into the lake to escape the blaze and looting. The furniture was stacked on a merchandise dock, which caught fire and burned.

Practically the whole business district of Marquette was reduced to ashes as the fire swept up the valley between Rock and Ridge Streets. All the docks in the harbor except the Cleveland Iron Company dock at the foot of Superior Street as well as the railroad buildings, burned. Fighting the fire was impossible. There was no water pressure. With the primitive equipment available, all efforts were turned to saving buildings that had not yet ignited. That part of the town on the ridge as well as the homes on Rock Street and south, were saved but, with no water, a stiff breeze and dry wooden buildings the devastation in the burned area was complete. Despite the size of the calamity, there was no loss of life.

There was no question but that Marquette would rebuild. It was the hub of a community which now consisted of three substantial villages. Negaunee had been incorporated into a village in 1865, when J. P. Pendill and the Pioneer Company made two separate plots. One was called "Iron" and the other was given the Indian name "Negaunee" for "Pioneer" or "first" (literally, the one who goes ahead). The year after the fire, Ishpeming was incorporated into a village. The first plot was laid out by Robert Nelson, who

Fridericus Baraga,

Top: Bishop Frederic Baraga.
Bottom: Alford P. Swineford (c. 1870). Courtesy of Mrs. Marriott. Mr. Swineford had worked for no less than twenty newspapers when he arrived in Marquette from Negaunee where he had been publishing the Lake Superior Mining and Manufacturing News.

also established a store at the Ishpeming House, built a slaughterhouse near Lake Bancroft, and set up the first meat market. "Ishpeming" was the Chippewa word for "high place" (or "heaven" as used by Bishop Baraga). Both the names "Negaunee" and "Ishpeming" were chosen by Peter White. Several new mines of great promise had been opened in Negaunee and Ishpeming after the Civil War, and by the time of the fire both iron and copper from the Upper Peninsula were in great demand. The finds of both metals were at last proving to be the greatest deposits in the nation. Men of vision and money, as well as experts in the field of mining, were being attracted to Lake Superior's south shore from all over Europe and America.

Alford Swineford and the New City

The new city, which literally sprung from the ashes, reflected the spirit of its citizens. The burning of the old village gave them a chance to correct the mistakes of the past. Rules were immediately adopted that all new buildings in the downtown area should be fireproof and have fronts of stone, brick or other masonry. Secondly, a new and powerful steam–driven water pumping station was planned away from the town. It was constructed on the beach just south of Lighthouse Point outside of the breakwater, so that the water would be cleaner and so that the pumping station would not be endangered again.

The vitality and ambition of the new community surprised everyone. Within 20 years it would be one of the finest cities of the midwest and would be called the "Queen City of the North."

The year before the fire, Alford Peter Swineford had come to Negaunee from Fond du Lac, Wisconsin. His hometown had been Ashland, Ohio and he had worked there and in Oshkosh, Wisconsin as a printer and reporter. In Negaunee the young journalist was printing and publishing a weekly newspaper called the "Lake Superior Mining and Manufacturing News." He was 33 years old, married, and had a young daughter, Nellie Flower Swineford.

Peter White recognized Swineford's abilities and realized that he was well qualified to run a newspaper. He too had followed the progress of the area with great interest over the years. Mr. White persuaded Swineford to set up his presses in Marquette after the fire and revive the Lake Superior Mining Journal. This was the oldest newspaper in the peninsula, having been started by John N. Ingersoll in Copper Harbor in the summer of 1846. The paper was later moved to Sault Ste. Marie, and then to Marquette. When

Upper left: Nellie Flower Swineford, who married E. O. Stafford in 1884 and lived at 430 E. Arch St. Courtesy Mrs. Marriott.

Upper right: Michigan counties 1856.

Bottom: Alford P. Swineford as Governor of Alaska. He published the Mining Journal in Marquette from 1868 to 1889. After going to Alaska he published the Ketchikan Mining Journal from 1893 to 1905. He is buried in Park Cemetery, Marquette. Photo courtesy of Mrs. Marriott.

Swineford took over, he changed the name to the "Marquette Mining Journal." Swineford soon became a great community leader, not only in the reconstruction of the village of Marquette but also by causing Marquette, Ishpeming and Negaunee to become home–rule chartered cities. He later served in county, state and the national government.

Mr. Swineford was one of Marquette's leading citizens. He became an expert in geology and mining problems. Like Peter White, he read law and was already a member of the Wisconsin Bar before coming to Upper Michigan. He championed the short–lived and unsuccessful Washington County.

Washington County was formed on February 15, 1867, with the Village of Negaunee as its county seat. The easternmost line of Washington County ran north and south, its north end coming out on Lake Superior just a few miles north of Granite Point. This put practically all of the present Powell Township in the new county. A lawsuit followed, in which the court found in favor of the plaintiff, nullifying the act of organization. Within a year or so of its inception, Washington County ceased to exist, but Swineford realized that Marquette County was too unwieldy and needed to be broken up. While this did not happen for some years, Alfred P. Swineford was elected to the House of Representatives in the Michigan Legislature in 1871. He was able to get bills passed which incorporated Marquette into a home rule charter city on February 21, 1871, and Ishpeming on March 9th of the same year. Negaunee's charter, although introduced in 1871, was held up over the fact that, as introduced, it gave the city council power to license brothels. It was finally granted in 1873.

Mr. Swineford became Marquette's third mayor, holding that office for two consecutive terms in 1874 and 1875. He was later nominated for Lt. Governor of Michigan but withdrew his nomination. Two years later he ran for the State Senate and was defeated.

When Swineford first moved to Marquette, he built a home on Palm St., an area which had not been destroyed by the fire. His first wife, Psyche Cytheria Flower Swineford, died on April 18th, 1880.

In 1882, Mr. Swineford started to build the huge, ornate home on Cedar Street at the corner of Michigan Street.

On January 11, 1886, he married Mrs. Minnie Marks Smith at Pequaming. She had a small daughter named Agnes. Mr. Swineford's daughter by his first wife, Nellie Flower, had married E. O. Stafford on February 6, 1884. They had one daughter, Ruth Flower Stafford, who was born on February 9th, 1890. In 1917 Ruth married Dr. R. C. Main, who was then the county health officer for Marquette County.

The Staffords lived at 430 E. Arch St., one of the finest homes in Marquette. It had been built in 1875 by Andrew Ripka. This beautiful sandstone home had the same architect, and was built at the same time and of the same materials, as St. Paul's Episcopal Church. In 1900 a Chicago architect, Donald Donnan, called this church "the most flawless piece of brownstone masonry in the world," and in 1956 an architect from Ann Arbor singled out 430 E. Arch as one of the architecturally finest homes in the city. Again in 1986 it received an award for the best kept premises.

In 1885, President Grover Cleveland appointed Alford P. Swineford the first resident Governor of the District of Alaska, and he left Marquette that year to take the position. James Russell took over as editor of the Mining Journal. The Swinefords lived in Sitka, Alaska at first, then later in Ketchikan and Juneau over the next 25 years. Alfred Swineford died in Juneau on October 26, 1909. Despite these many years in Alaska, he always considered Marquette his home. After his death his remains were returned to Marquette for burial in Park Cemetery, just across from Peter White.

When visiting Marquette after moving to Alaska, Mr. Swineford often stayed with his daughter at the lovely sandstone home at 430 East Arch Street. The big home on Cedar Street was sold to Mr. J. M. Longyear. Both of the homes are city landmarks.

Splitting Up Marquette County

From the time that the six original counties of the Upper Peninsula were formed in 1843 for the purposes of surveying and jurisdiction, nothing had been done with the huge Marquette County until the attempt to form Washington County in 1867–70. Marquette County included all the land it presently does, plus part of Iron County and all of Dickinson County, the county seat being Marquette. In 1885 Iron County was organized from portions of Menominee and Marquette Counties, with Iron River as the county seat, and in 1891 Dickinson County was organized and taken out of Marquette County with Iron Mountain as the county seat. As strange as it may seem, in 1887 the county records for Iron County were stolen during a poker game that was devised to divert attention. The plot was successful and the records were carried to Crystal Falls. A great argument followed which resulted in the call for an election. In 1888 the election was held and every rule in the book was broken but Crystal Falls retained the county seat by five votes.

Michigan Counties 1864

Top: Michigan counties 1864.
Bottom: The Negaunee Concentrating Works. Courtesy Marquette County Historical Society.

Baraga County was organized in 1875 from Houghton County, but the present boundaries were not defined until 1885.

The last county to be formed in Michigan was Gogebic. It was set aside from Ontonagon County in 1895, its lines set in 1897. It was nearly the turn of the century before the 15 counties of the Upper Peninsula stood as they do today. Marquette County is today the largest county in Michigan and the 14th or 15th largest county east of the Mississippi River.

Great Progress

When the little villages of Marquette, Ishpeming and Negaunee became cities, there were great strides in the growth and progress of each town.

Ishpeming's first Mayor was Mr. J. P. Mills in 1873, followed by Daniel J. Wadsworth the next year. The city succeeded in clearing and filling the impenetrable cedar swamp which is now its downtown district. Besides the Superior Mine and Cleveland Mines, Governor Samuel J. Tilden of New York was opening the New York Mine. William H. Barnum had opened the Barnum Mine, and the Salisbury, New England, Mitchell, National, Winthrop, Saginaw, St. Lawrence, Hematite and Norwich were soon in production. Then there were blast furnaces: the Excelsior in the city limits and another at Deer Lake.

At Negaunee, James P. Pendill was elected the first mayor, followed by Henry J. Collwell. C. G. Griffey inaugurated the Iron Herold in 1873 and ran it for many years. There were the Jackson, Teal Lake, Cambria and Bessemer Mines, and the huge Negaunee Concentrating works were about to be built. It was completed in 1882. This seven–story timber building was built against the bluff south of Teal Lake. Four stories were on the side of the bluff and three stories towered above it. The building was designed for the crushing and washing of the ores, much as it is done today in the modern pelletizing plants.

Marquette became a city exactly 200 years from the time its namesake, Father Marquette, made his last encampment on its shores before heading east to establish a settlement at St. Ignace. Henry H. Stafford, the pioneer druggist who established the drugstore at the corner of Front and Main Streets, where it was a part of the downtown for a century, was the first Mayor, and there were aldermen representing three wards. Among them were such locally famous names as T. T. Hurley, James Wilkinson, and Dan H. Ball. Francis M. Moore was the treasurer.

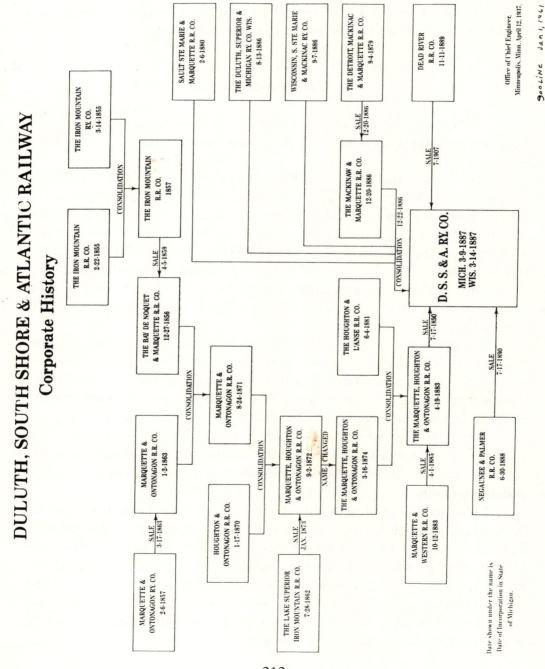

DULUTH, SOUTH SHORE & ATLANTIC RAILWAY
Corporate History

Part Purchased by Wis. Cen oct 11, 1887

Office of Chief Engineer,
Minneapolis, Minn. April 12, 1937.

Sooline Jan 1, 1961

In 1872, for the first time, Marquette was connected to the outside world by the laying of the tracks of the Chicago and Northwestern Railroad. That same year, the Marquette, Houghton and Ontonogon Railroad was incorporated and built the line from Champion to L'Anse. It then consolidated with the Houghton and L'Anse Railroad Company in 1883, forming the last link in a continuous line from Marquette to Houghton. With all this railroad activity, it is remarkable that there was still an operating dog sled mail route 180 miles long between Marquette and the Soo; it ran until 1881.

Wolf and Co. had taken over the Marquette Sandstone Quarry in 1870, when John Burt moved to Detroit after the great fire. The Wolf and Co. Quarry was owned and operated by John Henry Jacobs. He later opened the Wolf, Jacobs and Co. Quarry opposite the Wolf and Co. Quarry, which then became known as the Marquette Brownstone Company Quarry. Mr. Jacobs was the first to ship Lake Superior building stone through the Soo Canal.

Jacobs was born in Lorain County, Ohio in 1848. His parents had come from Germany. The family was known for its longevity, many of them living beyond the century mark. John was the sixth of nine children. After he moved to Marquette, he returned to Ohio for two winters to study a commercial course at Oberlin College. He had worked in stone quarries since he was eleven years old, starting in one near his hometown for 25 cents a day.

The first Marquette building to be built with Marquette sandstone after Jacobs took over was the First Methodist Episcopal Church on the northeast corner of Ridge and Front Streets. Mr. Jacobs had allegedly sold the lot to the Methodists providing they build with his stone. The quarry business flourished. It was soon employing between 500 and 600 men, and Marquette sandstone was being sent throughout the country and abroad.

In 1883 John Jacobs opened the Portage entry redstone quarry, while still running the Furst, Jacobs Quarry in Marquette. Later he opened the Kerber–Jacobs Redstone Co. Quarry at Jacobsville, in Houghton County.

Among the famous buildings he supplied stone for was the Dr. McKenzie Bank at Liverpool, England; the Hammond Building in Detroit; the Society Savings Bank Building in Cleveland, said to be the finest in the state; the Arsenal and Army Building in New York City; the Masonic Temple in Buffalo; the First National Bank (formerly known as the Lottery Bank Building) in New Orleans; the Court House in La Porte, Indiana; the Waldorf Astoria in New York; the City Hall and several other large buildings in Kansas City, Missouri; the City Hall in Omaha, Nebraska; the

Lumberman's Building and several others in Minneapolis; and the Germania Life Insurance, the German Bank, the Germania Fire & Life Insurance, the Manhattan, the Globe, the Soo and the Ryan buildings in St. Paul. The stone went to Canada too. It is in the New York Life Insurance Building in Montreal and the Royal Canadian Insurance Company in Toronto. High schools, post offices, trade buildings in Duluth, Superior, St. Louis, Vicksburg, Memphis, Jacksonville, Hot Springs and a score of other cities were all built of Marquette or Jacobsville sandstone. Other, smaller quarries opened in the area and the stone was sold to Mr. Jacobs to help fill his demand. There was one at Whitefish Point and another at Thoney's Point, neither of which lasted over a year. Gillett's Quarry at the Salmon Trout Bay was in operation several years. In 1876 the Rolling Mill Furnace, in cooperation with Mr. Jacobs, built a dock on Lake Superior at the north end of the lower harbor (where the Shiras Steam Plant is now) so that sandstone could be shipped in and out. Sandstone from other quarries, mainly Jacobsville, was shipped in for cutting and carving and then sent on.

There were other new docks also. After the fire of 1868, the Cleveland Company's dock had to operate 24 hours a day, and even then some vessels had as much as a two- and three-week delay in getting loaded with iron ore. In 1869 the railroad company rebuilt their dock, expanding it to 45 feet high and 25 feet from the mouth of the pockets to the water level. The 1870's were busy years for the Port of Marquette, with boats of all shapes and sizes, both steam and sail, hauling lumber, stone, iron ore and pig iron. There were always many ships sitting in the harbor waiting to be loaded. It was by far the busiest port on Lake Superior.

The Panic of 1873

While 1871 and '72 were important years for Marquette, 1873 and '76 brought hard times and panics. Negaunee and Ishpeming were hit harder than Marquette because mines shut down and furnaces went cold. Many new and struggling businesses closed completely. Marginal silver mines and three- or four-man operations had to close. Only the large, well-capitalized ventures weathered the panics, and in those times people became distinctly divided into the "haves" and the "have-nots." In 1874 the area had another severe blow when several of its largest furnaces burned and were closed.

Up to this time, most of the miners were German and Irish, and all of the mines were open pits. The miners of tin in Cornwall – that section of

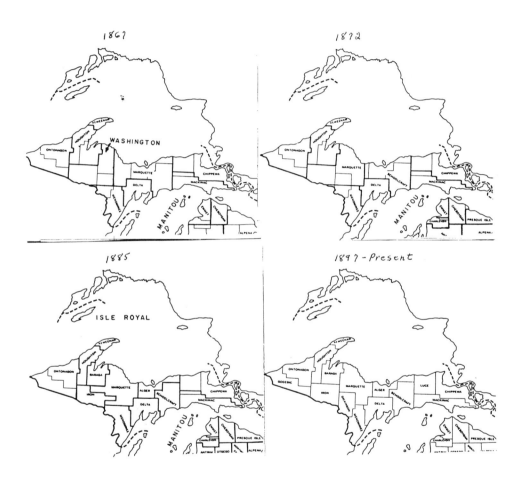

England that makes up its southwesternmost tip – were having difficult times as the tin was running out. As the high–grade ore on the surface of the Marquette Range was pretty well picked over, it became necessary to go deeper. Cornishmen and shaft–mining went hand in hand. No one on earth had more skill at this type of mining than the humor–loving, hard–working Cornishmen. As the copper and later the tin mines of Cornwall closed, the migrations away from that "little bit of Eden" increased. The migration started a few years after the American Civil War and continued up until the turn of the century. Nor did they come only to the copper and the iron deposits. Cornishmen showed up wherever there was a mine of any kind all over the world. They went to Australia, South America and Africa. In fact it was often said, "Wherever there is a hole in the ground, you'll find a Cornishman at the bottom of it." They brought with them their pasties, saffron buns, tea, Cousin Jack "wrassling," songs, stories and their alien way of speaking English. All of this was to greatly influence the way of life in the Upper Peninsula in years to come.

John Munro Longyear

It was a great loss to Marquette when John Burt left. He was one of the city's leading businessmen. He had been in on the surveys with his father, William A. Burt, when they discovered outcrops of the 13 most valuable mines in the peninsula, among them the Republic and the Lake Superior, at one time the largest in the world. Burt organized the Company and was one of the largest stockholders. He built the first sawmill at the mouth of the Carp River and was the first president of the railroad. He worked with Harvey as superintendent on the first canal at the Soo. He invented the underwater system of filling and draining the locks used there, and he brought the first paper to Marquette. John Burt owned the huge Burt Block on South Front Street, the largest building in Marquette, which burned in the fire of 1868. It was made of brick and was the first building to be rebuilt after the fire (although a bit smaller than the original). Today it is Getz's Store and in the third generation of that old Marquette family.

Now, there was another gentleman who came to Marquette who would soon take Burt's place of prominence in the community. He appeared about the time of the panic of 1873. It was young John Munro Longyear. Longyear's family had moved to Michigan from Ulster County, New York. His father was Judge of the United States District Court of Detroit. John was born April 15, 1850, in Lansing, where he attended the village schools. At

216

Upper left: Young John Monro Longyear (Courtesy Marquette County Historical Society).
Upper right: John M. Longyear and his bride Mary Hawley Beecher Longyear (c. 1883). Courtesy Mr. and Mrs. Philip Paul, descendants.
Bottom: Abe Matthews' house on Blaker Street. It was later Oats & Carter Funeral Home and (then) a Veterans' Center.

13 he entered the preparatory department of Olivet College. After a year there he went to Georgetown in Washington, DC, while his father was serving a two–year term in the House of Representatives. He returned to Lansing at 15 and went to work in the post office during the Civil War. John became an invalid for several years about this time, suffering from some sort of physical breakdown. He worked occasionally in a drugstore, a woodworking factory, and then scaling lumber and rafting logs in the Saginaw Valley.

It was during John's invalid period that the Longyear family bought a farm north of Lansing. While cutting wood on the farm, young John Munro had a serious accident with an ax. He cut his ankle and shattered some bones. The ankle never healed properly, and he walked with a slight limp for the rest of his life.

In 1872, Longyear went to examine a large tract of state–owned land for James Turner, who had been a friend of the family for years. Turner had a contract to make a timber appraisal on this land. John Longyear enjoyed the work, and landlooking became his chosen profession. He developed an eye for land use, timber and promotion. The work benefited his health and he loved it.

The next year he came to the Upper Peninsula to look at land. The panic of 1873 cut off his work, but as land prices fell he was able to purchase large blocks of it. Without much money, he turned at first to his friend Turner but later struck up a partnership with Abram Matthews, a resident of Marquette since 1866. Matthews was in the land, loan and real estate business and had a beautiful sandstone home on Blaker Street across from the Presbyterian church. At this time Longyear said he was "penniless and land poor." For some of his jobs he was paid in land.

As luck would have it, some of his land proved to be rich in minerals and while he continued to be a landlooker, both for his own interests and working for others, he was soon recognized as an authority on lands of the Upper Peninsula and was greatly sought after by investors in land, minerals and timber. Backed by the Norrie family of New York, he opened the Norrie Mine.

In "The Landlooker," a book which J. M. Longyear wrote about his early landlooking days, he tells of his discovery of mineral lands, of his friendship with the Indians of the area, and of his long treks through the roadless wilderness. Thus Mr. Longyear introduced himself to the Upper Peninsula as a young, energetic man. He was to profit greatly by these experiences in later life.

Moccasin Bill

There was another landlooker who came to the central Upper Peninsula a year of two after John Longyear. He didn't make as much money or become as famous as Longyear, but he was a diarist of backwoods experiences for thirty years, from 1874 to after the turn of the century.

His early entries, though short and to the point, tell a great deal about the life of a landlooker during that period.

In 1984–86 Moccasin Bill's diaries were transcribed verbatim by his grand–daughter–in–law, Mrs. Peter (Peg) Braamse and will eventually be published.

In his diaries we find many bits of information about the area's early entrepreneurs. He seems to have touched most of them and we will quote him occasionally in these writings.

Peg Braamse writes of him:

> Oliver's occupation, by his own definition, was a self–described "Explorer." and, more specifically, "timber cruiser,"–one who measures and scales the amount of timber available in and value of trees on a tract of land. While in the woods, he always did some trapping, hunting, and fishing. He also explored for ore deposits and gathered (mineral) specimens. His expertise became highly regarded as he was retained as an agent for large landowners and speculators."

"Moccasin Bill" got his name from the following excerpt, written on Sunday, November 1, 1874:

> This is the first day of the month and I laying around here (Ontonagon) with no news from home...no money...no clothes...no friends, ho, what a sad forlorn condition but "Moccasin Bill" is as happy as a clam at high water and have made up my mind to quit the bush after this winter and work in the mines if I can do what I think I can.

He didn't quit, of course; he remained in the bush nearly all the rest of his life.

Moccasin Bill Oliver made his own shoes, houses, canoes and did so with what he had in just a few days.

Consider the following excerpts:

To build a house:

January 06, 1874 – Resumed our journey arrived at our destination at about noon selected a place for a shanty choped wood pitched the tent etc– Mild. Wind SE little cloudy.

Jan 10, 1874 – Choped and split logs for our house baked etc snowed a little in the evening Wind NE

Jan 11, 1874 – Choped and split logs for our house it is to be 13 x 15 . Weather moderate. Wind westerly.

Jan 12, 1874 – Shoveled out the bottom of the shanty snow about 75 inches shoveled out about 72 inches of dirt and helped to build it up – cold.

Jan 14, 1874 – Cooked a little drawed some stone for the fireplace split some roofing etc Weather verry cold and clear. Wind northerly.

Jan 15, 1874 – Worked on the shanty all day We got it fixed so that we could stay in it at night – cold and clear wind westerly.

Jan 21, 1874 – I and Skip (a dog) drew some stones from the ____ to fix the fireplace tore the old one down because it smoked rebuilt the fireplace and I put another round on top of the chimney choped a tree for flooring and cut wood for night wether moderate wind southerly snow in afternoon.

To make some shoes:

May 15, 1874 – I went to the traps at twin lakes and fished in the forenoon, caught 4 bass after noon I got some dry wood and made a pair of moccosins Wether cool and cloudy Northerly wind.

May 19,1874 – I lost the powder flask or left it where I shot the deer at Beaver Lake.

May 25, 1874 – We arrived at twin L about 6PM old Bruin had been there but did not get in the shanty. I shot a bass and a RS and caught a bass with a hook. I found the flask at beaver lake. Wether clear and warm wind westerly.

To build canoes:

June 15, 1874 – We finished gardening and partly made a canoe choped and went to the traps nothing in them showery all day wind Southerly

June 16, 1874 – We finished the canoe in the forenoon Uncle David choped and I went to the traps nothing in them I caught 3 pike wheather cloudy warm wind westerly

Upper left: Charles Hebard. Courtesy Dan Sise Family (descendants).
Upper right: The Lumbermen's Monument on the Au Sable River in the Huron National Forest between Oscoda and East Tawas. The landlooker (center) is J. M. Longyear of Marquette.
Bottom: Moccasin Bill Oliver in his later years at Rock River. Courtesy Mr. and Mrs. Peter Braamse, (descendants).

Sept 17, 1874 – Worked at a canoe after I got done baking got it all done but the bottom _____. The river where we are camped is verry rapid about 10 foot fall in 15 rods large seynite boulders sticking up all along it with a few trap boulders.

Sept 18, 1874 – We finished the canoe and started down at 12 noon got about 60 rods and upset & got our packs gun and ourselves as wet as need be water 4 ft deep. We hauled the canoe out on the bank left the trap and went back to our camping place and dried up. The canoe is too small but is good for a trapping canoe and we will go afoot. Commenced raining at dusk.

Bill Oliver was hired as an assistant to landlooker Charles Cummings in 1875 and worked for Mr. Cummings off and on for several years.

Charles Hebard

Just a few years after John M. Longyear came to Marquette, a man named Charles Hebard arrived in the Copper Country. Hebard was born in Connecticut in 1831 and graduated from the Academy at Westfield, Massachusetts at 19. After some menial work as a bookkeeper and clerk, he was hired by W. E. Dodge of New York City. Starting as a clerk with that company, in two years' time (by 1853) he was made superintendent in charge of lumbering interests comprising over 45,000 acres of timberlands. He held this position for eleven years, finally resigning to become a partner of A. G. P. Dodge, the son of his employer. The new firm, operating under the title of Dodge and Company, became very successful as a lumber manufacturing plant at Williamsport, Pennsylvania. Mr. Hebard withdrew from the company in 1872 and moved to Detroit. Here he organized the firm of Hebard, Hawley and Company. While the company was based in Detroit, it ran a manufacturing plant in Cleveland, Ohio.

For a long time, Charles Hebard had known investors in the copper mines of the Keweenaw Peninsula. These friends were from Pennsylvania. Of course his friends kept asking him about the iron and copper boom in Michigan, and Mr. Hebard had to confess that he had never even been near that part of the state.

In 1876 he arranged to take a boat trip to the Copper Country with some friends who had investments there. As they approached the land forms of Michigan's Lake Superior country, most passengers were eager to see the much–talked–about copper mines, but Charles Hebard didn't even have to get off the boat to see what interested him. The huge white pine forests stretched on over the hills for miles. His life's work was cut out for him.

Immediately Mr. Hebard went to Marquette to look up a dealer in timberlands. He met with Mr. Henry C. Thurber, formed a partnership with him, and together they started the Hebard–Thurber Lumber Company. The company purchased a picturesque point on Keweenaw Bay (actually an island attached to the mainland by a sparsely wooded sandbar) about eight miles north of L'Anse. It had been the summer home for a group of Indians for many years. Here they built a large sawmill and a group of company houses, hiring the Indians who were living there and others from the nearby reservation. By providing housing far better than what they were used to and providing jobs, Hebard and Thurber had the admiration and cooperation of them all.

The point, as well as the village, complete with houses and company store, was called by its Indian name, Pequa–qua–ming Point. It was later shortened through usage to Pequaming.

At first Mr. Hebard lived in Baraga, on the west side of the Bay across from L'Anse, while Mr. Thurber remained a resident of Marquette. Thurber, being well–acquainted with the work of John Longyear, hired him to survey the company's timber holdings on the Keweenaw Peninsula.

This type of land–looking that John Longyear was engaged in is called "timber cruising" today. He also surveyed the timber land boundaries, blazing section lines to describe the property. To help with this job, Longyear had two faithful Indian packers well acquainted with most of the land from Marquette to the Keweenaw Peninsula. The men were Henry St. Arnold (pronounced "San–ti–naw") and Jim Spruce. St. Arnold was a tall, handsome, powerful, tireless man and the finest compassman Longyear had ever met. He had a keen eye and knew at least the Indian name for every plant, animal, and natural phenomenon in the forest; he was completely self–sufficient. Spruce was quite the opposite,– dirty and repulsive, but he was also faithful, honest, and steady. He and St. Arnold worked well together. Over the years, Longyear and Henry St. Arnold (Santinaw) became great friends, and Mr. Longyear gave much credit to the Indian for his widely recognized knowledge of woodsmanship.

Longyear's work with the Hebard–Thurber Lumber Company kept him in close touch with much of the lands that were granted to the Portage Lake Ship Canal Railway and Iron Company. This company had taken over huge areas of checkerboard sections of land, granted by the United States Government for the building of the ship canal from Portage Lake westward across the Keweenaw Peninsula. The portage itself was used by the Indians and Voyageurs for centuries, but did not go all the way through; the canal has had to be widened and deepened for almost its entire length to accommodate large ships.

The canal had been finished and the grant earned by the time Longyear joined the company, but there had been some years of litigation over the ownership. After the final settlement, John Longyear met with Mr. S. L. Smith in Houghton to complete what would seem, to ordinary people, like an almost impossible task. It seems that during the litigation, when things were in limbo, some timber trespasses had been made against the company in the Ontonagon River area, and it was Mr. Longyear's job to straighten them out.

Much of this land adjoined Thurber–Hebard land that Longyear had already been over, and he knew about some of the timber trespasses beforehand. With tact, knowledge and much luck, the report was completed in much less time than the company expected. Because this job was done so promptly and thoroughly, and because there was no other person as familiar with their lands and so otherwise qualified for the job, in 1878 John M. Longyear was appointed Agent of the Lake Superior Ship Canal Railway and Iron Company. This later became the Keweenaw Association. The company had been given 400,000 acres of land to dispose of, and Mr. Longyear was in charge of it.

With firsthand knowledge of these lands and others throughout the Peninsula, John Longyear soon became either the sole owner or else had the final say on huge areas of land in the Huron Mountain region, including the section between Pine Lake and Lake Superior containing the whole length of Pine River.

It was also about this time that Abe Matthews retired, so Mr. Longyear had to look for a new partner to finance his deals. Mr. Matthews had made out very well with Longyear, and with this very successful partnership behind him it was almost a matter of Mr. Longyear picking his own partner. He then teamed up with Frederick Ayres, a well–known wealthy Bostonian whose family had done well in the patent medicine business. Frederick Ayres, a close friend of the Norries, became Longyear's new financier, and to Longyear it seemed that he had almost unlimited funds to work with. Ayres would put up the money for land that Longyear felt was a good buy. They both made a tremendous amount of money over the next few years in this land dealing.

Incidentally, the winter of 1877–78 was known as the "winter of no snow." While some snow did fall that winter, especially in heavy–snow areas like the Keweenaw Peninsula, the Yellowdog Plains and some areas in the western Upper Peninsula, there was no snow on the ground anywhere else that year. There hasn't been another winter like it on record. [It was the opposite situation in the summer of 1669, when there was snow all summer.] Mr. Longyear always referred to the winter of 1878 as the "winter of no snow"; he was able to go about his land–looking unhindered by leaves, bugs or snowshoes.

The following year, with the future looking bright, John M. Longyear married Miss Mary Hawley Beecher, the daughter of Samuel P. Beecher of Battle Creek, Michigan. The Beecher Farm, with additional lands, was later taken over by the Federal government and Fort Custer was built there. The Fort, now called Camp Custer, became famous as a training site for soldiers in both World Wars I and II. It had been named for one of Michigan's favorite sons, General George Armstrong Custer. (Custer was actually born in New Rumley, Ohio, but claimed Monroe, Michigan as his home. He was killed in the battle of the Little Big Horn on June 25, 1876.) Miss Beecher was a schoolteacher in Marquette, and Longyear approached her to find a good student to copy some maps for him. After a proper courtship, they were married in 1879.

It was about this time that the Longyear–Matthews partnership broke up. Mr. Matthews was in poor health and retired. Longyear then teamed up with Mr. Frederick Ayres, the wealthy Bostonian whose family had done well in the patent–medicine business. Ayres freely put up money for land which Longyear would recommend for purchase on a speculative basis. They both made a lot of money in land dealing.

Other Loggers in the Area

While Charles Hebard was logging up and down the southern shore of Lake Superior from Ontonagon to Marquette, other smaller logging operations were going on. Some of the names were Hearsley, Powell, and Sullivan. Moccasin Bill Oliver mentions some of these camps in his diary. He had come to Marquette by stage and train in September of 1877.

On October 20, 1877 he wrote:

> I took dinner at Sauks Head with Mr. Hearsley went to his camp and got a loaf of bread and some butter and pork camped on a stream near L. Independence weather fine. (author's note: possibly Alder Creek)

Oct 21, 1877 – I got to Murry's camp about 8 AM stayed there till Grey came in and then after dinner we went and looked over the S 1/2 of SW 1/4 27 T51.27 weather fine.

Oct 23, 1877 – We started for Marquette got dinner at Powells & Hearsleys Camp camped Thonys' Stone Quarry.

In November of the same year Oliver was going to Grand Marais. He missed the boat at Marquette, so he started out on foot, stayed at the Halfway House near Laughing Whitefish River and caught another boat to Onota. On January 30, 1878, he got into the Whitedeer Lake Country.

I took the 7 AM Train to Champion (fare $2.25) up and back then struck North for 48.29 traveled till 3 PM and camped weather fine. The worst country I ever was in for traveling.

On February 6, 1878, he wrote,

I went down to Duncan Mattersons he was not at home Started at 20 minutes to 10 AM got back at 5:10 PM (24 miles) weather fine.

In June of 1878 Mr. Cummings and Moccasin Bill started in a small boat for Huron Bay. The first day they got about 4 miles past Sauks Head, about 24 miles from Marquette.

His diary reads:

Sun June 02, 1878 – we lay over remembered the sabbath to keep it Holy & baked weather showery till about 4 PM warm Blackflies beginning to show what they are good for.

Mon June 03, 1878 – we started at 5:30 AM got as far as Pine River about 17 miles blowed and rained so we camped commenced raining about 2 PM camped at 4 PM we went up the river to pine lake.

On their return trip Cummings and Oliver went to Pine Lake again. They went out to the lighthouse on Huron Island; then, on June 25, 1878–

we packed up and went to Pine River Headwind so we could go no faster then went up to Pine L and camped at 10 AM rained by showers all the rest of the day heavy Thunder I shot a duck

June 27, 1878 – we went in Boat to S. end of Pine L. then the trail to Ives Lake looked over NW 1/4 sec 51N.28W owned by S. J. Tilden NY city got back to camp at 8 PM I had my first swim weather hot.

June 28, 1878 – Breakfast at 5 AM went up the outlet of Mountain Lake 1/2 mile or so then packed up and went to our old camp of June 1st where we arrived at 8 PM Headwind all the way lay over 3 hrs at Salmon Trout River weather hot.

Gold and Silver

John Longyear had discovered, developed and continued to be a part–owner of the Norrie Mine in Ironwood. But not all mineral seekers were looking for iron and copper. Most of the lone prospectors in those days were looking for gold and silver. In these precious metals, the idea of the time was, one person working alone could strike it rich; a small investment could bring big returns. Indeed, gold and silver mines began to appear throughout the region, but mainly in the north part of Marquette County.

One of the early silver mines was the Herlock Mine just over the line in Baraga County between the two branches of the Big Huron River in Section 35, just above where Big Eric's bridge is today. There had been other mines of silver and lead in Marquette County before the '50s and '60s. There does not seem to be much pure silver in the native state except in the Copper Country, but silver with galena (lead ore), silver with copper, and pyrites (iron compound) has been found in several places. In fact, way back in 1845–46 the New York and Lake Superior Mining Company had worked the small silver–lead veins near the Cove at Presque Isle. Their claim included several offshore islands nearby, the largest of which was Partridge Island. Small amounts of high–quality asbestos are found there also. This silver–mining venture produced the first log buildings in present Marquette, which were used by the Amos R. Harlow family during their first winter here. The main shaft of this operation was 40 feet deep, dug by Cornishmen, and produced three tons of silver lead ore. There are stories that Alfred P. Swineford met this group of miners on an early trip to Lake Superior on the "Swallow" when it was delivering some cattle to the mining camp. He would have been only 13 or 14 years old at the time, if it is true.

During the Civil War, silver–lead mines were opened on the northwest end of Silver Lake in the north part of Marquette County, and on the north side of the Dead River Basin. The basin was not there at that time, and Silver Lake was much smaller than it is now.

In 1864, the Marquette Board of Supervisors appropriated $6,000 to build a road from Forestville, a town further down the Dead River, to the west end of Silver Lake. This was a wagon road for men and equipment to be hauled to and from the Silver Lake mines. There were eventually ten silver mines on the bluffs of Silver Lake, all in the vicinity of Silver–Lead Mine Lake. The area was referred to as "Smith's Lode" in 1863. The mining companies involved in Smith's Lode were the Marquette Silver Mining Co., the Detroit Silver Mining Co., the Chippewa Silver Lead, the Fortuna Mining Co., the Silver Lake Mining Co., the Lake Superior Silver Lead Co., the North Star Silver Co., the Eldorado Mining Co., the Northern Light Silver Mining Co., and the Nevada Silver Lead Co. The road followed the north side of the river all the way from Forestville and ended at a mining camp in an area now flooded by the Silver Lake Basin at its western end. Huge shiv wheels and ingenious, often homemade equipment was hauled up to the mines by horse and wagon. Power for the pumps and lifts was provided by oxen.

The Holyoke Mine was established by prospectors working on the supply road in 1864. The prospectors who recognized the ore were in the employ of a group from Holyoke, Massachusetts. A shaft was sunk, and an addit (a horizontal shaft) made the following year. Several hundred feet of sinking and drifting accumulated a small stockpile of galena, but hard rock and pinching out of the vein caused the work to be abandoned in 1866. An unsuccessful attempt had been made to smelt the ore in an adobe furnace built at the mine.

While the Holyoke Silver Mine could not be considered successful, one prospector claimed that there was a strike of much better potential in the same area which was never developed.

The Lost Silver Vein

Some thirty years ago Captain Williams, of Michigamme, was working at the old Holyoke silver–lead mine, some seven miles to the north of Ishpeming. That place at one time held many of the mining men of talent of this country. Messrs. S. S. Curry, John R. Wood, Wm. Oliver (Moccasin Bill), and many others were employed as miners. One day Captain Williams and two others were delegated to do something on surface in the way of fixing a highway. While thus engaged they cut a fine vein of silver–lead that assayed very high in silver. They decided to keep the matter a secret until such time as they could obtain possession of the land. The latter was hard to get. His two companions died, and finally, after a lapse of thirty years, Captain Williams decided, about a year ago, that he would go and

Upper left: The Holyoke Mine, north side of Dead River (1864).
Upper right: Julius Ropes (c. 1875).
Lower left: Henry Harwood (c. 1880).
*Lower right:*Ropes' Gold Mine as it stood in 1955. Author's wife, June Rydholm, in picture.

unearth the vein, and see how time had dealt with it. He was accompanied by a couple of trusted friends of this city, and thought he could go directly to the vein. So great was the change in the appearance of the country that he was unable to locate the spot. There were many old roads, trees had burned down, underbrush had grown up, and there was nothing familiar to be seen. He was very much disgusted, as he thought the finding of the vein would be but the work of a few moments after he had reached the old location. After searching for two days they left a couple of men to continue the search and, while they did considerable digging, nothing in the shape of a silver vein was uncovered. There is no doubt but that the vein is still there, and that it will someday be found.

> Ishpeming Iron Ore;
> December 13th, 1890–P.1, C.1.
> kdl

Gold was an even more sought–after element, and Marquette County has gold potential also. Although gold has been found in various parts of the Upper Peninsula, the northern part of Marquette County has had the only productive gold mine and by far the most promising prospects for future discovery. Over a million dollars worth of gold was produced and hundreds of feet of shaft sunk, as well as much underground drifting and an untold amount of surface trenching.

Julius Ropes

Mr. Julius Ropes' enthusiasm and perseverance in the search for gold led to the discovery of the Ropes Mine in 1880 on the northwest half of section 29–T48N–R27W. Ropes was born in Newbury, Vermont on April 22, 1835. He attended the St. Johnsbury Academy and then took up carpentry. Later he apprenticed as a chemist and went looking for gold and silver on the Pacific Coast and in the southern states.

Mr. Ropes came to Marquette in 1862. As a young man of 27, he worked for Mr. Henry H. Stafford, pioneer druggist and first mayor of Marquette. With mining and prospecting going on in and around Ishpeming, Julius Ropes moved there and went to work for Mr. B. S. Bigelow. Before moving to Ishpeming, Ropes married Eunice Rouse of Marquette on October

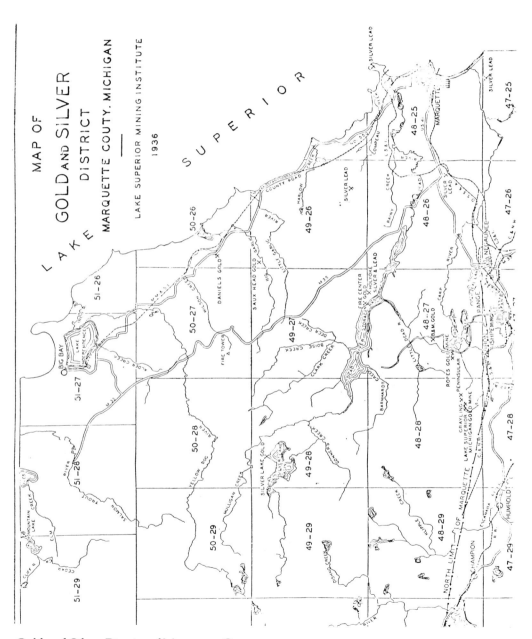

Gold and Silver District of Marquette County.

231

12, 1867. Miss Rouse had only recently come to Marquette, having arrived on the steamer PLANET, the second ship to lock through into Lake Superior that year.

In 1868, Ropes organized the Ishpeming school system. He applied for the charter and called the meeting to organize a school board. He was also elected its first member. This was three years before Ishpeming got its city charter. Julius Ropes proceeded to do prospecting throughout the area north of Ishpeming. He soon formed a small company of his own and started a drugstore. He became the postmaster of Ishpeming and operated the post office out of his drugstore for 20 years. He was known to be the finest analytical chemist in the entire mining community and did most of the chemical analyses for the mining companies and prospectors.

With more work than he could handle, Mr. Ropes hired a junior partner to help with the drug compounding and mineral analysis. This was a promising young Englishman named Harry Henry Harwood.

Henry Harwood had been born on the Isle of Wight off the southern coast of England on February 2, 1850. He had come to Toronto, Canada with his parents at the age of seven and had grown up there. He came to Ishpeming in 1869 and immediately went to work for Julius Ropes at the drugstore of Ropes and Co. Ropes taught Henry Harwood mineral analysis and drug compounding.

Henry Harwood worked as a partner with Julius Ropes during the next seven years, during which time Ropes discovered both gold and silver north of Ishpeming. The Ropes Gold and Silver Company was organized in 1881, and the following year a shaft was started. From 1883 to 1885 a stamp mill was erected, and by 1887 20 more stamps had been added. Due to the expenses involved, the mine eventually failed and was sold to the Calumet and Hecla Mining Co. This company increased the number of stamping machines to 40. In 1897 the mine was in financial difficulties again and had to close, but it had run continuously for 15 years, producing $647,902 in gold. In 1900 a cyanide plant was built on the site to treat the tailings, and still more gold was produced.

Exploration by drilling and drifting was resumed in 1935 by a new company. All the officers of the new company were from Wisconsin except Sam Cohodas of Ishpeming. Sam was a rising young businessman who was made vice–president and local agent of the company. No mining was done then. The crushers were dismantled and sold for scrap iron during World War II. By the 1970s there was some thought of opening the mine as a tourist attraction. This never came to pass, and the property was sold to the

Callahan Mining Co., which spent the years 1983 and 1984 in opening and developing the mine on a modern scale. It went into production again in 1985 and continues today on a grand and modern scale.

The discovery and development of the Ropes Gold Mine in 1880 attracted attention to this area, and in 1884 rich specimens of free gold were found in the northwest quarter of Section 35–T48N–28W, two and a half miles to the west. This "find" caused much excitement and a great deal of prospecting and trenching on this location, which they called the "Lake Superior Mine," resulted in the uncovering of some exceedingly rich ore.

The Michigan Gold Company began work there in July of 1887 and subsequently encountered several pockets of very rich ore, some samples of which are said to be the richest ever found. Although several shafts were sunk, a considerable amount of drifting done and nearly $18,000 worth of gold recovered, it was never a real mine. The ore was very spotty and only the first high–grade pockets were good. The Michigan closed in 1893. Underground work was resumed in 1933, when a small crushing mill was built and the mine was worked for two or three more years.

From 1887 to 1895, the land between the Ropes and the Lake Superior received a lot of attention, and many companies were formed to explore and develop quartz veins. Among these prospects were the Peninsular, Grayling, Brown, Case, Gitchigumme, Giant and Superior. Far to the northeast were the Kreig and the Daniels, these being at first opened as copper mines but running higher assays in gold and silver. Some gold was removed from all of them, but in most cases they could only be considered explorations.

The B & W, located in the northwest quarter of Section 21, 48–27, was another location prospected in 1896. Though good samples were obtained, it was abandoned two years later.

In 1890, Julius Ropes was responsible for another gold discovery. This time it was in the Dead River region near the Holyoke. The Fire Center Mining Company sank two shafts in Section 35, 49–27, and over $2,000 worth of ore was treated at the Ropes mill. The vein gave out and the mine was abandoned the same year. (For the establishment of the village of Munising, see Appendix A).

Mr. and Mrs. Ropes had four children: Leverett Smith Ropes, Eunice Luella Ropes, Ursula Elson Ropes, and Julius Bigelow Ropes. The family lived at 113 Euclid Street in Ishpeming. One of the daughters gave piano lessons in Marquette, Ishpeming and Negaunee for years, and another was a librarian in Ishpeming.

..COMMENCEMENT..

... OF THE ...

Ropes Gold Mine Public School,

....AT THE....

SCHOOL HOUSE,

Friday Eve., June 25, '97,

AT 8:00 O'CLOCK.

Top: Commencement Program of the Ropes Gold Mine Public School, June 1897.
Bottom: Ursula Ropes (1900). Rydholm collection.

234

A Sad Departure for James Pickands

We have already mentioned the business enterprises of Samuel L. Mather and how he and John Outhwaite, the Englishman from Cleveland, had founded the Cleveland Iron Mining Company and were its largest stockholders. They influenced Col. James Pickands to come to Marquette, and Pickands brought his brother Henry, his sister Caroline, and his friend Jay C. Morse. While Outhwaite only spent his summers in Marquette, Jay Morse married one of Outhwaite's daughters and James Pickands married another, and these families lived here the year round.

Samuel Mather and Peter White hired Stephen Gay to build the Bancroft Furnace on the Dead River, four miles from Marquette. Jay Morse became the manager, and it produced 2,400 tons of pig iron the first year.

The success of this furnace led to the building of the Munising Furnace by the same people in 1868, and the Bay Furnace opposite Grand Island in 1870. These were in what was then Schoolcraft County. They built at Munising because of the huge stands of hardwood there that they could use for charcoal. Today it is in Alger County. The Bay Furnace was designed by Lorenzo D. Harvey, who had built the Pioneer Furnace in Negaunee.

By 1873 they built the road from Bay Furnace to Marquette. It was the first road in, what is now, Alger county. It was too long a pull for one day and a halfway house was constructed at the Laughing Whitefish River that same year. (For the establishment of the village of Munising, see Appendix A.)

James Pickands followed Alfred P. Swineford as the fourth mayor of Marquette, and his brother Henry S. Pickands was the treasurer of Schoolcraft County. Henry later went downstate and built furnaces in Bangor and Freeport which sent the Northern Chicago Rolling Mill its first pig iron for conversion into Bessemer steel. When charcoal became scarce in the iron country, all the furnaces eventually moved south to the coal and limestone beds.

Miss Caroline Pickands opened a private school in a log building on what is now the corner of Arch and Spruce Streets. It had one wall stacked to the ceiling with wood, and the children sat on plank benches around the stove in the wintertime. Carol Watson Rankin attended there and told about it in a book called Stump Village.

When the public school opened in that area, Caroline Pickands took charge of it. The Kidder children, Alfred and Homer, whose father was in charge of the Champion, Angeline and Volunteer Mines, attended there. Alfred later became a famous archaeologist who worked at the Smithsonian Institution. He was the first to explore the cliff dwellings of Arizona and New

Upper left: Peter White 1830–1908. Picture c. 1890. The following tribute was read at a dinner given to establish a Peter White award by the Marquette County Historical Society in 1985:

"No man in the history of Marquette has so indelibly associated community withan individual as did Peter White. He has been gone for more than three quarters of a century but today, wherever one turns, there is vital physical evidence of his life and commitment to the place he called home.

"The First National Bank, Peter White Public Library, St. Paul's Episcopal Church, Park Cemetery, Northern Michigan University and Presque Isle...all bear witness, to a material degree, to Peter White's philanthropy and concern for his fellow citizens.

"History placed him in the right place at the right time to give full play to his potential, and it is uniquely fitting that the Marquette County Historical Society selects him as the symbol of excellence for those who help preserve the history he so strongly helped create."

Upper right: The famous Peter White signature.

Lower left: Fayette Brown.

Right: James Pickands' residence, sold to H. C. Thurber of Hebard–Thurber Lumber Co. Today residence of George Tomasi family.

Mexico. Another pupil was Frederick Eugene Wright, who became the head of the U. S. Geological Survey.

In 1881 and '82, James Pickands built a beautiful home on the north side of Ridge Street (455 East Ridge) next door to the Alfred Kidder, Sr. home and across from Peter White. His shipping business was flourishing, with vessels leaving Marquette regularly loaded with lumber from the mills, iron from the mines, pig iron from the furnaces and brownstone, and slate and graphite from the quarries.

The house James Pickands built was to be one of the finest homes in Marquette. It had seven fireplaces, beautiful doors of cherry and walnut, and everything in the home was of the finest materials and workmanship. He and his wife, Martha Outhwaite Pickands, had several small children and were anxious to get the house finished so that they could move into it.

Within a week after moving into their beautiful new home, Martha Pickands became ill and died. The official diagnosis was spinal meningitis, but the story that went around town for years was that the family had moved into the home before the plaster was dry, and that the dampness had caused pneumonia resulting in her death.

James Pickands never entered the house again. He sold it to Henry C. Thurber, Hebard's early partner and Marquette's tenth mayor, and moved to Cleveland, Ohio, where he proceeded to develop the Pickands Mather Steamship Company, which soon became the second largest on the Great Lakes. There is a story that Pickands built a replica of the same home from the original plans on Kennard St. in Cleveland. He did return to Marquette from time to time, but he never entered the house where his wife died.

Jay C. Morse became agent for the Cleveland Iron Mining Co., the Marquette Iron Co., the McComber Iron Co., Secretary of the Bancroft Iron Co. and, for a while, manager of the Bancroft Furnace. He was also President of the Lake Superior Powder Co. and a director of the Marquette Bank. He was also an early partner with James Pickands and Sam Mather, Jr. He ran his business out of Pickands Hardware, the sandstone building at the foot of Superior St. This was his office and his headquarters.

The Pickands Mather Co. was into everything that had to do with iron – mining, shipping and processing. They were soon doing the same for coal, owning everything to do with ships, docks, furnaces and so forth.

The Jackson Mining Company created the same situation on the Garden Peninsula in Lake Michigan. The company's manager, Fayette Brown, recognized that everything was present at Snail Shell Harbor – hardwoods for charcoal, a good harbor and a limestone bluff. All that was needed was iron ore and a furnace. In 1864 they purchased land at Snail

Shell Harbor and completed their first blast furnace in Fayette. By 1867 they had built a second blast furnace, kilns, and a company town. Raw iron was shipped on the Peninsula Railroad from Negaunee to Fayette and made into pig iron. The Company eventually owned docks, ships, furnaces and mines. It ran successfully for about 25 years.

The town was a completely isolated company town. Workers bought their food and clothing at the company store and went to the company parlor for a haircut. The company doctor cared for them when they were sick or injured, and the company made and enforced the laws in the town. Before a worker was paid, his charges at the company store, barbershop and other facilities were deducted, as were medical expenses. The doctor was paid a salary to care for anyone in need of his services.

As time went on, costs of production increased in Fayette, and steel from other parts of the country became cheaper. Then, in 1891, the company decided to close its Fayette ironworks. The town was abandoned.

Today, the Fayette townsite is owned and operated by the State of Michigan as a reminder of its industrial past. While many of the buildings have long since fallen in disrepair, others have been stabilized or repaired so that visitors today can experience life as it was in a company town of a century or more ago.

Horatio Seymour, Jr.

While coal, iron and limestone were all tied together in the steel process, land and timber were inseparable too, and there was much money to be made in these commodities. It was land that brought Horatio Seymour, Jr., to Marquette.

We are told that the Seymour family had no less than nine Horatios down through the years. Horatio Seymour, Sr. was the Governor of New York in 1852 and again in 1862. This Horatio Seymour had been a great political leader for many years in New York. In 1868 he gained national recognition when he was nominated for President of the United States on the democratic ticket. He lost the election to Ulysses S. Grant. This same Horatio Seymour had invested heavily in lands in and around the iron country, especially near the city of Marquette. He had formed the Michigan Land and Iron Company, which was strictly for speculation. It was a foregone conclusion that key pieces of land would grow rapidly in value as the area became more populated.

The elder Mr. Seymour sent his son (nephew, according to Mrs. Paul), Horatio, Jr., also of New York, to Marquette to act as agent for the company and to dispose of the lands. In the process, the younger Mr. Seymour was one of the first people in the Upper Peninsula to investigate what recreational pursuits could be connected with large tracts of land. After building a large home on the bluff overlooking Lake Superior (453 East Michigan Street, the grounds of which encompassed two whole blocks between Michigan and Ohio Streets, above and below the bluff; today there are some 15 or more homes on these grounds) he laid out the Upper Peninsula's first golf course in 1883. This was a three–hole course in the north part of Marquette, an area below the Prospect Street bluff which later became known as "Pine Plains." On this course one would tee off on the side of the hill, about where the corner of Prospect and Spruce Streets are today. The course was laid out toward Crescent, Park and North Spruce and the Lake Shore Boulevard in the vicinity of Picnic Rocks. This was mostly pine and blueberry plains in the 1880s and '90s.

More of Peter White

With all this talk of preservation, parks and recreation, Peter White decided to single–handedly do the impossible. He was going to try to get the federal government to give Presque Isle to the city of Marquette for a public park.

Mr. White had reached the pinnacle of political strength. As a practicing lawyer–banker–politician he was qualified to speak out on any situation. With his vast experience and seniority in the community, he had the support of the people. Peter eventually became an Episcopalian and had much to do with the starting of that congregation and building that church, and he had assisted in establishing nearly every other church in town. At first it was the Methodists, but he also helped the Presbyterians, Roman Catholics, Lutherans and others. He was dealing in lands and businesses, and was on nearly every committee from the school board up. He held all the positions in the early days: Postmaster, Registrar of Deeds, County Clerk and so on. He knew he was the only person who could possibly obtain a deed for Presque Isle, and he set out to do it.

First, Peter approached Congressman Moffatt, who assured him that a deed would be impossible to get. Mr. White then went off to Washington and spoke with the Committee on Public Lands, where he was also refused. However, this group did promise that they would agree to it if it was passed

Top: Peter White and City Library (c. 1893).
Middle: Peter White's road on filled land to Presque Isle.
Bottom: State Normal School, Marquette – Longyear Hall and Peter White Hall.

by the Senate. This was the spark Peter White needed, as he had a long–time friend in the Senate: Senator Tom Palmer of Michigan. Palmer made arrangements for Peter White to address an audience of Senators and, because of his reputation and speaking ability, many Senators were eager to hear his story. Eventually a bill was introduced by the Senate and passed by both houses. Mr. White stayed with the bill and personally carried it through each stage of red tape until it was ready for President Grover Cleveland's signature, which was finally obtained on January 12, 1886. White brought the deed home in his pocket.

The bill contained a provision that the park should be accepted and maintained by the city fathers. They rejected it, saying that the road and bridge which would have to be built would be too costly. They were sure that only the rich would benefit and the working man would get no pleasure from it whatsoever. Nearly all of the arguments finally came down to cost. Peter said, "If you will accept the park, I will personally pay the cost of its improvements and maintenance during the first five years." It was instantly accepted.

Peter White proceeded to build a road of over a mile on unclaimed beach land that was nearly a foot underwater. Fill had to be brought in for its entire length. The cost of this and the bridge was $30,000, with an additional $35,000 for the road around the island and other improvements. Over the years, the citizens of Marquette became increasingly grateful for this finest of all natural city parks.

While obtaining Presque Isle for the city of Marquette was one of Peter White's more noteworthy accomplishments, it certainly was not his greatest one. In 1893 he was appointed to the World's Fair Commission and later was appointed a master in chancery for the Pewabic Copper Co. He sold the Pewabic Mine to Mason and Smith for $710,000.

In 1900, the University of Michigan conferred on Peter White the title of M. A. In the newspapers it read L. L. D., which caused Mr. George H. Russel of Detroit, who later bought the Kidder Cabin at Huron Mountain, to write him as follows:

I have some misgivings and fear that the new title which comes to you will bring with it such added dignity that you must necessarily refrain from being the same old Peter White and give up your good French stories and other things and put on, as becomes a learned doctor of the law, a black stock, silk hat and cotton gloves.

In 1872, Peter White had started a little library for use of Marquette citizens. It outgrew its quarters and was moved into a portion of his banking building. With Mr. Longyear donating a piece of land and a few other citizens pitching in, a new library was opened in 1904, named the Peter White Public Library. With its $300,000 addition in the 1950s, it is now one of the better libraries in the country for a town the size of Marquette. Andrew Carnegie provided in 1903 the library for Ishpeming, which at the time had a greater population than Marquette. Marquette's population was about 9,000 inhabitants, while Ishpeming had over 11,000.

When the new Normal School opened its doors in Marquette just before the turn of the century, the Science Hall was named the Peter White Hall of Science. At the same time another Hall was named for Mr. Longyear, who had donated a large portion of the land that the school stood on. The two men were great benefactors to the city of Marquette.

First Thoughts of a Hunting and Fishing Club

Seymour, Peter White and John M. Longyear, who were all in the land business, became first business associates and then good friends. Seymour and Longyear were living next to each other when in 1886 Mr. Longyear bought the big Alfred P. Swineford home on Cedar Street. Swineford had been appointed Governor of Alaska and moved to Sitka at that time. Peter White lived on Ridge St., a block and a half away with no neighbors in between. He had drifted somewhat away from some of the original Marquette families, especially the Harlows, and had taken up with energetic newcomers like Longyear and Seymour.

J. M. Longyear purchased a steamboat named the CITY OF NEW BALTIMORE which made passenger runs from Marquette to Houghton. He often used it for his own parties to go anywhere along the shore from Houghton to Munising Bay. There was a fishing camp on the Anna River where Munising now stands. John Longyear went there for two– and three–day fishing trips in the 1880s.

It was also during these years (1886 and '87) that all three of these men took excursions into the Huron Mountains together. Longyear had done this since before 1880 and took great delight in showing his friends the area. It was on these trips that Horatio Seymour, Jr. brought up the idea of forming a fishing and hunting club. He felt that this beautiful, lake–studded mountain wilderness would be ideal for it. While this idea was discussed from time to time, Mr. Longyear says it was formally proposed by Mr. Seymour in 1887. However, many problems and questions came up also, and it was two years before any type of organizing was accomplished.

Tent camping was a common pastime in those years, especially by Marquette and Ishpeming people as well as groups from out east. It was not uncommon to see tent camps in the Huron Mountains or along the shore of Lake Superior on islands, points or at the mouths of rivers.

Abby Beecher Longyear was the eldest child of J. M. Longyear. She was born in 1880. In an interview, she told of the first Longyear family trip into the Huron Mountains which later became a tradition:

> My first trip up there was when I was four months old...I don't remember anything at all about it but I was told about it...that father had found this place, this wonderful system of lakes. He walked all over the Upper Peninsula on foot, you know, he knew all of it...but he found this place. He made several trips up there and he took a company party up there.
>
> I was a baby, I was born in March of 1880 and they went up in July and mother took me along in a clothes basket. She would park me out under the trees and I would lie there all day long watching the wind move the branches. You know the music of the wind in the Norway pines is something that's just built into me. It was the most beautiful lullaby I ever knew and it can always quiet me and give me a feeling of comfort. There's something about it that just enchants me.
>
> Mother felt very bad that she had to be tied down; she'd been a very gay girl and now to have to take care of a baby instead of going to the picnic with the rest of the people in the company party, she sat with very hard lines; she didn't enjoy it at all. She never really did enjoy the wilds or the company, and father was a master camper, you know. He had a crew of men who would go along and set up the most luxurious camp with a few tents and a couple of flies and things of that sort. Everything was just beautiful, but mother never liked it.
>
> There were about four men in the crew. One of them was "Pegleg" Marshall, and a couple of them were full–blooded Indians. Henry St. Arnold (Santinaw) was one of them.

Frederick Charlton

This trip was made in 1880. About five years later an architect named Frederick Charlton appeared on the Marquette scene from Detroit, where he was a junior partner in a large firm. His mission here was to design a prison. Utilizing the by then famous Marquette and Jacobsville sandstone, he

Top: Marquette Branch Prison, built in 1887. Picture c. 1900.
Bottom: Bishop G. Mott Williams and Frederick Charlton at a Shiras deer camp, c. 1910.

designed a both beautiful and practical building as a penal institution for the State of Michigan to be built near the Carp River. The building was completed in 1887.

Mr. Longyear immediately took a liking to both Charlton and his work. He convinced him that, if he should remain in the area, much architectural work would come his way. To make sure that he would follow his suggestion, he asked Charlton to design a massive 65–room mansion that should sit on a prominent bluff at the east end of Ridge Street. Besides doing a great deal of other work for Mr. Longyear, Frederick Charlton was eventually to become upper Michigan's most famous and respected architect, designing buildings for colleges, churches, banks, high schools and municipalities from one end of the peninsula to the other. In his later years, he even became a photographer of some note.

One of the most noteworthy accomplishments of Demetrius Frederick Charlton was the huge Longyear Mansion that stood high on the bluff in the center of the blocks surrounded by Lake Street (then called Walnut), Ridge Street, Cedar Street, and Arch Street. There were no other homes within these confines at the time.

Mr. Longyear first boarded and then bought homes until he built the mansion. He lived in the home at 328 East Ridge St., which he sold to lumberman and mill owner Edward Fraser in 1886. That year he purchased the Swineford home at 424 Cedar St. and added 18 or 20 rooms to the back of the house and had an elevator put right up through the center of the home, the first elevator in an Upper Peninsula home; it was run by counterbalance and handcrank. All of this was temporary, a place to stay while he had a home designed and built to his liking. Frederick Charlton worked with Mr. and Mrs. Longyear for several years, drawing up plans for the sandstone mansion which took three years to build. It was started in 1889 and the Longyears were moved into it by Christmas of 1892.

Abby Longyear gives us a little insight on the Englishman, Frederick Charlton:

> Fred Charlton, the architect, designed everything around here, and in certain ways he was a very, very good architect. But in other ways he was the most impractical man that was ever known. When he designed the Guild Hall (on High Street, 1907–1909) which had an indoor swimming pool and no dressing rooms, and no dressing rooms for the gymnasium, you see he had quite a few things like that. (Author's note: These facilities had to be added later after the building was completed by taking some space from the gym and pool

Top: Abby Longyear Roberts (1969). One of many Christmas cards to the author's family. *Bottom:* The 65–room Longyear Mansion.

area. The Guild Hall was removed from the premises on High Street next to the Morgan Memorial Chapel in August of 1987. It was demed too expensive to repair.)

He did design the big house (Longyear Mansion) but he had already been here some time, that was completed in '92. His wife and sisters were teaching me French. Cecil Grills was his assistant, she was teaching me French too, and her brother, Valentine Grills. Cecil Grills did an awful lot of work for Charlton. The Charltons were English and of course, in those days, anyone who came from England was like somebody from the moon out here.

People today just can't imagine why they built such large homes during the 1880s and '90s in Marquette. The Longyear house had 65 rooms in it. While it seems to us that it was just a sign of lavish wealth indicative of the times, Abby Longyear Roberts gives us a little insight into this also:

The Iron and Steel Institute used to have meetings up here in Marquette and various titled people from England used to come over and the Marquette people just fell all over themselves. The idea of having a real live natural–born Lord in your house was terrific, and we didn't have any good hotels in those days either.

It was not uncommon for these people to have large groups of houseguests for weeks at a time, and Mr. Longyear was well equipped to handle them with his large homes, his private steamboat, a smaller yacht, the ABBY, and many wonderful places and things to show them.

Logging and Homesteading Activities to the North and West

The very early loggers in this part of Lake Superior were Europeans who took pine from near the shore where it was easy to get. They brought this back to Europe in the form of square timbers for shipbuilding. By the 1880s, pine logging in the Marquette and Huron Mountain areas was gathering momentum. Dan Powell and Tom Sullivan were logging in the 1880s. There were sawmills in L'Anse and Baraga, and Hebard's mill at Pequaming. In Marquette, George Burtis had a big sawmill in the lower harbor below where Longyear built his big home, and Edward Fraser, Amos Harlow, the Pendills and the Reichels all had mills in or near Marquette.

Timothy Nester and Charles Hebard, the loggers, and Jim Redi, the jobber who drove rivers for logging companies, were covering the Huron Mountain area, eagerly looking at the pine and the best ways to get it out of the woods and to the mills. All of these people had to deal with John M. Longyear in one way or another. As agent for the Portage Lake Ship Canal Railway and Iron Co., he had control of every other section of land, and was in the best position to bargain for the opposite sections. Being a landowner, he was interested in what might be done with the land other than just cutting the timber. The hunting and fishing club seemed like a good idea.

One matter that had to be dealt with was the homesteaders. The loggers were not a problem, as they would just cut the trees and get out. They were usually glad to sell the land cheap when the timber was gone. The homesteaders, though, were there year–round hunting and fishing everywhere, living off the land.

Many homesteaders were residents of Marquette, and a few had businesses there. All homesteaders saw an easy way to own some land and many, living pretty much on their own, became very resourceful people. They made their way north along the shore in small boats, usually rowing but sometimes using a sail or poling their way on a raft. There were many of them over the years, but some will be remembered more than others as these left their mark on the land or had an important part to play in the history of Huron Mountain Club, Conway Lake, Big Bay, Birch or Buckroe. One name that still lingers is that of John Stewart.

Homesteader John Stewart

John Stewart was one of the very early homesteaders along the shore. His first intention was merely to have a hunting and fishing camp, near the lake for accessibility, mainly to use in the fall. He came from Canada in the late 1860s, made a few enjoyable hunting trips up along the lakeshore by rowboat, and decided to build a camp. He had located a beautiful cove in a sandstone bluff where he could easily land his boat and, since the weather in the fall was unpredictable, found himself trapped there more than once.

In 1872 he put up a cedar log cabin just above the cove, as it seemed to be an ideal spot. Besides being the only good place to land his boat, it was a good distance from town and was excellent hunting. There was also good fishing along the cliffs and at the mouth of the Garlic River just to the north of the cove. All of it was government land, except for a piece at the Garlic River that was granted by the government to the Madosh family. The

Top: John Stewart's Homestead. Stewart's Cove, Buckroe. Courtesy Mrs. James Redi.
Bottom: Amos R. Harlow Sawmill on Harlow Creek (c. 1890).

Madoshes lived there, but made no attempt to stop people from fishing the stream.

What a beautiful cove it was, large and hollow with round granite cobblestones graded out to coarse gravel where the cold, clear water constantly washed over them. The boat could easily be pulled up there for protection.

The sturdy log cabin had only taken a few weeks to build, but it was ready for hunting season, which was any time in the fall when a person chose to hunt. Everything for the cabin was brought up from Marquette in the rowboat and unloaded in the cove.

In 1859 Michigan established a hunting season during the last five months of the year, and in 1896 hunters were limited to five deer. However, since there were no game wardens in the U. P. until after the turn of the century, it was a foregone conclusion that these laws did not apply to the Upper Peninsula.

Several years later, when Amos R. Harlow bought all the surrounding sections of land from the government to supply timber for a sawmill he built on Harlow Creek, it just happened that the John Stewart cabin was on a tiny corner of Section 12, T49N–R26W, most of which was in Lake Superior. This section was not included in Mr. Harlow's purchase, though Mr. Harlow thought it was. He thought the cabin was in Section 11, and that he had purchased all of the shoreline. For several years John Stewart thought the same thing.

John used the cabin for hunting and fishing, as did others who discovered it. He soon found out that there was indeed a tiny strip of shoreline that was not in Section 11, and that his cabin was on that strip. While there was very little depth to the piece, there was actually over three quarters of a mile of shoreline in that small corner of Section 12. John immediately made his homestead claim on the property, which he proved up on over the next five or six years. In 1884, he was issued a deed to the property under the Homestead Act of 1862. The deed was over the signature of President Grover Cleveland, though it was most likely signed by an aide.

Over the next ten years John proceeded to make improvements to the property, adding a frame kitchen over a small cellar and building a sturdy cedar–log horse barn. Across the top of the cove he dragged two long cedar trees and constructed a picturesque cedar bridge, complete with railings. He got his water by lowering a pail into the lake from a platform on a high point next to the cove.

At times Mr. Stewart would go to camp on the old L'Anse road, which crossed the corner of his property as it went along the lakeshore toward L'Anse. To travel this road from Marquette with a team was sometimes difficult because of the steep sand hill at Sugarloaf Mountain. Sometimes it meant leading the horses up the hill or letting them go on their own after unloading the wagon. When the weather was good, the leisurely boat trip up the lake was very pleasant.

The Powder Mill Location

In the meantime, John Stewart got married and over the years had five children, two boys and three girls. John and his wife ran a boarding house at the Powder Mill on Dead River. This mill was established by the Lake Superior Powder Company in 1871 to make powder for blasting rock at the mines. Josiah G. Reynolds was superintendent. His father was a manufacturer of powder in the east, and J. G. had learned the business from him at the Bennington Powder Mills in Vermont. Mr. Reynolds was a pioneer in the manufacture of powder. Prior to his coming here, the iron and copper mines were using black powder or saltpeter powder. He introduced the nitrate soda powder and, in 1879, dynamite. He came to Lake Superior in 1871 and was connected with the powder company from that time on, as was his son M. K. Reynolds. M. K. Reynolds married Miss Jopling, daughter of Alfred Jopling and granddaughter of Peter White.

The Powder Mill was a small community of company houses about three miles north of Marquette, at what is now the Marquette Tourist Park. This land was annexed to the city in the 1960s and is now within the city limits. The mill itself was built right on the river for power, while the houses were in the woods a short distance away.

Besides helping at the boarding house, John Stewart worked at the mill from time to time. He also worked for Peter White doing various odd jobs. He worked for Peter White off and on for nearly 30 years.

The old Marquette–L'Anse road ran northwest out of Marquette, from what is now Presque Isle Avenue to the Powder Mill. It then continued on down to the river, crossing it on a wooden bridge, after which it wound its way up along a bend in the river and out toward the present railroad crossing on County Road 550. This is the L. S. & I. track which goes to the ore dock at Presque Isle. The road then went out along the lake to Sugarloaf. At Middle Island Point, this road is called the "old wagon road" and can still be seen plainly, as it can at the tourist park. At Sugarloaf the road appeared to run right into the mountain when it made a sharp left turn. It then went over a high steep hill at Sugarloaf and along the lake to Sauks Head outlet.

Top: The Powder Mill on Dead River. Courtesy Mrs. James Redi.
Lower left: Josiah G. Reynolds. Courtesy of Max Reynolds' family. Mr. Reynolds always drove a small, single–seat buggy with one foot hanging outside. Courtesy Mrs. Max Reynols, Jr.
Lower right: Residence of J. G. Reynolds (c. 1890).

Top: Powdermill Bridge.
Bottom: The Collinsville Furnace. Courtesy of Bob Clark.

Top: Forestville on the Dead River. Courtesy of Ken LaFayette.
Bottom: One of the many buildings at the Powder Mill.

Another road went west from the Powder Mill location to Collinsville on the Dead River, where a forge had been built by Edward K. Collins, who owned a fleet of ships on the Atlantic Ocean. Stephen Gay converted this forge to a furnace and ran it for some time under a lease agreement. Later, in 1891, Mr. Frohlingsdorf operated a flour mill there. The road then went on to Forestville where there was another furnace, sawmill and shinglemill. Forestville also had a good–sized school and was a thriving community. Beyond Forestville the road divided again, with one fork going to Silver Lake and the other to the mines in Negaunee and Ishpeming.

The small cluster of one– and two–family houses at the Powder Mill Location were quite substantial compared to the flimsy wooden buildings of the mill. There was a reason for this. The mill had blown up several times and each time had to be completely rebuilt.

Every precaution was taken to prevent an explosion. Copper tools were used instead of iron or steel so no spark could occur. The horses were shod with leather rather than iron shoes, and even these were glued on instead of nailed. But still the explosions did occur, and when they did, it was customary for the company to give the widows of the man killed a hundred dollars. This was a great deal of money in the 1880s and '90s, but then, the next–of–kin were expected to move out of the company houses.

North Along the Lake Shore

Up to this time, settlements along the Lake Superior shore from Marquette to Huron Mountain were few and far between. In summer tent camps could be found in various places on points and islands. Then there was Mr. Harlow's sawmill at Harlow's Creek, John Stewart's cabin at Stewart's Cove, and a few clearings on the shore where lumbermen were bringing logs down to the lake to be rafted to the mills in Marquette. One of these was called Freeman's Landing, another Wetmore's Landing, and there was a large storehouse and dock used by the Hebard Lumber Co. at the beach near the mouth of the Garlic River. Wetmore's Landing was quite elaborate, having a set of rails going back into the hills for a tram to take the logs out. At the mouth of the Salmon Trout River, Mr. J. H. Gillett was operating the largest sandstone quarry north of Marquette. The Thoney brothers later had a small one at Thoney's Point near Buckroe, but it only operated a year or two at the most. The Thoneys were stone masons and built a sandstone house near the quarry.

Top: J. H. Gillett residence on High and Arch Street, across from Dandelion Cottage. Owner of Gillett Quarry at Salmon Trout Bay.
Middle: Stone dock on Salmon Trout Bay (c. 1910). Much of the dock had washed away by this time. Courtesy of Shirley Rassmussen LaBonte.
Bottom: On the stone dock (c. 1910). Courtesy of Shirley Rassmussen LaBonte.

Top: A Le Claire cabin at Squaw Beach. Courtesy of Shirley LaBonte.
Bottom: Tent camp at Pine River (c. 1880).

The tug J. C. MORSE which had been sold to Frank B. Spear and was a familiar sight to Marquette residents for years, was used in his general merchandising business and for hire to loggers and quarrymen. By the mid–1880s it was purchased by J. H. Gillett to haul booms of pine logs to mills in Pequaming and Marquette. When he opened his quarry, the JAY MORSE brought men and supplies to Salmon Trout Bay and towed barges loaded with sandstone blocks to the Furst, Jacobs and Co. Quarry in South Marquette to be recut. Gillett had a camp of 80 or more men housed in a clearing south of the quarry. In 1884 they built a square timber and sandstone dock there and the following year the dock was enlarged to form a "T." It was equipped with a boomstick and a steam engine for loading the huge blocks of sandstone, 2 ft. by 3 ft. by 6 ft. and larger. There was a horse–drawn tram to bring the blocks from the quarry onto the dock. In some cases, these blocks were reloaded right from the Marquette dock (where the Shiras Steam Plant stands now) onto other vessels to be sent down the lakes to Chicago, Cleveland and Detroit.

At what is now known as "Squaw Beach" in Big Bay, there was a square–timbered home of Maurice Le Claire, a French–Indian voyageur who had built there as a squatter some time around 1865. Le Claire had an Indian wife and some children. There are only verbal records, and it is not known if Le Claire lived at that location before he built his first cabin. He was said to have camped there for some time in previous years.

These were the only things of a permanent nature along the shore from Marquette to Huron Mountain. There were loggers at the river mouths in the spring drives and some Indians in the summer. On rare occasions there would be a two– or three–day Indian gathering or encampment (pow wow) at Pine River or the Little or Big Huron Rivers.

From Big Bay to Marquette the summer tent campers were often local people, with a few groups traveling as far as the Huron Mountains. However, at this late date, the groups from the east – Boston, Pittsburgh and New York – were usually found west of the big bay at Salmon Trout Bay, Conway Bay, or at the beaches near Pine River and the Big and Little Hurons.

George Shiras I, II and III

Typical of the eastern campers, and by far the best–known, were the Shiras family. They started camping and fishing on Superior's south shore during Marquette's first year as a settlement.

Book One

George Shiras I was known to many as the angling patriarch of Lake Superior's south shore. He was married to the sister of Commodore Perry, hero of Lake Erie during the War of 1812 (in a book written by George Shiras III and edited by Winfield Shiras, she was claimed to be a cousin). This George Shiras was an ardent fisherman of brook trout in his native state of Pennsylvania, where his family was in the brewery business, but he had heard of the huge brook trout of almost unbelievable numbers that could be caught in Lake Superior.

Shiras arrived at Marquette in 1849 from Pittsburgh. He was advised to walk the shoreline north and that his best fishing would probably be near a group of rocky islands about halfway between Marquette and Presque Isle (Picnic Rock). He waded out to the nearest island and began to fish. When it was time to return to the boarding house for supper, he had so many large fish that he couldn't carry them. He had to wade back along the shore, dragging them in the water.

From that year on, the Shiras family returned every summer. The elder Mr. Shiras fished the south shore until he was 89 years old. It was his family that started the Pittsburgh group of campers who camped at Pine River long before Huron Mountain Club was ever thought of.

George Shiras' son, George, Jr., came to Marquette with his father in 1859. Even though he became a busy lawyer and eventually Justice of the United States Supreme Court, he never missed a summer on Lake Superior from then on. He fished and camped there until he was 92.

George Shiras, III, came to Marquette with his father and grandfather as an eleven–year–old boy in 1870. Following the family pattern, he returned to the fishing haunts of his ancestors, year after year. He watched the fish population drop sharply under the tremendous pressures of huge commercial fisheries, dams, log drives, and industrial pollution. He became a champion of fish and wildlife.

The Shiras family had known Peter White since they started their western vacations in 1849, and were very close friends with him. George Shiras, III, married one of his daughters, Frances P. White. This George Shiras, in his lifetime, became one of America's leading naturalists, and it has been said that he did more to develop wildlife photography than any other person. At the 1900 World's Fair in Paris his work took the first prize.

One of young Shiras' greatest experiences was exploring the area of the Laughing Whitefish River, east of Marquette. This later became the location of the famous Peter White Camp, where Shiras did much of his photographic work. He went there first with an Indian guide and he wrote fondly of this memory:

Top: A famous Shiras photo. It won several awards. Jack Deo collection.
Bottom: Hammer in the stern, George Shiras III in the bow doing some night photography on Whitefish Lake. Courtesy Jack Deo.

Fairly within the realm of romance were my two days' travel on foot, with an Indian guide, when I was 12 years old, through a pristine wilderness to a beautiful little lake hidden in the forest about 20 miles east of Marquette. The lake had been discovered by my guide the year before. I named it "Whitefish Lake" because a small river of that name entered Lake Superior at a point that made probable its origin in this lake, although this connection was not verified until a few years later.

To this secluded place I have returned for more than sixty consecutive years, first as a boy and later often accompanied by relatives and friends. The natural beauties of this woodland haven and the interesting wildlife inhabiting the surrounding forest undoubtedly had a governing influence in developing my career as a sportsman–naturalist. It was there that, as a youthful hunter, I shot my first deer. There I took my first daylight and flashlight photographs of wildlife, and there I became an observing field naturalist.

From these beginnings, young George Shiras, III, went on to be proclaimed America's most widely known field naturalist. In 1889–90 he was a member of the Pennsylvania legislature and took over his father's law firm in Pittsburgh in 1892. In 1903–05 George Shiras, III, became a member of the Congress of the United States, and during this period became a close friend of Theodore Roosevelt. He had a great influence on Roosevelt's thinking as a conservationist. Together they began a series of legislation to stop the slaughter of fish and game that was fast leading to the extinction of many species.

Of the Shiras migratory bird bill, Roosevelt wrote:

Washington D.C.
Feb. 1, 1905

My Dear Mr. Shiras:

I am very much pleased with your bill and am very glad we have in Congress a man taking so great an interest in the preservation of our birds and nature generally. I particularly wanted wild fowl to be protected.

With hearty congratulations,
Sincerely yours,
Theodore Roosevelt

Four Generations of the Shiras Family

George Shiras, Sr. 1805-1893 — George Shiras, Jr. 1832-1924

George Shiras, 3rd, 1859-1942 — George Shiras, 4th, 1889-1915

All Georges - All Sportsmen

Upper left: George Shiras II, Justice of United States Supreme Court. Courtesy B. S. Olds family.

Upper right: John Hammer. Courtesy B. J. Olds family (descendants).

Bottom: Four generations of Shirases. Couresty Jack Deo.

George Shiras photographed the animals, birds and scenes of the Upper Peninsula as no one has since. Nearly all of his best works were printed by the National Geographic Society Magazine. He became a member of the board of directors of the National Geographic Society, remaining on it for 25 years. He probably had a lot to do with the fact that the Huron Islands were among the first places in the country to be set aside as a wildlife sanctuary by President Theodore Roosevelt. In the course of many years, Shiras photographed and studied birds and animals before they became extinct. He identified several subspecies of common animals that had not been detected before. At least two of these subspecies were named for him, the Shiras moose and the Shiras bear, both of which were distinctly different from the rest of their species.

At the insistence of President Roosevelt, Shiras wrote a two–volume set of books which was printed by the National Geographic Society in 1935. Mr. Shiras did not like the way the first edition turned out, as an editor had made many unauthorized changes, and he would not autograph any of the copies. A second edition was printed in 1936, which was his original work. The set was dedicated to Theodore Roosevelt.

Shiras had his favorite woods guides from Marquette, who he took along on his many explorations to all parts of the globe. Among them were Jack La Pete, Jake Brown, Sam Noll, Fred Bawgam and John Hammer.

Sam Noll was a negro woods cook, and those who knew him claimed he was absolutely the best there was. Except for John Hammer, the rest were full–blooded Chippewas from in and around Marquette. Hammer was largely responsible for much of Shiras' photographic success. In this regard, he was more of a partner than an employee.

John Hammer

While George Shiras, III, has long been known as the father of wilderness photography, he was actually the leader of a team who developed this work together. For 45 years, he had at his side the trusted guide John Hammer, a machinist with an inventive mind. From the very beginning, Shiras and Hammer worked together on photography, and there are many who feel that because of the towering stature of George Shiras, III, in several fields, John Hammer may not have found his proper place in history.

Shiras and Hammer worked together for long hours trying to develop pieces of gadgetry to accomplish some particular task. Shiras had already perfected a flash technique for night photography by leaving the shutter open and then setting off a flash. Now they were working on the idea of having a flash go off simultaneously with the camera shutter. He and Hammer came up with a device after working long hours in the Shiras shop, but even then someone had to be there holding it. Shiras wanted it set up so that the animal being photographed would trigger the mechanism. Later an alarm or bell was added and timed so that the animal would look toward the camera before the light and shutter were tripped.

The inventive minds and tremendous patience of these two men solved one problem after another as fast as they presented themselves. By 1902 there were four or five different mechanisms, all designed by Shiras and Hammer and built by Hammer, to simultaneously explode a flash and operate the shutter as well as sound an alarm, and all tripped automatically by the animal to be photographed. These mechanisms and their various combinations were the first such ever devised in the world. George Shiras, having a legal mind and training, realized that all of these devices were worthy of being patented.

Getting a patent from the U. S. Patent Office was a project in itself. Shiras had blueprints of each piece of apparatus drawn up, then applied for the patents. Realizing that he could not have developed the inventions by himself, he had all the patents made in the name of John Hammer. Hammer received them in October of 1903 from France, England and Germany. In February of 1904 they arrived from Canada, and in June of 1904 from the United States.

Since George Shiras, III, was the only person who had ever used any of the inventions, he offered to buy all the rights to them for $300. Hammer accepted the offer and, following Shiras' advice, invested the money. Because John Hammer lived in the shadow of such a great man, he received very little recognition.

All of the original equipment which they designed and built is today in the possession of Hammer's descendant, the present owner being his oldest granddaughter, Mrs. B.J. Olds of Marquette. Some are still in working order but all are priceless museum pieces, the first of their kinds in the world. They were the first step toward the flash camera that is in such common use today.

John Hammer was far more than a guide to George Shiras, III. He was a companion who spent untold hours with him on his jaunts, not only to Whitefish Lake but to Mexico, Alaska, Newfoundland and Canada.

The "Midnight Series" printed by National Geographic Magazine which made Shiras famous as a photographer, were all "hand held" at night. It was this success which inspired him and Hammer to go on and develop their shutter–operating flashlight attachments for cameras. Besides winning first prize at the Paris World's Fair in 1900, Shiras also won the grand prize in photography at St. Louis in 1904. The third prize at the Paris fair also went to a Marquette photographer, Brainard Childs.

George Shiras, III, had a son and a daughter. The son died of pneumonia in Alaska under the constant vigilance of John Hammer, who fought the losing battle alone. The daughter became the second wife of Mr. Frank Russell, Sr., who had taken over the Mining Journal from Alfred P. Swineford and also published the Iron Mountain News. The Russells later moved to Iron Mountain.

After hearing about John Hammer from Shiras, Theodore Roosevelt begged Hammer to accompany him on an African safari. However, because John's wife was ill at the time, he had to refuse.

John H. Hammer had three sons and a daughter. Two of the boys, Arthur and Victor, died of the black diphtheria at just three and four years old. Morgan, the remaining son, became an engineer and worked in mining in western Upper Michigan. The daughter, Edith, became Mrs. Wilfred P. Murray of Marquette. She died at 91 in 1980.

John Hammer was born on November 29, 1858, in Oslo, Norway. He came to Marquette at 19 years of age and lived to be almost 99 years old. Mr. Hammer died in Marquette on July 15, 1957. Both Shiras and Hammer are buried in Park Cemetery in Marquette. The only public honor ever bestowed on John Hammer was after his death, when the Michigan Department of Natural Resources dedicated a public access site on the Laughing Whitefish River to him.

Early Homesteaders of the Huron Mountains

In the late 1880's there were several brothers from Sweden who moved in around Conway's Lake. Conway's Lake took its name from Conway's Bay, as did Conway's Point. When the Nelson brothers arrived there, they met a young trapper named Michael Conway who spent time there hunting and trapping. He had a rather small, crude cabin between Conway Lake and Lake Superior. The bay was named by Captain Taylor of the CITY OF NEW BALTIMORE and other supply boats that were asked to stop at "Conway's Bay" to drop off supplies or to pick up or drop off Conway himself as he traveled to and from Keweenaw Bay. Michael Conway was born on March 24, 1862. He had come from Toronto, Canada, where he was born, to L'Anse when he was just 16. For years he lived alone on a small farm on Keweenaw Bay. He never married and had no known relatives when he died

Upper left: Oscar Webster and Margaret (c. 1902). Courtesy George Webster.
Upper right: Hans Jensen. Courtesy Thelma Jensen, (descendant).
Bottom: John Nelson at Conway Lake.

Top: Hans and Julia Jensen at home at the homestead. Courtesy Thelma Jensen (descendent).
Middle: The Hans Jensen homestead below the skeet field.
Bottom: Pete Rassmussen's place on Conway Bay. It was moved to Conway Lake by Dr. Drury.

267

at the ripe old age of 93. Mike Conway passed away in 1956 at the Old Folks Home in Iron River.

The Nelson brothers who met Conway – Jacob, Christen, John and Barney – all took up homesteads around the lake. Back in the woods southwest of the lake was Oscar Webster. Jake Nelson built a place on the south end of the lake, Barney on the east side, Christ on the west side, and John out on the west end of Conway Bay. Pete Rasmussen, a Dane, bought a government lot from Jacob Nelson in 1892 and built a log home and barns toward the center of Conway Bay on Lake Superior.

Oscar Webster had been a saltwater sailor for a while and loved the sea. He liked sailing and sailboats but he didn't care for machinery of any kind. He had gone to work in a factory in the east and within the first few days on the job he got his arm caught between the gears of a large machine, crushing the bones of his elbow. The arm was saved but the elbow remained stiff and straight, a very awkward position when he had to do any work.

Oscar came up in a rowboat during the late 1880's and established his claim on the south end of Conway Lake. While part of the land grant represented by Mr. Longyear had claimed every other section of land, there were still government lands for sale or homesteading on the opposite sections.

Oscar made a few trips to Marquette in his rowboat, but the straight arm was such a problem that he had it broken again and set in a half–curved position to make it easier for rowing. He became good friends with the Nelson brothers.

Hans Jensen

Within a year or so after Oscar Webster had established himself near Conway Lake, Hans Jensen poled his way along Lake Superior on a large raft to a point about a mile west of the mouth of Pine River. Everything on the sand beach there was claimed by Mr. Longyear, so Hans, in order to locate his claim, walked inland to Rush Lake. He then paced back to a nice flat spot above a bluff that, according to his measurements, would be on his claim. He had filed the claim previously in Marquette and thought he was on it when he built his log house. A few years later, he was told by people from Huron Mountain that his cabin and the clearing he had worked so hard on were not on his claim.

There was no hurry about moving off the land so, taking his time, he lived in the old place while he carefully put together a beautiful frame house with storybook–looking barns and a garden below the bluff. The whole new place was tidy and beautiful. Since it was below the bluff, Hans and his brother, Otto, were able to pipe spring water into Hans' new home by gravity. Otto did the plumbing from the spring to the house, and helped build the house itself.

Hans Jensen and Oscar Webster married sisters and thereby became brothers–in–law. Hans' wife, Julia, already had a small son, Ronald, when they were married, and the boy was legally adopted by Hans. Oscar had four children: Margaret, born 1899; George, born 1902; Norman, born 1904; and Sylvia, born 1907. Norman fell in the icehouse at Huron Mountain. It was discovered that he had a brain tumor, and he died shortly thereafter.

"Pegleg" Marshall

Then there was "Pegleg" Marshall. His real name was William H. Marshall, but none knew him as such. His parents had come from Bordeaux, France. William, who was born in Oswego, New York about 1853, ran away from home when he was 16 years old and went to sea for 11 years. He settled in England long enough to marry his wife of 50 years, Ellen, and to have five children there. One, a daughter, died young in England, but he and Ellen brought four boys – Tom, Jack, Will and Charlie – to America in the late 1870's.

It was shortly after he arrived in Marquette that William Marshall began to work for Mr. Longyear, first as a woods cook and later as a chef. He made his first trips to the Huron Mountains with Longyear.

During the time that William Marshall was working for Mr. Longyear, he was walking on a railroad track of the Detroit, Mackinac and Marquette Railroad near Marquette. Hearing a train coming, he turned quickly. His foot slipped down between the ties, where it stuck fast.

As the slow–moving train bore down on him, William grabbed the front of the train and hung on to keep it from running over him. In doing so, his leg was shattered beyond repair. He was taken to Marquette, where the leg was amputated. They fitted him with an uncomfortable and awkward artificial limb, which broke within the first few weeks.

From a block of white pine, William carefully carved and fit himself a peg leg which he wore the rest of his days. From then on he was known as Pegleg Marshall. Apparently a Mr. Stephen Vickery "grubstaked" Pegleg Marshall to a homestead. This meant that a person would put up some money for a homesteader to live on while he proved up a homestead. In return for lending the money, the lender received title to the land. As the name Stephen Vickery appears on the records of the Pegleg Marshall homestead, we can assume that he grubstaked Marshall.

Pegleg and Ellen Marshall lived at the homestead west of Hans Jensen's, above the bluff, but every spring, Mr. Longyear would come and get him to work for him. Mrs. Marshall would hate to see Mr. Longyear come, but she said nothing.

Of the Marshalls' sons, the closest was Jack Marshall. He too went to sea, taking his young wife with him. It didn't work out as he had planned. His wife became pregnant by another man, and Jack refused to keep the baby. The baby girl was born March 13, 1901, and Pegleg and Ellen Marshall legally adopted her and raised her as their own. She was Ellen Mae Marshall, but became known to everyone as "Little Nell" and later "Nellie." Little Nell was brought up to the homestead west of the present skeet–field when she was three months old. She spent all her early life there.

The same year that Little Nell was brought to the homestead, Jack Marshall, the son who had given her up, was working on the Yellowdog River as a sawyer for logger Sam Durant. The first tree that was cut on the job that winter fell on him, killing him outright.

One of Nell's stories about the Pegleg Marshall homestead is the one about Sam Durant snowshoeing into the homestead on a cold winter's night in the deep, soft snow, arriving in the dark when the Marshalls didn't expect to see anyone, with the news of her father's death.

Pete Rasmussen

It has been mentioned that Peter Rasmussen, a Dane, bought the government lot between Conway Lake and Lake Superior in 1892. Before this, he had been a squatter at Squaw Beach behind Maurice Le Claire.

Pete owned a saloon and boarding house at 405 West Washington St. in Marquette. He built a log house back in the woods about a quarter–mile east of Maurice Le Claire around 1886. Neither of them took the time to get any legal right to the land.

Rasmussen's Saloon and Boarding House was no ordinary hotel, but the roughest bawdy–house in the county. It catered to lumberjacks, sailors, woodsmen and drifters. Deaths occurred for one reason or another, and raids were made on the place, often with brawls and fistfights in which furniture, fixtures and windows were broken. The raids were not always by the authorities – in fact, those were the exception. It was usually the crew of a ship or a gang from a lumber camp, or maybe just a crowd gathered by someone who had been beaten up a week or a month earlier. Sometimes the raid was carried out by angry friends of a "rolled" lumberjack who just wanted to bust up the place.

When the heat was on, Pete Rasmussen would close the place up and move out of town until things cooled off. This first cabin was back near the hill at Squaw Beach, practically in a swamp. By 1892 he moved on to the northwest to Conway's Bay where he purchased land from Jack Nelson, but he kept his saloon in Marquette for years. He built a cabin, horse barn and brewery at Conway. Mrs. Hazel Begole, age 91 at this writing, told about the Marquette place when she saw it in 1910 and '12. She said she wasn't accustomed to seeing such places and out of curiosity went there to sketch the place. She found herself most interested in the "funny people" who came and went, the tramps and roughnecks. In her words, "The place had a reputation for harboring the less fortunate."

Peter Rasmussen had two sons, Edward and Louis, who lived with him at Conway Bay.

When Louis married, he moved into the squatter cabin below the bluff at Squaw Beach, and Ed and his wife continued to live with Pete on Conway Bay. The sons and their wives helped out at the saloon in Marquette.

As time went on, Louie Rasmussen had a large family in Big Bay. There was Walter, Ruth, Peter, Pearl, Carl and Raymond, plus several children who died in infancy. Ed Rasmussen and his wife had only one boy, Eddie, Jr., who lived out his life at Huron Mountain Club.

Carter Harrison described Marquette as he remembered it in 1891:

As for Marquette, metropolis of this whole region, my most vivid recollection of the town in 1891 is Front Street's long row of saloons, broken only occasionally by a shoe store that displayed nothing but cruiser boots in its windows.

F. B. Spear owned the only non–ore dock; F. M. Spencer ran a gun and fishing tackle store; John Parker bossed the fish house on the waterfront where the Andersons later held forth; Ormsby and Atkins outfitted the male world of Marquette; the George M. Conklin Jewelry Store made a fine display on Front Street; Edward Stafford dispensed Marquette's drugs and two hotels, the Clifton and Marquette, were rivals, not only for patronage. but also for the reputation of serving the best planked whitefish.

271

Superior Heartland

Even as late as 1891, the water was so clean in Marquette harbor that trout were caught from the docks. I recall that a dock fisherman, eyeing the depths for trout, spied a fully clothed man 20 feet below the surface. The man was seated, elbows on his knees, and swaying gently, as though in a rocking chair. Minutes passed before the fisherman was shocked into the realization that he was gazing at a corpse. Lake Superior water is so cold that the bodies of drowned do not rise.

A Few of the Loggers

There were other homesteaders who arrived after the Huron Mountain Shooting and Fishing Club was organized, but we have dealt mainly with those who were around during the organization period from 1887 to 1892. Mr. Longyear had control of much of the land and had walked every inch of it. He had made camping trips to the area with Peter White, Horatio Seymour, E. W. Allen, and his trusted guide Santinaw.

One unknown early homesteader or trapper had apparently taken the time to turn out a beautiful dugout canoe on each of the largest lakes. Since all of the dugouts were of white pine, about the same size and shape, and all with similar seat construction, it seems very likely that they had a common builder, but this may not have been the case. Nevertheless, they were there for the trappers, campers, landlookers and loggers to use if they were fortunate enough to locate one on their side of the lake. Everyone knew enough to sink the dugout in the fall with stones, in shallow water to keep it from rotting. The end of the dugouts came when they were dragged up into the woods for a year or two.

Tim Nester and Jim Redi both used them. Nester and his brother came from Saginaw. He had been a pine logger there and had become wealthy. The Nesters moved to Marquette in 1882, where they again dealt mainly in pine lands.

Even before logging in the Saginaw Valley, the Nesters logged in Canada on a large scale. There are towns there today that were named for the family, one called "Nesterville" and another "Nester Falls." "Nestoria" in Baraga County, east of L'Anse is also named for the Nesters, as was the Nester School on Bluff St. in Marquette and the Nester Block on Washington Street. There were three Nester brothers, Thomas, Timothy and Patrick. Tom had a big home on Jefferson Ave. in Detroit and one in Baraga.

272

Top: One of John Stewart's party in the Mountain Lake dugout (c. 1880).
Lower left: John Stewart (and wolves) at Peter White camp.
Lower right: Jim Redi (c. 1910). Courtesy of Mrs. Redi.

Top: The Nester mansion in Saginaw. The home has been torn down (c. 1860).
Bottom: The Tim Nester home on top of Cole's Hill Marquette – became clubhouse for Marquette Golf and Country Club.

Patrick went to Oregon. Nestoria was on the D. S. S. & A. Railroad line, and was an important loading spot for pine. Tim Nester became the mayor of Marquette in 1887, following Henry Thurber.

Tim Nester logged extensively in the central U. P., including the Yellowdog Plains area. He drove logs on the Yellowdog River for at least two springs. The company had a steam tug on Lake Superior named the GEORGE NESTER after their father. It sank in 1909.

The Nester family had three mansions. The largest was in Saginaw but has since been torn down. The other two, much smaller but still impressive, were in Marquette and Baraga. Tom Nester's house in Baraga is on a hill overlooking the bay and is still in use. The home in Marquette stood high on Cole's Hill, just north of West Washington Street. It commanded a breathtaking view of the valley with the brewery to the west and Marquette Bay to the east. This was Timothy Nester's home. In later years, this house became the first clubhouse of the Marquette Golf and Country Club. The golf course was spread out to the south across Washington Street. This home was torn down in the mid–1930s.

Jim Redi also took the route from Canada to the Saginaw Valley and then to Marquette, and many of his best men followed him all the way. He too traveled the Huron Mountain Country from Lake Superior doing his own kind of landlooking. Jim was looking over the rivers and the terrain. In his job of bringing the logs out of the woods, he had to know the waterways and where to build dams, chutes, sluiceways, where to deck logs and other preparations necessary for the job.

Jim Redi was known throughout the logging community as one of the hardest–driving woods bosses in the north country, and any man who worked for him had to be tough. His reputation attracted good men. If they thought they were the best, they wanted to work for Jim Redi. He always told them that when they were fulfilling a contract, he had to work the men long and hard in order to make the job pay. If there was enough of a profit, he paid a bonus. And Jim set a good example. He laid out his own roads and took personal charge of the crew.

In 1885 Jim Redi built a tote road from the Marquette L'Anse road, where it turned west near the Yellowdog River, all the way to the outlet of Lake Independence and built a log dam there. Prosper Roberts took the tote road on up across the Salmon Trout and Pine Rivers and then west to the mouth of the Big Huron. He built no bridges, but forded all the rivers as far as the Big Huron. From its mouth he headed upstream on the high ground along the east side to the L'Anse Road again. Prosper Roberts was working for

Top: Part of the Hebard logging operation at Pequaming, Michigan. Keweenaw Bay (c. 1910).
Bottom: The DANIEL L. HEBARD at Pequaming.

Charles Hebard and Sons and built the road from the west to the Salmon Trout River.

Jim Redi's dam can still be seen underwater in Lake Independence, just above the concrete dam that is there now. The square–timbered sluiceway is still intact over a century later. This was the first dam that raised the level of the lake an appreciable amount, maybe 5 or 6 feet below what it is now. Many years later, a logging railroad was placed on Redi's tote road and a large "headquarters" camp built along it at the L'Anse cutoff. Today the L'Anse road from Sauks Head Lake to the headquarters camp clearing is called the "Peep O'Day" road because of a hunting camp of that name just south of that fork. Redi's tote road to the dam on Lake Independence is still there, but much of it is almost impassable. However, at the turn of the century this was the first road to Big Bay.

Redi also built the Reservoir Dam at Bulldog Lake (the beginning of the Yellowdog River), the Wylie Dam (named for Henry W. Wylie of Gaylord, Michigan, also a logger), and the Pinnacle and Hill dams between the two, all on the Yellowdog.

About 1900, Jim Redi married Emma Stewart, the oldest daughter of John Stewart of Stewart's Cove and the Powder Mill Location. The Redis had one child, who died of pneumonia at the age of two.

Charles and Dan Hebard

But it was the logger Charles Hebard who got into the Huron Mountains even more than Nester or Redi. Hebard drove the Salmon Trout for three or four springs between 1883 and 1889. He purchased much land and cut a lot of pine timber in the area. It was Charles Hebard who built the mill at Pequaming. The Hebard–Thurber partnership had dissolved, and the firm had been passed on to Charles Hebard and sons. Later, when Charles died, it became the Hebard Lumber Company, with Dan Hebard as president. His brother lived and died in Pequaming. His whole family is buried in the old Pequaming Cemetery. The Hebards had hired the powerful JAY MORSE while it was working around the sandstone quarry at Salmon Trout Bay, to haul logs to Pequaming. The Hebards finally bought it from J. H. Gillett. They used it as a log hauler between Ontonogon and Munising for many years. The Hebards started logging in the Huron Mountain region in 1882, some seven years before the club was organized.

The Huron Mountain Shooting and Fishing Club

On September 11, 1889, the articles of association were drawn up and signed for the Huron Mountain Shooting and Fishing Club. The signing took place in the office of Senator James McMillan in Detroit. Three and a half months later, on November 29th, the Huron Mountain Shooting and Fishing Club was incorporated under the laws of Michigan. Of the 12 men who signed the articles of association, four were residents of Marquette; the other eight were from Detroit. Not all of the ones from Detroit had even been to the property but all were enthusiastic; they had been sold on the idea by the powerful Marquette delegation. The Senator was included because his name was needed on the document while the others were friends and relatives used for the purpose of incorporation.

Horatio Seymour, Jr., who had suggested the idea several times, was interested in getting "his kind of people" into the organization. He thought of Marquette as a backwoods community, with the people nowhere near his standards. He did not want his children associating with Marquette people, even the Longyear children next door. He had high hopes for Huron Mountain as a summer resort.

Peter White had been in the central U.P. longer than any of them, and by this time it appeared that nothing could be accomplished in the area without his blessing. He ran the bank, the insurance company, and even the government when he wanted to. He was a powerful political figure wherever he went. It seemed he had a finger in every business, every church, every committee, every land deal. On the local level of government, Peter White was never elected to be Mayor of Marquette, although he ran for the position. The Harlow family, though never active in state or federal politics, had mayors from every generation. Harlow had been superintendent of the company town and then its first village president. In the next generation his son–in–law, Frederick Owens Clark, was the mayor and alderman, and Clark's son, Harlow Clark was mayor in his time, and his son James Clark in his time. But Peter White seemed able to see into the future. From his broad experience of the past 40 years during which the land had gone from wilderness to several thriving industrial communities, he looked on the Huron Mountain region as one that should be preserved and protected, an extremely valuable asset for future generations and a perfect spot for a fishing and hunting club. He envisioned the day when a place of this sort would be in great demand by people from the cities, a place where people could come and experience the northwoods as it had been in his younger days.

Ephraim W. Allen was different from the others. He was not wealthy, nor powerful, nor a woodsman. The son of a preacher, he had come from Salem, Massachusetts. He was sent to Marquette in 1880 to work as a bookkeeper for the Detroit, Mackinac and Marquette Railroad. Before it was completed, Allen was appointed cashier and paymaster of its construction by its prime builder, Senator McMillan himself.

The Senator found Ephraim Allen to be intelligent, hardworking, reliable with figures, and meticulous in keeping records. He came to depend on Ephraim a great deal, and they became good friends. In 1881, McMillan made E. W. Allen cashier and auditor of the railroad and stationed him permanently in Marquette. In this position he was now the highest representative of the railroad at the north end. To solidify his status in the community, Mr. Allen built a beautiful home at 343 East Arch St. in Marquette and in 1883 moved into it with his family.

The Allens' son, Hugh, and the Longyears' oldest son, Howard, grew up together as schoolmates and close friends. The two families became friends, and the Longyears showed the Allens the Huron Mountain country. They fell in love with the area on the first trip and Mr. Allen wanted his children to have the experience of hiking and camping in the Huron Mountains. It was through Mr. Allen and Peter White that J. M. Longyear became acquainted with Senator McMillan (before he was a senator), though through dealing with lands and railroads they had met before.

The four Marquette men, J. M. Longyear, Horatio Seymour, Ephraim W. Allen and Peter White, all traveled to Detroit on the Detroit, Mackinac and Marquette Railroad, where they met in James McMillan's office with James McMillan and Truman H. Newberry, the son of McMillan's partner John S. Newberry who had died two years before. The date was September 11, 1889. Also at the meeting was the brother–in–law of E. W. Allen, Mr. Hugh W. Dyar of Detroit. Allen had married Susan Dyar. Then there were McMillan's brother, Hugh McMillan, and Hugh's son Gilbert, McMillan's son–in–law William F. Jarvis and McMillan's sons William C. McMillan and James H. McMillan. These 12 men were the signers of the Articles of Association for the Huron Mountain Shooting and Fishing Club, and all were considered charter members. On November 29th of 1889 the incorporation was effected under the laws of the State of Michigan.

The reason for meeting with Mr. McMillan was twofold. He was the holder of huge tracts of Upper Peninsula land that had been granted by the government for building the railroad, and he was eager for support from Upper Michigan people in his bid for a seat in the U. S. Senate. He was elected to the seat held by Tom Palmer two months later. Upper Peninsula counties with representation in the state legislature formed the bulwark of the McMillan strength, with a double interest in machine politics. The east half of the U. P. wanted state offices, especially the lieutenant–governorship, while the western copper and iron districts wanted business favors.

Senator James McMillan

James McMillan's ancestors were Scottish. His parents, William and Grace McMeakin McMillan, came to Hamilton, Ontario before James was born in 1838. The father of Mr. McMillan, Sr. was a whaling captain.

Young James was born in Canada, the second child of seven sons and one daughter. In Canada the senior Mr. McMillan became prosperous working for the Great Western Railway. Of his eight children, three sons went to the United States – William to St. Louis, and Hugh and James to Detroit.

At age 13 James went to work in an Ontario mercantile business, and over the next four years he became familiar with railroads. Being a young boy observing the beginnings of a great industry, he was fascinated by the whole process. At 17 he went to Detroit in 1855 to work for the Detroit–Milwaukee Railroad. He soon married Mary L. Wetmore, the daughter of a prominent Detroit merchant. James and Mary McMillan had six children. The oldest, William C., worked closely with his father throughout his life, taking over much of the business when his father was elected to the Senate in 1890. The older daughter, Grace, married William C. Jarvis and they had one daughter, also Grace. Mrs. Jarvis died young in 1888, and the James McMillans raised young Grace as their own. The other children were James H., who also died young, and then Philip, Amy and Henry.

Early on, James McMillan tied himself closely to a partner, John Stoughton Newberry, whose family had come to Macomb County when John was only five. John graduated from the University of Michigan and went into Admiralty Law.

McMillan became a railroad–car contractor in 1862, which became a very lucrative business during the Civil War. In 1863 he formed the Michigan Car Co. He began renting and leasing rail cars to the rapidly

Top: J. M. Longyear residence in 1889. This home was built by Alfred P. Swineford. Mr. Longyear lived here while the mansion was under construction.
Bottom: E. W. Allen residence on East Arch Street (1889).

281

Top: Approach to the Cleveland Co. Dock – Ripleys rocks at upper left.
Bottom: Residence of the Honorable Peter White (1889).

expanding railroad system and he opened branches in London, Ontario and St. Louis, Missouri. His Michigan Car Works became the basis for a huge industry, the largest in Detroit. After joining Cornelius Vanderbilt to build railroads, he opened the Detroit and Cleveland Navigation Co. with large multi–decked steamships, the largest passenger ships ever used on the Great Lakes. In the 1870's, Hugh McMillan built the Detroit, Mackinac and Marquette Railway to the Northern Peninsula. In 1886 James consolidated the railroad, forming a syndicate capitalized at $10,000,000 to establish the Duluth, South Shore & Atlantic Railroad linking the two peninsulas.

McMillan, with his various railroads and steamship companies along with Vanderbilt and his railroads and the help of Senator Francis B. Stockbridge, built the Grand Hotel on Mackinac Island, which opened July 10, 1887. The same year, McMillan's partner, T. S. Newberry, died, not long before the meeting with the Marquette delegation to form Huron Mountain Club. McMillan had the industrial know–how and Newberry had the education, and they had worked well together. In 1878 James McMillan managed the Newberry campaign for congress. Newberry won, but found that he did not like politics – the handshaking, compromising or any part of it. He only served one term.

The McMillans bought downtown real estate in Detroit and eventually had a monopoly in street transportation and public utilities such as gas and telephone. Hugh McMillan was the first manager of the Michigan Bell Telephone Company. He was also involved with banking.

There is no doubt that the two most powerful political figures in Michigan – Peter White from the Upper Peninsula and James McMillan from the Lower Peninsula – had been in on the forming of Huron Mountain Club. The closest challenger for McMillan's position as head of Michigan's Republican Party was Governor Russell A. Alger, who also joined the Club in 1893. McMillan, Newberry, Vanderbilt, and George Seney, an officer in the railroad, all had towns named after them along the railroad line; only Vanderbilt is in the Lower Peninsula. In 1885 Alger County was set aside from Schoolcraft County and named for Russell Alger. They had all made a great deal of money from the logging business in the Upper Peninsula.

Mr. McMillan spent little or no time in the Huron Mountains. His family summered in Massachusetts but the family name will always be remembered in Detroit as its first industrial giant and most powerful political boss. He did much good there as an advocate of the purchase of Belle Isle park, and his many endowments toward Grace Hospital, the Detroit Museum of Art, the Shakespearean Library at the University of Michigan, the Chemistry Building at Albion College, the Pennsylvania Station, and McMillan Park, to name some of the more important ones.

McMillan died in 1902, and Governor Bliss appointed Russell Alger to succeed him in the Senate.

Activity at Huron Mountain

From 1889 to 1891, even with an organization on paper, there was very little increase in activity. A few of the members and some non–members camped and fished as usual, but there was no construction. One camping party from the east was the Shiras family. Just after the Civil War, an uncle of George Shiras, III, Col. W. R. Howe, had become a great influence on the camping group and had started his own trips to the Huron Mountains. Before this, the Shiras family camped no further north than the Garlic Islands, where they stayed for many summers. Under Howe's influence the trips began to move north to the Huron Mountains, and Howe's name became attached to the westernmost lake of the Huron group, previously known as Pony Lake. Howe also had a lake named after him near Peter White's Camp in Alger County – Howe's Lake. The other in Marquette County is called Howe Lake. Winfield Shiras, a younger brother of George ,III, was Carter H. Harrison's roommate at Yale Law School and it was this group that invited Harrison to the Lake Superior country for the first time in 1891.

Over the years the different Shiras parties had developed wilderness campsites at many places, but there were a few favorites. One was at the mouth of the Salmon Trout River. It was to this site that they came, with Carter Harrison as their guest. Others in the group were George Shiras, Jr., then a U. S. Supreme Court Justice; Albert Bigelow of New York; and Harry S. A. Stewart. The two Shiras boys, George, III, and Winfield K., were also on the trip. All of these people, including Col. Howe, joined Huron Mountain eventually, though by 1896 they had all dropped their membership except George Shiras, Jr. and Harrison, who did not join until 1897. He remained a member for the rest of his life.

There were two Indian guides on this trip, Don Mongoose and Jake Brown (nicknamed "Christ Jake") and Samson Noll, the famous negro woods cook from Canada.

The Club Farm

The oldest standing building on Huron Mountain Club property today is the homestead of Joe Paris. His real name was Evangelite Paris, but he always went by "Joe." He came to Second Pine Lake about 1890 and built a small cedar log cabin on the southwest quarter of Section 27. It was just south of the cranberry marsh and just north of the lake. Seven or eight years passed before Joe applied for his patent, which he received in 1899, but he had cleared a large field there and established a farm. In 1916 Cyrus Bentley bought the land for the club, in the name of Mrs. Bentley. For the next 35 years or so it was used as a farm to grow garden vegetables for Huron Mountain Club. Potatoes were one of the main crops. They were stored in a root house next to the ice house at the club, for use during the following season. Most of the crops, however, matured at the wrong time for club use and were used by the help or found their way to Big Bay. Any surplus of early produce was donated to Big Bay Health Camp in the 1930s and '40s.

The first gate was erected at the club farm in 1916. Blaine Nason raised a family there in the late 1930's and early 1940's. Eventually all the old buildings and the large barn were torn down, as well as the many additions to the original little cabin, but the cabin itself was left standing.

For the next 30 years the farm stood idle, the cabin slowly being eaten away by porcupines, sinking into the ground, and generally deteriorating. In the early 1970s there was serious talk of demolishing the place but because of its age and historic value, and since it was the oldest building on the property, one of the club carpenters offered to restore it in 1975 for the much–publicized U. S. bicentennial in 1976. Andy Heilala worked on his own time on weekends and in the evenings with materials supplied by the club. He did an excellent job and the building stands today, nearly 100 years old. Andy died of a heart attack while returning to Champion from Huron Mountain in March of 1979.

A Second Attempt at Organization

Around 1891 the State Legislature enacted a law which limited hunting and fishing clubs to an ownership of twelve and a half acres of land. This law was later repealed as being unconstitutional, but by this time Huron Mountain already had seven thousand acres under control and was negotiating for the control of two thousand more. It was assumed that this law would have no effect on the charter of 1889, and the pre–existing organization would be completely unique. Therefore, its charter prior to the restriction would be extremely valuable.

Mr. Longyear began running a steamboat service between Marquette and Houghton. It had the one vessel, CITY OF NEW BALTIMORE. This

Top: Choosing the site for the Club house, Oct. 9, 1892.
Bottom: Clubhouse site from across the river. Oct. 9, 1892.

286

Top: The new Club house, June 1893.
Bottom: The CITY OF NEW BALTIMORE with the WHAT'S WANTED alongside at the buoy of the Club beach. 1894.

was its name when he bought it. The boat served homesteaders along the shore, often picking up furs and fish or dropping supplies, campers, landlookers, prospectors or sports fishermen along the way. To give stability to his steamboat enterprise, Mr. Longyear had the idea of having other clubs along the shore. He organized one of them at the mouth of the Yellowdog River, now called the Iron River, in the 1890s called the Sosowagaming Club, and later he had a club house built there. It stood until the mid–1970s, when it was torn down. The building was made of huge upright white pine logs. Further east on a point near Sauks Head Island he proposed another organization, "The Tribe of Scribes," and on Partridge Island near Marquette in 1894 he built a pavilion for dancers and merrymakers from Marquette. To further enhance the business prospects, Mr. Longyear sold the old CITY OF NEW BALTIMORE and bought a new ship, THE CITY OF MARQUETTE in 1895. Sosowagaming was rented out to vacationers for several years and was later sold to the Tuton family from California. A son who became a high school teacher in Missouri ran a boys' camp there for many years under the name Camp Sosowagaming or "Camp Soso." The "Tribe of Scribes" never even developed as an organization. Mr. Longyear sold this property to the Payne family, who moved to Marquette from Grand Rapids. They built a large log cabin near the point.

The pavilion on Partridge Island only ran successfully for a few years. The storms and ice took the dock out, and people seemed to lose interest as well. In 1898, contractors Powell and Mitchell (established in 1883–84 by Dan Powell and his brothers–in–law, John and Edward Mitchell) moved the pavilion across the ice to Presque Isle for $600. A new hardwood floor was added and on July 9, 1898, the Swedish Crown held the first activity in the pavilion at its new location.

During these years, Mr. Longyear tried very hard to get the government to build breakwaters between Partridge Island and the mainland to form a 460 acre harbor of refuge. Eventually, the city purchased the pavilion for $2,070.

In the spring of 1892, Horatio Seymour, Peter White, and Mr. Longyear sent out a circular soliciting members to the Huron Mountain Shooting and Fishing Club. These were sent to friends, and friends of friends, in the Chicago and Detroit areas, especially to people who had some interest in the Upper Peninsula. They were also sent to the easterners who in some cases merely camped at Pine River on their way to the Copper Country. The mouth of Pine River had long been a favorite camping spot.

The organization was limited to 100 members and was to be a stock corporation with a par value of $100. Nobody could subscribe to more than five shares. The applications for membership were to be returned to Horatio Seymour in Marquette. While Mr. Seymour was the organizer, all the members knew that the club could not exist without the resources, knowledge and backing of Mr. Longyear.

The new group of incorporators met again in Detroit on November 7, 1892, to elect officers. Mr. Longyear was elected president, Peter White vice president, and Horatio Seymour, Jr. treasurer. Another Marquette man, Mr. Alfred R. Bennett, a stenographer for the Lake Superior Ship Canal Railway and Iron Co., and an employee and friend of Mr. Longyear's, was elected secretary because of his highly recommended ability. Mr. Bennett received shares of stock for his services, and when he resigned in 1903, he was given an honorary membership.

Two other directors were elected at the meeting – E. W. Allen and J. Everett Ball, the grandson of Philo Everett. Both of these men received stock for their services as Ball was a lawyer and Allen immediately took over the treasurership from Mr. Seymour.

On November 11, 1892, the officers and directors, all Marquette people, met in Marquette and elected 42 applicants to membership. Mr. Longyear had Frederick Charleton design a log clubhouse to be erected on the beach at Pine River in 1892. The house committee chose the location. Longyear's idea was to have each member own a cabin in keeping with the surroundings, an oasis in the wilderness where one could have the comforts of home to return to but the wilderness at his doorstep. In order to get things started he commissioned Charleton to design a cabin for him also, which he planned to build the following year. Longyear also encouraged others to get started on buildings.

From the book of Huron Mountain:

> In October of 1892, the house committee, accompanied by the architect, D. J. Charleton of Marquette, had visited Pine River, chosen a site, and staked out the clubhouse upon it. On the 12th of November (1892) a contract was made with B. J. Budd to build the clubhouse and to complete it by the 1st of May, 1893, for the sum of $2,313. In the end the contractor lost money, and the directors assumed the payment of certain bills for materials.

The first letter of advice to members, dated June 12, 1893, read as follows:

> The Clubhouse will be open, ready to receive guests July 1, 1893. The steamer CITY OF NEW BALTIMORE will leave Marquette

every Monday at 7:30 A.M., leaving the Club House on the return trip Tuesdays at 9:00 A. M. The distance is about 40 miles. (In addition to the regular trips the steamer will make such occasional or special trips as patronage of the boat may warrant.)

The facilities for bathing in Pine River and Pine Lake are excellent and it will be well for visitors to bring bathing suits. A few suits will be kept by the Steward, for rent.

"The fish to be caught are speckled trout, pike, black bass, landlocked salmon, perch and Mackinac Trout.

There is no shooting in the summer months, but in the Fall the following described game may be expected: deer, grouse, ducks and occasional geese and bear. Wolf, fox, lynx and some other shy animals may be found if looked for.

There are boats and skiffs belonging to the club, at the Club House, and skiffs on Pine, Trout, Rush, Mountain and Ives Lakes. No charge will be made for the use of the boats.

A team will be kept at the Club House for which a reasonable charge will be made for any service members or guests may require of it.

There are two men at the Club house who will act as boatmen, guides, etc., but in giving notice of intention to visit the Club House it will be well for members requiring a guide, part or all of the time, to indicate in advance their need of such services in order that if necessary, more guides may be sent to the house. Guides charge two dollars per day.

Each visitor to the Club House is advised to provide himself with a good pocket–compass and, in case of losing trails or becoming bewildered, to remember that a northeasterly course will surely bring him to the shore of Lake Superior from any point he is likely to visit while stopping at the house.

The charge for board and room at the Club House is one dollar per day for each person, settlement to be made with the Steward on leaving. Washing, team and bathing suits extra.

Members or guests desiring to use wines etc., must provide what they desire, as the Club has no license to sell such articles.

Mr. Longyear wrote an article about the building process that first winter of the reactivated organization (1892–93), explaining that a stable was constructed first and then used as a camp for the men working on the Club House. It was 16 below zero the day they abandoned their tents and moved into it. Today that stable, with many changes and improvements, is known as the carpenter shop. A boat shop has been added to it.

Then the men built an ice house and cut ice on Pine River to fill it. They did a poor job of packing it, and most of the first year's ice was lost. The Club House kitchen, the east wing and a bridge across Pine River were all completed by the time the first guests arrived on July 10, 1893. The west wing and a bathhouse with six stalls were built during July.

Of this first summer, Abby Beecher Longyear tells us the following:

Well, it was 1893 that we first went up there as a family. I was the oldest (1880), my brother Howard (1882) 18 months difference, my sister Helen, five years younger (1885), my sister Judith, six years younger (1886), then my brother Jack (10 years younger, 1895) and Robert, he was born in Paris in 1896, so there were six of us. Of course Jack and Robert weren't on this first trip." (author: actually there were seven children, the third child, John Beecher Longyear, died when he was 15 months old.)

The old Club House is still standing – that was there then. That was the first building on the beach and everybody went up by boat from Marquette – it was the only thing to do. There were a few camps here and there along the shore that the boat supplied because there were no roads at all." (this is not quite true, as there were the tote roads of Jim Redi, Prosper Roberts, and Bob Houghton, but Mrs. Roberts had no way of knowing about them.)

I think it was the CITY OF NEW BALTIMORE – the CITY OF MARQUETTE came a little later – when we had something to say about things. It wobbled like a duck in the water. We left Marquette early in the morning (7:30) and went around the breakwater. We loaded on the dock of what was the Burtis Lumber Company right at the foot of Ridge Street, and went around the breakwater and followed up the shoreline – we did get so we knew all the different points and knew how far you went and when, but we didn't get to Huron Mountain Club until about three o'clock in the afternoon. We stopped here and there along the way to leave supplies at camps and we stopped at Gillett's Landing, which is at the mouth of the Salmon Trout River. There was a camp there, and then finally around Pine River point and into the big bay there was this tremendous half moon of about two miles of beautiful sand beach. They came out in small rowboats to get us off, and I want to tell you that was a precarious job to get into these small boats. The next year they built a big scow–like

Top: Many early camping parties (not always Club members) were dumped on the beach for the day at the mouth of Pine River.
Bottom: Many small yachts were available to take parties up and down the shore (1890s). Rydholm collection.

boat there which, when everybody saw it, (they) said, "Well, that's just what's wanted" so that became its name; it was always called the WHAT'S WANTED. With that big scow they could take everything in one trip.

Well, as I say, that first year there was just the Club House and that was the dining room and what is now the Club Room. The kitchen was directly back of it and there were two wings, one was finished and the other wasn't. The one wing had two or three bedrooms where married couples stayed and the kids all bunked in the dormitory under the roof. There were no screens on the windows and I want to tell you the mosquitoes and the flies in those days were ferocious. Oh, to try to sleep at night you had to pull the blanket over your head until you nearly smothered, it was so hot up there.

Father got some pyrethrum – which was the first time we had ever heard of anything that would lick flies – and put it around in the kitchen after the help had gone to their camp. It's a plant, smothers them – gets caught in their spiracles – and Father put that around the kitchen. He was down early the next morning to see how it had worked. The cook said she took up eight dust pans full of flies. There wasn't any way to keep them out and of course the first thing they had to get was mosquito netting. It wasn't the kind of wire screen we use, it was a cloth you stretch across the windows and it wasn't any too efficient at that, because the flies were ferocious. They would hang on the screen doors, you know, so you could hardly see out the door. They were so thick, this was July. Those are the gray flies that are so murderous on the beach.

They just turned the kids loose on that beautiful, big, sandy beach and we started to investigate the country round about.

"There were about a dozen people. These were the Frederick Ayerses of Boston – the older boys were not there at the time but Louise was, and Beatrice, who grew up to be Mrs. George Patton (General Patton), my sister Helen was bridesmaid at her wedding, and Frederick, almost a baby at that time, just a very small boy. Then there was the three Kidder boys, Howard, Homer and Alfred – he was always called Teddy – and then the Dr. Dudleys from Chicago. I don't remember the Dudley children. They weren't my age and I wasn't interested in them. But they just turned us kids loose on the beach to play, it was a beautiful place, the beach now is only about a fourth the size it used to be. We played on the beach with pine cones, pebbles,

Top: Longyear Mansion, showing a part of the huge sandstone retaining wall (1890s). Rydholm collection.
Bottom: Longyear house from Ridge and Cedar Streets, 1890s. Courtesy Longyear Foundation Museum, Brookline Mass.

Top: Longyear family on the porch. Howard left, Abby, petting the dog, Helen seated on the floor. Judith in rear, Jack in rocking chair, baby is Robert. Boy on railing is a guest (1897). Courtesy Longyear Foundation Museum, Brookline.
Bottom: Howard and Abby Longyear (1897). Courtesy Longyear Foundation Museum, Brookline, Mass.

and built castles. The water would come and wipe it all out and we would start all over again. That first year we were just getting going.

The next year (1894) they had finished the other wing of the Club House and they moved the dining room into the other wing where it still is, and finished off the bedrooms on the second floor. Then people began to build their own cottages.

That first year at Huron Mountain – we always called it Pine River in those days, we didn't call it Huron Mountain – we went around to all the lakes. We went to Rush Lake, we went up to Mountain Lake, but we didn't go up to Ives Lake that first year at all, I don't know why. The next year (1894), Father said he'd bought this piece of property up there. Mother, as I say, hated camping, she hated roughing it and she wanted to be the queen bee at Huron Mountain Club. You can imagine her trying to tell these society gals from Detroit and Lake Forest and places like that what to do and how to dress. They didn't take kindly to it at all and Mother never felt that she was given the credit, the respect and honor and the deference that was due the wife of the president of Huron Mountain Club.

Father was president of the Huron Mountain Club for about 30 years, but about the third year Mother drew her toga around her with dignity and prepared to retire.

You must remember that the Longyears were now living in the huge mansion on the bluff overlooking Lake Superior, Lighthouse Point and the lower harbor in Marquette, which had been completed in 1892. The city had been laid out with 50–by–150 foot lots, or 17 hundredths of an acre per lot. Mr. Longyear's lot, in comparison, was just over 12 acres in addition to that part of the lakefront that was not included in the lighthouse reserve at Lighthouse Point. As homes go it was Charleton's masterpiece, among the finest in the land. It contained 65 rooms and was perched above a huge retaining wall of Marquette sandstone, originally 30 feet. high and 300 feet long, from Ridge to Arch Streets. Today this property contains more than 20 homes. The building was the first home to be planned with electric lights in the Upper Peninsula. It was built of the finest grade of Marquette sandstone known as "raindrop sandstone" with Arvon slate roofing, tower lookouts, first and second story porches, many fireplaces, and a recreational building complete with a fireplace and full–sized birdseye maple bowling alley. The windows were by Tiffany, the black walnut woodwork and bannisters were hand carved and all designed exclusively for Mrs. Longyear and under her direction. It was small wonder that she did not wish to leave her group of many servants to put in her summers at a wilderness forty miles to the northwest by boat.

Abby Beecher Roberts again:

So Father said that he had this piece of property which was right adjacent there (Ives Lake) and it would be very convenient and handy to the club and someday they'd have a road between the two places and either we would take off in rowboats down the Pine Lakes or walk over there.

Of that 1893 season it was reported at the stockholders meeting held on August 21, 1893 by Mr. Longyear that 73 percent had used the club – 25 members and 48 guests. At that time the club owned 460.9 acres of land outright. The piece where the Club House stood included 218.5 acres, but it claimed to control 11,543 acres. Purchase of other lands was being negotiated. Of 96 members and six honorary members, 16 were from Marquette, 61 from Michigan, and 21 from Pittsburgh. Even with this large group from Pittsburgh there were many who had camped at Pine River who did not join at that time, but a few joined at a later date. One of these families was that of Judge James H. Reed of Pittsburgh. His little son David played on the same beach as Abby Longyear in the 1880s. Years later David was a major in the field artillery and saw action in World War I at Verdun and the Meuse–Argonne drive. Still later, in the early '20s, he was appointed United States Senator from Pennsylvania to replace Senator Crow, who had died. Reed was the second youngest man in the senate. The Senator became a powerful figure in the upper house and was known as "Boss Reed." In 1936 Senator Reed built a beautiful cabin at Huron Mountain, and he returned summer after summer until his death in 1949.

In the winter of 1893 and '94, boathouses were built on Pine River, Pine Lake, Ives Lake, Mountain Lake, Trout Lake, Rush Lake and a guide camp, hen house, shop and the WHAT'S WANTED. Oscar Webster was in charge of her and, with Hans Jensen, usually took her out to meet the other ships. He had had much experience with the sea and with Lake Superior.

It was also in 1894, the Book of Huron Mountain tells us, that a lumberjack was angered at finding the boats locked and set a forest fire at both ends of Mountain Lake. The north fire spread across Trout Mountain, burned the Trout Lake boathouse and went on to Ives Mountain. Up until the 1930s Burnt Mountain, on the south end of the lake, was more rock and charred wood than anything else. The last 50 years has brought it back to beautiful greenery, however.

The year of this fire was also the year that Mr. Longyear first took his family up to Ives Lake. Abby Beecher Roberts tells us that story:

Top: J. M. Longyear with the Club's first deer. October 1893. Courtesy Huron Mountain Club.
Bottom: The flume or log chute from Ives Lake to Pine Lake (c. 1908). Jack Deo collection.

Father had sent his men ahead, and we went up the River Styx as far as we could go to the foot of the falls. We got out of the boat and climbed up a very steep slippery path. Finally we reached the flume. There was a beach where the water was raised to flood the logs down. The lumbermen had built a tremendous flume, you know the outlet has a beautiful waterfall there (about 125 foot drop through a rocky gorge), but it would break the logs to pieces when they went over it so the lumbermen had built out of white pine logs a tremendous flume from where the water made the dive over the lip of the falls down to the river and lake below, so that the logs would go down smoothly and wouldn't be damaged. They took all the logs down into Pine Lake and then rafted them down to the outlet of Pine Lake where there was another lumber camp and that was still there when we went up there in 1894.

Well, we made our way up that flume, which was very greasy and slippery – there was no water running down at that time – and at the top we climbed up over the ledge of rock. You just held on by your fingertips and here was this drop down below you. It was a little precarious in those days. I thought I could do everything and it didn't affect me at all, but the time was when I got a little leery about it, especially when the flume got to be very slippery with algae and so forth. If you lost your footing you would skid right down into the river below. At the tip we had this beautiful view all over.

Right at the outlet of Ives Lake, next to the flume, there is a crevasse that goes down just like that. We investigated it more thoroughly and discovered that the outlet is a geologic crack – a volcanic crack that lets the water out but when the lake was a little higher it ran down another volcanic crack a little off to the east from where it runs now and that is all full of broken boulders and things. We have made a trail down through there but it is not easy going for anybody and that rock there – that rock cliff has always thrilled me because I found growing on that rock the liverwort that every book in the world will tell you grows on the bark of living trees and here it is growing on a granite cliff. But, you see, there even the red trulenta grows. That's the only place in the Upper Peninsula I've ever seen it. It grows on this cliff because, you see, although it faces south, the cliff on the opposite side of the crack – the crack is just as straight as this up and down – throws a shadow over there and it's always damp. And there is negera and trulania and all kinds of liverworts and mosses growing on that cliff. The lake used to run down through the higher crack. When the new one opened, it fixed the lower level of the lake where it is now.

So then we came down off the thing there onto the beach and there we found Father's camp all set up by the little boathouse with Huron Mountain Club boats in it, and the lake, I thought, was the most desolate thing I had ever seen in my life.

So far as I know, they had just logged off the white pine there and it was all cut–over land and for sale for about a dollar an acre or something like that. We've always claimed that father went up there and scouted the place, and right where the point is, you know, where the house stands (Mr. Longyear's stonehouse), right there, there was a tremendous windfall of cedar. Father was climbing over this windfall and it tripped him up and threw him down to the ground. The family legend always has it that he rose up and shook his fist at it and said 'I'll lick you yet,' but that was family legend.

He bought I don't know how much land to begin with, but it had been burned over after the logging. Ives Mountain was practically a bare rock. There had been a strong wind that blew the brands across the lake and hit the mountain on the other side, and from what we call "Lookout Mountain" up to the top it was all burned and bare rock too.

The lumbermen had made a dam across the outlet and raised the water of the lake, which had been surrounded by large and beautiful cedar trees, and killed them all, so all around the lake there was a fringe of dead cedars. Then there was the bare rock of Ives Mountain with the fire marks still on it, the bare rocks of Lookout Mountain on the other side, but nothing had touched the point where the trees were. Father explained to me that lumbermen didn't like to cut white pine that grew on rock because it grew so slowly that it was very hard and would blunt their axes. They had not cut the pine on the rock, so that little knobs of rock stuck out in the lake and was about the only fresh green spot that was there. The lake was completely ringed with dead cedar trees, stone dead. To get around to the green point which was the one place where trees seemed to be flourishing on the lake, was practically impossible. There was a swamp between the end of the beach and the point where Father said he was going to build a house some day.

We spent the night there (at Outlet Beach) and I remember waking up in the morning – they had made beautiful balsam beds for us, in the tents – and I woke up in the morning and there was a nice little garter snake curled up on my breast here where it was warm. Fortunately, I knew that garter snakes couldn't hurt me. I was a little startled but not alarmed.

We stayed there, I think, well I don't believe we climbed Ives Mountain that day, that came sometime later, but Father kept waving his arms around and telling us what he was going to do and the rest of us just looked at him and said "Oh yeah," and we couldn't believe it; nobody could.

What he wanted to do was to take a piece of property and keep it, so his grandchildren would know what the country looked like when he first came up here – that was his theory – that he was going to let the trees grow up so that his grandchildren would be able to see what the Upper Peninsula looked like when he first came up here and fell in love with it.

Huron Mountain Blossoms

In 1894 the Dudley and the Kidder cabin were completed, both east of the Club House. Dr. Dudley was from Chicago and the Kidders were Marquette people. Mr. Kidder was the agent for several mining companies. Mr. Longyear had chosen the lot west of the Club House and was working on plans for the cabin with architect Charleton. He went to the trouble of cutting the lead growing stems of many young red pines so that in five years or so they would all be unique yet nearly identical for bannisters on the stairway in the cabin as well as other ornate woodwork.

By 1895 Mr. Longyear's cabin west of the Club House was completed, and the Ponds and the Rathbones both built cabins in a line stretching to the east, making five cabins in all. These cabins were started in the fall of 1894, worked on during the winter, and completed in the spring of 1895.

That same year, a new kitchen was added to the Club House and the old one made into a dining room. A second guides' camp was built south of the river and the boathouse on Pine River was doubled in size. In the winter of 1895 and '96 the east dormitory was finished off into rooms, an additional boathouse built on Pine Lake, and a small pavilion erected at the Rush Lake Spring. All the existing trails were cleared and new ones cut out where it was the consensus that they were needed. It was in 1895 that the raising of English pheasants for fall shooting was begun.

By now a little summer community was well under way. Horatio Seymour, its patron, had developed a bad hip and was using a cane. He was

Superior Heartland

Upper left: Kidder home in Marquette (1890s).
Upper right: Fireplace in Longyear Cabin. Bannisters and lyre above the mantel are made with Mr. Longyear's special red pine. It still exists the same today thanks to Mrs. Jon Clark.
Bottom: Picnic at the Rush Lake Spring Pavillion 1890's.

unable to do the necessary walking, and his business interests kept him in Marquette most of the time. Even Peter White had to make his visits short and far between as he became even more involved in Marquette projects and his own camp where he spent much time on the Laughing Whitefish River. Mr. Longyear had emerged as the true guardian of the club lands and the leader in the organization in both philosophy and action.

Most of the other Marquette members seemed to lack either the interest or the time, or were unwilling to spend the money to take an active part in the club activities, even though some were directors. It seemed there was an honest effort on the part of the early members to keep the club leadership in Marquette. There were several honorary members.

The early cabins at Huron Mountain were not very ambitious. Generally in the early days they were built by the homesteaders. Oscar Webster was the foreman. He was the man the owner dealt with and he held the responsibility on the job and hired what homesteaders or carpenters he was able to find during the winter. Among the very early carpenters who showed up to work the winters as well as summers were two French Canadians named Maurice "Ed" La Blanc and Alphonse Hetu. Alphonse came to Marquette from Canada about 1897 with three children, Ethel, nine, Joseph, six, and Archie, three. Relatives say that he came alone and then sent for his wife and children when he found work. Ed was single and lived in the guides' cabin, while Alphonse Hetu built a cabin for his family northeast of the Paris Farm (pronounced Perry Farm and later called by many the cherry farm) on the land that was being homesteaded by Reimi Fournier, another French Canadian. Reimi was a little hump–backed man with a strong French accent. His house was on the old road to the beach just east of Joe Paris's. He lived there with his cat (Mon Chat) for many years. He wasn't much of a carpenter, but drove team skidding logs and brought in lumber and supplies by wagon. Hetu was a good carpenter.

The member having the cabin built would discuss its size, location, and type of construction the year before, occasionally leaving a plan or just the dimensions. The logs were cut anywhere on the property, or any property where they could be found. There would be a cabin standing the following summer when the owner returned – not always what they expected, but at a total cost of $150 to $200. As time went on, additions and variations were made. The cabins, sometimes rather small to begin with, were always on post foundations, had no electricity, a hand pump and outdoor toilet facilities. They usually had a fireplace and a wood–burning box stove or two for heat. If the family required a helper around the place to do chores (later called a "cabin boy") they got him through the club management. If they had a

Upper left: Hemstead Washburne with children Hempstead Jr. (left) Clarke and Gratiot. 1896. Courtesy Hemstead Washburne (descendants).
Upper right: Alponse Hetu in his later years in Marquette. He built the home in the picture (Fourth Street.) Courtesy Hetu family.
Bottom: Huron Mountain Club families gathered on Club porch – Peter White left of post – 1895. Courtesy Huron Mountain Club.

favorite one, he returned year after year. A few of these cabin boys stayed in a tent out in back of the cabin during the summer months.

One of the Chicagoans who joined the Club was William M. "Bud" Le Moyne. He had chosen to build his own cabin in 1896 and '97, occasionally getting a little help here and there as he needed it. Then, having enjoyed the experience, he joined two more Chicago friends, Mr. D. R. Lewis and Mr. Kimball Young, in building a cabin for Mr. Young next door to the first one. This was in 1898. In 1917 this second cabin was sold to William P. Harris of Detroit and remains in that family today.

Still another Chicago family who built in 1897 and '98 was that of Carter H. Harrison II, who had been introduced to the Huron Mountains by the Shiras group years before. He became the mayor of Chicago that year, and remained in office for four consecutive terms before being defeated by Edward F. Dunne in 1905. Harrison was elected to a fifth term from 1911 to 1915. He was the son of Carter Harrison I, who was also the mayor of Chicago for five terms between 1887 and 1893. This Mr. Harrison was in office during the Haymarket riot of 1887, and was defeated that year and then re–elected in 1893 in time to host the Columbian Exposition. Harrison was assassinated while in office by a demented man.

One of the terms between the elder Harrison's was held by Hempstead Washburne (1891–93). He joined Huron Mountain in 1893 and built a cabin in 1896 next to Longyear's. The Harrisons were Democrats and Washburne was a Republican, but he and the younger Harrison were good friends. Hemp Washburne was the son of Elihu Washburne, who was Secretary of State under President Ulysses S. Grant.

Carter Harrison and Hempstead Washburne were both convinced that a trip by four fishermen to the Huron Mountains in June of 1896 was the event that put the club on the road to solid growth.

Harrison tells the story of Washburne's first trip to the club:

Hempstead Washburne was a member of the club but had never visited it, although he had fished and hunted in the region before the club was organized. Should he resign and save the $25 annual dues or retain his membership?

To help him decide, Hemp invited Horatio N. May, Dr. John B. Hamilton, director of the Marine Hospital, and myself – all Chicagoans – to take a fishing trip to the club's piney acres with him.

From Marquette we took the steamer CITY OF MARQUETTE (Mr. Longyear's new boat) to Pine River beach. For fellow passengers we had a crew of hard–boiled lumberjacks, who sat forward on their turkeys, smoked or chewed tobacco and spat.

At Hemp's direction, each of us had in his grip at least a quart of what our French cousins call vivifiants. In addition, Hemp had had a case of champagne and a case of Appolinaris water put aboard. Instead of 12 bottles, by mistake 144 bottles, or 12 cases, of the latter had been included in our luggage. Let me state that at the end of our six–day stay, the champagne was gone but 138 bottles of Appolinaris remained unopened.

The WHAT'S WANTED unloaded our impediments on one side of the river; the turkeys and supplies of the lumberjacks were piled high on the other. A hasty examination assured us that none of our goods was missing except the champagne. A search high and low, ashore and aboard the steamer, failed to restore it.

Hemp, wise in his day and generation, had a hunch. Almost simultaneously, my mind had a flicker of intelligence. We wandered across the sand beach to the lumberjack camp, where boxes of turkeys, canned goods, bags of onions and potatoes and what have you were dumped in utter confusion. Though their keen eyes were alert, the lumberjacks assumed attitudes of unconcern. One by one, articles were removed from their pile until Hemp yelled – "Ha! Ha! Eureka, I've found it!"

When the shining white case of Mumm's Extra Dry was recaptured (in Marquette anno 1896, no other label could it have borne and been classified as champagne) the lumberjacks spat in disgust and heaved sighs of disappointment, while Oliver Morris, their boss, muttered in well–feigned amazement, "Now, how the h – l did that happen?"

And Hemp grinned and answered, "Are you asking me?" (Author's note: these were men working for Dan Hebard, as Oliver Morris was a woods boss for that company for many years.)

After making camp, we fished two to a boat with Hans Jensen and Oscar Webster as guides. Two days fishing Lake Superior as far as Salmon Trout Point and including the dock, yielding on each day only 12 trout and averaging only a pound. And this was the first week in June. On the second day a 7 3/4 lb. lake trout was my prize. On another day May and Hamilton caught two pickerel (northern pike) and eight landlockers in Rush Lake, while Hemp and I got 16 brook trout at the lower dam of the Salmon Trout. Hamilton and Hemp caught seven trout in a day in Mountain Stream. In Mountain Lake,

May and Hamilton got a 2 3/4 lb. brook trout and 44 perch in the Perch Bed, now known as the Lily Pads, while Hemp and I took ten nice trout from Cliff River.

The report on Mountain Lake would be incomplete without the mention of a most glorious swim in the altogether of four gentlemen, middle aged or rapidly approaching it. Tap Gregory should have been on hand in search of wildlife subjects for his camera. As it was, a great picture, largely on the theme of tummies, was lost to posterity. Hemp's by degrees surpassed mine; May had Hemp beat by a city block and Hamilton took first place with one of Gargantuan proportions. The scene of the swim and the subsequent drying off in the sunshine with the bathers seated in a row on a log (took place) on the sand beach near the boathouse, which in those days was just east of the Norways.

Despite the poor fishing we all fell in love with the Huron Mountain country, and Hemp decided to retain his club membership. The outing had a fine sequel. For years the Washburne family had summered on Cape Cod, where their hotel rooms were already engaged for 1896. Shortly before the closing of school the hotel burned to the ground. Out of the upset plans came an inspiration. Whether it came from Hemp or the helpmate he loved to call Anne Marie, I do not know. Why not give Huron Mountain Club a tryout?

In July of that eventful year, when Hemp put Oscar Webster and Hans Jensen to work building "Driftwood Cabin," the club turned the corner from infancy to greatness. Before the end of the season the roof was on, and, Ethel Christy recalls, a house warming was celebrated with great eclat. She remembers vividly a punch bowl with maiden–hair fern trimmings. The Christy family that year occupied the J.M. Longyear cabin next door to Driftwood.

The Le Moynes completed and occupied their cabin early in 1897. In that same year the Rob Lewis, Horace Tenney, Theodore Sheldon, H. W. Longyear and Willie Hamilton cabins were built. S. S. Gregory became a member and frequenter of the club, although he did not build a cabin. I was elected to membership at the annual meeting in 1897.

Was the choice of Huron Mountain as a summer residence by the Washburnes responsible for the quickening into life of a club that had hitherto seemed doomed to acceptance of a moribund state? I believe so. Consider three facts: Mrs. Washburne and Mrs. Howard W. Longyear had been schoolgirl intimates. Hemp had no closer or older friends than Bud Le Moyne, Rob Lewis and S. S. Gregory. Theodore

Sheldon was another good friend, and Horace Tenney was the brother–in–law of Dr. Henry Favill, a lifelong friend of the Washburnes. They came, they saw, they were conquered. Five of these six families built cabins, and with the building boom the Huron Mountain Shooting and Fishing Club was off to a flying start.

More on the Shiras Family

George Shiras III had married Frances P. White, the daughter of Peter White, and they became members of Huron Mountain Club in 1892. Mr. Shiras dropped his membership in 1894 for several reasons. He had given up his gun for a camera by that time, and besides, he could use the club property as a guest of his father–in–law, Peter White, if need be. However, probably his main reason for dropping his club membership was that it was becoming very active, and he preferred the privacy of Peter White camp on the Laughing Whitefish River. He had had the Huron Mountains to himself for too long, and now he wanted Whitefish Lake to himself.

No one knew the Huron Mountain district better than the Shiras family, including George's uncle Col. William R. Howe, and no one ever fished it harder. Their first fishing excursion up the Salmon Trout River was in 1865 and the unbelievable success of that venture led to many more until the fishing was almost ruined in the river by the many log drives from 1885 to 1904. By that time the family camp at Laughing Whitefish was their main focus, and George Shiras III was fighting in Congress to save what was left. Peter White had purchased the land at Whitefish Lake and, after several years of camping in tents there, built the Peter White camp in 1884.

Probably Shiras' greatest shock was to see the great flights of passenger pigeons end so abruptly. In the 1860s and '70s the migration of these birds blackened the sky. On Open Rock Hill in Marquette (now between Ohio, Michigan, High and Pine Streets) men would load wide–mouth cannons with shot, gravel, chain, nails or anything they could get their hands on. When the sky was black overhead they would fire the cannon and everyone would run around with sticks, killing the injured or stunned birds that had been knocked down. They were the best of eating but many more were salted, packed in barrels and shipped off to the cities, as were tons of lake fish that were being taken at that time.

The last passenger pigeon in Marquette County was reported as being seen at Pine River in 1909. The last known one in the world died in a Cincinnati zoo in 1914. Even stuffed pigeons are hard to find. Apparently this bird was meant to live by the millions or not at all. George Shiras had seen the feeble attempts to save them fail. This experience prompted him to introduce his conservation measures in Congress which were eventually strengthened by the individual states.

Another of the favorite camping spots to which the Shirases returned for 40 consecutive years was Saux Head Island in Lake Superior (now called Garlic Island). This name is said to commemorate the massacre of a Sauk war party by Ojibways, under Chief Yellowdog. There are several versions to the story. According to one, the heads of the victims were hung in the trees around the island.

The point and island were owned by Mr. Longyear and were the site he had chosen for the "Tribe of Scribes" camp. He was going to invite reporters and writers to join this organization. However, when this club did not materialize, he sold the property to Mr. Hazel Payne who had moved to Marquette from Grand Rapids. For many years he worked for the D. S. S. & A. Railroad.

The Paynes had several children. They built a log cabin just back in the woods a short distance from the point and this put an end to the Shiras camp on the island, as it proved to be a popular spot for many guests of the Paynes.

The Kaufman Family

We have read of Sam Kaufman who married Juliet Adelaide Graveraet, the sister of Robert Graveraet. The Kaufmans had settled down in Marquette and raised a family of twelve children (one child died young). Sam had developed a dry goods and clothing store. It later became a kind of partnership with Isaac Neuberger who had his own store in the next block, and later on his own with the help of his sons. Neuberger had come to Marquette in 1873. The Kaufman store eventually became known as Sam Kaufman and Sons, Leading Clothiers, Gents Furnishings and Merchant Tailors. Sam traveled throughout the district selling his goods, and his store was well–known for miles around. Many of his friends jokingly called Sam "Cheap John."

The oldest Kaufman son was Nathan Myron Kaufman, born July 4, 1862. Nathan married Ed Breitung's widow and became the mayor of Marquette in 1893–94. He has been credited with being the prime mover in the building of the beautiful new sandstone and brick City Hall in the 200 block of West Washington Street during his term as mayor of the city. That

Top: Payne Camp at Sauks Head Point (present site of Granot Loma) (c. 1900).
Bottom: The Island at Payne Camp has been known as Saukshead Island, Garlic Island, and Daisy Island.

same year he took the whole City Council to the World's Fair in Chicago and met Carter Harrison I.

There was a lot of local controversy and indignation over the rise of Nathan Kaufman because he married into the Breitung family. However, it seems as though Nathan would have been destined to do well in life anyway, even without the Breitung money, as he was a tireless worker even at a young age. As a young boy, he worked hard in the clothing stores of Ike Neuberger and of his father. Since Sam was on the road for months at a time, Nathan had to bear much responsibility in the family and the business. As his brothers grew older and able to help, Nathan left Marquette at age 16 and, because of his store experience, went on his own as a traveling salesman for Wilson Brothers, a clothing manufacturer out of Chicago. He did well but the continual travel was a hard life. With the help of his family, Nathan opened a clothing store in Negaunee, but a few years later, in 1883, returned to Marquette and worked for his father again.

It was during this period that young Nathan became interested in exploring for minerals. There were well over a hundred small mines operating on the Marquette Range, some of them very small, but everyone was prospecting. He purchased mineral rights and became deeply involved in acquiring mineral lands. Among his investments, Nathan had obtained an option on the Blue Mine, which he later sold at a large profit.

Nathan, of course, knew the Breitungs in Negaunee and had done business with Mr. Breitung. Then the Breitungs built a large home in Marquette near the Kaufmans and got to know the rest of the family. The Kaufmans at one time lived on Lake Street, below the Breitung mansion, but later lived in several homes on Ridge Street, across the street from the Breitungs. Nathan had often done work around the house for the Breitungs. He took care of their horses for them on a part–time basis. The Breitungs were among the wealthiest people in town, and very influential. Between 1873 and 1887 Mr. Breitung was a member of the State Legislature, a State Senator, and a member of the United States Congress. He was also the mayor of Negaunee from 1880 to '83.

Because of Edward Breitung's innovative mining procedures, his introduction of shaft mining, his continual enlargement of his properties, and his general success in the mining business, there was a great influx of mining men into the area, both as employees and as observers. The Lake Superior Mine had become the Mecca of the iron–mining industry. Many men had to stay in Marquette hotels, as there were not enough accommodations for them in Negaunee and Ishpeming.

In 1878, a group of Negaunee businessmen headed up by Andrew Seass decided to build a fine hotel at the east end of Iron Street. The opposite end of the street was near the spot where iron was first discovered. They removed the old Ogden House and built the Breitung House, naming it honor of Mr. Breitung. For the first few years, although there was a boiler in the basement, water piping for two bathrooms on each floor, and gas piping for lights in every room, these utilities were not connected up. Their water came from a well in the backyard, heat from box stoves fired by wood, and each room had a kerosene lamp.

Over the years, young German girls had been brought up from around Milwaukee to work as chambermaids in hotels of the area. In 1870 Ed Breitung married one of them, Miss Mary Pulan, from Port Washington, Wisconsin. At the time, Miss Pulan was a waitress in a small boarding house in Republic where Mr. Breitung used to eat his meals when on business there. At 39, he was nearly twice her age. This couple had two children – Edward N. Breitung born November 1, 1871, and William M. Breitung, who died young.

Mr. Breitung moved to Marquette and built a huge home on the south side of Ridge Street, on the bluff above the old Kaufman house. It was built of the finest material money could buy, with parquet floors and handcarved mahogany columns in the library, and expensive tapestries. Whole walls were hand–painted on canvas, and German silver plumbing fixtures throughout the building. In the bathroom was a huge free–standing china bathtub on a raised platform. This was the age of elegance, and the Breitungs were not to be outdone.

As Mr. Breitung was away much of the time on business and politics, Nathan Kaufman efficiently took care of many small business details for him at home. Ed, Jr. was just a young boy at the time. Nathan's responsibilities increased when Mr. Breitung became ill in 1886.

On March 3, 1887, Mr. Breitung died, leaving the bulk of his estate, which included vast holdings on three iron ranges, to his wife and his son, Edward, Jr. The town gossips had it that Nathan Kaufman was seeing Mrs. Breitung even before her husband's death, and with Mr. Breitung's death Nathan was given even further control of the Breitung holdings. Later he was appointed officially as agent for the Breitung estate, a position he had held for several years and was said to have handled well.

It was during this period that Nathan became very active in the goings on of the city of Marquette. Among other things, he became the mayor and was responsible for the big city hall, a building the city could be proud of, and the Savings Bank Building. He became President of the Bank

Upper left: Sam Kaufman.
Upper right: Nathan M. Kaufman
Middle: Mr. and Mrs. Edward N. Breitung.
Bottom: The Breitung–Kaufman home, Ridge Steet, Marquette. (Jack Deo collection). There were two entrances in the front and two entrances in the back.

313

and joined with Frederick Owens Clark and another man to form the Marquette Street Railway, a fine set of trolley cars which ran from the Superior Hotel at the extreme south end of town to Presque Isle at the extreme north end.

On June 30, 1893, Nathan Kaufman married Mary Breitung, the widow of Edward Breitung, Sr., and moved into the big Breitung home at 334 East Ridge Street. When he took over the huge estate he stepped into the many positions of awesome responsibilities that went with it, but his years of experience in handling the Breitung affairs made him well qualified to do so.

Almost overnight Nathan Kaufman had become president of the Washington Iron Mine, director of the Republic Mine, director of the Arctic Mining Company, and secretary of the Negaunee Iron Mining Company. Within a few years, in the panic of 1893, Nathan purchased and became president of the Hammond, Whiting and East Chicago Railroad. He further stepped out on his own when he organized and became president of the Marquette County Savings Bank, placing several of his brothers on the board.

With his positions of authority and his vast new wealth, Nate Kaufman did a lot of traveling out east to New York, Boston, Philadelphia, Chicago and Detroit. He invited many of his new friends and acquaintances, many of whom were wealthy and influential people, to his beautiful home on the bluff for extended visits. His critics, of whom there were many, said that Nathan was seeing to it that all his younger brothers and sisters had the opportunity to marry well.

Marquette Blossoms

Nathan Kaufman and his brothers and sisters were all born and raised in Marquette, by then a small but thriving community of some three or four thousand people. Its fringes were the quarry and the Rolling Mill Furnace in the south, and Arch Street, with a road going out Fourth Street, on the north. To the west was the cemetery. The town was all clustered around Iron Bay and the lower harbor, which was completely industrial docks, the railroad yards, the Burtis Sawmill, the Grace Furnace, and various fish houses.

In their young lives, the Kaufman children had seen a wooded frontier port change to a solid home–rule city with many beautiful homes and buildings. These started in the early days after the fire, with the Hiram Burt (son of John Burt) home on Blaker and Ridge in addition to the Peter White home already there. The Burt home was copied from one in Paris, it was said, built with five– and six–sided sandstone blocks, extensive terracing, and an elegant interior. This was a very early sandstone building, and the only one of this style. About this time, the Marquette, Houghton and Ontonogon Railroad built a sandstone block building on the corner of Main and Lake Streets. It was also unique, with cast iron frames in the doors and windows, as was this same type of construction in the new sandstone First National Bank Building on the corner of Spring and Front Streets. Then there was the Methodist Episcopal Church on Front & Ridge, the First Baptist Church across the street and, in 1875, the beautiful St. Paul Episcopal Church on Ridge and High, built with the same stone as the other churches and the Burt house across the street from it. Donald Donnan, an architectural critic from Chicago, called this building "the most flawless piece of brownstone masonry in the world." Peter White, who was behind many of these sandstone buildings and chaired the committee to build this one, also had the Morgan White Memorial Chapel built in memory of his son Morgan Lewis White, who died in 1878 at 12 years of age. This building was attached to St. Paul's Church, to the north of it on High Street. It had a full basement and was all made of local material except the huge Gothic window which dominates the main room of the chapel, a registered Tiffany designed and made in London. The slate roof was from the Arvon Quarries, all the wood was from the local forest – floor of hard maple, wainscoting wall of oak, ceiling of red pine – and, of course, Marquette sandstone exterior.

There is a story known to many older Marquette residents that seems to have died with the passing of time. Peter White was an extremely energetic man with a great sphere of influence. His life, however, was not without tragedy. Peter had married the daughter of Dr. Hewitt, for whom Hewitt Avenue is named, in 1857. The couple had seven children. All but two of the daughters died of diphtheria when very young. The oldest daughter married Alfred O. Jopling in 1881, and the other married George Shiras III.

The legend, one of many told about town, is that Peter White had sold Sam Kaufman some land years earlier and had given him a bad deed. Now it seems that if anyone should have known how to make out a deed, it would have been Peter White, so it appeared that the act was deliberate.

One of Mrs. Kaufman's sisters, a Graveraet, put an Indian curse on Peter because of it. We must remember that these were different times, and an Indian curse was much dreaded and much believed. When his children came down with diphtheria, Mr. White was said to have begged on bended knee to her to lift the curse, but to no avail. All the male children of the

Top: The Episcopal Church and Hiram Burt home in the 1890s. By this time, the Burt house, built in 1872, belonged to Sidney Adams.
Middle: Terracing on the bluff behind the Hiram Burt home. Courtesy Marquette County Historical Society.
Bottom: Later in the 1880s, there were beautiful terraced gardens there. Burt home. Jack Deo collection.

 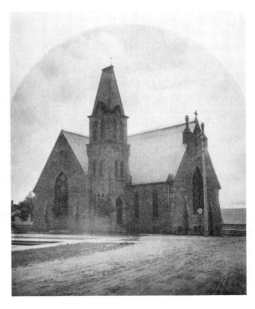

Top: First Methodist and Episcopal Churches, Ridge Street.
Lower left: Senator James McMillan, William C. McMillan and James T McMillan (in curls)
Lower right: The First Baptist Church, burned in 1963.

family died in the epidemic, and there was no one left to carry on the proud White name.

In the very early days Peter had embraced the Methodist Church and had personally helped build the first church on Washington Street, near where the St. John's Church once stood. (It was razed the Sunday morning before the Christmas of 1986,– very poor timing for the citizens of Marquette. Mrs. Merl Froney, who posed for the figure of St. Bernadette in one of the stained glass windows was still living at the time.) However, he then became influential in organizing the Episcopal Parish and, as was stated, a prime mover in building St. Paul's. One of the very early ministers of that church was Joshua Phelps. Shortly after the death of his sons, Peter White wrote a letter to the Rev. Phelps as follows:

> The good wife tells (me) you have a baby boy. Would you please name the baby Peter White Phelps. Anyone with that name should have something to start with. I am enclosing a bond for $2,000 which I hope will still be paying interest when he comes of age.

They named the child Peter White Phelps and Mr. and Mrs. White became his godparents. Peter White Phelps was a lifelong resident of Marquette. As a young man he worked as a bookkeeper in Peter White's bank and when Peter White died he inherited the Peter White Insurance Agency, the oldest insurance agency in Michigan. The Phelpses' daughter married Clarence Randall, who had been the District Attorney of Marquette County and later, for many years, the president of Inland Steel Company in its prime years. Peter White Phelps lived for many years in the beautiful home of Jacobsville sandstone at 433 East Ridge St. in Marquette. Although known to many as the Peter White Phelps house, it was built in 1892 by Mr. Fitch, the father of Mrs. Phelps and president of the D.S.S. & A. Railroad Co. It has been said that the rounded glass windows in the circular bay on the southwest corner of the house were a request of Mrs. Phelps, who had seen it in a military academy building in Indiana. Fred Charleton was the architect. In the den there was a balcony and when they gave elaborate parties, an orchestra would sit in one corner of the balcony and dancers could move around the house from one room to the other. The walls of the home were decorated with the same dark green velvet as the furniture, and this was never changed until after Mr. and Mrs. Phelps died.

Many other beautiful homes were built between 1880 and 1900 – the Seymour home; the F. W. Reed home on Arch Street, recently renovated by the Kiesbys; the Swineford home; the Pickands home; and the Dan Ball

Top: Alfred O. Jopling on Grand Island. Courtesy Mrs. Max Reynolds, Jr.
Bottom: Alfred O. Jopling at home. Courtesy Mrs. Max Reynolds, Jr.

home, to name just a few. Another remarkable home is the sandstone structure at 430 East Arch St., known to many as the Swinton home, recently renovated by Dr. Peter Kelly. This building was built about the same time as the Episcopal Church, designed by the same architect and built with the same materials. It was built by a Mr. Ripka but was later lived in by the architect who designed it, Mr. C. F. Struck, who also designed the Marquette Opera House for Peter White and Co. There was the still perfectly preserved and beautiful Dan Merritt house at 410 East Ridge, built of Marquette sandstone. The Merritts later moved to Duluth and became dock, bridge and marine contractors, building some of the largest of each in the world. Their descendants became a part of Merritt, Chapman & Scott Co. who, with the American Bridge Division of U.S. Steel Co., built the Mackinac bridge between 1954 and 1957. With the completion of the Longyear Mansion and Nathan Kaufman's Savings Bank, the architectural elegance spilled over into public buildings such as Nathan's City Hall, the waterworks building, the Marquette County Courthouse, the Peter White Public Library, and the great Hotel Superior in south Marquette. The City of Marquette, with its many parks, fine lighting, streetcar system (1891), two harbors and fine buildings had become the undisputed "Queen City of the North" and this was only the beginning.

This was the atmosphere of progress and development that Nathan Kaufman and his brothers and sisters grew up with. They had all seen it happen, and they were a part of it. With the wealth to accomplish just about whatever they wanted, they moved into the mainstream of the business world. Sam, Jr., the second oldest boy, born in 1864, married Una Libby of the Libby Packing Co. family. Bernard, born in 1865, married Miss Adelaide Lean. Bernie got into trouble and moved to Canada. Dan, born in 1867, married Lulu Kerr. Sarah, born in 1868, married Joe Jenkins. The sixth child was Louis Graveraet Kaufman, born in 1870. Charlotte, born in 1875, the seventh child, married Edward Nicholas Breitung, Jr., Nathan's stepson, thus keeping the Breitung interests intact. These later became the Breitung–Kaufman properties, which included the Mary Charlotte Mines numbers I and II, the Breitung Hematite Mines numbers I and II, the Milwaukee Davis mine, the Lucky Star mines in Negaunee and Ishpeming, and the Barron and Franklin Mines in Humbolt. There were also interests in the Athens Mining Co. and the Bunker Hill Mining Co. These properties were handled pretty much by Edward Breitung, Jr. and Harry L. Kaufman, the tenth child born in 1881. He married Hope Hamilton, who died at age 90 in 1985. The other children of Sam Kaufman, Sr. were Marion (1877), Callie Gladys (1879) and Maude, the youngest, who died at age five or so. Gladys married Samuel A. Morrison, and Marion married Dr. Edward J. Hudson, a

Top: The original Methodist Church, which stood on Washington Street about where the St. John the Baptist Society later built the St. John's Church in 1908. It was torn down in 1986 on the Sunday before Christmas. Courtesy Wilfred Fleury.
Bottom: City Hall and Post Office building. Courtesy Jack Deo.

Top: Dan Merritt home. Courtesy Wilfred Fleury.
Bottom: Queen City Band (c. 1890s). Rydholm Collection.

chemist who worked at the Cliff Dow Chemical Co. in Marquette. The Hudsons lived in another big, beautiful home on Ridge Street next to the Breitung home. This was one of the older elegant wooden homes, with a broad veranda covering the length of the house built back in 1871 by Mary E. and Matthew Maynard. In 1892 it was sold to the Breitungs and then to Mary Kaufman.

Dr. Hudson, years later (1929–1934), became the Mayor of Marquette.

Louis Kaufman

But it was Louis Graveraet Kaufman, the sixth child of Sam and Juliet, who distinguished himself more than any of the others and became even more prominent than his brother Nathan in the annals of Marquette County history. He was born on November 13, 1870 in Marquette. It was Louis G. Kaufman who became a national and even international financial and banking celebrity. When he graduated from Marquette High School he went to work in one of his brother's mines shoveling iron ore. At this time he was studying to become a mining engineer. It soon became apparent that Louis was better at using his brains than his back. After coming up with several ideas that would speed things up and improve efficiency, he was moved up to a boss's job. At the same time he still helped out, off and on, at his father's store. Before long, Louis was made superintendent of a mine. He was only 24 years old.

In 1893, Louis left the mine and went to work for his brother Nathan in the Marquette County Savings Bank. To teach him banking from the ground up, Nathan started his younger brother at the bottom of the ladder, reportedly as an errand boy. Within six years, Louis had advanced to the vice–presidency of the bank.

Many of the local people were still smarting from the rapid financial rise of Nathan and Sam Kaufman due to their marriages. They said that Louis could only have risen in the mine because of his brother and now, with Louis as vice president of the bank, the talk was renewed.

Then Louis married Marie Young, the daughter of Otto Young of Chicago. Otto Young was an extremely wealthy man. He was owner of the Fair Store in Chicago, which had the reputation of being the largest store in the country, if not the world. He had been buying up much of the downtown real estate in Chicago over the years, and owned the better part of the Loop. In Marquette the story was told about town that Otto Young had promised

Upper left: Louis G. Kaufman at age 16. Courtesy First National Bank.
Upper right: Louis G. Kaufman at 30. Courtesy First National Bank.
Bottom: Mr. and Mrs. Lous G. Kaufman and family C. 1920.

Louis and Marie a million dollars for every child they had, and there were eventually eight children.

When the Kaufman brothers purchased the controlling stock in Peter White's First National, Louis was made Vice President there. To many, this was the beginning of a struggle for financial control of Marquette.

A third bank in Marquette, started out on Front Street as the Citizens Bank, organized in 1871 by a young lawyer named James Milton Wilkinson. Wilkinson had come to Marquette in 1864 with a friend, H. P. Smith, who was right out of University of Michigan law school. The two of them set up a law office in town.

In 1879 Wilkinson joined forces with Ambrose Campbell to reorganize the Citizen's Bank as the privately owned Campbell Wilkinson Bank. Campbell had been in Marquette since 1855 in the mercantile business and had been a director of the First National Bank from 1864 to 1867. The bank did business until Campbell's death in 1890. However, just before Campbell died in Chicago on a business trip, he and Wilkinson had engaged the firm of Scott and Company, Detroit architects, to draw up plans for a new bank building to be placed on the northeast corner of Front and Washington Streets, across Washington from the County Savings Bank, known as Nathan's Bank. John Scott came to Marquette and hired Fred Charleton to act as local agent for the company. The building was built with ornately carved Jacobsville sandstone from Portage Entry and the then–famous Anderson pressed brick from Chicago, one of the finest brick products available. The design and construction showed a great deal of Charleton influence. A store front in the building north of the bank itself was occupied by George Conklin's Music and Jewelry Store. He moved there on the hill from 301 South Front St. Five rooms upstairs were used as offices by Mr. J. M. Longyear as agent for the L. S. S. C. Railroad and Iron Co. There were some other offices in the building. The new bank was known as the Marquette Savings Bank. The bank did a flourishing business against its two competitors, Nathan Kaufman's County Savings Bank and Peter White's and Louis Kaufman's First National Bank. Some businesses even went to Ishpeming to do their banking where Mr. Braasted was president of the Miner's Bank and to Negaunee where Mr. A. Maitland headed the First National Bank there.

On January 25, 1898, James Wilkinson died of a stomach ailment. It was a great loss to the city. Besides his banking career, he had been a civic leader for many years. He had been active in city government, served as state treasurer for a short time under Governor Luce for whom Luce County was named, and was on the board that selected the site for another beautiful classic sandstone structure, the Marquette Branch Prison which was designed by Charleton and built in 1887–88 of both Marquette and Portage Entry sandstone.

With Wilkinson's death, the Marquette Savings Bank closed its doors and the Boston brokerage firm of Paine, Weber moved into the building. By 1901 Wilkinson's estate was settled and the building sold. Depositors were dubious about getting their money, and there was a migration back to the Kaufman Banks.

A group of local businesses led by lumberman F. W. Reed, Fred H. Begole of the Lake Shore Engine Co., M. K. Reynolds of the Powder Mill, and Dan Powell, the lumberman, took up the cause to form a new bank.

Edgar H. Towar had been Vice President of Peter White's bank before the Kaufmans took over. Ed knew banking well. He was born in Lyon, New York in 1840. He organized the First National Bank of Hancock in 1874 and moved to Marquette to take over as Vice President to Peter White in 1889. Now the organizers of the new bank were asking Towar to help with their bank, as many people objected to doing business with the Kaufmans.

Edgar Towar announced his resignation from Peter White's bank in order to become associated with the new bank, which was to be called the Marquette National Bank. Then the organizers approached J. M. Longyear to be an officer and a director. He told them that he would take stock in it but that he did not want to be a director. Ed Towar told Longyear that he had resigned and been replaced by Louis Kaufman because "It was so unpleasant for me that I couldn't stand it."

When the Marquette National Bank was organized, Mr. Longyear was out of town and the board elected him a director of it. Several of the organizers had written to beg him to remain for a year to get things started. He consented, but only for one year. He also told Peter White and Louis Kaufman, when they asked him about the new bank, that he had "no intention of remaining an officer of the bank."

J. M. Longyear wrote in 1912:

> Before the first year was up I heard several times that the First National Bank people were telling businessmen that I had no confidence in the new bank and that I was going to get out as soon as possible. This obliged me to stay in. E. H. Towar was the first president. He removed to Utah and resigned. Mr. Frederick W. Reed was the next president. He died May 9, 1907 and again in my absence, on Sept. 30, 1907, I was elected President. I protested that the president should be someone who could be more active than I

could be, but the others said so many nice things to me that I accepted the office. It seemed safe enough, with Alton also on the board of directors and Sherman close by to look after it.

"Alton" was Alton T. Roberts who married Abby Longyear, J. M.'s oldest daughter, and "Sherman" was James Sherman, Mr. Longyear's right–hand man and confidant for many years.

Mr. Longyear continues:

I do not believe in directors who do not direct, but in several concerns I seem to be one of that kind.

The Kaufmans have seemed to feel much bitterness toward me on account of the new bank and they perhaps think they are justified, although, but for their own action in circulating erroneous reasons why I did not intend to remain on the board of directors, I should now be only a stockholder. They have purchased from weak stock holders nearly one quarter of the stock in the Marquette National Bank, paying more for it than it was worth. This has evidently been done with a view to getting control of the bank. The remaining stock, however, is held by people who do not wish to have the bank closed and it does not look as if they will be able to gain the control.

The Marquette National Bank has prospered and is now in flourishing condition.

On October 19, 1901, the following people were elected as directors of the Bank:

Hon. J. M. Longyear, who was also the president of Huron Mountain Club.

Charles Hebard, who had turned over his lumber business in Pequaming to his son Dan, who joined Huron Mountain in 1920 and later became its third president.

Edgar H. Towar, who was a member of Huron Mountain Club since 1899 and a director of it in 1900 to 1902. He dropped his membership when he resigned from the bank and went to Utah.

William G. Mather, president of the Cleveland–Cliffs Iron Co.

Walter Fitch of Beacon, who had mining interests.

F. W. Reed, a lumberman with large mills in Michigamme and at Eagle Mills near Marquette.

Dan W. Powell, for whom Powell Township was named, a lumberman and member of Huron Mountain Club in 1893 and '94. He held an honorary membership and was not active.

Frederick A. Begole, a nephew of a former governor of Michigan, who later built a camp at Conway Lake.

Frank H. Jennison, also a lumberman.

Peter White, who had sold his stock in the First National to the Kaufmans, was a charter member and Vice President of Huron Mountain Club, but he dropped his membership that year, even though his dues were paid to 1902.

Many people have wondered why the Kaufmans never joined Huron Mountain Club. Numerous answers to that question have been given, but never the above. This struggle was all behind closed doors.

The usual reason many people gave referred to the Kaufmans Jewish extraction. Descendants of the family now claim that they have researched this very carefully and found that Sam Kaufman was not Jewish but German. However, in the early days in anti–Semitic circles, the Kaufmans were always referred to as being Jewish. They did not practice the Jewish religion and Louis and Marie were staunch members of St. Paul's Episcopal Church in Marquette.

Another such misconception was that Daisy Kaufman, the daughter of Otto Young, was Jewish. Otto Young was actually Dutch and formerly his name had been "Junge."

A further misconception is that there have never been any Jews at Huron Mountain Club. In the past half century, several people of Jewish faith have married into Huron Mountain families, but to date there have been no full memberships.

This was not the end of the bank controversy. The owners of the First National, who later were all Kaufmans as Peter White died in 1908, owned about 25 percent of Marquette National stock. When the charter ran out, the directors decided against renewal and were about to transfer the assets from the Marquette National to the newly formed Union National. The Kaufmans brought suit to nullify the action, on the basis that no notice of these steps had been given to the stockholders and that assets should be sold at public sale.

In the 1921 lawsuit, the Union National tried to show that Louis Kaufman and his brother had acted as antagonistic shareholders and they were forced to reorganize the bank to exclude them. A decision was reached in favor of the Kaufmans in 1923, and the Union National Bank was ordered to make compensation for the Kaufman stock, "and for the good will of the bank and bank property." A bank spokesman made the following statement in response: "The result is cheap, even at the price. This city which we all love is not now and will not be, I hope, at any time under the financial control of any one man."

The "one man" they were referring to, of course, was Louis G. Kaufman, because he could easily have controlled Marquette and many other towns. It seems that Marquette was too small for him, but he never gave up calling it home. Nathan was into many things and on many boards also. He invested in the early automobile industry in Detroit for a time, then purchased the Congress Hotel in Chicago and remained there.

Louis was chosen to become president of the Chatham National Bank in New York City. This required a change in the Federal banking laws so that a person could be the president of banks in two different states simultaneously. This hurdle was surmounted and Louis Kaufman became the president of both banks, the one in Marquette and the one in New York. He became the talk of the financial world, and his financial genius blossomed. He started the novel idea of branch banking and introduced the trust system into banking. His New York and Marquette banks were the first in the world to have "And Trust Co." added to their name. He introduced many technical banking reforms, some of which had world–wide implications.

This was the Louis Kaufman who had purchased the Horatio Seymour home at 453 East Michigan St. and purchased the Payne camp which Mr. Longyear had formerly reserved for the "Tribe of Scribes." It is likely that Mr. Kaufman never would have gotten it from Mr. Longyear himself but, having gone through a third party, it became possible. The old Marquette–L'Anse road went right by the camp. Louis Kaufman made several additions to the camp as his family grew larger.

The Father Marquette Statue

During the early years of the Huron Mountain Shooting and Fishing Club, Peter White became embroiled in another controversy in Marquette.

An act of Congress was passed, allowing each state the privilege of placing a statue of its favorite son in Statuary Hall in Washington, DC. Michigan chose Lewis Cass, governor of the Michigan Territory. Wisconsin chose Jacques Marquette. Now Marquette is the most widely used name in the Great Lakes region. There are literally hundreds of things of all sorts named after the great explorer priest; they include towns, cities, counties, forests, parks, railroads, businesses, ships and universities.

There are Marquettes in Manitoba, Canada; McPherson County, Kansas; Clayton County, Iowa; Green Lake County, Wisconsin; Hamilton

County, Nebraska; and a Marquette Heights in Tazewell County, Illinois. Marquette County, Michigan is the largest of the 83 counties in the state, and also the first and largest city of all the Marquettes mentioned. There is also a Marquette County in Wisconsin. So it is evident that several states could have made some claim on Pere Marquette.

The bill, however, specified a "native son" and since Marquette wasn't born in Wisconsin, nor did he die there, nor had he lived there and he wasn't buried there, so he just could not qualify as a native son under any stretch of the imagination. After much argument, a special act of Congress allowed Wisconsin to place a likeness of Father Marquette in the Hall of Statuary.

About the time that all of this was taking place, statues were very popular and Ishpeming had only recently erected "Old Ish" in the center of their downtown district. The people of Marquette, 12 or 13 miles away, were very much aware of this fact, and maybe a little susceptible to the talk that was going around that Marquette should have a statue of its namesake, Father Marquette.

The prime mover for the Wisconsin project was General H. C. Hobart, who led the fight to have the famous Jesuit for Wisconsin's selection. An open contest of design was held for sculptors throughout the world. Geneotone Trentanov of Florence, Italy was chosen to do the job. He made a trip to Wisconsin to discuss the project and do some research on Marquette.

Alfred E. Archambeau was later to become a prominent businessman, with clothing stores in Marquette and Michigamme. At the time, he was a clerk in the store of K. Oshinsky in Marquette. He had been born and raised in Schwitzer Mills Location in Negaunee Township, and was at this time president of the St. John the Baptist Society (Societe St. Jean De Baptiste), a very active Catholic organization in Marquette. Mr. Archambeau wrote to Trentanov inquiring about costs to have a copy of the marble statue cast in bronze.

The marble statue was being done for a fee of $10,000, but Trentanov replied he could use it to make a mold for a copy to be done in bronze for $6,000. The St. John the Baptist Society decided to go ahead and have a funding campaign. They wanted it to be a city–wide project, not just the Society or just Catholic.

To get things off to a good start, Mr. Archambeau approached the most prominent protestant in the city, Mr. Peter White, for the first donation. Now Peter White was a generous giver, especially for something of this nature, but he was also a banker and the nation was then in the depths of the Panic of 1893. It is also possible that the project was not properly

Calumet and Hecla Band, Calumet, Mich.

Upper left: Bishop G. Mott Williams of the Episcopal Church. he was a good friend of George Shiras III and Fredrick Charlton and very active in Marquette activities and social events.

Upper right: Geneotone Trentonove ...sculptor of the statue of Father Marquette. Picture says Gaetano. Other records call him Geneotone.

Lower left: Old Ish in the Ishpeming town triangle...drawing by Bobbie Ameen.

Lower right: Calumet & Hecla Marching Band. Courtesy of Leo Fleury.

explained, or even that he was caught in a bad mood. Regardless, Mr. White felt that this was a poor time to be asking the public for money, and he was of the opinion that the campaign could not succeed at that particular time.

But Archambeau was committed and, though he was disappointed by Mr. White's attitude, he next approached G. Mott Williams, Bishop of the Episcopal Church, who enthusiastically started the fund with $50.

In January 1895, the sculptor himself visited the city of Marquette and talked with A. E. Archambeau and the Society of St. John the Baptist. He met with other community leaders, heard the legends and discussed all aspects of the project. He took pictures of Peter White and Chief Kawbawgam, about both of whom he had been told a great deal. Trentanov finally decided his price would include two bronze reliefs for the base of the statue: one of Marquette arriving at Lighthouse Point for the first time in 1669 and the other of Marquette preaching there in 1671. The Marquette sandstone base would be donated by John H. Jacobs, who owned and operated the quarry in South Marquette.

It was decided that the statue should be placed as near as possible to Marquette's favorite camping spot, but there was some discussion as to whether he should be looking toward the water as he would have in life, or if he should be looking at the city which was named for him. Peter White felt they were honoring the explorer priest and he should be looking at the lake, but others said that this would not be good because people viewing the statue from Walnut Street (now Lake Street) would be looking at the back of the statue. Most people did not know which way the statue would face until the actual unveiling, though the committee gave it away by holding the ceremonies on the side toward town under the face of the statue.

This was a beautiful part of town at the time. The huge Longyear Mansion stood high on the bluff before the likeness of Marquette. The new waterworks building of red Jacobsville sandstone was nearby and the premises could be kept very much like a park. It is true that there were ice houses, the old waterworks building and the Burtis Sawmill along the shore and Mr. Longyear's docking facility on pilings in the harbor, as well as some fish houses, but even at this date plans were being made to remove some of the eyesores. Mr. Longyear bought the sawmill which he did not like beneath his house, and it mysteriously burned one night.

And so, on July 15, 1897, the unveiling took place. The parade was led by the Calumet and Hecla Marching Band, which had once won an international championship. There were addresses by many dignitaries in Chippewa, French and English, and of course Peter White and Charlie

Upper left: Trentonove at the dedication 1897. Rydholm Collection.
Upper right: Marquette statue on Mackinac Island.
Lower left: Charlie Kawbawgam. The stately Indian chief impressed outsiders with his dignity. Jack Deo collection.
Lower right: Bronze relief of Marquette preaching to the Indians at Lighthouse Point. Sandstone base was donated by Mr. Jacobs, owner of the quarry.

333

Kawbawgam each delivered one. Trentanov, the sculptor, was introduced and he explained that Chief Kawbawgam's likeness was used twice in the bas reliefs, once as a young man in the canoe and once as an elderly person in the crowd at the mass. The activities went on throughout the whole day, starting at 6:30 in the morning and ending with the Grand Ball at midnight, held in the beautiful Hotel Superior at the top of Jackson St. Hill. One highlight of the day's events was the re–enactment of Marquette's arrival at Lighthouse Point by some local Indians. Since there were no good birchbark canoes available for use, they substituted some rowboats.

It proved to be a gala day in the history of Marquette, but amidst it all there were a few who were disappointed. Alfred Archambeau told several at the banquet that the statue was of Peter White and not Pere Marquette. Mr. White liked it so much that he ordered a second replica of it in bronze to be placed on Mackinac Island.

Peter White was a powerful figure on the Mackinac Island State Park Commission since its inception, and he felt that a statue of Father Marquette should adorn the Straits of Mackinaw – and what better place for it to do so than from Mackinac Island? When ordering the second statue, he specified that this statue should be the explorer priest with a map and compass in his hand, instead of a Bible as in the case of the original, and this one should most certainly be looking out at the water. And so, on a broad lawn which used to be known as the "potato patch" the great explorer–priest Jacques Marquette stands looking over the Straits. The inscription on the back of the sandstone base reads "This Memorial to the Pioneers of France in the New World is Due to Peter White of Marquette, Himself a Pioneer of Upper Michigan."

Mr. White had a plan whereby each school child in Michigan should donate one penny toward the cost of the statue. Whatever the amount, if any, that came in for the cause is unknown, but Peter White paid the lion's share from his own pocket.

As for the statue itself, no one alive had ever seen Father Marquette, and in his obscure life among the Indians no pictures were ever made of him. In the 1960's the Marquette County Historical Society received a drawing from a museum in Paris, which they claim was made of Jacques Marquette before he left France in 1666.

Father Joseph P. Donnelly of Marquette University in Milwaukee certainly one of the greatest living authorities on Father Marquette, says Geneotone Trentanov portrays the missionary as a "short, stocky ancient in his late seventies, at least." This could well describe Peter White at the time. The head, according to the sculptor himself, was copied from a portrait of

Top: Day of the dedication Peter White next to statue, Trentonove extreme right.
Lower left: Drawing of Pere Marquette from Paris, done before 1666.
Lower right: Marquette at Lighthouse Point (1897–1913). Rydholm Collection.

Father Pierre Francois Charlevoix when he was almost seventy, but some residents of Marquette were convinced that there is a striking resemblance to Peter White.

What did Father Marquette really look like? Well, we have a picture to go by now, but for three hundred years artists, sculptors and historians tried to guess. Father Donnelly made a scientific stab at it. We know Father Marquette was young – 37 when he died – wiry, rugged, and clean–shaven as all Jesuits were at that time.

Father Donnelly:

Let it be recalled that Jacques Marquette was born at Loan, a village just under thirty miles south of the Belgian border and not quite a hundred and fifty miles from the Rhine. The root stock of northern France was Saxon, Viking and Burgundian, all tall folk, fair–skinned and light–haired. Though Mediterranean French are dark, swarthy and small, northern Frenchmen are normally quite tall, rugged and sturdy. Interestingly enough, Marquette's collateral descendants, still residing in his native town of Loan, are all tall, blond, blue–eyed people who could readily be mistaken for Scandinavians.

In 1952, when Harry Wood was commissioned by the First Federal Savings and Loan Association of Peoria, Illinois to paint a new and more accurate portrait of Father Marquette, he visited Loan where he took photographs of Father Marquette's relatives. From these, Wood produced a portrait of Marquette which, in the absence of any contemporary painting of the man, is quite likely fairly close to the real man.

The pictures at the Historical Society and Wood's are two different people, but there are a few similar characteristics.

Wood shows us an obviously tall, rugged, partially bald, blond, blue–eyed missionary dressed in a travel–worn cassock, holding in his gnarled, callused hands an elaborately decorated calumet. Everything one learns from the mass of contemporary documents about Father Marquette seems to justify Harry Wood's concept of the man.

An article from a Sunday edition of the New York Times of July 25, 1965, gives still another view of the study of Father Marquette:

336

Frankfort, Mich – Because of Catherine Stebbins, both Ludington and Frankfort now contend to be the site of Jacques Marquette's death 290 years ago.

Ludington some years ago erected a granite monument topped by a stainless steel cross, to mark the spot where the French Jesuit and co–discoverer of the Mississippi River was buried in May of 1675.

However, Miss Stebbins, who lives in Traverse City, says Marquette died 50 miles to the north, at the mouth of the Betsie River near Frankfort.

The Michigan Historical Commission decided recently that quite possibly she might be right.

Miss Stebbins, who began her research in 1958, hunted through Jesuit archives in Quebec and traveled down the Lake Michigan shore for a firsthand study of every river from Ludington north to the Straits of Mackinac.

Frankfort officials, elated by the Historic Commission's acknowledgments, are planning to dedicate a marker and wooden cross to mark the spot cited by Miss Stebbins.

The people in Ludington, especially members of the Chamber of Commerce, are unhappy.

Dr. George May, research archivist for the Historical Commission, says both cities might be designated as possible sites.

'This is an historical question to which a definite answer will probably never be obtained,' he said.

Marquette is not buried in either place. Ottawa Indians removed his remains from the original grave in 1677 and reburied them at the Mission he founded at St. Ignace in Michigan's Upper Peninsula.

Some Historic Firsts

We have spoken about the Lake Superior Foundry Co. starting up in 1858, with Charles T. Harvey and Associates on the lower harbor. Then, as the Iron Bay Foundry, it opened again in 1867 under Dan H. Merritt and Col. C. Y. Osburn. They first called the company the Merritt–Osburn Foundry, then the Iron Bay Foundry, and later the Iron Bay Manufacturing Co. In 1886 Merritt went to Duluth, and that family has been in the dock and bridge construction business ever since. The Merritt Chapman Scott Co. built the Mackinac Bridge in 1957.

However, in 1886 the Iron Bay Manufacturing Co. reorganized as the Lake Shore Iron Works with J. M. Longyear, Charles Osburn, C. P. Sheldon, Alfred Kidder, Peter White, Nathan Kaufman, S. R. Holly, and William G. Mather as directors. In 1899 it became the Lake Shore Engine Works. Nathan Kaufman was president, and White, Longyear, Kidder, and Sheldon were all on the board. Fred Begole and C. H. Blomstrom were added later.

Up to this time, the foundry had been making heavy castings for mining machinery, but now, while they still continued with their former products, there was a trend toward engines of various sorts, especially steam and the brand–new internal combustion engines. The foundry became a pioneer in this field and it appears that much of the fame along this line rests mainly on the shoulders of one man, Carl (anglicized Charles) H. Blomstrom.

Blomstrom's family moved to Marquette in 1897 to work at Lake Shore, which at the time was housed in the long brick building that is still on the site at the corner of Washington and Lake Streets. Blomstrom was a cousin of Dr. Orin Youngquist of Marquette, and this may have been a factor in his coming here.

Charles had several titles while he was employed by Lake Shore; the highest seems to have been superintendent, although he was also a designer, chief engineer, and director. He was one of the great pioneers in gas–powered marine and automobile engines. He had scores of important patents in all phases of these mechanisms, especially in carburetors.

While Blomstrom was working at the Lake Shore Engine Works, he developed his Superior Marine Engine, and the company claimed the world market for this product. Many of the early experiments were conducted in the lower harbor, with the first engine being installed in a sailboat belonging to the Peter Anderson Fish Co.

Later, working with Captain Cleary of the U. S. Life Saving Station, Blomstrom installed the first engine ever to power a U. S. lifesaving boat. The boat was specially built, with a step in the bottom to accommodate the propellers. There was a patented system where one engine powered two propellers, one on each side of the keel. Both the lifeboat and the smaller surfboat were powered first in Marquette, and all experimentation carried out in Marquette's lower harbor.

Apparently Nels Flodin, another Swede and a pattern maker at the plant, got toying with the idea of an outboard motor, a portable motor that could be hung on a rowboat. He could not have come up with a completed engine out of the blue, alone. There are a number of Blomstrom ideas in it, and it is safe to say the entire concept was developed at the Lake Shore in

Top: Heavy Casting made at the Lake Shore Engine Works. Courtesy of Family of Nels Flodin.

Middle: Anderson Fish Co. sailboat which had the first Lake Shore marine engine in it. Marquette Lower Harbor 1890s. The Anderson brothers aboard. Left–right – Henry, August and Albert Courtesy Jack Anderson.

Bottom: Carl H. Blomstrom in one of his first automobiles built in 1897. Courtesy Marquette County Historical Society.

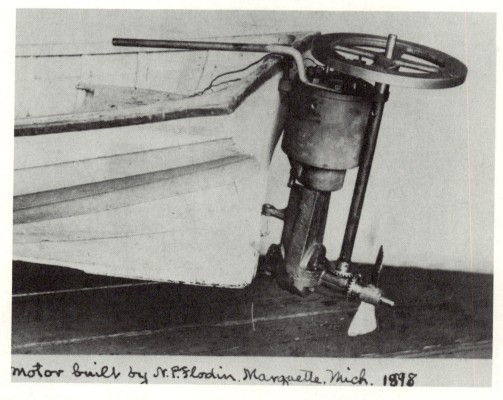

motor built by N. P. Flodin. Marquette. Mich. 1898

Top: Nels Flodin at his home on Arch Street (1920s). Courtesy Nels Flodin family.
Bottom: First Outboard motor, invented by Nels Flodin, 1897. Courtesy, Lake Shore
Engineering Ralph Houtala.

340

1897 and '98. Blomstrom never claimed any credit for it, but Flodin did. It was his baby and he carried the idea through until they had built an outboard motor, the first gas–driven outboard in the world. This motor was made in the same building at the foot of Washington on Lake Street.

In the summer of 1898, using some coils and a battery borrowed from the telephone company, the motor was finally started and it powered a rowboat across the lower harbor to the breakwater, better than a quarter of a mile away. As far as we know, the motor never ran again, and was given up as something to be worked on later. It eventually proved to be far in advance of the first commercially built outboards that were patented several years later by Cameron B. Waterman of Detroit, the son of Cameron D. Waterman of Huron Mountain Club. His were the first commercial outboards in the world.

Flodin had several patents of his own, including one for a self–oiling wheel also made at Lake Shore, and he may have had some type of patent, maybe just the idea, on the outboard. Years later Mr. Cameron B. Waterman told me that he was able to get all the patents of European countries but, because of a patent that came from Marquette, he had trouble getting a good patent in the United States. Mr. Waterman was a patent attorney.

For years there has been a story around Marquette that an automobile called the "Pioneer" was made at the Lake Shore before the turn of the century. According to the research of Robert M. Harris, formerly of Marquette and presently of lower Michigan, the auto was built in a barn behind a house on West Michigan Street by Charles Blomstrom. The parts for the car were made at the Lake Shore Co., but the car was made by Blomstrom independent of the company. Later the barn was made into a house and for many years was occupied by the George Millward Family. George was a blacksmith at Huron Mountain

Blomstrom's son says this car had no name, and that it was completely built in Marquette in 1897, some six years before Henry Ford drove his auto in the streets of Detroit.

Harris also tells us that Nathan Kaufman suggested Blomstrom move to Detroit to build automobiles, and, along with the Youngquists, financed him to do so. According to the Standard Catalogue of American Cars (1805–1942) by Beverly R. Kimes and Henry Austin Clark, Jr., C. H. Blomstrom made two early cars, both in Marquette – one in 1897 and the second in 1899. The first was experimental and had no name, and the second may have been the one called "Pioneer" and built at the Lake Shore.

Carl H. Blomstrom left Marquette in September of 1901, headed for the World's Fair in Buffalo, New York, where his lifesaving boat, the first to have an engine in it, was being demonstrated. The lifesaving crew would turn

1907 Blomstrom, roadster, WLB

1917 Frontmobile, roadster, AA

1909 Gyroscope, touring, WLB

1914 Rex, 2-pass. roadster, WLB

REX — Detroit, Michigan — (1914) — Whether the car itself or the m

Upper left: This is the four–cylinder Blomstrom made by Blomstrom.
Upper right: Blomstrom invented and put into production the first front–wheel drive in 1911.
This is a later model of the "Frontmobile."
Lower left: The Gyroscope Touring Car
Lower right: The Rex by Blomstrom.

the boat over in the water, at which time the engine would stop, and when the boat was righted the engine would start again. This was another Blomstrom patent.

President McKinley was shot on September 6th at the exposition and died there on the 14th. Because of his death, the exposition was closed before Blomstrom arrived. Carl went to Detroit and lived with his family in the Wayne Hotel until his furniture arrived from Marquette a month later.

The "Queen" automobile, first conceived and built in Marquette, was later built at the Blomstrom Car Co. in Detroit, with the first cars produced in 1903. Power boats were also made in the same building, and a Detroit News cartoon shows Carl Blomstrom holding a car in one hand and a boat in the other. Harris tells us there are other photos and that Bernie Kaufman is pictured in one of them.

A disagreement over financing between Carl Blomstrom and Nathan Kaufman ended in a court trial. Nate won the case, reportedly because of his "unlimited" funds, and the partnership broke up. Nathan acquired some other associates and went on to build the "Deluxe" car. Blomstrom started a new company which made the "Blomstrom 4 Cylinder Auto" and later the "Frontmobile," a front–wheel drive automobile. This front–wheel drive invention led to four–wheel drive, an idea drawn up by Blomstrom in 1911 and used in World War I vehicles.

Blomstrom's patents for the Superior Marine Engine came through on August 28, 1900, March 26, 1901, and August 6th, 1901. His son, Lowell C. Blomstrom, was an automotive pioneer in his own right, having closely followed the work of his father. Lowell was the Chief Engineer at Federal Mogul for over 30 years.

All in all, Carl Blomstrom was directly connected with at least eight early automobiles, and it was said that he was "never without new ideas." He was the inventor of the front–wheel drive and the four–wheel drive. There were two Blomstrom cars: a small single–cylinder runabout in 1902, of which he built 25, then in 1906 his new Blomstrom 30, a bigger car than was his former Queen. There were 1500 Queens produced from 1904 to 1906. He built 125 touring cars and 75 runabouts in 1907. These were described by the press as "the last thing in motor car design throughout." Then he became interested in his Gyroscope Car and the Blomstroms died through neglect. Later he was connected with the Griswold, the Page, and the Lyon, as well as the Frontmobile during World War I. He also built the Rex in 1914. He finally went with Camden Motor Corporation in Camden, New Jersey, which liquidated in 1922.

Upper left: 1899 Winton "horseless carriage."
Upper right: Pope Waverly.
Middle left: 1903 Olds.
Middle right: Mitchell.
Bottom: Pierce Arrow.

Book One

The "Horseless Carriage" in Marquette

When Blomstrom was building his car in 1897 in Marquette, there were no other automobiles of any kind in the Upper Peninsula. However, people had been experimenting with them for five or ten years in both Europe and America, and both steam and electric cars had been in existence for some time. The first commercially manufactured car, made by Panhard and Levassor in 1891, used the Daimler engine. The first automobile imported into the United States was a Benz, brought to the Chicago World's Fair in 1893. Charles E. Duryea built the first one in the U. S. in 1892, and Henry Ford built his first car in 1893.

Marquette's first commercial automobile arrived in 1899 (while Blomstrom was building his second car) when H. S. Pickands and H. B. Tuttle drove a "Winton" up from Cleveland. In those days they were called "horseless carriages." They had an adventurous trip and found the very worst roads between Rapid River and Carlshend. The trip was expected to take six days but they arrived nine days overdue, being pulled the last 16 miles into Marquette by a team of horses. Flat tires were common, and the machinery broke down often. When they drove the car through Marquette, crowds came out to watch it puff and blow its way up Front Street Hill amid smoke and strange noises. It had 30–inch wheels in front and 36–inch wheels in the rear. On the return trip to Cleveland, Tuttle and Pickands went by train and shipped the Winton back on a steamer.

By 1902 Bishop G. Mott Williams owned a car, and J. Everett Ball and Austin Farrell each bought an "Olds" the next year. In 1904 Morgan Jopling had a Stanley Steamer and Alfred Jopling purchased a Pope–Waverly electric car for use by the Light and Power Co. As this was a municipally owned utility, the taxpayers became very upset over what they saw as an extravagance.

By 1907 another six or seven cars had arrived by steamer, and there were more than a dozen around town. They were no longer such a curiosity. That year there were two Mitchells, two more Oldses, and a Pierce Arrow about town.

The Magnificent Hotel

As stated earlier, Senator McMillan and his Detroit & Cleveland Navigation Company and Cornelius Vanderbilt and their various railroads, through efforts of Senator Francis Stockbridge, built the Grand Hotel on

Mackinac Island around 1887. It was much smaller when it was first built than it is today, as it has been enlarged several times. However, some people in Marquette, including Mr. J. H. Jacobs, owner of the stone quarry, felt that Mackinac Island was only halfway to the promised land. You hadn't arrived until you pulled into Marquette, and it was in Marquette that a large hotel should be constructed.

Therefore, when he was approached by three young doctors to finance a sanitarium, he tried to persuade them to build a hotel instead. They liked this notion but, being doctors, they would not give up the idea of a sanitarium. After all, people with respiratory problems had been coming to Lake Superior for years to breathe the purest air in all the land, where you could sleep wet and not catch cold, and where the invigorating climate added years to your life.

With the doctors' promise to combine the two ideas, Jacobs became a prime investor in the "Lake Superior Hotel–Sanitarium Association." The doctors who took on the project were Dr. Markham of Marquette, Dr. Morley of Detroit, and Dr. Ide of Oxford, Michigan. They were counting on the delightful summer climate, the pure air, and the pleasant surroundings of the beautiful city to attract people from the whole country and abroad for health and rest purposes.

Two sites were proposed, one near Presque Isle and one high on the side of Burt's Peak at the west end of Jackson Street. As the Presque Isle site was too far from town, the Jackson Street site was selected. From here the hotel would overlook the entire sweep of Iron Bay, from Presque Isle to Shot Point. They had the idea that, as its reputation grew, people would flock here from all over the world.

One of the most famous architects of his day, Col. E. Myers of Detroit, was hired to design the building. He had built many hotels and even capitol buildings, including those of Colorado, Texas and Michigan, as well as homes and offices. Things got under way in 1891, with great hopes of being open for business in time for the Chicago World's Fair of 1893. With proper advertising at the Fair, people could board the Chicago & Northwestern train in the evening, sleep the night away in a Pullman berth, have breakfast on the train, and arrive in Marquette about 9:30 the following morning.

The Board of Directors was announced early in the spring of 1892. Dr. R. C. Markham was President; Dr. Henri G. Ide, Vice President; Mr. C. H. Call, Secretary Treasurer; and Dr. Charles Morley, Nathan Kaufman and Arch B. Eldredge, trustees. The foundations were built with Marquette sandstone and the building itself with fine, clear, Michigan white pine. The first floor rooms had fifteen–foot ceilings, and the guest rooms had twelve–foot ceilings. The structure, like the Brewery and Mr. Longyear's house, which had just been completed, looked like a medieval castle. It was complete with electricity, steam heat and sandstone fireplaces throughout the building.

There were already quite a few hotels in Marquette at the time – the Clifton Hotel on the corner of Front and Washington, the Bay View on East Superior, the Christie House, the City Hotel on Lake Street, the Cleveland House on Lake, the European Hotel, the German House, the Jackson, Madison, Mesnard and Summit Houses, the Marquette House on Spring Street, and others. None of these could even approach the grandeur of the Hotel Superior nor its size (241 guest rooms). The first guests, nine people from Detroit, arrived on August 30, 1892. The grand opening was held in mid–September of the same year.

Business was sporadic. Some local residents had Sunday dinner in the dining room, and there were parties, gala occasions and conventions, but not the crowds of long–term guests that had been anticipated. It could not make money as a stop–over place. In 1894 the Edison Company brought suit and the hotel was put up for public auction. Mr. Jacobs and Mr. Palmer, both of whom had invested heavily in the hotel, quickly purchased it in the names of their young daughters, Emmeline H. Palmer and Mary Ella Jacobs. It was then leased to two businessmen, Messrs. Evans and Julian, who ran it a few years, but still the beautiful hotel didn't get the attention it deserved from outsiders.

Mr. Evans requested some of the more famous guests who stayed there to write some testimonials for the hotel. Among those who responded were two gentlemen from Huron Mountain, Hempstead Washburne and Carter Harrison, both well–known throughout the midwest.

Hempstead Washburne wrote about the Hotel Superior as a health resort:

> The picturesque lakes of Switzerland, nestled around the base of the Alps, which have excited the admiration for centuries; the German dreamland, Schwartz Wald, whose every inaccessible mountain peak with its ruined Schloss speaks of a bygone but chivalrous age; that Holland Mecca, situated on the North Sea, Scheveningen; the seaside resorts of our own Atlantic coast, and that most attractive island on our continent, Mackinac, must all, in my judgment, fall below Marquette and its vicinity as a place for health, sport, attractiveness and climate. There is a vitality and purity about the air of Lake Superior to be found nowhere else. The locality is

totally free from any conditions which produce malarial disturbances, the water is pure, clear, cold and wholesome, while limitless forests of spruce, balsam, pine and tamarack fill the air with an ozone that restores the invalid and consumptive to robust health.

Lake Superior, the most beautiful body of fresh water upon this or any other continent, is an ever–changing object of interest. Its precipitous shores, standing out in irregular grandeur, capped with pine forests, receding into a horizon of unbroken hills and mountains, at all times and under all conditions present to the eye a landscape of unsurpassable beauty. Italian skies and northern sunsets, rendered famous by the pens of poets and letters of the traveled dilettante, do not surpass, and I doubt if they could equal, the depth, beauty and purity of our Superior skies, while the intensity of our own northern sunsets, as they illuminate the horizon with a crimson glory, are a fitting close to the days made perfect by an atmosphere purified by the mountains, by the vast unsalted seas, and by an almost unexplored wilderness of pines.

This region, so little known and yet so beautiful, the original land of Hiawatha (about which Longfellow wrote):

'With its legends and traditions,
With the odors of the forest,
With the dew and damp of meadows,
With the curling smoke of wigwams,
With the rushing of great waters'

is destined to become the Mecca to which thousands of health and pleasure seekers will make an annual pilgrimage, as soon as its beauties, sports and climate advantages become generally known.

It is easy to see from the above that Hemp Washburne had been completely wooed away from Cape Cod summers.

Then, not to be left out, Carter H. Harrison had this to say about the Hotel Superior and the vicinity of Marquette. His testimonial was written from the Mayor's office in Chicago on October 26th, 1897:

To whom it may concern – I have spent several seasons at Marquette, Michigan, with my family, and consider it one of the most pleasant summer resorts in America, the climate being excellent and the scenery unsurpassed. The Hotel Superior at Marquette, as conducted by Messrs. J. M. Evans and Co., is under first class management and deserving of patronage.

This type of enthusiasm was about unanimous among visitors to the area, and nearly every week in the Weekly Mining Journal of 1896 and '97 were letters praising the hotel and expounding the beauties of Upper Michigan.

One extravaganza tells of a complete trip by train from Chicago in 1896. Too long to be completely quoted here, the major portion of the story is as follows:

Leaving the heat of the bustling city (Chicago) I went to bed in the Pullman and was lulled to sleep by the gentle swaying of the rapidly moving train. Being called for breakfast, of which I partook while going toward my destination at a rate of forty miles an hour. The last hours of the journey were past innumerable little lakes and streams that were alive with beautiful, speckled trout, through woods where game abounds in abundance and a veritable paradise for the nimrod, into an atmosphere that is a sure specific cure for hay fever and all kinds of malarial diseases, and where every breath one draws adds strength and vitality to both mind and body.

I was awakened from the reverie inspired by the grandeur of the country through which we were passing, by the shrill sound of a whistle, and seconds later the well modulated voice of the trainman, crying out – –Marquette! Marquette! I had reached the promised land.

Alighting from the train, I inquired for the best hotel and was told if I wanted the best obtainable, here or elsewhere, to go to the Hotel Superior. Handing my satchel and luggage checks to the gentlemanly porter who was near, I stepped into the hotel bus (horse–drawn) and in a moment was bowling along over a lovely road, which in most cities would go under the high–sounding title of boulevard, but here, I observed, was just plain Jackson Street. (author: our tourist has undoubtedly gone up Blemhuber St. to Altamont, following the streetcar tracks and then turned right onto Jackson.)

Turning a corner the fine hotel burst out on my astonished eyes in all its truly splendid magnificence. I had in times past spent weeks buffeting the ocean waves in search of medieval architecture, while here, within a day's journey of my home is a structure which, for beauty of design, impressive appearance, picturesque location and lovely surroundings is equal to the best and in some respects superior to anything the old country has to offer.

Arriving at the hotel, I was received with a cordiality that is characteristic of the people of the house as well as the citizens of Marquette. If the exterior of the hotel was surprising the interior was even more so. All other resort hotels of my acquaintance seem to have been constructed with a view to economizing space as well as money. Here everything about the house is suggestive of comfort and luxury. The finish and decorations are equal to those of a high–class city hotel; the ceilings are high; the hall, the corridors, the public rooms, the family apartments and chambers are all spacious, elegantly furnished, electric lighted, steam heated, electric call bells; the floors are hardwood, polished profusely, decorated with oriental rugs. There are bath and toilet rooms on every floor; and Turkish baths for those who desire them. It requires no stretch of the imagination for one to say of the house that it provides the comforts of a luxurious home. After divesting myself of my traveling garments I paced the entire length of the long corridors and promenades of the entire seven stories of the building, new beauties unveiling themselves at every rise. The grand climax, however, was not reached until I had ascended the tower, which rises to a perpendicular height of some two hundred feet. What I had seen before was grand, but this, awe inspiring. Like the Queen of Sheba, I was ready to exclaim, 'The half hath not yet been told.' Before me was spread out the clear blue waters of the earth's greatest lake; to the right rises green–crested Mount Mesnard, to the left, overlooking the city, far–famed Presque Isle stands out prominently from the waters of the lake, while in the rear and on the east and west, stretch out miles of hills and valleys, brooks and rivers, interspersed here and there with finely cultivated farms and an occasional village. I see spread beneath my feet the means for many weeks of enjoyment and rare entertainment, and for the hundredth time I thank my luck–star and chance acquaintance on the train for the treat I am just now beginning to taste.

Our writer orders a team and visits Presque Isle, where he rents a rowboat to explore its shoreline. He then describes Marquette as a summer resort of 12–15,000 thousand people. He calls it a well–groomed city and "by all its odds the best built, the handsomest and wealthiest city on the south shore of Lake Superior." The writer says visitors at Mackinaw hear of these fishing grounds and come up here in droves every summer. So abundant are the trout in the vicinity that an unsuccessful expedition after them is almost unknown.

He then goes on to describe Negaunee, Ishpeming, the Copper Country, and mines of iron, gold, and silver. He continues with Munising and Pictured Rocks, waterfalls, stagecoach rides, and finally back to describing the Hotel Superior.

The Hotel Superior is, in fact, the finest resort hotel, as I have said before, within my knowledge, certainly the best on the great chain of lakes between the cities of Buffalo and Duluth. The rooms are exceptionally large, ventilated both at top and bottom with independent flues. Rooms may be had single or en suite, and the furniture of the rooms is above the ordinary of even the best of our city hotels. Brass bedsteads and hair mattresses are found in every sleeping room in the house. The house is brilliantly lighted by electricity throughout, and many colored lamps in the public rooms and on the promenades give it a most pleasing effect. The culinary department is located in an entirely separate building, back of the hotel proper, and the help are all roomed on the upper floors of this hall. There are Turkish baths, electric baths, shower baths and tub baths, which are conducted under the supervision of the house physician, no better than which can be found in America.

A porch or veranda, 16 feet wide, extends clear around the first and second floors, affording guests of the house a promenade and afternoon resort that affords a fine view of land and sea that is unparalleled and beggars all attempts at description. To render the scene still more charming, an excellent band dispenses music during both morning and evening hours.

What is one of the strongest features of the house, one that will be among its greatest recommendations to the public, is the farm and garden that is a part of the hotel property, and from which the milk, cream and eggs are obtained, and where the produce and vegetables are grown, that are used on the tables.

Very extensive grounds surround the house, which like everything else here is a departure from the ordinary kind. Just back of the hotel and almost in the center of the grounds is a ledge of rock, or miniature mountain, that rises to an elevation of about one hundred and 50 feet. On one side the rise is perpendicular, but the ascent is gradual from the rear, and is covered with a fine growth of trees, shrubbery and grass, except at the summit where the rock rises

Top: Hotel Superior (1894). Courtesy Ella Jacobs.
Bottom: Marquette Hotel. Courtesy Marie Shaw.

abruptly. The view from this summit is an inspiring one, as it is the highest point for miles except Mount Mesnard. The grounds are beautifully laid out in walks and drives, which in some places have been cut through the rocky ledge.

Daily excursions are made by steamer or by train, to places of interest for sightseeing or fishing; and for those who choose less exciting sport, swinging in the hammock, playing tennis and croquet, lounging or reading under the shade–trees, lunching on the rocks are among the pleasant midday pastimes here, while for the evenings after the six o'clock dinner, there is music, promenades, dancing, card parties or almost anything in the way of innocent amusement from which guests can select their own mode of entertainment.

The house and grounds are so spacious that there is always a quiet nook for those who are less sociable in their inclinations or prefer an evening of quiet conversation with friends or acquaintances.

Special excursion tickets, making low–fared round trips, are on sale by the leading railway and steamboat lines, west, south and east, providing for a land and water route, affording visitors the greatest possible diversity of scenery while on the way. The hotel bus meets all trains and boats, and the electric cars make trips every five minutes from the hotel to the depot and through the city.

These frequent runs may have taken place for a short time or special occasions, but most old–timers agree that normally the run up Blemhuber and Jackson Streets to the Hotel Superior was on a half–hour schedule. These were the Marquette Street Railway streetcars which started in 1891 and ran until 1935. Their electricity came from a generator on Presque Isle and Hawley St.

The principal organizers and owners of the street car company were Frederick O. Clark and Nathan Kaufman

Even with all this service at rates of $2.50 to $3.50 per day, and such a beautiful setting, the hotel did not prosper. After a year or so, when the hotel closed its doors completely, it was leased in 1900 to the former owner of a Chicago hotel, Mr. George Ross. Ross made $15,000 worth of improvements which included an elevator, private baths, tennis courts and bowling alley, but the hotel closed again in 1902.

Over the next few years there were some attempts to purchase the building by outside interests. One such group wanted to start a private school but decided it was too large for that purpose. The W. C. T. U. (Women's Christian Temperance Union) tried to negotiate a purchase or lease to use it as a home for homeless and wayward girls. This plan did not materialize either, and for the next 25 years the building was left to deteriorate.

Clyde Steele tells of going into the rooms with a bunch of boys (about 1915–16) and collecting about 300 pillows filled with chicken feathers, which they took to a nearby roller rink to jump in. The project ended with a huge pillow fight and feathers all over south Marquette. Caretakers lived in the building from time to time, but the vandalism was severe and the huge wooden building, once the pride of Marquette, deteriorated rapidly. In 1929 it was torn down. The aged, clear white pine from the early 1890s was perfect for pattern wood, and much of it was salvaged and sent to Chicago for that purpose. It was sold at top price by the wrecking company from Green Bay that demolished the great hotel.

The land was sold off with the exception of Burt's Peak itself, which was retained in one piece of ten acres (the original site was 15 acres). A short time after the hotel was torn down, the hill and peak became known as the "Giant's Foot" to local residents, and the name "Burt's Peak" was lost. A wooden 10,000–gallon water tank had been constructed on top of the peak to supply water pressure to the hotel in 1892. About 1974, the City of Marquette purchased the ten acres and constructed a one million gallon steel tank in the same place. At the time, some city officials attempted to make a park in the ten acres, with the thought that the tank itself could be used as a lookout tower for the public. Liability problems that swept the nation in the 1960's seemed insurmountable, and the park idea was dropped.

Some people have speculated as to why the hotel did not flourish. There were those who said it was built for the wrong purpose – a sanitarium, a place for sick people – and others would shy away. Others said there were so many places to go and things to see that people did not want to stay around in a large building listening to music. John Hallam, the brother of Henry Hallam, contractor and partner in the Schoch and Hallam Jewelry store, said the hotel grounds were mostly behind the problem. To be sure, the view from the veranda was breathtaking, but if one dropped his gaze a little, the view, according to Hallam, left something to be desired. Instead of forest, flowers or lawn, the viewer looked down on Jackson Street with the backyards exposed, complete with woodpiles, outhouses and the laundry hanging out. He felt people staying in the high–class Hotel Superior didn't want to see that. Whatever the reasons, such was the fate of what some said was the largest summer hotel in America.

Another hotel of some note in Marquette was the Mesnard House at the corner of Rock and Front Streets. It faced Front St. and had a

Top: Vierling Saloon in Detroit. Courtesy Louis Vierling.
Bottom: Vierling Saloon in Marquette. Courtesy Louis Vierling.

Carter Harrison, the fisherman (c.1900) Courtesy William Manierre (descendent)

commanding view of the bay and lower harbor, especially from its second and third floor verandas. The building was erected in 1883, where an older hostelry called the Mesnard House had been built in 1875. The new Mesnard House was considered the finest hotel in Marquette until the Hotel Superior was built. Its proximity to the downtown shopping district was evidently the main drawing card, along with steady management and a good reputation. At any rate, this hotel was used more than any other by guests and traveling men who wanted good accommodations. In 1891 the Mesnard House was purchased by Charles Dean from William Walker and the name changed to the Marquette Hotel. More often than not, Huron Mountain Club people who came in by train would stay overnight, and on rare occasions up to a week, at the Hotel Marquette. The Mesnard House had the comfort and hospitality provided by the wonderful Mrs. J. A. Busch and later, as the Marquette Hotel, that same reputation was taken over by John Lewis, who later leased and then purchased the hotel.

Hempstead Washburne and Carter Harrison were both becoming well–known in Marquette, especially Mr. Harrison. He had great charm. People who had never met him felt no embarrassment in approaching him for a conversation. Many in Marquette looked forward to seeing him each summer. He usually stayed at the Hotel Marquette, sometimes for a day or two waiting for a boat. The energetic Mr. Harrison was in and out of the stores and saloons downtown, chatting with proprietors and lumberjacks and townsfolk. He loved to talk fishing with the local people, and would stop regularly at Vierling's Saloon at the corner of Front and Main.

One story often told by Louis Vierling, Martin Vierling's grandson, concerns Harrison's fishing involvement.

Martin Jacob Vierling had come to Marquette permanently in 1862. He built a saloon on the corner of Lake and Superior Streets, about in the location where Mr. Amos Harlow's first house once stood. This eventually became a very rough part of town. Martin Vierling moved to Detroit and built a fine saloon there but, longing for Marquette, he and his son Louis returned to Marquette and built the Vierling Block on South Front at the corner of Main Street. Much concern was voiced in the Detroit papers at the time over the fact that a great collection of paintings and objets d'art were being removed from Detroit.

It was reputed to be the finest saloon in town, filled with stained glass and fancy woodwork, and one area had numerous machines to test the strength and prowess of the patrons. On the wall was a huge moose head that was bagged in the Seney swamp in 1888, said to be the largest moose ever shot in Upper Michigan.

Carter Harrison had come into the saloon carrying a pail of frogs that he had purchased from a local boy to use for bass fishing. One or two of the frogs managed to escape in the toilet room where he had left them. A strange little gentleman named Johnny Hume worked around the saloon cleaning and emptying spittoons. He went into the men's room to clean. In the dim light, Johnny bent down to pick up what he thought was a cigar butt behind the toilet and just as he was about to touch it, it jumped. Just short of complete shock, he dashed out and grabbed the bar, shouting for a drink. The story, with variations, was told for many years, but the main character was not Johnny Hume – it was Carter Harrison.

Some Huron Mountain Recollections

There was a handsome young Irish lumberjack seen occasionally around Marquette in the summers who had earned the respect of many of the town's businessmen. They had come to know him for his strength, Irish humor and strong qualities of leadership. Having been highly recommended by Mr. Vierling, the young lumberjack, who was casting about for summer employment, was hired by Hempstead Washburne as a guide to work at Huron Mountain. The fellow later became famous at the club. His name was Jack Cassidy.

Jack went to the club the first time in the summer of 1900. He was a master woodsman, having been taught by his father since he was a small boy.

Jack Cassidy was a partner of John O'Rourke, alias "Jack the Ripper," in the pine camps of Marquette County and the central U. P. In the early days the two of them were never very far apart. It was only natural, then, that O'Rourke should show up at Huron Mountain within a few years after Cassidy arrived. They both worked in the lumber camps during the winters until about 1907 or '08. They both became famous, and later infamous, at Huron Mountain. There was, in those years, a good number of lumberjacks who became regulars at the club.

Almost all of the homesteaders would work at the club at some time or another. Some, like Oscar Webster and Mrs. Rasmussen, as well as Hans Jensen and Peg Leg Marshall, worked pretty continuously. There were a few homesteaders who didn't like the club people, and the club people didn't like them. They worked for the club once or twice, or not at all.

We have met the Nelsons, who were well established at Conway Lake while the club was just starting. Carter Harrison mentions John Nelson in his account of one of his own early trips to Huron Mountain in 1891, when he camped on Salmon Trout Bay:

Upper left: Jack Cassidy in later years as a guide at Huron Mountain. Courtesy of William Manierre.
Upper right: Grandma Nelson and two granddaughters. Daughters of John Nelson (later Mrs. Keough and Florence Gallagher).
Lower left: Granny Rasmussen, wife of Ed. Sr. The "Rasmussen Trail" from Conway Lake to Huron Mountain Club was named for her. Courtesy Shirley LaBonte.
Lower right: The John Nelson Homestead.

One day Jake Brown (a Shiras Indian guide) rowed Win (Shiras) and me to the west end of Conway Bay. We had towed along a flat bottomed skiff, which we packed across the narrow strip of sand to Conway Lake. Finding the Conway fish singularly obtuse to our trolling, we hid the skiff in the brush and rowed back to camp.

After dinner Win suggested that I go back to Conway Lake with Jake and get a buck 'under the light' as he put it. I objected that deer were out of season and that shooting 'under the light' was illegal. To which Win replied, 'Either you or I will kill a deer tonight. Which shall it be?'

Not wishing to show the white feather, I had Jake row me over. By the time we reached Conway Lake and had set the headlight in place, it was dark. Within an hour from camp I had bowled over a 5–prong buck. The horns were still in the velvet.

Jake cleaned the buck and we packed the carcass across the sandspit to the lake. But my shot had aroused John Nelson, one of the three Nelsons living in cabins nearby. As he began to lecture us on the enormity of my offense, Jake, with his favorite expletive and a string of oaths, approached Nelson and growled, 'I'm guessing you ain't above getting a piece of meat when you need it?'

Nelson, recognizing that a scrap was brewing, made tracks.

Jake, as a precaution, put me in the skiff and paddled us a good distance up the shore where we packed the skiff inland and hid it in thick brush. Packing the deer through the Cimmerian darkness of the tangled forest was no easy chore, and with my lawbreaking and its discovery I found it an eerie row back to camp.

A week later Win and Jake went back to Conway Lake, but although they searched high and low, the skiff was not to be found.

On the day we broke camp, Jake sighted a Mackinaw under sail toward Marquette. He guessed the Nelsons were on their way to collect an informers' reward from the game warden. I had counted on taking home the head of this, my first buck, but it now seemed prudent to bury it instead.

Conscience had made fools as well as cowards of us. Off Salmon Trout Point we met the Mackinaw, which had gone to pick up supplies unloaded on the beach from the tug that had come to meet us in the Big Bay.

Now for the aftermath. Seven years had passed. One day I walked to Conway Lake, where I met John Nelson, now a summer guide. He was puttering around on his dock, where a weather–worn skiff was tethered.

'By golly, John, that skiff is a dead ringer for one that was snaked from me one August night in 1891. How about it?' I asked.

John flushed, grinned and walked away.

John Nelson's homestead was on the west end of Conway Bay. He gives us some insight as to the life they led there in a letter he wrote in Swedish to his brother, Ollie, in Detroit. (Translation by Rev. Savaried of Grace Methodist Church in Marquette, and Roy Froling of Marquette)

Conway Bay
December 21, 1893

Dear Brother Ollie,

I don't know how to begin but I'll say thanks for the letter of August 28, 1893 which I received the seventh of this month. I received four letters – all written during the summer, they have laid in Marquette a couple of months. After that a Frenchman got ahold of them and sent them to me. At last they came up here and I read them all. When I understood that you would have come here in October, then I got mad and if I could have gotten ahold of that Frenchman I would have given him such a licking that he would never get up. But you shall have a rest this winter.

It isn't so nice up here but if you want to you may come if you so desire. All of us here are well. Mother is at the clubhouse two miles from here. There is a fellow from Galltomming (a town in Sweden) and a Dane (Ed Rasmussen, Sr., son of Pete Rasmussen). These two together are the watchmen there. They milk the cow, but I do not know how long Mother will be there. She was home on Sunday and she wishes she was through. She has become somewhat old and childish in the last ten years but she still has her pride and her good health.

Now I must tell you what we have done this fall. Jacob was fishing and I was with him, but boy oh boy, we had dirty weather. It was so stormy every day that we had to give it up. We only got 1400 pounds of fish and all the nets in a mess.

Now I am doing a little trapping all alone and I caught 9 beavers, 2 fishers, 14 muskrats, a marten, a fox, a mink and an otter. I hope I can get some more later on or maybe I'll take a job chopping wood. There are five (logging) camps around here and some are only two miles from here. The wages are 26 to 30 dollars a month and there is lots of work in the winter and they are building railroads all around here. It looks like this will be a wonderful country.

And once more I must thank you for the letter and your good thoughts concerning me...I would like to see you and would like it if you could come here. It wouldn't be good for me to go down where you are because I couldn't afford to. The next time I'll try to write to Maria, your wife, and Emma.

I am trying to get a grip on myself and send something. Jacob will go to Marquette tomorrow to buy something for Christmas but I'll go out and get a beaver instead.

My girlfriend is a little timid and fair, but I am dark complectioned.

Merry Christmas and a happy New Year to you all, wished from your faithful brother.

Drop a letter in the post office addressed to John N. Nelson, 405 Washington St., Marquette, Michigan.

This was the address of Peter Rasmussen's saloon.

Some years later Jacob Nelson died of a broken neck in the same saloon. He was said to have fallen down the stairs. The Nelsons never heard much detail of the circumstances of Jacob's death, and they always felt he had been "rolled" and pushed down the stairs. What actually happened is not known.

John Nelson married the fair, timid girl he spoke of, and she bore him three daughters.

During these years, the whole Nelson family assembled at Conway Lake at one time or another. John had a log house and barn at the west end of the bay where he lived with his mother, wife and daughters. Barney Nelson built a log cabin with Jacob's help on the east side of the lake, where it stands today (1985), although somewhat the worse for wear. The building is owned by Mr. and Mrs. Donald Oates. Jacob built a cabin at the south end of the lake, which later became the Stanton Bice property. Nels Christen Nelson homesteaded but left and sold out to Bill Johnson of Marquette. The fifth brother, Ollie, did not homestead. All of the other boys together built a cabin, a small barn, some storage and woodsheds and a garden plot for their mother on the back of John's property, as she was difficult to live with. This was near a grassy spot on the northwest tip of Conway Lake. She lived there alone for several years. The grassy spot later became known as "Grass Lake." In wet years there is water in it, but usually it is a field of grass.

Book One

Huron Mountain Becomes a Little Village

During the summer of 1896 the Washburne cabin was completed and the Le Moyne cabin begun, both west of the Longyear cabin. In the winter of 1897, the Le Moyne cabin and five others were completed. There was the Lewis cabin between the Washburne and Le Moyne, and then to the east, the Tenney, Christy, Sheldon and Hamilton cabins were constructed. Five more cabins were started in the spring of that year making more than a dozen cabins on the beach by 1898.

It was in the 1897 season that the dining room was enlarged to hold ten tables, and even so, during the month of August this was found to be inadequate. A writing room was made of four rooms in the west wing and furnished with bookcases, two writing tables and one round table, all made at the club. A "timber walk" to Pine Lake was built early that spring for the comfort of the walkers, who often complained about the loose sand, and also a walk of boards to the bathhouse. Never in any previous season had the bathhouse been so popular. It was recorded that there were five cows, four dogs, a horse, a donkey, and a greatly increased number of pheasants at the club that year. The pheasants were being raised in captivity. The donkey was a Texas burro named Don Quixote which was bought by Ashley Pond of Detroit for his ailing daughter, Florence, to use around the property. As she improved, the donkey roamed around the property more and more. Pond was one of the early members of the club who arrived early and stayed late every summer.

The Keweenaw Cabin

Those who knew Carter Harrison II could readily testify that he had a lot to say on any subject. His was one of the finer cabins when built in 1897–98, and we quote his own story of its building:

> The cabin was made from a pencil sketch I made while on a fishing trip at the Tourilla Club in the Laurentian Mountains in Canada with Graham H. Harris of Chicago. The sketch was brought to scale by a German architect, who claimed wide experience in the construction of log cabins in the northwoods.
>
> Among other things I instructed him to plan a fireplace wide and deep enough to take a 40–inch log and equipped with a crane to carry an old–fashioned iron kettle.

Top: The Washburne Cabin. 1898.
Middle: LeMoyne, Hodges, Washburne and Longyear cabins from Pine River.
Bottom: Keweenaw cabin from Lake Superior 1910.

'O.K.,' was his reply. 'I've built dozens of 'em.'

His sketch was turned over to the contractor, a Marquette firm of carpenters, who agreed to do the log work and carpentry for the large sum of $1,450. Masonry and plumbing were not included. For cutting and hauling the Norway pine logs, I paid an additional $45.

From whose land the logs were cut I do not know. (author: they came from the club land) I was busily engaged that winter in managing the affairs of the city of Chicago and I could not spare any time to keep watch on the building of our cabin. Moreover, the Washburne, Christy, Sheldon, Tenney, H. M. Longyear and Hamilton cabins had just been built, and the logs for all of them had been cut as mine were. When in Rome, do as the Romans do, was the advice I got when I made inquiry about the source of the logs. Since I had plenty of company in this respect, I reconciled my conscience through some pure casuistry.

The plumbing contract was unquestionably let to the Sink Shop, pioneers of that trade in the north country. In my sketch I had included a bathroom equipped with hot and cold water and the usual conveniences. So had Nathaniel T. Guernsey, whose cabin was going up on the lot next to mine.

When word of our plans reached the clubhouse veranda, something like a riot broke out there. A bathtub with hot and cold water was an innovation that threatened to undermine the simple life of the rugged mountaineers. A toilet might be tolerated, but not a bathtub! Perish the thought! One of the veranda mountaineers declaimed that the enervating luxury of the baths of Caracalla had led to the downfall of Imperial Rome. Preparatory anointing and massage, hot air sweating in the Colderium, the plunge in the Frigidarium, the rubdown, reanointment and wrapping in warm wool blankets, rest on a marble couch with languid conversation and slow sinking to sleep – none of these I would have. Mr. Sink's pine board enclosure on my back porch will lack the seductive elaboration of the Thermae of Diocletian.

But my words were drowned out by the stentorian objections of Messrs. Pond, Christy, Le Moyne, Washburne, Hamilton, Alfred Kidder and even the medical team of Dudley and Longyear (Dr. Longyear, brother of J. M. Longyear). Not a word was said in my behalf, not a friendly look.

Above the tumult Hemp Washburne's squeaky voice objected 'There's Lake Superior at your front door; if she's too cold there's Pine River in your backyard.'

Washburne was mayor of Chicago from 1891 to 1893. According to the Chicago Tribune, the city "had a tendency in this era to elect a reform Republican every other term to clean up the city's vice operation." Washburne was the son of Elihu Washburne, secretary of state under President Grant. Carter Harrison was a staunch Democrat.

Carter Harrison again:

Browbeaten and bullied, I beat a weak–kneed retreat. Keeping my plans in the dark, for fear of another uprising from the veranda, I included a cold water shower in my plumbing estimate. Maurice "Ed" La Blanc, a French Canadian, ingeniously arranged the flooring for the galvanized iron shower in four triangular sections that slanted to a vent. This emptied the shower water on the bare earth.

La Blanc was a capable assistant to the pair of carpenters who built the cabin. He had the amazing skill of the "habitant" with an axe. In an extremity I believe he could have cut a keyhole with the small, tomahawk–headed axe all French Canadian woodsmen carry in their belts.

I wanted a large lamp swung from the roof rafter in the center of the living room. The rafter was at least 25 feet from the floor.

'How can it be done?' I asked.

'That's easy,' replied La Blanc, who at the time was three sheets in the wind.

He and a helper lugged indoors the clumsy ladder made of two saplings that had served in building the cabin. With two nails he made fast a 12–foot plank to its top. When the ladder was upright, he carried a stepladder to the balcony, mounted it, and nailed the top of the board to a pine log that helped support the roof. La Blanc then climbed the big ladder and, balancing on an upper rung, screwed into a roof joist the stout hook from which the lamp was hung by a chain.

While he was on his perch, my heart was in my throat, not only from fear for his safety but also for the cabin, should the heavy, awkward ladder fall against the log wall.

For 48 years (88 years at this writing) the hook has been in place, holding up a heavy kerosene lamp that has been handled by all kinds of servants. Are the hook and the timber still sound? Now that La Blanc is gone, who is left to get up there and look? La Blanc's last years were darkened by blindness as a result of drinking bad liquor in the early days of prohibition. (Not quite accurate; Ed La Blanc's true story in Books II and III.)

The first fully equipped bathroom at Huron Mountain Club was installed by Nathaniel Guernsey in the cabin next door (east) to Harrison's in 1898. it may have been his undoing, as the Guernseys only belonged to the club for a few years. Some said they were eased out. In 1907 the cabin was sold to the Samuel T. Douglas family, an old name on Lake Superior, as Samuel's father had traveled on the "Algonquin" in the 1840's to Ontonagon, Isle Royale and elsewhere in search of copper. There was animosity between Mr. Le Moyne, a Harvard crew member from the class of 1881, and Guernsey, a Yale crew member from the same year. Each had rowed four years, and Yale won all four.

Up to this time, the club had been raising the English pheasants in captivity in hopes of building a large enough flock so that they could be released to fend for themselves in the wild. In 1897, for the first time, they were released in the hope that they would go into the woods and multiply. Also that year, in the early spring, because so many cabins had been built, a water tower was erected east of the clubhouse to provide pressure for running water piped to all the cabins. This was Mr. Longyear's idea. He had a small naphtha engine to pump the water from the lake to a tank high on the wooden tower. It was well accepted and added much to the convenience of the clubhouse.

By 1898 the Huron Mountain Shooting and Fishing Club had become a well–established social community. However, much of its continued success rested on the shoulders of one man, Mr. John M. Longyear. Up to this time the club had depended almost entirely on the steamship CITY OF NEW BALTIMORE and in later years on the newer CITY OF MARQUETTE for transportation of food, supplies, and people. Even with all this freight, the steamboat business, right from the start, was losing up to $25,000 per year. To try to make it pay, in 1898 Longyear had gone ahead with his project of having some buildings constructed at the mouth of the Iron River, near Big Bay Point, in hopes of starting the Sosowagaming Club there. He took the name the Indians had for Lake Independence, meaning "yellow water" or "yellow lake." Sosowagaming Club operated for a year or two on a small scale, but when Mr. Longyear terminated his boat service in 1900, it was also the end of Sosowagaming Club. The buildings were rented out to local people for the summer. One of the best customers was Charlotte Kaufman Breitung, Nathan's sister, who had married Edward Breitung, Jr. Carter Harrison had visited them at the Sosowagaming Hotel a few times.

Carter Harrison tells a story that mentions the Sosowagaming Club in these years. This is not a direct quote, as a few geographical corrections have been made:

Top: Water tower at Huron Mountain Club. Courtesy Shirley La Bonte.
Bottom: Steamer – CITY OF MARQUETTE.

Top: Charlotte Kaufman Breitung at Sosawagaming Hotel. Courtesy Marquette County Historical Society.
Bottom: Club House at Sosowagaming Hotel. Courtesy Marquette County Historical Society.

None of my experiences is more vivid testimony to the primitiveness of the Huron Mountain region in those days than a trip from Marquette to the club in August of 1899. I had reached Marquette from Chicago one morning only to find a stiff wind blowing out of the northwest. The captain of the THOMAS FRIANT forecast a three–day blow.

The thought of loafing that long in Marquette had no appeal. I hired a two–horse buckboard and set out with a 16–year–old driver at 9:50 A. M. on a 45 mile trip to Pine River. It was my companion's first run over the tote road. Near Sugar Loaf, rain began to fall. It stayed with us through the trip.

Slipping and sliding on the wet mud road and climbing over the swath at Sugar Loaf was hazardous enough. But that was trivial compared with negotiating the four miles of corduroy east of the Yellowdog. The rain had swollen the swamp to a lake. Had the buckboard slid off the narrow corduroy roadway, there was little to check it this side of China. As it was, the log road sank under the weight of our rig until water covered the floor of the buckboard. At 6 P. M. we knocked at the kitchen door of Sosowagaming Club, drenched to the skin. We ate standing because water was streaming from us.

Dusk was creeping on, the clouds were heavy and low, and the light was fading fast. The night was black as Erebus long before we reached the Salmon Trout ford at Dead Man's Bend. As we drove on, I became convinced that something was wrong. I got out finally to scout the road ahead. Over the beating of the rain, the low murmur of falling water was audible. I stumbled on through ankle deep mud and soon found out that we were but a short way from the lower dam (up the Salmon Trout River). We had strayed from the tote road (Prosper Roberts Trail).

The driver and I unhitched the weary team and, by brute strength, lifted and turned the rig toward the main road. We had to trust to luck that we would know when we reached it again. The gods were on our side. By sheer intuition the driver jerked the team to the left at the right place. From then on it was easy sailing, for that is almost literally what our mode of locomotion had become in the rain. We passed Joe Paris' squat cabin and turned right off the main road toward the Huron Mountain beach.

The tote road passed between the Fournier and Hetu cabins, reached Pine River near the Tea Banks, and followed the river back of the club cabins. Mine was the second one. I dragged my weary bones to earth there at 2:15 A. M., after 16 hours and 25 minutes on the road, gave the young driver a stiff slug of whiskey and sent him on his way back. As for myself, I piled into bed at once.

The Longyear Tragedy

It was a crushing blow to Peter White to lose five of his children to disease, but there was no dramatic change in his behavior. He did build the beautiful Morgan Memorial Chapel on High Street attached to the Episcopal Church, but emotionally he seems to have taken the devastating loss pretty much in stride. His life went on as before.

However, J. M. Longyear and E. W. Allen also suffered similar tragedies which seem to have resulted in great changes for the city and Huron Mountain. There are several related stories that have been told many times, many ways. With the first hand accounts of Mrs. Abby Roberts, the facts can be sorted out. No one had more knowledge and empathy for the situation than Mrs. Roberts, the oldest daughter of Mr. and Mrs. Longyear.

The series of events began when Hugh Allen, son of E. W. Allen, and Howard Longyear, son of John M. Longyear, were drowned in Lake Superior while canoeing to Huron Mountain Club in the summer of 1900.

Mrs. Roberts:

It was in 1900 when my brother Howard and his friend Hugh Allen were drowned. We were at Huron Mountain at the time it happened and Mother sent me (I was 20 years old) back on the boat with the younger children to the house (Longyear Mansion) and she and father walked from Huron Mountain back to Marquette along the beach – hunting every inch of the shore for any trace of those boys. (There are nearly 50 miles of shoreline between Marquette and Huron Mountain Club). It took them three days, and by the time they got to Marquette the canoe had been found and the Coast Guards were dragging for the bodies at the north end of Presque Isle. It was seven days before they found them, they were about 500 feet from shore. The side of the canoe was broken.

What had happened was, my brother had come back from college – he had been rowing on the freshman crew at Cornell – and had come from college back to Marquette about the 6th of July. Mother had a few servants in the house keeping it running because we were back

Top: Howard Longyear the year of his fatal accident.
Bottom: The Stonehouse at Ives Lake. Courtesy Howard Paul.

372

and forth on the boat to Huron Mountain. We had been up to Huron Mountain for the 4th of July. She had servants in the house and they took care of Howard. In the morning he got his friend Hugh Allen and they started off in the canoe.

Marquette Harbor was perfectly quiet. They went around the end of the breakwater and out past Lighthouse Point and past Picnic Rocks up to Presque Isle. There was a wind coming from the west at Presque Isle and they couldn't get past the granite point of the Island to the black rocks. We had to reconstruct this, you see, afterwards, but evidently as they approached the black rocks, the wind and waves upset the canoe, which was pretty well laden, a canvas canoe, a very light canoe, bright green – looked like a pea pod, but it would turn over in a whiff. I know because I've been in it when it happened, right down at the foot of Hewitt Avenue. Yes, I was in the canoe when it rolled over with us one time, nothing that we had done apparently, it just rolled over.

Howard, the eldest son of the Longyear family, had been a great source of pride to them. He was always very popular during his high school years in Marquette. Everyone liked him, and he had everything to live for. He was handsome, intelligent, wealthy, adventurous, a good athlete and had a pleasant personality. Howard had been in the last class to graduate from the old Union School, a sandstone building constructed about 1875 on about two and a half acres on the corner of Ridge, Pine and Arch Streets. The building burned the following year, the fire thought to have started in the chemistry laboratory. No one was hurt.

Mrs. Roberts:

Yes, the Coast Guard was looking too, and did find them, but only 500 feet from shore – Howard was a good swimmer, but it was the cold water of Lake Superior and trying to help the other fellow, I suppose, but that was the way it was and as I say it just broke Mother's life in two.

But they had found the canoe floating in the cove at Presque Isle with a hole broken in one side; all the flowers, mail, laundry and everything else and the baggage the boys had and the paddles of the canoe were over at Shot Point.

The canoe evidently got far enough around that the wind steered it into the cove, but a man from Ishpeming found it there. He never said anything about it to anyone, he just took it on the train and went up to Ishpeming. When they began to put articles in the paper about what had happened to these boys, then he came back with the canoe.

After that, Mother never wanted to see Huron Mountain or Ives Lake or anything again, because she knew that that was the place that Howard loved to be and where he wanted to be and when he was happy there, then she was happy. So anyhow, Mother was practically out of her mind. The curious part of it is, as I look back on it now, she had no intimate friends in Marquette. I never heard anybody but her own sister and father's family call her Mary. Everybody else always called her Mrs. Longyear. She just shut her mind and soul against sympathy of any kind. That was something she just couldn't stand — to be pitied. She liked to be envied, she liked to be looked up to and that sort of thing, but she couldn't stand to be pitied. She just would receive people when they came to make visits of condolence. It was, well, it was pathetic, you know, because she was so thrown back on herself and according to her, she was the only one who had suffered any loss — the rest of us didn't amount to anything. It hadn't meant anything to us, she thought, or even father, but I have seen father at the little morning lessons that we had every morning after breakfast, break down and cry when he read a verse in the Bible that touched him, and that never meant anything to Mother at all. She was — the loss was — the loss was hers, you see, she was the mother. She always thought I'd never lived because I'd never lost a child. She always considered me as untrained and unregulated, well I was perfectly willing to stay as I was.

The next year (1901), she went to Chicago and spent the winter in a dingy little hotel and she began to do some painting at the art institute. She got very much interested in that and went on to develop it all the rest of her life. I was in college that winter and I went from there to Lansing for Christmas. Mother took the whole group of children out shopping, I had lots of young cousins in Lansing. Father sent most of them through what was then Mining School — that was the mining school at Houghton. He sent most of them there. I had six cousins there at once, one year, and they came around the three daughters. Jack was such a little boy he didn't count, but us three girls (the Longyear daughters, later Mrs. Roberts, Mrs. Paul and Mrs. Lyethe) why we were — the boys would stick around us like bees around a honey pot. And we went over to Battle Creek and saw the place, the farm where Mother had been brought up. We had dinner in one of the big farm houses there. And the old neighbors of

Mother's – I know the old farmer took father off aside and he says, 'Munro, them young folks of yours is real ladies and gentlemen. Why they ate Mother's dinner as if they really liked it.'

It was the most marvelous farm cooking, you know, and they set out this table that reached through most of the big living room there and the table was completely covered with cakes and pies, jams and jellies and dishes of this, that and the other thing. It was delicious, although, well, you couldn't see the tablecloth – just the plates around where you sat yourself and the rest was just covered with everything. And of course we'd been all day frolicking around out in the fields and seeing the little schoolhouse where Mother first taught school and all, and I want to tell you, we were really hungry. There were about 16 of us and we really cleaned up on her dinner.

Then after that, Mother still didn't want to go back to Marquette, she couldn't bear it. So Father planned a cruise trip. He had heard that there was coal in Spitzbergen and iron in Norway. He was always looking around. He knew the iron mines here were not going to last forever. He was always looking for something to take their place. When the Mesaba began to peter out he kept looking ahead more than any man I've ever known.

He kept trying to get Marquette to do things that it took them 50 years to grow up to. They couldn't see the point in those days, if it wasn't right under their noses. They were bogged down with today; and tomorrow, which was what Father was always building toward, they couldn't see. Well, he thought, when there's good coal up in Spitzbergen and iron in Norway, perhaps we can get some lime somewhere and build some furnaces and do some business up there.

So we took that cruise trip along the Norwegian Coast and then along the North Sea to Spitzbergen and father found his coal all right. Wonderful coal, it burns almost without any ash. Then we came back. We left the cruise boat at Bergen and drove (with horse and carriage) across to what was then Christiania (now Oslo), then over to Wuir and Gotteburg. We took the steamer up the Gotte River to Stockholm. You climb through 79 locks, you go up one mountain and down the other side. It's a beautiful trip. Beautiful little passenger boats there that just fit in the locks and of course when we'd run through a place where there were lots of waterfalls, why we'd have to get out and walk. We did that every day. We stopped occasionally at a little farming village as we went along – between fields, you know, it was almost like being on a road, then down the other side to

Stockholm. Then from there I went out on the Island of Bisby and saw where there had been a very flourishing Hensa town which had been wrecked by traitors in the early dark ages. Then back to the mainland of Sweden and down to Copenhagen. Oh, I fell in love with Denmark. That was the most lovely place.

From Denmark we went down to Berlin and then across and took the boats down the Rhine (summer of 1901) and we finally got to Paris.

Before Mother had left Marquette, some of the businessmen had come around there talking about putting a railroad along the shore of Marquette. Father had decided that one thing that kept her busy and interested was construction and if he could find something for her to build, she would be happy. He had the idea that to get her back interested in Marquette, he would buy the land between what is now Flanigan's warehouse out to the breakwater and then from Lighthouse Point along the shore to Picnic Rocks. He would get all that land and make a 'Howard Memorial Park.'

Mother heard all this pointed out.

What a time Chicago had had, to overcome the fact that they gave their waterfront to the railroad. How they had to spend millions of dollars to build out beyond the railroad and sink the Illinois Central railroad tracks out of sight. She wanted Marquette not to make that mistake but to keep the shoreline for the people of the City of Marquette. And the idea of a Howard Memorial Park – they were going to have a swimming pool there with supervised swimming and dressing rooms just north of Lighthouse Point. They were going to have a small boat harbor behind the breakwater. They were going to build paths and gardens and picnic places all the way out to Picnic Rocks – and they were going to have a restaurant there.

Well, Mother was enchanted. She loved the idea, and that would be a lot better than the lumberyard we had had under the house ever since it had been built. This was the big house up on the hill. We moved into it in 1892. I was 12 years old when we moved in there – you know I have one of the Christmas tree balls that was on the first tree we had in there. One of the maids was so impressed by it that she swiped it. She left it to her niece after she died and I met the niece downtown one time. She told me she had it, and gave it to me.

The first Christmas tree we had in that house was in 1892, with the first electric lights on any Christmas tree in Michigan. They weren't very effective. They were round – little, little round globes with a

Top: Longyear Mansion as viewed from Arch Street. Rydholm collection.
Middle: The Longyear Mansion in Brookline, Mass. Courtesy Mary Baker Eddy Museum and Longyear Historical Society.
Bottom: Solarium in Longyear home, Brookline. Courtesy of Mary Baker Eddy Museum and Longyear Historical Society.

terminal on each side and each had to be connected with a little piece of wire to the next one and of course if any one went out it threw the whole circuit off. But anyhow, we had our own electric light plant down in what was then the bowling alley, it's now an apartment.

These were the first electric lights in Marquette. The plant was not in the house, it was down on the edge of the bank. There was a big fireplace and a bowling alley on the top floor and then the lower floor was the electric light plant, which put–putted so that everybody could hear it all over town. There was a great big rough stone fireplace built out at one end of the bowling alley – the whole south end of it. I remember the slogan they had carved in the beam that went across to hold up the mantel shelf: 'Pleasure and action make the hours seem short.' They had a lot of fun there.

Father was the mayor of Marquette at the time and kept thinking that Marquette should have electric lights. They were just coming in. So he and his chief clerk, James Sherman, got to talking about things and they finally built a dam and a power plant on Dead River at what was called "Collinsville" in those days. The houses are still there that Father built. They had a flour mill jut below the dam. You can still see some of the walls there, and every Sunday of his life Sherman would walk from his house on Spruce Street, just one house short of Hewitt Avenue, out to that power plant and look it over. James Sherman was the first light and power superintendent.

When Mr. Longyear and the City of Marquette were going to build a power plant and dam, there were several companies eager to build the plant and run the business. Mr. Longyear's attitude was, if it's going to be such a profitable business, let the city build it and own it and the profits can go to the city in the form of cheap electricity. The city built the dam and the plant, and set up a power board to run it.

Mrs. Roberts:

Father quietly went around – he realized that that one plant was fairly temporary – electrical power was due to grow and he wanted to safeguard Marquette so that they would always have the power of the Dead River which he realized was a rather extraordinary stream – they just about went out and developed every bit of power there was on it, you know. But he built that first dam and then he quietly bought up all the land all the way up to Silver Lake where the river started. Because no one was aware of what he was doing, he got the land for a very good price. It was cut–over land and he got a good bargain on it. He offered it all to the city of Marquette for just what he paid for it. Well, those people stood up on their hind legs and screeched that he was trying to "Jew the city down." He was trying to take advantage of them, why he was a Czar, why they called him all the names they could think of – you can't imagine all the abuse he got for that. They would have nothing whatever to do with it.

That one reservoir which has blotted out the old horseshoe bend where we used to drive around on Sundays – just blotted out that beautiful curve in the river – that's at the bottom of the city dam there (at the present tourist park) – and why they just screeched and hollered that they weren't going to be taken in by any such nonsense as that. One electric plant was plenty for all the electrical power that Marquette would ever need.

Mrs. Roberts is saying that there was plenty of power for four more electric plants upstream, and that they wouldn't have to develop the one in town. Marquette developed one more downstream and then had to turn to diesel. Cliff Power and Light developed the power upstream that could have belonged to the city. Before Marquette went to diesel generation, it and Niagara, New York had the cheapest electricity of any cities in the United States, and at the same time the utility was turning money into the general fund of the city. In 1935 and '36, when new street lighting was installed all over town, it was known as the best–lighted city in the world.

Mrs. Roberts:

I must say I get really wicked satisfaction now when Marquette has to buy power from Cleveland–Cliffs, because they could have had everything, the whole thing.

Well, as I say, these businessmen got up to Mother and they said they had really no intention of building a railroad, but the South Shore freight rates were really much too high and they thought if Mother made a gesture of cooperation and all that they would come down on their freight rates and make things more reasonable for Marquette, but of course they had no intention of really building the railroad. All they needed was permission and the right of way and the rates would come down immediately. It might not be built for 20 years, or maybe never, but they didn't want Mother to stand in their way with ideas of a Memorial Park and they soft–soaped her. She wouldn't want to be the person to affect the economy of Marquette, to lower the economy and make it non–productive and all the rest of it. She must want the progress of Marquette to continue, etc., etc.

Mrs. Roberts does not discuss the fact that the railroad went into condemnation proceedings to put the track along the lake and along the property of the Longyear Mansion and actually condemned the land on which Howard Memorial Park was to be built. Nor does she mention the fact that Mr. Longyear paid the railroad to survey a tunnel which would go under the bluff at the curve on Lake Street, where Flanigan Storage is, emerging north of Hewitt below the bluff on Hewitt Hill, and still be below ground level at Prospect. While the tunnel was family legend among the Longyears, documentation for it was recently located by L. S. & I. Railroad officials, the engineering report, and a copy is at the Marquette County Historical Society.

Mr. Longyear offered to pay for this solution to the dilemma.

He also worked out another route across town which had little or no incline and had only one diamond, a crossing going to the South Arm Lumber Co. Either route was shorter and would eliminate what Mr. Longyear contended would be the sharpest curve on a main line of any railroad in the country.

Mrs. Roberts:

> Mother finally admitted that she did not wish to cramp Marquette's economy or anything of that sort. She listened to what these men were saying. They were just using it as a threat to bring the South Shore and Marquette and Southeastern down in their rates and she signed a group of papers that were put before her, one saying she had no objection and words to that effect. She truly planned, however, to go through with the park.

The park idea was very important to Mrs. Longyear. The beautiful Park Cemetery had just been completed on the west side of town and, with industry pretty much confined to the lower harbor, Marquette, with its beautiful buildings, spacious homes, outstanding churches, harbor out to and around Presque Isle and its many wealthy benefactors, Marquette which had already been classified as the unconditional Queen City of the north, could well have been on its way to becoming the most beautiful city in the United States. There was no city in the north to compete with it at that time.

At the turn of the century, starting with the death of Howard Longyear, the pendulum began to swing the other way. This went virtually unnoticed by the local citizens, who were too close to each detail of the various situations. In 1900 the population was about 9,000 people.

Mrs. Roberts again:

Well, as I say, we were abroad all that next summer and when we finally got to Paris, we got the first mail that we had had since leaving New York.

Father's mother and his sister (Ida Longyear) were living in the big house that summer. There was a letter from Grandmother saying that the blasting for the railroad was so severe around the house it was knocking the pictures down off the walls.

Mother suddenly realized she had been tricked and she went absolutely crazy – absolutely berserk – for an hour she had hysterics and cried and howled and screamed. Finally Father got her a little quiet. He went down and got a phaeton to take her for a drive. He thought it possible that would calm her down.

He told the cab man, he said, 'My wife has had a terrible shock, but I think if you take her for a drive up the Champs Elysees, I think it would calm her down. And the Bois de Boulogne, that would possibly quiet her.'

So mother, with the tears streaming down her face, sat in one corner of the cab – an open carriage, you know – and they made their way up toward the Bois de Boulogne, around the Arc de Triomphe.

Finally Mother said, 'Monro, I'll never go back to Marquette again. I can never go back and live with those people who tricked me like that and destroyed the precious dream of my life. I just can't do it.'

And Father answered, 'Well Polly, I don't know that I blame you. I'll do everything I can to help you.'

They sat quietly for a time and after a little while she said, 'But my house, my beautiful house. I can't bear to think of anybody else living in it, or having anybody take it and not love it the way I do.'

Without hesitation Father said, 'Well, Polly, I'll tell you, I built that house, and I can take it down. We can put it anywhere you want to put it in the United States. I'll put it there.' That was how come. It was done as a gesture of love to my mother.

He said, 'I can't leave Marquette myself, all my roots are there, it's where I make my money, where I pay my taxes and I will have to keep doing business in Marquette.' Which he did for 22 years. That's something that's never considered when people talk about moving the house. They think Father went with it, but he didn't. He was in business here for 22 years after, until he died.

189. *John and Mary Longyear.* Relief medallion portrait from reverse side of *Spirit of Life Memorial.* Location: Longyear Foundation, Brookline, Massachusetts.

Top: "Spirit of Life." Bronze figure at poolside at the Longyear home in Brookline. A memorial to Mr. and Mrs. Longyear, created by Dallin in 1928. On the back of the stella is a bronze medallion, a relief of Mr. and Mrs. Longyear. (Inset).
Courtesy of the Mary Baker Eddy Museum and Longyear Historical Society
Lower left: Family room, Brookline (c. 1917). Longyear Home. Courtesy of Mary Baker Eddy Museum and Longyear Historical Society.
Lower right: Mrs. Longyear and her secretary.

To fill in a few details of the Longyear house, just for the record, there were two contractors who bid on its construction – Mr. Van Iderstine and Mr. Hallam. The low bid was from Van Iderstine and he constructed the house out of the finest grade of Marquette raindrop sandstone. They set up a stone–cutting shed on the job, 150 feet long, and hired over 50 stonemasons during the course of the project.

The Longyear family was living in the Swineford house at 424 Cedar St. during the three years it took for construction.

While we were in Norway, Father decided that since Mother didn't want to come back to Marquette and be where she could look out at the end of Presque Isle (where Howard had drowned) every day, that he'd build a house up at Ives Lake. That was large enough for us, pleasant and comfortable. The little log cabin there was getting pretty shaky by that time and incidentally, full of bedbugs too, and you can't get those out of a log cabin.

So he had that house built out of native rock there. They cut it out of the outcrop that sticks down to the lake on the far side across the lake and blasted it out in chunks and loaded it on sleds. Not toward the mountain, but at the end of the little beach where the boathouse was. That's where the rock came from that the house was built of. They brought it across the lake and chipped it into shape and built the house. Mother had never seen the plans or anything else, but when she was in Norway she got interested in what Father was talking to her about.

Gus Anderson, his brother Albin and four other men hand–drilled the rock, blasted it and brought it across the lake on the ice. He later became known throughout the Upper Peninsula as "Cement Gus" or "Concrete Gus."

Mrs. Roberts:

How Mother always resented that anybody would furnish a summer cottage with cast–offs! When she was in Norway she was enchanted with the Norwegian furniture and she sent home any amount of it, carved and painted and decorated and all for the new house that she had never seen. I think she sent home 22 different consignments of goods, including one complete Viking ship with a red and white lateen sail. Hip–high in the prow and in the stern, sent that back to Ives Lake.

I remember when we got to Steboreng just before we took this beautiful river trip. When we landed there in front of the Hotel it was full of little booths. We found that the peasants were having an annual fair, bringing their handiwork down to sell. Mother never went up to see the rooms in the hotel. She asked the gentleman at the door how to say "How much" in Swedish, and with "Hur mycket" as her entire equipment she sallied forth to the fray. Well, she had the time of her life. She'd seen a bolt of handwoven cloth with beautiful little dancing figures and things on it, you know, all she'd say was "Hur mycket" and the woman holding it, well they'd tell her but they could see right away that Mother couldn't understand what they said. Mother would take out a few paper kronig and they would shake their heads "no" and she'd add more or else they'd take off a few, and that's the way she went. Well, everybody was following her around. Here was this woman and the only Swedish words she knew were "How much" and she was buying like a drunken sailor. We bought towels and draperies and bolts of weaving – bolts and bolts of weaving by the yard. The next day we found a Swedish shop where they had some particularly delightful things and went in there. Father had gone to the bank to get some more money. He had been depleted by this session the day before, because we children were all running like ants back and forth, you know, carrying loads of things back to the hotel that Mother had just bought. Father came into this shop and we said, "How did you know where we were?"

'Oh,' he said, 'I looked for a place that appeared to have been struck by lightning.'

They had to take everything out of the windows, Mother was buying the whole works. And so she got the foundations for the Ives Lake place.

When we came home (1902) we didn't see it that year. Mother stayed in Paris that year. I came home and lived with Father's sister (Ida) in a little apartment in Cambridge. I studied singing and took some courses at Radcliffe – courses in creative writing under the famous Charles Townsend Copeland. In the spring Father took his mother and his sister and me on a cruise ship down to Jamaica. He had a beautiful trip going down there. Then Mother came home from Paris and she started to find a place where she wanted to put the house.

The news had gotten to the newspapers by that time, and we were offered property clean to Albany. Mother wanted to go to Boston because she knew Mrs. Eddy was there. She thought that maybe Mrs. Eddy could tell her why this terrible loss had happened to her and reconcile her to God. She thought God had punished her unjustly. She thought if she could talk to Mrs. Eddy things would work out better. And she did talk to Mrs. Eddy. She got to know her family well, and Mrs. Eddy did help her.

She found two pieces of property on the top of a hill on the edge of Brookline, Massachusetts. Look toward Boston and from that property you could look way down across Boston Harbor on a clear day. That was about twice a year, but it is a magnificent view. There was a road right across the top of the hill and there were two separate pieces of property for sale up there, two lots – and Brookline is still run by town meetings, you know. They will not come into Boston, they are not a part of corporate Boston – they have their own firemen and their own police. They are very haughty indeed. Corporate Boston surrounds them completely.

So they waited for the town meeting to come up and they presented their request for the town officers to vacate the street so they could buy the two properties and throw them into one. There was no question about it. That was a wonderful place for us because we had all the utilities. We built the house right across what had been a street, you know, and we had the sewer and the water and gas pipes and electricity and everything right under the house there.

It took four years to take the house down and move it to Brookline and rebuild it there. Mother had lived in it long enough so that she knew that she wanted certain changes. The house as it stands now in Boston is twice as big as the house that was here.

Mrs. Longyear had sought out Mary Baker Eddy, the founder of the Christian Science religion in Boston. She spent much time with Mrs. Eddy, and the two of them became great friends over the years.

The dismantling of the huge, 65 room, Marquette sandstone home was let out on bids. Again there were two bidders for the job, Hallam and Van Iderstine. This time Hallam made the low bid, clearly and decisively, by a great deal of money. But Mr. Longyear felt that the task could not be accomplished for such a low price and since Van Iderstine had built the house, he should be the one to take it down. The contract was awarded to Van Iderstine.

Every stone was numbered and wrapped in straw and cloth, every door and window and every timber had to be coded and marked. But through the course of the dismantling, Mrs. Longyear made change after change and addition after addition.

It took 172 freight and flat cars to move the house the 1,300 miles to Brookline and we can only guess at the cost and the cost of rebuilding the house skyrocketed. Because of the many changes, the original quotation of Van Iderstine meant nothing, and it had to be rebuilt on a cost–plus basis.

The home that was constructed in Brookline had 100 rooms; a whole new wing was added. No quarrying was being done in Marquette by 1904–05 and Mr. Longyear had to have a search conducted for a new vein of matching raindrop sandstone. The vein was found and ample stone was removed to complete the new wing. This was the last building to be built of newly quarried Marquette sandstone, completed in 1906. The Marquette County Courthouse was completed in 1904 from both Marquette and Portage Entry Sandstone.

It has often been said around Marquette that Mr. Van Iderstine never did another contracting job and that he retired after moving the Longyear house. This is not quite so, as he did do work in Big Bay for Mr. J. B. Deutsch as late as 1912 and '13. However, during the period the house was being moved, there was a Van Iderstine son in dental school at the University of Michigan. This was Dr. William Van Iderstine who had been born on December 6th, 1861. He finished dental school and returned to Marquette to set up a dental office in the Savings Bank Building. The doctor became noted for doing as little as possible for his patients. He became known by many of the townfolk as "Cotton–battin', come again." Throughout his dental career the doctor often had his cronies in his office for cards and such. Dr. Van Iderstine belonged to the Peep–O–Day Camp and hunted out of there for many years. He also occasionally hunted out of the old lumber camp on Lumbermen's Bay on Mountain Lake in its later years.

It has been said that Dr. William Van Iderstine owned about nine houses on Spruce Street in Marquette and retired comfortably on the rent from these houses. Later he was forced to sell or mortgage them for his income. He lived in a beautiful old home on the corner of Spruce and Prospect Streets, high on a hill overlooking Lake Superior. In his last years the doctor had a bad fall down the stairs in his home, breaking his arm so badly that it had to be amputated at the shoulder. At about the time his money was used up, he died, on August 22nd, 1964. He was 92 years old.

Mr. Longyear claimed that in the entire moving of the house, only one piece of marble was broken. He said they had done a perfect job.

And so the Longyears lost their son, Howard (1900), moved their big home to Brookline (1902–06), built the stone house as a summer home at

Ives Lake (1901–04), established a successful business in Spitzbergen (1907–08), and started the main city on that island, known as Longyearbryn. Mr. Longyear claimed the Island of Spitzbergen for the United States, but at the Treaty of Versailles, which opened on January 18, 1919, it was given to Norway. However, Norway had to purchase Spitzbergen from Mr. Longyear for $40,000,000, which they did shortly before his death.

It was around the time that Mr. Longyear decided to move the house to Boston that the massive new Marquette High School, manual training building and grade school complex on Ridge, Arch and Pine Streets was completed. The School Board, one of whom was Peter White, hoping to offer some small consolation for the loss of Howard Memorial Park to the Longyear family, named the new school the Howard High School, and a picture of Howard Longyear was hung in the entranceway for all to see and never to forget.

E. W. Allen had also lost his son, Hugh, at the same time and under the same circumstances, but that tragedy was seemingly overshadowed by the loss of Howard Longyear, the boy who showed such promise. He would have been a sophomore in the first Forestry class at Cornell University. All of his classmates became leaders in the federal forestry programs but Howard would have had his own lands to practice on. At one time the Longyears had a million and a half acres of land in Michigan, Wisconsin and Minnesota.

The Allens, both father and son, loved the Huron Mountain country dearly. Mr. Allen had been a charter member of the club, and a director from 1889 to 1900. He had not paid any dues but received his stock for taking care of the Club bookkeeping. On Hugh's death, Mr. Allen retired from the Club, but as a gesture of sympathy he was given an honorary life membership and was invited to use the club and its lands until his death in 1916.

The Seymour Story

The tragedies in the lives of Longyear, White and Ephraim Allen have been well remembered by the older inhabitants of Marquette. Horatio Seymour, the fourth signer from Marquette of the Huron Mountain Charter, had a different type of disaster. For him it was possibly just as tragic as the others, but to a certain degree he brought it upon himself.

It seems Mr. Seymour wanted only the best for his children, sending them away to schools in the east but not knowing just what to do with them in the summer. He did not want them around Marquette associating too closely with children their age in an unsupervised situation, nor could they spend the whole summer at Huron Mountain.

The Seymours had not built a cabin there and due to health reasons did not plan on doing so. In the mid and late 90's, Mr. Seymour was developing a condition in his hip that was fast making him a cripple. In the last few years before being confined to a wheelchair he found the trip to Huron Mountain and indeed the life they led there too rigorous for a man in his condition. His alternative was to have a little place of his own close to town where the children could stay for the summers.

He owned a piece of land southeast of Wetmore's Landing. The land, obtained from Cleveland–Cliffs, was 100 feet wide from the top of the mountain down to the lake. There was a clearing there that had been used to deck logs, and near the clearing was a corral, ice–house and stable that had been used by the lumbermen. Mr. Seymour hired Henry St. Arnold, (Santinaw), Mr. Longyear's trusted Indian guide, to build a little camp further to the south, beneath Sugar Loaf Mountain on a tiny harbor. It was a beautiful spot, very isolated, yet could be reached by road or by lake. The little natural harbor was a perfect place to moor a small boat.

The Seymours had Moccasin Bill Oliver build a fishing camp for him on the Sturgeon River in Baraga County during the 1880s. While still maintaining this camp, the family tent–camped near Little Presque Isle in the late summer of 1890.

William Oliver speaks of it in his diary:

Sun. Aug. 31, 1890 – Mr. Seymour came to see me about 5 PM he wants me to go to Harlows Mill tomorrow and put up tents etc. to get ready for himself and family – am to go to his house about 8:30 AM tomorrow.

Mon. Sept. 01, 1890 – I got rig of Hodgkins and loaded up by 11:50 AM and came to Pickerel Lake (Harlows Mill) Durphy and I.E. Farmer took the boat up the shore – we got all the stuff across the lake to where we will put up the tents at 6 PM and got our tent up to sleep in the dark.

They were still putting up the tents the next day and bringing supplies in. There were six tents in all.

Mr. and Mrs. Seymour, Miss Johnson, a sister of Mrs. Seymour, Mary and Horatio and Mary Fagan, a nurse, all camped there for a week. Mrs. Johnson, Mrs. Seymour's mother, came for the last day.

Fri. Sept. 12, 1890 – Geo Reed's Livery team brought Mrs. Johnson out to camp she stayed till after dinner they all excepting Durphy started for home and all seemed pleased with the time they had. We have had nice weather and have boated, fished and hunted till camp broke up. I have made five trips to Marquette since we came out and I expect tomorrow to finish the sixth and last. In the PM after the crowd had gone we got about half packed up put everything in the dining tent.

During the following summer, Santinaw built the cabin below Sugarloaf which Oliver refers to as L. Presque Isle. They would fish Lake Superior, Harlow Creek and Harlow Lake from there. Bill Oliver did a little work in the cabin also.

> Tues. Sept. 01, 1891 – Today we fixed up around the camp – put railing around the porch boarded up around the foundation – put shelves up. Got lumber across the lake – put up the Flag etc.
> Wed. Sept. 02, 1891 – Today I monkeyed around the house some – went with Mrs. Seymour to get some ferns – chinked up a couple of cracks – took the kids out boating etc.

Later on that fall, Bill Oliver built a barn there.

The first cabin Santinaw built was completed in the fall of 1891. The next year he built a second cabin behind the first as a kitchen–dining room. One room was for sitting and sleeping, the other for cooking and eating. Later these two cabins were joined together by a breezeway.

Santinaw was asked to stay and look after the Seymour children as he had done while working on the buildings. There was a boy, Horatio ("Raicky"), about nine or ten years old and his sister Mary, 13 or 14. The Seymour children spent several enjoyable summers with Santinaw at the little cabin beneath Sugarloaf Mountain while Huron Mountain was in its formative years. Santinaw taught them an appreciation of life that they had never known before. He taught them about the woods and animals, the herbs and Indian medicines, and they liked him very much. He even made a trail from the cabin right to the top of the mountain so that he could take the ailing Mr. Seymour up to the summit to see the magnificent view. It was an awesome trip dragging the heavy wheelchair with Mr. Seymour in it up through the woods, but with Santinaw's strength and patience he succeeded, and in so doing endeared himself even more to the children.

Mr. Seymour's disaster struck in 1900 when Mary Seymour, age 20, crept down the back stairway of the big home in Marquette to elope with Henry St. Arnold, age 50. Santinaw's first wife had died some years before and his children were grown.

Upper left: Moccasin Bill Oliver, years later at Rock River. Courtesy Mr. and Mrs. Peter Braamse (descendants).
Upper right: Santinaw.
Bottom: Mary and the baby. Courtesy of Marquete County Historical Society.

Horatio Seymour was notified that the couple was seen boarding the train to L'Anse together. Santinaw had a home there. Seymour had them taken from the train and detained until he could arrive by a special train to talk them out of the marriage. Mary said that it was mostly her doing, and that she was determined to go through with it, which they did a week later in Marquette. The Seymours were shocked and infuriated. Besides completely disowning their daughter, they sold the big home to the up–and–coming Louis G. Kaufman family and as soon as arrangements could be made, moved bag and baggage back to New York. The whole thing was just too much for the frail and failing Mr. Seymour, who died a few years later.

The townspeople had a field day with the scandal, which might have been ignored under other circumstances. They knew the situation perfectly, and sided with Santinaw. He was always highly respected by all who knew him, as a woodsman but also simply as a person. He was tall, handsome and wore a long beard. Even though he was half French, he was proud of his Indian blood. He lived as an Indian and referred to himself as one. In the days when it was against the law for Indians to be served liquor, many had seen him walk into the Vierling Saloon on the corner of Front and Main and ask for a glass of whiskey. Mr. Vierling would look him straight in the eye and slightly shake his head. Without ever a change of expression, Santinaw would turn and leave the premises.

For a few years Santinaw and his wife Mary, along with their little daughter, who was the talk of the town, lived on the east side of Seventh Street, just down the hill from Park Cemetery. Henry's work was in the woods and he spent long periods of time away from home. When the child was approaching school age (Mr. Seymour had died) Mrs. Seymour returned to Marquette and stayed with her daughter a few days. In the absence of Santinaw she enticed Mary to take her daughter and return to New York with her. The story about town was that Mrs. Seymour had brought someone with her who forced Mary to go back to New York.

They left without even a note of explanation. Only the story from an observing neighbor enlightened the bewildered Santinaw. He told his friends that it was probably all for the best, as they could offer her far more than he could.

The little daughter was brought up as an easterner in fine schools, knowing little of her proud Indian background. The story was told around Marquette that she eventually married a young man who fulfilled all the high standards the grandparents would have demanded. He was said to have become a prominent lawyer and later gone on to politics. One source claims he became governor of New York.

Upper left: Mary Seymour St. Arnold and her daughter about ten years later. Marquette County Historical Society.

Upper right: Clipping of the event from an Eastern newspaper. There are errors in the ages. Santinaws given age range from 60 to 75 in different reports, but courthouse records say he was 50. He lived 35 more years and died at 85.

Lower left: Mary St. Arnold (late 1920s). Courtesy of Marquette County Historical Society).

Lower right: Santinaw in his last years. Courtesy of Byron Healy.

Henry continued to work in the woods between Marquette and L'Anse, often for members of Huron Mountain Club and later for the Club itself. His long black beard turned pure white and he was a familiar figure on the Salmon Trout River in the 1920's where he worked as a guard to discourage poaching.

In his early 80s Santinaw became quite ill and was staying with a daughter in L'Anse. When it looked like death was about to overtake him as a result of pneumonia, Mary St. Arnold was notified in New York. She returned to L'Anse to be at his side. The powerful Santinaw recovered and he and Mary spent four or five years together before his death at 85 years of age.

The Seymour Camp, which later was called "Cove Cottage," stood vacant for a few years. It was finally sold to the F. B. Spear family of Marquette, who spent ten or twelve years enjoying the place. The children were in on the building of the Bart King Memorial at the top of Sugar Loaf in 1920. A few years later the cabin was purchased by Doris King (Bart King's sister) and Gladys Campbell.

Miss Campbell came to Marquette in 1918 to teach in the high school. She and Miss King purchased the C. F. Button camp at Button's Cove near the Seymour place. Charles Button's son Kenneth drowned there in 1912, and Charles decided to sell the place and move to a sand beach. The Button Camp was destroyed by fire and Miss King and Miss Campbell bought the Seymour Camp in the early 1920s.

John Tobin was a young fellow who enjoyed hiking along the rocks beneath Sugar Loaf. It is beautiful there, with the crystal clear water and the clean white rocks and tiny coves. It was sometime in the early 1920s that he first discovered the cabin there. It was alone, as the neighboring places were gone. Tobin returned again and again and ate his lunches on its porch. Then one time during a terrible rainstorm, John broke into the place and spent the night. After that he made the place his headquarters but knew nothing about its history.

One time when John Tobin arrived at Cove Cottage he found the two owners there. He explained that he had been using the place, and offered to do repairs and look after it if he could use it in their absence.

The women had been looking for an arrangement like this, and accepted. John Tobin became the official caretaker of Cove Cottage. He had many good times there, alone and with his friends. He even lived in the cabin one winter.

About 1930, Tom Kelley, a good friend of John's, had a nervous breakdown and had to quit his studies for the priesthood at St. Norbert's Seminary. Tom's father, who owned the Kelley Hardware Store on South

The deaf-mute daughter of Henry St. Arnold with whom he lived in L'Anse. Her children were taken from her and sent to an Indian school in lower Michigan. They resent this to this day. Courtesy of the Brisson Family.

Front Street, asked John to take Tom up to Cove Cottage for a long rest and a chance to relax. They had a wonderful time. It was in the depths of the Depression and they could live there for about $12 a month.

It was during this time that Mary St. Arnold was living with Santinaw in L'Anse. In the summer she visited old friends from the early years of her marriage. She also made a pilgrimage to Cove Cottage where it had all started. Learning that John Tobin was the caretaker there, she contacted him, and they soon became good friends.

After Santinaw's death Mary moved to Marquette, at first staying with the Tobin family and later moving in with an old friend, Kate O'Neal. In the 30 years or more that Mary had been away, she had had a brilliant career as a botanist. She had worked for the Smithsonian Institution and had done botanical studies for them. She did the early studies in hot spring algae and discovered the red snow algae of the west. She claimed this was all a carry–over from her childhood days with Santinaw.

During the few years after Santinaw's death that Mary Seymour lived in Marquette, she did much exploring. She couldn't take in enough of the woods and waters. She located a cabin cruiser for sale in Marinette, Wisconsin and hired John Tobin and a commercial fisherman named "Inga" Summers to bring it around through the locks into Lake Superior. They had a terrible time. Besides having trouble with the six–cylinder Oldsmobile engine, they came into a storm like nothing they had seen before. In the vicinity of Poverty Island Light, it looked as though the NEPTUNE would be smashed to splinters on the rocks, but as they readied themselves for the crash a huge wave lifted the boat into a quiet bay.

Mary had often wanted John to take her up beyond the Huron Mountains to L'Anse, but he had learned his lesson and they had to be content with trips between Marquette and Munising.

Mary St. Arnold eventually returned to New York to live, and the Seymours, while having left their mark many places in the county, were not heard of in Marquette County again.

The Middle Island Point Association

About the same time that Santinaw was building the cabin at the foot of Sugar Loaf, a small group of people began constructing simple rough camps on a piece of land west of Presque Isle, now known as Middle Island Point.

The first of these cabins was built in 1891 by a group of friends of Mrs. Alice M. Adams. She knew the man in charge of the Government land office in Marquette, and he assured her that this was reserved land and that his office had no jurisdiction over it. Her intention was to build a small temporary–type camp near the bay where Compeau's Creek has its outlet. One of her friends who helped construct the first camp was Dr. R. W. Boyer, a dentist from Marquette. The following year the dentist, using many of the same men, built a second cabin of their own, high on a rocky knob on the northwest side of the point. These two camps and the activity around them probably did as much as anything to discourage the various tent camps that had been at that location off and on for decades. The tent campers preferred to move up the shore.

By 1895 a group of railroad men built a third camp in the area, and that same year still another group put one up on what is now known as Second Beach, to the west of the point.

As more people found out that there was apparently no objection to building on the government reserve, several camps went up over the next few years. Among the owners of these early camps were the Frederick Charletons; the Hagers, prominent furniture dealers and undertakers; and Arthur Delft, a grocer. These and another dozen camps of one sort or another appeared on or near the point over the next decade. The only other prominent camps between Middle Island and Stewarts Cove were the Charles Button camp and the Seymour place at Sugar Loaf.

It was in 1894 that Mr. Longyear built his dock and pavilion on Partridge Island, which he serviced with his steamboat, CITY NEW BALTIMORE. Dances were held there during the warm months, with music supplied by orchestras from town. For two years the Partridge Island venture proved to be a big success, to the point that it was during this time that Mr. Longyear purchased the much larger CITY OF MARQUETTE in anticipation of the crowds. But by 1897 the novelty had worn off and the dances ceased. Mr. Longyear offered the pavilion to Marquette City to be used at Presque Isle. It was placed on skids and moved over the ice by horses early in 1898.

On Hallowe'en Night of 1911 the steamer D. LEUTY hit a reef several hundred yards off Lighthouse Point in a bad snowstorm. All attempts to free her over the next several days failed and the ship was finally abandoned as she began to sustain irreparable damage to her hull.

A crew who had been employed to extend the breakwater in the lower harbor was hired to salvage the cargo of lumber and sell what they could from the wrecked ship. Two cabins and part of the deck were removed and mounted on a scow. They sat in Marquette's lower harbor the winter of 1912, tied to the dock of the abandoned Grace Furnace.

Three young men, Dr. J. P. Whitmore, an osteopath, Karl Way, an engineer, and Barney Welch, an insurance agent, contracted with the salvage boss James Wanlass to purchase the largest cabin and have it moved to Middle Island Point. A few years later Dr. Whitmore bought out his two partners and remained the sole owner for many years. He spent his summers there for over 50 years.

By the time the cabin of the D. LEUTY was in place, there were many cabins and cottages, some quite unique and substantial, on or near the point, and there was rising concern over the ownership and regulation of the land. It all came to a head when some Detroit people who were familiar with the situation tried to build on some islands in the Detroit River that had been set aside as lighthouse reserves. They were denied permission but, after they pointed out that a number of responsible citizens had camps on a lighthouse reserve near Marquette and had been there some time, an inspector was sent to assess the state of affairs at Middle Island Point. His recommendation to Washington was that the reserve be abandoned and the land sold to the highest bidder.

The group got together and chose Dr. Boyer to be their envoy. He was armed with three checks of different amounts from which he could choose, depending on the number of bidders. In July of 1917, Dr. Boyer submitted a bid of $1,505, his lowest check, as there were no other bidders. The bid was accepted and the deal closed. The Middle Island Point Campers Association was formed into a stock company, with shares valued at $25 each. The association purchased adjoining land from time to time and today is a going concern of over 50 memberships.

The Beginnings of Big Bay Village

In the last decade of the 19th Century, activity began to increase around the big bay between Salmon Trout and Big Bay Points. Though the name came from the big bay itself, the village has always been centered closer to Lake Independence, and until recently most of its inhabitants have depended on the lumbering industry.

At one time Lake Independence was much smaller than it is today, but the various raisings of the water levels due to the height of the dam at the beginning of Iron River has greatly expanded its size. The Iron River, which connects Lake Independence to Superior, is actually a continuation of the Yellowdog. This river was formerly called by the French the "St. John" or in French, the "St. Jean." It has been suggested that the ornate lettering on

Top: Early buildings at Sosowagaming Club. Courtesy Huron Mountain Club.
Bottom: "Pa" Louis L. Touton (1886–1946).

Top: The McGifford Log Loader that was responsible for the death of little Alice Burns. Courtesy Milton Tompkins.
Middle: First Big Bay Mill. Courtesy Milton Tompkins.
Bottom: Big Bay Lumber Company Mill (1901–1908) Courtesy of Milton Tompkins.

these old maps was misread and the the "S" in "St." became "L" and the "J" an "I," thus "La Iron." Others say the name referred to the dark color of the water. Sosowagaming is the Indian word meaning yellow water.

The earliest family known to have lived in Big Bay was that of Maurice Le Clair. He was the French–Indian who built a cabin at Squaw Beach sometime in the 1860's. This was a squatter's cabin, as he had no rights to the land, but sometime after that in the 1870's, he built a beautiful, two–storied hewn log house which remains there today. He lived there with his family.

One of Le Clair's daughters married an Indian named Montgomery, by which marriage there were two children, Patrick and Mary. It has been said that Montgomery left the area without a trace. In 1885, Charles A. Burns, an Irishman, showed up at Squaw Beach. He had been born in Toronto, Canada and must have migrated to the United States with the lumbering operations of the early 1880's. He moved into Le Clair's house, adopted the family, and fathered four more children, Joe, Christina, Albert and James. The first Mrs. Burns, Montgomery's widow, died and Burns married her sister. After this marriage there were nine more children, Frank, Flossie (Florence), Victor, John, Beana, Forrest, Jennie, Alice and Margaret. Margaret died in infancy and Alice was killed as a young girl, run over by a self–propelled McGifford log loader, right in front of their house at Squaw Beach. Pat Burns married a Bowers. Patrick and Jim both took their turns living in the square timber cabin at Burns' Landing.

In 1885 Jim Redi built the dam and wooden log sluiceway at the head of Iron River, which was used by several logging companies. He built his tote road to the dam from the Marquette–L'Anse road that year.

Then, in the winter of 1895, six Swedes were hired by several lumber companies to build a dock at Big Bay. One of them later worked for Gus Anderson and explained how they did it. They squared a bunch of pine and spruce trees and dragged them out on the ice at the north end of the sand beach, a few hundred yards north of Charlie Burns' place. They built a cribbing on the ice which they filled with rock, brush, sand and gravel. In the spring, when the cribbing sank, the men continued to crib above the water level, about four feet high. The dock became quite popular, and was used not only by the lumber companies but by anyone else who chose to use it.

That same year, 1895, Bill Bushey, whose name was really Henri Goulette (he changed his name after serving a prison term), took up an 80–acre homestead where Hungry Hollow now is.

In April of 1897, Henry Sylvester Smith homesteaded a quarter of a section on the Pine River road leading to Huron Mountain.

In the winter of 1897, Mr. Longyear built the Sosowagaming Club at the mouth of the Iron River. At that time a bridge was constructed across the river there so one could drive a wagon all the way to Huron Mountain as Carter Harrison had done in 1899. To do this, one would take Redi's tote road from the Marquette–L'Anse road and go to the Sosowagaming Club. One would then follow the Prosper Roberts Trail. This was also a tote road used by lumbermen. It followed the lake west to the Big Huron River, fording the streams it encountered until at the Big Huron it followed that river upstream to the Marquette–L'Anse road again. There were other tote roads off of the Prosper Roberts. Bob Hautton, a supplier for pine camps, had a supply road heading to lumber camps west of Ives Lake. Because of the distance involved and the tremendous difficulty of getting supply wagons or sleds over the gap at Sugar Loaf, water was the easiest mode of travel and the main reason for the dock at Big Bay. There was also a halfway cabin near Crary's Farm on the south side of Saux Head Lake, and the Hebard Lumber Company had a dock and storehouse at the Garlic Bay.

In 1898, Prosper Beerman homesteaded along the Pine River Tote road with his family. Like the Burnses, the Beermans are still found in Big Bay. Both Burns and Beerman carried the mail the first years after the village started.

In the spring of 1898, 6,000 invitations were sent out asking people to look over the Sosowagaming Club. A grand opening was held on July 12, 1898 and, despite the excitement generated by the Spanish–American War, they had a successful summer. William O. Butler was the Steward. The financial backers, mainly Mr. Longyear, were so pleased that they decided to build more cottages the next year. The Sosowagaming Club only lasted a few years, but it ran successfully as the Sosowagaming Hotel until about 1913, when business slacked off and the idea was abandoned. In 1927 it was sold to Louis L. "Pa" Touton, a high school then Junior College teacher from Kansas City, to run as a boys' camp.

Red Town

In 1899, Andrew McAfee of Grand Rapids, Michigan purchased 12,000 acres of fine timberlands south and west of Lake Independence. Some pine was taken from the property and boomed to Marquette but, because of the tremendous amount of hemlock and hardwoods, it was decided to seek further capital and build a mill at Big Bay.

In 1901 the McAfee brothers got additional funding from the Pennypackers of Wilmington, Delaware and organized the Big Bay Lumber Company with a capital stock of $100,000.

Marquette businessmen tried to get the company to build in Marquette, but without a railroad the company decided to build on Lake Independence. They planned to cut all kinds of wood and leave the land in good condition for farming.

A preliminary survey for the railroad had been made the year before McAfee purchased his land, as it was a known fact that a railroad would eventually be needed for the large timbered area surrounding the big bay and beyond.

A first hand account of the survey was given by Edward C. (Ned) Watson in 1964:

> On January 2nd of 1899 the survey party was collected at the Marquette and Southeastern Railroad consisting of the following men: J.F. Deiniling, chief engineer; Northrup, surveyor; Frank Jenks, engineer; Fred Perry, guide and landlooker; W.F. Morgan, levelman; W.H. Brown, head chainman; Charles Charland, rear chainman; T.F. Sullivan, stakeman; William Urich, rear rodman; Mike Layne, axeman; Andy McGann, axeman; George Fraser, packman, cook and chore boy.
>
> Loading our equipment, snow shovels, tents and camp equipment, we started out with four sleighs with double teams.
>
> Our first stop was at Compeau Creek, just about where the road to Middle Island Point crosses the Creek. The ground was covered with two feet of snow and we cleared a spot with axes and shoveled out places to pitch our tents. It was a cold, gloomy day, and we had the tents set up by dark.
>
> We then cut balsam trees and used the branches to make beds on the frozen ground. Fred Perry showed us how to make them as we were all green at camping out during the winter.
>
> At daybreak we got up and washed ourselves with icy water and trooped into the cook tent for breakfast.
>
> After breakfast, we all put on our showshoes and started back toward town to make a start on our survey.
>
> All I can remember of the first day was how awkward Frank Brown was with his snowshoes. He had the hardest job of all and was the clumsiest man for the job, falling down repeatedly and having to be helped to his feet. Bill Urich had the loneliest job, way behind with his rod for a back sight. He was cold all the time, being unable to move around and keep warm.

We axemen didn't suffer from the cold much as we were busy cutting down the trees and brush on the line about three feet wide. When we ran into a maple tree two feet thick, we all chopped on it until it fell, sometimes taking 15 or 20 minutes to do. It was very vigorous exercise and we all got heated up pretty well while the rest of the gang stood around and froze.

Our second camp was at Pickerel Lake. While running the line there, Mr. Northrup, our surveyor, a very heavy man, walked along the shoreline of the lake, rather than staying on the line. He broke through the ice and we had to cut poles to get him out. We thought sure that we would have the rest of the day off as it was a regular blizzard and cold, but no, he stayed the rest of the day at his instrument with a cap on his head and no mittens and suffered the cold until night.

At Eagle's Nest we swung west and went up toward the Dead River Plains.

Our third camp was near the Little Garlic, way up in the hills.

For some reason we came back to Eagle's Nest and started north along the lake to Buckroe then turned northwest to Birch and Big Bay. (author's note: they returned to Eagle's Nest because they were getting into high, hilly country, while the route along the lake proved to be quite level.)

Our fourth camp was on the Little Garlic River, this was the last camp.

Six years later, Ned Watson was an engineer who ran the work train building the branch line to Big Bay. He was the first engineer who traveled the track from the west yard to Pickerel Lake.

In June of 1901, ten men were sent to Lake Independence to clear the millsite. The McAfees owned a circular-saw mill at Lakeview, in Montcalm County. It was dismantled and shipped by train to Marquette, and then up to the Big Bay dock by scow. This mill was set up to cut lumber for town buildings and for a larger mill. They also erected several log cabins and a shingle mill that year.

By 1902 there were 65 men working for the Big Bay Lumber Company. The dock was lengthened to 300 feet and raised to a level of six feet above the water. A tram was built at the mill.

Besides a group of company-owned houses there was an electric plant, a boarding house, a general store and a post office, all made of flat lumber and all painted with red lead. It quickly took on the name "Red

Town." The Mining Journal reported that there were no brawls because the employees consisted "of a better class of people." The men slept, not in bunks but rather in beds with springs and mattresses.

Apparently there was no market for lumber and later that same year the mill closed and the town became all but deserted.

Meanwhile, Trouble at Huron Mountain

While 1897 had been a high point in the history of Huron Mountain Club, with the completion of the Le Moyne Cabin and the building of the Lewis, Tenney, Christy, Sheldon, Hamilton and Harrison cabins, 1901 turned out to be a very bad year. The deaths of Hugh Allen and Howard Longyear had cast a pall over the place. Many of the Marquette members dropped out at this time. There was the trouble with the Kaufmans, Peter White and Munro Longyear that year, and Peter White even dropped out. Mr. Longyear terminated his steamboat service after Howard's death, saying it had been a losing proposition from the start. He had wanted to give it up earlier, but now he had a few reasons to take the step.

Of the Marquette members, only J. M. Longyear kept his membership after this time, and that was because he was the president. Even his presidency was almost solely on an honorary basis. He had turned his attention almost entirely to Ives Lake which, although it was in the heart of the Huron Mountains, was separate from Club lands and was Longyear's personal property.

William C. Busch, lumber manufacturer, George Conklin, jeweler and piano dealer, A. B. Eldridge, lawyer, Irving Hanscom, owner of a harness and saddle shop, Horatio Seymour and George Shiras III had all left the club before 1900. E. W. Allen retired when Hugh drowned, but was granted an honorary membership for the rest of his life. He did not use the property. L. M. Spencer, sporting goods store owner, W. W. Manning, who ran the government land office, and Alfred Kidder all retired in 1901. Dan W. Powell, lumberman and chairman of the County Board of Supervisors, had a membership until 1904 but never used the property, as well as Alfred Bennett, who retired in 1905. Dan H. Ball and his son Everett did not use the property either, but they had received stock in the club for legal services rendered.

From the Marquette standpoint it looked as though the club was about finished. It was out of the question for guests to consider traveling to Huron Mountain by horse and wagon

Upper left: George Judson Gillett (1893). Courtesy Hannah Gillett (descendent).
Upper right: The ALABAMA of Marquette, G. J. Gillett boat thrown on the beach south of Big Bay: storm 1897 – then he bought the CLARA MAE. Courtesy Hannah Gillett.
*Bottom:*The A. J. FREEMAN – seemed like dependable transportation. Courtesy Hannah Gillett.

Without Mr. Longyear's CITY OF MARQUETTE, smaller, less convenient boats had to be relied upon. Some guests arrived on the Booth Fisheries boats, the MABEL BRADSHAW or the C. W. MOORE. The Booth Line was based in Chicago but their boats made irregular runs up the shore, picking up tons of fish from homesteaders and fishermen along the way. Some hired the harbor tug SCHLENK, the excursion steamer THOMAS FRIANT or one of the boats of the U.S. and Dominion Transportation Company. You had to go on their schedule, often causing a long wait, and it was costly.

One enterprising gentleman who took advantage of the fact that Mr. Longyear's boat had gone out of service was George Judson Gillett (no relation to J. H. Gillett who owned the JAY MORSE and worked the sandstone quarry at Salmon Trout Bay between 1887 and 1892).

George J. Gillett came from New York State to Traverse City, and from there he moved to Marquette in 1891. Being aware of the demand for transportation up the shore on a regular basis, he bought a small boat in 1900 and started taking people and goods, first on a hired–trip basis. Realizing his boat was too small to command the respect of some of his passengers, George ordered a larger one to be made for him by Mr. A. J. Freeman of Marquette.

Before the new launch was ready, his first boat was washed ashore in a bad storm. Luckily George, who was alone at the time, escaped safely.

The new launch was christened the CLARA MAE, and again George was in business, now on a regular–run basis, making stops with passengers and supplies at Huron Mountain, Big Bay, Sosowagaming Hotel and several homesteads in between. Most of his passengers were lumberjacks.

Again Lake Superior took her toll and the CLARA MAE ended up as a wreck on the beach of Salmon Trout Bay. George had a second, still larger launch built by A. J. Freeman. This one he named the A. J. FREEMAN. The Freeman became quite dependable transportation for the next several years.

Cement Gus

While the cornerstone on Mr. Longyear's stonehouse at Ives Lake says 1901, that is actually the year work was started on it. They cut and peeled poles, blasted out a foundation and got a start on the lower part of the basement in 1902.

The Longyear family had a log cabin and a barn, a blacksmith shop and a men's camp on the property. The log cabin was strictly a camp and Mr. Longyear, from the very beginning, had the idea of building a fine summer

Left: George Gillett had the first taxi cab in Marquette when he gave up his boats.
Right: George J. Gillett at his familiar post on Front Street – Marquette. Courtesy Hannah Gillett.

home on the point, which was the only green spot on the lake after the devastating fire.

Young Howard spent the best years of his life there, exploring the valleys and the mountains, swimming, fishing, canoeing, and making the area his own. He discovered a cave made by the glacial piling of several giant boulders. They were piled so as to form two or three rooms with as many entrances. He went there often, by foot and by boat, swam from the rocks beneath the cave and spent many happy hours. It is the one thing at Ives Lake today that is still Howard's and is known as "Howard's Cave."

The children loved the hearty lumberjack food and went to the camp kitchen often for lemonade or one of the giant sugar cookies that were baked three times a week.

After Howard's death the family did not return to Ives Lake or Huron Mountain for three or four years. Their first trip there was when the stone house was complete and ready to move into.

In the fall of 1902 a foreman from the Ives Lake camp contacted Gus Anderson, who had only recently arrived from Sweden. The foreman had been told that there was a powerful Swede working that summer, poling ore on the South Shore ore dock. These men stood high on a little platform beside the chute up on the dock, jabbing at the packed ore in the pocket. It was a low–paying, dirty job. But this fellow could empty a pocket in no time, rain or shine, and then work a ten–hour shift in the stone quarry.

Gus was asked if he would come to Ives Lake that winter and break stone for the stone house. Gus said he'd do better than that, he'd contract the job, hire his own crew and have all the stone they could use piled on the site by April 1, 1903.

In the late fall Gust hired Lud Swanson and his boat to deliver his little crew to Gilletts Landing. They had rock drills, hammers and powder. Otto Torsat and Ellison were old time rock men; Ellison had worked on the Big Bay dock. With packs that would have crushed some men, they walked the five or six miles to Ives Lake and went to work. On the flume side of the lake, across the lake from the stone house, there was a granite ridge extending to the lakeshore. Here they started in teams of three men, one holding the drill, two men hammering. Each time the hammer struck the drill, the holder would turn it.

The six men – Torsat, Ellison, Johnson, and three brothers, Albin, Martin and Gus Anderson – drilled and blasted and moved rock all winter, carrying the huge pieces down to a big sled and taking them across the ice to the building site.

Top: The first Longyear camp at Ives Lake. Courtesy Huron Mountain Club.
Bottom: Gus Anderson in Sweden with his parents (1886). Courtesy Gus Anderson.

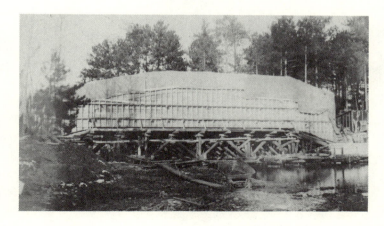

Top: Mr. and Mrs. E. L. Dixon of Detroit and Mr. and Mrs. Gust Anderson of Marquette – "Cement Gus" at the spot where the first discovery of iron ore was made in the Lake Superior region. (c. 1925) The Pyramid has been moved due to caving ground.
Middle: Tourist Park Dam. Courtesy of Gus Anderson.
Bottom: Building the Dead River bridge 1924.

410

When the breakup came in the spring, the crew had a six o'clock breakfast, bade farewell, and started down the road to Marquette. They followed the road around the northeast side of Lake Independence across the Sauks Head Plains to Crary's Halfway House. L. P. Crary was there alone. It was a rough place with several old barns. The men pushed on.

At two o'clock they reached Stewart's Cove; Gus Anderson called it "Jim Redi's Halfway House." John Stewart wasn't there – he was working at the County Poor Farm in Marquette – but his sons John, Jr., and Hugh were there, along with their brother–in–law Jim Redi. Jim had married their sister Emma. A few years later young John and his brother Hugh started a stagecoach run to Big Bay. They had a big livery in Marquette. The men pushed on again.

Instead of going down the road to the Powder Mill and then into town, Gus and his friends followed the path along the lake to Presque Isle, where they caught the last streetcar into town. They arrived in Marquette at 10:30 that night.

For Cement Gus, this was the beginning of many years of work around Big Bay. He built the concrete vault which still stands by Pine River at Huron Mountain Club. He also built the first sewer system at Huron Mountain and the first Bentley breakwall that was made out of cement. Concrete Gus built the cement dam on Lake Independence, the sidewalks in Big Bay, the foundations for all the mills, and the massive cement bridges over the Dead and Yellowdog rivers on the Big Bay Road. Gus had the reputation of laying more cement than any other man in the Upper Peninsula.

Gus Anderson was born in Dalsland, Sweden on October 16, 1881 and came to Marquette alone, arriving on the 9th of May in 1900 at the old depot on Baraga Avenue. He was joined a year later by his two brothers. His first job was poling ore on the South Shore dock. Then he worked at the South Marquette quarry taking out brownstone. He worked there until it closed that fall. No more brownstone was quarried in Marquette after that, except when they opened up a vein to add the wing to Mr. Longyear's house in Brookline.

Then Gus loaded stone at the roundhouse rock cut for the L. S. & I. Railroad, and worked eight months for the Copper Range Railroad. In 1902, the Negaunee Mine caved in and the railroad went with it. Gus helped rebuild that spur, worked the winter at Ives Lake, then drilled rock on the Mesabi Range for the Great Northern Railroad. He was soon back in Marquette working for the city. Later he was a cook and then a bartender before spending five months in South Dakota building a post office. From

1906 to 1912 Gus worked for contractors Lippsitt and Sinclair, who did many big construction jobs around Marquette. They worked on the prison, the brewery, the coast guard station and the Pioneer Furnace (Cliffs–Dow) to name a few.

In 1912 Gus Anderson decided to go into business for himself. It was then that he really started pouring cement. Gust married in 1906; his first wife died in 1946 and he married again in 1957. His second wife, Ethel, died in 1966.

Emblagard

Mrs. Roberts tells us of the first trip to the stone house at Ives Lake:

The first time we went there we stopped at Gilletts Landing and they sent the team of heavy work horses down with the dray. They had brought lunch, and we ate lunch there. We had come by boat, you see, as far as that. Then we climbed in the wagon and rode over a sand road up to the Five Forks and beyond the Five Forks up a road that was very steep and deep sand. And so we got to Ives Lake toward the end of the afternoon, we had done this for a number of years.

This old steep road, west of the Breakfast Roll Mountain, has long been abandoned but can still be seen. It was even steeper than the Sugar Loaf hump and everyone had to get out of the wagon, and sometimes a man had to get on each wheel to help the horses get over the hump.

...and so we settled down and we just loved the new house – in fact the family took to it with great vigor and enthusiasm. Mother never did – it was too close to where Howard liked to be and, as I say, she never got over his loss.

The Longyears lived between Ives Lake and Boston pretty much from then on. Abby, the oldest, married Alten T. Roberts who became president of the Union National Bank. He and Mrs. Roberts remained in Marquette and expanded the Ives Lake property into a grand farm in about 1908–09. They started the Emblagard Dairy (Elm Garden in Norwegian) and brought in the best Holstein cattle money could buy. They traveled around the country to fairs and shows and purchased the champion cows, paying large amounts of money for them. One cow from England had cost $10,000 and had

Top: Ives Lake Farm (c. 1910) Courtesy Elsie Mayhew.
Bottom: Some of the prize herd of Holstein cattle – Ives Lake Farm (1910). Courtesy Elsie Mayhew.

413

tuberculosis and had to be killed. The herd wasn't large but it was said the barn they built was the largest in the Upper Peninsula and they had a milker, a young man, for each of the champion cows.

In 1910 they started to deliver milk in Marquette from Emblagard at Ives Lake. The milk was brought from Ives Lake to Big Bay in an express wagon with a big team driven by Henry Gardner. Henry drove the express wagon the entire seven years Emblagard operated out of Ives Lake. The wagon met the train at Big Bay and the milk was delivered to homes in Marquette that same afternoon. The dairy at Ives Lake closed in 1917.

Mr. Longyear built the Longyear Building on Blaker and Front streets in Marquette. It had a fine apartment upstairs where he could live comfortably while his family was in Boston.

Huron Mountain Weathers the Storm

From Marquette, things at Huron Mountain looked very bleak just after the turn of the century. Many were sure the club could not survive. But the solid group of Chicago people, a beautiful clubhouse, awe–inspiring lakes and vistas, waterfalls and rivers, made it imperative that the remaining members retrench and overcome their setbacks.

To keep things progressing, Charles A. Du Charme of Detroit had a cabin built in 1901 and '02. The Du Charmes were an old French family who landed in Montreal in 1620. They gradually moved west, settling around Detroit in the 1800s. Charles Du Charm's father joined with three other men and founded the Michigan Stove Works, which became the largest manufacturer of stoves and furnaces in the world. This company later became the first to produce and sell electric cookstoves and ranges.

The Du Charmes were delighted with the north country. They built next door to the Tappeys, who had been the first to choose a cabin site on the south side of the river. Their lot was across the river from the cabin of Kimball Young, the one which had been built by Bud Le Moyne and D. R. Lewis; however, by the time the Du Charmes were building in 1901 that cabin belonged to Henry Hooper of Chicago.

Also that year, John F. W. Whitbeck of Rochester, New York built a cabin just east of Nathaniel T. Guernsey's. The Guernsey cabin had been sold to Samuel T. Douglas of Detroit. The Douglases had been long–time visitors to Lake Superior. The Whitbecks seemed to have lost heart in these bleak years, and did not use the club much. In 1906 they sold out to John R. Russell of Detroit.

Top: First Club Bridge – east of the store. Courtesy Huron Mountain Club.
Bottom: Later club bridge – west of the store. Courtesy Huron Mountain Club.

In 1902 it looked like there would be no other cabins built for a while, at least until some regular transportation could be established. There was talk that the railroad would soon be coming as far as Big Bay, but for now, the little resort community was very isolated.

Tom Gallagher

In 1902, homesteader John Nelson drowned near a little dock he had constructed on Conway Lake.

According to Mrs. Keough, a daughter of John's, it was a hot day in July and her father dove from the dock into shallow water, hit his head and died.

Quite a different story came from George Webster, son of Oscar Webster and the Nelsons' closest neighbor. George drove team at the club for years and about 1918 drove the first Model T the club owned. His partner, Charles Alvord, Sr., continued to drive the team in 1918 and '19. The Nelsons and the Websters knew each other well.

According to George Webster, it was the 4th of July and John had been drinking heavily, which he had been known to do, and fell from the dock and drowned.

While we will never know which story is true, it may help us to hear another story George Webster tells in the same breath. The two families would visit each other once a year or so. The Websters believed that one time when the Nelsons came to visit, Mrs. Nelson had several bedbugs wrapped in a piece of paper. They said she released the bugs in the Webster place during her stay there. While bedbugs were common in those days, especially in log buildings, the Websters claimed they never had them until after the Nelson visit. It seems not to have occurred to them that the bugs could have come by accident.

Tom Gallagher was a tough, wiry Irishman who had come out of the river drives to the Huron Mountains. He was a foreman in the woods and was given the job of foreman at the Club. Men had a habit of doing what Tom Gallagher told them to. He was firm, honest and all business. Tom didn't know the Nelsons, but he knew of them. When word was received at the Club that John Nelson had drowned and was somewhere in Conway Lake, Tom gathered his crew, walked to Conway and took up the dragging operation. They found the body not far from the dock in the weeds.

Tom was single and about 38 years old. Apparently he thought part of life had passed him during his rough years in the pine camps, and here was a

Top: Mr. and Mrs. Tom Gallagher on a Sunday at Huron Mountain.
Middle: T. Gregory, L.D Smith, T. Gallagher, W. Hodges - Conway 1906
Lower left: Tom Gallagher and the Nelsons at the Conway Lake cabin.
Lower right: Mary Hamilton at Huron Mountain about 1916.

ready–made family. Within the year, Tom Gallagher married the widow Nelson, adopted the three daughters and moved into the homestead.

Tom was also very thrifty. In his book "Growing Up With Chicago" Carter Harrison wrote about Tom Gallagher. He wrote: "Uncle Adlai reminds me of Tom Gallagher, a north Michigan lumberjack. Fifty years ago in the dead of winter with snow two feet deep on the level, he hoofed it going and coming on the tote road 45 miles from Pine River to Marquette. I knew the road was traversed thrice a week by a four–horse bobsled "bus." The fare was $1. I asked Tom why he had not "raised the wind."

"'I had the money all right,' said Tom, 'but I didn't know a better way to make two American dollars!' Tom was Scotch–Irish."

Besides being thrifty, Tom was a real opportunist. He turned out to be a good father and husband for his adopted family. Tom already had a homestead on the north shore of Howe Lake. He brought the family there to live for the summers during the early years of the marriage while he was still working at the club. He had jumped a claim to obtain that homestead. When Jake Nelson died in his accident in Rasmussen's saloon, Tom bought out Barney's half of that homestead on the south end of Conway Lake.

The new Mrs. Gallagher, whose maiden name was Blake, had a brother, George, and a sister, Mary. Mary was married to Elmer Batty of Detroit, who had a homestead on the north shore of Rush Lake, in a beautiful little bay surrounded by a stand of white birches. Tom Gallagher had acquired other lands in the area also.

One would think that with all the homesteads and land available to him, Tom Gallagher would have lived in one of them while working at the club, but they were all too far away and he built a little house on the west–end beach where he lived summers with his family.

Both the Gallagher homestead on Howe Lake and the Batty homestead on Rush Lake were later sold to the club and the buildings burned. Tom sold the Jake Nelson homestead to Stanton Bice of Marquette and the John Nelson homestead on Conway Bay to Mr. William P. Hamilton of Detroit, a member of the Club. There was some talk at the time of a hotel company wanting to purchase the spot to build a resort hotel on. Mr. Hamilton purchased the land to protect the club. He had the building put in good repair for use by his daughter, Mary Hamilton.

Mary became known by her friends as the "Countess of Conway." She was a poet and an artist of some renown. She loved to do miniatures, some of which are on display today in the New York Museum of Fine Arts. Mary painted a little mouse in a prominent place on each piece of furniture in the Conway Cabin and added other little unique touches of color and decor. Her poem "The River," with some accompanying artwork, hung in the children's dining room at Huron Mountain for many years.

It was a pleasant outing for Mary Hamilton and her friends to walk the trail around Conway Point to the Hamilton Cabin for tea, spend the afternoon, and return by a shorter trail through the woods. This trail was later known as the "Granny Rasmussen Trail" as for many summers Ed Rasmussen's wife would walk it to work at the club every morning and return on it every evening.

When Mr. Hamilton died in March of 1929, the land he owned went to Huron Mountain Club. He had been an ardent supporter of the club since he joined it in 1896. For many years he had been a director, and he became the second president in 1922 after the death of Munro Longyear. Mr. Hamilton held that office until 1926, when it passed to Dan Hebard of Pequaming.

And What of Peter White?

When Peter White dropped out of favor with Mr. Longyear due to his selling out to the Kaufmans, he also dropped out of Huron Mountain Club. All of this was common knowledge to the tight–knit group of monied people in the community. To the housewife, the miner, and the laborer nothing had changed. Most of them didn't know or care who owned the bank. However, the many benevolences of Peter White were always present and he was continually in the news. The new library bearing his name was most impressive, being the only building in town made of beautiful gray Indiana limestone. The opera house, the churches, the college, St. Luke's hospital and Presque Isle all had the power and money of Peter White behind them.

When the Normal School was dedicated, it was brought out that although Peter White had given $5,000 to the art department, they had named the Science Hall for him instead.

Don M. Dickinson, for whom Dickinson County was named, spoke at the dedication ceremony. He said that people came from across the country "not to dedicate a new branch of an educational system, but to see an honor done to Peter White."

Dickinson suggested that "a colossal bronze statue" of Peter White should be placed at the entrance of Presque Isle Park. Dr. H. C. Potter wrote that he had long believed that if there had been no Peter White there would have been no Upper Peninsula.

Top: Northern Normal School.
Middle left: Peter White Spring – Horse watering trough – Lake Street – Marquette.
Middle right: Road to Presque Isle. (c.1902)
Bottom: St. Luke's Hospital (forerunner of Marquette General)

One of Peter White's last great honors was presiding as Admiral of his own flagship, the "Marigold" at the Sault Canal Semi–centennial Celebration in 1905, attended by such dignitaries as William G. Mather, J. H. Sheadle, John Russel and Miss Betty Poe, daughter of General Poe. Charles T. Harvey himself was the chief marshal. The Peter White flag was presented to the Marigold by Henry M. Campbell and flown at the bow of that vessel during the celebration. U. S. Vice–President Fairbanks and Governor Warner of Michigan headed the list of distinguished visitors in the parade.

Peter White returned from that celebration in August of 1905 to face a great sorrow, the death of his beloved wife of 48 years. He had lost five of his seven children, and now his helpmate and constant companion was gone.

On June 13, 1908, the Mining Journal printed a Peter White Memorial Edition of its weekly newspaper. The entire front page and more was filled with the highlights of the famous man's life, and the two columns on the far right side of the front page told the story of his death due to a heart attack in Detroit's downtown. The body was returned to Marquette on a special train and was met by a great crowd of sorrowful people.

Peter White had gone to the Detroit City Hall on business. While in the building he complained of indigestion and decided to walk back to his room at the Hotel Pontchartrain. He was midway between the Woodward Avenue entrance to City Hall and the corner of Fort and Woodward Avenue when he staggered and fell. The Mayor of Detroit had seen it happen from a window in his office. Mr. White was carried into the Mayor's office but he was already dead.

The Lombardy Poplars

Peter White had spent a lot of money building the road to Presque Isle. The area along the lake was all marsh, underwater and subject to severe wind damage. After the fill was made the road would wash out, often becoming impassable.

George Wilson had learned about trees and landscaping from a Detroit firm with which he kept contact. He suggested to Mr. White that trees be planted along the road. It would beautify the scenery and help hold the soil. The Detroit firm had told George Wilson that the only tree that could withstand the winds and waves of Lake Superior and grow almost anywhere was the Lombardy poplar. Peter White sent for 500 seedlings,

Perry Hatch – The father of Boy Scouting in Michigan, lover of camps, woods and waters. Courtesy Martha Hatch.

imported from Italy. This tree is noted for being a hearty grower, easy to plant, growing under extremely adverse conditions in poor soil, and it has a life span of roughly 65 to 85 years. The tree, "populus nigra," comes from the mountainous regions of northern Italy.

John Stewart was given the task of planting the trees on either side of the road to the island in 1904. He had many more than he needed. Peter White gave some of the surplus to friends. Some found their way to Ives Lake, where Mr. Longyear planted mostly elm but also some other ornate varieties. John Stewart took some to the Poor Farm (now Brookridge) where he was superintendent after 1902. He planted some in Harvey, where Mrs. White owned some land, at the Powder Mill where he and his wife had the boarding house, and he gave them to friends in town. John planted some at Stewart's Cove along with a few black locust, some of which he planted at the Powder Mill also. Many of the original Lombardy poplars are dead now, but their descendants have spread. Just a shoot in the ground will start a new tree. They are found in many places around Marquette today.

Many people said the trees would never make it through the first winter. Perry Hatch, outdoorsman and lifelong resident of Marquette, wrote a poem as a young boy about the Lombardy poplars.

> They planted them there a month ago
> Not being too sure if they would grow
> But they leafed right out like early spring
> So the birds could sit at evening and sing.
>
> Of happy evenings on Presque Isle Bay
> Where mothers and children come to play
> On picnics and parties the summer long
> With feverish haste, 'ere it is gone
>
> I wondered last night if the poplars knew
> What the fall would bring, what they'd have to go through
> With storms from the north and waves piled high,
> With howling winds and dark cold sky.
>
> When the ice will form around their trunks
> And the sea runs past with great big chunks
> Of everything, logs, ice and stones
> Hurled at them to break their bones.

I'm glad they're young, I'm sure they don't know
What the future is, what will happen and so
As they are there now in orderly rows
I hope they grow strong for the future blows.

Perry Hatch is famous in the peninsula as having started the first Boy Scout Troop, possibly in the nation. It was started as the Junior Epworth League of the First Methodist Church in Marquette in 1909, some months before the officially recognized troop of scouts in America. As soon as the scouting movement was heard of in this country, the group was organized as Troop I in Marquette. This was in 1914. Eventually, Perry Hatch also became widely known as the second oldest Scout in the United States, with his 64 years of service to the Organization. He died December 30, 1975 in Marquette.

The McCormicks and the Bentleys

By 1902–'03 the Marquette and Southeastern Railway was beginning to buy right of way for a railroad to Big Bay. Even though it looked like the railroad would become a reality within a few years, there were two members of the club who didn't particularly care if it went through or not. To them the isolation became a delightful challenge. These were two more prominent Chicago residents, Cyrus McCormick and Cyrus Bentley. McCormick, whose father had invented the reaper, had been tent–camping off and on for many years on an island in a lake about 25 miles south of Huron Mountain. In 1902 he and Bentley formed a partnership and decided to develop a rough permanent camp at the south area and make a trail north across a virtually unbroken wilderness into Huron Mountain Club. The rough camp would have all the charm of the club itself but would add to it a vast area of wilderness more challenging than what the club could offer, the kind of challenge and intrigue that Cyrus Bentley thrived on. This lonesome, rough camp on an island offered even more isolation than the club did. In fact, to Cyrus Bentley, the difficulties caused by the lack of transportation made Huron Mountain Club seem even more inviting. The trail he planned in 1902 was completed by 1905.

In 1904 and '05, Bentley built his cabin at Huron Mountain. It has a unique location, right on the point of land at the end of the sand spit between the mouth of Pine River and Lake Superior. McCormick was a member of the club for some 20 years but never built a cabin there.

Top: Mrs. Carolyn Watson Rankin, children's author. Courtesy Marquette County Historical Society.
Bottom: The Bentley cabin on the sandspit between Lake Superior and the mouth of Pine River. Photo by Don–Ball Keillor.

Buying the Right of Way

No sooner was the Bentley cabin under construction than the Hamiltons snatched up the last lot between the Bentleys and the Henry Hooper cabin between the river and the lake. The Hamiltons sold their old cabin to the John L. Shortalls of Chicago, who had recently joined the club by purchasing the stock of Fayette Brown of Cleveland.

The Hamiltons and the Bentleys were very close friends and some years later the Bentleys' daughter married the Hamiltons' son. They just would not miss the opportunity of having their cabin next to the Bentleys. The Fayette Browns were in the smelting and shipping of iron ore and had built the little town of Fayette, Michigan, which is now a state park. Their descendants returned to Huron Mountain and come there often today.

By 1904 most of the railroad right of way had been purchased, and plans for the railroad had solidified. The track had been laid along the Marquette lakeshore right by Lighthouse Point, the Father Marquette statue, the beautiful waterworks building, and in front of the big Longyear home and the way was clear to head up to Big Bay. Because of this, Mr. Longyear had made arrangements with the contractor Van Iderstine to move the house to Brookline, Massachusetts. With this obstacle overcome, the Marquette and Southeastern Railroad Co., with William G. Mather as President, was ready to start laying track the following year.

The years of 1902, '03 and '04 saw Ernest Rankin, Sr. of Marquette purchasing right of way for the railroad company. Up to this time nearly everything had gone in and out of the little settlement at Big Bay by water. The incentive to build the railroad came from the fact that there was already a mill there and 12,000 acres of timberland waiting to be cut. It was agreed that everything would be shipped by rail after the first year.

With the prospect of the railroad coming into the village, people prepared for expansion. That year, the dam at Lake Independence was rebuilt out of logs, and by 1905 a few people were moving back into the houses at Red Town. Summer transportation was by water and stage, and winter transportation by sleigh. They used Jim Redi's old tote road which crossed the Iron River at the Sosowagaming Hotel. The stage and sleigh were run by John Stewart's sons, John and Hugh.

Ernest Rankin, the right-of-way purchaser, had married Caroline Watson. They were an old Marquette family. Her father, Edward M. Watson of Marquette. His father, Jonas Watson, who had married Emily Wood, was aboard the steamer Independence when it blew up just a mile out of the Soo on November 22, 1853. Jonas' life had been saved as he was reportedly blown into the air and came down into some baled hay. Four people were killed while the survivors clung to floating wreckage and bales of hay. The ship sank in 18 feet of water.

Jonas' son, Edward Watson, Caroline's brother, came to the Soo from Cleveland in 1852. He was hired by J. P. Pendill and moved to Marquette in 1860. He joined the army and was assigned to the First Michigan Cavalry. By the time the Civil War broke out, Ed Watson was a captain. He was wounded by saber at the second battle of Bull Run, shot through the neck at Morristown, Tennessee, and finally taken prisoner. He eventually returned to Marquette and went into business with his father. After his father's death he was joined by E. B. Palmer in a store at 310–312 South Front St., Watson & Palmer. They sold general merchandise, dry goods and groceries, and had a good business with lumber camps in the district.

After Jonas Watson died, his wife, Emily, built the home at 219 East Ridge Street in 1877. This is on an extension of their original lot of a former home facing the harbor, down below the hill on Lake Street. The new home has been occupied continuously by the family for well over 100 years. The present owner is Ernest and Carol's daughter, Phyllis.

Mr. Rankin obtained signed right of way agreements from all but two of the land–owners along the right of way. While John Stewart gave the company verbal permission to cross his property, he refused to sign anything. They finally let it go at that.

A little further up the line at Buckroe, Rankin ran into another problem. The Madoshes, some of the famous Indian family who were living along the shores of Lake Superior long before the first white settler came, had been granted 160 acres of their age–old fishing site at the mouth of the Little Garlic River. There was a beautiful stretch of sand beach there with some cobblestone beach, low sandstone cliff at either end, and the river mouth. About the center of the beach was a large warehouse and a dock as well as a small cabin and a horse barn, which previously had been built by the Hebard Lumber Company. The problem here was that the Madoshes wanted to sell the whole 160 acres, not just a right of way. Their price was $1,000.

Now Mrs. Rankin had been writing some short stories for several magazines on a national basis and was a well–accepted authoress. She wrote for Harpers, Ladies' Home Journal, Gardening Magazine, Century, Youth's Companion, and Mother's Magazine. In the latter she had articles under three pen names, all with initials C. W. R. The pen name did not reveal whether she was male or female. Mr. Rankin explained the situation to her. They knew the spot well and had fished and camped there. Mrs. Rankin had $1,000 of her own money hidden away in a cigar box. It was from her writing.

They decided it was too good an opportunity to pass up and that they would buy it themselves. Mr. Rankin took the money and headed downtown.

On his way down the hill on Front Street, he met his good friend, William S. Hill. Hill was a lawyer and had been the city attorney for Marquette. Ernest had known him in Detroit. He offered to put up half the money, as he knew the place well and wanted to be a half owner of it. They bought the property together, to the dismay of Mrs. Rankin. They each owned an undivided one–half interest. The deed, replacing an earlier one for just the right of way, was executed on March 12, 1902 between David Madosh and his wife Maggie, George Madosh and his wife Jane, and Thomas Madosh, all heirs of David Madosh, deceased; and Caroline Rankin, and William S. Hill.

In 1918 Thomas and Bessie Gowling made a deal with Mr. Hill for his half of the property. Mrs. Gowling was Hill's secretary. Mr. Gowling was a stonemason and later worked for Longyear and Hodge.

David Madosh was the son of Madosh, a Chippewa chief who was part of a band of Indians who lived in this area for generations. He was one of the signers of the Treaty of La Pointe. David had been a volunteer scout during the Civil War and had made many scouting forays behind enemy lines. David had been given a medal by President Abraham Lincoln for bravery in action and had been granted 160 acres of land of his own choosing after the war. The piece of land he chose was that portion of a quarter section which encompassed the mouth of the Garlic River. It had been the age–old fishing grounds of his people. Members of the Madosh family lived in the area for many years before they sold the land to Mrs. Rankin and the Hills. In modern times there has been some doubt as to the legality of the transaction of 1902, since it was the custom for Indian lands to be held in trust by the Federal Government, and the question has been raised as to whether the Madoshes had a right to sell it. Apparently, Madosh had a deed to the property, or it could not have been sold.

Birch

The work on the railroad went on all during the year of 1905. There was a massive sinkhole between Sugar Loaf and Hogsback Mountain which had to be filled. No one realized how deep it was or how much material would disappear into it. Rock, gravel and criss–crossed tree trunks from the right of way were laid in the mud across the 100–foot–wide area. Ties and track were laid on the timbers, but within a day all evidence of them had sunk from sight. Tons and tons of rock and more timbers were hauled from the mines; all would disappear in the depths of the mud hole. Again load after load of rock from the mines was dumped into the hole until everyone was sure the foundation was solid. However, when the first 50–ton locomotive passed over it, everything sank again. After more fill, the engineers finally devised a cable system, tying the cables to rocks and trees on either side of the sinkhole. To this day, no one is sure if the cables did the trick or if the hole is finally filled. Some of the cables are still visible.

Ned Watson told the story in 1964 as follows: The track had been laid and he was the engineer on the train expecting to travel the line.

> We came along and found 300 feet of track sunk under water in one of the swamps. We hauled more rock and gravel until we had a new roadbed above the water. We cut the old track and there it stays today, under the roadbed fastened to a tree by a big steel cable just south of the rock cut.

Thomas McKenna was the foreman of the track laying crew.

Sometime before the laying of the track was started, the Northern Lumber Company was organized. It had a capital stock of $300,000 and the company planned to cut lumber, lath and shingle from 20,000 acres they had purchased in the Sauks Head Lake area.

There were already a few inhabitants nearby. Besides Judge Crary, who had his farm on the southeast side of Sauks Head Lake, and the Halfway House, which was just an overnight building for anyone to use, Frank Krieg and Captain Martin Daniels each had been operating mines in the area. Frank had been the first to locate his mine and he also had bought a homestead with a sturdy log cabin and a nice garden from John Frazier who settled there in 1895. He had done some prospecting in the area as early as 1891 and staked out a claim in 1892. Frank was doing his prospecting while he ran a grocery store at the corner of Third and Washington streets in Marquette during the 1890's. While up in the woods prospecting he had found some rock bearing copper and silver. He exposed the area further and dug some test pits. In one pit, the deeper he went the better the prospects looked. Frank soon discovered samplings of gold in the same rocks with the copper and silver.

Over the next few years Frank Krieg made great preparations to open a mine on the location in the near future. We can only imagine his frustration when a newcomer came into the area and announced his

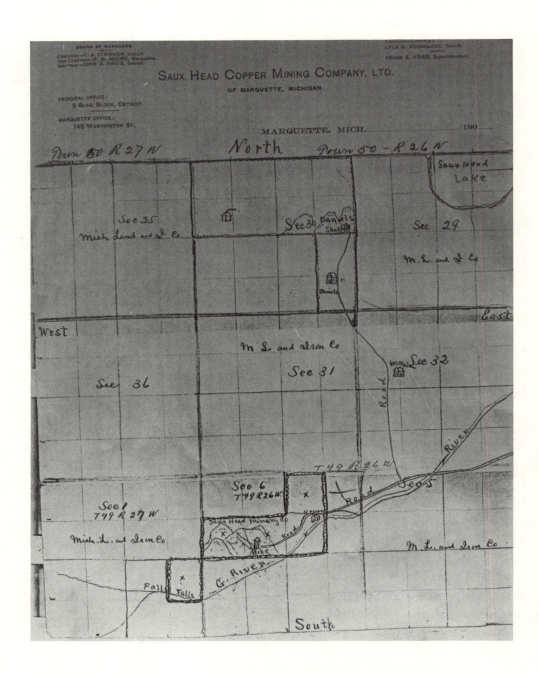

Frank Krieg's map of the Krieg and Daniels Mine. Courtesy Laura Lockhart (daughter).

Top: Saux Head Copper Mining Co. stock. (1905) Courtesy Mary Paquette.
Bottom: Kriegs' Mine near Birch. (1902) Courtesy Laura Lockhart.

intentions of opening a mine also. The new adventurer was Captain Martin Daniels of the schooner MYSTIC. Daniels hauled any kind of merchandise anywhere for anybody. The MYSTIC even took a few loads of sandstone from the Gillett Quarry at Salmon Trout Bay, and was one of the few ships that would carry explosives up and down the lakes. He had even taken Frank Krieg and his brothers to Saux Head beach a few times, and had learned of their plans to open a mine.

By 1898 Frank was ready to start his mining operation. He ordered a big steam boiler out of Cleveland. The boiler arrived by boat at a Marquette dock, but Frank would have nothing to do with shipping it up to Saux Head because of his rivalry with Captain Daniels.

Frank had the huge boiler loaded on a heavy wagon with an eight–horse hitch and he and his little eight–year–old daughter, Laura, started up the old L'Anse road to his mineral claim.

At Sugar Loaf Gap they spent several days cribbing the wagon up so that the boiler would fit between the rocks. They had to get another team and several more men to negotiate the hill and the rock cut. Having conquered Sugar Loaf, Frank and Laura and the eight–horse hitch continued on alone. At the south end of Sauks Head Lake they turned west and cut their way, making a road as they went, several miles up to the mine location. The whole trip from Marquette to the mine took over two weeks.

Working with Frank's brother Charlie and a few hired men, they set the boiler up and built a shed over it. They also built several other buildings in the area. By 1899, when the mine was in full operation, they could hear Captain Daniels blasting on his claim just a mile and a half north of the Krieg mine. The Daniels Mine was in the southwest forty of Section 30, while the Krieg mine was in the southeast quarter of the northwest quarter of Section 6, T49N–R26W.

Both mines were quick to report good news. Some of Krieg's samples assayed higher in gold than in either silver or copper. Daniels called his mine the Saux Head Mine Ltd., but it was usually referred to as the Daniels Mine. The Krieg Mine was called the Saux Head Copper Development Co. but it is usually referred to as the Kriegs' Gold Mine.

When the Krieg mine was in full production in 1901 there were about 22 men working there. Frank Eugene Krieg had four brothers – Ed, John, Charlie and Henry – all of whom worked at the mine at one time or another, but Frank was always in charge and owned the property. To get operating capital, he turned the operation into a stock company and then Frank became known officially as the superintendent.

Top: Mining crew at the Kriegs' Mine 1902. Courtesy Laura Lockhart.
Middle: Kriegs' Store at Birch, Kaufman's St. Bernard. Courtesy Vera Wilson.
Bottom: The early houses at Birch. Courtesy Frank Smith.

Upper left: The second set of houses at Birch. Krieg home left. Courtesy Frank Smith.
Upper right: Second school at Birch. Courtesy Milton Tompkins.
Middle: Down Town, Birch. Courtesy Milton Tompkins
Bottom: Lumber piles at Birch. Courtesy Milton Tompkins

In July of 1902, Daniels reported finding the main ore vein at 60 feet deep and was getting copper ore "three times as rich as ore being stamped out in the Copper Country." The value of gold in the ore was $13.75 per ton of rock, while silver was valued at $3.99 per ton of rock. In the same year, the Krieg Mine was producing $125 in gold per ton at the 38–foot level.

By the end of the summer of 1902, the company had spent more than they had made, but Frank Krieg knew that the ore was getting richer as the mine went deeper. He always had the feeling that they would soon reach the "Mother Lode" which would surely turn the mine into a paying proposition.

Just before Labor Day of 1902, at about the 120 foot level, the Krieg Mine began filling with water. The pumps could not handle it. The miners had to quit working and on the Labor Day weekend the whole crew went down the road. The fire went out in the boiler and the mine filled with water. The men never returned, and that was pretty much the end of the Krieg Gold Mine.

Frank Krieg did everything to try to raise money to get another crew – he was sure that pay dirt was within reach – but there were no takers. The stock company that had been formed was called the Sauks Head Copper Mining Co. Ltd., with all the officers in Detroit and Marquette. The address of the principal office was at 5 Buhl Block, Detroit, and the Marquette Office was at 149 Washington St. The secretary of the company was John G. Krieg of Detroit.

When the Northern Lumber Company started to build a company town between Frank Krieg's place and Saux Head Lake, Frank was staying at his homestead summers, and he and Lillie had four or five children. They eventually had a family of fifteen. He had also built a camp at the south end of Sauks Head Lake where they would go so that the children could go swimming and boating.

The company had hoped to be able to use the railroad, but since the tracks were not laid yet, everything the first year (1905) had to be hauled by horse and wagon from the Hebard Dock on Rankin Beach at Buckroe. This was to avoid the steep hill at Sugar Loaf.

The company hired William Froelingsdorf of Collinsville to build the first 20 houses, a hotel and the store. Mr. Froelingsdorf had come from Germany to St. Paul, Minnesota in the late 1880s. He moved to Marquette about 1890 and was employed as a miller by the Marquette Valley Milling Co., who owned a large, three–story flour mill on Dead River at Collinsville. The mill closed about the beginning of 1905 due to lack of water in the Dead River, and Froelingsdorf went into the contracting and carpentry business. The sawmill and iron furnace at Collinsville were all shut down by then.

Top: Jim Malone (crew) on Gillett's new boat the A. J. FREEMAN. Courtesy Hannah Gillett
Middle: Heading into a rocky shore. The A. J. FREEMAN. Courtesy Hannah Gillett
Bottom: Huron Mountain guests headed for Huron Mountain. Courtesy Hannah Gillett

Top: The A. J. FREEMAN in Pine River 1905. Courtesy Hannah Gillett
Middle: A. J. FREEMAN headed for Birch. 1905. Courtesy Hannah Gillett
Bottom: Furniture headed for Birch.

Frank Krieg was hired to run the store. He also ran the post office out of his store, so he became the Postmaster and eventually was on the Township Board and the School Board. Frank, his wife Lillie, and their growing family moved into house no. 6 as soon as it was completed in 1905. Mrs. Krieg had a child there, but it died in infancy. Frank buried it up on the hill on the northeast side of the new millpond, thus starting the Birch Cemetery. It eventually had about 30 graves in it, mostly children.

In 1906, when the railroad and the mill were operating, the company hired contractor Hallam to build the second set of houses. A much larger home was built for Frank Krieg and his family at that time, house no. 36, and he moved into it. When Frank applied for the Post Office permit he chose the name "Birch" for the new settlement because they had so many birch trees. The little village had a sawmill, a shingle mill, a general store, a town pump, a hotel and 20 houses that first year, all built out of green lumber.

The land that the company had purchased was described as a solid block of timber, beginning at a point two miles south of the Little Garlic River, extending north to Sosowagaming Club Preserve and west to a north–south line through Hill's Dam on the Yellowdog River. The president of the company was Rush Culver, of Marquette; vice president W. W. Miller of Wellsboro, PA; secretary W. F. McKnight of Grand Rapids; and treasurer F. J. Jennison of Marquette.

George Gillett had built up a good business bringing men and supplies up to Birch that summer of 1905, as well as bringing a few guests to the Sosowagaming Hotel and Huron Mountain Club as well as Big Bay. This had been his most profitable year so far. Right at the peak of his rush season, around the first of September that year, there was a terrific storm and George again lost his boat and nearly his life. The force of the storm threw the A. J. FREEMAN on the rocks north and west of the Iron River's mouth. Even though this was the third boat of George's that had been tossed on the beach by the cantankerous lake, he lost no time in procuring another one.

In the Mining Journal of Sept. 7, 1905, it stated in part:

George Gillett has purchased from John Wachter of Munising a new gasoline boat which he will use in carrying freight and passengers to the resorts north of the city.

For five years Mr. Gillett ran his little boats up and down the shore, making a profit even after losing three boats, while Mr. Longyear's larger steamers had lost money heavily. The difference was that Gillett's was a one–man operation. In the winter, George would make snowshoes in the front room of his home on South Lake Street.

In the fall of 1905 the Northern Lumber Company installed a portable mill so that enough lumber could be cut immediately for the construction of the permanent band mill and the other necessary buildings. The portable mill arrived in Marquette from Port Huron, but the railroad was still not ready to handle it. It was transferred to a scow and unloaded at Saux Head Point. By that date, everything shipped by water was coming to Saux Head Beach and the dock at Buckroe was abandoned. Rankins built an addition on a caretaker's cabin that the Hebards had at the dock clearing.

They cooked in the shed, but usually slept in tents for the first years. Over by the mouth of the Garlic, the old Madosh shack still stood for a number of years. The Gowlings later built there. There were also the remains of two old Madosh cabins out near the road.

At Birch, temporary camps, large enough to house 200 men, were put up that fall and work was started on the main mill, the shingle mill and the other buildings. The lumbermen assumed that the Garlic River and Wilson Creek were large enough to drive logs close to the mill on a head of water from the back country.

The work on the railroad was all but completed right to the mill at Big Bay by December of 1905, but the trains did not start running regularly until the next year.

Reorganization at Huron Mountain

Further up the shore at Huron Mountain the same year that Birch was being organized, there were some other kinds of organization going on. Up to this time in the Huron Mountain Club's history, in order to live up to the requirements of the state laws in effect at that time, a partnership association, "The Pine River Co., Ltd." had been formed to hold title to the lands used by the Huron Mountain Shooting and Fishing Club. But on April 2, 1905, all that changed and a new organization was formed. It encompassed all the lands, assets and liabilities of the other two organizations. Membership was reduced from 100 members, which seemed unwieldy, to 50. Old stock was surrendered and a membership in the "new" club issued in its place. At this time, the name was officially changed to "Huron Mountain Club," which was already being used by many. With prospects of the railroad starting up the following year, the club had survived its infancy and was off to a running start.

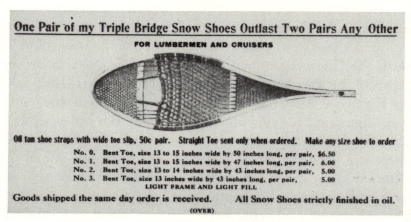

One Pair of my Triple Bridge Snow Shoes Outlast Two Pairs Any Other

FOR LUMBERMEN AND CRUISERS

Oil tan shoe straps with wide toe slip, 50c pair.   Straight Toe sent only when ordered.   Make any size shoe to order

No. 0.   Bent Toe, size 13 to 15 inches wide by 50 inches long, per pair, $6.50
No. 1.   Bent Toe, size 13 to 15 inches wide by 47 inches long, per pair,   6.00
No. 2.   Bent Toe, size 13 to 14 inches wide by 43 inches long, per pair,   5.00
No. 3.   Bent Toe, size 13 inches wide by 43 inches long, per pair,   5.00
LIGHT FRAME AND LIGHT FILL

Goods shipped the same day order is received.   All Snow Shoes strictly finished in oil.

(OVER)

Top: The end of the A. J. FREEMAN Sept. 2, 1905. Courtesy Hannah Gillett.
Middle: George Gillett's living room. Courtesy Hannah Gillett
Bottom: George Gillett's snowshoe tags. Courtesy Hannah Gillett

Book One

The Wreck of the IOSCO and OLIVE JEANETTE

The fall storm that had wrecked George Gillett's little ship near the mouth of the Iron River left another memory at Huron Mountain. In general, the fall storms at the club are often violent and destructive to the unprotected beach. Because some of the older cabins are so close to Lake Superior, the storms are imprinted deep in the memory of many a fall visitor. A few of these storms have become famous. The club has had pilings driven and groins built to protect the cabins and save what little beach is left.

In the recorded history of Lake Superior for this century, there were probably six or eight storms of historic significance. Four of these stand above the others, and each one of them is claimed by some witnesses to be the very worst. They are the "blow" of 1905, the famous 1913 storm, and the storms of 1975 and '85.

While no ships went down, on December 1st and 2nd of 1985 was probably the most destructive storm ever for the Lake Superior shoreline. Three unusual conditions culminated in the loss of thousands of huge trees and many homes and cottages near the water.

First, there was no protective ice buildup along the shore; second, the water was at its highest in recorded history; and, third, the storm came out of the northeast and swung around to the northwest thus sparing nothing on the south shore.

At Huron Mountain, the Harris cabin and the H.M. Campbell cabin were devastated and all the others lost their front porches, except for the Bentley's, saved by the breakwater but encased in a four–inch coat of ice.

Of the first three storms, many old–time sailors who were sailing during the first two claimed the 1905 storm to be the worst. However, most people believe – and the facts seem to bear this out – that more ships and lives were lost during the 1913 storm, and it lasted twice as long. Some modern sailors argue that any storm that could tear an up–to–date, scientifically constructed double–hulled ship like the EDMUND FITZGERALD into two or three pieces, like the storm of November of 1975 did, just had to be a strong contender for first place. Others say it was a freak condition just at the wrong time.

While many ships were wrecked in the famous 1905 blow, this particular storm was a late November storm, around the 26th, 27th and 28th. It had little effect on Huron Mountain, as there were no guests there at the time, and destruction of the property was no worse than in other years. But the 1905 storm that wrecked the A. J. FREEMAN is the same one most old–time Huron Mountain people were referring to. It occurred on a weekend around the first of September.

A few days after the storm, Harry M. Campbell, Jr. of Detroit, a college student and son of member H. M. Campbell who had purchased the Rathbone cabin in 1901, was running down the beach as he had done daily in the mornings for most of the summer, when to his great astonishment he encountered a body floating near the water's edge. It was a gruesome sight. He dashed back to tell someone, only to find out it had already been reported and preparations were under way to retrieve it. It seemed, however, that the body had two locations. Confusion reigned momentarily and false reports were circulating until it was eventually realized that there were, in fact, two bodies. Then people began to notice the unusual amount of debris floating in the water. Soon, search parties and patrols, by foot and motor launch as well as rowboat, were organized.

By then the beach fairly hummed with stories. Several people said they noticed the lights of a ship headed west during the heavy blow. It had seemed to some to be moving at a slower and slower pace. A few people observed that, at times, it seemed to be actually losing ground.

Horace Kent Tenny of Chicago, a long–time summer resident of Huron Mountain, brought the first reports of the drownings to Marquette. The county coroner, Judge Crary, who owned the farm at Sauks Head Lake, came to Huron Mountain by motor launch to hold inquests for the bodies.

When the facts were sorted out, it was discovered that the steamer IOSCO, with the schooner OLIVE JEANETTE in tow, was headed downbound or east from Duluth, both ships heavily laden with iron ore. Somewhere out from Salmon Trout Point they had made the decision to turn around, possibly because the steamer had lost her tow and they were looking for her, or else they were headed for the protection of the Huron Islands or Huron Bay to wait out the weather. In any event, the IOSCO and the OLIVE JEANETTE had become separated in the high sea and both vessels had foundered.

All in all, there were 27 people lost between the two ships. Over the next year most of the bodies were found strewn from the beach west of the Big Huron River in Baraga County all the way to Big Bay.

As the body count rose, club carpenters were instructed to build pine coffins, at first just a few and then a dozen or more. Stories were told for years how the carpenter shop at Huron Mountain was so full of pine coffins that there was hardly room to work.

Each day, reports of the findings at Huron Mountain were brought in by campers returning to Marquette. H. J. Lobdell, a bookkeeper for the Burtis

Lumber Company, was the resident agent for Huron Mountain at the time. He was the son of a long–time Marquette resident, and proprietor of the Marquette Steam Laundry and City Express Line. The younger Lobdell lived with his parents at 213 East Arch St. Lobdell brought reports to the Mining Journal as they came in, and the paper reported that the club had been extremely helpful and cooperative during the search.

Soon representatives of Hawgood & Co. of Cleveland arrived. These were the owners of both vessels. It was learned from them that the schooner OLIVE JEANETTE had been built in 1890 by F. W. Wheeler in Bay City, Michigan and the steamer IOSCO by the same company a year later. The IOSCO was insured for $65,000 and the OLIVE JEANETTE for $40,000. They also said that in 1900 the steamer J. R. DOTY was lost while towing the OLIVE JEANETTE from Chicago to Buffalo. The schooner survived that storm, while the steamer DOTY was never heard from again. No bodies or wreckage were ever found. They felt that the OLIVE JEANETTE was a jinx and a hoodoo.

Hawgood & Co. hired J. J. Behrendt, a homesteader living west of Moyer, to patrol the beaches in the area and watch for looters.

One body was found at Big Bay near the Big Bay Lumber Co. dock, one at Conway Bay, four along the club beach and west to the Flatrocks, two more on the east Huron River beach, and seven further west in Baraga County. One man must have reached shore alive near the club, as he was found well up on the sand and had left a trail of blood from the water's edge. Dr. Stockwell, a guest at the Club at the time of the disaster and a member of one of the search parties, gave his opinion that the man had reached shore alive, but had not survived the shock.

A Mining Journal sub–headline read, "Ex–Mayor Washburne of Chicago Tells of Finding Bodies on the Beach at Huron Mountain." The story, a grisly one, was told in detail. In it, Mr. Washburne said the sight, particularly of a woman, believed to be the only one on board either ship, was "One of the worst sights I have ever witnessed." He told of the people in his boat observing a black cloud that seemed to hover, appearing and disappearing near the rocks west of Pine River Point. As they drew closer, they realized that it was flies over the woman's body, entwined in the roots of a tree washed up on the shore. There were stories of finding a doll's clothing and a child's coat, leading searchers to believe that there may have been a child on board one of the ships, although the official roster did not list any.

Such were the events at Huron Mountain that late summer of 1905. The coroner made several trips to Huron Mountain that fall, bringing five and six bodies back at a time. More bodies found late in the fall were put in

Top: Hank Havery hunter-trapper of wolf and bear. Courtesy of Mrs. Hank Havery. That's Hank on top.
Bottom: Hank Havery guide—Mountain Lake. Courtesy of the Huron Mountain Club.

Top: Hank Havery homestead on Howe Lake, wife and children. Courtesy Mrs. Hank Havery

Bottom: Hank Havery hunter–trapper, wolf and bear. Courtesy Mrs. Hank Havery

coffins and buried high on the beach near where they came ashore, to be picked up the next summer.

More Homesteaders

Homesteaders were still arriving in the years of 1903, '04 and '05. In 1903 Hank Havery took up a homestead on the south side of Howe Lake which included the spring and the island there. A little later, Joe Krinke homesteaded 80 acres way up on the side of the hill, south of Howe Lake. He never proved up properly and became a squatter, with no rights to the land except that he used the cabin there. His was a trapping shack. Joe worked for several of the members of the Club as a private guide, but generally few people knew him. Many were the mysterious stories concerning Joe Krinke and his gold mine that was supposed to exist over in the valley of the Little Huron River.

Hank Havery had a farm on Lake Superior along the highway in Marquette where the Garden Room Restaurant now is located, but he lived for long periods at the homestead; he hunted and trapped there, and made maple syrup in the spring. He also worked many summers for the Club.

Along the Prosper Roberts tote road north of Rush Lake were homesteaders Jensen and Marshall. Later, around 1905, came Moyer and Mulhauser, both cigar makers, and Bernhardt. Moyer had a cabin made out of huge white pine logs, about four or five to a wall. The remains of his place can still be found near the corner where the road turns north to the Flat Rocks. Mulhauser eventually sold his land to the club, except for five acres which he sold to Charlie Reidinger of Marquette about 1914. Elmer Batty, brother–in–law of Tom Gallagher, took over 40 acres filed by Earl Sharp and proved up that homestead about 1904. Gallagher jumped a claim at Howe Lake from a fellow who built a small cabin there but never showed up again. Tom built his cabin, further west on the north shore of Howe Lake but still on the same claim, and took it over. He sold that homestead to Bryant Walker of Detroit, a member of Huron Mountain Club.

To the east of Huron Mountain Club were the Frenchmen, Antoine Hetu, Reimey Fournier, and Joe Paris. In 1904 Oscar Webster started a new, enlarged cabin on the club tote road and abandoned the old one near Conway Lake. The new building was still on his original claim. He also built a little frame bungalow at 508 E. Hewitt Ave. in Marquette. That home was just five or six houses up the street from Lake Superior. Down the club road just west of Big Bay, Charlie Burns made a claim right across the road from Smith's homestead and just west of the cemetery where all the Le Clairs had

Top: Dutch John's homestead cabin (1950) built 1910.
Bottom: Dutch John (Gottlieb Rudot) at Stonedock about 1912. Courtesy of William Manierre.

been buried. This became the first Big Bay cemetery, which was later moved to its present location in the village.

Christianson homesteaded on the southeast side of Conway Lake. This place was sold to Victor Swanson in 1927, though Vic had used it for years before that. In 1906 Myron Perkins homesteaded out by the Conway Lake gate on the Club Road, north of the Breakfast Roll. Myron had several daughters. His homestead consisted of a log cabin, a roothouse and a woodshed. His land went part way up the mountain to the south, and he put the trail up the mountain there. It used to be known as "Perkins' Mountain."

Just east of the Perkinses was Theodore Leach, who homesteaded around 1909. Then, a year later, Gottlieb Rudat received his patent on 160 acres just south of a big marsh east of the Salmon Trout River. He worked at the club regularly, first along with Oscar Webster and then for Mr. Bentley and Mr. Le Moyne. Gottlieb Rudat became known to everyone as "Dutch John." He spoke with a deep, growling German accent. John had come right from Germany, done some sailing on the ocean and then on the Great Lakes. He was followed to the Big Bay area some years later by Anna Rudat, his niece from Germany. Anna became known as "German Annie."

Up on the Salmon Trout River, at a truly beautiful location, was Murphy's cabin. Many assumed it to be his homestead, and he guarded the river as if it was his own for many years. In truth, this was a cabin built by Huron Mountain Club for Murphy, who was a guard on the river from just after the turn of the century up into the 1920s.

Murphy was a big Irishman with a red handlebar mustache. He always had a bottle of whiskey to share with his friends and always expected one if he had done someone a favor. Murphy had a swinging bridge on cables across the river near his place, and he patrolled both sides of the river from it until he was an old man. The location is still known as "Murphy's."

George Hager's homestead was 3/4 of a mile west of the Salmon Trout bridge. About 1890 he built a substantial frame building there. He is said to have brushed out a road from Ives Lake over to the Salmon Trout upstream from his place, where the state road M–35 later was to cross. His cabin was later almost completely eaten by porcupines.

The Five Forks cabin was built as a guards' camp on the Salmon Trout about 1920. At this point, there was the Pine River Tote Road which constituted two roads, one east and one west. Then the road from Gillett's Landing at the Salmon Trout Bay came to a fork there for a third road, and a road went up along the west side of the river to the dams for a fourth. The fifth fork took off to the west, just south of the club road, curving up a grade and can still be seen, though it is unused and overgrown today. It went to a

Upper left: Delia Murphy – spent much time at Salmon Trout with John. Married 1875 – had family of about 8.
Upper right: John Murphy.
Bottom: John Murphy ran a saloon on South Front Street in Marquette before going to the Salmon Trout about 1910.

homestead claimed by Frank Nason, the father of Dave and Blaine Nason. Dave was a young fellow of 12 or 13 when he and his dad built a cabin about a quarter mile up from the Five Forks in 1906. Blaine later lived at the Paris Homestead when it was the Club Farm.

Golf at Huron Mountain

There were several attempts to build a golf course in the early years of Huron Mountain. The only first hand account we have is from the pen of Carter Harrison, who tells us it was a five–hole course for the express purpose of trying to get Mr. Rob Lewis to join the club. He says that Lewis cared nothing for the fishing and could see no point in choosing a summer home where golf could not be enjoyed daily.

Mr. Harrison: "Between the club grounds and Pine River Point lay a huckleberry patch of such fame that, until the club acquired and posted it, a family of Chippewa Indians camped there annually throughout the berry season." This is believed to be some more of the Madosh family, a remnant of the Marje Gesick band who spent summers at Pine River and springs near the mouth of the Garlic River, where they fished and made maple sugar in the woods north of Echo Lake. In the 1890's John Hallam encountered them in a log cabin in the woods, back from the mouth of the Salmon Trout. They gave him boiled fish to eat and let him sleep on the floor of their cabin. John had been selling watches to the men in the lumber camps at Ives Lake. He got lost at night in the winter and happened onto a trail to their cabin. There was a Charles Madosh, another son of Chief Madosh and brother of David Madosh, who had received a medal from President Lincoln.

The next day, John Hallam followed a sleigh road to Granite Point where he went out on the clear blue ice of Lake Superior. With the wind at his back, he opened his coat and, taking little runs, let the wind blow him 60 to 80 feet on the ice, using his coat for a sail. He did this all the way to Middle Island Point.

Harrison:
What did countless messes of succulent huckleberries count with Hemp when they stood in the way of getting Lewis to spend his summers at the club? The directors consented to the building of a five–hole course. Axes soon laid low the scrub Norway and jack pines on the tract. No effort was made to clear away the luxuriant huckleberry growth. Rob was told about the links, and in the winter

Top: Golf links at Huron Mountain. Courtesy Huron Mountain Club.
Middle left: Herb Perkins in England (1901).
Middle right: The Perkins at Huron Mountain Club 1911. Courtesy Mrs. Perkins
Bottom: The Perkins at Huron Mountain Club 1910. Courtesy Mrs. Perkins

of 1897–98 he joined the club and authorized Le Moyne, cabin builder in chief at Huron Mountain, to throw up a cabin as quickly as possible. For the sake of speed it was built of real planks instead of logs.

On entering the living room of the clubhouse on my arrival in 1898, I saw a conspicuous bulletin announcing formation of the Huron Mountain Golf Club. Below it were spaces for signatures of applicants for membership. To my surprise, I found myself already enrolled and pledged to pay the $25 membership fee. Indeed, like Abou Ben Adhem, my name led all the rest.

Now I was not a golfer. I had joined the Skokie club and tried the game, riding my bicycle 21 miles to Glencoe, playing 18 holes and riding back to Chicago. But I had not joined the Huron Mountain Shooting and Fishing Club to play golf. I explained my position and objected to finding my name on the list. But to what avail were expostulations with good old Hemp, who had a way with him that rarely failed?

A few days later, equipped with all the tools, I was led to the slaughter. On the second hole I found my ball with difficulty in the huckleberry thicket. Gone was its spic and span newness, its gleam of white. Had the head of the last Indian family that beached his Mackinaw here let his eagle eye catch sight of my ball, down on his knees he would have dropped to worship Manitou and to thank the Great Father for the last blessing to his tribe. My golf ball in his eyes would have been a glorified huckleberry.

Rob Lewis must have had no more pleasure out of the hastily built golf course than I did. His membership was short–lived. With his cabin it passed into possession of Charles H. Hodges.

Golf was never played much at Huron Mountain. With a few feeble attempts by a small group that year and the next, it died a natural death. There was one more attempt at golf in 1924 and '25 when Dr. Tappey had a very rough nine–hole course between his cabin and Pine Lake. There were too many trees and too much brush then, and this was the end of Golf at Huron Mountain.

Early Club Stewards

While there were work trains back and forth from Marquette to Big Bay all winter, it was not until the spring of 1906 that the first passenger train came into Big Bay. This marked a specific milestone in Huron Mountain history in more than one way, for on this first train were two passengers bound for Huron Mountain who had come all the way from England. They were Mr. and Mrs. Herbert Perkins.

Before this time, one of the most important responsibilities at Huron Mountain Club was that of Steward. Seeing that the members and guests were fed well was of prime importance to the success of the club, and the planning involved in procuring food, preserving it and preparing it in the right amounts at the right time was tremendous. The supply of meat and fresh vegetables depended entirely on the irregular arrival of the CITY OF MARQUETTE. The meat purchased from "Bill the Butchers" slaughterhouse in Marquette was liable to be an old bull or a worn–out cow. A lot of vegetables were wilted when they reached Marquette and they usually had to lay over a few days before being sent on to Huron Mountain.

Carter Harrison used to say, "Club board in its infancy was $1 a day and it was not worth it." The one meat that could be counted on was fish, either from sportsmen or purchased from local fishermen.

Dan Sullivan and his wife, both from Marquette, were the first manager/steward combination at the club. Dan had run the Clifton House and that, along with the Hotel Marquette, was considered the best eating establishments in town. Dan was a heavy drinker, though he was careful to stay out of sight when he was not sober. Mrs. Sullivan was a kindhearted, motherly soul but, according to some, a little unkempt and careless.

When the Sullivans left, one steward after another was hired over the next several years. Some lasted a full season, but others either threw up their hands in the middle of the season or were let go. Up to 1906 only the Sullivans had kept the job more than two seasons.

Herb Perkins, a tall, distinguished Englishman, took over the job as steward and Mrs. Perkins was put in charge of the waitresses and kitchen help. Gradually, over the next six or eight years, Mr. Perkins' job took on greater proportions. At the same time as Mr. Perkins' job was shifting away from the dining room and food responsibilities, Mrs. Perkins was taking them over. By 1916 she was in full charge of the commissary, hiring kitchen help and waitresses and taking full responsibility for them, planning the menus with the help of the members, making food purchase lists and running the whole commissary department. Mr. Perkins became the manager of the club in general. The dedication of these two people for the rest of their lives went a long way in establishing a delightful and smooth–running organization over most of the next half century.

Oscar Knuusi at Huron Mountain

The second train that pulled into Big Bay that summer of 1906 had young Oscar Knuusi aboard. He was bound for Ives Lake to work for Mr. Longyear. Oscar was 28 years old and had come all the way from Merikarvia, Finland. The son of Heikki and Elizabeth Alaknuusi, his name should have been Franz Oscar Alaknuusi, but in order to make it more pronounceable to Americans, he dropped the first two syllables in his last name.

At Ives Lake, Oscar did bull work and rough carpentry. However, later in the summer there was a shortage of guides at Huron Mountain and Mr. Longyear asked Oscar to go there and help out. He became a guide for the Tuttle family. When Oscar first arrived, he knew no English at all. He learned it little by little, but even in later years many people found him difficult to understand.

The first time Oscar was asked to do carpentry work, it was to help build some more coffins for bodies that were still turning up from the shipwrecks of the previous fall. Again the coroner had to make a couple of trips to collect bodies, digging up some that had been buried on the beach that summer and some from the previous fall.

Oscar Knuusi, like the Perkinses, was destined to have a great influence on the club in the years that followed. He started building boats in 1914. In his lifetime he built over 200 boats for use on the club property, a phenomenal accomplishment considering he never used an electric tool in his life. He also worked on about 15 or 16 of the cabins on the club property, at first as a laborer on the Arthur L. Farwell cabin in 1909 and then as a carpenter on the Tuttle cabin in 1910. In 1912 there were four cabins built, three of logs and one of lumber. Oscar Webster was the foreman during this period. The cabins were built for George A. Carpenter, a judge from Chicago; Edwin Denby, Secretary of the Navy under Roosevelt, Taft, Wilson and Harding; Francis C. Farwell of Chicago and Dr. Theodore A. McGraw. Francis Farwell was a great friend of Cyrus Bentley and Cyrus McCormick. He had built up a dry goods store business in early Chicago which he later sold out to Marshall Field.

In 1913, a cabin built for Victor Elting of Chicago was the first and only cabin ever built by Club members that had the bark left on the logs. Cedar is the only wood with which this can be done, and the matched straight cedars in this cabin are perfect. The cabin stands today, three quarters of a century later, as a fine example of this kind of construction. That same year, Dr. Russell A. Hibbs of New York had a cabin built on the

Top: Elizabeth Mattila (far right) in Finland with the rest of her family. (c. 1908). Courtesy Albert Knuusi
Middle left: Franz Oscar Alaknuusi in Finland. (Oscar Knuusi). Courtesy Albert Knuusi
Middle right: Mr. and Mrs. Oscar Knuusi and children Allan (baby) and Helen at Huron Mountain. (c. 1916). Courtesy Albert Knuusi
Bottom: An "Oscar Boat" at Canyon Lake landing. Courtesy Albert Knuusi.

east beach. It was of red pine, but again, the matched size of the logs, non–tapering, could only be duplicated artificially today. By this time, the log work at Huron Mountain had taken on a pride of workmanship that made it an art, and the collection of buildings there formed a museum of log work unequaled anywhere. Many of the cabins put up between 1910 and 1930 were done by Marquette contractors.

It was in 1913 that the Du Charme cabin, which had been completed in 1902, burned to the ground. It was replaced the following year. The new cabin, built by the same family, was more substantial than any other at the club. It was the first to have a full basement of poured cement, its own well, and a central heating system. It later became the first to be electrified, with its own light plant. Obviously the Du Charmes planned to come to Huron Mountain in the fall and winter.

From about 1914 to 1944, Oscar Knuusi became the boat builder. He always had one or two boats in the process of being completed, but some years he completed as many as ten or twelve boats in a year's time. Unlike most boat builders, Oscar's boats were of various sizes and shapes, though usually of the lap–strake construction. Some time after World War I, Oscar settled on a rather heavy and broad, double–ended boat of his own design. It was similar to the fishing boats used years ago in his native Finland. He built a form and made many boats from it. It became the standard Club rowboat, found on all the lakes. There must have been as many as 40 of them in use at one time. By the late 1940s, these boats became known as "Oscar boats." They got tremendously hard use, often left on gravel beaches or swaying gently for hours on a jagged rock. They were a pleasure to row, wide enough for two long oars without having them bump, and every stroke provided the exceptionally long glide characteristic of a properly trimmed boat. With constant seasonal use, some of these boats lasted over 50 years. At present there is a 65–year–old Oscar boat at the Marquette Maritime Museum. It was a boat that had been given to Albert Knuusi, Oscar's son, by Huron Mountain Club. The boat was meticulously restored in 1984 and '85 by Peter Braamse of Marquette, grandson of landlooker "Moccasin Bill" Oliver.

On November 11, 1911, Oscar Knuusi married Elizabeth Mattila, also from Finland. Oscar built a log house that year back in the woods about a quarter of a mile west of the mouth of Pine River. At first, Oscar lived at Huron Mountain and his wife lived with a family in the 300 block of East Arch Street in Marquette. The Knuusis had three children – Helen, Allen and Albert, who was born with spastic paralysis. In 1919, Oscar bought Oscar Webster's four–room bungalow at 508 East Hewitt and rebuilt the whole thing. He cut the roof free by hand, jacked it up eight feet, and put four

Top: Oscar Webster Homestead before north addition (c. 1910) (note violinist) Courtesy Richard Bentley
Bottom: Shinglemill at Birch. c. 1909.

bedrooms and a bath on the new second floor. The family lived there from then on during the winter so that the children could attend school. Oscar still spent winters at the Club, building boats or working on cabins.

Oscar Webster moved to Detroit with his family after retiring from Huron Mountain. However, he returned every summer to live at his homestead on the club road just outside the gate.

In the early 1930s Henry Ford purchased the Oscar Webster homestead and turned it over to the Club.

Activity in Big Bay and Birch

With the railroad running a daily schedule in 1906, the towns of Big Bay and Birch were prospering. In Big Bay a planing mill was constructed which employed 40 more men. Later in the summer there was dissension among the stockholders which caused them to close the mill again and the town went into a slump for a few years.

Birch, however, was booming. Around the first of April, 1906, the big three–story sawmill, which had been under construction all winter, was put into operation. It was a double bandsaw with the capacity of 120,000 feet of hemlock or 80,000 feet of hardwood per day. In about six months' time a boom town had grown out of the wilderness. That spring there were 33 buildings and a population of over 300 people. There was a general store, machine shop, warehouses, barns and boarding houses. Forty acres of land were cleared at the mill site and there was a network of side tracks from the mainline that covered a quarter of a section. Streets and alleys had been surveyed and the streets named. Eighteen houses were built on what was known as Front Street and a large public park was provided for. All businesses were on one street, while the residences and the school were on the other streets.

Frank Krieg had experience running his grocery store in Marquette before opening the gold mine in 1901. Being Birch's first citizen and having his store background, he was placed in charge of the company store when it opened in the fall of 1905. Frank still worked occasionally on his mining operation along with his brother Charlie, but he was also the Birch Postmaster, member of the school board, and the Powell Township's treasurer.

The mining operation went on for another five or six years on a small scale. After two more unsuccessful shafts were started, Frank and Charlie decided to run an adit into the ore body from a valley a hundred yards or so

Wedding day of Walter Raish at Birch 1907. Mrs. Raish left. Courtesy of Mrs. Ivan (Kathy) Raish.

west of the main shaft. They went in about 40 or 50 feet before terminating the venture, and the mine never opened again.

Freeman Raish, Sr. was the superintendent of the Northern Lumber Company operating at Birch. He was also a stockholder in the company. Gust Anderson described him as a good man to work for. He had a bottle in one hand and a Bible in the other. The Raish family had come from Pennsylvania.

The railroad had brought a lot of hunters and fishermen into the area for the first time, and Frank Krieg was appointed the first conservation officer in Marquette County.

In the middle of July of 1906, a forest fire broke out not far from Birch. Frank Krieg, already in the employ of the state, was made fire warden. After several days of unfavorable winds, it looked as though the new town of Birch would be doomed to ashes. The company sent an urgent call for help to Marquette, and a group of firemen and volunteers with a thousand feet of hose and other equipment was dispatched by special train. While the crews were bringing the fire under control, a timely rain drenched the whole area on the 26th of July and the last element of danger was removed. The threat of destruction had lasted over 40 hours.

The first houses to be put up by Froehlingsdorf were all made of green lumber, as was the first school, which opened with 50 students, right after the holidays at the beginning of 1906. Later the homes and other buildings were more substantial, with plastered walls and ceilings.

The board of directors of the Northern Lumber Company by then was made up of three lawyers and two bank cashiers, all from Pennsylvania. They thought the best method of getting logs to the mill, one that was used in the hills of Pennsylvania, was to make hardwood slides in 16-foot sections that could be connected together. Four or five logs were put on the heavily-greased slide and horses walked alongside pulling the last log, thus forcing the others ahead of it. This method was practical when all hills led down into the mill, but proved to be a failure at Birch and was abandoned.

In a few years the population reached over 500 and a new contractor from Marquette, Henry Hallam, who had bid on the Longyear house, built a large new store, a 30-room, two-story hotel, and more houses. The store had a spacious second floor where dances were held once a week, as well as silent movies and other entertainment.

W. F. McKnight's part of the holdings was sold to another Pennsylvania group in 1908 and a great deal more money was spent in the now quite sizable town. An imposing two-story school was completed up on the hill. In the fall of 1909, the school even boasted a small football team.

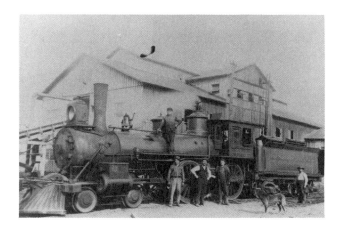

Top: Pete, Ed and Leonard Raish (brothers) at the first camp the Raishes built at Birch 1905.
*Middle:*Mill at Birch and Northern Lumber Co. engine 1910.
Bottom: A Raish camp at Birch 1910.

Top: Birch 1907 – They raised pigs, kids sat on the woodpile and watched.
Middle: Flanagan's dray – Mary Raish on trunk July 20, 1911. Flanagans started dray service in 1872, later went to busses and moving and storage.
Bottom: Theodore Schneider right, Henry center, Paul left on Ridge Street, Marqette.

Book One

A Shot in the Arm for Big Bay

The village of Big Bay had gone into a slump after 1906, and had not pulled out of it. It was in this condition when the Brunswick Balke Collander Company of Chicago sent Theodore Schneider up to cruise the maple timber in the area.

Schneider came from Seney, where he had been in the lumber business for some time. He and his partner, Fred Brown, found plenty of the finest maple they had seen, a high percentage of it birdseye. They were sure there was hardwood of a high enough quality to support a larger town and a larger mill.

The Brunswick Balke Collander Company bought the timberland, the mill and the village of Red Town. They immediately laid out a new and larger townsite up on the hill above old Red Town, overlooking Lake Independence and Lake Superior, and hired Contractor Liephart of Munising to put up 30 or more houses. All of the earlier houses had been down on the flat below the hill. By 1909 there were over 300 men employed by the new company. It was called the Lake Independence Lumber Company, and was a subsidiary of Brunswick.

Most of the construction went on between 1909 and 1914. The first new house completed on the hill was a large one for Theodore Schneider and his family, and he was made superintendent of the mill. His partner, Fred Brown, was a millwright. The last building to be completed was the school in 1914. The boilers for the new improved mill were constructed by a Mr. Prescott of Menominee.

By 1910 Jay Brunswich Deutsch, the nephew of B. E. Bensinger, who was president of the Brunswick Balke Collander Co., moved to Marquette to take over the operation of the business. Deutsch had gone to Heineman, near Antigo, Wisconsin, right out of college to learn the lumber business from another uncle, Mr. Heineman himself. Heineman's son later bought the Chicago Northwestern Railroad. When J. B. Deutsch moved to Marquette County, he brought several families with him to Big Bay.

Phil Aird's family had come from Antigo. Phil ran the company store for Deutsch, arriving in Big Bay in the fall of 1910. A few years later, in February of 1912, John B. Tompkins ("Jay" Tompkins) came to Big Bay as walking boss for the Lake Independence Lumber Co. He had met J. B. Deutsch in Heineman.

Deutsch proceeded to plan and build a huge home overlooking Lake Superior, high on the bluff above the dock at Squaw Beach. This home, built in the years 1912 and '13 by Liephart of Munising, was truly a showplace for

Top: New hotel in Big Bay (c.1910). Courtesy Milton Tompkins
Middle: J. B. Deutsch home on the bluff just north of Big Bay.
Bottom: Butcher Hardings Brush Runabout (c.1911). Allegedly the first car in Big Bay.
Courtesy Milton Tompkins

Big Bay in that day and age. The full basement was constructed by stonemasons of Van Iderstine who had moved the Longyear home. They quarried the sandstone right on the site at the edge of the cliff. It was a large basement, complete with wine cellar, servants' toilets, furnace room and food storage and preparation rooms.

The frame of the home was of white pine and the flooring of the first and second floors was laid in what was known as "bedstock," one–inch birdseye maple made specifically for bowling alleys. The wallpaper in the living room was handpainted and had come from France. There were two large fireplaces, the one in the big living room being made of uniform Lake Superior boulders and the dining room fireplace being made of brick. Across the front of the building and part way along each side was a wide, screened–in veranda.

Workers and gardeners kept the grounds immaculate. There was a winding concrete driveway through the trees, sturdy white fences, walkways, hedges and flower gardens everywhere. There was even a sunken concrete pond with water lilies in the front yard at the edge of the bluff near a gazebo, and a beautiful stairway descending the bluff to the dock and beach on Lake Superior. Halfway down the 119 steps was a round open porch with built–in seating all the way around the railings. One could take a pleasant and needed rest in the shade of the huge trees in the bluff after climbing the sixty or so steps to the ringed seat.

When J. B. Deutsch moved into the beautiful home early in 1913, there was already one car in Big Bay. It was a 1911 Brush Runabout that belonged to "Butcher" Harding. But Mr. Deutsch's 1913 Cadillac was the talk of the town as it was unloaded from a flatcar down near the mill. There was only about two miles of road he could travel on in the whole village, but he hired Max Vogel to be his chauffeur and be responsible for the automobile. His main trips in 1913 and '14 were from his home, which he called Bay Cliff, to the mill and company office.

Leiphart's men worked over two years constructing the company houses. In August of 1912, Cement Gust Anderson staked out the new part of the Big Bay Mill and began to pour the foundations. Deutsch had the log dam at Lake Independence bolstered with logs again that fall. When it continued to leak in 1913, he made arrangements with Cement Gust to pour a concrete dam there the following year.

Brunswick had bought out the mill at Birch in 1912 and much of the machinery was moved up to Big Bay. The mill at Big Bay was now made up of the finest and most modern machinery of its day. The Prescott portion of the mill had a non–releasing Corliss engine. According to Milt Tompkins it was

Top: J. B. Deutsch and his 1913 Cadillac. J. B. driving, Max Voegle, his chauffeur beside him, Jay Tompkins marked with an x, Big Bay hotel in background.
Middle: The two stack mill at Big Bay.
Bottom: Company houses in Big Bay constructed 1912–14. Courtesy Milton Tompkins

one of the finest engines ever made, and of course the Clark equipment was the top of the line. The Clark engine was a 500 horsepower steam engine from the Birch Mill.

The construction went on all winter and all the next summer of 1913. There was a serious setback just about when the construction began. It was the burning of the pin warehouse in 1912 when 100,000 bowling pin blanks – that is, unfinished pins – went up in smoke. Firemen poured in from Big Bay, Marquette, Ishpeming and Negaunee, along with 100 volunteers, but the best they could do was contain the fire to the warehouse with the pins inside.

On New Year's Day of 1914, the new three–stack mill went into operation. There were two ten–hour shifts, each shift producing 125,000 board feet of lumber as well as bowling pins. That summer, under contract with J. B. Deutsch, Gust Anderson brought his crew and the huge cement mixer they had used on the mill foundations, over to the dam on Iron River to build the concrete dam that is there today.

Incidentally, one of Gust's crew who worked all that summer on the dam was a young fellow from Marquette known as "Cotton" Johnson. It was his hair that gave him the name; his real name was John. Gust and "Cot" became great friends on the job, as they each admired one another. They were both Swedes and both hard workers. Cot was a smart young fellow with two years of college behind him. He had a two–year teaching certificate from the Normal in Marquette and was already the principal of the Diorite school during the winter. Cement Gust knew that young John Johnson would go places. Gust was right; John Johnson later became vice–president of General Motors of Canada.

The building boom in Big Bay that started in 1912 continued for three or four years. When it was completed, there was an impressive, sizable town laid out south of the main buildings on the bluff: the hotel, the big Schneider home, store and company office building. Red Town was gone. Only the mill and depot were down below the hill.

The Logging Railroads

Back in 1909 and 1910, when the Brunswick Company was first getting started in Big Bay, they built logging camps all over in the woods surrounding the town. There were as many as eight and ten camps operating at one time. When the timber was gone from an area, the camp was moved or abandoned. Railroad grades were pushed through the rough terrain of

Top: The three stack mill went into production January 1st, 1914. Courtesy Milton Tomkins
Middle left: "Cotton" Johnson – later became vice–president of General Motors of Canada. He lived out his retirement years in Skandia. Rydholm Collection.
Middle right: New houses in Big Bay (1914).
Bottom: The main street in Big Bay boasted the hotel, Company office building and Company store and the big superintendent's home after the building boom of 1914–18. Courtesy Milton Tomkins

virgin hardwood forest in every direction. Each camp had a railroad grade heading back to the mill at Big Bay. When a camp had to be moved, the track was extended further into a new timber area and away from the mill.

Powerful, vertical–piston Shay–type engines, nicknamed "Limeys," were used to haul the logs to the mill. These engines were built by the Lima Locomotive Works in Lima, Ohio. They were strange looking compared to a conventional locomotive. The boiler was offset to one side to make room for three upright pistons on the other side, and there was a double universal joint. The engine was short and maneuverable, and could climb grades and take sharp curves that would be impossible for a regular engine. In fact, they had a reputation for being able to run on no track at all. Of course this was an exaggeration, but the tracks were laid in sections 30 feet long that could be unbolted and a great piece of track, as many as 20 sections at a time, ties and all, could be picked up and loaded on cars to be relaid somewhere else. The Limeys sounded like they were traveling through the woods at 90 miles an hour when you heard one coming, but when they swung into sight, they were hardly moving. The engine was geared down so low for power that top speed on the main line was 18 or 20 miles an hour, but on the curved and often poorly laid track in the woods, they would only go three or four miles an hour.

By 1913 and 1914, the loggers had started taking the timber from behind Birch back to Big Bay.

When the mills at Birch were closed and dismantled, the schools and other facilities, store, saloon and hotel were all closed. The Brunswick people pushed railroads out of Birch up into the hills to get the timber out with the Limey engines. Back in the woods just beyond the Bass Lakes they lost a Limey engine and never retrieved it. It settled into a sinkhole and was almost out of sight when reported in 1950. The Limeys brought the timber down to the main line at Birch, where it was transferred to the big Baldwin engines to be brought up the Marquette and Southeastern line to Big Bay. There were some interconnections and Brunswick had some arrangements by which they were, at certain specified times, able to use the Marquette and Southeastern tracks. In 1922 this was bought out by the Lake Superior and Ishpeming Railroad, L.S.& I.

Tom Williams was an engineer for Brunswick on the Lima engines and Herman Bystrom drove a conventional switch engine around the mill for Brunswick. There were few routine days. It was always an adventurous life on the logging railroads. Herman Bystrom had a camp on the Yellowdog River, and a homestead which is still in the Bystrom family. He had been involved in a bad wreck while working for the D.S.S.& A. Railroad. After the wreck

Top: Lann Bryant, a close friend of Vera Blue, standing beside a Limey engine – note the boiler offset to one side to make room for the pistons on the other side. Courtesy Vera Wilson

Bottom: Another "Limey" showing the three cylinders on the right side. Courtesy Orvil Bystrom; Picture taken at Conway Lake; Train crew: Tom Green, Roy Lowe, Joe Kluseck; Spectators: Dave, Cleo, Naomi and Betty Tripp, Alice Prosen.

Top: Limey with load of logs, Birch 1909.
Bottom: Huron Mountain Club wagon at Big Bay depot 1910. Courtesy Shirley LaBonte

he went to work for Brunswick, where he worked for years until the days of the colorful logging railroads ended in this part of the country.

It was a little later in 1913 that another car appeared in Big Bay, a Ford owned by Dr. Webster, the company doctor. By 1914 people were beginning to drive cars all the way from Marquette to Big Bay and during 1914 and '15 in the summers it was not uncommon to see several cars around town. By 1916 there were two or three more Fords owned by Big Bay residents. Bill McGeorge, the head filer at the mill, and Oliver Hall, the master mechanic, both had them.

Natpo

There are many reports of log schools for three to five pupils and churches that were built in small lumbering settlements with no written records. This was much the same as in some small, short–lived mining communities and charcoal kiln communities of an earlier era.

One such place was called "Natpo," near Birch. In the spring of 1911, Walter W. Jones and Frank Brown built a road into the woods from Birch for the National Pole Company (thus Natpo) to a location where they built two cabins and a large bunkhouse for the company. It was an independent organization and sold timber to the mill at Birch. The men stayed at Birch the first year in a house that had to be fumigated for bedbugs, until the families were able to live in the new settlement in the woods. A small, one–room log cabin was built, which was used as a school during the week and a church on Sundays. Walter W. Jones was the clerk at Birch in January of 1912.

In 1909, the population there was 600; in 1911 it was 500. Big Bay in 1911 was listed as having 40 inhabitants. In 1913 Birch went down to 100 people and remained there for several years, while Big Bay had grown to 400 by 1915. Natpo lasted three years, until 1913. Many of the people in Birch had come from Tioga County, Pennsylvania.

As the population figures show, most of the families who lived at Birch moved away, but some stayed on. Frank Krieg and his now grown family was one that stayed, as did his brother, Charles, and his family. Freeman Raish, Sr., who had been superintendent of the mill, had a son Freeman, Jr., "Pete," who remained in the area and went logging. Pete Raish built camps and logged at Harlow Lake, the Kaufman land where they cleared fields for Loma Farms and all around Birch, Antlers and Big Bay. He logged for 45 years (1913 to 1958) in the Birch, Big Bay and Huron

Top: Mary Raish, Dorothy French, Blanche Perry, Edie Bingham, Ruth Bingham – at top Diane Britton 1922 – When Birch closed this building was used as the third school.
Middle: Raish home at Birch, Grandpa Raish on porch.
Bottom: Northern Lumber Co. engine near Birch 1907.

Top: Decking logs at camp 4 Big Bay 1912, Bowers – camp foreman next to three teamsters, Dad Tompkins center of logs. Courtesy Milton Tompkins
Middle: The Krieg girls: Violet, Laura, and May at Sauxhead Lake.
Bottom: Louis Kaufman's old camps built and added on for ten years between 1905 and 1915. Courtesy Jack Martin.

Mountain areas. In the 1930s, '40s and '50s, Pete Raish had his own mill on a small lake across from the Tourist Park on what is now Sugar Loaf Avenue and County Road 550. The lake became filled with sawdust. It is the present site of the D. J. Jacobetti Skill Center, a unit of Northern Michigan University.

Mr. Kaufman eventually purchased the Birch property and all of the cut–over lands that were available. He gave some of the larger buildings at Birch to Cement Gust Anderson to tear down. Gust took them down but most of the lumber was no good. It was hemlock and splintered badly.

Of the many other residents of Birch, the Linblads, Riopelles, Crains, Robertses, Stevenses, Farrells, MacFaddens, Daileys, Elmers and Gauthiers moved to Big Bay. The Fritzes, Galinas, Gillespies and Pages went to Marquette. The Hudsons, Heslips, McKenzies, Crotherses and Kriegs stayed in the area and even today some of these are found between Marquette and Big Bay.

Frank Krieg lived in Birch longer than anyone else. He lived there from 1897 up to 1935, and then lived on the Big Bay road for the rest of his life. His daughter, Laura, also remained in Birch. She married George Ecket, who tended bar in Big Bay. During the flu epidemic of 1919 they all came down with it. The Town Hall, across from the Catholic Church in Big Bay, was turned into a hospital and was full of flu victims. Ecket died there. Laura later married Bill Lockhart, who worked for L. G. Kaufman, but they still lived in Birch. It was 1929 before the Lockharts moved to Marquette and Bill went to work at the college.

Louis Kaufman Becomes a Celebrity

It was during the period of the closing up of Birch that the Kaufmans became quite active in the area. Actually the last family to live in Birch was the Loy Ellis family, which lived in the depot until 1953. When they moved out, the building was torn down. It was the last building in Birch to go.

Louis G. Kaufman had purchased the Payne Camp on Lake Superior in 1905 and made several other buildings over the next ten years. He was a familiar sight in and around Birch in its heyday, especially in the summer and fall. He picked up his mail at Krieg's Store and bought groceries there. Then, around 1915, Louis Kaufman's older brother Sam bought 1,100 acres of land from Judge Crary at Sauks Head Lake, including the Judge's whole farm and the lake outlet. Sam built a beautiful lodge there with logs that were shipped

Top: Louis J. Kaufman with six of his children. Courtesy First National Bank of Marquette.
Middle: The Crary Farm, Sauxhead Lake (1905).
Bottom: The Sam Kaufman Lodge 1917.

into Birch by train. The area's camping community had never seen such a fine camp; most people called it a lodge.

There is an age–old tradition of camping in the U.P. going back to the time of the voyageurs, but the permanent camp idea did not start until the 1890s. Today, everyone steeped in the traditions of the Upper Peninsula just has to have a camp of his own back in the woods somewhere, or at least one of a friend that he can go to. Some U.P. camps later become homes if their locations make this possible, and some are in the fourth, fifth and even sixth generation. As early as 1892, Nathan Kaufman had built a large one on Silver Lake, four miles south of Onota in Alger County. Landlooker Bill Oliver gives details of the locating and building of it in his diaries. The camp was a few miles southeast of the Shiras III or Peter White Camp at Whitefish Lake. While Nathan's camp was originally a hunting and fishing camp, he eventually turned it into a farm where he kept cows and chickens and where caretakers lived year–round. They produced far more eggs and milk than they could use, and gave most of it away or fed much of the milk to the pigs.

The story was often told that Louis Kaufman's big old rambling camp, with no plumbing and no electricity, was mouse–infested and rotting. Louis' wife was very jealous of the fine new S. R. Kaufman lodge and was determined to have one bigger and better. There is also a story that Louis made some overtures to join Huron Mountain Club and that, getting no encouragement, he purchased six forties of land on a blind slew near the mouth of the Salmon Trout River so that he could at least have access to that stream for fishing. Word got around that Louis had been put off the river several times by Huron Mountain guards. They always claimed he had a big gob of worms on his hook, while club members were restricted to flies only.

Did Louis G. Kaufman have the wherewithal to become a Huron Mountain Club member? Well, yes, he could have supported the club handily if they had let him in.

After becoming president of the First National Bank in Marquette in 1906, he was soon elected president of the Michigan Bankers' Association, an office of great prestige for such a young man. He held this office for two years and was one of the youngest men to hold it at the time. He later became active in the American Bankers' Association and served for some years on its executive council. Through the speeches and papers he delivered while president of the Michigan Bankers' Association, his genius was soon recognized and he became the talk of the banking world. His services were sought after by an old and well–established New York bank, the Chatham National. While he was interested, Louis did not wish to give up the presidency of his own First National Bank in Marquette. However, by special permission of the Comptroller of the Currency, he was able to accept the new post in addition to the old one, presumably the first in the country to be president of two banks in different states at the same time.

Louis Kaufman was 38 years old when he was elected president of the Chatham National Bank in 1910, succeeding George M. Hard who was retiring. The gentleman who had sponsored his appointment was Judge Elbert H. Gary, chairman of the board of the U. S. Steel Corporation and a major stockholder in the Phoenix National Bank in New York. Gary had been much impressed, as were many others, when he heard Mr. Kaufman address the Michigan Bankers' Association.

In 1911, Louis engineered the merger of two old and respected banks, the Chatham National and the Phoenix National, making the new Chatham and Phoenix National one of the largest banks in New York City, with combined resources of 20 million dollars. Over the years, the large bank then swallowed up over a half dozen more small banks in New York: the Century Bank, Jefferson Bank, Security Bank, People's Bank, and the Union Exchange National Bank, to name a few. The Chatham and Phoenix Bank soon boasted resources of over $200,000,000.

Mr. Kaufman was very proud of his board of directors, which now included, besides Judge Gary, the brother–in–law of then–president Woodrow Wilson. Other prominent directors were John Ringling, August Belmont and Pierre S. Dupont.

In 1914, deposits in Mr. Kaufman's New York bank were approaching $300,000,000, a staggering sum for that day and age. William Crapo Durant, who had put together the huge General Motors Corporation by purchasing many automobile companies in their infancy and had been its president from the very beginning, had just been eased out of the company altogether by the money holders.

In 1913 Durant was in New York desperately trying to stage a comeback. He had tied in with the Chevrolet brothers and planned on building a plant in New York to make the Chevrolet automobile. He knew of Louis Kaufman from Marquette, and Louis Kaufman knew of Willy Durant from Flint.

Durant went to Kaufman for money and sold Louis on the Chevrolet. Louis backed Durant in his Chevrolet venture and got him back into the very competitive automobile business. Through the efforts of Kaufman and Dupont they put up enough money to take over General Motors, reorganize it and reinstate Willy Durant as president in 1918, and the Chevrolet was added to the General Motors line. Louis Kaufman was a member of the Board of Directors of General Motors from 1914, reorganized the company in 1915, and was the chairman of its finance committee from 1916 to 1922. During the period from 1918 to 1926, the Chevrolet was the first automobile to seriously challenge the Model T Ford and within a decade, General Motors was fast becoming the largest industry in America.

Louis Kaufman was also doing what he could for Marquette. He was influential in having the wooden parts for the Buick made in J. B. Deutsch's plant at Big Bay and had a car named the Marquette reintroduced by Buick (General Motors) in 1930. There were two or three other companies that made a car called the Marquette as early as 1904. Buick (Willy Durant) made Marquettes in 1912 also. Kaufman's aim was to eventually have a Chevrolet plant located in Marquette as iron was still being processed here and wooden parts had a good source nearby, but this plan never materialized.

In 1918, an act was passed that allowed national banks to maintain branches or branch banks. It came about due to the fact that Louis Kaufman's huge bank in New York already had branches throughout the city since 1915 when they were maintaining the smaller banks they had purchased. The Louis Kaufman bank was the first to develop branch banking and his competitors often facetiously stated that he had a branch on every corner in the city.

Louis Kaufman did not stop there in his active development of the American banking system. Under his leadership, in 1925 the Chatham and Phoenix Bank consolidated with the Metropolitan Trust Company and Louis incorporated the trust system into banking. The Chatham and Phoenix Bank was the first in the world to have "and Trust Co." added to its name, and Louis' First National in Marquette was the second. The incorporation of the trust system into banking has spread worldwide. The president of the Metropolitan Trust Co. at the time of the merger was General Samuel McRoberts. He had formerly been the treasurer of Armour and Company, the meat packers in Chicago, and was well acquainted with Louis Kaufman's father–in–law Otto Young and Louis' older brother Nathan, who had become a part of Chicago life after building the famous Congress Hotel there.

Louis G. Kaufman also became a director of the Chicago and Erie Railroad and had his own private railroad car. His personal fortune was estimated at $150,000,000 during World War I, but all this was not enough to get him into Huron Mountain Club. They had rules and standards and if there were no memberships open, no one could get in. Henry Ford had to wait for years to join.

So Louis Kaufman started to buy up land adjacent to his own at Sauks Head Island Point. He bought the Thoney place at Thoney Point and the quarry property to the south along the shore and the town of Birch – that is,

WILLIAM CRAPO DURANT.

for Economical Transportation

This boxy 1925 Chevy mounted the first serious challenge to Ford's Model T

Top: William Crapo Durant.
Bottom: The 1925 Chevrolet.

Top: Louis Kaufman and Tin Can Sullivan at the Lido Club on First Bass Lake – Courtesy Marquette County Historical Society
Bottom: Building the foundations for Granot Loma c.1919. Rydholm collection

what was left of it – and all the land in between. After the death of his brother S. R. Kaufman in Chicago in 1922, he took over the Crary land at Sauks Head Lake and the lands to the northwest three miles up along the Lake Superior shore and lands west to, and including, the Bass Lakes. But in purchasing all the lands adjacent to the old Payne camp property in three directions away from the lake, there were still 160 acres surrounded by Kaufman lands that Mr. Kaufman could not purchase. It was the old Blemhuber Farm, run down, rocky and overgrown with brush, but Bob Blemhuber refused to sell out to the Kaufmans.

The houses at Birch were slowly dismantled over the years. Some were moved to Big Bay, Lake Independence and Marquette. Others were torn down for lumber, or burned. Two or three were left standing and slowly rotted into the ground.

The Kaufmans started a place called the "Lido Club" up on the First Bass Lake. The name was a parody on the fancy club that Mr. Kaufman knew in New York and Paris by that name. The Bass Lake Lido Club was just a backwoods hunting camp, a log cabin in the back country to hunt out of. For all the splendor of city life and the hubbub of his own camp on Lake Superior, Louis loved a backwoods camp; he loved to fish for brook trout and hunt partridge. He stayed at the Lido Club occasionally in the fall to satisfy this longing. To keep things in shape and in readiness for him, he hired a fellow known as "Tin Can" Sullivan to be his caretaker there. Tin Can lived at the Lido Club for a few years and became a good friend of Louis Kaufman.

Granot Loma

When the Great War was over in 1918, Louis had his old camp torn down. Some said it was to outdo Huron Mountain Club, but Louis said it was to demonstrate to his brother Sam what a real camp should be like. It was about this time that Nathan died in Chicago and Sam went there to take over the running of the Congress Hotel.

Mr. Kaufman hired the famous architect, Marshall Fox, to draw up plans for a palatial summer home. Before Mrs. Kaufman was through planning, 21 other architects had been involved. They cleverly chose a name for it by using the first two letters of their childrens' names, the children known as the "million dollar babies." "GR" came from Graveraet Young Kaufman, born in 1901, "AN" came from Ann Elizabeth, born in 1902, and "OT" from Otto Young, born 1904, making the word "Granot." Then "LO" came from Louis Graveraet, born in 1906 and "MA" from Marie Joan, born in 1907, making the word "Loma." There were three other children born later. Granot Loma proved to be a very distinctive name for a very distinctive place.

Granot Loma Lodge was started in 1919 and held a grand opening in 1927. There were nearly 300 workers involved in the construction and a number of contractors. Cement Gust Anderson did the concrete work, Hilmer Levine did the plumbing, and Rudy Walin got a good start for Walin's Electric by doing the wiring. If a contractor couldn't do what Mrs. Kaufman wanted, he was let go and a new one was hired.

When construction was under way, digging a foundation down into solid sandstone on the point, Michigan passed Prohibition and the Kaufmans made provisions for two liquor storage vaults, solid cement with steel vault doors, modestly referred to as the "wine cellar," one his and one hers.

To stock them, Mr. Kaufman bought out an entire liquor store in New York and had its contents shipped to Granot Loma before the deadline when liquor could no longer be legally transported. The foundations for the building went down into the rock four feet, and were made of cement and steel seven feet thick and faced with another foot or more of washed stone from Lake Superior. On this tremendous foundation was constructed a steel "I" beam frame with cement and steel floors and ceilings. Over the cement and steel frame were laid tightly fitted logs. The building had a basement room with a machine shop, heating system, baths, saunas and massage rooms and a place for a dozen or more boats to be stored. There is a track leading down into a miniature manmade harbor enclosed by two cement breakwalls.

The main floor consists of a large kitchen and a spacious dining room overlooking the lake at one end, then ascending a few steps. This leads to the main sitting room – 80 feet long, 40 feet wide, and 36 feet high. From the center of the ceiling hangs an enormous peeled white pine root, each branch of which has been painstakingly hollowed out for wires so that it can serve as a northwoods chandelier. With study, numerous carvings can be seen among the maze of roots. There are a moose, a snake, a coyote, a grasshopper and many other carvings in it. On the lakeside of this room there are huge windows presenting the view of the island which used to be known as Saux Head Island or Garlic Island. The Kaufmans renamed this "Daisy Island" after Mrs. Kaufman, who was called Daisy, and a granddaughter, also Daisy, who was born to Joan Kaufman in the lodge.

Opposite the windows is a tremendous stone fireplace built by Ernie Riopelle and his crew. It is 24 feet wide, with the stonework covering that wall to the ceiling. Beside the hearth, which can hold six–foot logs, is a stone fireplace seat and room on the opposite end for wood storage. The mantle is

Top: Facing the foundations with Lake Superior stones. Rydholm collection.
Bottom: Starting up with the log work. Granot Loma. Rydholm collection.

made from the keel of the steamer INDEPENDENCE, salvaged from the explosion of 1853 at the Soo.

Continuing west through the living room, or great hall as it is called, there is a stairway going up to a balcony and a few steps descending into another large but low–ceilinged room with two or three pianos, including a nine–foot grand selected for the lodge by George Gershwin himself. This room also contains a pool table and a very valuable mineral and natural crystal collection. The combination of the great hall, the dining room and game room is an open area 170 feet long. From the game room there is a hall leading south to a unique room of Indian decor known as the "Teepee Room." The paintings, artifacts and design are Indian, but the center of attention is the teepee fireplace, certainly one of a kind.

Above the Teepee Room is the master bedroom, with a beautiful view of Daisy Island through a window over a fireplace. Smoke from the fireplace is cleverly routed through the sides of the window. Attached to the bedroom is a birch–log lined bath and dressing room, also with a fireplace. A hallway passes down a large two–story wing of bedrooms, each with its own distinct style and lined with rustic native woods, each with its own hidden source of central heat and each with its own fireplace. There are said to be about 40 or 50 fireplaces on the property, and over 30 in the big lodge.

There is artwork throughout the building in the form of root furniture, hand–carved chairs, tables and bannisters, and oil paintings on log ends and in half–hidden places. There were artists in residence who did paintings and carvings. One of these was Orie Kelly who, years later, received an Oscar as a Hollywood producer. Even dishes were handpainted, as were the walls in some of the bedrooms. The children's room wall was painted by some of the Kaufman children.

The huge kitchen, with some of the very early custom–made stainless steel sinks, was staffed by 20 to 25 working people, cooks, waitresses, dishwashers, and others, many of whom were housed in the upstairs rooms above the kitchen wing, but nearby were servants' quarters which could house 28 more people. An eight–car garage was filled to capacity, including a 1914 Rolls Royce limousine. Old Mr. Bingham, patriarch of the Bingham boat–building family, was the chauffeur/mechanic. Mrs. Kaufman had her own private garden just south of the lodge, and two full–time gardeners.

Just back in the woods, some of the Kaufman children had ornate log cabins, camps of their own. These were private places with ornate log work, running water, fireplaces and basements. Beyond Thoney Point to the south, Mr. Kaufman's private physician lived with his family in the old Thoney

Top: The great hall with 24 foot fireplace opening – Granot Loma. Photo by Tom Buchkoe.
Bottom: Granot Loma Lodge from the air. Jack Deo collection.

sandstone house, and still further south at Buckroe, Joan Kaufman built a white painted dreamhouse.

As Louis Kaufman got older, and the fishing wasn't as good as he remembered it, he had the old Birch millpond fenced off with eight–foot–high cyclone fence with three strings of barbed wire at the top to keep poachers out. A sign is never enough, as poachers are always ready, like flies at a screen, to get into every nook and cranny where there may be a trout left. But this was to be Louis' private pond, and he figured that if he were to put a lot of beaver in it, they would build a huge beaver dam there and enlarge the pond to a sizable lake. So that the beavers wouldn't dig under the fence to escape his 40–acre enclosure, the fence had to extend six feet underground. This would make a magnificent beaver dam, and Louis had always had good luck fishing beaver dams. He bought live beaver from anyone in the area who would take the time to live–trap the animals and bring them to him to be released in the pond. He bought a tremendous number of live beaver but did not seem to realize that many of them were trapped in his own pond and sold to him over and over again.

Toby Pascoe, from an old Negaunee family, had been a coal miner in Kentucky. He came to Marquette as a young man after World War I and went to work for Mr. Kaufman at Granot Loma. One of Toby's jobs was to row Mrs. Kaufman around in Lake Superior near where the lodge was under construction to find large, pretty stones to face the fireplace with. A dredging firm had procured most of the stone from the lake bottom, but the outer stones and keystones were all to be selected by Mrs. Kaufman. When she would see one she wanted, Toby and his partner would dive to it or hook it with a rope sling and get it to shore.

One day Mrs. Kaufman spotted a beauty in about 30 feet of water. The men told her they couldn't get down to it, but that with luck they might be able to hook it. After many tries they took Mrs. Kaufman ashore and returned to the stone to work on it. They soon discovered it to be an impossible task, and decided to give up on that particular stone. When Mrs. Kaufman found out that they had not retrieved the stone, she told them to go out the next day and work on it.

By noon the following day the men had become very discouraged. When they came ashore Mrs. Kaufman told them to go back and keep trying. Toby's partner became very disgruntled. He wanted to quit his job and go down the road. However, he got quite a lecture from Mrs. Kaufman. She insisted that this stone was very special and just the right shape. It was to be the keystone in one of the big fireplaces.

At the end of the third day, the men were coming ashore in the late afternoon. They had done little that day but row around in the boat and complain to each other. Toby was standing on a large rock at the water's edge, pulling the boat up. They had given up any hope of getting the rock Mrs. Kaufman was insisting on. She appeared over the top of the bank and shouted down to them, "Did you get the rock?"

"Yes, Mrs. Kaufman, it's right here," answered Toby without the slightest hesitation.

"I knew you'd find a way if you kept at it long enough," said Mrs. Kaufman, and Toby always claimed that the rock he was standing on, which had been on the beach all along, is the keystone in the center of one of the fireplaces.

The Mausoleum

About the same time that Louis Kaufman decided to tear down his old Camp and build Granot Loma, he also decided to build a beautiful mausoleum for the family in Marquette's Park Cemetery. The setting near one of the small lagoons is absolutely beautiful. It lent itself well to a building of a very formal nature.

Possibly the idea of building the mausoleum was brought about by Nathan Kaufman's death in Chicago in 1918. Much interest was aroused in the community when it was learned that Nathan had left all his assets to the Kaufman side of the family and none to the Breitung side. Nathan's wife, the former Mrs. Edward Breitung, Sr., encouraged by her long–time friend and housekeeper Miss Nellie Merritt, went to court to break the will. So many things of a derogatory nature about Nathan were brought out in the trial that Mrs. Kaufman decided to divorce him posthumously. The most shocking revelation was the rumor that Nathan had been keeping a mistress on the tenth floor of his hotel. Mrs. Kaufman divorced Nathan posthumously and had her name changed back to Mary Breitung. Much animosity developed between the Breitung and Kaufman sides of the family at that time.

And so in 1918 Louis Kaufman had the beautiful Kaufman Mausoleum constructed. It is a scaled–down replica of the Parthenon in Greece. Its cost was said to have been around three million dollars, but folklore has brought it as high as five million dollars over the years.

One story about the tomb's construction was that the roof is made of just two huge marble slabs, shipped from Italy. When they arrived in Marquette, one of them had a bad scratch on it, and it was returned to Italy

Upper left: Miss Helen (Nellie) Merritt friend and companion to Mrs. Breitung Kaufman.
Upper right: The Grand Wedding – Mr. and Mrs. George Drexel Biddle at Granot Loma.
Courtesy First National Bank.
Bottom: The Kaufman's Mausoleum, Park Cemetery, Marquette. Jack Deo collection.

Anthony Drexel Biddle, Joan Kaufman and George Anthony Drexel Biddle. Courtesy First National Bank.

for a replacement. The immense slabs of marble were brought up Lincoln Avenue Hill on rollers by many horses, according to one workman on the job. He said it was "like building the pyramids of Egypt."

One window in the tomb was made of colored leaded glass by Tiffany. It depicted the same scene that would have been seen through a clear glass window in the same place: grass, blue sky and white birches. Some time around 1980 the window was stolen from the Mausoleum during the night, apparently by professionals.

Sam Kaufman, Sr. had died in 1900 and was buried in the Kaufman plot near the mausoleum. His body was not moved into it. But on October 25, 1919, both Juliet Graveraet Kaufman, Louis' mother, and Nathan Myron Kaufman, Louis' brother, were interred in the new mausoleum, as were other brothers and children of Louis in years to come.

More U. P. Connections

As president of the huge Chatham and Phoenix National Bank in New York, Louis G. Kaufman was put in touch with the great bankers of the east and midwest. The name of one of the great banking families of Philadelphia struck a familiar note for him; it was that of the famous Philadelphia Biddles.

Louis Kaufman's ancestors on his mother's side had lived on Mackinac Island at the same time that Edward Biddle, a cousin of the banking family, had lived there. Both Louis' grandfather Graveraet and Edward Biddle had Indian wives. Edward Biddle had bought a house on Market Street just a few doors down from the Northwest Fur Company in 1782. He had become a fur trader and a leading citizen on Mackinac Island. The Biddles and the Graveraets were well acquainted there.

When Louis Kaufman and the Philadelphia Biddles finally got together in eastern banking circles, they found that they had much in common, as they both had ancestors of almost identical backgrounds. Anthony Drexel Biddle had a famous name in banking, but his son George had come onto hard times. Louis Kaufman had the wealth and the know-how but for some reason his name in banking had not quite reached the pinnacle of fame that the Biddle name held. Many felt that fate had brought these two families together, one on the way up and the other on the way down. Eventually, George Anthony Drexel Biddle with the name and Joan Kaufman with the money, were married. It was a grand wedding, held at Granot Loma.

The couple lived at Granot Loma in the summer and at the Kaufman home in Marquette, known as the Horatio Seymour house. It was during this time that the George Biddles built the storybook white cottage at Buckroe on Lake Superior, just a half–mile or so south of the Granot Loma property. People who knew the couple well said it was not a good marriage. There are claims that Joan was often mean to George and belittled him in public, but he was always a gentleman. The Kimballs of Marquette were hired as caretakers at the Buckroe Cottage.

Joan and George Biddle had children, one of whom was born at Granot Loma. The marriage, however, ended in a divorce.

At Granot Loma, things continued on an even grander scale. Great parties were held, with guests from Chicago, Philadelphia and New York. Hundreds of guests at a time arrived by train, and whole troupes of entertainers from New York, some of the biggest names in the entertainment world of the day, performed in the great hall. Madam Alma Gluck and Irene Castle were among them. The polo field and two teams of polo ponies were available to provide daytime amusement, and many of that game's best were on hand to excite the guests. George Gershwin became close friends with the Kaufmans and played the fine piano he had selected. Bill Tilden, the great tennis champion, came for extended stays at Granot Loma. He designed the tennis courts there and gave lessons to the children. Opera stars sang from the balcony and orchestras were on hand for dancing, both indoors and outdoors. Private trains brought the guests to the private railroad station.

Meanwhile, at Bay Cliff

In the meantime, up at Bay Cliff in the 1920's J. B. Deutsch had expanded his beautiful home into a large dairy farm. He called it Bay Cliff Farm. While he had the usual farm animals, the mainstay of the farm was a fine herd of Jersey cattle which had been imported from England with their herd master, Blake Arcoll. To increase the herd, Mr. Deutsch had also purchased a fine bull from Marshall Field III for $10,000. This bull subsequently produced some record butterfat–producing cows.

These were good years for Big Bay and for J. B. Deutsch. He had men and women from Big Bay work at his farm as laborers and servants. He also had purchased a French "Minerva" automobile with an open chauffeur's seat and a closed passenger cab, speaking tube and all. It was the greatest elegance possible in an automobile, complete with two Japanese uniformed chauffeurs whose quarters were above the garage where the Minerva was kept, just back of the main house. There were gardeners, the private railroad spur at the bottom of the bluff, which used to go to the dock, and the finest of everything.

The last big contract the Lake Independence Lumber Company had was in 1924. This was for floorboards and other wooden parts for Buick, a part of General Motors. It was an arrangement helped out by Louis Kaufman.

In 1926, what was known as the mill's "body plant" burned to the ground. One thing led to another, and the Lake Independence Lumber Company was forced into bankruptcy. Mr. William Boniface of Escanaba was appointed the bankruptcy referee.

J. B. Deutsch went to Louis Kaufman in Marquette and borrowed as much money as he was allowed, putting up his fine herd of cattle for collateral. With the money he reopened the Big Bay Mill as the J. B. Deutsch Lumber Company.

Louis Kaufman could see the writing on the wall. Mr. Deutsch was not going to be able to make a go of it, and Kaufman had lent him more money than he should have, considering the market price of the herd. As fine as they were, they could not pay their way. Mr. Kaufman came to the conclusion that he was going to end up with a herd of Jersey cattle and no place to put them.

Louis Kaufman was still building. He had hired the Bartlett Construction Company out of Eau Claire, Wisconsin to build a new First National Bank building to replace the old sandstone structure on the corner of Front and Spring Streets. The new location was on the southwest corner of Front and Washington. Since Washington Street had now become the undisputed business district of the city, the town was pushing north. This would make three bank buildings on that corner. This new bank would not only be the finest bank in town, it would be the finest building in all of Michigan. In fact, it was considered the most expensive building in the nation on a per–square–foot basis up to that time. He also built a fine store building next door on Washington Street, which he could rent out and ensure the bank a good neighbor of its choosing. Now, over a half–century later, both buildings are still in use, the building next door to the bank still occupied by its first tenant, the J. C. Penney Co. Louis purchased the land from the Frei Family and donated the site for the bank. It was formally opened on October 15, 1927.

It was while these buildings were being constructed that Louis Kaufman found himself in desperate need of a farm to house the Bay Cliff herd of Jersey cattle. The Bartlett people were sent up to Granot Loma to build a farm. This was the time when the Kaufmans needed the Blemhuber property so badly but could not obtain it. They couldn't wait but decided to build on the hill above it. The Bartlett people were told that for every day they could make up to finish the job ahead of schedule, they would be paid a sizable bonus.

The work started in April. The digging of the foundations was all pick–and–shovel work in the rocky soil. Many workers had to quit the job and move on, but the Loma Farm buildings were completed on time in about six months, and the bonus was paid.

At least one of the workmen who arrived in Marquette to work on that job became a successful contractor in his own right. He was Franz Menze. He has made an enviable record and built some of the city's finest modern buildings over the past 60 years.

No one had ever seen anything like Loma Farm. There had been some fine farms in the area, starting with Nathan's at Onota with its big three–story house and giant fireplace, then Mr. Longyear's farm at Ives Lake with its beautiful setting and fine cattle, and finally Bay Cliff Farm, connected with the J. B. Deutsch mansion at Big Bay.

Louis Kaufman had to go some to put up a better place than these, but with the advantage of modern techniques, the barns were constructed of cement and brick, with insulated shingle roofs. The insides of the buildings were plastered and some of the buildings were built of glazed tile; the cow barn was lined in white glazed tile. In fact, the cow barn was the showpiece of them all; all the floors of the stalls were cork, even in the holding pens for the bulls, and the building was capped off with a huge clock that could be seen and heard from nearly anywhere on the farm. There was also a fine horse barn, a piggery with indoor and outdoor pens, and quarters for a full–time veterinarian on the premises. There was also a slaughterhouse, a creamery for processing milk, a boarding and rooming house for the men, and housing for ducks, goats, sheep and about 1,200 chickens. The herd of Jersey cattle from Bay Cliff Farms was moved down to Loma Farm and Blake Arcoll, the herd master from England, went with it.

Loma Farm sat in a picturesque setting, high on the side of a hill on the opposite side of which was Granot Loma Lodge, out of sight from the farm. For 50 years it could easily be seen from the Big Bay road, miles to the west, but in recent years the forests in the area have grown to such an extent that the buildings are no longer discernible from the Big Bay road. Beneath the farm were great fields that were hurriedly cleared and expanded over the next several years.

Peter Raish cut the timber, and then there was the awesome job of pulling stumps. They used every method known at the time to get the job done, eventually a huge stump–puller.

Top: A sketch of the Bay Cliff Farm. 1920's. Courtesy John Vargo.
Bottom: Loma Farm – cow barn and creamery. c. 1920's. Courtesy George Johnson.

They tell the story of how a fire broke out when the men were clearing the fields. The state was paying about 25 or 30 cents an hour for firefighters at the time, and their progress left a lot to be desired as far as Mrs. Kaufman was concerned.

She offered a dollar an hour to get those fires out. Well, fires started popping up all over the property and crews were coming from all over when a conservation officer had to explain to Mrs. Kaufman why the fires were not getting put out when she was paying these high wages.

There was only one flaw in the setting: the Blemhubers' 160–acre farm that occupied a key spot just beneath Loma Farm on the side of the hill that was constantly in the way. The Kaufmans always had to work around this land. They had purchased all the land around – 9,000 acres, but they could not purchase the Blemhuber land.

Who Were the Blemhubers?

The Blemhubers were highly successful farmers who had emigrated from Europe. Henry Blemhuber came to Marquette from Germany in 1860 and married Miss Catherine Schmidt, also from Germany, that year. They had four children, one of whom was Robert Blemhuber, also a farmer, the one son who followed in his father's footsteps.

In 1866, Henry bought 15 acres of timberland in Chocolay Township to cut cordwood for the Marquette, Houghton and Ontonagon Railroad as fuel. He built a house on the land and started farming. Henry subsequently purchased surrounding land until the farm was 400 acres. Due to hard work by Henry and his son Robert, the Blemhuber farm met with phenomenal success.

Henry took his son in as a business partner in 1883 and they farmed together. They raised apples, apricots, peaches, pears, plums, grapes, mulberries, blackberries, raspberries, strawberries and cherries. No other farmers in the area could even approach their production figures. In one season they produced 1,000 bushels of apples and 1,000 bushels of strawberries, besides other immense crops of vegetables that supplied the markets of central Upper Michigan. Potatoes produced enormous yields. In 1904, 660 bushels were produced on just five acres of land, and in 1912, 2,800 bushels were grown on seven and a half acres.

But Blemhuber drew some startling conclusions about farming in the U. P. which are difficult for us to believe today as farming in this area of rock, poor soil and short summers is often considered a bad risk. He claimed he had

Upper left and right: Henry Blemhuber and Katherine Schmidt. Courtesy of Werner Weiland family (descendents).
Bottom: Bob Blemhuber – late 1940's. Courtesy Werner Weiland family.

traveled extensively in many portions of the country and became convinced that no part of the United States is better suited to growing as many different varieties of fruits and berries as in Marquette County and other parts of Upper Michigan. Mr. Blemhuber backed up his conclusions with amazing evidence. At a land show in Chicago in 1911, one of his exhibits was a peach, grown in Marquette, which was ten and one half inches in circumference.

While Bob Blemhuber had a green thumb the likes of which may never be seen in this area again, he found it easier to make money by buying and selling land. He bought land at tax sales and from people who needed money badly. He owned a lot of land near Sauks Head Lake and around Blemhuber Lake in the Granot Loma area. He bought 40 acres in Marquette City and subdivided it, and bought and sold many single lots and houses beyond that. There were two streets in Marquette named for him. Actually, one was a street and one was an avenue. To avoid confusion, one of them was changed to Tierney Street by the city commission in 1970. Mr. Blemhuber owned a lot of land east of the city in Chocolay township as well, much of it along the Chocolay River.

This was the Bob Blemhuber who owned what he called the North Farm, which was surrounded by Kaufman lands.

Clyde Steele tells a story that gives us a little insight into the kind of man Bob Blemhuber was. Bob had given up farming by 1929 and was maintaining a little feed and seed store on Third Street, next to his home on the corner of Ridge and Third. He was doing well buying and selling land, but that line of business didn't take up much of his time and Bob was a hard–working man. It wasn't beneath him to go out on small labor jobs if he could make a few dollars, although he was rich enough to buy and sell most of the people he worked for on these jobs.

They rode up to Saux Head Lake, late one fall, on the back of an open stake–bodied truck. There were about five workmen in the crew, none of whom knew each other very well. Bob was in the group, probably looking a little seedier than the others, with his lunchpail full of sauerkraut as usual, going to do a day's work on a short labor job along with the others.

At lunch time the men were warming themselves around a fire in a steel barrel and the conversation got around to the Kaufmans, whose land was nearby, and besides, they were a favorite subject of conversation around Marquette. One of the men told the story of this stubborn old German fellow who owned a piece of land surrounded by Kaufman land. Mrs. Kaufman approached him to buy him out. She asked him how much he would take for the land, which at that time had a few rotting buildings and was growing up in brush and trees.

"Thirty thousand," was the quick reply.

"That's ridiculous," said Mrs. Kaufman, "It isn't worth ten," and it wasn't at the market price at the time.

Mrs. Kaufman left, but returned a few days later with a check for $30,000. "I'm sorry," said the old German, "The price has gone up to $40,000."

Mrs. Kaufman was furious. She argued for some time before she finally left. A week or so later she returned with a check for $40,000.

"The price has gone to $50,000," said the farmer, and refused the check.

"Well," said the storyteller, "Mrs. Kaufman couldn't believe her ears, and this went on for several months and that guy raised the price $10,000 every time she came with the money. She finally came to him with a check for $90,000 for that little piece of no–good land, and do you know, that dumb S. O. B. said it wasn't for sale...not at any price, and he turned her down flat."

At that, old Bob, who had been listening intently to the story with a twinkle of anticipation in his eye, chimed in with great enthusiasm,"and do you know who that dumb S. O. B. was? Me!"

Bob Blemhuber never did sell the land to the Kaufmans. It became a part of the Loma Farm tract long after Mr. and Mrs. Kaufman and Bob Blemhuber were dead. Dana Varvil, who had worked at Loma Farm, eventually bought it from Ray Anderson, who was a son of Bob Blemhuber's sister. Through a trade agreement with Jack Martin, who was married to a Kaufman daughter, the 160 acres finally became a part of the Loma Farm.

The Fate of Bay Cliff Farm

With the loss of the dairy herd as well as the herd master, J. B. Deutsch moved out of Bay Cliff Farm in 1927. He turned the place over to his sister Edna Corsant and her husband, Dr. Charles Corsant, a dentist. The Corsants moved into the big house and decided to run the farm again, but not as a dairy farm. They had several other ideas. They experimented with a breeding program of chickens, dogs, rabbits and goats. They changed the name of the place from Bay Cliff Farm to "Chedna Farm," taking the idea from Granot Loma and using the combination of Dr. and Mrs. Corsant's first names, Charles and Edna. Pewter sugar and cream pitchers are still in collections around Marquette with "Chedna Farm" engraved on them.

Top: "Mink" Milton Tompkins Fox Farm just north of Big Bay.
Middle: Big Bay Hotel, Company store and theater (1923)
Bottom: The old Theater in Big Bay. Courtesy Milton Tompkins

The Corsants were only at the farm five or six years, as their breeding projects were not at all successful. Dr. Corsant wanted to breed horses and donkeys to get mules. The donkeys were hard to handle and were left to wander. They were liable to show up anywhere in the Big Bay area. Edward Fish was a son–in–law who raised chickens, but he too had trouble. It seems there was something lacking in their feed, and the chicks reverted to cannibalism.

Joe Melville was a bartender from Canada who married Evangeline Berry from Marquette. She had formerly worked at the Hotel Marquette. This couple worked at Chedna Farms, Joe taking care of the rabbits and Evangeline working in the big house as a housemaid for the Corsants.

Milton "Mink" Tompkins lived on the old Smith place up the Club road from Bay Cliff. He had a fox farm and later a mink farm there. Mink was the projectionist at the theater in Big Bay. He said they couldn't start the movies until Mr. and Mrs. Deutsch and the gang had arrived from the farm. Mink described Mr. Deutsch as a handsome man and Mrs. Corsant as having so much makeup on that her face that it looked like it was made of china.

When Chedna Farm was operating and the donkeys were running loose all over the place, Mink slid into one on the slippery, snow–covered road when he was traveling to Big Bay in his 1931 Chevy coupe. The door handle hit the rear quarter of the donkey, leaving a deep wound. There were some caustic words over the incident, but finally Tompkins was given the donkey for fox food.

The Corsants' stay at Bay Cliff extended into the days of the Great Depression, and it was inevitable that Bay Cliff, or Chedna Farm as it was then known, would have to be sold. It was put up for sale while people lived on in the big house.

J. B. Deutsch had moved to Detroit where he lived on Chicago Boulevard. He died there some years later. When the Corsants finally left Bay Cliff about 1934, they went back to Chicago.

Louis Kaufman in New York

Mr. Kaufman's bank building in Marquette turned out to be one of the most beautiful and impressive buildings in the city. It still stands with its classic design and rich interior. The outside is beautiful, almost–white Kentucky limestone, while the inside is polished Italian lava. The huge brass doors are hand–chased into intricate classical designs. This building, in its

501

Top: First National Bank Building. Courtesy Ellwood Mattson
Middle: New York Governor Al Smith.
Bottom: Interior First National Bank. Courtesy Ellwood Mattson.

prominent location, is more of a tribute to Louis G. Kaufman than is his mausoleum in Park Cemetery.

On June 19, 1929 the Board approved the lease of the Nathan M. Kaufman coin collection to be housed in a prominent spot in the new building. Several banks and museums had asked if they might display it, but Louis G. had acquired his brother's collection and gave the First National the first refusal on it.

It was while the First National Bank building was being built in downtown Marquette that another famous visitor arrived at Granot Loma. He was Al Smith, the governor of New York and Democratic candidate for president of the United States. He arrived with an entourage of businessmen and architects, and a request for help from Louis Kaufman. Governor Smith unrolled a huge set of plans on the big slab table in front of the fireplace at the lodge. It was the plan of what, for the next half century, would be the tallest building in the world. It was to be called the Empire State Building.

Al Smith asked Louis Kaufman if he wanted to be one of a committee of four New York financial leaders who would take the responsibility of financing the 102–story building to be built in New York City, right in midtown Manhattan, ironically on land that had already felt the influence of the Lake Superior region on two occasions. It was to be placed on the site originally graced by the home of Mrs. Astor, whose wealth had come from the fur trade.

William Backhouse Astor who had lived on Mackinac Island was the one who had outfitted his wife, Caroline, in a necklace of 44 remarkable and large diamonds with another 282 marginally smaller ones and Marie Antoinettes diamond stomacher – all worn over an encrustation of gold along with other jewelry, which helped to distinguish her as "the" Mrs. Astor.

The Waldorf–Astoria hotel was later constructed on that site. It was built of Marquette sandstone from the quarry in south Marquette, and it became the gem of the Astor estate. The old Waldorf–Astoria had recently been dismantled. The home and the site were sold to the Empire State Building committee for $7,560,000. Al Smith assured Mr. Kaufman that if he would be part of that committee and lend his financial prestige and know–how to the project, everything else would fall into place.

Governor Smith was completely taken by Louis Kaufman's summer palace. He left an autographed picture of himself and some documents which are displayed in Granot Loma today. He had finally seen Louis Kaufman's real home. Up to this time, Al Smith thought of Louis Kaufman living year–round in his apartment in the Ritz–Carlton Hotel in New York, which was described as a "plush suite if there ever was one." Nor did he realize that the Kaufmans had built a beautiful home in Palm Beach, Florida, where they subdivided the land and sold lots to many wealthy people from the east. It was here that they were friends with Joe and Rose Kennedy. In fact, their daughter Joan was a flower girl for the Kennedys' wedding. Joan, it was said, also rode her horse for the King and Queen of England as a girl. It was in Florida that Mr. Kaufman had organized the "Breakers" club and had entertained General Douglas MacArthur, General Eisenhower and Admiral Halsey as house guests. Then, of course, Louis still owned his home in Marquette, the Horatio Seymour house with its beautiful, spacious, park–like grounds that he always called home; Granot Loma was still camp. The Florida property was referred to in the family as "Palm Bitch."

Louis Kaufman offered his full cooperation to the project in New York, and they built the Empire State Building. Harvey O'Connor wrote:

> And so the tallest building in the world arose on the old Thompson farm which William Backhouse Astor bought in 1827 for $20,500. That done, finis seemed written on the development of 350 Fifth Avenue: beyond the Empire State Building men's minds could imagine nothing grander, as perhaps in the 1890s could have imagined nothing taller, bigger or more splendid than the Waldorf–Astoria.

In an article entitled: "Cloudbuster" for a 1943 issue of WNYF, the magazine of the New York Fire Department, Peter J. Maker reflected that "when almost everything else was coming apart and tumbling earthward with the stock market – the Empire State, with its gracefully curved mast 1,250 feet in the sky, became a reality."

Patrick Walsh, a New York Fire Commissioner recalled these lines in his annual report. He also recalled the wonder and the paradox of the period from 1929 to early 1931: "While the Western World was slipping deeper and deeper into economic stagnation, the Empire State Building was rising higher than any other structure in the world."

Among the network of big money men, the leader was John Jacob Roskob who had risen to wealth in the Du Pont empire and, through Coleman Du Pont and his cousin Pierre, well knew Louis Kaufman from the days when the same group was reorganizing General Motors. It was these men who prevailed on Al Smith to bring Louis Kaufman into the group. They well knew his financial genius.

It was at the end of August of 1929 that the announcement was made that an organization headed by former Governor Alfred E. Smith would tear down the elegant but fading Waldorf–Astoria Hotel at Fifth Avenue and Thirty–fourth Street and replace it with the world's tallest building. Six weeks later the stock market began its catastrophic plunge.

Many sizable ventures were abandoned, but the Empire State project did not falter.

Graveraet High School

At this same period Louis Kaufman was a financial advisor to President Hoover, for which he received a medal, and a member of the school board in Marquette. The board was about to build a new high school. They had come up with a plan to close the Ely School on Bluff Street and move the seventh and eighth graders from there into the Howard School, which for 25 years had been the high school. Then the high school students would move into the new building. Both of these buildings were sandstone, solidly built and familiar landmarks. The Ely School was made of Portage Entry sandstone from the Jacobsville Quarry, and the Howard was of high–grade Marquette sandstone.

Louis Kaufman, as president of the school board, donated the land for the new school. He personally put up the $25,000 that was needed to purchase the lots, and the dozen or so homes on the property had to be moved. He gave the land in honor of his mother, Juliet Graveraet, and asked that the school be named the Graveraet High School for her.

Sidney Adams had been a real estate broker in Marquette and the vicinity for many years. He built the Adams Hall on the east side of Front Street after the fire of 1868, and added a building to the Main Street corner and sandstone facade to the whole thing about 1887. In 1928 this was purchased by Frank Karobetsus and made into the Adams Hotel. Sidney lived in the big Burt house across from the Episcopal Church on Ridge and Blaker. At the time the new school was being built, Mr. Adams had died, but Mrs. Adams owned the property on the corner of Hewitt and Front where the Sidney Adams Gymnasium stands today. The story is that Mrs. Adams would only sell the property to the school board on the condition that the gymnasium would be named for her husband. So today it is known as the Sidney Adams Gymnasium.

Willard Whitman was the Superintendent of Schools in Marquette at the time of the building of the Graveraet High School. He was a Harvard graduate and had a special interest in dramatics. Great care was taken to have the auditorium's acoustics and lighting perfect. No expense was spared as Mr. Kaufman gave extra money to cover these costs. He also donated a fine grand piano and the finest velvet stage and window curtains, in the school colors of Harvard – crimson lined with white. The Auditorium was named the Louis G. Kaufman Auditorium.

Louis Kaufman then started an endowment fund which provided scholarships and graduation awards, money which was presented to graduates who were deemed outstanding in different fields of study. The fund also provided for a Lyceum of famous artists and lecturers who spoke or performed in the Kaufman Auditorium. There were news columnists, politicians, singers, instrumentalists and ensembles, as well as people like Amelia Earhart. The children of Marquette are today still reaping the benefits of the fund.

Louis Kaufman was the first person in the country to endow a high school, and Graveraet High School was the first public high school in the United States to be endowed. The Graveraet building was also the last piece of architecture in Marquette that Frederick Charlton was a part of. He worked in an advisory capacity along with other architects on the building, which is still in use over a half–century later.

The class of 1927 was supposed to be the first to graduate from the new school. They held the ceremonies at the laying of the cornerstone in the summer of 1926, and their names are in the copper box behind the cornerstone. However, the school was not quite completed in time for the class of '27 and the first graduating class was actually the class of '28. Even though the class of '27 didn't graduate from Graveraet, they were part of a grand party that was given to three classes, 1927, '28 and '29, at Granot Loma lodge as a graduation present from Mr. Kaufman.

It was also in 1927 that a colossal, weekend–long party was held in honor of the grand opening of the lodge. A private train with an eight–piece orchestra of black musicians from Chicago aboard, played during the day. The train made trips day or night, whenever necessary, from Marquette to the Loma Depot and back. From the depot the guests were transported by carriage to the lodge. There were no invitations, but everyone was welcome. Friends invited friends to stay as long as they cared to.

Before the opening of Graveraet High School, a large bronze plaque mounted on a large marble slab arrived from the officers of the Chatham and Phoenix National Bank and Trust Company. It was sent to the Board of Education at the opening of the school. The engraving on the bronze plaque reads as follows:

Louis Graveraet Kaufman

Whereas Our President, Louis Graveraet Kaufman, has generously presented to his home city of Marquette, Michigan, in memory of his mother, a site for Graveraet High School...

And Whereas the city of Marquette recently completed and opened a monumental high school upon the land so presented, and Whereas the Board of Education of the Public Schools of the City of Marquette, by resolution adopted on May 18, 1927 has given to the auditorium of the new high school the name of Louis Graveraet Kaufman Auditorium and Whereas the officers of the Chatham Phoenix National Bank and Trust Company in New York City are desirous of giving some expression of their pleasure in being associated with the man whose energy created the banking system he heads and where ideals permeate and stimulate the organization he leads – Therefore, the official staff of Chatham Phoenix National Bank and Trust Company has caused a bronze and marble tablet to be procured, suitably inscribed and transmitted to the Board of Education of the Public Schools of the City of Marquette, with the compliments of the officers of the bank and be it resolved that the president of the Board of Education be informed that this tablet is sent to the city of Mr. Kaufman's birth from the city where his financial genius has made him a towering figure as a token of admiration of the unfailing skill and the unflagging zeal that have raised him to his enviable position in the financial councils of the nation, and as a pledge of loyalty which bears his name.

...the Officers of the Chatham Phoenix National Bank and Trust Co., New York, N. Y.

The resolution was signed by 62 officers of the bank. Today the huge bank that Mr. Kaufman built in New York City is called the Manufacturers Hanover Trust Company. Its main offices are at 140 East 45th Street in New York.

Even this doesn't fully cover Louis G. Kaufman's exploits in the financial world. Certainly books could be written about him, but they are yet undone. The splitting up of this great wealth caused controversy and family bitterness as time went on. But this was the boy, born and raised in Marquette and educated in its public schools, who rose to such prominence in the financial world, and who the old–time Marquette natives used to like to say, "I knew him when he was the first kid in town to take his shoes off in the spring and the last one to put 'em on in the fall."

Henry Ford in the U. P.

We all know of the phenomenal climb of Henry Ford, from the first car he put together in 1893 to the first one of actual production that he drove through the streets of Detroit in 1903. What many people don't know about is the tremendous amount of time and money he spent in the Upper Peninsula after 1910. It was some time after he had created the assembly line that Henry Ford quietly began to explore the idea of being the owner–producer–handler of all the natural resources that went into making an automobile.

In 1910 he sent timber cruisers into the U. P. seeking the kind of timberlands he was looking for. His first decision was to set up an operation at Manistique because of the year–round open harbor there, but apparently the quality of the hardwood timber was better further to the west. He had purchased land in Manistique in the early days, however.

The story is often told that Mr. Ford made an attempt to join Huron Mountain Club in 1917, the year he ran for Senator from Michigan. Although he was unable to join the club, he had friends and acquaintances who were members, and he continued to be on mutually friendly terms with the organization. He purchased 350,000 acres of timberland near Iron Mountain for just under three million dollars and in 1920 personally came to Escanaba in his steam yacht, the SIALIA, to look over the property.

Ford had a relative in Iron Mountain, Edward G. Kingsford, who owned the first Ford distributorship in the U. P. The business was housed in the Lake Superior Carriage Works Building at 700 Champion Street in Marquette. Mr. Kingsford's wife was a first cousin to Mr. Ford. This dealership was said to be the seventeenth in the country. After two years, Mr. Kingsford moved the business to Iron Mountain, which was his home town. Ford decided to start an operation in the area. South of Iron Mountain, Henry Ford built one of the world's finest sawmills, which by 1921 was shipping lumber to Dearborn to be used in the Model T Ford. Each car required 250 board feet of wood.

In 1923, this establishment became the Village of Kingsford, where Ford built 100 houses for married workers, and bunkhouses and mess halls for single men. The operation employed 2,000 men. That same year, Ford also built a 400–foot wide dam on the Menominee River and a hydroelectric

Upper left: Henry Ford (c.1917) Courtesy of John Wheat. Enjoying the cool waters – From the collections of Henry Ford Museum and Greenfield Village.
Upper right: Ford about 1915.
Bottom: Edison, Ford and Kingsford playing cowboy in the U. P. early 1920s. Jack Deo collection.

plant which provided 25 million kilowatts of electricity for the plant. By 1925 the plant was employing 3,000 men and was producing 100 tons of charcoal briquettes daily. The charcoal briquette was invented by Henry Ford himself, to make use of the powdered charcoal. He thought of adding a binder to the charcoal powder so that it could be pressed into a briquette. By 1925 Kingsford housed 7,500 people, and Ford later had 8,500 employees in the area. Kingsford was incorporated into a city in 1947.

It was about the same period that Kingsford was being developed that Mr. Ford started looking at the possibilities of developing a dam and power facilities on the Mississippi at Minneapolis and St. Paul, as well as making industrial developments in Mexico and Canada. With all this going on, one would think Mr. Ford would have little time to pursue still other interests in the Upper Peninsula. While these Upper Peninsula developments received little attention in the news, the Upper Peninsula had become his playground, and he couldn't seem to get enough of it. He was enjoying great popularity at the time, and was even being considered to run for President of the United States. He could do just about anything he wanted with his bank balance, variously stated at between 150 million and 220 million dollars. It was during this period that Ford spent a lot of time, both summer and winter, traveling all over the U. P., often by train. He became well acquainted with people in the small towns up and down the railroad lines. For two or three summers he took junkets accompanied by his friends Tom Edison and Harvey Firestone, and at least one of these years their wives went along.

Way back in 1880, Edison had experimented with a beneficiation plant at Humbolt, west of Ishpeming, which proved to be unsuccessful. The trouble was, he was about 75 years before his time. With plenty of high–grade iron ore around, there was no real need for such a plant. Since the 1950's, four similar plants have been built on the Marquette Range, and many elsewhere.

In 1920, Henry Ford purchased the Imperial Mine west of Michigamme. This mine had been opened in 1881, but closed down in 1913. In running the mine after 1920, he spent far more money on it than the value of the ore which was removed. In 1926 he bought the Blueberry Mine northwest of Ishpeming. Ford named it the "Blueberry" himself because his son Edsel had had a good time picking blueberries at the site on one of their earlier camping trips. The Blueberry didn't start operating until 1929.

All during the 1920s, Ford and his friends would visit his different properties. His lumber camps around Sidnaw were the finest in existence. They had indoor toilets, running water, electricity, showers...no lumberjack had ever seen such camps. There were even dining and recreation rooms at the camps, and laundry was taken care of each week.

Henry Ford at Huron Mountain

It was also in 1922 that Mr. Ford really began to close in on the Huron Mountains, very possibly in anticipation of eventually joining the club. That year, he bought a sawmill and docking facilities at L'Anse and 300,000 more acres of timberland reaching right up to what is the Huron Mountain Club land today, though when this purchase was made, Ford land and Huron Mountain land didn't touch. He built the Ford Railroad from L'Anse to the Cliff River for logging purposes. The Cliff River flows into Mountain Lake. At the same time he purchased most of Dan Hebard's holdings at Pequaming – the mill, the town, the Hebard 14–room bungalow and the tugs, including the Jay C. Morse, the famous boat that sank on her maiden voyage with Peter White aboard. The powerful little ship was still around. In the same purchase was some Hebard land right in and around the Club itself. Mr. Ford later turned a lot of this land over to Huron Mountain Club.

Dan Hebard sold almost all of his holdings to Henry Ford and retired. That year, he built a beautiful cabin out of white pine on Pine River and vowed to spend his summers at Huron Mountain and go back east for the rest of the year. Through extensive land and timber dealings, Mr. Ford and Mr. Hebard had become close friends and a few years later, in 1926, Dan Hebard became the president of Huron Mountain Club, following Mr. Hamilton. It is only natural that Mr. Ford and his party were regular visitors at Huron Mountain in those years.

This is the time when Henry Ford really fell in love with central Upper Michigan. He couldn't wait to get up to the clean air and enjoy the most beautiful summers in the world. It was a time when the Ford Motor Company was at its greatest relative potential. It was the largest automobile manufacturing organization in the world, and was being run by one man with an iron hand. It had its own coal mines, iron mines, forests and fleet of ships, to say nothing of docking facilities and sawmills. After a short–lived involvement with the Ferguson tractor people of England, Ford perfected an efficient and economical farm tractor which soon drove all competitors from the market. Everyone had heard of Henry Ford. His influence was being felt throughout the developed countries of the world. Between 1923 and 1924, Herbert Perkins, who was then the treasurer of Marquette County, reported

Top: Clara and Henry Ford left on platform. E. G. Kingsford extreme left with foot on platform. At right, Mrs. Edison and Mr. and Mrs. Firestone – Imperial Mine near Michigamme. From the collections of Henry Ford Museum and Greenfield Village.
Middle: Ford lumber camps at Sidnaw. Jack Deo collections.
Bottom: Henry Ford put Ford tractors on the farm like he put Ford cars on the road.

512

Top: The J. C. MORSE – still working over a half century later – now belonged to Henry Ford. Courtesy Mrs. Mary Morris.
Middle: Gust Lintula.
Bottom: Tom Edison and Henry Ford camping near Sidnaw 1923 – from the collections of Henry Ford Museum and Greenfield Village.

an increase of 1,339 automobiles in operation in the county. In 1924, 5,629 licenses were issued in the county, whereas in 1923 only 4,390 plates were sold. Almost half of these cars were Fords. These were the years that Mr. Ford desperately wanted to become a part of Huron Mountain life, but apparently there just were no openings in the club at that time. While this was the apparent reason, many members didn't want Henry Ford in the Club because of his tendencies to take over, change and develop wherever he went.

Largely due to Mr. Ford's flivver, the Model T, automobile touring was coming into vogue in the mid 1920s. So it may be said that Mr. Ford was indirectly responsible for the fact that the state of Michigan, in 1925, announced a plan to extend Highway M–35, which then went north as far as U. S. 41, halfway between Marquette and Negaunee. The plan extended the highway in a northwesterly direction, across the Dead River, over the Panorama Hills, then west past the Elm Creek swamp, along the south side of Burnt Mountain, across the Cedar Creek, the Cliff Stream and out past Cliff Lake to Skanee and L'Anse. The new road didn't really go to any new places, but would have been a more direct route from Marquette to Skanee and would have opened up a lot of back country. There is no doubt that it would have ruined the wilderness aspect of the Huron Mountains. Also, with the prospect of the road came the threat of a resort hotel on the south end of Mountain Lake by Mr. William C. Weber of Detroit, who owned the property there.

The proposed road would only cross a few forties of club property at the upper Salmon Trout River, but would cross a sizable portion of Longyear property. Mr. Longyear had died just a few years earlier (May 28, 1922) and his estate was being handled by his son–in–law, Carroll Paul, who had married Helen Longyear. The Pauls now owned Ives Lake and were spending their summers in the Stone House. They were also members of Huron Mountain Club.

There were many who objected to the road – hunters, campers, hikers, fishermen and some landowners – and there seemed to be no great groundswell of sentiment in favor of it, but it looked as though the die was cast and nothing could be done to stop it. A survey was completed in 1926 and work got under way that year from the south end. By 1927 the road clearing and grading had reached the Salmon Trout River.

Finally, amidst the objections, an Attorney General's opinion was handed down, stating that if two–thirds of the property owners along the right of way objected to it, they should stop the construction of the road. Mr. Ford's property would make up more than the required two–thirds. Possibly by coincidence, that year Henry Ford was granted a membership in Huron

Mountain Club and the highway, in 1928, was swung out to the north, where it connected to the Big Bay road. The few miles of the road going to the Salmon Trout River, complete with guard rails and cement culverts, has been known as "Dead End 35" ever since.

The following year (1929) Mr. Ford built a beautiful white pine hewn log cabin at Huron Mountain. Reports of its building cost ranged from $80,000 to $100,000. Henry and Clara Ford traveled to Europe that year but left the details of the building in the hands of the famous architect from Detroit, Albert Kahn. He had the complete trust of Henry Ford and had designed nearly all of Ford's buildings, both industrial and otherwise. In fact, Albert Kahn became known as one of the world's greatest industrial architects. He designed over one thousand buildings for Mr. Ford, including the Ford plant at Highland Park and the huge River Rouge complex. He was also the designer of the General Motors buildings in Detroit, as well as Angel Hall and several other buildings on the University of Michigan campus at Ann Arbor.

Building the Ford Cabin

It was early in the spring when they started to construct the foundations of the Ford Cabin at Huron Mountain. The weather was unbearably hot that year, and the early–season blackflies tormented the workmen. At the end of their ten–hour workdays, the men went swimming naked in Pine Lake. This raised a chorus of objections from Club members, and Ford's people were told they could no longer be housed on the property and would have to commute from Marquette. This was a harsh judgment at the time, considering the Model T transportation and 45 miles of curving gravel road. In compensation, the men were paid a staggering wage. In a time when $1 to $3 a day was the going rate of pay, Ford was paying the cabin workmen $9 a day. When they were told that they had to drive back and forth to Marquette, their work day was reduced to 9 hours and their pay increased to $11. The men pooled their rides and couldn't believe their good fortune. There were 30 to 40 employees working on the Ford cabin all that summer and fall.

The stonemasons who put up the huge sandstone fireplace were Ernie Riopelle, Tom Devonshire and Charlie Swain. They had all worked at Granot Loma. There were some other men splitting stone for them. When the fireplace was about five feet above the mantel, Mr. Kahn, the architect, told them that the rock work was too perfect. He wanted it rough and rugged looking. He said any mason could build a smooth–looking fireplace but it took experts and artists to make it rugged looking. He told the men to tear it down and start over. They were furious, but did what they were told.

In the big living room where the fireplace stood, the carpenters were using lumber that had been planed on one side. Naturally they were putting the planed side out where it would show. Again Mr. Kahn emphasized that he wanted the inside and outside of the cabin rugged looking; he wanted the rough, unplaned side of the boards exposed. The boards had to be taken off and turned over, rough side out.

Louis Vierling came to be known, on the job, as the "Jackknife Carpenter." He was the son of Louis Vierling and grandson of Martin Vierling, who owned the Vierling Block and saloon in Marquette. Louis did all the grill work over the hidden radiators and all the hidden light switches. A lot of the finishing touches had to be done with a jackknife.

The building was constructed a lot like Granot Loma except that instead of a steel frame, it was built on a frame of 2 x 6 inch lumber. Each of the huge white pine logs was selected from the 200,000 acres of Ford land around L'Anse and Pequaming. A road had to be cleared out to each tree that was selected, the tree cut and taken to the L'Anse mill, where it was slabbed. Then men worked the log over with a broad ax to give it a hand–hewn effect. The logs were half–lapped at the corners and lag screwed to the frame. Mr. Dan Hebard became very upset when he was told that Ford was going all over the property selecting the largest white pine for his cabin, as he had taken rather small pine for his own.

The heavy asbestos shingles were specially designed for the cabin by the Johns–Manville Company at the request of Albert Kahn for Mr. Ford. They were put on with copper coated eight–penny nails over wide, heavy–gauge copper flashing in the gutters.

The head contractor was John Godwin from Marquette. He had done a lot of fine work at Huron Mountain Club over the years. Among his best carpenters were Joe Oulette, Ronald Dorrow, and Gust Lintula. Gust Lintula was a good log worker. He was in charge of the work in the library, a beautiful room facing the lake with a fireplace. This room was lined with perfectly matched white birch logs with the bark left on. Unlike the birch logwork at Granot Loma, though, the logs were used whole and had no way of drying properly, as birch bark is air–tight. Though it was absolutely beautiful, in a few years the wood shrank and all the bark wrinkled and tore. The bark was peeled but, because of the trapped moisture, the wood did not look good. The birch was removed and the room was redone in peeled red pine logs. This room has a double thickness of logs, hewn on the outside, round on the inside. The walls are nearly two feet thick.

The porches and rafters are made of 10 x 10–inch white pine square timbers, and the porch floors are Arvon slate laid in cement.

Late in the fall of 1929, Joe Eiseman and a small crew set the laundry tubs and did the weather stripping. The building had a large coal–fired central heating system and was well insulated with balsam wool and so was completely winterized. The only other winterized private cabin on the club property was the second Du Charme cabin.

The following year, when Henry and Clara Ford returned to Huron Mountain, Mr. Ford didn't like what he saw. He said the cabin looked like a big naked barn and that, while he had hoped for a place that would blend into the forest, the untreated white pine stuck out like a sore thumb. Albert Kahn assured him that the condition was temporary. Left to weather six or eight years, it would blend comfortably into the surroundings, and wouldn't look nearly so big. The only thing that could be done to help matters right then was to plant trees around the cabin, especially in the large bare places where logs had been piled. It was ten years or more before the beautiful effect that Kahn was speaking of came to be.

The Famous Indian Jim

Mr. Longyear turned his first cabin over to his brother, Dr. Howard Longyear, in 1904 and moved his family over to the Stone House at Ives Lake. In 1916 Mr. Longyear proceeded to build a second cabin way down the beach west of the river mouth. Some said he built there to get away from the other cabins, but Mr. Longyear claimed it was to encourage more building on the south side of the river. He was still using the Stone House at Ives Lake, but wanted a place at Huron Mountain on Lake Superior.

The one unique thing about his new cabin was that it was really three separate buildings, all connected by a large porch and all under one single large roof. This cabin later became the property of his daughter, Mrs. J. M. Richardson Lyeth. Mr. Lyeth was a corporate lawyer from New York.

Then, in 1920, Charles Denby, a brother of Edwin who was also in the diplomatic service, had a frame cabin built south of the river. In 1921 Allen F. Edwards of Detroit had a very fine log structure put up next door. Mr. Edwards owned a company that made automobile parts. He sold out to the Chrysler Company and was put on their board of directors as a vice president.

Also in 1921, Cameron B. Waterman, the inventor of the outboard motor, and son of Cameron D. Waterman, brought the first prefabricated building in the U. P. from Detroit. The pieces were made in New York State and brought first to Detroit and then on to Huron Mountain by boat, where it was assembled just west of the Edwards Cabin.

When Dan Hebard sold out to Henry Ford, he had taken some matched white pine logs from the property before the sale. They were all wrapped in burlap and delivered to a site at the end of the line of cabins on the south side of the river, east of the Elting Cabin. The logs were not large, as white pine go, but they were all perfect, straight and of uniform diameter. No one was allowed to use a pike, cant hook or any kind of tongs. Dan Hebard wanted the logs kept perfect.

Mr. Hebard had run the Village of Pequaming single–handedly for years. He had a brother who lived, married, raised a family and died in Pequaming, but it was Dan who took over the leadership role and ran the business and the company town. The Methodist Church that he built in Pequaming was later moved into L'Anse and covered with washed Lake Superior sandstone. They used to tell the story about how Dan Hebard even ran that church. He was always there on Sunday morning, sitting in the same pew. Sometimes if the preacher got a little long–winded, as some preachers are wont to do, Mr. Hebard would pull the big gold pocket watch out of his vest pocket and look at it. The watch was at the end of a heavy gold chain. The first move was silent, but if the hinged watch cover was closed in a certain way, the click could be heard all over the church. When this signal was given, the well–trained minister would immediately shout out "and in conclusion..."

Mr. Hebard brought with him to Huron Mountain two daughters, a son and a famous Indian guide. It was the daughter, Mary Hebard, who took over her father's membership after he died and returned every summer until her death. The Indian guide was Jim Dakota (relatives living today spell the name DeCota).

Jim was born a Menominee (Chippewa) Indian in 1873 or '74, in White Cloud, Michigan. The records of his birth were lost in a fire there, but his sister, figuring back from her own age, gave this information to a court for legal purposes. He worked for Charles Hebard in lumber camps from Menominee to the Keweenaw Peninsula. In his younger years, Jim trapped and snared and traveled throughout the central Upper Peninsula and guided for literally hundreds of hunting and fishing parties. Through his guiding for a group of Detroit doctors year after year, he was brought to the attention of

Top: Ford cabin at Huron Mountain Club. Courtesy Dan H. Sise Jr.
Bottom: Jim Dakota in the 1940's. Courtesy Huron Mountain Club.

519

the Hebards, who took Jim with them on several extended trips to the Canadian shore of Lake Superior.

When Jim returned to L'Anse, he was given the title of "the World's Greatest Guide." Though it was given in jest, Jim never forgot it, and it was a title he wore proudly and was quick to reveal. As the world's greatest guide, he was often sought out by traveling or vacationing reporters looking for something different to put in their city papers. It seemed, at least in some cases, that they would print almost anything Jim told them. But whether they printed it or not, they always got a story out of Jim.

It was Jim who, maybe three–quarters of a century ago, started predicting the intensity of the winters by the flight of geese, the thickness of the fur on animals, the wood supply of the beaver, and other such indicators like the woolly bear prediction. Jim also relied heavily on the direction of the horns of the moon, whether it "held water or not," and whether a chew of tobacco would float against the current. He had several other indicators that were less scientific.

Jim Dakota became Dan Hebard's personal guide and, as such, always arrived at Huron Mountain a week or so ahead of Mr. Hebard and remained a week or so after he had gone. For years Jim spent his summers around the Hebard house at Pequaming. After the Hebards sold out to Ford, they moved to Philadelphia permanently, but returned to their cabin at Huron Mountain for the summer months after 1922. Jim spent his winters in Zeba, a part of the Keweenaw Indian Reservation, but knew when the Hebards were expected each summer. He always walked the 22 miles from L'Anse to Huron Mountain to be able to get the cabin ready for the Hebards, so that they could walk in and have everything just as though they had been living there all year. There was always a lot to do to get the cabin into that kind of shape.

After several years of finding a better route while making this trip to and from Zeba, Jim developed a trail. Sometimes it was a two or even three–day trip, depending on the weather and other circumstances, and his experiences, real or imagined, became the basis for many stories at Huron Mountain for years to come. There were times when Jim's storytelling around a campfire could outdo Mark Twain, Hans Christian Andersen, or Will Rogers but, unfortunately, his audiences were small, often a few lumberjacks or children, and his stories went unrecorded.

Everyone liked Jim. His simple ways, his proud optimism, his witty answers, made him loved by young and old alike. When asked to entertain at a campfire, he went to great lengths to make it good. Mr. Hebard paid Jim's sister, a remarkable woman in her own right, to make a beaded buckskin suit for Jim to entertain in. He liked to wear the suit and did so on many

Top: There were many cars in Big Bay by 1918. Courtesy Milton Tompkins.
Bottom: Henry on the Christie bridge 1937. Courtesy Shirley LaBonte.

occasions, singing, dancing all the Indian dances alone and without drums, explaining and telling the story of the dance as he went. At evening gatherings of the club employees, he would have the whole group dancing and whooping and all having the best time of their lives. Jim could cure headaches, toothaches, warts, moles and nearly any sickness with his magic. As the children he knew grew up, he was sought after by some of them for advice on a number of things. He planted many trees and bushes at Huron Mountain just because he felt that "there ought to be something growing there." One thing Jim impressed on people early in a conversation was his love of life, both plant and animal. He could tell a whopping lie in such a way that you found yourself believing him and yet, when he was telling the truth, it often came out in the most unbelievable forms.

Jim will always be remembered at Huron Mountain by those who knew him, and even by some who didn't know him but had heard about him. After the death of Mr. Hebard in 1939, Jim remained at the club doing various jobs for another 15 years or so.

Early Gatekeepers

Henry D. Sheldon of Detroit, who was married to Governor Alger's daughter Caroline, had joined Huron Mountain Club in 1893. He was a descendant of the Hiram Walker family. Henry dropped his membership in 1895, along with many others. His brother, Theodore Sheldon, joined in 1896 and sold out in 1901. Then in 1920, Henry Sheldon came back to the Club and in 1923 and '24 built quite a large cabin on the beach a few lots beyond the last cabin to the east. Later he made the cabin even larger by adding a wing to provide rooms for domestic help. Mr. Sheldon arrived with a chauffeur, as did many others in those years. There were so many chauffeurs coming in that a chauffeurs' quarters had to be provided by the Club. They moved the old laundry from behind the shinglehouse, or women's quarters, over next to the ice house. There was not quite enough room to bring the building between the help's recreation hall and the little Delco electric plant there, so a corner had to be cut off the eave of the plant building. It remains that way today, over 60 years later, causing those who notice it to wonder why. The chauffeurs' quarters, for years, also housed a small library and a doctor's office.

The first automobile had showed up on the Club road about 1914. By 1915 they were not an uncommon sight and it became obvious that the Club location which, for a time, had been too inaccessible, was now becoming too

Top: Dan Hebard and his grandson Dan Sise 1939.
Bottom: Johnny Freeman, seventeen years at the old club gate. Courtesy Shirley LaBonte.

accessible. By 1916 nearly everyone in Big Bay owned some kind of a car, and trespassing on the Club grounds became a common practice; boats were used and not cared for, often abandoned at the pleasure of the user, and Sunday and holiday picnics were held all over the Club property. In the summer and fall, two and three–day camping trips on Pine Lake were still arriving from as far as Ishpeming.

A gate was placed at the Club farm in 1916, but it proved inadequate over the next two or three years. People parked at the gate and walked in. When an authorized person showed up, sometimes after five or ten minutes of shouting and honking, they would have to hunt up the farmer to let them in.

In 1920, a little gate cabin with a screened–in porch was built just west of Oscar Webster's place on the Club road. John Freeman was the first gatekeeper. He remained at his post for eight months of the year, from 1920 to about 1936. Carter Harrison wrote about him:

> The first Cerberus at the roadway gate was John Freeman, a retired lumberjack of uncertain age and seemingly mild manner. But rub John's hair the wrong way and sparks would fly. When tooting an auto horn roused John from his cabin, he would toddle to the gate, key in hand, and pause for a nearsighted squint at car and passengers before making any move to insert the key in the lock.
>
> John received bed and board from the Club for eight months' service, besides lumberjack wages paid as a lump sum at the end of the resort season. He handed over almost all his wages to a couple with whom he lived in the four winter months. In return, he got board and lodging, and a promise that when he retired, the couple would return enough money to care for him in his old age.
>
> After a generation as gatekeeper, John retired and asked for a modest sum.
>
> 'No,' the couple told him, 'Your money was lost in the stock market.'
>
> So John spent his last days in the county poor farm.
>
> But if John was not as sharp as he might have been financially, he had his woodsman's wit. One day a rough–looking fellow summoned John to the gate.
>
> 'Important telegram for Jack Cassidy,' he announced.
>
> 'Lemme see it,' countered John. The stranger took a Western Union envelope from his pocket, showed it, and pocketed it again.
>
> 'Lemme read it,' said John.

'Why, man,' said the stranger, 'It's a private telegram. I've got to give it to Jack personally.'

'Unless I see it, I can't let you through,' said John doggedly. 'Unless I see it, you can't deliver it. That's flat.'

The stranger snarled, 'Okay, you win.'

Passing through the foot gate, he led John behind the cabin, took out a bottle of whiskey from his hip pocket, pulled the cork, and handed it to John.

'That's the telegram,' he said. 'Can you read it?'

John took a slug of the whiskey, but the stranger wasn't allowed through the gate.

The next gatekeeper was Jerry Kane. In 1937, there was a big automobile strike in Detroit. Henry Ford spent the month of August at Huron Mountain as he always had, but to the newspaper reporters he had gone there to hide. They hung around the gate for several days waiting for Mr. Ford to come out so they could get some kind of statement out of him.

Jerry Kane could spot a reporter with little effort and, no matter what their story, he wouldn't let them in. None of the reporters wanted to leave without a story after having come so far for one, so they made their own story. They borrowed a shotgun, put it in Jerry's hands, and took his picture standing in front of the Club gate. It was in the Detroit papers, stating along with it that Mr. Ford was hiding behind locked gates with armed guards. The reporters never saw Henry Ford, but they got their story.

Jerry Kane died in the guide house at Huron Mountain in 1939. They burned his mattress, an old lumberjack ceremony. An ex–convict from Marquette Prison, Bill Saunders, took over.

Ivan Ryan

Herb Perkins added to his relatively quiet life at Huron Mountain with hobbies of politics, dogs and racehorses. He was treasurer of Marquette County for a time, and supervisor of Powell Township. It seemed like everyone knew Herb Perkins and liked him.

The Marquette County Fair Grounds on the north end of Lincoln Avenue had a half–mile track built for sulky racing, although it had been used for track and field meets by the high schools and college, and as an automobile race track at times. Many of the sulky drivers considered it one of the best tracks in the midwest. There were large stable facilities nearby, and it

Upper left: Onnie Aho (c.1930) – Onnie worked at the club for an unprecedented 65 summers. Courtesy Mrs. Eimert Salminen.

Upper right: Ivan Ryan in his elderly years. Courtesy Mrs. William Ryan.

Lower left: Herb Perkins also did some flying in the early days. Courtesy Mrs. Eimert Salminen.

Lower right: Mamie Kivela Ryan left, Alma Pierce right. (Mrs. Howard Pierce) c.1920's. Courtesy Fannie Salminen.

was a great meeting place for race horse owners. Herb Perkins took his horses around the peninsula and even into Wisconsin sometimes. He owned two, three and four horses at a time, and was always buying, selling and trading in search of a faster horse.

Tom Ryan lived on a farm in Greenup, Illinois. He raised sulky horses all his life. His wife died, and their little son, Ivan, had gone to live with his aunt on an adjoining farm. Ivan was brought up with horses, stables and racing. There wasn't much he didn't know about these things.

Mr. Perkins made a few horse–buying trips to see Tom Ryan in Illinois. About 1922, young Ivan hand–delivered some horses to Mr. Perkins at Huron Mountain. It was fall and Ivan had never seen such a beautiful place in all his life. It was a sharp contrast from the flat, treeless prairies of Illinois. When Mr. Perkins asked him if he would be interested in coming back and working for him the next summer, taking care of his horses, young Ivan jumped at the chance.

Onnie Aho

Onnie Aho's father, Matt Aho, also trained and raced horses. Matt was from Negaunee. He and his wife, Mary, had nine children. Two of these children were twin boys, born in 1905. One of the boys died when he was nine years old. The remaining twin was Onnie.

Onnie loved to hunt and fish and he did a lot of it, but he was a hard worker too. When he was a young boy, he took any job that came along for a few cents. Onnie used to talk about working in the coal bins under the sidewalks of Iron Street in Negaunee, leveling the coal as it came down the chute from the wagon. He would be under there, black as the ace of spades, pushing the coal back into the corners of the bin. His pay was 50 cents a load.

After high school, Onnie attended the Northern Normal School in Marquette. It was during his freshman year that he met Mr. Perkins at the race track at the fairgrounds. Mr. Perkins had known Matt Aho in horse racing circles for some time. Onnie was looking for a summer job, and Herb Perkins invited him to Huron Mountain. This was in 1924, when Onnie was 19.

There was a young girl who showed up at Huron Mountain that year as a waitress. She was Mamie Kivela, right out of high school in Negaunee. A lot of young girls came to work at the club from Marquette, Ishpeming, Negaunee, Palmer, Republic, Big Bay and the other nearby towns. Many of them were of Finnish descent, and in those days nearly all of the Finns knew the mother tongue. Mamie and Onnie knew each other, both being from Negaunee.

Ivan Ryan took on the full responsibility of tending, training and racing Mr. Perkins' horses. He also, at times, worked for the club.

Onnie worked in the kitchen, mainly as a fireman. His job was to fire up the five big wood–fired cook stoves in the club kitchen and two more in the bakery, along with a fireplace in the dining room and another in the club room. His work started at 4:45 in the morning. Through the day he kept the stoves hot, hauled and piled wood, filled wood boxes and split kindling. He attended to a few coal–fired water heaters also, but his day was through when the dinner was on the table in the evening.

Mamie Ryan

In 1927, Ivan Ryan and Mamie Kivela were married. They had two sons, born about a year apart. They were Ivan, Jr., the older, and Billy. It was a Huron Mountain family, and the boys were raised there.

There were a lot of Huron Mountain families like the Alvords, the Rasmussens, the Jensens, the Cardinals, the Hytinens and the Grosses.

The Ryan boys attended school in Big Bay through the eighth grade and then had to go 45 miles to Marquette in a school bus for high school. When they got into athletics they stayed in Marquette with the Hytinens. Vic Hytinen had been an electrician at Huron Mountain for years, but they made their home on Fitch Avenue in Marquette.

Billy eventually married Patty Hytinen. Herb Hytinen, Patty's brother, was named after Herb Perkins.

After the crash of 1929, Ivan Ryan worked for the Club pretty much full time, and Mamie became about the finest cook anyone could find. She had a brilliant mind when it came to who liked what, where everyone was eating or who wasn't eating, what was left over, what should be used up and what should be ordered. It was all in her head, no lists or paper work. She was never caught following a recipe, but made up many that any cookbook would be proud to feature. She never measured anything – just a handful of this, a few shakes of that. When people asked her for a recipe she would say, "Well, I like it with lard, and kind of light and fluffy," and really thought she was telling them her secret, but usually to a recipe–follower her hints meant nothing. Mamie could make up a delicious meal out of almost anything. She cooked for the Club crew for years, and later for the Club members.

Book One

The Rescue by Henry Ford

In 1926, Onnie Aho worked in the Club store, a little log building built on the edge of the river, just across from the Club kitchen, where the canned goods and staples were stored. Then for about five years he was a private guide for Mr. Edwards. In 1932, Onnie went to work for Dr. Tappey of Detroit. The Tappeys had been long–time members of the Club, having joined in the initial solicitation of 1892.

The second ARGO had a Gray engine and a Johnson outboard drive. This was considered to be about the first inboard–outboard drive there ever was. Dick Durant was in charge of the ARGO and kept her in good running order.

The launch, with Mr. and Mrs. Ford and Mr. and Mrs. MacNeff aboard, had just returned from the Salmon Trout. They stopped in front of the Ford cabin and dropped off the Fords and MacNeffs, both elderly couples. While the people were disembarking, Onnie set the carburetor a little leaner, as the engine had not been running quite right.

The ARGO swung out from the shore with Onnie at the wheel and Dick back by the hatch tinkering with the engine. The boat made a large circle in the bay while the adjustments were being made. Suddenly there was a loud bang and the whole boat started to break up.

Onnie heard Dick yell "We're on fire!" He grabbed a little fire extinguisher attached to the gunwale near the wheel and turned toward the stern. His assessment took only a second. "We have to bail out," Onnie shouted to Dick.

Dick Durant couldn't swim. There were six pillow life preservers in the boat. Onnie grabbed two of them and jumped overboard. A moment later he looked over his shoulder at the ARGO and saw Dick with a large fire extinguisher in his arms shooting a stream high in the air; a second later he jumped in the lake with it.

"Onnie, don't leave me, I can't swim!" shouted Dick. Onnie started back to Dick and took hold of the struggling man. He gave him a cushion and told him to hang onto it and calm down.

In the meantime there had been several observers on the beach who had seen the episode unfold. Most of them thought they were too far from the scene to be of any help, or didn't know what to do. They stood helplessly by. However, Henry Ford and Harry MacNeff, who were closest to the action and had seen the explosion, immediately ran over to the river, about 100 yards away, picked a canoe out of the water, and carried it over to the Lake Superior beach.

529

Muggsy, or Muggins (left) Tin Can Sullivan (right). Courtesy Orvil Bystrom.

The canoe reached Onnie first, but he told them he was okay and sent them on to pick up Dick Durant. When they had pulled Dick into the canoe, they returned for Onnie, who hung onto the stern. By the time they were halfway to shore, a second canoe appeared and a third was leaving the beach.

Dick Durant was cold and in shock. Someone gave him a shot of prohibition booze and wrapped him in a blanket. When Onnie reached shore, he ran as fast as he could for the Guidehouse.

By this time, the beach was swarming with people, some just looking, others running up and down shouting. When the fire reached the gas tank, there was a huge explosion and Dr. Tappey's beloved ARGO II slipped quietly under the surface.

For years after the incident, Onnie Aho would remark in passing, "Henry Ford saved my life one time," or more often when there was time for a good story, "Did you ever hear about the time Henry Ford saved my life?"

Tin Can Sullivan

There was a character who showed up at Big Bay around 1910 and became known far and wide. He had come originally from Seney. Familiar with mills and logging, he went to work for the Lake Independence Lumber Company for a while, but had a little too much of the free spirit and could never stay on the job too long. His name was Tom Sullivan, but from the very beginning in Big Bay, he couldn't get along with his bosses at the mill and always called the company "a tin can outfit, if ever there was one." He used this term "tin can" so often that he soon acquired the nickname of "Tin Can" himself. Anything he didn't like was "tin can," even people.

Tin Can Sullivan built a shack which still stands today, down near Herman Bystrom's camp just off the Yellowdog River. It is just off the road that goes past Bear Lake, which is a piece of the old Marquette–L'Anse road of 1857. Tin Can became a hunter for lumber camps and a trapper, first for furs and bounties and later for the state as a state trapper. He spent a few years as a caretaker of the Lido Club for L. G. Kaufman, at the first Bass Lake west of Birch. On all of these jobs he was left pretty much alone, and that was the way he liked it.

Tin Can Sullivan's best friend was his horse, Muggsy, on which he went everywhere. He became a familiar sight with his big cowboy hat and reddish mustache. Sullivan was liable to show up anywhere from Granot Loma to the Andersen Homestead on the Yellowdog Plains. No one ever had

Top: Leach homestead at bottom of Breakfast Roll 1919.
Bottom: Reimy Fournier homestead.

to ask who he was, because he was the only one who rode a horse everywhere at that late date. He was well–known at Huron Mountain Club and was seen around Birch a lot. Tim Maney and Frank Krieg and Herman Bystrom were three of his closest friends. They knew enough to leave him alone most of the time. He also associated with Bill Bushey and Dave Nason. Dave had a farm and a couple of rows of hardwood forties at Homier.

There were also a few boys who liked to go and visit Tin Can. The Laurich boys used to visit him. They lived on a small farm just down the stream and across the river. Orville Bystrom was another boy who was fascinated with Tin Can. He, too, would always go over to see Tom Sullivan when he was a young boy staying at his dad's homestead, which was only a short walk from Tin Can's shack. Orville used to like to hear Tin Can talk and criticize everybody. He'd always say, "Wouldja like a cup 'a java?"

Tom Sullivan met an awful death at his own hand in 1927, but they still talk about him in Big Bay, a half–century after his death. He had become despondent and decided to end his lonesome life. The old shacker poured kerosene around in his cabin and rigged up a candle device that would burn the place down after he was gone – a kind of a tin–can timing system. Then he lay down in his cot and put the barrel of his shotgun under his chin. But due to his inexperience, the first shot wounded him terribly but didn't kill him. He had to get his pistol, load it and finish the job with that. Even the candle setup didn't work.

About three or four weeks later, young Orville Bystom, then fifteen or so, went to visit his cantankerous friend. It was a hot August afternoon, and Orville found the shack locked from the inside. Upon opening the door, he came upon the whole terrible scene. All the evidence was there...the shotgun, the blood, and the smell of kerosene...to tell of the end of Tin Can Sullivan.

Another Drowning at Conway

In 1919, Edwin Denby had five dozen Chinese pheasants sent to Huron Mountain from mainland China. They were in a dozen large cages piled back in the woodyard, which at that time was a corral for Mr. Perkins' horses. There were five birds in each cage. Bill Tompkins, Mink's brother, was working for Mr. Maund in the Club store. It was his job to feed the pheasants every day.

That same spring, Theodore Leach, his brother–in–law Nathaniel Brown, and their nephew, Paul Brown, were staying at the Leach homestead near the Conway Lake turnoff on the Club Road. They were looking for a buyer for the property. Their intention was to stay there until it was sold.

The building they were staying in had four log walls and a tent roof. They lived in it that way for two summers and a winter. It was during this period that 19–year–old Paul became acquainted with young Eddie Rasmussen. He used to see him once in a while coming down the road on the back of a Club wagon. Sometimes Ed would hop off there and visit with Paul, and Paul would walk with him to the Club. The two of them, with no one else their age around, became friends.

Paul loved living in the deep woods with his uncles. He thought every boy should spend a year or two in the woods while they were young.

The first time Paul had been to the homestead was when he was only five years old, in 1905. He tells that story:

> We came up to Uncle Theodore's from Fenwick, Michigan . . . Mother, Dad and myself on the train to Marquette, then by boat up and around Big Bay Point to the Club grounds. The cook on the boat took me to the galley and gave me a big sugar cookie, I can remember that plain. Also the tin cup with a chain on it that we drank with right out of Lake Superior.
>
> Uncle Nat came out in a small boat and got us from the steamer and took us ashore and then went with us east to Conway Bay, across Conway Lake in a boat, and to Uncle Theodore's.
>
> When we came home, we came to Marquette from Uncle Theodore's by horse and wagon, stayed all night at Saux Head Lake (the Crary Halfway House) and then on to Marquette.

Paul Brown was only four or five years old in 1905, but in 1919 his recollections were far more vivid. He tells us some of them from that period in his life:

> My two uncles must have been about 70 years old then. Uncle Theodore went over to Ewen to sell his land there at this time. I would enjoy seeing the Club grounds, Mountain Lake, Canyon, Cliff, etc., where the beaver fought on the snow at Mountain Lake outlet until the snow was red for rods and rods in all directions, where I killed a mammoth buck as he jumped across Mountain Lake outlet. Where the wolves about scared me to death on the north side of Pine Lakes as I was coming back from looking at mink traps on Mountain Stream. And I would like to know just how far I ran that night, just

how far I carried the bear trap up the Salmon Trout River before we set it in a log triangle baited with a skunk carcass.

There was a lumberjack that came by the cabin one day. As it was very unusual to see anyone at all, we invited him in to eat cabbage, beans and venison, all cooked in one kettle. He accepted and said he was from L'Anse and going to Big Bay for work in the mill. Wondered if we had found the cabin on Conway and if we had noticed the grave in the front yard, a little over 2 feet square. He said he had found the man drowned on the shore, had been dead for some time, so put him in the ground in front of his cabin. He put four stakes, one on each corner, to mark it. They probably lasted about a year. Said he took his rifle for his work. The cabin was closed when we were there but not locked, we looked around inside, maps and maps all over, a pair of snowshoes and a pair of skis in the loft, handmade. We took a frying pan and a lamp that we needed and locked it up as good as we could when we left. We found the old boat, a dugout, about halfway around Conway on the south side.

Theodore Leach and the two Browns had gone looking for the cabin the stranger had told them about. It was Barney Nelson's place. They didn't know Barney and had never heard of him, but they assumed it was the owner of the cabin who had washed up on the beach in front of it and had been buried there. But the dead man was not Barney Nelson...he died in Long Beach, California, many years later. It was his son who had drowned, and Barney never returned to Conway Lake. His brother, John, had drowned there also, and his other brother, Jake, had died of a broken neck. The drowned man was actually a stepson of Barney's. Barney had married the widow Beckman, who had a 19–year–old son, and it was this stepson who had drowned. Barney decided to sell the place when he could. There were three other brothers, Christen, Charlie and Ollie, who were all in Manistee along with a sister.

The three men looked over the Nelson cabin. They noticed a salt lick near some birches in the clearing, and two holes through the chinking between the logs facing that way. Barney could get his winter meat without having to drag it very far.

Before leaving the premises, the three men made a crude birch cross and planted it on the grave. Then they started walking south along the edge of the lake. Near the south end they found the dugout, floating upside–down near the shore. It was undoubtedly the one Barney's son had been using and, incidentally, the last one reported on any of the lakes. They pulled it up into the woods in a kind of swampy area there, and that was the end of that.

As the three men started toward their homestead, they thought they heard shots far to the west. With their curiosity piqued, Mr. Leach and the two Browns rounded the end of the lake and headed toward the sound. In time there were more shots, unmistakably a shotgun, and much closer now. The shots continued.

They soon came to the Club farm. At the far side of the clearing there were still more shots. They walked toward the shooter.

At the edge of the woods on the west side of the farm clearing they found a little hump–backed Frenchman, Reimy Fournier.

"What are you shooting at?" they shouted.

"Phea–sánts," he replied in a strong French accent.

"What?" They couldn't believe it.

"Phea–sánts," came the reply again. "Come here, I show you."

"There aren't any pheasants around here," said the astonished Theodore Leach.

"A–há," sang out Reimy, "You come to my cabéen, I show you."

They went a few hundred yards further through the woods to the northwest, where they came upon the whitewashed cabin of Reimy Fournier. Once inside, they saw evidence of pheasants everywhere. He had been plucking them, skinning them, canning them, cooking them, eating them, and there must have been 18 or 20 lying in two rows on a table in the middle of the room.

The homesteaders were flabbergasted. They had never seen a pheasant in the woods before nor since that incident, and Reimy didn't know where they had come from either.

Over at the Club, a mile or so away, they had been releasing two cages full of pheasants every day for a week, hoping that they would survive the winter and nest in the spring. The official conclusion was that the winters of the northern Upper Peninsula of Michigan were just too harsh for pheasant. They never knew what happened to them, but there wasn't so much as a feather of a pheasant seen the next summer.

It must have been just one more bewildering experience for young Paul Brown. He never knew what to expect next in this new, wild land. He never found out who the dead man was who drowned in Conway Lake, nor whose cabin he was buried in front of, though whoever it was had been his closest neighbor. He had many bone–chilling experiences during the year or so that he spent in the northwoods that he never forgot.

Apparently, Reimie Fournier didn't get all the pheasants that were turned loose that fall of 1919 nor did the winter kill them, for at least one bird survived that winter and the next.

536

Top: Wiipola and neighbors opening the road to Ishpeming with a six horse hitch. Courtesy Mrs. Dewey Tippit.
Bottom: On the Wiipola farm – 1920 Moline tractor – Front William Ollila, Center row – Nels Wiipola and unknown boy, back row – Aate Ollila, Emil Wiipola (diarist) Henry Nisula. Courtesy Mrs. Dewey Tippit.

Upper left: Standing on the well cover – Wiipola farm, Otto Wiipola left. Courtesy of Mrs. Dewey Tippit.

Upper right: Emil and his 1924 Chevy truck – he used several inventions so he didn't need air in the tires. Courtesy of Mrs. Dewey Tippit.

Bottom: The Wiipolas – Center in white shirt Abram Wiipola – seated center with baby – Kaisa Wiipala – baby Nels Jacob died at 1–1/2.

Emil Wiipola the diarist is standing at left in front of John Hautakangas. (c.1900) Courtesy Mrs. Dewey Tippit.

About 30 or more miles to the southeast of Huron Mountain at what was known as the Fire Center Location north of the Ropes Gold Mine, the Wiipolas were eeking out a humble but enjoyable existence on their farm that they had carved out of the jack pine woods. The boys trapped, cut wood, hunted, fished, ran the farm and kept track of their cows. Emil was keeping up his diary, although he had become a little lax as far as daily entries were concerned unless something out of the ordinary happened. During the month of October of 1921 there were only four days accounted for and the longest entry was on the 16th. It read as follows:

On the 16th, Sunday, we found a dead wildcat in the woods,– some animal probably killed it. It weighed 9 lb. 2 oz. On the 16th Pappa got with a rabbit snare a pretty bird that we have never seen the likes of its kind and probably will never see again. From the tip of the wing to the other 2 ft. 5 in. From its beak to its tail was 2 ft. 4 in. Its tail was one foot seven inches long. (Legs) and feet 9 1/2 in. long. Beak 1 inch. 5 1/4 in. around the head. Length of wing 1 foot 1/8 in. Tail 17 feathers,– 2 feathers were 1 ft. 7 in. long. Weight was 2 1/2 lbs. Eyes red. White ring around neck,– other color blue black or navy blue around head and neck,– around the lower part body pinkish and gray. 17 day Oct we opened a line around a new piece of land (40 acres) that we bought $12.02, the price of the land, NE 1/4 of SE 1/4 Sec 4 – 48N – 27W. 17th day the Social Service brought for Mother bed clothes, mattress and two blankets– price $10.00. (She had probably been sleeping on straw.)

The Wiipola Family, Abram and Kaisa Kreeta (Juntela) and their four children: Franz Emil, Niilo Ariel, Otto Abram and Hilda Katarina took a farm homestead about 1887. A fourth child died young. Three generations live there today and are the best authorities on that area.

Emil lived his entire life in a huge square building that was part barn and part house of a type still found in Europe. Emil kept a diary off and on from 1910 to the 1950's; it is a classic of rural life in Northern Michigan.

More Writings of Paul Brown

Paul Brown wrote some more about his experiences at Huron Mountain in a letter years later:

Then one night, after a freezing rain, I was awakened by a scratching on the tent about midnight. I nudged Uncle Theodore and he nudged Uncle Nat, we slept three in a bunk. We got up and went out as quietly as possible, but he had heard us and vanished into the dark. The next morning there was clawmarks on the canvas much higher than I could reach.

About twice or three times a month we would hear the cry of a lynx and that would cause goose–pimples.

One night just after finishing supper and doing the dishes, the door opened and a man walked in. He took in the whole layout with one glance; saw the three rifles and three men there. We asked him what he wanted and he said he just stopped in. Well we knew he hadn't 'just stopped in' because there was nobody in the woods in the night and also no place to go, either way, only to Big Bay. He didn't say a half–dozen words until he said he guessed he would go, and opened the door and was gone.

We jumped up and put out the lamps. Uncle Theodore and Uncle Nat took their rifles and went out in the dark. They told me to shoot anybody that opened the door unless they whistled first. More goose–pimples. But after about half an hour they came back, whistled and came in. They said there were four men in all, they had a little fire built down where the little creek crossed the road east of the cabin and that after quite a lengthy conversation with the man that came back from our cabin, they put out the fire and started back east to Big Bay. We wondered what would have happened if there had only been one there instead of three in the cabin.

About once each week Dutch John or, as we called him, 'Greasy John,' would come by the cabin about mealtime and would 'just happen to be going by' from looking at his mink traps, that he never took up from one year to the next, only to change sets. He would come in and eat with us. We didn't have much variety in our meals, as all our food had to be carried in from Big Bay, from the Mill Store or Company Store as it was called then. I walked to Big Bay twice each week to get the mail and bring back more beans, potatoes and cabbage; very filling. We had our own venison across the road in a pit in the ground under a brush pile.

As the Game Law Digest said you could kill partridge from October 15th to November 15th inclusive, we had lots of 'pats' to eat, and were they good, until one day, in walked two game wardens from Marquette. They had dinner with us and then asked us if we had killed any pats while we had been in there. Of course we knew something was wrong because we had just eaten 'pats' for dinner. We told them yes, we had real good luck.

They said, 'All right, you will have to go to Marquette with us, as it is illegal to shoot partridge in Marquette County this year.' It said you could kill them in the Digest but in the 'big book' it said you couldn't kill them. The supervisors had closed the county because pats were very scarce in some places, but not where we were. As we came into the woods early, we didn't see it in the papers and were very innocent. I guess it showed, because the wardens said they would talk to the judge and maybe get us off.

I went to Marquette with them on Saturday, paid our fine, which was $10 apiece and costs, and came back to camp on Monday. They were fining some of the fellows $100 and costs that year, so I guess we did get off easy. The game wardens then always traveled in pairs everywhere. I heard a man from the lighthouse invite them to come out and look his place over if they didn't care about coming back. They didn't even answer him. This happened in the depot when we were waiting to go to Marquette to pay our fine...scared me half to death.

We had a few fish to eat, but just on special occasions. I walked up to the first falls on the Salmon Trout one day and took two beauties from just below the falls. I stood on the big flat rock just at the foot of the falls and cast out in the foam. I didn't have any trout equipment, just a casting rod and a 'pikey minnow,' regular pike equipment, but it was November and they would strike on anything that came under the foam from the falls.

On my birthday, November 2, we took a walk from our cabin down along Pine Lakes to the Club, then around Pine Lake to the Mountain Stream outlet, up that stream to Mountain Lake, along the east side of Mountain Lake to Canyon Lake, then back home by way of Ives Lake. There was about a foot of snow, wet, and my new leather shoes, 'high–tops' that I bought in Petoskey, just couldn't stand it and were wet through. By the time I got back to camp I had a beautiful blister on each big toe, clear across the toe and then wore it off, so I really had two sore feet for a few days. I realized for the first time that my two uncles did know something about footwear after all. They both advised me against buying the leather shoes in the first place.

The next day we were going to Bulldog Lake on the Bentley Trail, but my feet were so sore I couldn't even get my shoes on, so I had to sit by the stove and make expanding and collapsible fans out of cedar. They are beautiful, have you ever done it? It is a wonderful time—consumer, and that, at the moment, was what I had most of.

The above quotations are from a long letter which Paul Brown wrote to me. It was written at his farm in Ionia, Michigan on August 2, 1963. Paul died about five years later.

The Doctors Drake, Drury and Bennett

It was in the spring of 1921 that Dr. Drake, a dentist living in the 300 block of East Hewit Avenue; Dr. Drury, the city health officer who lived on Spruce Street; and Dr. Bennett, a physician who had purchased the F. W. Reed home on Arch Street, went to Conway Lake to look over the Barney Nelson homestead that had been put up for sale a few years earlier when Barney's stepson drowned. Dr. Drake did not get in on the financial part of the deal, though he used the camp regularly, but Dr. Bennett and Dr. Drury jointly purchased the place from Barney.

That summer, the three men went up and cleaned out the cabin and built a log addition on the back of it for a kitchen. Though Dr. Drake was at the camp off and on in the early years, he eventually quit making the trip because of his age. The other two men had large families, and they both spent more and more time at Conway Lake as time went on.

Dr. Drury was the city health officer from 1917 to 1924, following Dr. Main. When Henry Ford became established in Iron Mountain, the Drurys moved there and the Bennetts pretty well took over the camp at Conway. After eleven years in Iron Mountain, the Drurys returned to Marquette in 1936 and the doctor resumed his former position with the city, which he then held for many years.

When the Drurys returned to Marquette, both they and the Bennetts had five children, and there just wasn't enough room for the two families in "Whoabuck," as the Nelson cabin came to be called. Dr. Drury purchased land at the northeast end of the lake and had a friend from Iron Mountain, Nick Gustafson, who was actually a former patient, dismantle and move the Rasmussen cabin and the old log horse barn from the beach to the Drury property on Conway Lake. The move was less than a quarter of a mile. By 1937 the Bennetts and the Drurys each had their own separate camps and were both well established on Conway Lake.

More about the Early Camps on Conway

While Pete Rasmussen had a rather bad name in the community because of the saloon, his sons, especially Ed, were well respected. Louis, too, preferred to live in Big Bay to keep his children clear of the questionable place of business. Ed, Jr., Ed's only child, didn't want anything to do with the saloon. He didn't even want to go to Marquette, for fear of people associating him with the saloon, and told his parents so. He refused to go to school in Marquette beyond the Eighth Grade. Young Ed was a life–long resident of Huron Mountain. He lived his entire life at the cabin on Conway Bay and at Huron Mountain Club. After Ed, Sr. died at only 47 years old of Hodgkins Disease in 1922, Eddie, Jr. and his mother sold the lot on Conway Bay to the Club and later secured a forty on a secluded bay on the southwest end of Conway Lake. When Huron Mountain Club installed their first electric plant, Mr. Perkins sent Ed, Jr. to the Coyne Electrical School in Chicago. With the knowledge he gained there, he was placed in charge of the maintenance and operation of the whole electrical system at Huron Mountain. In 1932 Ed built a log cabin on the bay on the south end of Conway.

There were four other early camps on Conway which should be mentioned. Three men who used to hunt together in the Conway area were Oliver Hall, Ed McGeorge and Ed Thompson. All were from Big Bay and worked for Brunswick. These three formed a Club called the "Fin, Fern and Feather Club," for fishing, camping and hunting. While the group had been active in the area since the early 1920s, and had a camp on land they purchased from J. B. Deutsch, it was in 1933 that Oliver Hall purchased a piece of land from Louis B. Nelson. Louis was a Nelson brother who did not remain at Conway. Oliver was considered quite a character by all who knew him. The first camp was a log cabin and he later took down the old Big Bay Saloon, a frame building that had been built around 1906, and rebuilt it back in the woods on the same property as the old camp. The Hall property passed to his daughter, Mrs. Williams, and then to her daughter, Mrs. Sakota. Oliver Hall was one of the regulars around Conway Lake. He spent a lot of time there.

Fred Begole of Marquette purchased his land from J. H. Austin Corporation in 1924. He had a camp built there and loved to be there alone. He would explore constantly. A unique feature of the Begole camp was the back seat of an old automobile which they put in the corner of the camp and threw a rug over for a couch. They later built two smaller camps on the property for the grandchildren.

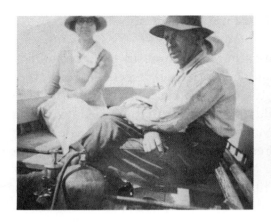

Upper left: Ed Rasmussen Sr. – in an inboard launch at Huron Mountain. Courtesy Shirley LaBonte.

Upper right: The new house (c.1935) Halls second camp at Conway. Courtesy Mrs. Marion Sakota.

Lower left: Oliver Anton Hall and daughter Maude Iren Hall (Williams) and granddaughter Helen Marion Williams (Sakota) Conway Lake 1929. Courtesy Marion Sakota.

Lower right: Fred Hurlburt Begole (c. 1890)

Book One

The Begoles were an old Marquette family. Fred Begole was born on the farm of his father, Charles Myron Begole, near Flint. His grandfather, the Hon. Josiah W. Begole, was the Governor of Michigan from 1883 to 1885. Fred's son, Charles, was born in Marquette in 1892. Charles married Hazel Wheatley in Marquette. Miss Wheatley was the daughter of Captain William Henry Wheatley, keeper of the Marquette light at Lighthouse Point.

Captain Wheatley met a tragic death by drowning in April of 1896 and the story was told for years by older Marquette residents.

A group of women walked from town to a camp at Middle Island Point. Mr. William C. Brandon, who lived in the house next to Dandelion Cottage and was a typesetter at the Mining Journal, asked Captain Wheatley to bring him up to Middle Island in his sailboat to meet the group after work on a Saturday. There was a lot of spring ice in the bay west of Presque Isle and a stiff breeze from the north. A line became tangled and the boat capsized in the rising wind. Will Wheatley, an excellent swimmer who often practiced with Captain Cleary's lifesaving crew, told Brandon to strike out for shore while he was going to dive under the boat and loosen the tangled line and attempt to right the boat. It was a small boat that he had made himself. Captain Wheatley never surfaced again.

Mrs. Brandon and another of the women decided to take a walk along the beach to see if they could make out the boat coming. They spotted something moving on the beach. As they drew near, they could see it was an exhausted William Brandon, who survived to tell the story.

A month later, two boys discovered Wheatley's body.

Mrs. Hazel Begole, Wheatley's daughter, now residing in Marquette, is 93 years old at this writing. She remembers well being awakened by her mother and Mr. Cleary as she slept in her parents' bed, waiting for her father to come home. Mr. Cleary brought the news of the drowning and did his best to console the family. Mrs. Begole was the youngest of the three daughters. There is a window in the First United Methodist Church of Marquette in memory of Captain Wheatley. Fourth and fifth generation descendants of the Wheatleys and Begoles live in Marquette today, and still return to the camps on Conway Lake. The Begoles sold a piece of their land on Conway to Dr. Bolitho and his family, who built a camp there in the 1950s.

The Austin Holding Company also sold a piece of land on the lake to Thomas L. Collins in 1945. He, too, had been a frequenter of Conway Lake country for some time. Later, in 1956, his brother, George Collins of Negaunee, bought out the Victor Swanson place, which adjoined the other Collins property. These Collinses were relatives of Hans Jensen. Mrs. Collins' father was Otto Jensen, Hans' brother. It was Otto Jensen who moved the John Nelson cabin from Conway Bay to Ives Lake for Munro Tibbitts.

Finally, there is the little white pine cabin on the west side of Conway Lake on a single forty of land. The forty is surrounded by Huron Mountain Club land and one corner of it touches the lake when the water is high. Normally the corner of the forty is eight to ten feet from the water's edge. This is known as the Johnston cabin. Billy Johnston used to hunt the Conway Lake area from a tent camp, starting the year the railroad was completed to Big Bay, 1906. His party usually consisted of the County Sheriff, the Chief of Police, Registrar of Deeds, the County Clerk, Frank Jenks, and other city and county officials. Bill Johnston himself was the fire chief in Marquette.

They discovered an abandoned log cabin near the lake that had been built by Christen Nelson before the turn of the century. Christ Nelson, another brother of the Conway Nelsons, acquired a homestead deed to the land on July 30, 1900, but the cabin had been built at least five years earlier. William C. Weber of Detroit paid the back taxes on the forty and was in the process of gaining title to the land by that means, as he had done with thousands of acres in the north part of Marquette County over the years. Before the allotted time had run out, Bill Johnston bought the forty from Christ Nelson, who then reclaimed the property by paying Weber his money plus interest and issuing a warranty deed to Bill. After Johnston's death, the property went to Bill's son, Jim Johnston, and at his death to Jim Johnston's wife. It is still the original camp with no changes, the oldest one on the lake. It has always been used as a hunting camp. For the last 30 years or more, Wes Jenner, who for years was the president of the Cliffs Dow Chemical Company in Marquette, has had a party hunting out of the Johnston camp.

Lumber Camps

It was in 1914 that things really began happening in Big Bay. That's when the Brunswick–Balke–Collender Company, an old organization started back in 1840 by these three men, put up about ten lumber camps throughout the area. By then, the company was headquartered in Muskegon, Michigan, with their factory offices at 1700 Messler Street.

This is when the Lake Independence Lumber Co., under Jay B. Deutsch, was building. Railroads were constructed to every camp, the mill was enlarged, and the concrete dam built to replace the old log one at Lake Independence that was failing.

Theodore Schneider was living in the big house next to the company office, store and hotel. The Schneider house had been originally designed as

Top: Headquarters Camp Lake Independence Lumber Co. – "Big Ole" Cook – 1920's. Rydholm collection.
Middle: Mill at Big Bay 1922.
Bottom: Camp 6 – Lake Independence Lumber Co. (1920's). Rydholm collection.

the Big Bay Athletic Club. It had eight bedrooms and a large recreation room on the third floor with a pool table in it. However, it was always called the Superintendent's house, and the mill superintendent lived there. There was also a big hall upstairs in the office–store building that was used for dances, meetings and movies. Dr. Webster was the physician, Carl French was a log scaler, Marie Flanigan had moved up from Birch and was a schoolteacher, and John Bunyan Tompkins, "Jay," was in charge of logging operations.

Jay Tompkins had come from Wausau, Wisconsin in 1912, with his wife and five children. A few years later, in 1918, the Tompkinses bought the Smith farm across the road from the Burns homestead, and lived there for years.

Fur farming had come into vogue in the area. Herb Perkins had invested in it as a silent partner with the Coxes' Fox Farm west of the Brewery near Marquette. One of the Tompkins boys, Bill, had a skunk farm when he was young. He operated it for about three years. Peter Raymen, who worked for Brunswick, took a trip to Alaska in 1923 and brought back some blue fox breeding stock. He also had a silent partner who helped finance the operation. The partner was Garrett John Scholtus, a stonemason with years of experience in Marquette County. He had worked on the original Longyear mansion, helped take it down and worked on it again in Brookline. He also worked on the Marquette Waterworks building and others around town.

Pete Raymen bought forty acres adjoining Big Bay, just west of town, and started a fox farm there in 1924 with his brother Ray as a partner. Bill Tompkins later raised mink and fox on his farm. These men also made some attempts at raising silver fox, as did others in the area, but the breeding stock was too expensive and at about that time, the fur market went to pieces. However, the Tompkinses sold some silver fox breeding stock to be sent to Sweden for $5,000. They called that buyer "Santa Claus."

The Harry Hansens

There was a Moberg family that came to Big Bay from Wisconsin in 1912. Mr. Moberg was a lumber inspector and the family first lived in Red Town. Hearing about an opening for a secretary in the company office, they sent for their 18–year–old daughter, Judith, who was working in Chicago. Judith Moberg got the job.

By 1916, everybody in Red Town had moved up to the new houses that Leiphart had built on streets laid out west of the main street. Red Town was dismantled.

Harry Hansen had been an ardent sport fisherman, fishing the environs of Big Bay for years. He first came to Big Bay to work as the payroll clerk for the lumber company, moving there in 1915. The company had built a big warehouse on the main railroad line at Antlers. It was seven miles north of Birch and six miles south of Big Bay. Antlers was a busy place. All the logging railroads came to the warehouse there, and supplies were coming in every day from Marquette.

Harry Hansen, the fisherman, was put in charge of the big warehouse at Antlers. He married Judith Moberg and moved down there with her. The couple lived at Antlers for five years. For their convenience, the company gave them a four–cylinder gasoline car that had been made in West Allis, Wisconsin. The car had railroad wheels and ran on the tracks, which went everywhere Harry wanted to go. There was a problem, however. The car was always broken down. Harry was forever ordering parts for it, which took weeks to arrive. If and when they came at all, they were usually the wrong ones, or if they were the right ones, there would be a piece missing. At any rate, the car was always out of commission. But the company brought them wood and ice, as they did for everyone in town who lived in a company house. The ice was cut on Lake Independence and the wood was slabwood from the sawmill or cull bowling pins from the pin mill, all of it the highest grade of hard maple.

It was a big job supplying food and materials for ten lumber camps of 40 to 80 men each. Tuesday was supply day when trains came into Antlers from all the camps. The meat car was sidetracked near the warehouse and was usually empty by the end of the day.

Camp 1 was at Birch on the Garlic River, Camp 4 was about 2 1/2 miles south of Big Bay on the main road, and Camp 6 was on the Yellowdog near where County Road 510 crosses it today. Camp 7 was a mile and a half west of Big Bay, and Camp 8 was up by the Pinnacle Falls. Camp 10 was three or four miles south of Big Bay, and Camp 11 was up at the headwaters of Alder Creek. Later, Camp 10 was between present roads 550 and 510 on Alder Creek. The headquarters camp, originally down by Kaufman's camp, was moved up near Peep O'Day. It was later moved up toward the lighthouse. The camps moved when the timber was gone or out of reach. Some kept the same number when they were moved, and some were given a new number.

About 1915 the company obtained a steam skidder. The huge machine was first used in back of Birch and later moved just out of Big Bay on what is now known as County Road 510. Later, two more skidders were purchased. A skidder was a big steam engine with a drum containing a mile and a quarter of steel cable on it. A team of horses would pull the cable into

Top: Harry Hansen and two friends at a beach picnic. (1920). Courtesy Mrs. Marion Sakota.
Middle: Old Camp 8 on the Yellowdog River. (1930's). Courtesy Mrs. Marion Sakota.
Bottom: Pete Raymen – made skis at Birch and was head of the clothespin operation at Big Bay. (c.1944) Courtesy Milton Tomkins.

the woods. They could pull logs out of all kinds of places. Sometimes the log would get hung up and a cable would snap. There were serious accidents.

One skidder was being used out of Camp 2 at the foot of Bald Mountain. It worked well in the hills there. There were also camps to the northwest as far as Ives and Conway Lakes, and railroad tracks leading to both places in the 1920s. By 1926 and '27, much of the hardwood had been logged off.

Something New Every Year

During the ten years from 1915 to 1925, the automobile had come into common use, World War I had been fought, the Prohibition Amendment had been passed, and there had been great epidemics of typhoid fever and Spanish Influenza, locally known as "Wartime Flu." While many people were desperately ill and thousands died across the state, miraculously Big Bay only lost five people, all told, to the epidemics.

During Prohibition, moonshining became commonplace in Big Bay, and booze was being sent to Marquette regularly. One method of smuggling it was in a tank built right into the frame of a taxi cab. Some wondered why the driver didn't seem to care if he had any passengers or not.

The government cracked down on the company. They said that the moonshiners were living in company houses and the company would have to pay. J. B. Deutsch told his employees that if they insisted on making and selling illegal alcoholic beverages, they would have to move out of the company houses. He would give anyone who wanted to move a lot a few miles down the road in what became known as the "hollow," where they could build their own houses and take their own chances. A small suburb of Big Bay appeared down in the hollow within a year or two. The bootlegging business proved to be quite lucrative, and those involved with it were dubbed "hungry" by the other inhabitants of Big Bay, who began calling the little community "Hungry Hollow."

The Fleurys

Archie Fleury (Oct. 2, 1889–Nov. 30, 1975) came to Big Bay in 1918 as agent for the Marquette and Southeastern Railroad. He was one of eight children born to Mr. and Mrs. Abraham Fleury, who had moved to Marquette from Three Rivers, Canada. There were five boys and three girls, all born in

Top: Mr. and Mrs. Abraham Fleury fresh from Canada. (1880's) Courtesy Leo Fleury.
Bottom: The Abraham Fleury family – front row – Agnes (became a nun), Mrs. Fleury, Abraham Jr., Archie, Abraham Sr., back row – Wilfred, Clara, Clem, Louis (Bureau), Leo. Courtesy Leo Fleury.

Top: Archie Fleury family raised in Big Bay. Top left – Lowell, Evelyn, Emerson, Dorothy (raised by the Fleury family), Clem. Front row L – Grace, Mrs. Emma Fleury, Archie and Doris Beerman (remained in Big Bay).
Bottom: Emerson Fleury family – raised in Big Bay. From L, Fred (doctor), Barbara (Nunn), Mr. and Mrs. Emerson Fleury, Margaret, Emerson, Jr., and Peter (not in picture).

Marquette. Leo Fleury, Archie's brother, went to Big Bay first on September 16th, 1916 with the railroad. Archie was an auditor for the railroad and was sent up to Big Bay to look at the books.

Joe Madigan had just left Big Bay as station agent for the railroad, and his job was open. He went to Munising and opened the Munising Hardware Store. He was known to have had several money–making schemes going on the side, one of which was giving as little as eight dollars back for cashing a $10 check. The Railroad was looking for a station agent.

When Archie was told about the job and realized all the fringe benefits, which included free quarters upstairs in the depot, he took the job himself. As station agent at the depot, he sold magazines, candy and eggs. With no bank at hand, he could cash checks for a small percentage, which saved the men a trip to town and they appreciated the service. With this start, Archie Fleury later became known as Big Bay's most famous storekeeper. He would own several in the years to come. Archie used to boast that he never spent a night away from Big Bay after he moved there.

The McKenzies

Herman Ellis McKenzie was a wood technologist, an engineer of national acclaim when he first came to Big Bay as a consultant for the Lake Independence Lumber Company in 1920. He came from old New England stock that had its roots in the little fishing village of Jonesport, Maine. The McKenzie family was looked on unfavorably there, due to an incident concerning the religious migration to the Holy Land by a group of people. Great–grandfather McKenzie, who helped plan the trip, ultimately did not go, but took over some of the lands of those who did. The fascinating story is told in a privately printed book that at present is only in the hands of McKenzie descendants.

Herman McKenzie was recommended to Jay B. Deutsch by the Brunswick people as a man who could help reduce the number of cull pins caused by cracking, through better drying techniques. He was already considered an expert in this field, and had done work all over the country.

Mr. McKenzie had received a Bachelor of Science degree from the University of Maine in 1907 and an advanced degree from the Yale School of Forestry. He had also done laboratory research at Yale and had worked for the U. S. Forest Service.

In 1915, Herman McKenzie authored the rules of logging for the California State Board of Forestry which are still in effect there today. In Big

Bay, his first assignment was considered a complete success. He redesigned their kilns and revised their wood–drying techniques to the extent that it reduced the loss of pins from 50 to seven percent. He was even able to salvage a huge number of culls by eliminating the cracks by using a process that put moisture back into the wood. For this first venture, McKenzie received $2,500 from the company.

Herman McKenzie left Big Bay for 13 months to work for the W. H. Mason Company in Laurel, Mississippi, during which time he developed Masonite for the company. The new product was patented. He already had seven other patents in connection with the wood industry. At the time, no one realized how important masonite or any other artificial board would eventually become. As a result of these and other developments, Mr. McKenzie was listed in "Who's Who in American Scientists."

"Mac" McKenzie married Geneva Wagner of Williams, Arizona in 1915. The couple met and were married in Sacramento, California, where Mrs. McKenzie was working as a nurse. In Big Bay, Mrs. McKenzie became the company nurse. Prior to this, the closest person in town to a nurse was Mrs. Jay Thompkins, Sr., who was a midwife on many occasions. Many was the night that Nurse McKenzie was roused from her bed in the wee hours of the morning to sew up a pair or more of brawling drunken lumberjacks. She would spread newspaper on her dining room table and have them laid out on it for the surgery. They never failed to get a severe lecture during the whole procedure. Everyone in the Big Bay area, whether or not they worked for the company, depended on Mrs. McKenzie in emergencies, and she had a heart of gold when it came to giving of her time. For some years she became the nurse at Huron Mountain Club, as did Hilda Carlson, who had been the school nurse in Marquette, covering all the schools in town on foot after the street cars were discontinued in 1935. Hilda was the school nurse for nearly forty years.

The McKenzies lived, for the most part, in a house that had been moved up from the company supply depot at Ransom. The warehouse was moved from Antlers to Ransom, a few miles toward Big Bay on the track, in 1924, and then from Ransom to Big Bay in 1926. The warehouse at Ransom was moved up to Big Bay and Charlie Draver, who came from Ewen, was to move it into place with a big tractor. It was to be used as a hospital. There was a lot of trouble with the skids sinking into the sand. After finally laying crossties for the skids to ride on, the job was accomplished and the building was made into a residence for the McKenzies. They later moved into the big superintendent's house.

Top: Brunswick letterhead (c.1924).
Lower left: Four stack mill at Big Bay after 1924. Rydholm collection.
Lower right: Herman Ellis "Mac" McKenzie. (1930's). Courtesy Don McKenzie.

Book One

The End of the Lake Independence Lumber Co.

With the production of bowling alley stock and the increase in bowling pin and duckpin production, the future of the company looked good. The "dimension plant," which made wooden parts for General Motors, Buick division, required an extra two boilers. These were added in 1924, and a fourth stack was erected at the mill. Even with the extra boilers the load proved too heavy and another crew had to come in and finish the pins at night. Wood was shipped out regularly to the Buick assembly plants in lower Michigan.

This all came to an abrupt end when in 1926, there was another big fire at the mill and the company was forced into bankruptcy. It was the dimension plant and some kilns that burned.

J. B. Deutsch had recently been building up his fine herd of Guernsey Frisian cattle at Bay Cliff Farm. It was then that he went to L.G. Kaufman and mortgaged his herd so that he could keep the mill operating as the J. B. Deutsch Lumber Company. They kept only two camps open to supply logs.

After a matter of six or eight months, things were worked out and the Brunswick people took over until the early years of the Depression. However, J. B. Deutsch left Big Bay shortly after his herd was moved to Granot Loma.

It was impossible for the company, even on a reduced scale, to weather the bottom of the Great Depression and it closed its doors in 1931. The lights went out in Big Bay.

The following year, all the lumber that was piled in the mill yard was sold to the Kerry and Hanson Flooring Company of Grayling, Michigan. Herman McKenzie was put in charge of the disposing of the holdings, and his family moved into the superintendent's house. He took the pin finishing plant to the Brunswick properties in Muskegon and set up a ten pin manufacturing plant in the Schneider Mill on the Dead River in Marquette.

When the company store closed down in 1932, William L. Katz, who had a clothing and dry goods store at 116 West Spring Street in Marquette, purchased all of the canned goods and some of the other stock and turned his place into a department store in Marquette. Archie Fleury bought the remainder of the stock and the furnishings, and went into business for himself in the company store. Joe Columbo[1], who later became Joe Borro, had a little store down in the Hollow, but Mr. Fleury saw the chance to take over what business there was left in the village. He had the north half of the building, a long narrow room and another room in the rear where he could set up a bunk, office and temporary living quarters. He still lived upstairs in the depot for many years. The Asselin Creamery of Marquette bought all the

[1] Columbo or Columbus: see Supplementary Appendix C

refrigeration equipment, and Archie had to go back to using ice and kerosene lamps. He bought a home at 1007 North Fourth Street in Marquette, where the family could live so that the children could go to school there.

Harry Burk, a scrap metal dealer from Escanaba, bought the company railroad. Two good Limey engines went to Panama, the rest were cut up, and everything else was loaded on flat cars and shipped to Japan.

Don McKenzie, son of Herman, says "a few years later they shot it all back at us" in World War II. There were a few places where some rails were left in the woods and were removed during and after World War II.

Herman McKenzie, now superintendent, made plans to sell lots on Lake Independence. He drew a beautiful map of the lake and plotted lots around it. The McKenzie family thinks that when he drew this map, he named a few previously unnamed places for reference, and put his family name on a beautiful bay now known as McKenzie Bay. But Mink Tompkins, the earliest resident of Big Bay living today, claims the bay was called McKenzie Bay before the McKenzies ever came there. He believes that it may go back to early loggers or surveyors.

Herman McKenzie began to sell off the lots around the lake, as well as the company houses from the village. At the time, the company owned 97 houses; of these, 45 houses were sold and moved from the west end of town. The lots on Lake Independence sold for 50 to 75 cents per front foot, depending on the depth and quality of the lot, and the houses sold for $45 for a one–story house and $65 for a two–story house.

Charlie Draver moved the houses, most of them down to lots on Lake Independence or down along the Big Bay Road. Nothing very large could be taken to Marquette because of the two cement bridges with their high sides. They tried it with one large building, jacked it high over the Yellowdog bridge, but the Dead River bridge was too much. They brought it back to a lot on the Big Bay road near the Middle Island turnoff where Phil Aird opened a little store, today the "550" store.

Pete Raish was apparently able to take six of the smaller houses over the bridges and put them in a line on the east side of Holy Cross Cemetery in Marquette.

Joe Borro turned his store in the hollow into a tavern, and Joe Rose tore down the school at Birch and used the lumber to build a tavern up where the lumberjack tavern stands today. With some changes, it is still the same building.

Mac McKenzie had a select, hardworking crew that took out contracts to empty the kilns of bowling pins. It was a hot job. Joe Stuper, Ludwig Prosen, John Barber and Martin Grady were on the crew. They were all making good money. Joe Rose worked his way in with these fellows and was able to buy the land where he built his tavern.

Lowell Fleury, Archie's son, rented the little place in the Hollow from Borro after he gave up his business.

These were bleak years for Big Bay, and there was talk that the town might die. But other things were happening. Cottagers were beginning to settle in around Lake Independence, Bay Cliff Health Camp opened its doors, and a CCC camp was built on Alder Creek. The real boost came when, in 1936, the Kerry and Hanson people came back and purchased the mill, what was left of the company town, and the timber that had been left by Brunswick. It was mainly in two areas, up around the hills near the Hairpin Fire Tower and between Big Bay and the Salmon Trout River.

Albert Lewis was the first Superintendent for Kerry and Hanson, and they hired William Burklund out of Fence, Wisconsin to do contract logging for them. At the same time, Victor Makela started opening up a big pulpwood operation up on the Yellowdog Plains. Big Bay was humming again, and wood was piled at the mill.

Kerry and Hanson were taking the last of the Brunswick timber up along the Sullivan Creek Truck Trail and the Club Road out to Lake Superior. This was the last to go.

The Garlic Locks

In 1927, when the Kaufmans were having their great parties with guests from Chicago, New York and elsewhere, as well as the parties for the graduating classes of the high school, they decided to bring an elaborate canal system up to the railroad depot by way of Saux Head Lake and the Garlic River. The Lake Superior and Ishpeming Railroad – L. S. & I. – had taken over the Marquette and Southeastern Railroad in 1922, and it was an L. S. & I. train that was making the daily runs to and from Big Bay.

Each year Mr. and Mrs. Kaufman had given each other hilarious and often bizzare birthday gifts. They had started some years earlier, rather innocently, but by 1926 the gifts had reached gigantic proportions.

In 1926, Mrs. Kaufman had decided she wanted to bring boats across Saux Head Lake and up the Garlic River. She had an engineer draw up elaborate plans, which included three locks, each of which was to be a large pond to berth the vessels of their guests.

The surprise birthday present was to be a great explosion, which would start the project.

A car load of dynamite was secretly ordered from the Dupont Powder Company and brought up to the Loma Depot. This is where the three locks were to be placed. The charges – hundreds of them – were placed at intervals on both sides of the river and in concentric circles outward.

On Mr. Kaufman's birthday, November 13, 1926, Mrs. Kaufman took Louis to the top of the highest hill behind the farm – some call it Saux Head Mountain. At exactly 12 o'clock noon the earth shook with a terrifying explosion that was heard for many miles; the whole carload was set off at once. Needless to say, it took Mr. Kaufman completely by surprise!

At this point Cement Gust Anderson was brought in to clean up the mess and complete the job.

Mrs. Kaufman talked to the contractor "Cement Gust" and explained the plan. They would build two sets of locks at the outlet of Saux Head Lake and have it so yachts from Chicago and elsewhere could pass from Lake Superior into Saux Head Lake. Then they would dredge the Garlic River and raise the lake level to a point where quite a large vessel, say 50 feet, could travel up the river through two or three more locks to the train depot. Here there would be docking facilities where the boats could be left and the people could be transported to the lodge by the same wagon that met the train.

Gust Anderson was given the word to go ahead with the work. Elaborate engineering had already been completed, and there was no question that the scheme could be carried out. One piece of equipment that was essential was a large crane. The job, Gust figured, would take about three to four years. He picked out and purchased a huge crane just right for the job. It cost him well over $100,000. The idea was that this one project would just about pay for this one big piece of equipment.

Gust went to work in 1927 dredging the river. He started at the upper end with the low water. His crew made log mats which would act as a foundation to give footing to the heavy crane as they drove it along the river bank. Cement dams with gates were constructed near the polo field and further downstream. As the machine worked its way down the river, the mats from behind were taken up and thrown ahead of it. Bends in the river had to be straightened out, and at a few places the course of the stream had to be completely rerouted.

Cement Gust was ahead of schedule and the work was going well. Suddenly Gust was told to stop work, as they were not going to complete the project. He asked for an explanation, but none was forthcoming. He was told that maybe if he waited a few months he could proceed again. Gust was bewildered. He had done a lot of work for the Kaufmans and had never had anything like this happen before. He could not figure out what had gone wrong, and his entire livelihood was tied up in that big new machine. He had made the down payment and about six monthly payments. Interest costs would mount rapidly and he owed over $75,000 on the principal.

The problem that had developed behind the scenes, which Gust Anderson knew nothing about, was that the Michigan Department of Conservation had ordered the project stopped. The Kaufmans had not presented their plan to them for approval, and they would have to have permission to change the course of the river. They assured Mrs. Kaufman that such drastic changes in the river would not be allowed for private purposes, nor would they be allowed to tamper with the lake level to that degree under any circumstances. The Kaufmans could cite several lake levels that had been changed, and since they owned the stream and all the land affected, they felt there should be no problems. They were sure that permission to continue would be granted in due time. While this was one story, another was that the plan was not feasible, engineeringwise, and had to be terminated.

Permission was never granted, and Cement Gust was left with a big machine and a big debt. The project was halted in 1928. A year later, the crash came and the country was thrown into the Depression. The best Gust could do was to pick away at his huge debt from other small jobs. During the Depression he was forced to rent out his big crane for a dollar and a half an hour.

The Kaufman's had spent over $100,000 on a project that couldn't be completed. If one views the scene today, there is always great wonder as to what went on there with three cement dams in place,– three ponds close together and the little river flowing down between them and into the alders.

By 1938, Gust still owed $40,000 and the big crane was almost worn out. It always needed expensive repairs and parts. In 1939 Gust went to Greenland to work in the iron mines there. They were crying for men, and paying big money. Cement Gust was not worried about going all that distance and not getting a job, even though at nearly 60, he would be the oldest man working there. He assured everyone he spoke to that he could outwork any two 25–year–olds they put beside him, and all he asked was a chance to prove it. But Cement Gust, the man who broke stone for Mr. Longyear's stone house 40 years earlier, even did them one better than that. Within a few months on the job, he took on another eight–hour shift. Gust worked 16 hours a day for several years. He didn't stop until he had paid off his debt and had a stake to come home and start in business again. Gust returned home before World War II was over.

Too Much Toilet Paper

Daisy Kaufman spoke with a slight Chicago accent that was not familiar to folks in Marquette, and, besides, a voice could easily become garbled over the phone line from the Loma Farm to Marquette.

Apparently, they were going to need a boxcar load of tarpaper to put on all the roofs at Loma Farm as an undercourse to the asbestos shingles on the various farm buildings.

Always a little impetuous, Mrs. Kaufman called an agent in Marquette and told him to order a carload of tarpaper. The agent thought she said toilet paper and questioned her on it.

Mrs. Kaufman was indignant: "I mean exactly what I said. I want a carload of tarpaper."

Well, when the carload of toilet paper arrived, at first there was shock, then peals of laughter, and it made a great story which they were still telling twenty years later, as there was still plenty left even then.

The Drowning at Pine Lake

Many young girls from all over the area went to work at Huron Mountain over the years as waitresses, cabin girls and cleaning girls. They all had a wonderful time. Mrs. Hodges took it upon herself to hire a recreation director for them who organized picnics, hikes, bonfires, taught them swimming and planned parties. Some of the parties were hilarious. A few members had donated a recreation hall around 1923 and '24 for the help, and parties and dances became regular forms of entertainment. Music was provided by Eddie Rasmussen on the accordion, or by the old windup Victrola.

The highlight of any party was to get Jim Dakota to lead the crowd in a war dance. Everyone would join in. There was no doubt that Jim was at his best if he had been in town a few days before the party.

Two of the girls who couldn't swim were Gertrude Martila from Rock and Tyne Suo from Negaunee Township. In fact, very few of the working girls in those days could swim, but they enjoyed going to Pine Lake. They didn't even own bathing suits, and swam in their slips.

Tyne and Gertrude had often gone down to Pine Lake in the afternoon, walked out to the raft, which was usually in water about chest deep, and sat there in the sun for a half–hour or so. The two girls took off their dresses, and Gertrude took off her stockings also. Tyne noticed that she

562

was wearing some kind of a girdle to keep her tummy in. Gertrude was secretly pregnant by her boyfriend in Rock, and had told only a few close friends. She planned to get married as soon as possible.

It was Tyne's first summer at the Club. She came with her father, Simon Suo, who worked as a carpenter. Though neither of the girls could swim, they had no qualms about walking out to the raft, but unknown to them, a bunch of boys from the Club had been swimming there the night before and had moved the raft out to deep water.

When Tyne got to the drop–off she made a lunge for the raft and climbed up on it. She could hear Gertrude, who had also stepped off the drop–off, struggling behind her. Tyne quickly pulled off her slip and tried to throw one end of it to the drowning girl, but every time she came up she seemed to be further away.

Tyne screamed for help from a girl in a canoe a few hundred yards away, another waitress. The girl in the canoe was terrified because she was using a member's canoe and was sure she would be fired if it became known. She had secretly been seeing a young married member and had his canoe, and was afraid that if she stopped to help, the whole mess would have been exposed. She paddled as fast as she could for the boathouse and ran for help.

Oscar Knuusi, Victor Johnson, Simon Suo and Joe the baker arrived in a truck with a boat in the back. Joe was a wonderful swimmer. He retrieved the body.

The whole episode was a terrible shock to everybody. It was the main reason for the swimming lessons the following years for all non–swimmers or poor swimmers. Many of the members took the drowning very hard, and did everything they could in the way of condolences and paying all the funeral expenses.

Many members who attended the funeral were taken back to see the coffin set up in the sauna, a small separate building on the family farm. This was an old Finnish custom. When the mother saw the dead body of her daughter, she was so grief–stricken that she ran screaming into the field. It is very likely that the girl had also been born in the same sauna, which was also a common practice on the old–style Finnish farms of Upper Michigan. Tyne Suo later married Uno Kivela, a brother of Mamie Ryan.

Ives Lake Farm in the 1930s

The dairy farm at Ives Lake had not worked out. It was too far from a good market, although a wagon met the early train in Big Bay every day and

Upper Left: Carroll Paul
Right: Mrs. Helen Longyear Paul.
Lower left: Roosevelt Dam, Arizona – Carroll Paul helped design this dam and was an engineer on the job.

the milk reached Marquette in a few hours. But it was a lot of handling, and besides, there was difficulty raising enough feed and hay for a very large herd. They had also tried to raise sheep and pigs. The Emblagard Dairy was moved to Marquette, just west of the present golf course on Grove Street, and was taken over by Frank Vandenboom. The Ives Lake Farm had been built by Mr. Longyear and was later taken over by Alton T. Roberts, his son–in–law.

The Robertses had built a beautiful home behind a stucco wall on Longyear land, on the corner of Arch and Cedar streets in Marquette. Before that, they had lived in the Case house on East Ohio Street, where they had entertained Presidents Taft and Roosevelt.

Alton and Abby Roberts separated and later divorced, and Alton left Marquette. While they were married, the couple purchased a large parcel of land west of Marquette which they named "Deer Track." Mrs. Roberts often told of the first time they had walked through the property at the beginning of Whetstone Creek, and a deer had run through ahead of them – thus, the name.

In 1935 Mrs. Roberts contracted with Frank Lloyd Wright, the famous architect, to design a home for them which would be built at Deer Track. The home, constructed there in 1936, is unique and very beautiful, as one might expect, but there were many problems that needed to be ironed out. To eliminate ice buildup on the eaves, Mr. Wright experimented with slanting the roof inward, a type of construction unheard–of in the North. The ice built up anyway, and there were problems with a leaking roof. Mrs. Roberts, with her jovial spirit, was quick to make fun of the many leaks and the expensive changes that had to be made. She called it "El Fiasco" and had a little bronze sign with that name placed under the doorbell. She opened her home for many charitable functions.

In 1911, Helen Longyear married Carroll Paul, a Commander in the U. S. Navy. Commander Paul's father, Henry Martin Paul, was an astronomer of some note. He was a professor of astronomy and mathematics at Annapolis, and was said to have selected the site for the Naval Observatory in Washington, DC. He also spent two years in Japan, during which time he set up an astronomy program for the Emperor.

Carroll and Helen Paul first lived on the island of Guam and then spent three years in the Philippines. Mrs. Paul took on a lot of responsibility in both places, especially Guam. She designed the flag of Guam, which is used to this day, and started a fair there similar to the county fairs that were so popular in the American midwest.

Carroll Paul was a graduate of Dartmouth, and Helen had attended Smith and the Massachusetts Institute of Technology. In her freshman year at

Smith, her roommate was Beatrice Patton, Mrs. George Patton, wife of the General of World War II fame. They became lifelong friends. Helen was one of the very first women to graduate from the MIT School of Architecture. Commander Paul was a civil engineer and designed the steam plant and heating system at Paris Island, South Carolina and the Yorktown Mine Depot at Yorktown, Virginia, among other things. Mrs. Paul designed the gates that are still in use there today.

When Mr. Longyear died in the big home in Brookline, Massachusetts in 1922, Carroll gave up his Navy career and came to Marquette to manage the Longyear estate. He started a going concern which is still in operation today as the Longyear Realty Company. The Pauls spent their summers at Ives Lake Farm and were members of Huron Mountain Club. Mrs. Paul's other sister, Judith Folger Longyear, had married John M. R. Lyeth, and they were also members of the Club. The Lyeths purchased Mr. Longyear's second cabin at the west beach at Huron Mountain.

The youngest son, Robert Dudley Longyear, became a diplomat serving in Central America and elsewhere around the Caribbean. They told an interesting story about Robert's early days in the service. During World War I, Robert joined the Navy and found himself doing duty as a cook on a ship. Mr. Longyear felt that this was a little beneath his station and sought to do something about it. He called Washington and offered to buy the Navy a ship if they would put Robert in charge of it. They agreed, and at their recommendation, Mr. Longyear purchased a minesweeper and Robert was made an officer.

John Munro Longyear's dealings in his lifetime would be impossible to equal today, and are very difficult even to list. He dealt with high government officials and men such as J. P. Morgan, the Rockefellers and the Pillsburys in vast commodities of minerals, timber, land and government projects. He dealt with James J. Hill, the builder of the Great Northern Railroad, and bumped heads with firms such as U.S. Steel over conflicts of interest. Mr. Longyear more often than not won these disputes, because he said he would never go to court unless he had his opponents on his own turf. His coal mines in Spitzbergen became some of the largest producers in the world, and his iron mines on three ranges are still producing after almost a century. At one time, Mr. Longyear owned over a million and a half acres of land in Michigan, Wisconsin and Minnesota. After his death, the states of Michigan and Massachusetts argued as to who should tax the estate. The question went to court. The Michigan stance was defended by the Marquette law firm of Eldridge and Eldridge. A. B. Eldredge was a former director of Huron Mountain Club. In that trial, it was proven that Mr. Longyear resided most of the time in Michigan, voted in Powell Township, did his business out of Marquette, and was a resident of Ives Lake Farm.

Mrs. Longyear died in 1931 and the big home in Brookline was left to be a museum to the Christian Science Church and to Mary Baker Eddy, although still owned by the Longyear Foundation set up to maintain the house and premises. It was opened to the public in 1937. In 1985 the home was featured in a television show as a setting for a fiction story. Many items and furnishings from the big home are in the hands of Longyear descendants who live in Marquette.

With the death of Mr. Longyear in 1922, Carroll and Helen Paul also took over the running of Ives Lake Farm. They built a new, smaller chicken coop in back of the hay barn, kept work horses, about 50 beef cattle, some pigs, a half–dozen or more milk cows, and some ducks, geese and turkeys. It was still a farm, but on a smaller and calmer level of production. It was used more for a summer gathering place for the Longyear family and friends, all of whom kept in touch with Huron Mountain through the use of the Lyeth cabin there and by an exchange of friends and guests between the two places. The grounds, buildings and fields of Ives Lake were beautiful during these years.

The Pauls adopted four children – Beatrice, named after Mrs. Paul's friend, Beatrice Patton; Howard, Judith and Philip. Phil tells a story about Mr. and Mrs. Ford's visit to Ives Lake for a dinner one Sunday noon. Phil had the bedroom right above the dining room in the Stone House. Judy and Phil, the two youngest, were fed ahead of time and sent upstairs. Phil opened the register so he could see and hear what was going on downstairs and, in doing so, dropped dirt and dust all over Mrs. Ford, who was seated in the chair below. As Phil remembers it, Mr. Ford had a good laugh over the incident.

A few years later, when Phil was 12 or 13, he and his brother Howard went to the Club to get something one evening from the Club House office. It was a dark, moonless night and as the two boys ran along the Club House porch, Phil stumbled over the feet of someone who was seated in a chair back in the shadows against the wall. As he went sprawling, the gentleman jumped to his feet and picked him up. It was Mr. Ford.

Black Bart

There was some confusion about who was who when a man named Carl Paul showed up to work at Ives Lake and the Club farm. Ten years later, Carroll Paul came back to run Ives Lake. The only connection that was ever

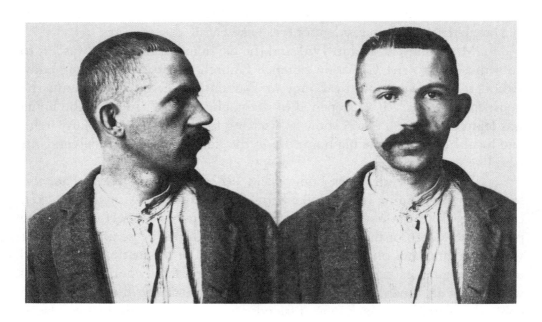

Top: Black Bart. Courtesy Ike Wood.
Bottom: Murphys taken by photographer Black Bart.

568

made between the two was that the Club employee adopted the name when he was released from Marquette Prison in 1914. Three years earlier, the name of Carroll Paul was much in the papers when the handsome Naval Officer married the beautiful Helen Longyear in a grand wedding at Ives Lake. The ex–convict may have chosen the name then, or it could have been pure coincidence.

Carl Paul had no choice but to change from his original name if he was to remain anywhere in the midwest. He had been Reimund Halzhey, a train and stagecoach robber known to many as "Black Bart." In fact, he was famous, or infamous, for being the last stagecoach robber east of the Mississippi. He had held up a stagecoach at the little resort town of Lake Gogebic in the western U. P. on August 26, 1889. He shot two bankers in that holdup, Donald Marcarcher of Minneapolis and Adolph Fleishbein of Belleville, Illinois and reportedly took $10 or $15 from the wounded men. Marcarcher recovered. A $5,000 reward was placed on Halzhey, dead or alive, and a massive manhunt took place. Later it was discovered that he had committed at least two train robberies, and the railroads hired the famous Pinkerton Detective Agency out of Chicago to track him down. On August 31, 1889, Bart Halzhey was captured in Republic and, avoiding a lynch mob, was sent to Marquette Prison, where he spent 25 years. While there, he went berserk and held one prisoner hostage and threatened another with a knife. The prison warden shot the knife out of his hand, and Halzhey was left with only a thumb on his right hand. He said he had blank spells when he was unaware of what he was doing.

Halzhey was sent to Ionia for observation and it was discovered that a boyhood accident had caused pressure on his brain. He had surgery and a silver plate was put in his head, after which he became mild–mannered. He worked in the prison library and edited the prison newspaper.

Alton T. Roberts was a member of the State Board of Corrections, and James Russell was the warden of the Prison. Through the efforts of Alton T. Roberts, a proposition was made to the governor, whereby one of Halzhey's life sentences was commuted and good conduct time was granted for the other. He changed his name to Carl Paul and was secretly brought to Ives Lake to be a cook's helper at the Farm. Abby Longyear's husband, Alton Roberts, was running the farm at this time. Carl Paul spent his first night out of prison alone on the end of the point where the Stone House is at Ives Lake.

Carl Paul later ran a photography shop in Marquette, but when his true identity leaked out, he had to leave the city. He then went to Huron

Mountain again, where this time he was employed by the Club as a photographer. Later he became a fishing guide and then, for a long time, he was a guard, living at the Five Forks Cabin on the Salmon Trout River. The stories about "Black Bart" just hummed around the river and lingered in the woods long after he was gone. Carl Paul was alone most of the time, but many said if you were walking on a trail in the woods with him, he was always the last in line. No one ever got behind Black Bart. There were those who wouldn't trust him, and of course there were many stories about the money he had stolen. Some said he had it stashed away. There was supposed to be a lot of money from the train robbery that was never found. Whenever Carl Paul went somewhere, they were sure he had gone to pick up the money. Howard Treado was a schoolteacher in Big Bay and was selling insurance on the side. He sold Carl Paul a $100,000 paid–up insurance policy.

But Reimond Halzhey had another side to him at that late date, and any threat of violence was really all in the minds of the observers. He had several cameras and did some beautiful photography around the Club and the Salmon Trout River. Winston Elting, who spent all his boyhood summers at Huron Mountain, had fond recollections of Carl Paul. He described him quite differently than others did. Winston first knew him about 1915.

(Carl) Paul had a mustache. His hat was always too big and came down over his rather large ears. In the woods he always carried an axe. He was, despite his right hand, very proficient with it. He loved the forest and got to know it well. He was a good paddler but could not row. He was a good cook. He could quote Shakespeare or Spengler by the hour. His humor was keen and his broken English picturesque. He talked of 'volffs' and 'schwamps' and his laugh was always 'he–he–he.' He smoked a corn–pipe. No reference to his former life was ever made to him – or by him. He was with us many years at Mountain Lake Camp (the Eltings were regular campers on Elting Point there) several years as a guard on the Cedar Creek; several years as a guard on the Salmon Trout River. Along with the earlier Hank (Havery) he was my great favorite. He was quiet, intelligent, thoughtful and efficient in his work. We felled many dead trees together on Burnt Mountain and pulled them across the lake to use as firewood. He would rig a sail on one of Oscar's boats and hope for a tailwind. Otherwise he would paddle. He loved to tell stories from the books he had read, and we would sit around the fire at night listening to him.

Book One

The Desormier Girls

A group of sisters began working at Huron Mountain in the 1920s, and some remained there many years. These were the Desormiers. They came from a family of 13 children born to Julius and Emma Desormier, who had come, like most of the French in Marquette, from eastern Canada. There were three boys and ten girls. Three of the children died young. Two of the girls married Decembers, and a brother and a sister married Strielmans. Isabelle and Olive Desormier married Joe and Ray December, and Phillip Desormier married Ann Strielman, and Jeanette Desormier married Joe Strielman. Joe was the Superintendent of Schools at Big Bay for many years, and ran the Club store in the summertime. Four of the girls worked at Huron Mountain as waitresses – Leona, Virginia, Isabelle and Jeanette.

Leona, the oldest of the Desormier girls at Huron Mountain, married Ed Rasmussen, Jr. They had four children. Bobby, who was born January of 1927, drowned in April of 1929. Shirley was born in 1928. The Rasmussens were living in the log home that Oscar Knuusi had built at what was known at the West End, but which he had vacated when he bought Oscar Webster's house on Hewitt Avenue in Marquette. After that, Oscar, when at the Club, lived at the Guide House.

Leona Desormier Rasmussen came to Huron Mountain July 17, 1921, as a waitress and continued as such until 1936. From 1936 to 1940 she was the head of the cabin crew and from 1940 to 1948 was the Head Headwaitress. She then managed the dining room until her death in 1964.

The Jensen children and the Rasmussen children were playing on the icebergs of Lake Superior along the shore. They were all very young. The children knew better than to play on the icebergs, but sometimes they would stray out and climb up and slide down the side toward the shore.

An article in the Mining Journal of April 2, 1929, explained that Mrs. Rasmussen had come out of the house and spoken to young Bobby and then went into a nearby house for a few minutes. When she returned, she asked where Bobby was; the children said that he had run off toward the lake, a few hundred yards from the home. They followed the tracks out onto the icebergs, where they disappeared. Myrtle Jensen went to the Club to get Ed and Ronald to retrieve the body. The body was retrieved in slush ice with pike poles. Bobby had been in the water between three and four hours and had no water in his lungs. On December 16th of the same year as the accident, another boy was born. This second son was named Edward James but was always called Bobby. The last child, Carol, was born March 31, 1933. By then, Ed was running the light plant and the family had moved to a

Upper left: Some of the fourth generation of Rasmussens at Huron Mountain – Shirley and Carol Rasmussen.
Upper right: The Desormier family.
Bottom: Charles B. Burns School. 1930's. Courtesy Milton Tomkins.

duplex at the Club proper, opposite the Ryans. This duplex also had a double outhouse, with one side for each family.

Ronald Jensen, stepson of Hans, had lived with his uncle and aunt, Oscar and Julia Webster, in Marquette on Hewitt while going to school. He married Myrtle Thompson, daughter of Ed Thompson of the Fin, Fern and Feather Club. Ronald and Myrtle had four children, all brought into the world by Mrs. Jay Thompkins, who acted as midwife for all of the births. First there was Jean, born in 1922. She was born with a bad cleft palate, and they were sure it was from Myrtle watching something like a chipmunk too much during the pregnancy. Then there was Ronald Lyle, born in 1924, Thelma in 1925, and Betty in 1927.

Ronald, Jr. was killed during the noon hour at school in Big Bay when he was about nine years old. The kids had learned to grab the bumpers of cars and trucks to go for a ride on the icy roads. Young Ronald hung onto the back of an old army transport truck that was under contract to scrape the roads for the county. The truck belonged to a Mr. Johnson who was living at the Tonella Farm at Buckroe. He was in front of the Presbyterian church and about to turn around. Not seeing the boy, he proceeded to back up, running over young Ron. The Jensens and the Rasmussens had a certain kinship for some years, having each lost a son. Both of these families were raised at Huron Mountain.

Another Fire at Big Bay

On Dec. 31, 1936, the Charles B. Burns School in Big Bay burned to the ground. Mr. Perkins, who was the Powell Township Supervisor at the time and a friend of Henry Ford's, called Mr. Ford in Dearborn. He told Mr. Ford what had happened, and that they could provide for the children of the lower grades in the churches, the township hall, jail and the teacherage, all within a hundred yards of each other, but that the older children would have to travel to Marquette and a school bus was badly needed.

The swift reply was "I'll have one driven up tomorrow." The bus arrived and the students didn't miss a single day of school. Mamie Ryan's son Billy, who was in about the first or second grade at the time, tells of going to school in the Powell Township jail. There was an article about it in the Detroit papers.

...and Fires at Huron Mountain

Fire has always been of great concern at Huron Mountain and Big Bay. I have mentioned the burning of the first DuCharme cabin in 1913. Then there was an early fire in the Club Room which destroyed a beautiful birch–bark ceiling put there by early steward Dan Sullivan. That fire took place on September 23, 1925, and the Club House itself was nearly lost. The fire broke out in the east wing. There was also a fire at Ives Lake where a long nursery room attached to the Stone House by an overpass from the second floor burned. No one was hurt in that fire either. The heroes of the Club House fire were Herb Perkins, chef Jack Bodine, Victor Johnson, Tappan Gregory, and Douglas Stewart. A classic remark has lingered down through the years from that fire. It came from Victor Johnson as he stood on the Club House roof, flames bursting around him, and he with an empty hose, "Less talk, more water!"

Ten years later, in 1935, the Le Moyne cabin burned to the ground. The story was around at the time that Bud Le Moyne invented the heatolator, and the fire that did the cabin in was caused from an overheated heatolator.

Mr. Le Moyne had died and Mrs. Le Moyne was too feeble to come to the Club any more. Percival Dodge of Detroit was very anxious to buy the cabin, but Mrs. Le Moyne was reluctant to have anyone but herself stay in it. Under some heavy coaxing, she finally acquiesced, and the Dodges had many repairs made on the aging cabin before they planned their first stay in it.

The story goes that the day before Mr. Dodge was to arrive, the carpenters hurriedly finished their work and cleaned up the scrap ends of lumber and piled them into the fireplace to burn. During the night the cabin burned to the ground, and the fire seemed to have started from an overheated fireplace.

The haunting tale that went with the burning of the cabin was that in the last weeks, Mrs. Le Moyne had some second thoughts about selling the place. She could not bear the thought of someone else using her cabin. That night, before the Dodges arrived, Mrs. Le Moyne died in Chicago, at about the same time the cabin burst into flames. When Mr. Dodge arrived the next day, there was nothing but ashes.

But the greatest fire in the Club's history occurred on a night in May of 1939, when a fire, thought to be electrical in origin, started in the Bell cabin and quickly spread to the Shortall cabin next door. It jumped two cabins east to the Russel cabin.

Mamie Ryan was making her way from her home, the Ryan–Rasmussen duplex, to the Guide House to start breakfast at about 4:30 that morning. The sky to the northeast was unusually brilliant for that time of the morning, but it was still some time before the sparks in the air made her realize that it was not an early sunrise, but a great fire.

There was a stiff wind out of the west and by the time men and equipment had arrived, the second building was burning. Everyone was afraid that the seven cabins to the east might go. Men were stationed on the roof of Mr. Harrison's Keweenaw cabin to the east, to put out any brands that might land on it. The two burning cabins were deemed hopeless, so the firefighters concentrated their efforts on saving the cabin next door.

Just when it looked like success was theirs, the cry went up that the Russel cabin up the beach was in flames. Many felt that if the wind hadn't died down, there would have been a much greater loss. All three of these cabins were replaced in 1939 and '40.

The result of this great fire of 1939 was a much improved fire–fighting system, fire drills and alarm system. Since that time there have been many fire precautions, fire hydrants, fire trucks and fire inspections. Several fires since that time have been caught and extinguished, but nothing got away from them again at Huron Mountain.

Oscar the Builder

It was several years after the completion of the Ford cabin in 1929 that Oscar Knuusi was made construction foreman at the Club. He was now an institution there, with over 25 years of service as a boat builder and rustic furniture maker. Everyone had great confidence in Oscar as a builder. While he had worked on several cabins, the first one he had full responsibility for was the Willard M. Clapp cabin. The Clapps were from Cleveland, Ohio.

If Oscar was going to be in charge, then he was going to be in charge, and nobody was going to tell him what to do. He made change after change in the architects' plans – subtle changes, but changes. At first these were over the objections of both architect and owner, but they soon realized that Oscar always had good reasons for any change. However, there was much ado over his audacity in making changes, often without saying anything. It was soon learned that this was a part of Oscar's personality. They would have to either fire him or learn to live with his ways, because Oscar wasn't going to change. His genius was soon recognized. The Clapp cabin workmanship was above reproach.

Top: Oscar Knuusi the builder. Photograph by Dr. Fredric Schreiber. Courtesy Huron Mountain Club 1942.
Bottom: Building the Clapp cabin (1931). Courtesy Knuusi Family.

A few years later, in 1935, Oscar was in charge of building a 22–room log cabin for Senator David A. Reed of Pennsylvania. He was given free rein, and again the finished product was outstanding. The people of Huron Mountain found it much easier and less expensive to work with Oscar than it was to hire a contractor from town whom they didn't know. More than any other foreman, he put himself into the project, doing much of the work himself.

When the Le Moyne cabin burned in 1935, there was a restriction on taking logs from the Club property. Oscar suggested jackpine from the Yellowdog Plains. Mr. Dodge left it up to Oscar. Oscar completed this cabin in 1938 and then replaced the three that had burned in 1939. These three cabins, completed in 1940, were the last full cabins Oscar was in charge of, and these were the last years he built any boats. He was still foreman when additions were made to the Haffner cabin and the sitting room added to the River cabin. These were all log constructions, and the last complete log buildings ever built at Huron Mountain. Log work became too expensive, and the next cabin built at Huron Mountain was of frame construction. It was built in 1947 for Mr. and Mrs. Wendell C. Goddard of Detroit, and Franz Menze of Marquette was the contractor.

The log cabins of Huron Mountain are as much a treasure of the Upper Peninsula as are the sandstone buildings of Marquette. It seems like the sandstone buildings should outlast log buildings, but this has not always been the case.

White Deer Lake Country

Up until this time (World War II) some of the members and guests of Huron Mountain Club had enjoyed, to a limited extent, the use of a sister camp to the south. It was a continuation of Huron Mountain, just as large, with more but smaller bodies of water, far more secluded. Most people knew little or nothing about it. With over 100 miles of beautiful trails, a history that went back beyond that of Huron Mountain Club, and owned by two of Huron Mountain's members, it was still, to most people, a place that just didn't exist.

In all the writings of Huron Mountain Club – and there have been many down through the years – not so much as a word was ever mentioned about the White Deer Lake country. In 1929, the Book of Huron Mountain was published in a very limited edition by the Huron Mountain Club Conservation Committee. The organizer and writer of the history portions of the book was Bayard H. Christy, who was himself a frequenter of the White Deer Lake country and knew it well, but again, not one word was mentioned about it in his history.

How could such a beautiful spot go unnoticed, and who could support such a place? In the 1930s both of its original owners, Cyrus H. McCormick and Cyrus Bentley, died and the property passed to a son of Mr. McCormick. Then in 1967 the property passed to the Federal Government under the jurisdiction of the U. S. Forest Service.

Just who were these people, and what is the story that has been kept so quiet that it is about to be lost to time? It is real backwoods history of our central Upper Michigan. There are many local people with ancestors who were in some way connected with this almost mythical heaven deep in the woods, and who would like to know something of their life there and the story of the place.

Let's look back into the history of this unknown land to the south of Huron Mountain Club, and the history of some of the people connected with it. Let's look into some of the stories of the forgotten past.

White Deer Lake Country. 1930's. Rydholm collection.

Book Two

White Deer Lake Country:
The South End of the Bentley Trail

Book Two

R obert McCormick, the father of Cyrus Hall McCormick, emigrated from Ireland and settled in Rockbridge County, Virginia, just after the Revolutionary War. He was more than just an ambitious farmer; for years he was dedicated to the improvement of agriculture. He constantly worked to eliminate the backbreaking drudgery of harvesting grain, particularly wheat. He envisioned the development of a reaper, a machine designed to automatically cut and stack grain in one operation. Robert made several models of a reaper, but none proved successful.

Robert's son, Cyrus Hall McCormick, was a brilliant, hardworking, and determined young man. At age 22, after studying his father's records of failure in his designs for a reaper, he proceeded with some new ideas of his own. His ambition was rewarded when in 1831 he successfully demonstrated his reaper to a small group of farmers gathered at his father's farm near Steele's Tavern.

Cyrus continued to improve on his invention until finally he perfected it. He built several models of the reaper himself, eventually obtaining a patent in 1834.

A few years later, Cyrus went into the pig iron business with his father. However, the effects of the panic of 1837 nearly wiped out this venture in 1839. Trying to make an income from his invention, McCormick sold the first reaper in 1840. As business prospered, the McCormick reaper came into use in New York and Pennsylvania. A few got as far as Indiana, Illinois, and Wisconsin, and even Tennessee and Ohio. By 1844 more than fifty reapers had been sold for $100 each.

Cyrus McCormick might never have tried to obtain a patent for his reaper but for the fact that he had read an account of another inventor, Obed Hussey, who also developed a reaper in the autumn of 1833.There was another reaper invented in England in 1826 that seems to have gone unnoticed. It was built by a Reverend Bell, and with a few changes was in use until 1868. Because this machine was in Europe and there was only one built,

Top: Cyrus Hall McCormick. Inventor of the reaper (1880).
Middle: The blacksmith shop in which Cyrus McCormick built his first reaper in 1831. It still stands today on the family farm, Walnut Grove, in Rockbridge County, Virginia.
Bottom: The Bell Reaper (1826) invented by the Reverend Patrick Bell. Reportedly it could cut one acre per hour. Now in the British Museum of Science.

it never got into the McCormick–Hussey competition. The original Bell reaper stands today in the British Museum in London.

Although Cyrus and his father were skeptical about the commercial value of the reaper, Cyrus was determined to protect his interests, and took the proper steps to have his machine patented. In the meantime, Hussey had been producing and selling his reaper under a different patent. This not only inspired McCormick to produce reapers, but the competition also gave him the impetus to promote and advertise his own product.

After the harvest of 1844, McCormick traveled to New York state and through the western states, where the vast expanse of flat country astounded him. From this observation he began to realize the immense potential market for his reaper. Returning to Virginia, he sold a license to manufacture reapers to two business partners, Seymour and Morgan, in Brockport, New York. He also sent his younger brother Leander to Cincinnati, Ohio to begin production of the reaper there.

In 1847, McCormick moved to Chicago, where he built a large factory on the Chicago River and continued to improve his machine, obtaining patents to cover modifications in 1845 and 1847. The simmering battle between Hussey and McCormick erupted, and as a result the courts denied an extension of his patent. McCormick had lost the first of a great many lawsuits which were to continue for the next thirty years.

In 1851, McCormick confronted the partners Seymour and Morgan in a lawsuit. McCormick sued because of several damaging newspaper articles stating the inferiority of the harvester bearing the McCormick name but built by Seymour and Morgan. After two years of litigation, McCormick was awarded $9,354 in damages. As a result, Seymour and Morgan were no longer competitors.

However, McCormick's greatest competition during these years was another brilliant farm boy from New York, John H. Manny. Manny organized and led a large group of lesser reaper manufacturers against McCormick, who countered by filing suit against them over infringements of the 1845 and 1847 patents. Among the host of attorneys arguing the Manny case was Edwin M. Stanton, who later became Secretary of War, and a younger lawyer named Abraham Lincoln. It was Lincoln's first big case, and for the first time he earned a fee of a thousand dollars. Later it was said that it was Stanton's oratory in the case which inspired Lincoln toward the Lincoln–Douglas debates and thus perhaps led him to seek the presidency. Stanton became Secretary of War under Lincoln. It was said that the two men admired but never liked one another.

Other manufacturers entered the field of building reapers, and all were challenged by McCormick. Some were bought out, but always the McCormick reaper won the admiration of the farmer. McCormick forged ahead, always working with the farmers to improve his machines.

The huge factory he had built on the Chicago River was greatly expanded in 1849. This was about as close as anyone had come to mass–production of a large item at this time. McCormick was shaping the way of American industry and establishing wheat instead of corn as the basic American grain crop. Cyrus Hall McCormick is acknowledged to have been the world's leading industrialist at the time.

McCormick continued to strive for perfection in his business. He realized how important it was to his reputation to have all McCormick machines manufactured in his own factories. To retain control, he issued no more production licenses when existing ones ran out.

In 1857, when Cyrus McCormick was 48 years old, he met Nancy Fowler, who was visiting friends in Chicago.

Nancy Marie Fowler, "Nettie" as she was usually called, was born to Melzar and Clarissa Spicer Fowler on February 8, 1835 in Brownville, New York. She had two brothers – Anson, who died in infancy, and Eldridge, who was just a few years older than Nancy. He was to remain very close to her in the ensuing years.

When Nancy was but seven months old and Eldridge two years, their father was killed in an accident, kicked by his own ill–tempered horse. For the next seven years Nancy lived with her mother and brother in Depouville, New York.

In 1842 Clarissa, who had been ailing, died, leaving the nine–year–old Eldridge and seven–year–old Nettie orphans. The children went to live with their grandparents in nearby Clayton, a small town jutting out into the St. Lawrence River. Here they lived closely with their uncle, John Fowler and uncle–in–law, Eldridge C. Merick. They had the companionship of cousins near their own age. The families were all very religious.

Nettie attended three private schools, leaving home the first time when she was 15. Nettie taught school on two or three occasions during the next five years. At one point she became quite ill and spent a few months working at a "water cure" in Elmira, New York. She was there with two of her cousins, Ermina Merick and a Mrs. Lyon. Nettie was the first to fully recover, and after visiting a school friend in Lima, Ohio, she returned home to Clayton. She then accompanied Mrs. Lyon to Chicago, where she cared for her cousin's two children. It was while in Chicago that Nettie happened to meet Mr. McCormick, already a famous and wealthy man. McCormick, at that time, was spending little time in Chicago due to his business with patents and lawsuits in New York and Washington. His business in Chicago was, for the most part, being looked after by his younger brothers, William and Leander, all under Cyrus' direction by letter.

Nevertheless, the meeting of Cyrus Hall McCormick and Nettie Marie Fowler did occur and on January 26, 1858 a grand wedding was held in Chicago, the bride age 22, the groom 48.

About the time of the Civil War, two young farmer brothers named Marsh produced a machine they called a harvester. It did some extra steps beyond the reaper in the harvesting of grain. It not only cut and bound the wheat, but it also separated the grain from the stalk. The new machine immediately made the reaper obsolete. Cyrus McCormick had no choice but to begin making harvesters, and his knowledge made him the supreme builder. McCormick later added a binder that could be used for any grain to his growing line of farm equipment.

On May 16, 1859, just prior to the Civil War, their first son, Cyrus Rice McCormick, was born. He was named Cyrus for his father and Rice for Dr. Nathan Rice, a friend of Cyrus and Nettie who had officiated at their wedding. As a teen–ager, Cyrus Jr. dropped the Rice and took his father's name in full.

When he was a few months old, Cyrus and Nettie McCormick took young Cyrus to Rockbridge County, Virginia, the home of his ancestry. They visited many relatives and friends, who became immediate beneficiaries of the newfound McCormick wealth. Returning to Chicago in the fall, the family lived in a fine new hotel, the Richmond House, on Michigan Avenue. Cyrus referred to his son as "Young Reaper."

The McCormick industry – that is, the reaper and Cyrus McCormick as its inventor and largest manufacturer – drew much credit and praise during the Civil War. Secretary of War Stanton, who by this time had become a great friend of McCormick's, said, "The reaper is to the north what slavery is to the south." Stanton believed that without the harvester, the wheat crop could not have been gathered at all or, if the North had relied on manpower alone, its fighting strength would have been critically reduced. In either case, Stanton reasoned, lack of food or lack of men could have lost the war and broken the Union.

Cyrus, being from Virginia, was a southerner who had adopted the north. His wife Nettie was a born northerner who shared his philosophy about the war. They believed in the abolition of slavery but felt that it should occur gradually and by law, with restitution being made by the government.

Nancy Marie Fowler "Nettie McCormick."

They abhorred the war and the idea that the country should be split in two. They would do anything in their power to end the war and reunite the north and south.

Their second child was a daughter, Anita, who married Emmons Blain, the son of James G. Blain, who had been Secretary of State under Garfield and who had been defeated by Grover Cleveland for the Presidency.

Cyrus and Nettie were present at the inauguration of President Lincoln in March of 1861, only months before the birth of their second daughter, Mary Virginia.

In 1860, probably to further his cause against the war, Cyrus McCormick bought two Chicago newspapers, the Chicago Herald and the Chicago Daily Times, and combined them into the Daily Chicago Times. Within a short time he sold part interest to a Wilbur F. Stoney and gave the remaining interest to his brother–in–law, Eldridge Fowler.

McCormick, a staunch Democrat all of his life, entered politics. He ran in the primary for Mayor of Chicago but was defeated. He also thought about running for governor, senator, congressman, and even vice–president, but never held a public office.

On October 8, 1871, the main McCormick factory, as well as the entire business district and a large portion of the residential district of Chicago, burned in the Great Chicago Fire. McCormick immediately took over as one of the main forces to rebuild the city. His courage and stamina prevailed more than ever in this time of holocaust.

At the time of the fire, Nettie McCormick was in New York with the three children. She spent much time in upstate New York, hoping the children would benefit from country life. She did not like living in hotels. Cyrus McCormick had gone to Chicago on business and was there when the fire occurred. When Nettie and the children went to the telegraph office to send a message to Chicago announcing their departure for home, they were told, "There is no Chicago."

On May 5, 1872, during the early days of the reconstruction of Chicago, Harold Fowler McCormick, their fourth child, was born.

A year later, with reconstruction nearly complete, McCormick and others opened a huge exposition building on the Chicago lake front to show everyone that Chicago had recovered.

Mr. McCormick was a man of great wealth at this time and was of retirement age but, rather than stand aside and allow others to take over, he began several more projects. He rebuilt the plant,along with many huge warehouses. He also purchased a great expanse of prairie land outside the Chicago area for future expansion. Cyrus McCormick was continually looking toward the future.

The expansion proceeded rapidly into all types of farm equipment and machinery. The influences of Cyrus McCormick now extended to the furthest reaches of the agricultural world.

All in all, Cyrus and Nettie McCormick had six children: Cyrus, Anita, Mary Virginia, Harold, Stanley, who had mental problems at an early age, and Alice, who died very young.

Although he never held a political office, McCormick was a great politician. An intimate friend of the great journalist Horace Greely, McCormick is given credit for having inspired Greely with his wisdom.

McCormick acted as a counselor to hundreds of people up until his death in 1884. It had been his practice to see, hear, and help if possible, anyone who came to him. Inventor, industrialist, developer, philanthropist, Cyrus Hall McCormick was one of the great men of his time.

Cyrus H. McCormick

Cyrus H. McCormick, the eldest son of the inventor Cyrus Hall McCormick, took over as president of his father's company at the age of 25. He was at Princeton at the time. Nettie McCormick, his mother, could easily have taken over the operation by virtue of her knowledge and ability, but she chose to maintain control through her eldest son rather than violate a society rule of the 1800's that women did not participate in business ventures. Actually, she received a great deal of help from her brother, Eldridge Merick Fowler.

Eldridge had gotten married the same day as Nettie. He had moved with his wife to Bay City, Michigan, and was in the logging business when he heard of McCormick's death. He gave up the logging and moved to Chicago to help Nettie run the business. The title "President" passed to Cyrus, Jr., when he returned from Princeton, but it was some time before he actually took over that position.

Competition in the field of harvesters during the 1890's had become intense and bitter. Every means, both fair and foul, was used to sell a piece of farm equipment. Smaller and weaker companies fell by the wayside as the larger companies undersold each other. Lawsuits continued, and the market became flooded with farm machinery. The future looked bleak. It soon became evident that the competition should join forces.

McCormick and Deering, the two largest companies, made an early attempt to amalgamate and then backed out due to insurmountable problems. Later, an attempt to combine ten harvester companies under the name of the American Harvester Company was undertaken, but this too fell through. Many leaders felt that such a merger would not have stood up under the Sherman Antitrust Laws.

Finally, in 1902, at the suggestion of the famous New York financier J. Pierpont Morgan, five companies – the John Deere Company, the Deering Company, the Milwaukee Harvester Company, Champion, and the McCormick Company – joined together to form the International Harvester Company. The title "International" also was a suggestion of Mr. Morgan. J. P. Morgan was so interested in this business venture that the House of Morgan purchased one of the amalgamating companies, the Milwaukee Harvester Company, and became one of the partners in the newly formed International Harvester Company. Much of the tremendous amount of legal work was carried out by a staff of lawyers under the direction of a brilliant attorney, Cyrus Bentley, who represented the McCormick interests in the merger.

Cyrus Bentley was from an old Chicago family. His father, also named Cyrus Bentley, had started practicing in Chicago in 1847, the same year the McCormick industry had moved to that city. The families had known each other for years, and the McCormicks had carefully followed the brilliant career of young Cyrus Bentley over the years. He had graduated from Yale University in 1882 at the age of twenty and from Union College of Law two years later, and was admitted to the Chicago Bar while still a student. He began practicing with the firm of Bentley and Quigg, of which his father was senior member. Upon the death of his father in 1888, young Cyrus became a partner of Colonel Quigg. The Colonel retired in 1898 and Bentley formed a partnership with Edward B. Burling, under the name of Bentley and Burling. It was at this time that he was hired by Mr. McCormick.

In his early years, Cyrus Bentley had tried many important cases. He was an expert in the laws of real estate, wills, trusts and the administration of estates. He had also become especially skilled in corporate law. To Cyrus McCormick, he was the obvious person to organize the huge International Harvester Company.

With the amalgamation of these several companies, the harvester war had finally come to an end. The capital of the newly formed company exceeded $120,000,000. Cyrus H. McCormick, at age 36, was president of the firm, and Charles Deering was named Chairman of the Board of Directors.

From 1913 to 1918 the International Harvester Company was under continuous attack in various state courts and by the federal government on the grounds that it was a monopoly. In 1918 it was legally decided that this was true, and the International Harvester Company agreed to divest itself of

Upper left: Cyrus McCormick.
Upper right: Cyrus Bentley.
Bottom: William Cunningham Gray (1830–1901).

592

the Osborne, Champion, and Milwaukee lines of harvesting machines and to maintain only one dealer per town.

At the reorganization of the company in 1918, Cyrus McCormick became Chairman of the Board of Directors, and the presidency of the company was turned over to his younger brother Harold. Four years later, after 90 years of McCormicks at the helm of the leading farm machinery company in the world, the presidency passed out of the family to Alexander Legge, who had for many years been general manager of the company.

In recent years, Fowler McCormick and Brooks McCormick have taken their turn as company presidents, but these men are descendants of brothers of Cyrus McCormick I and II. The Cyrus McCormick II line has run out.

History of the White Deer Lake Country
(since 1967: The Cyrus H. McCormick Experimental Forest)

The McCormick Tract

The history of the McCormick Tract begins in 1884 with the death of Cyrus Hall McCormick, inventor of the reaper. This was the year in which Cyrus H. McCormick, eldest son of the inventor, succeeded his father as president of the McCormick Farm Machinery Company, and also the year in which he decided to go on his first camping trip.

As a student at Princeton, the young millionaire McCormick met a professor, Dr. William C. Gray of that university. For many years, Dr. Gray had been selecting wilderness areas from an atlas, then traveling to the town or village nearest this point, where he would hire an Indian guide and go camping in these spots.

It soon became Dr. Gray's method to look for an area which had the headwaters of two or three streams or rivers flowing in different directions and several small lakes relatively close to one another. Areas which fulfilled these requirements usually proved to be excellent camping grounds with unusually abundant game.

Gray's camping junkets had taken him to many regions of the United States. He had established a permanent camp on an island in a small lake called Island Lake in Bayfield County, Wisconsin. Between 1875 and 1900 he invited many people to his retreat, including the McCormicks, with whom he became great friends. Because of the location of his camp, his trips narrowed down in these years to locations scattered throughout the Upper Peninsula and northern Wisconsin.

William Gray was an ardent outdoorsman, and took pride in his knowledge of the trees, wildflowers, food, medicines, and fauna of the areas he had explored on his camping expeditions. He developed a personal philosophy of man's relationship to nature which he shared with his students and friends. According to Gray, there was nothing in the entire world better for health and peace of mind than a week or two "roughing it" in the forest–fishing, hiking, exploring, and canoeing.

Professor Gray (1830–1901) was the author of Campfire Musings. He was a pioneer spirit who brought an original and lively approach to everything he did. In 1875 he became the first columnist and introduced to newspapers a special reporting technique with his story of the Northern Pacific Railroad's completion in 1883. His paper made almost the earliest regular use of half–tone newspaper illustrations in 1891, and installed the first typesetting machines in 1892. He was one of the first to print photographs taken in natural colors in 1897, and one of the first special writers to carry his own camera for picture reporting, for the Lapland Reindeer Expedition to Alaska in 1899.

Dr. Gray writes:

> Pile on the pine and hemlock boughs,
> Send up the starry shower
> Ten days of wildwood friendship be
> Concentrated in this hour.
>
> Perchance, when the last battle's fought
> In the last evening's damp
> Our earthly thought of Heaven's rest
> Will be this island camp.

When Cyrus McCormick accepted Dr. Gray's invitation to accompany him on a camping trip north, Gray secretly met Nettie McCormick, Cyrus's mother, and arranged for some of Cyrus's personal possessions to be sent to the campsite before they arrived, so he would be sure to feel at home in the woods.

Gray had selected a region in the Upper Peninsula which encompasses the headwaters of the Yellowdog, Peshekee, Dead, and Big Huron rivers and Mulligan Creek, to bring young McCormick camping. This area met all of his specifications, including the numerous rivers, lakes, timber, islands, rugged terrain, and abundant fish and game. Beyond all these natural elements, this area was undeveloped and uninhabited, which provided the seclusion he desired.

Dr. Gray had probably come to this spot earlier and scouted it out before he would invite a novice like Cyrus McCormick to camp with him, and it can be assumed that Dr. Gray thought of this as a very special place.

Traveling from Chicago on a railroad which had only recently been extended north to connect the Marquette Iron Range with the outside world, McCormick, a companion, and Dr. Gray stopped at the small mining community of Champion, Michigan, situated near the eastern end of beautiful Lake Michigamme.

The three men and the French–Indian guide they had hired followed an Indian trail up the Peshekee River to the lake region north of Champion. Expecting that Dr. Gray had arranged a primitive, wilderness–style campsite for their trip, Cyrus McCormick was pleasantly surprised when, venturing near the edge of a beautiful, nameless lake, he came upon a spotless white tent, bed with sheets, new fishing pole, and an assortment of his own personal effects. His first exclamation was, "My mother!"

When he saw the strong, light rowboat, painted gleaming white with his favorite sister's name, Anita, neatly lettered on the bow, he said, "My sister!"

McCormick's first stay in the Peshekee Country was a pleasant one. He explored the lake country on foot and in a rowboat. He brought down a white–tailed buck with his first shot. He found peace and serenity in the forest, a welcome change from the pace of the city and business life.

In the ensuing years, McCormick returned to this northern area from time to time. He explored the area more thoroughly, and became well acquainted with this portion of the wilderness and soon began to feel at home there. It became a place of refuge for him.

About this same time, the country began to open up. Logging companies were beginning to take the white pine from the region. Charles Hebard and Sons from the L'Anse side, Jim Redy from the Yellowdog River, and F. W. Read and Co. from the Peshekee River area were beginning to cut white pine and float it down the river. Redy had made a dam at Bulldog Lake, and Read had several dams on the Peshekee and a big mill on Lake Michigamme. A steam tug was operating on the lake to bring the logs to Read's mill, which was cutting up to 75,000 feet of lumber a day.

However, with the exception of building roads, dams, bridges, and camps in the fall, logging was for the most part a winter operation. McCormick and his party, who were summer visitors to this region, had little contact with the lumbermen.

The Iron Range and Huron Bay Railroad

In 1890, another operation got under way which further penetrated the rugged northern wilderness along the Peshekee River valley. This was the construction of the Huron Bay Railroad grade.

Milo Davis, an entrepreneur from Detroit, had observed the spread of the Marquette Iron Range from Negaunee westward to the Taylor Mine, seven miles east of L'Anse.

Champion was located at the center of the western end of the ore field, and from an overall view on a map it was only twenty–five miles to a beautiful, natural harbor at Huron Bay on Lake Superior. Davis envisioned a railroad heading north through this rugged wilderness which would carry all of the iron ore from the western end of the range – that is, from the Champion, Michigamme, Republic, Ohio, Beaufort, and possibly the Taylor mines. Davis was also confident that iron, copper and other minerals would soon be discovered in the rocky hills to the north.

It was speculated that a railroad in this area would develop the logging business. Gold, silver, lead and zinc mines had already opened near the iron range at Silver Lake north of Ishpeming, and along the Dead River Basin, and Davis was sure that others would open up soon.

In 1890, several slate quarries were operating near the little village of Arvon, four miles south of Huron Bay. Slate quarrying was an established business, and a four–mile horse–drawn tramway extending from Arvon to Lake Superior was already in use. The railroad was planned to go through Arvon and link the slate production with the main railway. This would make it possible to lengthen the slate quarrying season since the slate could then go by either rail or ship and would not necessarily be limited to the summer shipping season.

S. C. Smith first drew attention to slate in 1868, when he carried samples from Arvon to Marquette. They were sent to Vermont for examination and analysis, and all reports were favorable. In the years that followed, more and more slate samples were analyzed and determined to be of a quality that could be quarried profitably.

W. L. Wetmore; M. H. Maynard, lawyer and school board member of Marquette; Peter White, banker, politician and also a school board member; William Burt, land dealer and son of William A. Burt; and F. P. Wetmore, grocer, organized the Huron Bay Slate and Iron Company. Besides the company town of Arvon, the company owned a well–built wooden dock extending 200 yards into Huron Bay.

Top: The huge, modern pocket dock built on Huron Bay by the Iron Range and Huron Bay Railroad Co. No ore was ever deposited or shipped from it.

Bottom: The Christopher Columbus, the only "whaleback" passenger ship ever built. She carried more passengers than any other Great Lakes ship during her career. Built in 1892, the 400th anniversay of Columbus' trip to America, it arrived at the Columbian Exposition in Chicago 1893. In this picture it is docked at the Huron Bay ore dock on its first trip to Lake Superior. She stopped at Marquette many times. The Christopher Columbus was scrapped in 1937, her steel sold to Japan.

Top: The largest of seven rock cuts along the Huron Bay Grade.
Bottom: I. R. & H. B/ engine number 301 ready to go – it never went.

In 1874, the Clinton Company, a group of men from Houghton and New York, established a quarry nearby. T. T. Hurley of Marquette opened another quarry, and the Michigan Slate and Mining Company opened still another, all within a mile of one another, in Arvon Township.

The slate was of high quality. After being quarried, much of it was shipped to various companies to be processed into material for billiard tables or roofing. Some shingles were made on the site. However, due to the small demand and excessive costs of processing, the businesses failed entirely in 1880.

By 1882, a group of men from Lansing had taken over all the slate companies and invested thousands of dollars in improvements, and the new Michigan Slate Company was flourishing while plans were being made for the Iron Range and Huron Bay Railroad.

Milo Davis, superintendent and construction engineer for the railroad, had estimated that the entire project would cost $15,000 to complete. He later upgraded his estimate to $50,000, but five years later he had spent $2,000,000.

Capital for the booming copper and iron mines of the Upper Peninsula was relatively easy to come by in the 1880s and '90s. Mr. James M. Turner, one of the owners of the Michigan Slate Company, became a heavy investor in the proposed railroad. Milo Davis had used the slate quarries and timber stands as selling points to lure investors and had successfully attracted wealthy, optimistic men to provide the outlay necessary to begin construction of the railroad.

In July of 1890, the Iron Range and Huron Bay Railroad was organized, and the Board of Directors enthusiastically granted permission to begin work on the grade immediately. Nearly a thousand men were employed to begin grade work. It was anticipated that the tracks would be in place by the end of the year.

About this time, still another event occurred which was to have a great influence on drawing Cyrus H. McCormick back to the North Country. The Huron Mountain Shooting and Fishing Club – organized in 1889 by Peter White, Horatio Seymour, and J. M. Longyear – had reorganized in 1891, and was distributing brochures to many of the most prominent people in the Chicago area. McCormick and many of his associates received copies of the brochure which solicited membership to the Club, which was situated about 25 miles directly north of the camping grounds McCormick had visited with his friend Dr. William Gray.

While some Chicago residents responded by taking a trip to the Huron Mountain Shooting and Fishing Club within the next few years, McCormick was not interested in this at that particular time because he had his own private campsite, and continued to camp occasionally at his wilderness retreat.

Before the railroad, wagon roads and winter roads had been crudely developed in the Peshekee River valley, deep in an area which was difficult to penetrate by any other route because of its extremely rocky and hilly terrain. The Peshekee River was a natural highway to float pine to the mill at Michigamme during the annual spring floods. Primitive dirt roads, slashed out during the summer or fall, provided access to various dams and camps along the river and on the lakes. These roads were used by the McCormick party to reach their base camp, located on an island that looked out on a high rocky fortress on the north side of the lake. McCormick had named it Fortress Lake.

The course which the Iron Range and Huron Bay Railroad would take followed the Peshekee River valley, a little west of due north, climbing as it approached the headwaters and then, unbeknownst to Milo Davis or anyone else at that time, extended into some of the highest land in Michigan – over 1,700 feet above sea level. It was not until the Coast and Geodetic Survey of 1956 that information about the extreme height of this region was officially recorded. After reaching its maximum height, the land sloped off abruptly at a grade that was almost impossibly steep for a railroad. In this high country the railroad would head almost due west after it crossed the fifth correction line, then north again to the village of Arvon. Then it would start the grade down to the waters of Huron Bay. Using this route, the original 25–mile estimate had been stretched to nearly 40 miles. On the Champion end, the roadbed crossed and recrossed the Peshekee River eleven times before finally leaving the valley.

Work proceeded rapidly in the spring of 1890, but soon bogged down as one difficulty after another was encountered. Many holes and swamps had to be filled, timber bridges and trestles had to be constructed, and camps to house the seven or eight hundred workers had to be built along the right–of–way. In addition to the tremendous construction tasks, expenses mounted rapidly, exceeding all expectations. Two million feet of fine timber were used in the construction of a huge pocket ore dock of the most modern design at Huron Bay, at a cost of over $250,000.

Work continued into the winter of 1891. In 1955, a first hand account from 1891 was given by Mr. Arthur W. Moore, a ninety–year–old gentleman from Marquette, Michigan. According to Mr. Moore,

> My partner and I set out north from Clarksburg (near Humboldt, about eight miles west of Ishpeming) on snowshoes and pulling a toboggan to do some trapping on the Yellowdog River...

After we reached the river we set up our camp to stay a few weeks. Every day we heard blasting, and after a week or so we were out of provisions. The blasting sounded so close and our curiosity got the best of us, so we set out to find it. It sounded like it should be only a short distance away, but we covered many miles before we came to a large camp of men – over a hundred of them. They were hand drilling and blasting a big cut in the solid rock for the Huron Bay Grade. They gave us our meals and all the food we could carry – flour, sugar, lard, crackers, everything.

It is impossible to pinpoint exactly where Art Moore came onto the grade, as there were several rock cuts; one giant one, sixty feet deep in places, is where the grade swung north above the fifth correction line. They worked nearly a year on this cut alone.

There were many other problems. Typhoid fever broke out; many men died, and the Champion hospital overflowed with patients. Some were put in a house next door, and some taken to Ishpeming by team. Wagons hauled away the dead each night. Then there was the panic of 1893, when work on the grade ceased altogether. On several other occasions there was trouble with the stockholders.

In 1894, it looked like the railroad would begin to run within a year. Two brand–new first class locomotives and twenty flatcars, plus other rolling stock, were stored at the Huron Bay end of the line under the watchful eye of Sam Beck, who could steam them up at a moment's notice. The locomotives weighed a hundred tons apiece. Storage sheds, a blacksmith shop, a machine shop, a fine interlocking plant, and the huge ore dock were all in readiness.

By 1895, 5,000 tons of heavy–gauge rail had been laid in place, connecting the Marquette, Houghton and Ontonogon Railroad in the south with the dock at Huron Bay, and the engine crew was ready to make a test run. All admitted that it was a steep grade up from Huron Bay, but the fact that the train would be traveling empty should have made it possible.

Natives of Marquette and Baraga Counties well know the famous story of Sam Beck's $2,000,000 ride. Sam lived in Baraga for years after, and told the story a thousand times.

"I was in the cab with the engineer and we had proceeded just a short distance up the grade. We were only on the line about twenty minutes. There was a long curve, and a steep grade. A piece of road bed gave way and the engine rolled over on her side. From that moment, the Iron Range and Huron Bay Railroad ceased to exist."

This was the greatest railroad debacle in Michigan's history. It was later figured that the grades were just too steep for a railroad (over 8 percent) and should not have been used. Escaping the wrath of the stockholders and creditors, Milo Davis and his brother fled to Mexico, and were never heard from again.

Tom Belanger, a resident of Champion, tells of traveling to the McCormick base camp by handcar, and of driving a team up the track, hauling supplies on a flatbed wagon equipped with railroad wheels. The only train ever to go over the track was a small Michigan–type engine borrowed to pick up the rails, which were sold to the Detroit Electric Railroad and used to complete an electric line from Grand Rapids to Holland, from Oxford to Flint, and from Rome to Imlay City. The engines, the rolling stock, and the massive ore dock were sold downstate. Over 2,500,000 feet of white pine was salvaged from the dock and taken to Detroit.

While there appears to be no written record of how often McCormick and his party returned to the Peshekee Country before 1902, he did return often enough to establish two stopover tent camps on the Peshekee River and the base camp on the island in Fortress Lake, at the head of the Yellowdog River. It appears that the tents were set up at these camps each year, or at least when Mr. McCormick sent orders to do so.

During those years prior to 1902, it was Mr. McCormick's custom to have local men set up a camp of several tents on different lakes in the area. In later years, the camp was on the island on Fortress Lake. If there was a chance of McCormick's returning several times in the summer, he would leave the camp set up all summer and would have a watchman or camp keeper remain there. It was not uncommon to have several men and a few teams involved in bringing boats, supplies, and equipment to and from the base camp. From the Grade, the supplies were transferred to a wagon if lumber roads were available, or else were backpacked to their destination.

On its southwest end, Fortress Lake has a high island covered with white pine. The lake is wide at that end, and the island a mere 75 or 100 feet from shore. The lake then tapers to the northeast, past a tiny rock island with a few cedars on it, then tapers even narrower past the fortress to the very narrow northeast end, which at that time ended abruptly with an immense beaver dam. The overflow from this dam made its way through six or seven hundred yards of smaller dams and grassy marshlands. Beyond this point it opened up to another large shallow lake, which had been named "Bulldog" by the lumberjacks who had dammed it earlier.

The lakes in this area had not been officially named at this time, and were virtually unmapped. Landlookers and lumbermen knew where the lakes were, though, and had given them names that were well–enough known to make them stick. An example is Bulldog Lake. "Bulldogging" was a term for hard work, and Jim Redy's men worked hard indeed when they built a sluiceway and dam about 50 yards long at the foot of the lake, the beginning of the Yellowdog River, in about 1885. The dam, while not used now, still remains there in remarkably good condition. It was called "Reservoir Dam."

Bulldog Lake also received drainage from another lake with a large island in it, appropriately named Island Lake, and also from another secluded and beautiful lake with picturesque rocky and wooded points. This lake was originally called Lake 32, being in that section, but was renamed "McKinley Lake" in 1901 because a fire broke out there the day President McKinley was shot, September 6, 1901, and was extinguished on the 14th, the day he died. The lake was named by Robert Bruce, a lumberman who at the time ran a camp near the lake for F. W. Read. Today the lake is known as Lake Margaret. It has a small outlet going east to Mulligan Creek, which drains to the Dead River.

This complex of lakes all empties into the Yellowdog River, which originates at Bulldog Lake and cascades through its rocky course to the north. A mile or so below Bulldog Lake, the river falls 220 feet in a distance of 220 yards. This falls, known as the East Falls, is located at the extreme end of the east branch of the river, which joins the west branch further downstream. The Yellowdog then makes its way east through the tag alders along the south edge of a large swamp, then over another falls and on to Lake Independence.

By the 1880s, several loggers had driven white pine down this mean and treacherous river. Among the lumbermen, the Yellowdog had the reputation of being the toughest river in the state to drive.

Jim Redy of Marquette had built the reservoir dam at the outlet of Bulldog Lake in order to form a reservoir which, when released, would send a torrent of water racing down its course and crashing over the East Falls, giving depth to the normally shallow stream and making it possible to float the huge pine logs.

In the 1880s, Jim Redy's crew had built another dam in an impressive hole on the extreme eastern end of the Yellowdog Plains, where the water of the Yellowdog River dropped though a 50–foot chute as it passed a huge pinnacle of rock, then dropped abruptly over smooth granite about 35 feet to the rocky bed below. From the hole at the bottom of the falls, the sheer rock cliff rose straight up over 150 feet to the wooded pinnacle. This falls was consequently called the Pinnacle Falls, and the dam which was constructed there the Pinnacle Dam.

Top: Cyrus McCormick (right) Jack Grove to his right at lumber camp on the Peshekee river
– early trip.
Middle: An early trip (before 1900) into Pesheekee country by Cyrus McCormick.
McCormick left – Jack Grove next to him
Bottom: An early picture of Bulldog lake looking west from the rocks on the north shore. The
water was raised by Redy's dam killed the trees in the Island Lake outlet.

The crews tediously drilled and blasted away the rocks at the top of the natural chute and built a set of heavy white pine chutes to carry the logs over a 15–foot deep water hole above the falls. The sides of the chute were built up with more white pine backed with rock and earth to form a sluiceway.

At the beginning of the sluiceway was a set of six–foot sluice gates, designed to hold back the water as the snow began to melt in the spring. High on the north side of the pond formed by the dam, the loggers had cleared a large landing. During the winter, it was to this landing that the white pine was hauled on iced roads and precariously decked on the landing some two hundred feet above the pond. In the spring when the pond was full, they were rolled down the steep hill into the water, and when the sluice gates were opened in the spring flood, the logs would nuzzle their way through the gate on the head of the water and slip down the chute over the falls. The men worked rapidly with peaveys and long pike poles in the icy water to keep the logs in mid–stream and prevent them from following the flood into the woods along the stream, where they could be hung up forever.

Between the Reservoir Dam at Bulldog Lake and the Pinnacle dam at the east end of the Yellowdog Plains was the Wylie Dam, named for a lumberman from Grayling in Lower Michigan. The Wylie Dam had been built around 1893. Using horses and men, the loggers had built two earthen wings which swept out from either side of the dam to hold back the water. These wings fanned out from the sluiceway for eighty or one hundred feet on each side.

Then, many miles below the Pinnacle Dam was the Hill Dam, named for Dan Hill, the foreman of the crew that built it, or more likely for Arthur Hill of Saginaw, also a logger.

From the Hill Dam, the river flowed on to Lake Independence, where in 1885 Jim Redy had raised the lake level with a fifth dam. This was the beginning of the Iron River, which led on to Lake Superior.

Back at the headwaters of the Yellowdog, some forty or fifty river miles from Lake Independence, there is the source of another watershed. Just a few miles west of Fortress Lake, the Peshekee River flows south to Lake Michigamme and on to Lake Michigan via the Michigamme and Menominee Rivers. The Big Huron River flows almost directly north to Lake Superior, and the Dead River (River du Mort) flows east to Silver Lake, then continues slightly south of east to Lake Superior.

During the formation of the International Harvester Company in 1902, Cyrus H. McCormick had worked closely with, and had eventually come to depend on Cyrus Bentley. Mr. Bentley was a brilliant attorney, and while he had been paid well for his work from a monetary standpoint, Mr. McCormick felt deeply indebted to him for the outstanding job he had done during the McCormick farm machinery battles and the organization of the International Harvester Company.

During their leisure hours after grueling, tension–filled days, their conversation often centered around the Peshekee River country.

Both the Bentleys and the McCormicks were good friends of many Chicago members of the Huron Mountain Club on Lake Superior. While Mr. McCormick had come to the Peshekee River country off and on to camp, it was Mr. Bentley's idea to make a permanent camp in this area and to push a trail across to the Huron Mountain Club.

Whether the idea of a permanent trail was there at the very beginning of the partnership is unknown, but at any rate something like this was in the planning stages for a long time, for no sooner had the snow left the ground in the spring of 1902 than the pair were off to the Peshekee country ("Pechekeme," Mr. Bentley always wrote it) to select a spot for a permanent camp and to hike through to Huron Mountain, a trip Mr. Bentley was to make over a hundred times in the next 25 years.

In his journal, Mr. Bentley describes how he and Mr. McCormick traveled to the McCormick Camp in 1902 to select a site for a permanent rough camp.

Being a corporate lawyer and a very meticulous man, Cyrus Bentley kept thorough notes, far too detailed to quote in their entirety. However, portions of them are very interesting and shed some light on customs and behavior of the time.

The Bentleys had probably been to the Huron Mountain Club at least once before this time. Quoting Mr. Bentley's journal, "7 May 1902 – Cyrus McCormick (written CMcC) and Cyrus Bentley (written C. B.) left via the Chicago & Northwestern RR. at 8 P. M. to travel by compass from Michigamme through to Lake Superior, for the purpose of getting an idea as to the character of the country with a view to possibly establishing a camp in this district.

8 May – We arrived at Michigamme at 9 A. M. and found that our trunks had been left behind at Negaunee. We telegraphed for them, and they were forwarded by special train reaching us bout noon. As a preliminary to our northward journey we decided to explore the country around Michigamme and after luncheon in the Dining Car, we started out about 1 P. M. With us were Gordon Young, who is

camp keeper at the McCormick Camp; Schwindeman, a land looker living in Michigamme; and Picot, a cook.

This gives us an idea of how McCormick and Bentley traveled. They went on foot and carried light packs, but also had a packer, cook, and guide.

First, the group walked west five or six miles to a lake in Section 34 in Baraga County. They spent the night in an old cabin in Section 29 on balsam branches spread on the floor of the cabin. They had breakfast at 5:45, and walked to Three Lakes (today Beaufort, Helen, and Ruth), then returned to Michigamme by train.

Again quoting Cyrus Bentley:

We set out (as yesterday our baggage and supplies going with us in a wagon) upon our journey northward. We followed the county road from Michigamme to Champion, to its intersection with the abandoned grade of the Iron Range & Huron Bay Railway, when we traveled northerly along the grade through wild and rocky country, along the Pechekeme (pronounced Pe che ke) River, to the Rock Dam. We camped near the Dam, sleeping in a tent with a big fire in front of it. Found Coles, the damkeeper, at the Dam. Our party was the same as yesterday with addition of Johnson.

10 May – Last night was not so cold as the night before. We were up at 4:30 and after drinking a cup of coffee with a cracker, we started to get through a bad place in the road covered with water which Coles told us might become impassable if the flood from the upper river (the dams on which were to be opened early this morning) arrived before we got past. CMcC, Gordon Young, and C. B. poled themselves past the low point in the road on a raft through the high water where a trestle had formerly connected land ends of the grade. The rest of the party went through with the team. We on the raft carrying on our backs our clothing etc., got through alright, but the wagon box floated off at the high water point in the road carrying all of our food supplies and much of our baggage which finally were submerged. We recovered everything except one bag of C. B.'s containing some extra clothing and ammunition (which came to light a few days later when the water went down), but our provisions were much the worse for the water. The driver lost heart and left us, but an empty team came along opportunely and after we had dried our clothing etc., we went on up the grade, stopping at the tents (about half a mile from the ford) for lunch; in the afternoon, leaving

the tents about 1 P. M. after having been there an hour, we traveled by wagon and on foot over a very bad, rocky and muddy road, from the tents to Camp 1 in Section 33–50–29. Here we spent the night in the office of the camp, meeting Robert Bruce, foreman, and Jim Scanlon, bookkeeper, etc. The Camp is owned by F. W. Read or the Read Lumber Company. We had supper and breakfast in the camp kitchen. A bear got into camp in the evening, but we did not see it.

Up to this point the McCormick and Bentley party had come about five miles northwest from the Peshekee River, traveling on a lumber road south of Fortress Lake, Bulldog Lake, and Lake Margaret. Mr. Bentley had never seen these lakes, nor the McCormick camp on the island of Fortress Lake.

11 May (Sunday) – Left the Camp at 9:30 A. M. beginning our real northward journey on foot. We traveled at first uphill, then up and down for an hour through beautiful hardwood groves and some swampy spots, a distance of about two miles; then for about a mile and a half we traveled through marshes, watching a doe for 15 minutes which fed in the open after we came close to her, though not close enough to get her picture. We finished with the marshes about 11:30 and then, after walking 20 minutes more, we reached a lake with an island in it just off a lumber road which we were following. We went down to the shore of the lake; the island seemed from an eighth to a quarter of a mile distant and was thickly covered with spruce and cedars. It stood high in the water very near a point on the shore of the lake between a quarter and a half mile to our right. The lake appeared to be about three quarters of a mile wide at its widest part and not far from a mile long, though Schwindeman told us that it stretched away where we could not see it, for another mile. CMcC suggests the name 'Cedar Island Lake'.

This lake is the present "Island Lake" just over the county line in Baraga County Section 25. It does "stretch away" for a mile to the east. At the time of Bentley's writing, there was a great deal of logging going on in the area. Schwindeman and possibly McCormick had been to the area before.

Their route had taken them around the present Lake Margaret, across the upper Yellowdog River, and east to Island Lake. We must remember that in 1902 the section lines had been laid but most lakes had not been mapped or, in many cases, even named.

Top: Jim Redy's dam from the old pine logging days. The dam can still be seen underwater and tag elder growth today on Bulldog lake.
Middle: Robert Bruce's men logging near McKinley Lake (1903).
Bottom: Mrs. Cyrus McCormick and Mrs. Cyrus Bentley heading into camp (1903).

We left the lake (Island Lake) at noon and at 1:15 we reached, just beyond a little creek, a piece of high ground in Section 30 T50 R29, just about on the West Township line. Here we pitched our tents. According to my pedometer, we had walked between five and six miles during the morning. The sun had been warm and the air cool – a delicious morning for a walk. In the afternoon Schwindeman, Gordon Young, CMcC and C. B. started for a lake of which Schwindeman had heard, lying southeast of our camping ground, and called "McKinley Lake" or Lake 32 (from the section on which it lies). We first went through a cedar swamp – not a bad one – then over ridges of hardwood which must be beautiful in leaf. We came upon a pretty lake in Section 31 and crossed on an awkward dam at the foot of the lake; after that there were more hardwood ridges and then we came to Lake 32 which had pretty rocky shores with many coves and points; its outlet is through a creek at the west end. The vegetation of the lake had been much disfigured by recent burnings.

The lake in Section 31 is Bulldog Lake, so named by Jim Redy's lumbermen when they built the "awkward dam" at the foot of the lake about 15 years before. Schwindeman and McCormick had both been to this lake before, but this was Mr. Bentley's first view of it. None of them had ever seen Lake 32 ("Lake McKinley" or "Lake Margaret"). The short–lived name "McKinley" had been given by Robert Bruce, the F. W. Read camp superintendent. Mr. Bruce had immigrated to the Upper Peninsula of Michigan from Edinburgh, Scotland, and had run lumber camps in the Champion and Big Bay areas. He later lived in Marquette and had two sons, Robert and Leo. Descendants of Robert Bruce still reside in Marquette today. He is buried in Park Cemetery. The shooting of McKinley, who was also of Scotch–Irish descent, undoubtedly had a special significance to Robert Bruce.

We returned to Camp by the same route, reaching camp about 6:00, having walked about five miles during the afternoon, according to the pedometer. In the evening clouds came up and the moon was obscured, and we were finally driven into our tent by rain.

12 May – Rain fell until I went to sleep. Cloudy morning with mist and rain at intervals. Breakfast at half past six. CMcC and I remained in camp until half past eleven when we walked north along the county line (between Township 50–29 and 50–30). Finding the walking good we returned to camp, lunched at noon, packed up and

started north at one, following the county line which was heavily blazed. The traveling was very easy except nearly half a mile of corduroy through a swamp in Section 19 (the south half, I think) 50–29 and one or two other short pieces of swamp – one in Section 13–50–30. We found no good drinking water except one very pretty creek just north of Section line between 7 and 18–50–29. We camped for the night near a deserted cabin in a swamp in Section 1–50–30, not far from the line which separates that section from Section 6–50–29. The cabin stood just off the L'Anse road which we first reached (and crossed) about an eighth of a mile before finding the cabin. We went into the camp about 4:45, having dispossessed and killed the party in possession of the cabin when we arrived – a porcupine.

During the last two days we have seen a few deer (yesterday on Lake 32) and some partridges today. We have found no flowers so far, and the trees are only in bud. The ground has been quite wet and rain has been falling most of the afternoon. We sleep tonight on hemlock boughs over corduroy. CMcC's idea.

Cyrus Bentley goes on to tell how the party, five in all, traveled the next three days to the Huron Mountain Club on the shore of Lake Superior. Their route took them to Cliff Lake, where McCormick and Bentley had an icy bath, and then to Mountain Lake, where a boat had been left for them. Mr. Bentley states that he suffered a great deal with rheumatic pains and held the others back.

We have had no bread since day before yesterday and are out of jam, condensed milk and coffee. Oatmeal is getting low, but we have plenty of tea and bacon.

The party spent the last night at Dudley Point on Mountain Lake, sending one man to the Club for provisions and also getting some from the lumber camp on Lumberman's Bay on Mountain Lake.

The last day, they climbed Mount Homer and followed Mountain Stream Trail to Pine Lake, and thus to the Club.

On May 16th, McCormick and Bentley slept in the Kidder Cabin (later owned by Albert W. Russel of Cleveland, then Francis C. McMath of Detroit, then Arthur Dixon; the present owner is Mrs. Richard H. Turner of Grosse Pointe, Michigan).

As if they had not had enough walking, they proceeded to Mrs. Nelson's cabin on Conway Bay, returned, and then climbed Huron Mountain back over to the Fortress on Pine Lake.

On May 17th they went to Marquette by the FRIANT and took the evening train to Chicago.

The tent camp on Fortress Lake was maintained in 1903 and, although no records are available, Mr. McCormick probably visited it some time during the summer.

On August 20th of that year, Cyrus Bentley, accompanied by a Mr. Frank M. Bailey, arrived from Chicago aboard the Chicago, Milwaukee & St. Paul Railroad at Champion.

Knox, who had been sent up to the lake in Section 1 (Fortress Lake) from Lake Forest, was at the station. He had killed a bear the day before in the lake and was unwilling to stay longer alone on the island. We passed Dishno (a horse), driven by C. H. Lavigne in his spring wagon, at 9:50. A spring on the wagon broke as we went on to the grade. At 11 we passed the road leading to Dishno Creek, where Lavigne says the fishing is good. There were ripe raspberries along the road. At 11:55 we passed a brook on the left, at 12:01 a spring on the left a little off the road, reaching the Ford at 12:05. Here we left Charley who went on to the camp by road, Bailey and I going up Baraga Creek.

The two men, wanting to see the Baraga Lakes and at the same time avoid the last several miles by wagon, went looking for a more pleasant, but longer, route to Fortress Lake.

Gordon Young had blazed a trail from Baraga Lake to Fortress Lake, but they could not locate it. There were logging roads throughout the area.

They spent the night watching the Aurora Borealis by a big fire at the south end of the Baraga Lakes. They slept little that night on the hard ground, and were up at 4:30 the next morning. Unable to find the trail they were looking for, they went east by compass and the sun to Fortress Lake the next day.

Mr. Bentley's description of the island on Fortress Lake at that time (August 1903) is as follows:

"The Island was covered with blueberries. I rowed around it and saw that its shores were quite rocky with mud bottom here and there. Two large platform tents stood near the eastern extremity of the island, and in the middle two more, one for a kitchen and one for a

612

dining room. Two or three smaller tents were pitched between the middle and the east end, and between the kitchen tent and the west end were a couple of tents for the men.

Mr. Bentley goes on to describe a trip through the "waterway," with its beaver dams and snags, to a spot on Bulldog Lake near Jim Redy's dam that had a sand bottom. Here they took a good bath and returned to "our lake" for supper and bed at 8:15. Lavigne had shot a deer on Bulldog Lake the night before.

Two days later, they left for Chicago. The journal reads "We left the island about one and drove (team) all the way to Champion. Rain began to fall just before we started and deluged us on the journey. We were wet before we got into the wagon and became extremely cold before we got to Champion."

According to Cyrus Bentley's journal, Gordon Young blazed the original trails in the vicinity of Fortress and Bulldog Lakes.

Mr. Bentley recorded another trip made on September 30, 1903. It was made by Cyrus Bentley and Cyrus McCormick, who were joined a few days later by their wives, Elizabeth King Bentley and Harriet McCormick. The party, as usual, stayed in tents on the island in Fortress Lake, but did a great deal of hiking in the surrounding area. They were accompanied on these excursions by Gordon Young and "Black Tom" Belanger, and a man referred to only as "Herman." Later they were joined by Jack Grove, whom they had met in the woods and who knew the country better than anyone else. There was also Archie LaCosse, a cook from the tent camp on the island.

At this time, McCormick and Bentley were definitely planning to build a permanent camp somewhere in the area and, even then, had the idea of buying up a large parcel of land as it became available. They were looking at the different lakes with building in mind, noting where there were beauty spots, sand bottom, or good timber.

From October 3, 1903:

We spent all day in camp, but Gordon Young went out and got us some venison. The barometer fell very low – to 28.15 (though our barometer has never been adjusted). There was a terrific wind late in the afternoon which would have blown over the dining room tent if four of us had not hung on to it. The wind held from the southeast all day and evening but during the night changed to the northwest without, however, making the air much colder."

Upper left: Mr. and Mrs. Cyrus Bentley (front) and Cyrus McCormick tent camping on the island at Fortress Lake 1903.
Upper right: Harriet McCormick and Elizabeth Bentley at Fortress Lake (1903).
Bottom: McCormick tent camp on Fortress Lake.

October 6, 1903: "We breakfasted at 8:30 and started at 10 for Island Lake. Black Tom and Gordon Young going on in advance to improve the raft which was made the other day, or build another. We reached the lake at noon, having seen four partridge and a porcupine. We crossed to the island by raft and found stumps of many large and handsome trees which were cut last winter – most, if not all, good sized pines. The island is large but no longer attractive though there are a few good white birches standing on it. After lunch E. K. B. (Elizabeth King Bentley) and Gordon Young walked over to Picnic Point on Birch Lake and on our way back went to Clear Lake which is a tributary to Lake Michigan while Island Lake, very close to Clear Lake (both can be seen from a point between) feeds Lake Superior. H & CMcC (Harriet and Cyrus McCormick) with Tom preceded us home, we returning by Tom's new trail to a dock which he has built on the north shore of the lake of our camp. We reached the island a little after 4:30. Went to bed early.

Mr. Bentley's notes go on in detail, telling of each trip he or Cyrus McCormick made, where they went and with whom, meticulously noting times and distances whenever possible. On a trip with Jack Grove on October 10, he mentions Mr. McCormick's naming Trout Lake and Evergreen Lake. These two names were accidentally reversed on the U. S. Coast and Geodetic Survey map, and now on other maps of the area. On the same trip with Grove, McCormick named it "Bleak Lake;" in 1908 he renamed it "Flag Lake," and on today's maps it is called "Lake Phillip."

By the late fall of 1903, it was decided that any planned buildings would be in the general area of the original McCormick base camp on the island of Fortress Lake. Probably Mr. McCormick had already made up his mind about this but wanted to give the meticulous Mr. Bentley a good look at the other possibilities first. And, realizing his place, Cyrus Bentley was willing to let Cyrus McCormick do all the naming of lakes and places.

After all their searching for building sites, it was to the McCormick base camp that they returned, deciding it was the best place to build after all. Once the decision was made, the two men went to Robert Bruce, the foreman of the F. W. Read camp, to discuss the cost of hiring men on a permanent basis. Bruce assured them that they should be able to get a good man for the camp for $35 per month, and that the cost of feeding men in lumber camps was, including the cooks' wages, 30 cents day; that one man can live pretty well on $8 or $10 per month, and two for about $14 a month.

It was about this time that an option was picked up, and Bentley and McCormick purchased 160 acres of land which included the southwest end of Fortress Lake plus the island.

Two men, Lambert and Murphy, were hired to remain on the property for the winter and told to build two cabins, both on the mainland just southwest of the island. One, for themselves, would be located on the side of the hill near the road. It was to be about 12 feet square. The other, a little over twice that size (14 by 24 feet) was to be for guests, and would be closer to the lake.

In March of 1904, McCormick and Bentley arrived from Chicago by train to inspect the cabins. The temperature was sixteen below zero when they traveled by snowshoe to Bruce's logging camp south of the property. On this trip, they were joined by a local surveyor, Charles Cummings, and his assistant Beaudoin. Cummings and Beaudoin pulled a toboggan loaded with supplies.

Jack Grove had come from somewhere out of the north to meet the party at the logging camp. He was what we might call a shacker or a squatter nowadays, and had become highly respected as a woodsman and a man who knew the land better than anyone else. On the trip from there to Fortress Lake, Jack Grove broke trail, followed by Beaudoin and Cummings pulling the toboggan. Fourth was Cyrus Bentley and finally Cyrus McCormick, who carried a small handbag. The position of the hikers in this trailbreaking routine was established automatically by order of importance and gave the last man the easiest walking. Each man knew where he belonged in the pecking order and fell into position without discussion.

When they arrived, Bentley and McCormick seemed satisfied with the cabins, as crude as they were. Murphy, Lambert, and Tom Belanger were there. In these first two cabins at Fortress Lake there was no thought as to architecture. Only the size mattered now. They were places to work out of, put up guests and crew, and store material for later projects.

It was on this trip early in 1904 that the land was carefully surveyed and the lines laid out. On snowshoes, Cyrus McCormick and Cyrus Bentley, along with the surveyors and Jack Grove, walked the boundaries of their 160–acre plot.

They left orders to build another cabin – on the island, this time. But now location was of prime importance, as there would be additional buildings there in the future.

Mr. Bentley had made trips in May and June of 1904 without commenting on the new cabin while it was under construction. That August, though, the new cabin was complete, and he made his first comments about it.

Top: Murphy and first cabin and storage shed on mainland. March 1904.
Bottom: Murphy and Lambert, March 1904, guest cabin in rear.

We found Ed McLean and Frank LaCosse at the island. The new cabin seems well and strongly built. It is about 14' x 24', I think, has two doors, one toward the east and one toward the south, and it is placed where the ladies' tent and mine were last year, having small porches to the east and to the south. Ed has built a small boat house on the side of the hill close to the road. The island cabin is chinked with moss and lime cement or mortar on the outside; it should be chinked with plaster inside also and a second floor should be laid over the first which is not very tight. We spent a little time arranging the cots, air mattresses and blankets (we have no sheets) and moved some things from the mainland.

LaVigne arrived about 3:15 with a load of provisions and supplies.

The children are first mentioned on August 6, 1904, when Mr. Bentley states that Cyrus McCormick, Jr., went into the lake that afternoon. It was also on this day that a tradition was started that was to be repeated many times over the ensuing years: the Talking Machine Concert. Mr. Bentley writes,

> The evening was spent listening to the talking machine which arrived and was set up this afternoon. The favorite pieces were Anona (orchestra) and Du Bist die Ruh (sung by Gadski).

The next day they crossed the trail to Huron Mountain via the forty–foot falls on the Cliff Stream. The trail was not yet completed, though after many crossings a route had been decided on, and the trail would be completed the following year. Six people made this particular trip: Cyrus McCormick and Cyrus, Jr., Cyrus Bentley, LaVigne, LaCosse and McLean. Grove had met them north of Bulldog Lake. A boat had been left for them in the Cliff Stream so they could row Mountain and Pine Lakes. Mr. Bentley made the trip again a few weeks later with Ralph Dillenbeck of Chicago, and still later with Ed McLean.

The proposed trail was laid out by Mr. Bentley with the help of woodsmen like Ed McLean, Frank LaCosse, and Tom Belanger. It began at the Sawyer Goodman Lumber Camp on the north shore of Bulldog Lake, headed north on a tote road from the camp and, crossing the east branch of the Yellowdog River, followed the valleys to the west end of the Yellowdog Plains, called at the time the "Sand Plains."

The planned trail would then drop down from the plains through a stand of beautiful virgin hardwoods to the valley of the Cedar Creek.

Following the clear, cascading stream to the point where it entered a swamp, the trail would climb abruptly over the west end of a rocky prominence named Burnt Mountain, affording a magnificent view of Mountain Lake. The trail would then drop down to the southern tip of that lake.

Cyrus Bentley called it the Huron Mountain Trail. However, it was "Mr. Bentley's Trail" to the workmen, and it later became widely known as such, despite the fact that it was still called the Huron Mountain Trail on the maps of that time.

The Bentleys had joined the Huron Mountain Shooting and Fishing Club in 1902, and at once started making plans to build a cabin there.

The cabin at Huron Mountain was to be built on the very end of the sand spit between the mouth of Pine River and Lake Superior.

Up to this time, the mouth of the river had moved up and down the beach several hundred yards, and many onlookers felt there was a strong chance of losing the cabin to the force of Lake Superior or, at best, having it stranded on an island.

Chosen to design the Huron Mountain Cabin was James Gamble Rogers, a prominent architect at the turn of the century. He had designed the Harkness Tower at Yale University. The head carpenter was Ed LaBlanc who, after working two years on the cabin at Huron Mountain, was brought to the "Rough Camp" at Fortress Lake, where he became the head carpenter for many years. The Huron Mountain Cabin at the north end of the Bentley Trail was started in 1904 and completed in 1905.

That same year, the trail was finally completed from the Rough Camp on the island of Fortress Lake to the Bentley Cabin at the mouth of the Pine River on Lake Superior. It was also this year that Cyrus McCormick joined Cyrus Bentley in the Huron Mountain Shooting and Fishing Club, although their motivation for joining the club was not the shooting and fishing. The intrigue of walking the trail had become their great delight.

It was also in 1905 that Mr. Bentley ordered a long, light rowboat from the Rushton Company, well–known boat builders in New York state. These light, strong, and graceful boats were famous throughout the United States. The new boat would be about 22 feet long, with high sides and a little deck extending all the way around. It was to be equipped with three rowing seats and a fantail. Typical of Rushton boats and canoes, it would be constructed of unpainted but thoroughly oiled quarter–inch cedar.

Also available on Fortress and Bulldog Lakes were sailboats and rowboats that had been purchased by the Bentleys and McCormicks. Several club rowboats, to be used by the trail–crossers, were maintained at the Huron Mountain end of Pine Lake. Mr. Bentley's Rushton longboat would be kept

Top: F. C. Farwell 1904.
Middle: About to start for Huron Mountain Club – Miss Hooper, Elizabeth King Bentley, Frank C, Farwell – Sept. 8, 1904 Fortress Lake Camp.
Bottom: Along the Forty–foot Falls trail to Mountain Lake.

Upper left: Along the trail (1905).
Upper right: Cyrus and Harriet McCormick near Fortress Lake (1904).
Bottom: Hamilton Cabin (left) – Bentley cabin (right) at Huron Mounatin as viewed from the ice on Lake Superior.

in a boathouse on Mountain Lake, the longest lake to be crossed, and was to be used exclusively by hikers crossing the trail.

Cameron D. Waterman of Detroit, a member of Huron Mountain from 1899 to 1910, had a son, Cameron B. Waterman, a law student, who had been tinkering with an outboard motor on Pine Lake. Bentley and McCormick inquired about it and found that he was building and selling 25 a year. Mr. Bentley bought two of them, one for Mountain Lake and one for Fortress Lake. As it turned out, no one at Huron Mountain appreciated the racket and smoke and smell, which detracted from the clean tranquility they had learned to love. Efforts were made to stop Mr. Bentley from using his motor, but since he already had it and was only using it to cross the trail, a rule was made that no outboards could be used on any Huron Mountain lakes except Mr. Bentley's motor, and this only on trail crossings – probably not more than a dozen times a year.

The Club blacksmith fitted the longboat with a couple of iron brackets that supported a two–by–four upon which the motor could be mounted. Mr. Bentley was very careful that none of his people broke the rules.

The trail to Huron Mountain had to be worked on continually. It had to be reblazed and brushed. Corduroy and hewn logs had to be laid in the swampy land which divided the Yellowdog and Big Huron Rivers, as well as some hewn cedar bridges over three or four creeks. The first bridges were crudely made but their replacements were more substantial, picturesque and equipped with railings. Ed McLean was hired as a foreman to see that the jobs were done properly, and when Mr. Bentley was in Chicago the station agent in Champion acted as his local contact.

During the first trips across the Huron Mountain Trail in 1905, it was noted that sometimes the boats would be at the wrong end of the lake for the hiking parties. Also, at times it was next to impossible to travel against the wind in a boat, especially on Mountain Lake. As a result, Mr. Bentley took it upon himself that summer to visit a little family of homesteaders who in 1902 had established themselves in the southwest corner of Section 35, out on the Sand Plains.

The homesteader, Nels Anderson, his wife, and their son Jim, a powerful boy of 15, had been discovered by trail crews that summer and had been hired by Mr. Bentley to do some work on the trail. They were found to be honest and hard workers.

Mr. Bentley asked Nels if he would build a trail around the east side of Mountain Lake, a distance of about two and one–half to three miles of the most difficult terrain. A contract was agreed upon, and Nels promised that he and Jim would finish the trail that fall.

Top: Bentley cabin at Huron Mountain from the river side – Hamilton cabin far right.
Bottom: Mrs. Bentley and Cyrus McCormick, Mrs. McCormick in back, tent camping 1903.

Nels and Jim cut the trail from what soon became known as Bentley Point on the extreme southwestern shore of Mountain Lake, all along the shore and on the sides of the rocky slopes of Mt. Homer (named for Homer Kidder) to Mountain Stream on the extreme northeastern corner of the lake. There was already a trail from the camping spot called "The Iliad," just north of Mount Homer on the lake shore, but it had no permanent structure. There was a winter logging road there that went out on the ice to a logging camp in Lumberman's Bay, which saw its last use that year. From the Iliad, the trail walkers used the road if they were unable to come by boat.

In those days, everything Mr. Bentley thought and did was centered around the trail. At the south end, all costs were split by Bentley and McCormick. On the north end, Bentley assumed full responsibility for all expenses. He was very pleased with the cabin at the mouth of Pine River, and Mrs. Bentley was just delighted with it. She was a very kind and unassuming lady who really did not take too well to the rough camp, and much preferred the lifestyle of Huron Mountain. Although she had hiked the trail several times in 1904 and 1905, she would just as soon stay at Huron Mountain, where life was less strenuous and more social. Therefore, Mr. Bentley decided that the Huron Mountain Cabin was to be for his wife, and plans got under way to build a cabin for Bentley and McCormick on the island at Fortress Lake.

The Bentley–McCormick cabin arrangement was a compromise that took care of any potential disagreement as to who would get what site, which cabin should be built first, and so forth. It was started in the fall of 1905 and completed in the fall of 1907. Built right next to the original camp on the island, it faced southeast. A wall completely divided the cabin through the middle. One half was Bentley's, the other McCormick's. The only way to get from one side to the other was by a porch. Since it was constructed around a huge rock chimney, it was called the "Chimney Cabin."

The Chimney Cabin, built on the placid Fortress Lake, was never endangered by the elements. A stone foundation was laid about 25 feet from the water's edge. In contrast, the Huron Mountain Cabin was constantly battered by the fall storms on Lake Superior. There were those who said it wouldn't last ten years, and indeed, within a few years of its completion it was obvious that a row of pilings would have to be driven in front of the cabin to control the relentless washing away of the shoreline and undermining of the cabin. The row of pilings held the cabin intact for a while. Some years there was a huge expanse of beach, reaching 40 or 50 yards out to the water's edge. In the winter great mountains of ice, up to forty feet in height, would protect the cabin. But in the fall, when the lake was at its highest level and the storms were at their worst peak, the whole beach would disappear. Before the ice formed, severe damage occurred to the walkways, steps, and railings, and often the log structure itself was threatened. Mr. Bentley decided to have a log breakwall built. This task was undertaken in the summer of 1915 and completed a year later.

In September of 1905 there was a terrific storm, but the cabin was protected from damage by the wide beach in front of it. It was during this storm that the OLIVE JEANETTE and the steamer, IOSCO, foundered in Lake Superior. Mr. Bentley and Joseph Swanson left Chicago on September 1st on the Chicago, Milwaukee & St. Paul Railroad, and Mr. Bentley recorded the events of his trip over the next few days.

> There was a heavy storm of wind and rain in the evening of 2 Sept. We were an hour and a half late in Champion. Leaving there with two wagons we found the long bridge over the Pechekeme had gone down in the storm. We were delayed by this from 11:40 until after 2:00, but finally pushed our wagons across the railroad bridge, the horses fording the river. We reached camp at 5:30 finding the road from the hill in very bad shape. Rain fell all day with high wind but our "automobile cape" rain coats were very good protection. The rain and high wind continued all evening – just as we reached camp two trees on the island blew down.

They left on foot for Huron Mountain the next day and it rained all the way. They went through without stopping. He wrote that there was water everywhere.

The weather caused other hardships; from Bentley's journal of November 13, 1905:

> When we awoke this morning there were two inches of fresh snow on the porch of the men's cabin and a real blizzard was raging. LaVigne considered it useless to attempt dragging the wagon out so it was left in camp and we walked to the Ford (3 1/2 miles) dragging our baggage on a sled. LaVigne took the horses through the river and came back with an old sleigh which had been left on the road, which we took through to Champion.

A few more details were mentioned in the journal for May 18 and 19, 1906, the year the new railroad was opened from Marquette to Big Bay. Cyrus Bentley and Frank Farwell rode it to Big Bay on the 19th, and it seems that

Top: Unknown guest, Cyrus II, Gordon and Cyrus III. 1904–05.
Bottom: Mountain Lake from the south as viewed from Burnt Mountain.

Top: Mr. and Mrs. Bentley on Fortress Lake.
Bottom: Mrs. Cyrus Bentley didn't enjoy walking the trail (1905).

on arrival they fully realized the impact of two fall storms the year before. Journal: "Went by the new train to Big Bay in two and three quarters hours, running through the scene of very recent, disastrous forest fires, especially at Birch. We went by wagon from Big Bay to the Club. We spent the afternoon and evening in our cabin discussing the best way of protecting the cabin and the site from storms."

It was cold at night in the cabin, but with a kerosene stove in the hall and hot irons in the beds, they were able to keep warm.

The next day Mr. Bentley and Ed LaBlanc, the carpenter, hiked the trail to the rough camp, where LaBlanc went to work making furniture. He made a large table for the sitting room while another carpenter, Willett, made a corner sofa.

Cyrus McCormick walked the 16 miles into camp that spring and joined Bentley and Frank Farwell in making trails. Harry and Fanny Tuttle also arrived.

The trail that had been cut in 1905 approached Mountain Lake from high on the end of Burnt Mountain and afforded a magnificent view of Mountain Lake off to the northeast and Mt. Ida, Fortress Mountain, Trout Mountain, Mt. Homer and the east end of Huron Mountain in the distance. Burnt Mountain was denuded of trees due to a recent forest fire, said to have been started by some irate lumberjacks who had been asked to leave Club property.

On June 25, 1906, Steve Lowney and an assistant named Sullivan arrived from Marquette to start mapping the Huron Mountain Trail. Mr. Bentley later went over the trail with the map and meticulously corrected errors, inserted place names and made additional notes. He soon found a way of showing elevations on the map also.

That summer, they invited a Dr. Davis from the University of Michigan to camp. While Professor Davis was primarily a geologist, he had many ideas about ecology, which was relatively unheard–of in that day and age. He had a barometer which he could set at a known elevation and detect other elevations relative to his setting. Dr. Davis and Wetmore Hodges recorded elevations along the trail all the way to Lake Superior with the barometer, later checking them by using a transit and rod starting at Lake Superior, known to be 602 feet above sea level. Another place Dr. Davis and his barometer helped out was in obtaining drinking water. This had been the concern of Mr. McCormick and Mr. Bentley for some time. Up to this time water from the lake had been suitable, but with the increased use of the place a better solution was desperately needed.

Book Two

They had discovered a beautiful spring area in the hills some distance southwest of the camp. Dr. Davis again took elevations and learned that the spring was 65 feet above the level of Fortress Lake. The ceiling of the second floor of Chimney Cabin on the island was only 28 feet above the lake, so plans were made to put 12 well–points in at the spring site and bring the water down by gravity with iron pipes to the camp.

When measurements of elevation were being taken it was found that this was extremely high country, certainly the highest in Marquette County and possibly the highest in the state of Michigan. The highest point on the trail was 1,770 feet. The hill west of the camp was found to be 1,835 feet, 200 feet higher than Huron Mountain. In 1954 it was discovered that the highest point in Michigan, today called Mt. Curwood, is some 12 or 14 miles due west of the camp, but the McCormick–Bentley property is still the highest spot in Marquette County[1]. Some residents say Arvon Hill is eight feet higher than Mt. Curwood.

Professor Davis had some other suggestions to make the Island and the camp a little nicer: put peat in the outhouses for disinfection, and sprinkle kerosene over the garbage to help get rid of flies. He said peat could be obtained from the bottom of the lake near the shore, and in the bottom of the beaver pond between Fortress and Bulldog Lakes. He suggested that all the cans be buried, instead of left exposed on the ground; also, everyone should avoid trampling on the small growth of the island. The bushes and flowers were very delicate, and paths and walkways should be established and used so that the flora could grow undisturbed.

The main goal of the summer of 1906, besides cleaning up the place, was the drawing up of plans for the new Bentley–McCormick cabin. Two other incidents also took place which are well worth noting. Late in June, a terrible thunderstorm struck. A single blast knocked down all the men working on the men's quarters on the mainland and burst open a hemlock on the island. The other event was Ed McLean's sighting of an albino deer on August 28, 1906. It was a doe, perfectly white with black hooves and pink eyes. Other workmen – Alden, Jay, Theodore Pomeroy, and Hebert, a cook – also saw the white deer that summer.

Margaret Bentley and Elliott spent several days drawing up plans for the cabin. Later, Mr. Bentley, Harry Tuttle and the boys spent a few days' time making corrections and additions. The island cabin would not have a professional architect like the Huron Mountain Cabin. This cabin would not

[1] In recent years it is said that some tremendously high tailing piles near Palmer in southern Marquette County have exceeded the 1,982–foot Mt. Curwood. These Empire pit tailings will be well over 2,200 feet in the future, we are told, making them the highest point in Michigan.

629

show; it was in the backwoods on an island, and utility was the main aim. Nevertheless, the best thoughts of many people went into it. Of course Mr. Bentley made the final recommendations, but it still had to go to Cyrus McCormick for final approval, though he generally agreed with what was being done. The men had been hauling rocks for the new cabin the whole summer of 1906. The stone foundations were already under way in August, and the log work started in the fall. They worked on the Chimney Cabin through the winter of 1906–07.

By 1907, only a few purchases of land had been made near Fortress Lake, but there were many options and agreements arrived at, and Mr. Bentley made sure they were ironclad. Logging operations were still taking place in their vicinity, and in the spring the Bentleys and McCormicks were shocked by the aftermath of the winter logging. The loggers had devastated one area after another. Wherever possible, Mr. McCormick would purchase whole forties of pine and in some instances even individual trees near trails, lakes and beauty spots, to be sure they would not fall to the loggers.

In his negotiations with the loggers, Mr. Bentley had seen to it that the logging crews would be finished cutting in the immediate area of Fortress Lake in a year or two. It must be remembered that these were winter operations, and in the winter months steam tractors and horses were hauling logs down Bulldog and Fortress Lakes on iced roads, and were using the McCormick and Bentley Camp road to the Peshekee River. There had been several purchases by 1907, but due either to neglect or, more likely, to the desire for secrecy, no land had yet been recorded in the name of McCormick and Bentley at the County Court Houses in L'Anse or Marquette.

On July 15, 1907, Mr. Bentley noted the arrival of the first fresh cream at Fortress Lake. It was a day of celebration, as he loved fresh cream on his berries and in his coffee.

At this time the new cabin was under roof, and the shingling by Ed LaBlanc and Frank LaMora had got under way. A telephone line had been set up between the cabins on the island and the men's camp on the mainland, though they did not connect with the outside world.

On July 19, at 4:00 A.M., Ed McLean telephoned Mr. Bentley that the white deer was at the deer lick, and everyone in camp got up to see it. A slight noise frightened it away. Off and on, for a year or two, the white deer was observed as it came to the water's edge at Fortress Lake. Guests of the McCormicks and Bentleys were told of it, and were constantly on the lookout for the unusual creature. Such an animal had been heard of, but none of the guests or crew had ever seen one before. The early rising, the quiet stalking, the anxious waiting in the early morning mist for a fleeting glimpse of the ghostly creature fascinated everyone.

Top: An early island cabin.
Bottom: Elizabeth McCormick and Margaret Bentley 1904.

Mr. Bentley gave the teaming job to Jim Hinton of Champion that summer, taking it away from Dalphis LaVigne. He had not been pleased with the way LaVigne was doing his job. He had purchased a new wagon for camp, and hoped Hinton would take good care of it.

Mr. Bentley was delighted with the progress on the new cabin. He worked hard himself along with the men, getting sand, mixing cement and mortar, and even breaking rock for the chimney. He went with the men on a barge to the far end of Bulldog Lake, where he helped screen and bag 87 bags of sand to be used by the masons. He counted and measured constantly, keeping track of everything – he noted, for instance, that Elliott, who was cutting the holes for the doors and windows, had cut through 32 feet of logs with a crosscut saw.

They all had their enjoyments too. One weekend three of the crew hiked to Summit Lake and caught 32 trout in the pool above the dam going into the Big Huron River. The dam had been placed there in 1902 by the Heinz Lumber Co. The remarkable thing was that the crewmen had left early in the morning, caught the fish at high noon under a bright sun, and returned before dark.

The guests had been enjoying regular Talking Machine concerts, but on July 31, 1907, a brand new Talking Machine arrived in camp. These concerts had already become an institution, and were looked forward to by young and old alike. The new machine was the finest that could be obtained, and became an heirloom in the Bentley family.

Emerson Tuttle, from Huron Mountain, spent several days mapping the lakes around the property, while Mr. and Mrs. Bentley walked the trail north. On August 19th, they returned with a party including two former mayors of Chicago – Carter Harrison and Hempstead Washburn – along with Clark Washburn and Kent Tenny. It was a warm day, and they all went in for a swim when they arrived. That evening Mr. Harrison gave the Talking Machine concert, making a specialty of the Red Seal records.

Mr. Harrison had been mayor of Chicago five times after the assassination of his father, who had preceded him. Like any good politician, he made it a point to talk to all the workmen, especially to Ed LaBlanc, who had been a carpenter on his "Keweenaw Cabin" at Huron Mountain.

There was a bustle of activity in August of 1907. Fifteen workmen were in camp, in addition to the Andersens of the plains and Pat Cleary, the stonemason who had built the fireplace and chimney at the Bentley Cabin. Carter Harrison had known him there and seemed very glad to renew acquaintance with him. The other mason was a man named Gover. Besides the Chimney Cabin, these men put a fireplace in the small sitting room

Top: Trail through the swamp west of the Sand Plains 1905.
Bottom: F. W. Reed bridge across the Peshekee river (1905).

cabin, while Mr. Bentley and Clark Washburn hauled sand for them. Clark Washburn worked on the maps also.

There was a near–disaster on August 24th, when the swimming raft broke loose with Mrs. Bentley on it and, according to Mr. Bentley's journal, she nearly drowned. She went under, but a life preserver was thrown to her and she was saved.

On August 29 Ed McLean, Cyrus Bentley, and Frank Farwell lit the first fire in the new sitting–room fireplace, the first fireplace on the island. To their dismay, it smoked very badly. They tried it several times without success. A galvanized smoke deflector was placed at the top of the fireplace opening, which helped a little, and later seven or eight feet of chimney was added. It still smoked occasionally, but was much improved.

There were many comings and goings that fall, but Mr. Bentley stayed right through to the latter part of November, except for a few days in Chicago. Many different groups crossed and recrossed the trail, and some more land was purchased. Mr. Bentley led a rigorous life at camp, going into the lake morning and evening for a bath, even when the temperature was in the 30s in late October. He once wrote that he had to walk to the water's edge on iced planks.

That fall, besides finishing the Chimney Cabin and constructing a boathouse on the mainland, they got a good start on a new dining room on the mainland. Both the boathouse and dining room were planned by Mr. Bentley and built by Ed LaBlanc. Though Ed had helpers, all work on the buildings stopped whenever he left camp for a few days.

In November, Cyrus McCormick arrived to discuss the camp plans. On November 21, 1907, McCormick and Bentley decided to call their lake White Deer Lake. Up to this time they had usually referred to it as "Our Lake," though the official name given to it by McCormick years before was "Fortress Lake." The thrill of the white deer had impressed them both, so the name "Fortress Lake" dropped quietly out of use.

Margaret and Richard Bentley had spent much time at Huron Mountain and at the rough camp that summer and fall. For the most part they stayed with their mother and preferred to walk the trail with her – she had a slower pace, rested often and was more understanding of children's ways. Richard enjoyed sailing on White Deer Lake and shooting at a floating target he had made. He often went on hikes with Ed McLean and the other woodsmen. In late September, Ed took Richard down to the Huron Bay Grade along the river to hunt ducks. Ed told Richard that his father had named a nearby lake for him that Richard had never seen. The two went over to look at it. This was Richard's first glimpse of Lake Richard. Ed had

Albino deer from Marquette County – George Shiras III took pictures of several at a time. This one at Presque Isle 1988. Courtesy Richard P. Smith.

put this name on a map of the camp lands which he had made, and it was the name used by automobile maps of Michigan up into the late 1940s. Later owners of the lake renamed it "Four Island Lake," the name it bears today.

Mr. McCormick had named another lake off to the northwest after his old woods cook and companion from Champion, Antoine Hebert. This lake was changed to Lake Herbert, but recent steps by descendants of Hebert have corrected the error.

In the spring of 1908, work was started on a channel between White Deer and Bulldog Lakes. The past winter had witnessed the end of the logging in the Bulldog Lake area. The Sawyer Goodman camps on the north shore of the lake were abandoned, and the land and timber rights in that area passed to McCormick and Bentley. That winter, the crew that remained in camp saw the last of the huge steam tractors with runners on the front and tracks behind. These giant machines would pull trains of ten and twelve sleds loaded with logs across Bulldog Lake, down the channel and across White Deer Lake. They would climb the big hills out to the Peshekee River on iced roads, then travel down the Huron Bay Grade to the mills.

When logging operations ceased, it meant the last winter that the crew at White Deer Lake would be in contact with the outside world. This was the last winter they would be able to go and visit the lumber camp at the Bulldog Lake clearing, and have available a nice iced road to Champion during the winter.

For as long as there had been a winter crew at White Deer Lake, there had been a lumber camp on the north shore of Bulldog Lake. The weather and snows were nearly always severe, and had been especially so in these years. Many of the loggers were ill–prepared to put up with great hardship, and waited only for the day when they had accumulated enough money to leave. The call was always out in the cities for more men to work in the woods.

But now that the loggers were through, the channel work could be started. The idea was to make a channel between White Deer and Bulldog Lakes that could be maneuvered by barge, canoe, or motorboat. The work on the channel was slow and hard. A raft was built with two upright poles attached to the edge. These stakes slipped up and down in iron brackets so they could be jammed into the mud to stabilize the raft. Once the raft was anchored in the proper location, a long–handled shovel was put into use, handled by two men. The shovel was on a sling arrangement between two upright poles.

As camp foreman, Ed McLean always tried to have someone working on the channel, and he never had to worry about having too little work for the men. When other work was slack, there was always channel work to be done. The workers would row the length of White Deer Lake early in the morning. The camp cook would prepare coffee and a lunch to take with them. They would pole the raft into position, drive in the anchoring poles and attach the huge shovel to the sling. The back–breaking work would then proceed all day long.

The process involved lowering the shovel down into the mud, levering it up by the weight of the two men positioned at the end of the handle, and depositing the scooped mud on the raft. Even a small deposit of the heavy mud made the raft unsteady, so the men would frequently have to throw the mud to the side of the channel with long–handled shovels or else pole to deep water and push it into the lake.

In this manner the entire 1,900–foot channel was dug by hand between 1908 and 1916. The log dam at the far end of Bulldog Lake was opened and the water lowered for this work. Later, continuous maintenance was necessary – marking the spots that needed attention, driving posts to mark the main channel, cutting weeds, grass, and water lilies, and moving or breaking up an occasional floating island. The depth of water could be adjusted by adding logs to the dam, to be sure there was enough water for navigation with outboard or inboard motors.

Another important and continuous job was the laying out, cutting, and maintenance of trails. The trail crews' work was never done. Trails were made to every lake in the area and around most of them, and along streams. Nor was one trail to a lake ever enough; the trails were cut from lake to lake in a network system, and to outstanding points of beauty and other places of special interest. Crude but picturesque benches were built on every prominence that afforded a view. Boathouses were built on the larger lakes, and light, graceful rowboats were carried to each lake to be housed in the boathouses during the winter. Bridges were built over rivers, along cliffs, through swamps, and over dry gulches. And then, of course, Mr. Bentley's Huron Mountain Trail always needed perfecting.

By 1910, White Deer Lake and the surrounding lands had been transformed into a dream world for those who loved the out–of–doors. These were still construction years, and the work crews were large. The summer crew usually ran between 15 and 20 men, and the winter crew from five to eight men. The workmen were housed in the "Guide House" on the mainland, one of several buildings, including woodshed, storehouse, ice house, and barns.

Winter work consisted of general maintenance, such as shoveling snow, cutting and putting up ice, and cutting, splitting and piling firewood.

Top: Cyrus McCormick, the hiker 1906.
Bottom: Cyrus McCormick – excited about the trail shows it to a group of ill–prepared guests (1905).

638

Foreman Ed McLean made daily records and reports until 1908. After 1908, a member of the crew would snowshoe into Champion to mail the reports to Mr. Bentley in Chicago. Jim Scanlon, who had worked for Bruce at the logging camp south of Lake 32 some years before, took over the job of reporting from 1908 to 1912, and George Belanger, brother of Black Tom, took over in 1912.

These Belanger brothers used the French pronunciation of their name at the time, but since it meant "baker" in English they later changed their name to Baker.

As a further check of the comings and goings at camp, Mr. Bentley kept close contact with the station agent in Champion, who also sent in regular reports. By getting his information from two sources, the meticulous Mr. Bentley had an excellent picture of what was going on.

The Chimney Cabin, the exclusive quarters of the McCormick and Bentley families or their very special guests, was by far the most imposing structure on the island at White Deer Lake. It stood facing southeast, where it got the full blessing of the morning sun. The former "men's camp" and "ladies' camp" became housing for guests when a crowd of young people arrived. There was quite a large building, at first called the "Library" , then the "Ladies' Camp," and later, "Birch Cabin." It was capable of housing eight or ten people and perched high on the north side of the island. In 1910 a recreation room, or "sitting room," was built on the northeast tip of the island, jutting out over the water. Beneath it was a boathouse which housed two boats, as well as a canoe or two. Directly above the boathouse, attached to the recreation room, was a screened–in porch surrounded by an outside porch with an ornate wooden railing. The recreation room itself was divided into two parts. The front section housed books, curios, comfortable furniture, beautiful kerosene lamps, some very ornate hand–painted globes, and the Victor Talking Machine. The Talking Machine and its collection of fine records was the center of interest of the entire building, which eventually became known as the Victor Room.

The Victor Room was Mr. Bentley's spot for relaxation. He spent many hours playing his records there while gazing out at the changing moods of White Deer Lake. From the room and the screened porch he could look out to the northeast, past Gull Island (a tiny island said to straddle the county line between Baraga and Marquette Counties, named for the gulls that nested there) and the impressive natural fortress rising abruptly from the water's edge, to the channel in the distance. Out of view from the Victor Room porch, but always present in Cyrus Bentley's mind, was the channel stretching away to Bulldog Lake. His thoughts would constantly travel down

Top: A picture of the Bentley Victor Talking Machine. Courtesy Richard Bentley.
Bottom: F. W. Reed steam hauler. (1908).

Top: 1910 – Island boathouse, sitting room and library.
Bottom: Sitting room and ladies camp.

the trail to Huron Mountain, making changes and improvements. He always had the feeling that the trail wasn't quite right yet...but how could it be improved?

In the fall of 1910, Mr. Bentley had a rather unfortunate experience during one of his trail crossings. As his hiking party was traveling north along the trail just west of the Yellowdog Plains, they chanced upon a stranger. Mr. Bentley challenged the man rather severely, as he usually did any stranger he encountered on his trail. He soon learned that the gentleman was Mr. William C. Weber of Detroit, who had been buying up tax titles in the area since before the turn of the century. To make matters worse, Mr. Bentley learned that at the moment he was on Weber's land.

Another similar incident occurred which did not sit well with Mr. Bentley. Part of his trail crossed a long stretch of land owned by Mr. Smith and Mr. Hall, lumbermen and flooring manufacturers from Grayling. Over the years they had acquired some of the finest pockets of hardwood timber in the north country. Loggers and homesteaders familiar with the area had a little ditty that they liked to recite: "If it's any good at all, it must belong to Smith and Hall."

Smith and Hall had received reports from their timber cruisers that the Bentley Trail passed through some of their holdings. They asked Mr. Bentley to provide a firewatch along the trail during the dry season of the year. They were afraid that hikers could easily start a forest fire by smoking or campfires. Mr. Bentley would have been glad to comply with their request, except that their virgin hardwood was far less susceptible to fire than either the cut–over part of his own lands or the jackpine plains which the trail crossed. This hardwood country required less maintenance than the other areas, and the men would have little to do there but sit around or patrol. The whole idea of dealing with other people concerning his trail bothered Cyrus Bentley a great deal. It was at about this time that he began discussing a whole new route with some of his better woodsmen. There was plenty of virgin country north of Bulldog Lake, and various routes were considered through a four or five mile wide corridor running northeasterly.

*   *   *

A typical guest routine of 1910 would originate at social functions in Chicago or New York, or through mutual friends when the subject of camping and vacations was discussed. Bentley or McCormick would extend an invitation to friends and, after making tentative plans, they would correspond at length during the winter before the trip. Plans were made down to the finest detail. The camp had to be notified well in advance as to who was coming and when they should be met, where each would be housed, what men and guides should be available. From many experiences of guests arriving ill–prepared for the experience that awaited them, Mr. Bentley provided each guest with the following information.

Everyone should come provided with two stout pair of walking shoes or boots. The heels should be hobnailed. It is better to have nails in both heels and soles, unless the nails in the soles are troublesome to the feet. Most woodsmen prefer shoes much too large for them, with plenty of stockings inside, but this way of dressing is not popular with city people. In addition to the walking shoes there should be a pair of light shoes for camp wear.

Everyone should have a rubber coat of some kind – the best kind is an 'automobile shirt.'

Everyone should have a sweater – the high–neck style is best.

Old soft felt hats are most serviceable for both men and women.

Flannel shirts for the men and flannel shirt–waists (or something like them) for the ladies are orthodox. Short skirts are indispensable and leggings, while not necessary, are on occasion desirable, especially for fishing.

Everyone should bring a bathing dress.

There are absolutely no dress requirements. Old clothes are the rule and the camping outfit should be assumed before reaching Champion, as it will be needed as much during the four miles just before reaching camp as at any time after.

The nights are likely to be cold, though they may be occasionally quite warm. There will probably be both cold and warm days. It is best to provide underclothing of moderate weight, with light and also heavy nightwear.

Everyone who intends to make a serious business of fishing should bring his or her own tackle, though there is plenty of tackle (such as it is) in camp for all who wish to fish.

Mail sacks are the best means of carrying clothing into the woods. The articles of clothing should be protected by smaller bags or wrappings.

Along with these instructions, each guest was given a cloth–backed map in a fine black leather case. In fact, each map was personalized with the

Top: First built as a library, then called the "Ladies Camp" this building was later known as Birch Cabin.
Bottom: Chimney cabin 1908.

guest's name or initials neatly lettered in gold block letters on the case. Each guest also received a gold–lined collapsible metal drinking cup engraved with the words "White Deer Lake." Each came in a sturdy leather case. These final touches of luxury and hospitality were the ideas of Cyrus McCormick. It was probably at his request that Mr. Bentley wrote out the clothing suggestions, as more than once Mr. McCormick had invited a group of business associates to White Deer Lake for a woods outing, only to have them walk out on the trail in their hard collars, suits and street shoes.

Over the next five or ten years some guests, even with the explicit instructions in their hands, still came ill–prepared for the wilderness. They just had no idea of what life would be like in the woods, and no amount of explaining could convince them until they had been there. Many did not own the needed types of clothing, fishing equipment, and footwear; nor did they know what to buy that would best fill the bill. To take care of this situation, a store room was started that was stocked with boots, rain gear, and clothing of all types, all neatly classified by size. Soon skis, snowshoes, fishing equipment, and other items were added to the store.

The camping parties would arrive by train in Champion, to be met by a team and wagon which had come down the grade the night before. The 16 miles from Champion to White Deer Lake was a day's trip, sometimes taking six or eight hours.

In anticipation of the guests' arrival, George Baker would climb a tree that afforded a view of a distant bend in the road, where he could see the team approaching. The guests would all be housed on the Island in one of the various cabins, but would eat in the guests' dining room on the mainland. No meals were eaten on the Island; in fact, there were no food service facilities there at all.

As the wagonload of people and baggage swung into view, George would blow the old bugle. As it was used for no other occasion, everyone knew what it meant. And it was no sharp melody he blew, either; just a loud BLAT which signaled the crew that the guests were arriving.

This was what the men had been waiting for. This was the main reason for being there all the long winter hours. Excitement ran high and everyone was at his best, especially if they expected Mr. Bentley or Mr. McCormick to be arriving with the party.

The members of the crew took special pains to look good. Their khaki pants were clean and showed a sharp crease in front and back. Blue work shirts were ironed to perfection. Everything on the grounds had been washed, polished, raked, arranged and rearranged several times in preparation for the arrival. Even the rope that stretched between the Island and the mainland had been scrubbed with strong soap and hot water.

Top: Island boathouse, also called the Victor room or Living room cabin.
Bottom: Victor room porch – White Deer Lake 1912 – Courtesy Richard Bentley.

Everyone stood at attention as the wagon pulled into view. George would clamber out of his perch in the tree and run ahead to ring a little set of chimes as the wagon pulled to a halt.

While the foreman exchanged greetings with Mr. Bentley or Mr. McCormick, the men on the crew would grab suitcases, duffle bags and packsacks and run down the wooden steps to the raft, quickly transfer them out to the Island and return the ferry before the guests had walked to the water's edge. Later on, the ferry barge became known as the "Good Ship Piffle."

After freshening up, the guests would return to the mainland for an elaborate dinner in the dining room. Fireplaces were lit if there was the slightest chill in the air. For the first few days, meals were usually planned by the cook, though sometimes special requests had come by mail. Later, people in the party would usually make suggestions. Even without any guidance, the cooks often outdid themselves. The food, while often plain, was delicious. It was usually a hearty breakfast, a very light lunch – often just a sandwich or a trail lunch – and a scrumptious evening meal. If there were big eaters in the party, the meals became even more lavish. The guests made every effort to explain why the food tasted so delicious – the crisp invigorating air, the long hikes, the wood stove, the cook, and so forth.

George Baker, besides being the winter cook and camp secretary, was also the Island Boy. If anything was needed on the island, George would run the errand, managing to keep out of sight at the same time. When no one was around he would sweep the porches, fill the wood boxes, make kindling, and lay the fires in the stoves and fireplaces.

One of the favorite evening pastimes during the stillness of the late summer twilight was for the guests to go out on the lake in a boat or canoe to sit and listen while Mr. Bentley played records on the Victor Talking Machine in the screened porch of the Victor Room. Strains of Liebestraum or Harry Lauder's "There's a Wee Hoose Mong the Heather" carried out over the open water. The men on the crew had many a good chuckle over Mr. Bentley's opening the screen door so the music would carry further. It never entered their minds that the screen could actually have a dampening effect on the sound. During the still, quiet summer's evening the soft music of the Victrola flowed from the huge graceful horn to every distant shore of the lake, its sound magnified by the heavy air. Since this was usually a moonlit night, it was an experience every guest remembered.

During their stay, which generally lasted a week or two or even up to a month, the guests would do a great deal of walking and fishing. They would often make it a point to see every lake in the vicinity.

One favorite was Summit Lake, located in Section 22 in Baraga County, about three miles northwest of the camp at White Deer Lake. "Summit" became its name when people realized that it was about the highest large body of water in the area. The highest lake in Michigan was later discovered to be Island Lake, some eight miles east on the Mulligan Escarpment. Summit Lake covered well over a hundred acres and was quite deep, with an irregular shoreline. Even today it is known for its huge bullfrogs and smallmouth bass. A boathouse had been built at the south end of Summit Lake in 1908 and a light boat carried in to be kept there. Whenever a boat was to remain at a lake, a log boathouse was built and the boat was kept in the water in the boathouse all summer, taken out of the water in the fall, and hung in the boathouse for the winter.

Two small lakes to the east and southeast of Summit are actually higher, as one drains down into Summit, but they are only about forty acres each in size. Both of these lakes are on the section line between Sections 22 and 23, and about a half–mile from Summit Lake. The one to the south is called Trout Lake because Jack Grove, the long–time squatter in the area, stocked it with trout from the Yellowdog River. He built a cabin at the northwest corner of Trout Lake around 1890. This lake could easily be seen from the Summit Lake trail, but was never much used by the guests.

The other small lake to the north of Trout was in the general area of hardwoods, but was mostly surrounded by evergreens, so Cyrus McCormick named this lake "Evergreen Lake."

Evergreen and Trout Lakes had their names mistakenly reversed on maps printed by the U. S. Geological Survey in 1956 and again, probably because of the first error, by the U. S. Forest Service in 1968, when they were in the process of acquiring the property. This has resulted in some confusion regarding the lakes. The maps, made from aerial photos, are very accurate as far as topography and size, shape and location of water bodies are concerned, but the field work in this area was sketchy and inaccurate when it came to inlets and outlets of many lakes.

Evergreen, Trout and Summit Lakes form the headwaters of the Big Huron River, which flows north. In 1898, the Hines Lumber Company put in a dam at the north end of Summit Lake. A half–mile or so north of Summit Lake, the main,or "west," branch of the Big Huron River picks up a river from the west which drains the same area that is also drained by the south–flowing Peshekee River.

In 1898, Hines had also built a log dam where the west branch of the Big Huron River meets the Summit Lake outlet. This was known as the Reservoir Dam, and it formed a head of water for logs being floated north on the Big Huron to Lake Superior.

The tributary from the west actually flows from Lake Charles. (A cabin in the same section is called "Charlie's," but the owner's last name and identity are unknown.) This is another very high body of water, and its marshy seepage flows south to the Peshekee River. Recent maps show two branches flowing from the west to the Big Huron, but not the main branch, which flows out of Summit Lake.

Below the Reservoir Dam, the river truly becomes the Big Huron River, flowing almost due north, picking up a small east branch which also drains little Trout Lake in Section 23. It then flows northeasterly to what was once known as "Flag Lake,' and then about two and a half miles north, near Tuttle's homestead, where it joins the main river.

Christ Andersen and Cyrus McCormick came onto Flag Lake for the first time in 1908. A deer standing near the edge of the lake took a quick look at them, threw up his tail or "flag," and disappeared over a windfall. Mr. McCormick exclaimed, "We'll call this lake "Flag Lake" from now on." Years later, though, it appeared on the maps as "Phillip's Lake." While there is no documented source as to the origin of this name, we can assume that it was later renamed by either McCormick or Bentley for a friend.

To the north, the Big Huron River goes into such wild gyrations that the Hines people had to build 22 bridges in order to cover one mile of territory on a road they had built from the Reservoir Dam just north of Campbell's Creek.

The Big Huron River had five dams in these upper parts built by the Hines Lumber Company between 1897 and 1901, and a sixth called the McLeach Dam, built by the Campbells in 1904. Hines built the dam at Summit Lake, the Reservoir Dam just below Summit Lake, the Upper Dam above Hines Camp I, the middle dam near the fifth correction line, and the lower dam above the McLeach.

The McLeach Dam was built on the property of a Mr. McLeach, a homesteader who reportedly had a farm in Skanee but resided near the dam site from 1903 to 1907.

As far as Bentley and McCormick were concerned, the Big Huron country was relatively unexplored in 1911. After a fishing trip that summer in the McLeach Dam area, they realized that the Prosper Roberts Trail, a winter logging tote road, followed the stream all the way to the mouth of the river. Then it cut along Lake Superior, past the Huron Mountains, to the Salmon Trout River. Prosper Roberts was an old pine logger who worked for Charles Hebard, and this road had been built in the 1870s. Mr. Bentley decided to explore the possibility of using this route for a new trail from White Deer Lake to the Huron Mountain Club.

Top: A group at the ford – Old lumber camp on the Peshekee 1910.
Bottom: Guests on the trail – Dr. Hibbs (center) (c. 1910).

Top: A wagon load of guests leaving Champion for White Deer Lake camp. (1910).
Bottom: The very early raft setup to the island. (1910)

651

In September of 1911, Alphonse Gamache blazed a trail from Bulldog Lake to the Prosper Roberts Trail and a month later ten men, led by Christ Andersen, set out from White Deer Lake to clear a direct trail to the mouth of the Big Huron River. Two Indian packers, Jim DeCota and his cousin, carried a tent, food, and cooking utensils. One of them carried a grindstone which was set up whenever a stop was made so that the men could sharpen their axes.

When the crew reached the mouth of the Big Huron in the late afternoon of the second day, they were wet and cold due to an unexpected snowfall which had hampered their work. While the rest of the men set up camp and remained at the mouth of the river for the night, Christ Andersen took one man and went on to Huron Mountain for supplies.

Christ and his partner stayed overnight in the Huron Mountain Guide House, picked up their supplies early in the morning, and returned to the mouth of the river, some ten miles west of the Club. They found the Prosper Roberts Trail to be in excellent condition from the Club to the River, so there was no need to bring the trail crew further. The entire crew returned to White Deer Lake that day. All in all, Christ and his partner had traveled over 60 miles in three days' time, 30 of it on the last day. The other members of the crew had covered only forty miles, but had worked two of the days, one day in heavy, wet snow.

Despite these labors, the second Bentley Trail was never used to get to Huron Mountain. The main reason was that it was just too great a distance and too far out of the way. In addition, the bad experience and tired condition of the trail crew hadn't enhanced the report they gave Mr. Bentley. Finally, there was the fact that over half of the new trail was Prosper Roberts Trail, all down the east side of the Big Huron and along Lake Superior. Mr. Bentley wanted a better trail, and one of his own making.

An interesting side tale was related in 1970 by Mr. Howard Marks of Marquette. He was born and raised in Michigamme, just seven miles west of Champion. His father had made a homestead claim of 160 acres in the hardwoods west of the Sand, or Yellowdog, Plains. They had made several trips on foot up the Grade from Michigamme to the McCormick and Bentley Camp. From there, they took the old Huron Mountain Trail north to the parcel of land they had claimed but not actually "proved up."

On all the previous trips, Howard and his father had been treated rather coldly at White Deer Lake Camp. However, when a teenaged Howard made the trip alone in 1912, he found things quite different.

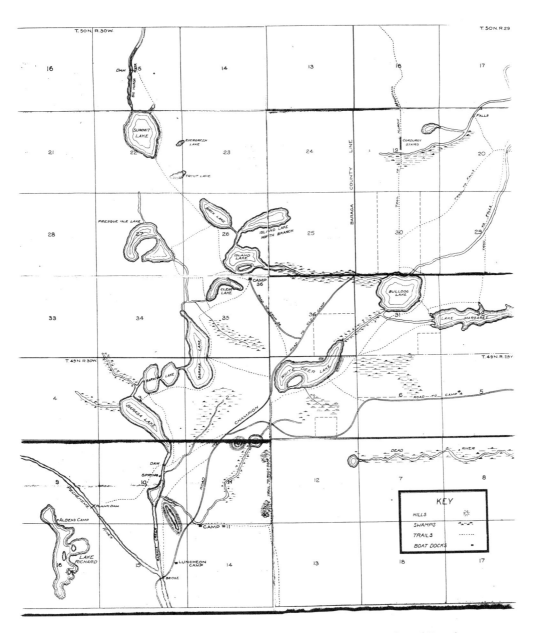

Leather bound, cloth backed map, given to each guest by McCormick and Bentley.

When he introduced himself at the McCormick Bentley Camp, he was treated royally. He was well–fed and given a boat to take down the lakes. When he approached his father's land, he realized the motive for his polite reception. Bentley's new trail had cut a swath clean across the Marks' 160 acres.

Upon further inspection, Howard discovered a new trail heading east from the Bentley Trail, seemingly right out into the jackpine plains. Out of curiosity he decided to follow the new but already well–worn trail. Soon he discovered a strange set of log buildings in a clearing. The first was a two–story log building. The upper story was obviously a hayloft, but in the center of the high–peaked roof was a little cupola with a walkway and a railing around it. Thirty or forty yards to the east was a hodgepodge of a two–story log building with a small lean–to attached to the far side.

This was the Andersen homestead, and Mr. and Mrs. Andersen were in. Again Howard received a royal welcome. The Andersens invited him to dinner and bade him stay for the night. Howard had expected to rough it in the depths of this backwoods country – had expected to sleep cold, hungry, and uncomfortable – but there he was that night, well–fed and sleeping in a warm, comfortable bed between clean sheets. In the morning the Andersens were reluctant to have him leave, but after a good breakfast they sent him off with a trail lunch under his arm.

Over the next year or two, several new routes were explored in the hope of finding a better trail to Huron Mountain, much to the chagrin of Cyrus McCormick, who felt that one trail was enough. He was content to remain in the White Deer Lake area, and would just as soon have left the rest of the forest undisturbed.

Mr. McCormick enjoyed walking, but did not need a destination. He would often picnic at the North Falls or a delightful setting at the top of the East Falls. McCormick enjoyed the view from the "Acropolis," a high prominence north of Island Lake, and especially the view from the "Crow's Nest" between the North and East Falls. He had benches and lookouts made on other high spots, where he would bring his guests to enjoy a panoramic view.

In the meantime, Mr. Bentley, who had taken some guests as far as the Big Huron River on his new trail for a fishing expedition, decided to set up a summer tent camp along the river. The camp could serve two purposes: it could be a fish camp, as these proved to be the finest trout waters in the area, and it could also be used as a stopover en route to Huron Mountain. He later decided to have a permanent building erected at the fish camp site. Christ Andersen would watch the place during the summers.

Top: Cyrus McCormick having lunch in "luncheon ravine" near the headwaters of the west branch of the Yellowdog.
Bottom: White Deer Lake crew 1909 – George Baker second from right.

Top: Trail hikers 1910 – Mrs. Hibbs (center) and Dr. Hibbs (2nd from right) easily identifiable.
Bottom: Tents on the Big Huron River 1910.

Book Two

Jack Grove

In the fall of 1911, Jack Grove came into the White Deer Lake camp to stay, unannounced. Everyone in the woods knew Jack Grove. Mr. McCormick had encountered him on an excursion before the turn of the century, and both he and Bentley had depended on his knowledge of the area. He had been their guide several times. They knew he was living somewhere out in the woods, and had told many of their guests about this mysterious man.

Cyrus Bentley had taken a picture of Grove in 1904, and another several years later at Christ Andersen's pond. These seem to be the only pictures ever taken of Grove, and both by Cyrus Bentley.

Jack had been a mineral prospector in Canada before coming to Michigan in 1885, a fugitive from the law. These stories, told to Nels Andersen shortly after the turn of the century, had come piecemeal from several lumberjacks who had known or heard about Grove in Canada. At least some of the tale was confirmed to Christ Andersen by Grove himself.

It seems that as a young man, Jack Grove had taken a partner into the woods with him on one of his many lengthy prospecting expeditions and, after a year or two, had returned without him. The family of the missing partner, having heard that Jack Grove was around, tried to contact him about their relative. Grove acted very suspicious, and eluded everybody who wanted to question him.

In order to get some information before he disappeared again, the family contacted the Royal Mounted Police, who immediately began a concerted search for Grove. Getting the word that he was being sought from all corners, Grove left the country.

Traveling by foot and raft, or by boat when he could borrow or steal one, he went from Blind River, Ontario to Sault Ste. Marie. There he crossed illegally into the United States.

Jack Grove worked his way west along the south shore of Lake Superior until he reached Lake Independence and the mouth of the Yellowdog River, now known as the Iron River. He found much activity there in the fall of 1885, with Jim Redy's crews building dams and tote roads. He followed the river south and west until he arrived at the very source of the west branch of the Yellowdog River, a small spring lake set down in steep timbered hills. Here he built a crude shack about ten feet square from unpeeled logs of various softwood species.

Within a few years, lumbermen moved into his Shangri La, dammed up his lake, and began cutting his pine. Of course, Jack Grove had no claim

Top: Jack Grove. Picture taken by Cyrus Bentley in 1904. Grove had been living in the area nearly twenty years at this time.
Bottom: Unidentified picture of an early work crew. Third from right is "Black Tom" Belanger (author's opinion). The shack in the picture has to be Jack Grove's second camp. Jack is not in the picture.

to this land, but rather than move on, he built another cabin on the opposite side of the lake, very near the clearing where a set of logging camps had been erected. This second cabin, though crude, was an improvement over his first, as he had gleaned some flat lumber from the camp bosses for roof boards. For chinking he used moss, earth, cloth scraps, and old blankets. Inside, the cabin boasted a makeshift chair, a two–by–three foot table, a stove, a bunk, and a few shelves, as well as one door and one window.

The camp was situated about 30 feet from the crystal–clear waters of the little lake which the loggers by now referred to as "Jack Grove's Lake." Along a small beach in front of the camp, several fast–running, clear, cold springs flowed into the lake. Jack took some hollow cedar logs and, following some of the larger flows, sank the logs down into the mud, providing him with clear, cold spring water several inches above the lake level. This system worked well even in winter, as the flowing spring water did not freeze.

Jack had brought three guns with him from Canada. One was a single–shot .32 caliber rifle, his constant companion in the woods. It was very light and easy to carry in one hand, ready at all times. He sometimes carried a nickel–plated Smith and Wesson .32 caliber six–shot revolver in a holster, or sometimes in his pack. For bird hunting he used a shotgun which the British had manufactured for the Zulu War in Africa The Zulu War took place in 1883–84. The Zulus were fierce fighters, not intimidated by normal weapons. Death meant nothing to them. The Zulu shotgun, designed to literally blow away parts of the body, had great psychological effect and was said to be instrumental in the final British victory over the Zulus.

An overproduction of these guns in Britain was sold in Canada, where Jack had obtained his. He often carried this gun on his back with a sling arrangement when he was carrying the other rifle, but in later years the Zulu gun usually stood in the corner of his little cabin.

During the year or two that the lumber camp was located at Jack Grove's Lake, Jack provided supplemental meat for the camp table by hunting deer and small game. In exchange, the lumbermen gave him staples such as flour, sugar, and salt, as well as odds and ends of lumber, tools and nails. The woods boss, traveling the iced roads by horsedrawn cutter, would occasionally bring Jack an item or two he requested from town.

In the early days (1885–1905) Jack Grove had a reputation for being resourceful, intelligent, and extremely clever, but in his later years he was the dirtiest, greasiest man that Christ Andersen had ever met. He washed neither himself nor his clothes, and his huge black mustache was always dirty. He had all the known species of body bugs. Fortunately he did not crave human companionship, for only the hardiest of men could bear to be close to him for

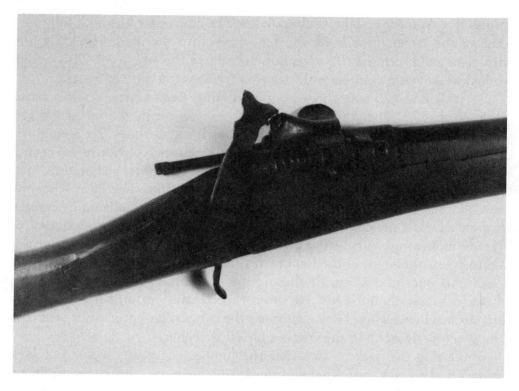

Jack Grove's Zulu shot gun (1883 model). Picture by Jack Deo.

very long. He kept his lonely vigil anywhere within six or eight miles from Grove's Lake, hunting, prospecting, and scavenging for food. Guests at White Deer Lake found him a curiosity, and loved to spin tales about him. The younger folks always held the hope of seeing this living legend.

The local woodsmen mistrusted Jack, and rightly so. One of his favorite tricks was taking pot shots at strangers with his single shot .32 rifle; he would knock the bark from a tree above their head. Several folks from Champion and Michigamme who had received this treatment had blamed the Andersen boys, who also were much talked about but seldom seen. Stories of their heroic tasks and Jim Andersen's uncanny marksmanship were spread throughout the land by the lumberjacks who poured out of the woods after the spring drives.

Grove claimed to have struck gold in two or three places within a few miles of his camp. All of these places turned out to be on land owned by William C. Weber of Detroit. Upon learning this, Grove contacted Weber by mail with the help of the people at White Deer Lake. Jack requested half–interest in any gold that was taken out, in payment for the discoveries. Weber replied that he didn't see why he should pay half, as he rightfully owned it all. Jack ended the matter by saying, "Then go ahead and find it!"

Jack did his level best to see that neither Weber nor anyone he sent would ever find the gold. Weber prospected the area himself for years after that, but was never able to find gold. Jack never bothered Weber, Bentley or McCormick, since Weber owned the land, and Bentley and McCormick had been good to Jack, hiring him as a guide when they had needed his talent and letting him pick up supplies at White Deer Lake. But strangers were another story. He guarded "his" gold and his territory for the rest of his life.

At least once, Jack passed – or tried to pass – some counterfeit coins in L'Anse. He was even rumored to have tried passing counterfeit diamonds made from sugar crystals. He became known as "the Counterfeiter" and was seldom seen near L'Anse again. The local authorities never went after him; they did not take his attempts seriously, and besides, they had no idea where to look for him.

In 1909 or '10, Grove built a third cabin near one of his gold strikes at Trout Lake, and he had still another outpost camp north of the Yellowdog Plains. Three of the four places – one at Trout Lake, one at Grove's Lake, and one north of the Plains – were all livable at the same time, and he would travel between them, spending most of his time at the two lake cabins. Trout Lake had no name when he built there, but Jack later claimed to have stocked the lake with trout from the Yellowdog River.

The Trout Lake cabin was his last and best. It was constructed of cedar logs and, like his previous cabins, had a lean–to roof, one window and one door. At first it was heated by a sheet metal stove, and later by a small, ornate cast–iron box stove. As the cabin became cluttered with tools, extra cooking utensils, and other items, Jack built a small storage shed nearby.

It was here at Trout Lake that Jack spent many of his last winters, without any contact with other humans. Each day he had to scrounge for food and fuel. Items which should not be allowed to freeze, such as potatoes, he kept in a burlap bag or a water–tight crock, and shoved through a hole in the ice. Although Jack wasn't a trapper as such, he did set snares and small home–designed or Indian–type traps, and once in a while would even sell a few furs.

One winter, Jack built a cedar log raft on the ice of Trout Lake. He used the raft to fish for trout year round. No bird, large or small, was safe from his Zulu shotgun. No plant or animal was overlooked if it proved edible. It was said that Grove ate ferns, song birds, and even mice, frogs, and worms, as well as all the larger animals. Though he did obtain some food from the McCormick camp, he was a master of scavenging.

The Andersens had come from the west and established themselves on the Yellowdog Plains before Jack had realized it. After taking a shot from ambush at each of the Andersen men, hitting a tree just above their heads without scaring any of them, he gradually made friends. He later went to visit them at the homestead. While he was always cordially welcomed in 1910 and '11, he began to make a pest of himself. On one occasion Grove stayed for a week, and Nels had to ask him to leave, a thing he had never before had to do to any visitor. It seems that the good cooking and warm atmosphere at the little Andersen homestead were just too pleasant for Jack Grove.

Christ Andersen had spent a night at each of Jack's lake cabins, and hadn't enjoyed either visit. One time, in the dim light of an oil lamp, Christ found himself staring straight down the barrel of Jack's loaded .32 during one of Jack's stories.

Jack became extraordinarily sociable in 1910 and '11. While he couldn't be considered old by today's standards, small ailments were major problems for him in his hermit–like existence. To live the type of life he did, a man had to be secure in the thought that he could handle any situation, and had to be in good physical condition. In his early fifties, Jack was beginning to feel the effects of old age. When he wasn't feeling good he wanted to be with other people, but of the few available, none seemed to desire his company.

In the late fall of 1911, Jack appeared at the Guide House at White Deer Lake Camp. He had broken trail in the deep soft snow all the way from one of his cabins, a challenge for a much younger man. From time to time, Jack had walked this distance before and had stayed with the crew for a few days, often as a stopover on his way to Champion. Some of the crew wondered why Jack had tackled the fresh, soft snow, since he usually waited for a hard–packed snow or a firm crust. But here he was, with no apparent business and no obvious reason for making the visit. Following the unwritten law of the woods, the foreman took him in, gave him shelter, and set a place for him at mealtimes, the same as he would for any other traveler.

A tradition throughout the northwoods lumbercamps that carried over to places like White Deer Lake was that no one spoke at the table. The men ate in silence. Under these circumstances Grove was unable to communicate his plight to the men, even if he had wanted to. As soon as the meal was completed, the men either left to work or purposefully ignored Jack.

The days of the long winter stretched into weeks, and the weeks into months. Jack neither worked nor offered to help with chores at the camp. He ate and slept. None of the men had anything to do with Jack, but if a stranger happened to arrive at the camp the men would arrange it so he sat next to Grove at the table. Then they would sit back and enjoy their little joke as the stranger became aware of Jack's uncouth table manners and offensive odor.

By the spring of 1912 the crew had had enough of Jack Grove. They began to complain to the foreman, Alphonse Gamache, in hopes that he would ask Grove to leave. Alphonse was a reasonable man. He understood the men, but was reluctant to turn Grove out until the weather was good.

It was a beautiful day in early May when Gamache made his move. Early in the morning just after breakfast, he presented Jack with a bill for quite a large sum of money.

"What is this?" exclaimed Grove, taken completely by surprise.

"It's a bill," said Alphonse. "You can stay here whenever you want for a meal, or for a few days or even a week if you're sick, or if the weather is bad, or the snow too soft to travel, or any other excuse you can dream up, but nobody stays here all winter without either working or paying. If you're going to stay here like this, you're going to have to pay."

Jack was shocked. He had no one to turn to for sympathy. He looked again at the bill. After some hesitation, he mumbled, "All right...I'll pay."

He gathered together his few belongings and walked down to the lake. It was a beautiful spring day. The sun shone brightly on White Deer Lake, and a light spring breeze played from the southwest. The lake was clear of ice, and what snow was left in the woods was melting fast. The men followed Jack out, staying some distance behind him. They solemnly watched as he climbed into one of the McCormick rowboats and threw his turkey, or little bundle of belongings, into the bow. Jack rowed out past the island, then headed a little south of east across the lake. One of the men came out of the Guide House with a glass to get a better look at him disappearing into the distance. Through the glass he saw Jack pull up on the far shore, pick his turkey up out of the boat, and vanish into the woods. No one ever laid eyes on Jack Grove again.

Life at White Deer Lake

Life for the men at White Deer Lake in those years was isolated and hard, but not without its pleasant compensations. While the loggers had left the immediate area of the camp, most of the crew well remembered the hard life in the logging camps – the long hours, bitter cold, and wet, soggy snow. The river drives, sometimes pictured as romantic and adventurous in Canada and lower Michigan, were more often miserable and dangerous in the small fast rivers of the Upper Peninsula. On the drives many of the "river hogs" were wet to the waist in icy water nearly every day, and their lives were in constant danger. When a man drowned, he was buried where they found him and, more often than not, no record was kept. The crew at White Deer Lake remembered the smelly bunkhouses with their coarse woolen blankets and straw ticks. If a man wasn't strong as a bull, or mean and tough, or had a friend that was, he found himself at the mercy of the pranksters and the bullies.

By comparison, life at White Deer Lake was much better. Food was plain, but nourishing and bountiful. Bunks were made up with clean sheets which, in later years, were changed every week. The pay was a dollar and ten cents a day, compared with less than a dollar in the lumber camps. The bosses were more understanding and easier to work for, and the crew smaller and more close–knit – in short, the job at White Deer Lake was much more desirable.

Mr. Bentley had compiled a list of eighteen rules to be memorized by each man hired to work at White Deer Lake. These rules explained exactly what was expected of the workmen, including how to behave, and what areas were off–limits. Some of the rules were so strict or specific that they are quite humorous by today's standards. One stated, "If you are walking by the ladies' camp on the island, you may look straight ahead or away from it, but you may not look toward it."

Top: One of F. W. Reed's camps on the Pechekee (1890s) Notice an ox right rear.
Bottom: Champion (c.1905–1910) – The streets were packed down with horse–drawn roller after a heavy snow fall.

Each week, a progress report consisting of daily summaries was mailed to Mr. Bentley, who assumed the position of overseer from his office in Chicago.

Once a week, a man or two would set out on snowshoes from White Deer Lake to travel the sixteen miles to Champion with mail and other messages. This trip was extremely important, as it was their only link with the outside world.

Dr. Dudley of Chicago, a friend of Bentley and McCormick and a long–time member of Huron Mountain Club, had left medicines and medical instructions for the men in case of emergency. These special instructions covered such maladies as sore throats, pneumonia, appendicitis, and a wide range of accidental injuries. For years they hung in the foreman's office for all to see.

In the winter of 1914, one such emergency arose while Christ Andersen was staying at the camp. While few people in the vicinity of Champion had actually seen him, nearly everyone had heard of him. Stories of the Andersen family living somewhere in the big woods north of the McCormick–Bentley camp were told, and often exaggerated in the telling, throughout the small community. The Andersen boys were famous for their feats of strength, daring and perseverance. Many of those who had only heard of the Andersens were a little apprehensive or even afraid of them, and few wanted to penetrate their country. Another common but erroneous belief was that the Yellowdog country was the home of several large packs of wolves, and that a man would have little chance of surviving if he encountered them. The Andersens heard wolves regularly, but seldom saw them.

Christ Andersen had beaten all the lumberjacks in arm wrestling and finger wrestling, and no one could match Jim's skill with a rifle. Men who saw Jim shoot were amazed at his accuracy, but Jim regarded it as routine. He never showed off, but was always reserved, quiet and humble. Christ and Jim were as close as two brothers could be. They defended each other verbally, and everyone was certain that they wouldn't hesitate to defend each other physically if necessary.

Although by 1913 Nels and Johanna had left the original homestead, and Jack Grove had mysteriously disappeared, trappers still did not enter the Andersen country without good reason. This fear was unwarranted, for Christ and Jim would never intentionally harm anyone. Both men were slow to anger and extremely kind and gentle but, like the bear or wolf, their great strength was known and as a result they were feared.

The son of the White Deer Lake foreman was ill and on the verge of pneumonia. Medicines specified by Dr. Dudley's list of instructions were unavailable at the camp. One of the men was scheduled to return to Champion the next day for some time off. It was decided that he would obtain the medicine and the following day either bring it back halfway or else send someone else by snowshoe to meet Christ Andersen, who would relay the medicine to camp. This way, no one would have to travel more than the sixteen miles on snowshoes which was considered a day's work.

Christ started out from White Deer Lake at five in the morning, following a fresh snowshoe trail. Within a few hours the wind picked up and a wet, heavy snow began to fall. Later the temperature dropped rapidly, and Christ's trail was soon covered with blowing snow. Christ plodded on, step after step. The fierce wind and new snow made the going tough, but Christ was never concerned about losing his way. He became a little anxious about the person he was supposed to meet, though; who would it be, and how far would he get? What Christ didn't realize was that no ordinary man would ever continue in such a storm.

The messenger from Champion had turned back early in the morning, just after the blizzard struck. Never in his wildest thoughts did he expect anyone to come all the way from White Deer Lake under these conditions.

Christ pushed on into the wild gusts. For long moments he could see nothing at all. Christ had been nearly blind in one eye for most of his life. He had acquired the habit of peering through the good eye and keeping the poor one shut, and in bad weather he would squint his good eye so tightly that an onlooker would think he had no vision in either one.

Then, too, his ankle had been crushed in an accident in Denmark when he was just a boy. The ankle never seemed to bother him much after he was warmed up, though he always limped slightly. Many people thought this limp was just a confident swagger.

Before 9 A.M., Christ reached the Rock Dam on the Peshekee, about nine miles from White Deer Lake. He kept up his pace. By the time he reached the fork where the West Branch joined the river, he realized that the man from Champion had very likely turned back. Christ's only choice was to keep on going.

Christ arrived in Champion around noon. The town was at a standstill, except for a few men who had gotten as far as the saloon. It was the only place open, and a place to get inside.

When Christ swaggered into the saloon, the place was electrified. To the group of men assembled there, boasting of their bravery for having been able to reach the saloon in such a blizzard, Christ had accomplished the impossible. They had all heard stories of the Andersen brothers which had sounded like wild exaggerations, but now here stood the great Christ Andersen before their eyes, having come sixteen miles on snowshoes in a blinding blizzard for a bottle of medicine!

Christ had never been a drinker. He had been taught never to consume alcohol, except for medicinal purposes. But he had also been brought up to believe that if he entered a man's place of business he should oblige him with trade, Christ ordered a shot of whiskey. Downing the first glass in a swallow, he ordered a second, thereby establishing a long–standing reputation as a heavy drinker.

No one in the saloon said a word until Christ had left. A few hours later, their amazement was increased when they learned that, without even stopping to rest, Christ Andersen had taken the bottle of medicine and immediately set forth again for the White Deer Lake camp in the waning storm, which was now accompanied by huge snow drifts and intense cold.

Christ was beginning to feel the wear and tear of his long hard tramp. The return trip was all uphill. The storm had subsided toward evening, but his trail had disappeared, and any warming effect the whiskey had had long since worn off. Christ plodded on, a little slower now, in the gripping cold. Darkness had fallen, and he had miles to go.

A short distance off the grade was a trapper's shack that he could have headed for, but he had long passed that without a thought of it. The idea of the warm stove at the Guide House kept him moving.

It was late at night when he finally reached Spring Hill, just a mile or so from camp. In 18 hours he had broken trail for over 30 miles. Despite his strength and incredible endurance, Christ was exhausted.

He sat down in the snow and soon fell asleep. This could easily have been the end of Christ Andersen. Stories are widespread of men in the northwoods succumbing to cold and exhaustion who finally went to sleep in the snow, never to wake again. But at this point Christ had a strange dream.

He dreamt he was in a huge cathedral back home in Denmark, looking up through tall stone pillars at a bright light beaming down at him through stained–glass windows. An organ was playing loudly. Away from the scene and surrounding it, all was black. The picture suddenly changed, and Christ became conscious of the bitter cold. The sound of the organ turned into the howl of a timber wolf. As Christ looked up at the streaming heavenly light, it became a full, cold moon pouring its light down between the tall pines.

A shock ran through his entire body. He tried to get up but found he couldn't move. His fingers were completely numb, and they rattled like bones when he shook them. With great effort he managed to get to his feet and take a painful step forward, then another...and another. As he staggered along in the deep snow, fear seized him and he broke into a run. As Christ told it years later with a twinkle in his eye, he couldn't walk, so he ran all the way back to camp.

Christ Andersen, called by some people "The Great Dane," had accomplished the impossible. He had snowshoed 32 miles in terrific winds, a blinding snowstorm, and unrelenting cold all in a day's time, and successfully returned to camp with the bottle of medicine. Whether it was the medicine itself, or the effort of will required to bring it, the foreman's son recovered.

Woodsmen's Impression of the City

The position of foreman, later called manager and then superintendent, of White Deer Lake Camp, passed from Ed McLean to Jim Scanlon in 1908, and then to Alphonse Gamache in 1911.

Spring, summer, and fall visitors were very common in those years, but winter visitors were unheard–of. No bathing facilities had been provided for the year–round crew and this concerned Mr. Bentley a great deal, although the men themselves didn't seem to mind.

Possibly Mr. Bentley was being pushed by his friend Dr. Dudley, who was always on the lookout for the welfare of the crew. Besides leaving the medical kit and instructions at the camp, he also listened to complaints and tried to treat the men himself whenever the need arose.

Because of his concern for the men who worked at the camp, Dr. Dudley asked for, and received, permission from Mr. Bentley to make a winter trip to White Deer Lake. It took three days for the teams, working in shifts, to break a road from Champion to the camp.

When Dr. Dudley and Mr. Delano, the president of the Wabash Railroad, arrived in Champion, they were met by a sleigh and team and taken up the newly opened road to White Deer Lake. The crew waited on them, treating them like summer guests. Dr. Dudley soon announced that he and Mr. Delano wanted none of the folderol that had been accorded them. They had come to the camp in order to live with the men, in the same style as the men. They even insisted that they wanted to eat the same food and even eat with the men. The crew at White Deer Lake never ate so well as they did in those two weeks!

Dr. Dudley made arrangements for two of the men to come to his office in Chicago for surgery. The trip was scheduled for April.

George Baker was one of the men to make the trip, and it was he who later related the story.

According to George, it was in April when he and another man set out from camp on a crust of snow at about four in the morning. By leaving early and traveling before the sun got too high, they planned on the crust holding until they could reach town. They arrived in Champion in time to board the train for Chicago. They left their snowshoes with the station master but took their heavy Duluth packs with them, since these contained all their worldly possessions. Once settled in the train car, they took off their heavy sheepskin–lined canvas mackinaws and settled down for the overnight trip to Chicago. Propping their feet up on the opposite seat, they slept comfortably after their long snowshoe trek.

The train arrived in Chicago bright and early the next morning. Shouldering their Duluth packs, the two woodsmen walked out into the streets of the city.

In contrast to the ten–degree temperature at White Deer Lake, the men found Chicago bathed in warm sunshine, the heat reflecting from stone and concrete. While their camp was still locked in the dead of winter, the city was in the heart of spring, with grass turning green and buds bursting on the trees.

Passers–by on the street stopped to stare at the strangers, who looked as if they had just been transplanted from the Klondike.

George liked absolutely nothing about the whole trip. Even the basic reason for it was distasteful – surgery on both ends of his alimentary canal for enlarged tonsils and hemorrhoids. When the doctor told him how long they would have to remain in the city for treatment, George and his friend refused their operations and boarded the northbound train as quickly as possible. They had seen all they ever wanted of the city.

In the spring and summer, Mr. Bentley wrote constantly of the water system. It was fairly easy to get pressure from the springs to the Island by gravity, but the Guide House was so high that it presented a real engineering problem. After much debate, the old fellow Mr. Bentley had hired to work on the project finally said, "Well, Mr. Bentley, let's give up on this thing. I haven't had a bath in 60 years, so I guess I can get along the rest of my time without one."

"What?" cried Mr. Bentley, holding his nose. "Get out of here, get out, I tell you!"

But finally the water system was installed. Twelve large points were driven into springs on Spring Hill, and gravity brought the water down to the buildings on the mainland and the Island.

The other problem which occupied much of Mr. Bentley's time in 1913 was the trail to Huron Mountain. He was dissatisfied with each of the three routes which had been attempted, and discussed the trail system off and on all summer with Alphonse Gamache. That fall, Alphonse blazed a trail across to Canyon Lake, just south of Mountain Lake. He sent a rough map of the route to Mr. Bentley, who became very enthusiastic. Up to this time, he had purposely avoided this eastern route for several reasons. First, he wanted to come in at the west end of Mountain Lake in order to take full advantage of crossing the lake by boat, and second, the new route could not avoid the huge Yellowdog Swamp south of the plains and the Cedar Creek Swamp north of the plains.

The more he pondered the new layout, the more confident Cyrus Bentley became that this was finally the best solution. Since he could no longer avoid the swamps, he would hit them head–on and take the shortest route through them. He would make this new trail superior to all the other trails. He would bridge the swamps.

Walter McClintock

In the winter of 1914, Bentley wrote to the son of Oliver McClintock of Pittsburgh, Pennsylvania, a member of Huron Mountain Club. McClintock's son Walter was a famous Indian scout, the adopted son of "Mad Wolf," a well–known Blackfoot chief of the Rocky Mountain region.

Walter McClintock was considered to be one of the world's great woodsmen of his day. He first went west with the government timber survey party which was to report on the extensive timber holdings of the U. S. in the west. In 1890, he left the survey party and traveled with an Indian guide to join Mad Wolf and his tribe, the Blackfeet, who had been forced west and north into the Canadian Rockies and were appealing for help. McClintock was taken into the Blackfoot tribe and then adopted by Mad Wolf himself. He spent 15 years in this rugged frontier life. In 1910, he returned to the east and wrote a book, "Old North Trail," about the plight of the Blackfeet and about Indian life in general. For the next several years, he carried the message of the Blackfeet throughout the United States and Europe. His lectures kept him almost continuously before the royalty of Europe, especially Denmark, Germany, and England.

McClintock could mimic the sound of every bird or mammal in the wild so perfectly that after a lecture in Germany he submitted to a physician's examination of his mouth for any device that made such sounds. He was at the peak of his fame in 1914.

In 1923, he wrote a second book called "Old Indian Trails." Both books are rare glimpses of authentic rituals and Indian life.

(This Walter McClintock was no relation – no close one, at least – of the McClintock family from Marquette, who also had a son named Walter about a generation later.)

Mr. McClintock planned to be at Huron Mountain, and promised to spend time on the trail in the fall and make what suggestions he could to Mr. Bentley.

In Chicago, Mr. Bentley and the McCormicks spent much of that winter discussing plans for the new trail. With all this talk and planning, even the McCormicks became enthusiastic about the new trail. All three decided to go up to White Deer Lake just as early that spring as the weather and snow would warrant. They could seldom plan on getting into the woods much before the middle of May, and even then there could be much snow left in the shaded places.

On May 14, 1914, Cyrus and Harold McCormick and Cyrus Bentley arrived, intending to look over the land between White Deer Lake and Huron Mountain Club, east of the old trail. They had arranged to have Christ and Jim Andersen accompany them on the trip. It was an ideal time to go land looking. The snow had gone and there were no bugs. There were no leaves on the trees to hinder one's vision. They wasted no time getting into the woods.

After the trip down the lakes and the long hike to the Yellowdog River along the south side of the Panorama Hills, the party plunged headlong through the big Yellowdog Swamp. As Mr. Bentley grappled his way through the tag alders that blocked his way and tore at his clothing, he exclaimed, "This is worse than the jungles of Africa!"

The swamp seemed to stretch endlessly ahead of them. Christ Andersen explained that the time to go through the swamp was in March, when the snow was deep and had a good crust on it. You were above the water and the mud, and halfway up the tag alders. Bentley and McCormick suggested that the Andersens take some time off from trapping and complete the trail through the swamp the next winter.

It was a welcome change when they walked out into the tall jackpine and white pine stumps of the Yellowdog Plains. They kept their northeasterly course and came out onto a pleasant little pond. Looking about, they found another small pond further east. All of them agreed that these ponds would be a nice stop over for hikers when the trail was completed.

Top: May 18, 1914 – Jim Andersen, Cyrus Bentley, Christ Andersen and Cyrus McCormick starting out to look for a new route for the Bentley Trail. – Picture taken by Harold McCormick at the edge of the Sawer–Goodman clearing on the north side of Bulldog lake.
Bottom: May 18, 1914 – Christ Andersen, Jim Andersen and Cyrus Bentley on the south side of the Yellowdog Plains scouting a route for a new Bentley Trail. Picture taken by Cyrus McCormick.

Top: October 6, 1914 – Jim Andersen (left) and Walter McClintock begin to lay out the New Bentley Trail. Picture taken by Cyrus Bentley at White Deer Lake.
Bottom: Ruben Swanson, Mr. Bentley's private secretary at the west pond on the Sands Plains, en route to Huron Mountain Club – May 25, 1914.

The group continued to a point where the land dropped off sharply. From the edge of this escarpment they saw the familiar Huron Mountain and Mount Homer, which appeared to be guarding Mountain Lake. The route seemed to be a good one and, knowing that they would still have to carefully work out the exact course of the trail, they returned to White Deer Lake.

That summer, plans were initiated to build the new trail along the eastern route. Mr. Bentley planned to follow the contours of the hills, gouging the trail out of the hillsides. He would corduroy the swamps or stretch great hewn logs across them for a walkway. Where it was impossible to follow the hills' contours, he would build steps. He would have a boat carried into Canyon Lake from Mountain Lake, only a quarter–mile away, for use by the trail hikers.

In the spring of 1914, an incident occurred which made Mr. Bentley furious. He took a party to his fishing camp on the west side of the Big Huron River below the McLeash Dam. When the fishing party arrived, they found the cabin a mess. It looked as though trappers had used it for shelter all winter long. The door was broken, items had been stolen, and the cabin itself was a complete shambles.

Then and there Mr. Bentley decided that he would have the camp burned down. He felt that in this dilapidated condition it could only breed contempt from everyone who saw it, including those who owned it and those who had used it illegally.

At the time Cyrus Bentley was contemplating destroying the fishing camp, he was also planning the construction of an overnight camp out on the Yellowdog Plains, secluded from trappers and fishermen.

On October 6, 1914, Jim Andersen and Walter McClintock set forth to lay out the New Bentley Trail. Although Bentley himself never referred to the trail by his own name, it was truly "his" trail in every sense of the word.

The New Bentley Trail branches off the old one about a half–mile north of Bulldog Lake, heading slightly to the east. The trail traverses the high country and hardwoods on one of Sawyer Goodman's old logging roads, then swings east, following the sides of some low hills, to a little valley which Mr. McCormick named the "Luncheon Ravine." The trail follows this ravine to where it deepens into a long, turning, picturesque gorge, then gradually leads the traveler down to the west branch of the Yellowdog as it comes out of a large, marshy pond.

Generally following the river valley, crossing it twice on log bridges, the trail winds around a rocky outcropping, past the point where a stream from Grove's Lake joins the river. Here the waters of the river narrow down

Top: Looking east on the Christ Andersen pond. (c. 1914).
Middle: The shallow lake now known as Bentley Lake. The New Bentley Trail passed along that far shore in the picture.
Bottom: October 20,, 1914 – The first day of work on the new trail. L–R Christ Andersen, Jim Andersen, Frank LaCosse near the North Falls.

to three feet or so as they travel through a crevasse at the bottom of a rock cliff. The trail follows the river to the top of the North Falls, where the river rushes down a gorge over about 70 feet of sloping rock to a narrow pool below. After this, the trail gradually eases away from the river and heads through a forest of spectacular giant white pines toward the Yellowdog Swamp.

The west end of the swamp contains two bodies of open water four or five acres apiece in size, connected by a small channel of open water. The pond to the northwest was Christ Andersen's Pond. It is four or five feet deep and is very long and narrow, with a beautiful black spruce island near its north shore. In periods of high water, this pond drains into the Big Huron River. To the southeast the pond drains through the channel and grasslands to the other little body of water, a round, shallow lake formed by beavers many years before. This became known as Bentley Lake, the name it bears today.

Bentley Lake drains through the huge Yellowdog Swamp to the Yellowdog River. Raised humps of dry ground or "swamp islands" are dotted through the entire marsh. These mounds have an assortment of vegetation ranging from leather–leaf and labrador tea to tamarack, jackpine, soft maple, ash, white birch and white pine.

Along the eastern rim of Bentley Lake, and forming a part of its shoreline, are five such islands between which beavers have built their dams to form the lake. The New Bentley Trail was laid out to cross these islands in the middle of the swamp. Then, upon crossing the last piece of open swamp, the trail comes onto the jackpine area known as the Yellowdog Plains.

On October 20, 1914, Christ and Jim Andersen and Frank LaCosse, another of the White Deer Lake crew from Champion, began work on the trail to Mountain Lake north of the Yellowdog Plains. They planned to complete the brush work that fall and then do the sidehill gouging the following spring, after laying the corduroy through the swamp during the winter.

In March of 1915, Christ and Jim each carried a load of supplies out to the homestead on Christ's pond. Using the homestead as a base camp, they started work on the marked trail through the swamp. Each morning before daylight they would start down through the snow to Bentley Lake. Walking on snowshoes, they worked their way from island to island with ax and saw, cutting trees and dragging them to the route of the trail. It took the two men three weeks of hard work to lay out a boardwalk which extended about three–quarters of a mile. Each day they cut, dragged and hewed the logs, placing them where they could be arranged after the snow had melted.

Throughout May, until the mosquitoes and flies became thick in the woods, the men worked all day in the swamp. Along with a few members of the White Deer Lake crew, they managed to get the heavy, green logs in place. Where the water was deepest they drove cedar posts into the mud and nailed crosspieces to them. In some areas they laid stringers in the mud and nailed half–logs, about two feet long, next to each other in corduroy fashion, and in many places they built actual bridges, complete with railings.

At the same time another crew of fifteen men, hired by Mr. Bentley from Huron Mountain Club, began work at the other end of the trail. They built a boat landing at Canyon Lake and laid a hewn log walkway through the big cedars in the Canyon Lake Swamp.

The Canyon Lake Swamp was just a few hundred yards of seeping water at the south end of Canyon Lake. Toward the south end of the Jim Andersen–Walter McClintock part of the trail there was a walk of about three hundred yards through a stand of beautiful giant maples, then a single giant basswood that stood right next to the trail. It stood 50 feet above the surrounding forest and had a giant knot or swelling at the base, about 17 feet around, after which the trunk tapered just like a normal tree base.

Just over the knoll from the basswood, the trail passes through the clearing for an old pine camp, known as Peterman's Clearing, on the edge of a pond known as Peterman's Pond. Upstream, the pond was fed by Elm Creek, which also flows into Ives Lake. The trail then crosses Elm Creek on a hewn log walk and passes between two giant white pine, alone in the middle of the swamp. After coming out of the swamp, the trail follows Elm Creek to its source, then heads east through a forest of giant hemlock to the line between Sections 24 and 19. Another hewn log trail follows the section line through the swamp then, heading straight south to the hills, works its way up the hillsides to the Bowl.

Jim Andersen and Walter McClintock had discovered the Bowl when they were working out the trail from the south. As they came to the north edge of the plains, they passed through about a mile of hardwoods which ended abruptly at a steep, wooded hill. Looking for the best way to get down the hill, they realized that this was the top rim of a huge natural amphitheater almost a quarter–mile across. From where they stood on the top rim, Lake Superior was plainly visible in the distance. They could only describe the place as bowl–shaped, and thus it got its name. Near where they stood, about 30 yards from the rim of the Bowl, was the remains of an old cabin. It was a homesteader's camp whose ownership has never been determined. They found a trail, barely discernible, leading from the door of

Top: The "Ripper" at Huron Mountain 1915 – Boatshop and blacksmith shop are behind him, guidehouse center, laundry to the right.
Bottom: The east pond – with a close look, Sharron can be seen on a raft clearing the pond of debris (1915).

the old cabin straight down the wall of the Bowl to a clear, ice–cold spring, literally gushing out of the bottom of the Bowl.

Skirting the west rim of the Bowl, they made their way down the crest of a hogsback between the ravines down to the section line.

There was a rumor at White Deer Lake that one of the men at the camp, formerly from L'Anse, had advised the Sicotte brothers, Octave and Edward, who were storekeepers in L'Anse, that McCormick and Bentley were going to cut a trail across the Yellowdog Plains. The rumor further stated that for this reason the Sicotte brothers had bought up a large area of land from the federal government at $1.25 an acre. This was called a "stone and timber" claim. Federal lands that were not dedicated could be either homesteaded or purchased in this way. The logical basis for the rumor was: Why would anyone spend money on land way out on the middle of the Yellowdog Plains unless they had got a tip that it would be worth something soon?

The facts, however, contradict this rumor for, according to courthouse records, the Sicotte brothers and their wives had purchased the land in 1910.

Whatever the case, the land was sold to Cyrus H. McCormick and Cyrus Bentley on April 3, 1915 for $15 an acre. The purchase took into account all the lands surrounding the little ponds. After purchasing the property, Bentley proceeded to lay out plans for constructing a stopover or "halfway" house near the ponds.

The job of gouging out the hillsides for the trail went on all summer and into the fall. Trail crews were assigned to this duty almost every day at each end of the trail. From the south, Frank LaCosse and the two Andersens did a great deal of the work, along with Tom and George Baker and Victor Johnson. From the north, the sidehill gougers included John O'Rouek, known to all as "Jack the Ripper," and Gottlieb Rudat, known as "Dutch John." The trail crews from each end never met, nor did they know what was going on at the opposite end of the trail.

Some years later an interesting sidelight about the side–hill gougers developed. An English teacher at the Northern State Normal School in Marquette in the 1920s sent her students into the lumber camps of the area to get some tall tales. One of the tales collected was the story of the Sidehill Gougers of New Bentley Trail fame. No one knew of any others in the world.

Dr. Bowman, head of the English Department, used some of these tales as a basis for his Paul Bunyan stories which were published a few years later. Although the Sidehill Gougers did not show up in the original works, they did crop up in Paul Bunyan stories later on, and many felt that the Bentley Trail was their origin.

Top: Dutch John and Oscar Webster on Huron Mountain beach (1914).
Bottom: Crossing the trail July 25, 1915 – Dr. and Mrs. Hibbs and Emerson Tuttle – all long time summer residents of the Huron Mountain and White Deer Lake country.

Bentley envisioned a perfect trail. He used to tell the men that he wanted it cut wide enough so that he could walk with his arms outstretched, high enough so that he could carry an umbrella, and smooth enough so that he could ride a bicycle over it. While it was impossible to attain this standard of perfection for 25 miles of wilderness trail, it was the established goal and Bentley expected all of his men to strive to achieve it.

The Perambulator

Cyrus Bentley was very exacting. Years before, when the elevation of the land had been taken with a barometer, he wanted it checked and corrected with a transit. Even then, he had areas checked again if he found reason to question the figures. Fifty years later, when the government made its official survey of the area, they found that Bentley's accuracy was uncanny.

Now that the general elevations had been established from the old trail, he turned to measuring distances on the new one. Map distances generally meant very little. At times, the actual walking distance was half again as far as it appeared on the map, even on relatively level terrain.

Walter McClintock's parents knew of Bentley's passion for accuracy. They had a very special "perambulator," a measuring device for long distances, designed especially for him, and sent it to him as a gift shortly after their son crossed the trail with Jim Andersen. The perambulator was made up of the front part – handlebars, fork and front wheel – of a bicycle. The handlebars were narrow, with leather handgrips. It had a light metal frame and a wooden–rimmed wheel with a small, solid rubber tire. Near the axle was mounted a small odometer which, by the turning of the wheel, would measure up to 9,999.9 miles.

Cyrus Bentley was as elated as a young boy with a new toy. This perambulator proved to be far more accurate than his pedometer, which was worn on the belt. This wheel made precise measurements, and for the next several years he was rarely in the woods without it. Besides measuring and shortening his trail, he used the perambulator to improve the crudely drawn maps of Gordon Young, Ed McLean, and Alphonse Gamache. He measured the trail from end to end several times, changing the route a little to take in a beauty spot, cross a creek at a different point, or straighten out a curve. He even pushed the wheel down the Huron Bay Grade all the way to Champion.

Many snide remarks and humorous anecdotes were told about Bentley and his perambulator.

Left: Herman Piikela and Victor Johnson at White Deer Lake.
Upper right: Dr. and Mrs. Hibbs of New York on the landing at the south
end of Canyon Lake – July 26, 1915.
Lower right: September 28, 1915 – Beginning of the Halfway cabin on the Sands Plains.

The first time Victor Johnson saw the wheel, he couldn't imagine what it was for. Vic was a Finn who spoke very little English. He was the brunt of a lot of jokes himself, but was a happy–go–lucky fellow, and none of it bothered him much.

In his younger days, Vic had sailed with the Russian Navy. Later he worked on a schooner that plied the waters between Sidney, Australia and Valpariso, Chile. He told of being out of sight of land for 145 days on one trip from London to Valpariso.

Victor Johnson jumped ship in California and worked in the woods there and in Oregon. He then made his way to the midwest where all the West Coast loggers had come from. Vic followed the timber cut from Wisconsin north through Upper Michigan. He planned to go through to Lake Superior, but decided to stop for a while at White Deer Lake. In a few years, though, he did end up at the shores of Lake Superior – at Huron Mountain Club.

When the men made fun of his rolling, bowlegged gait, Vic would explain in his heavy Finnish accent that he got that way from being at sea so long. His accent added to the humor of his stories, which were a constant entertainment to the men. He would tell about the times his ship would cross the International Date Line and have two Mondays. Since they always had pea soup on Monday, they would have it two days in a row. All the men on the ship would work six days and rest the seventh, but each man had a different day off. Going the opposite direction across the Pacific, they would skip a day and Vic would have to work 12 days in a row, as it was always his day off that they skipped. His stories were educational too – whales, porpoises, storms, sea lore – but what the men liked the most was Vic's imitation of Mr. Bentley. With his accent it always came out "Mr. Pentley."

One story he told concerned the perambulator. Vic and Mr. Bentley had set out early one morning to measure the trail again. He had measured it twice and had gotten two quite different mileages, and was determined to see which was correct. In Mr. Bentley's mind this measurement had to be exact, but Vic didn't even understand what their mission was.

"Victor," as Mr. Bentley always called him (Vic said this "Wictor") was carrying the pack and a hand ax. Mr. Bentley went along behind, pushing the wheel. After about five miles of exact measurement, he asked to take the ax, as he noticed some brush that Vic, who was about 20 yards ahead, had not trimmed to his liking. Taking the ax, he gave Vic the wheel and went on ahead trimming. Vic dropped behind and, not knowing what the wheel was for, picked it up and put it under his arm. Cyrus Bentley trimmed on for the next 20 minutes or so, unaware of what Vic had done.

Top: October 5, 1915 Ed LaBlanc, Victor Johnson, F. C. Farwell, Sands Plains cabin.
Bottom: Victor Johnson at work 1915.

Top: Mike Jarvis scoring jackpine to hew – Yellowdog Plains 1915.
Bottom: October 11, 1915 – Ed LeBlanc, Victor Johnson.

Suddenly he turned around and saw Vic walking along with the perambulator under his arm. At this point in the story, Vic would mimic Mr. Bentley's look of mixed rage and despair, and the men would roar with laughter. The two men returned to White Deer Lake.

Years later, Vic still told the story in such a way that you weren't sure if even then he knew what Bentley had been trying to do, or why he got so mad.

Another story came from "Dutch John," a homesteader from a big swamp he called "Mein Schwamp," east of Huron Mountain. John was acting as compass man while Mr. Bentley measured the shortest distance between two lakes, hoping to correct a map. Bentley was walking with his head down, intent on the wheel, but noticed that their course seemed to be hedging to the left. He severely reprimanded Dutch John, telling him to stay on course or he would find someone who could. What Mr. Bentley didn't realize was that he had given John the wrong course to begin with. John knew where the second lake was, and was trying to steer for it without alarming Mr. Bentley. After this verbal whipping, John stayed on Mr. Bentley's reading, right past the second lake. Half an hour later, when Mr. Bentley began wondering why they hadn't reached the lake, John told him. Mr. Bentley flew into a rage.

The summer of 1915 was filled with endless work on the trail. There was constant improvement, changing, grubbing and straightening. Even the guests at Huron Mountain were pressed into service. While some were eager to help out, there were those who didn't like the idea at all. When Cameron B. Waterman was handed an ax and invited to walk the trail, he refused outright.

The channel between White Deer and Bulldog Lakes could now be navigated quite well with an outboard motor. The crew had repaired Jim Redy's old dam on Bulldog Lake, and closed the gates to raise the water level in the channel. Every morning the crew would go down the lakes, hike north on the new trail to the site where they had cached their tools, and proceed with their work.

Christ and Jim Andersen spent an entire day searching for the narrowest point in the swamp north of the Yellowdog Plains. They eventually decided that the original section line, which had been chosen first, was the best route.

Though the new trail was not complete by the end of July 1915, it was crossed by a party of guests including Dr. and Mrs. Russell Hibbs and Emerson B. Tuttle. The trip was made on July 25 and 26. The Hibbses had also been among the first people to cross the original trail to Huron Mountain, some 12 or 13 years before.

Top: Ed LeBlanc carpenter – Sands Plains 1915.
Bottom: Sir Lancelot II and Dishno – Sands Plains 1915.

The most pleasant time to work in the woods is September and October, when the nights are cool and the days warm. Even on the Yellowdog Plains there are few bugs that time of year, so it was on the first of September that work began on the Halfway Cabin. It was to be in keeping with the new trail – superior in every respect. Ed LaBlanc would be in charge of building it. It would be made of hewn jackpine logs, lined with wainscoting, and have a brick chimney, hardwood floor, and a screened porch.

A spot on the north end of the eastern pond was selected so that the cabin would face south. While the trail came very near the west side of the west pond, it was felt that a building on the east lake would be even more secluded. The east lake was also the larger of the two.

A new branch of the trail was made that skirted the west and north side of the west pond and went down to the cabin site on the east pond. From the cabin, the trail headed north and rejoined the main trail. With repeated use of this branch, the main part of the trail became overgrown with blueberry bushes, and within a few years had disappeared.

A crew of about seven men worked off and on that fall, building the Sand Plains Cabin (at this time, the Yellowdog Plains were still called by their old name, the Sand Plains). Though Ed LaBlanc had been the head carpenter on the larger buildings at White Deer Lake and on the Bentley Cabin at Huron Mountain, this relatively small cabin was a real challenge to him. Not only was this cabin to be hewn out of the wilderness, and everything that could not be obtained from the woods had to be carried a long way, but also Ed had gone partially blind a year or so before when he had accidentally drunk some wood alcohol. He could see to the side well enough, but could see nothing he tried to focus on. Ed knew he was not the man he used to be but, taking his time and using his crew wisely, he did a beautiful job on the cabin.

Mike Jarvis and his partner, who had arrived in Republic from Finland just a few years earlier, were hired to cut, peel, and hew the big jackpine to be used for the cabin. Mr. Bentley also rented a horse, Lancelot II, to help with the skidding, and the men had the "come along" to handle the logs also. He later purchased Lancelot II for $95.

The jackpine was hewn with a broad ax on two sides to a thickness of six inches. While Jarvis and his partner did the hewing, LaBlanc did the actual fitting and dovetailing with the help of Victor Johnson, Alphonse Sharon, and sometimes Antoine Brunette or Dishno. George Baker was the timekeeper and cook. The crew stayed at Christ Andersen's homestead, about two miles from their job, and sometimes Christ helped with the cooking.

Top: Sharon about 1911.
Bottom: Sands Plains cabin – F. C. Farwell, Ed LaBlanc, Victor Johnson – October 15, 1915.

Christ Andersen recalls that the men used to refer to Alphonse Sharon behind his back as "the crazyman." Sharon had done some strange things while working at White Deer Lake. For example, said Christ, he had stolen a cookstove in Humboldt and carried it the four miles to Champion. The victims of the theft discovered he had taken it, and as punishment the sheriff made Sharon carry it all the way back to the owners. Another time, Sharon had leaped off a bridge over the ice–choked Peshekee River and landed on the back of a big buck, killing the animal with his jackknife. A nephew of Sharon's said that the deer had broken through the ice and was helpless, but it had still put up a terrific struggle. The nephew also said that when he and his brother were about ten years old and weighed about a hundred pounds each, Sharon's favorite trick was to let out a yell out of the clear blue sky and lift the two of them, one in each hand, high in the air, giving them a good scare.

All agreed that Alphonse Sharon was a brute of a man – hardworking, certainly, but crazy. They said that the time he was carrying the stove, he climbed up on the slippery railroad tracks for most of the four miles. He walked the eight–mile round trip from his home to work all winter. One day when he was on the track, the train came along. Alphonse climbed the snowbank to get out of the way, but the train had two big wing plows cutting the top off the bank, and one wing caught him and threw him 30 feet. The train stopped down the track and some trainmen pulled Sharon out of the snow, a bit bruised but able to continue to work. The story got around and when a fellow said to Alphonse, "I hear you got hit by the train's wing plow," his quick answer was, "Yah, I geeve him good jar."

Christ Andersen claimed that all the men's suspicions were later borne out when Sharon eventually ended up in the "crazy house."

Work, Workorders, and Other Letters

All the jackpine used for the Halfway Cabin was cut nearby, but none came from any place where it could be noticed – that is, near the trail or within sight of either pond.

When the hewn logs were put into place, the top of each log was cut down a little and the bottom of the next log above was trimmed so they would fit tightly. The ends of the logs were dovetailed using a square, mallet and chisel, a technique common in those days but seldom seen today. The only flat lumber used on the building were the roof boards that had been salvaged from the vandalized fish camp on the Big Huron River before the

Top: Sands Plains cabin – William H. Parsons with Bernette, LaBlanc and Victor Johnson, October 15, 1915.
Bottom: October 22, 1915 – Ed LaBlanc and Frank C. Farwell at the Sands Plains cabin.

rest of the building was burned. It was a tough job hauling that much lumber nearly six miles through the woods, much of it without a road. It was accomplished by using a travois, or triangular drag, pulled by Lancelot II.

In the daily reports written by George Baker to Mr. Bentley, every detail of each project was spelled out. Every man's responsibilities were accounted for:

October 15, 1915

Mr. Cyrus Bentley

Dear Sir,

The following are work notes from the 11th to and including the 14th, October 1915.

11th – LeBlanc and Victor (Johnson) worked at Sand Plains Cabin. Dishno and Sharon hauled lumber with the horse from the Big Huron to the new cabin. Christ (Andersen) had packed a load of supplies from Sec. 19 to his shack. Gagnon and (Jim) Hinton with his team hauled wood at camp. Raiche worked on the Bulldog tote road and hauled lumber from the shop to the wood dock at W. D. L. (Author's note – White Deer Lake). Frank (Carrier) carried a pack of supplies to Sec. 19 and worked on the tote road with Raiche. Tom Baker worked on the Island in the A. M. and planted strawberries in the camp garden in the P. M. (Author's note – the camp garden was at the Sawyer–Goodman camp clearing at Bulldog Lake). George Baker worked on the Island and cleaned the men's quarters. Mrs. Sorensen did the cooking. Sorensen worked in the kitchen. Hall (butler) worked in the dining room. Blair returned to Champion.

12th – LeBlanc and Victor worked at the cabin. Tuffel Dishno and Sharon hauled lumber with the horse from the Big Huron to the new cabin. Christ went to Sec. 19 for supplies and did the cooking. George and Tom Baker worked on the Island. Sorensen worked in the kitchen and Mrs. Sorensen did the cooking. Frank (Carrier) Gagnon, and Hinton (with his team) hauled lumber, tile, roofing paper and etc. from Bulldog Lake to the swamp in Sec. 19. Raiche returned to Champion. Joe Cardinal, father of station agent Louis from Champion "teamster" came to camp with supplies for Mr. Bentley.

13th – LeBlanc, Victor, and Antoine Brunette worked at the cabin. Dishno and Sharon hauled lumber with the horse from Andersen's place to the cabin. All of the above men worked (at the cabin) in the afternoon. Blair in the forenoon. Gagnon and Frank packed lumber and etc. across the swamp in Sections 17 and 9. (This is on the new trail.) Christ went to W. D. L. for supplies and returned to his shack and did the cooking. George and Tom Baker worked on the Island. Sorensen worked in the kitchen. Mr. Sorensen did the cooking. Hall (the butler) worked in the dining room. Hinton and Cardinal returned to Champion.

14th – LeBlanc, Victor, and Brunette worked at the cabin. Dishno made two trips with the horse to the swamp in Sec. 19 hauling lumber and roofing paper. (Author's note – these heavy items were taken on the old trail in the big swamp in 17 and 9 of the new trail.) Sharon packed roofing paper from Bulldog to the plains. Gagnon and Frank worked with Dishno and helped the horse along through the swamp in Sec. 7. Christ did the cooking. Tom and George Baker worked on the Island. Sorensen worked in the kitchen. Mrs. Sorensen did the cooking. Hall worked in the dining room. Hinton came to camp (from Champion with his team) with supplies for Mr. Bentley.

Very truly yours,
George Baker

We notice in Baker's work report for the first time, a man named Hall working in the dining room. This gentleman was an elderly English butler and, though his presence at White Deer Lake seems insignificant in this report, he and his family were to change the whole character of living at the camp, until it could no longer be called the "rough" camp.

"Hall," as George wrote it, was Henry Walter Halls, born in Highham, England. He had married Louella Elvira Miller in 1895, and the couple had three children, Mildred, Quentin and Gordon.

Mr. and Mrs. Halls had worked for the McCormicks and their friends on occasion in Chicago. Now in a sort of semi–retirement, they had moved out of the city to Wisconsin. Having been asked to come to the northwoods to be the butler, Halls was a little apprehensive, but this first trip to White Deer Lake proved to be a new and wonderful experience for him. And, in his own unassuming way, he did a great deal to enhance the quality of life at camp. He had apprenticed as a butler in England, and knew exactly how everything should be done. In addition, his wife was a very good cook.

Top: Trunks and supplies head for White Deer Lake early in the spring.
Bottom: Christ Andersen and his floating bridge.

After this first successful venture, the Halls were invited back again and again. Their children would occasionally come and visit them at camp, and eventually came to help out as employees.

In these years, even though the Great War was going on, the activity at White Deer Lake was reaching tremendous proportions. Family and friends – and, in the case of Huron Mountain, friends of friends – were using the place. The McCormick and Bentley children were coming of age, and there was ever–increasing use of the camp by groups of young people.

September and October became especially active in these years. This was the finest time to be in the woods. Generally the days were warm and sunny and the nights crisp and invigorating. Good food, good friends, and the warmth of the fireplace as the evening cooled, were pleasures surpassing anything that could be bought in the city. In the fall there were none of the seasonal problems that stamp the north country as severe or hostile, namely intense cold, deep soft snow, and bugs.

Around late August or early September, all the colors of the woods begin to brighten. This is especially noticeable from the lakes. The color increases in intensity until it reaches a grand climax near the end of September or the beginning of October. During this period even the sky becomes a special brilliant blue, the haze of summer clears, the waters sparkle and the whole country takes on an unsurpassable grandeur. These were the days that both the Bentleys and McCormicks most wanted to be in the north country.

In mid–October, the brilliant color quickly subsided to the gray, cold days of November, when the chores of preparing for the long hard winter took precedence over all else.

At White Deer Lake Camp, this preparation kept four teams of horses going steadily with supplies and people. The four teamsters owned the horses and the various rigs they pulled, but McCormick and Bentley did own some wagons, drags, and skids.

The loads coming into camp ranged anywhere from a few hundred to well over a thousand pounds, and sometimes even a ton or more. Some average loads would be as follows, again reported to Mr. Bentley by George Baker.

Oversupply was the rule. Anything that might be needed during the winter had to be thought of months in advance. Experiences of running short on food were long remembered, and the items brought in went beyond the basic staples of sugar and flour to things like broom handles, dishes, and can openers. Mr. Bentley took time to scrutinize each item on every list as he sat in his Chicago office. Often his return letter would question specific items or amounts.

Book Two

White Deer Lake
15 October 1915

The following are the loads received at Camp.
Teamster – John Blair – 10 October
    4 bales hay 466 lbs.
    5 rolls deadening felt 240#
    1 roll wire screen 80#
    1 bundle galvanized tin 140#
    66# granulated sugar
    1 bunch – 3 handles for brooms 3#
    1 emery wheel grinder 45#
    200# of flour
    100 paper plates)
    3 chambers)
    6 candlesticks) 40#
    3 brush brooms)
    1 dustpan)

The load averaged about 1200#

(s) George Baker

Joseph Cardinal – Teamster – 12 October 1915

    M chops – Mutton
    Quarter leg lamb
    2 heads lettuce
    4 bunches celery
    10 bread
    4 bunches brussels sprouts
    4 lambs
    1 box dry goods for Mr. Farwell
    1 syrup mug and saucer (glass)
    12 quarts cream
    6 quarts milk
    8 salt shakers
    8 pepper shakers
    1 doz. after–dinner cups and saucers

Top: The new Andersen Homestead cabin, pond and floating bridge.
Bottom: The crew at White Deer Lake (1915). L–R Christ Andersen, George Baker (kneeling), Ed Turenne (cook), Jim Hinton (teamster) and dog, Jewel Gagnon, Frank LaCosse (foreman).

2 fruit bowls
2 cream pitchers
The load averaged about 500#

(s) George Baker

Teamster Hinton – 14 October 1915

1 silver syrup pitcher (from Burley)
1 pkg for Mr. Farwell
2 doz. eggs from Champion
1 box candy (Woods)
"Stanton # Co."
3 casava melons
2 baskets Concord grapes
2 doz. apples
2 baskets peaches
1 doz. pears
2 bu. oats
300# hay
40# fresh meat (for men)
10# cheese
16# cabbage
1 sweat pad

The load averaged 550#

(s) George Baker

Teamster Raiche – 15 October 1915

4 doz. eggs)
10 qts. cream) Roycroft
6 qts. milk)
1 pkg. – record (for Mrs. Clement)
2 kegs spikes 200#
V chops
6 chickens
2 soup chickens
2 P. H. steaks

1 rst. beef
10 tomatoes
5 head lettuce
1 jar cream cheese
2 bunches celery
8 bread

The load averaged about 400#

(s) George Baker

Then there were the many letters that came in regarding the camp, the land, or the men, that all required some kind of answer. Mr. Bentley turned over this job to his private secretary, Reuben Swanson, who came to White Deer Lake with him several times over the years. He was at Mr. Bentley's elbow many hours of the day, and one time the two of them stayed a whole week at the Halfway Cabin. Mr. Swanson would carefully discuss each item with Mr. Bentley, and Mr. McCormick too if he was present. He was then given time to write up and send out the various answers.

One of Swanson's unique answers was sent out on October 19th of that year:

Dear Madam:

Your letter of 18 October received. Yes, Mr. Sharon is temporarily employed at this camp, but he is working in the woods about seven miles from here and may not be into camp here for a week or so. When he does come in or if anyone goes to where he is working the matter will be taken up with him. His wages for October have already been drawn on so that he has very little coming to him at present. However, we will do the best we can for you.

Very truly yours,

McCormick & Bentley
R. S.

Similar complaints had come from other people and places, the nearest being Jake LeVine in Champion. When confronted with the

Top: One of the old railroad bridges on the Pechekee river.
Bottom: The Rock Dam on the Pechekeme (as Mr. Bentley always wrote it). The road is off to the right of this picture heading north.

complaints, Sharon said he didn't owe any money. LeVine called the sheriff and when Sharon was tracked down, it took a deputy and six men to handle him, and even they had some trouble.

Other recorded documents include the letters for supplies to Montgomery Ward's in Chicago, and another set of work notes for the next week.

White Deer Lake
22 October 1915

Mr. Cyrus Bentley,

Dear Sir:

The following are the work notes from 15 to and including 20, October.

15th – LeBlanc, Victor and Brunette worked at the cabin. Dishno and Sharon worked with the horse hauling roofing paper and lumber from Sec. 7 to the cabin.

Author's note: There was a swamp in Section 7 on the old trail which was almost impossible for the horse to get through. Heavy items were taken as far as the swamp with the horse, then the men carried the roofing and lumber the half–mile across the swamp. Then the horse was used to take the material on the old trail to the Marquette road, then east 2 miles on the Marquette road and south on the new trail to the cabin. George Baker's notes continue:

Hauled one load of the above material from Sec. 19 to Sec. 7. Christ did the cooking and went to Sec. 19 for supplies. Tom (Baker) packed supplies out of the trail in the morning and worked on the Island in the afternoon. Geo. worked on the Island. Frank, Gagnon and Hinton with his team hauled wood at camp. Sorensen worked in the kitchen. Mrs. Sorensen did the cooking. Halls worked in the dining room. Raiche came to camp with supplies for Mr. Bentley.

16th – LeBlanc, Victor & Brunette worked at the cabin. Dishno hauled roofing paper and lumber with the horse from Sec. 7 to the cabin and hauled logs for the porch floor of the cabin. Sharon helped Dishno in the A. M. and went to Bulldog and packed a load of oats to

Christ's place. Christ packed a load of supplies from Sec. 19 and did the cooking. Frank, Gagnon and Hinton with his team packed supplies on the Mt. Lake Trail for the cabin, lumber, chairs, linoleum, & etc. Tom packed supplies out on the trail & worked on the Island. Geo. worked on the Island. Halls worked in the dining room. Sorensen worked in the kitchen. Mrs. Sorensen did the cooking.

17th – (Sunday) – Raiche returned to Champion with Mrs. Platte (guest from Huron Mountain Club).

18th – LeBlanc, Victor & Brunette worked at the cabin. Frank, Gagnon, Dishno & Sharon packed with the horse from Sec. 19 to Christ's place. Christ did the cooking and filed a saw. Tom went to the new cabin with some letters in the morning and returned to camp and worked on the Island. Geo. worked on the island. Sorensen worked in the kitchen, Halls worked in the dining room. Mr. Sorensen did the cooking.

Author's note: The one sentence, "Tom went to the new cabin with some letters in the morning and returned to camp," meant that Tom Baker had rowed White Deer Lake, the Channel, and Bulldog Lake, or else had walked the two and one–half miles around them, then hiked four and one–half or five miles out on the new trail and back, a walk of some 14 or 15 miles, then worked the rest of the day on the Island. This seems like a formidable task, but to these woodsmen a walk of this kind, carrying only letters and a light lunch, was considered an enjoyable day. It was certainly preferable to many other chores he could have been assigned.

19th – LeBlanc, Victor, Brunette, Gagnon & Sharon worked at the cabin. Dishno hauled supplies for the cabin from Christ's place. Frank worked with Dishno in the morning & in the afternoon he worked around the lake near the cabin, cleaning it out. Tom packed the trail in the morning, went to Bulldog garden in the afternoon and dug up the carrots (1 1/4 bu.) and took back (36) strawberry plants and planted them in the camp garden, – and so on about Geo. – Sorensen and his wife and Raiche & Hinton coming from Champion for camp and Mr. Bentley.

20th – LeBlanc, Victor, Sharon, Brunette & Gagnon worked at the cabin. Dishno & Frank with the horse hauled brick from the Big Huron (fish camp) to C. Andersen's place. Christ did the cooking and cut wood. Tom & Geo. worked on the Island. Sorensen worked in the kitchen. Mrs. Sorensen did the cooking. Halls worked in the dining room and ret'd to Champion. Raiche & Hinton ret'd to Champion with Mr. and Mrs. Parson, Mrs. Bentley & Mrs. Clement & their baggage.

Yours,
Geo. Baker

And so on go the daily reports, month after month, specifying every detail of the men's activities and responsibilities.

During the construction of the Halfway Cabin, the crew stayed at Christ Andersen's homestead, some two miles from the work site. The men would walk the trail north from the new cabin to the old Marquette–L'Anse road, which had gone into disuse years before. They would walk west on the old road to the homestead, where Christ would have a meal prepared for them. During the day Christ would have packed supplies all the way from Bulldog Lake. Other men were dismantling the Fish Camp and hauling brick and lumber from the Big Huron to the Halfway House with the horse. Still others were shuttling supplies including building material, either by scow or boat or by foot or team, from White Deer Lake to the garden spot on Bulldog Lake. Another crew was working daily transporting wagonloads of supplies from Champion or Marquette to White Deer Lake.

Christ Andersen welcomed the change in having the men stay at his camp. To him, it was like getting paid for staying home. He enjoyed working around his own place. Christ would often pack a double load from Bulldog Lake or Section 19 by carrying a pack on his back and pushing another load in a wheelbarrow. He would clean his cabin, cut and haul wood, and work on his floating bridge. When there was a big task like some wood to carry, he could generally get help from some of the men before breakfast or after supper.

At this time Christ had two cabins. His first one, very crude with a lean–to roof, was on the west side of the pond near the old Bentley Trail near Mr. Bentley's pump, and his new one was east of the pond. Christ used water from the pump once in a while, and also used the old cabin for storage. However, now that they were building the Halfway House, four men slept on the floor in the old place, and another four in the new cabin. Between the two cabins Christ maintained his floating bridge, as the lake was too big to walk around, and he had no boat. In the winter, when the lake iced up, there was no problem.

Work continued on the Halfway Cabin in the fall of 1915 until the outside was completed. The roof was on, windows and doors were in place and shuttered, and all the debris had been cleaned up and hauled away into the woods. Even the lake had been raked clean to the water's edge. The pond was very low at the time, so in reality much of the bottom of the lake had been raked out. In short, everything had been made fast for the winter.

Cyrus Bentley, his guest Frank Farwell, and his secretary Reuben Swanson had arrived from Chicago to make a final inspection of the place before winter set in. They stayed only a few days and, satisfied with the work that had been done, left by team for Champion and by train for Chicago on the 28th of October.

A few days later, on November 1st, the Sorensens left, the foreman Frank LaCosse went on vacation, and the part–time men went home. Christ Andersen was put in charge until LaCosse returned, George Baker took over as cook, and a small crew of four or five men holed up to await what became an especially long, cold winter.

A typical load of winter supplies – this one arriving in camp the day before Mr. Bentley's departure – is listed here:

2 bales of hay	1 case peaches
2 bu. oats	70# ham
1 bag of laundry	12 stove pipe elbows
4 cases milk (canned)	50# lard
8 sash	6 lemons
2 qts. milk (Roycroft)	1 box DOM sugar
4 qts. cream	veal chops
1 barrel lime	1/2 peck sweet potatoes
2 doz. eggs (Champion)	2 heads of lettuce
2 bts. 3–in–1 oil	2 bunches celery
7 pkgs. shoe nails	tomatoes
1 bt gun oil	1 eggplant
3 strips leather	1 bskt. pears
1# cinnamon	2 bskts. grapes
1 box codfish	spinach
Porterhouse steaks	6 pkgs. yeast
1 bag powdered sugar	40# fresh meat

George added, "The load averaged #1000 lbs. George Baker."

Another interesting letter gives the monthly pay for the entire crew working on the Halfway Cabin. It should be remembered that these men received room and board also.

The letter was sent to Mr. F. A. Steuert, an accountant in Chicago.

White Deer Lake
30 October 1915

Mr. F. A. Steuert,

Dear Sir,

The following is a statement of the Men's time for the month of October 1915.

Oct. 1st	Frank LaCosse to Oct. 30th	$60.00
Oct. 1st	Jules Gagnon to Oct. 30th	40.00
Oct. 1st	George Baker to Oct. 30th	50.00
Oct. 1st	Christ Andersen to Oct. 30th	40.00*
Oct. 1st	Tom Baker to Oct. 30th	40.00

Earl Arsenault – two (2) days @
$25.00 per month   1.92
Tuffel Dishno – 18 1/2 days @
$40.00 per month   28.49
Alphonse Sharon – 25 1/2 days @
$40.00 per month, less $5.00 payment
to Nellie Huber (butcher shop)   34.27
Antoine Brunette – 22 1/2 days @
$40.00 per month   34.65
Ed LaBlanc – 27 1/2 days @
$2.00 per day   55.00

*Christ Andersen wishes to have $20.00 turned into the company, and $20.00 returned to him.

Very truly yours,
George Baker

One observation that can be made from looking over this list, and one which held true for many years at White Deer Lake, is that every man on the roster except Christ Andersen was a French–speaking Frenchman. They read only a French newspaper called "L'Independant," published in Fall River, Massachusetts, which arrived by mail nearly two weeks late. The men invariably spoke French to each other, and while men who were not of French origin often came to work at White Deer Lake in these years, they'd usually felt like outsiders. Even the easygoing Victor Johnson felt more comfortable at Huron Mountain Club, and ended up working there full time. Those who couldn't speak French didn't stay very long, except Christ Andersen. He had a way about him that enabled him to be liked and looked up to by everyone who got to know him.

A trip to the camp with a team cost $4, and the teamster was fed free while in camp. A charge of $1.25 per day was made for a team's board at camp. If any of the crew had things shipped up the Grade on the camp wagons, the charge was a penny a pound. The Andersens worked under this agreement for years, but by 1915 Nels Andersen and his wife had moved to Menominee, Jim was working at Huron Mountain, and only Christ depended on the McCormick wagons now and then. In the fall, he would have a hundred pounds or so of supplies brought up the grade, which he would pack into his homestead to prepare for his return in the late winter to do some trapping. In the meantime, he would be the foreman at White Deer Lake.

Ed La Blanc Ends His Career

During November of 1915, thousands of pounds of supplies were brought by team and wagon up the Huron Bay Grade in preparation for winter. Plowing and planting of Timothy hay was done on a small piece of land, later called the Baraga Plains, near the ford on the Peshekee River. The size of the winter crew varied depending on the weather. In good weather a few part–time crewmen were brought up from Champion.

Ed LaBlanc, the head carpenter, had completed his last job for Mr. Bentley. He had worked for McCormick and Bentley for ten years. He had been a good carpenter, if not a truly expert one, working at Huron Mountain since the first buildings in 1892, and had been in charge of the Bentley cabin at Huron Mountain, Christ Andersen's second camp, and the new Halfway Cabin. The last was the only dovetailed, hewn–log or square–timbered cabin of them all, and it was really very well done, especially considering the fact that Ed was nearly blind when he built it.

In 1910 or '11, Ed LaBlanc was staying at a boarding house in Negaunee. He had been feeling ill for several days, "under the weather," as they used to say. One of the common woods remedies of that time was balsam pitch in grain alcohol. Lumberjacks were known to eat it straight for venereal disease. They used to say you could tell if someone had been eating balsam pitch, as the odor of it in their urine would fill the woods. The pitch was tediously collected from balsam blisters which, according to some woodsmen, were largest during the full of the moon. The pitch was mixed with ethyl or grain alcohol, about half and half. The mixture was thoroughly shaken and allowed to settle, then some of the top layer drunk. It acted as a strong physic and general cure–all.

Ed had gone to a drugstore and asked for some grain alcohol, but by mistake he received wood or methyl alcohol, which causes blindness in small doses, and is fatal in large amounts.

LaBlanc took a dose of his remedy before going to bed, awoke early the next morning, dressed in the dark as was his custom, and went outside. It seemed pretty dark to Ed as he felt his way out of the house to the front porch. A dog was chained to the porch of the boarding house near the steps, and Ed found himself tangled in the dog chain. Even then he thought it was still dark, as he could see neither the dog nor its chain. Finally, as he scrambled around on the porch, he realized he was blind.

Although after this Ed could not read a word, he managed to continue with his trade with the help of Antoine Brunette and his other assistants. However, the Halfway Cabin was a difficult and discouraging job and, while everyone was patient and understanding, he decided to give up carpentry. Bentley and McCormick were quite willing to keep him on, but he had made up his mind.

On the 30th of October, 1915, just two days after Mr. Bentley went to Chicago, George Baker sent the following letter to Reuben Swanson, Mr. Bentley's private secretary in Chicago:

> White Deer Lake
> P. O. Champion, Mich.
> 30 October, 1915

Mr. Reuben Swanson

Dear Reuben,

Ed has returned to camp and I gave him the package you left with me. He also said that he received his bank book OK, and has Mr. Bentley's check ready to be retd. to him. I am enclosing a card to you from A. Mathews rec'd 30th which I read to Ed and he "Ed," wanted the deed sent direct to him here and wanted me to write Mathews about it. I told him I could do that, but I said since you knew all about the matter it would be just as well to let you finish it up, but I gave him his choice so he thought the latter was the best.

Very truly yours,
George Baker

Ed LaBlanc stayed on that winter, but in the spring of 1916 he quit White Deer Lake, never to return. He bought a horse and forty acres of land in Carlshend, about 25 miles south of Marquette. Several years after that, he sold out and took up a homestead in Colorado.

The Trials of George Baker

November and December of 1915 were spent preparing for the winter. Correspondence was heavy between George and Mr. Bentley, George and Reuben Swanson, and George and all the places of business where supplies were obtained, from Marquette to Champion.

George Baker was under a huge responsibility and, while he was always conscientious about his job, he always seemed insecure. He was forever apologizing for his lack of education, and constantly tried to improve it on his own. Though he had worked for Mr. Bentley since 1908 and had been given many responsibilities, there was never any thought of making George the foreman. Mr. Bentley seemed to sense that George was not of the right temperament, and had gone as far as he could at White Deer Lake.

George was born in 1888 in Marquette, but his family moved to Champion when he was just a baby. His boyhood was spent in poverty, and there were times when he would actually scrounge through garbage bins to find bones with meat on them, which he would bring home and recook for a meal.

At the age of 13 he went to work as "cookee" at F. W. Reed's camp on the north shore of Lake Michigamme. Here he learned the hard life of a lumberjack, and longed secretly for something better. White Deer Lake was, for George, the pinnacle of a dream. There could be no better place to work in the whole world. His honesty and capabilities were soon recognized, and responsibilities were heaped on him.

He was the "Island Boy," timekeeper, trail cook, men's cook in the winter, secretary, and purchasing agent. George was often put in a position of having to make decisions, but always felt that he had no authority to do so.

He would study hard, using whatever books were available to him. He often read the dictionary and reference books. Even while washing the dishes, George would have a book of poetry open on the windowsill, which he would read and memorize. Eventually he became able to recite poetry literally by the hour.

He was often moody, and the added responsibilities sometimes made this worse. Any criticism hurt George deeply. Some of the men found him quite hard to live with, and complaints about him often got back to Mr. Bentley.

In the early days at White Deer Lake, it was one of his jobs to keep the outhouses clean. On the Island, they were built with a little rear door where a sand box could be placed under the hole. When guests were in camp, George would get up at 4:30 A. M. and, while all but the cook slept, he would empty the boxes from each outhouse, taking the contents down the lake in a rowboat and climbing a steep hill in the woods, where he would dispose of the waste. He resented this task a great deal.

By 1915, complaints from the men had mounted against George. Then a ham disappeared from the carefully inventoried supplies that went out to the Halfway Cabin crew.

George knew it was gone and had a pretty good idea where it was, but said nothing. He was quite surprised, then, to receive a letter from Mr. Bentley questioning him as to the whereabouts of the ham.

One of the men working at the cabin lived in Champion and had a family of four children. The ham was quite an event in the lives of these children, and they had told their friends about it. The station agent, who corresponded regularly with Mr. Bentley, had reported the incident to him, and as a result George was put on the spot. Mr. Bentley may have suspected George of actually stealing or giving away the ham, but at any rate he felt it was George's job to at least know what had happened to it. He had to get to the bottom of it so this type of thing would not become a practice. As absentee owner, he scrutinized every item listed for purchase even more closely than a regular owner might, sometimes noting some things as "too good for men," or "priced too high at this time."–He pushed George for an explanation on the issue of the ham, but none was forthcoming.

Despite the long association between George Baker and Cyrus Bentley, a little mistrust was beginning to appear. All this upset George very much, and Mr. Bentley sent a letter reprimanding George – or at least questioning him specifically. George kept this letter for many years, but eventually it was lost or destroyed. However, George's answer to the letter is recorded here:

710

Book Two

Mr. Cyrus Bentley,
Dear Sir,

I have received your letter of 29 December, and 3 January. With two cheques enclosed to my order it was alright to send me these cheques as I had paid for the supplies and express bill.

I see that you are strictly against buying from Leffler in Ishpeming, and also from Quinn in Champion, that part is alright and I understand what you mean by this, before I bought any supplies in Ishpeming, I mean, the last purchase I made, I went to Cudahy's and Swift's packing houses and asked about their prices, they demanded pay for the supplies at once and they also refused to show me the goods I wanted. I got beat on such a deal as this last year so I still remember it. Leffler asked the same prices as the packing houses did and he let me examine the goods all I wanted to so I knew what I was getting. If I got beat I didn't get beat both on quality and prices, because I knew what I was getting. I do not want to be insulting or too quick in my meanings and I hope you will understand what I mean as "I am not in bad humor."–If you think you are any "money out" since I have been buying supplies for camp, please let me know, I am not rich, far from it, but I am willing to spend my last cent in order to be in my right. I have always done the best I could for the camp since I have been here, which will be three years the 10th of May, all of this work is entirely new to me, if I were to handle the pick and shovel then I would be working at my trade. You could expect good work of me then but as it is now I can only "do the best I can" and I think I have explained this to you before and your answer to me was satisfactory. Now to come back to the subject of buying meats; If I were to run short towards spring, I do not know where to get any in small quantities, such as the men would have to carry up on their backs, because you do not want me to get any from Quinn, and I have told you before that the packing house in Ishpeming sells only by the quarter and all orders are C.O.D. so you can see I am completely in the dark. Will you please give me some detail on this subject when you write me.

I have more to tell you in order to make myself understood but I cannot do it in writing – for lack of education. But I hope I will be

711

fortunate enough to meet you this spring so that we can talk the matter over, this seems to be very serious to me.

At the present time everything is going on fine at camp, and everyone is enjoying good health. The cake of spring ice is about half finished.

I am,

Yours truly,
George Baker

George had been quite diplomatic in the wording of this letter, which was meant to convey to Mr. Bentley his honesty and loyalty without mentioning the stolen ham. This letter probably would have set very well with Mr. Bentley but George, having written it, lost his courage and never sent it. In fact, he felt so strongly about it that he kept the book of carbon copies containing this letter so it would never be seen by anyone connected with White Deer Lake. In telling his story, he gave the book of carbon copies to the author some forty–five years later.

In the book of carbon copies was another letter written the same day, very curt and reflecting a complete change of heart. This is the letter that Mr. Bentley received:

White Deer Lake
3 February, 1916

Mr. Cyrus Bentley,
Dear Sir,

I have received your letters of 29 December and 3 January with two cheques enclosed to my order. I wish to thank you for these cheques. The supplies were all ready paid for so it was right for you to send them to me. I have nothing to say in regards to your questions on your letter of 29 December, I did what I thought was right.

Yours truly,
George Baker

Mr. Bentley had pressed George for an explanation and had not gotten it. A rift was beginning to form between the two which could only get worse.

The cake of "spring ice" George referred to was quite a project that went on for several winters. Since 1906, ice on White Deer Lake had been cut by hand. First, it was scored using a horse with caulked shoes, pulling a special blade much like a plow. This blade cut a groove three or four inches deep in the ice. At one end of the groove, a hole was punched all the way through the ice with a spud or long chisel and one end of a two–man crosscut saw inserted through it. Christ Andersen, the foreman at the time, always said with an elfish smile that it was hard to find a man to take the lower end of the saw. The long groove was sawed all the way by hand, but all the cross–grooves needed was one blow with the spud, and the ice block would break on the score. The blocks, about 32 inches to a side and weighing about 200 pounds each, were pulled out and taken by sleigh to an ice house insulated well with sawdust, and kept for summer use.

The block ice kept the iceboxes cold and was satisfactory to use in drinking water for the men, but the idea of the brown water of White Deer Lake appearing in cocktails or drinking water for the guests was repulsive to Mr. Bentley. The answer was the cake of "spring ice."

Early in the winter, George would nail four ten–inch–wide boards into a six–foot square enclosure. He would then take a few pails of spring water and pour it inside the enclosure, where it would freeze like a tiny ice rink. As the weather grew colder, he would add water more often. When the water was frozen solid to the top of the boards, George would pry them off, move them up, and continue adding water.

Toward the end of February there was a huge six–foot cube of pure spring ice. It was George's pride and joy. The block was cut and put in a special place in the ice house, to be used exclusively for cold drinks for McCormick, Bentley, and their guests.

One very cold night, the Guide House cat was perched on top of the spring ice block, deftly balanced on the two–inch–thick board around the top. As the water froze, his fur too became frozen into the ice. When the cat jumped free, he left two or three big tufts of fur stuck in Mr. Bentley's ice, which George had to chisel out. George was sure Mr. Bentley would never put a piece of ice in his drink if he found this out, and he would have to start the whole cake over.

Another episode took place some years earlier while George was the "Island Boy" during the summer.

At five o'clock every morning he would go down to the raft, which was guided by a cable between the mainland and the island, and pull his way over to the Island by a rope. This setup was later replaced by a hand crank device attached to the guide cable itself, which took a little less effort. Mr. Tonkin, the superintendent for many years, called the device the "Armstrong Motor."

Having reached the Island, George, working very quietly so as not to disturb the sleeping guests, would go about his chores in the various cabins – picking up glasses, coffee cups, and ash trays, cleaning the outhouses, setting the fireplaces, filling the wood boxes, carrying out ashes, renewing the wood piles, sweeping the porches, and any number of other things that had to be done.

Working at the Chimney Cabin one morning, George suddenly felt the urge to relieve himself. There was no time to go all the way over to the raft and pull it across the channel – this was something that needed to be taken care of right away!

George wouldn't think of using one of the toilets on the Island; he was a working man, and they were for the guests. In his rush to meet the emergency, he grabbed a newspaper that he was about to set a fire with and, spreading it on the ground beneath the front porch, he accomplished the task there. Without much forethought, George wadded up the paper and threw it out into the lake, expecting it to sink. The matter thus taken care of, George went about his chores.

Later in the morning, he was splitting some kindling in front of the Chimney Cabin when he heard Mr. McCormick, Mr. Bentley, and Mr. Farwell come out on the second deck of their cabin in their pajamas, and begin doing some setting–up exercises before dressing. George was directly beneath them and could hear every word they said. Something white floating out on the lake had caught their attention.

"What is that out there – a piece of birchbark?" asked one.

"No, it's the seagull that's always sitting out there every morning," said another.

"It looks to me like a blob of that white foam formed by the waves every night; the morning's change of winds often takes it out," commented the third.

"I'm pretty sure it's that seagull," came back the second.

"Well, my eyes are very good when it comes to distance, and it certainly looks like a piece of birchbark to me," said the first.

"Let's go take a look at it in the boat before breakfast," said one of the voices, and George froze. As the men continued their exercises, George waited beneath the porch in a state of terror. It seemed to him that they would never go in.

As soon as they did, however, George sprang to life. He dashed madly over to the boathouse beneath the Victor Room, hopped into a boat, and rowed over to the drifting paper, which still floated bearing its ominous cargo.

Telling the story years later, George exclaimed, "I took the oar and sunk the 'goldarned' thing!"

Struggling for Privacy

One winter job that always had to be taken care of in this land of deep snow was shoveling the snow off the roofs of the buildings. The roofs were usually strong enough, but not always, and the build–up of ice, besides its weight alone, could also cause leaking and subsequent rotting of the cabins themselves.

The official record for deep snow presently goes to the little settlement of Herman, some 15 or 20 miles west of White Deer Lake, though there is regularly deep snow throughout the Copper Country and in Munising. While no snowfall records were ever kept at White Deer Lake Camp, a Drapers recording thermometer recorded below–zero temperatures every day for thirty–two days straight one year. It is not uncommon to have the snow on the roofs built up to five, six or seven feet, and the fact that there are five rivers flowing out of one small area attests to the fact that there is heavy rain and snowfall there. Often there is still some snow in the woods as late as June.

The summer of 1916 brought many changes in the lifestyle of the people at White Deer Lake, most of them as a result of the automobile. A few drivers had tackled the Huron Bay Grade, and Mr. Bentley had a gate put up at the Rock Dam on the Peshekee River to keep the intruders out. Over at Huron Mountain, the problem was even worse, and Mr. Bentley purchased the Joe Paris homestead north of Second Pine Lake so that a gate could be erected there.

Mr. Bentley later donated the land to the Huron Mountain Club. His idea was that since the Joe Paris homestead was the club farm, the men working the farm could be there to let the occasional automobile through the gate when necessary.

The idea was tried, and proved successful as far as Huron Mountain was concerned. A gate was put up at the east end of the farm clearing. People arriving would honk their horns, or sometimes have to walk over to the farmhouse or out into the field to find someone to unlock the gate. Within a year or so, it was discovered that people from Big Bay would drive as far as the gate at night, park the car and walk three miles to the club to pick up the young waitresses. After a few years of fighting this night traffic, Bentley finally had the gate moved in 1919 another two miles toward Big Bay, a few hundred yards east of Hans Jensen's burning and about 200 yards west of Oscar Webster's homestead. A little gatekeeper's cabin was built on the side of the road about thirty yards inside the gate, and a full–time gatekeeper put in charge there. This setup lasted for the next 50 years, when in 1970 the gate was moved out to the Salmon Trout River.

Mr. Bentley's gate on the Huron Bay Grade did not work out quite so well. This one had some more determined people to deal with. People had been using the Huron Bay Railroad Grade to get into the north country for years, and they were not about to let Mr. Bentley put an end to it now.

Some railroad bridges were in bad repair to the point of becoming unsafe. Mr. Woodward, the owner of Four Island Lake (formerly Lake Richard), had shared Mr. Bentley's concern and had hired Christ Andersen to blaze out a new road along the Peshekee river that would eliminate two dangerous bridges by staying on one side of the river. Bentley had asked Christ to do the same job. When Mr. Woodward learned that Bentley and McCormick had the same idea in mind, he dropped the matter completely, realizing he would get his road completed for nothing.

Several of these bridge–eliminating roads were built, with McCormick and Bentley sharing the cost equally. The first such work was carried out in 1915 and '16. Having built and paid for the road, Mr. Bentley felt he had a perfect right to put a gate on it, which he did at the Rock Dam in 1916, just a little too close to Champion.

Trappers, hunters, and fishermen who traveled up the grade from time to time were very indignant when they discovered the gate, and word of it spread like wildfire through the area. The accompanying rumor was that Bentley didn't own any of the land there, nor very much even around the camp. At that time, even land that Bentley and McCormick actually did own had not been filed in County records.

The gate was dynamited, repaired, and dynamited again. The talk at the time was that the Bulley brothers, Henry and Louis, had done the job with some of their friends, but nobody knew for sure. Several men were heard to say that they would have done the job themselves, if the Bulleys hadn't got there first.

With the advice of local employees, Mr. Bentley gave up on the idea of a gate this far south, but had one put up off the grade east of the Peshekee, just a few miles from camp. Even then the gate was usually left open unless guests were in camp. There was no trouble with this gate.

Book Two

Arbutus Lodge

1916 proved to be a banner year for the whole McCormick and Bentley project. The channel between White Deer and Bulldog Lakes was completed and the old log dam at the end of Bulldog repaired, so that water could be raised in the two lakes and the channel. The new trail to Huron Mountain was put into top shape that year, and the Halfway Cabin was completed.

The snow wasn't off the ground that spring when a crew was sent out to do the final work on the cabin. Fir doors and screening, as well as screen doors, were carried from Bulldog Lake. Maple flooring was used inside the cabin and the fir, which was rot–resistant, was nailed over the hewn log floor of the porch.

The men working at the cabin stayed right there in a tent this time, rather than walking to and from Christ Andersen's homestead.

On May 14, 1916, Mr. Bentley and Frank Farwell made the hike out to the cabin for an inspection tour. They left early in the morning, spent several hours at the camp, and returned in the evening. It was a bright crisp day and the air around the cabin was filled with the fragrance of arbutus, that lovely little pink or white flower found so abundantly on the Yellowdog Plains when the sun's warmth first penetrates the ground in the spring.

The little flowers were so prolific and had such a delicate aroma that Mr. Farwell could not resist picking a whole box of them around the pond. In fact, it was on that very trip in 1916 that they named the lake "Arbutus Lake" and the little cabin "Arbutus Lodge." Mr. Bentley was very impressed with the whole place, and agreed that the name was most fitting.

While the trailing arbutus is still a highlight of a trip to the Yellowdog Plains in the early spring, it is now a protected wildflower by the Michigan Department of Natural Resources.

By late summer Arbutus Lodge was nearing completion. It was the culmination of years of planning by Mr. Bentley. His friends and employees could see the delight in his countenance. His trail was approaching his exacting standards.

The cabin was fitted with wainscoting on the inside. It had two rooms, with three doors and two windows in each. The front door of each room led out to the screened porch which extended across the entire front of the cabin. The porch, which was actually a room of the building, had a single door in the center, and opened to a set of steps about eight feet wide which led down to the grass on the north shore of the pond. The wide steps gave the otherwise plain cabin a certain elegance.

Top: Halfway cabin or Sands Plains cabin (spring 1916) George Baker and John Carrier.
Bottom: May 14, 1916 – Frank C. Farwell picking arbutus at Arbutus Lake – so named this very day.

718

Top: Sitting room of Sands Plains cabin or Arbutus Lodge showing double doors to bedroom. 1916.
Bottom: Wash basin sink and side east window of the Arbutus Lodge bedroom.

The second door in each room led to the outside at the back of the cabin, and the third connected the two rooms. There were two doors in the door frame between the two rooms, and each could be locked from its respective side. The central wall between the two rooms was made of solid, six–inch hewn logs with each side covered with building paper and then wainscoting. The double doors made the walls soundproof. Mr. Bentley's liking for privacy was apparent in the construction of the cabin.

Above the two rooms was a small attic which could be entered by a small door eight feet up on the wall inside the porch. One end of the attic was lined with galvanized sheet metal where pillows and blankets could be stored without damage from squirrels, chipmunks, or mice.

At first, one side of the cabin was called a sitting room, while the other was used as a bedroom. Later they wanted more sleeping accommodations, and one side was called the men's side and the other the ladies' side, the only difference between the two being the size of the dressers. Mrs. Bentley had picked out a matching man's and lady's bureau set in Chicago and had it sent by train to Champion. The set was brought by wagon to White Deer Lake, scowed down the lake, and carried to Arbutus Lodge on men's backs. The Lodge had sleeping accommodations for four, two in each room, and if there were more in a party, they slept on the porch or camped out in a tent.

There was a single brick chimney in the back of the cabin. Each room had a small sheet metal stove connected to it and, for the first time, some late fall trips could be undertaken knowing that a warm, clean room was available halfway along the trail for the weary hikers.

The cabin also had wash basins, kerosene lamps, table and chairs, but no cooking facilities. Cooking was always done outside over an open fire. There were men's and women's outhouses off in the woods, complete with sandbox and rear door.

On the northwest corner of the pond, about forty yards from the building and a short distance up from the water's edge, a well point was driven. A box was built next to the pipe and lined with galvanized sheet metal, with a water–tight tin container in the center. Between this container and the outside wooden box was a four–inch space. When a party arrived during warm weather, the guide's first job was to pump the ice–cold water into the space surrounding the center container, which could then be used as an icebox. Both guests and crew often remarked about how good and cold the water was.

Book Two

Drama on the Plains

It took nearly all that summer of 1916, with four or five men working constantly, to complete everything, and it was during this period that George Baker's life reached a turning point. In retrospect it may have turned out for the better, but it all started when he had a complete falling–out with the rest of the men.

George and four other men had been working as a crew to finish the Arbutus Lodge. George's duties were to take charge of the supplies, do the cooking, and make out the daily work reports, but it had been made clear to the men that he was not in charge of them. However, it was difficult for George to do his job without giving some orders, and sometimes he acted as if he were completely in charge. George did what he could to cut corners on expenses and still do a good job. He tried hard to please the men with his cooking, but was highly sensitive to any criticism. He thoroughly enjoyed this work, though, having been swept up by Mr. Bentley's enthusiasm for the various projects which were just now coming together into a clear, magnificent picture. He loved the woods and the newly constructed trail through it, and most of all he felt a part of it – he felt important.

Often while at the Sand Plains, he would rise at dawn, grab his fishing pole and creel, and walk the trail south to the pool at the base of the North Falls. In about 15 minutes he would have from a dozen to 20 nice brook trout. An hour later he would be back at the cabin cooking the fish over an open fire in a big frying pan.

Breakfast was served at 6:30 sharp. It was a big meal, usually consisting of oatmeal, bacon, eggs scrambled in the huge iron frying pan, and French toast. George liked to prepare French toast, as it was a favorite with the men. The mornings that George served up fresh brook trout, however, were the best. On these mornings George was king, as it is hard to beat the taste of brook trout right from the stream.

But there were other days when the men seemed only to pick on George. They enjoyed getting his dander up, and they felt they could do it without fear of reprisal. One evening the men's muttered insults grew into loud name–calling. It was four to one, but George didn't care; he had reached the breaking point. He grabbed an ax, stepped outside, and shouted, "Why don't you come out here and call me that!"

There was breathless silence. George stood in the darkness with the ax raised. No one stepped through the doorway.

The moment passed, but after that things weren't the same between George and the others. Eventually Christ Andersen and the others at White

Deer Lake heard about the standoff. Christ had known George a long time, and tried to defend his actions. He realized that George took his job seriously and that he had a sharp temper. Christ also knew that in this case George had gone too far, and that if one man had stepped out the door that night, he probably would have been killed.

Mr. Bentley heard the story from several sources during his next trip to White Deer Lake. He called George aside and told him that the men led far too isolated a life at camp, and that someone who could not contain himself had no place there. Therefore, George was fired.

George Baker was stunned. He had only held two jobs in his entire life, his first at the F. W. Reed logging camp, and this job at White Deer Lake. For him, this had been the pinnacle of success. He had no other place to go.

His lumber camp experience during the log drives on the Peshekee River had been a rough one. Many of the men were rough and mean. George's mother had sent him off to work with new all—wool winter underwear and clean white hand—knitted socks and mittens, handmade shirts and woolen pants.

In his first unhappy experience, the men had just come in off the river cold and wet. George had been working all day preparing the meal with the cooks. The hungry men devoured everything in sight, shoving the empty platters at the hapless boy as he ran back and forth from the stove with new supplies of food.

At night the big stove in the center of the bunkhouse was fired up and all the men's wet boots, socks, pants and underwear were hung around it to dry. Though George's clothing was not wet, he hung it around the stove too, thinking that this was the right thing for him to do.

All the bunks near the stove were taken, so George looked for one toward the end of the long row. Here were two empty, cold, double—decker iron bunks with lumpy straw ticks. George took one and decided to make it his own. The warmth, light and activity all took place down by the stove. Here in his bunk it was cold and dark. He went to search for another blanket.

As he made his way down the aisle between the bunks, one of the lumberjacks spat tobacco juice at George's feet. George jumped and yelled. This brought the sport to the attention of the other men, who were all chewing Spearhead plug tobacco. On his return trip many joined in, spitting at George's feet as he danced his way down the long aisle.

Alone in a rough place, George had nowhere to turn. He dreaded the run down the aisle in the morning. On the verge of tears, he fell asleep.

To George it seemed as though he had hardly shut his eyes before a gong rang, alerting him to come to the kitchen. He tried to get down the

Top: The Breitung Hotel (1932). The Hotel burned while being restored in 1988. A vagrant built a fire on the floor.
Bottom: Mrs. Perkins about 1910 at Huron Mountain Club.

aisle quietly to his clothes, but soon everyone was spitting at his bare feet again, amid roars of laughter. When he reached the stove he discovered that his new hand–knit socks and mittens were gone. In their place were some hard, stiff socks with holes in the heels. There was nothing George could do. He started back. The tobacco juice flew again and the men laughed loudly at his plight.

Suddenly there was a roar that shook the rafters. A voice like a bull's bellowed out, "That's enough!"–The men quickly quieted down.

"If anyone wants to spit on someone, try spitting on me," roared the voice.

George's eyes quickly met the piercing eyes of his rescuer. He recognized the man – he had only seen him once before, but who could forget him?–It was Jack the Ripper. There he stood, completely bald, with a big nose and fiery, piercing eyes. Even more than his fierce appearance, it was his voice which commanded respect. George had heard about Jack the Ripper and had seen him loading logs with Dan McOlly at Toma Siding about 1903. No one knew his real name, but he was not alone – he had a friend, a big man standing near him who added, "That goes for me too."

Those two men made life in the lumber camp bearable for young George. He would never have made it without them, and when he left the camp some years later, Jack the Ripper and his friend were what he missed most. The rest of his experiences there had not been endearing ones.

The White Deer Lake job was his second. He had come there at about nineteen years of age and had worked his way up to be Mr. Bentley's trusted right–hand man. He had studied hard, practiced reading, writing, figures, and memorizing, and he thought the future was bright. Now his dreams had crumbled. Suddenly, at age 28, he was fired.

The Grand Reunion

George gloomily packed his packsack, said a few farewells, and was about to leave when he was told Mrs. Bentley wanted to see him.

Unknown to George, Christ Andersen had talked to her and explained the situation. Mrs. Bentley was a kind and understanding lady, loved by everyone. Most people thought there was only one authority above Mr. Bentley at White Deer Lake – Mr. McCormick – but Christ Andersen knew of another, and he had gone to her. Mrs. Bentley told George that what he had done was wrong, but that he had been faithful in the past and his work had been good. She had therefore decided to hire George to work at her cabin at Huron Mountain. He could go there as soon as he wanted. Mrs. Bentley had always been fond of George and didn't want to see him go, but she knew how badly he was getting along with the rest of the crew. She had discussed her wise decision with Mr. Bentley earlier.

The next day, George walked to Champion and took the train to Negaunee. After a night at the Breitung Hotel, he went to Marquette and boarded the Marquette and Southeastern train to Big Bay.

Arriving in Big Bay, George set out on foot for Huron Mountain Club. While he was resting along the sandy road in the big timber just east of the Salmon Trout River, a team and wagon came along that was headed for the Club, and George got a ride.

He was filled with wonder as he was let off near the "Shinglehouse," a place where the waitresses and laundresses stayed. There was a long set of steps leading to a screened–in sitting porch on the second story. It was a warm day, and there were several young girls sitting on the porch talking and laughing. They called to George.

Now, George Baker was 28 years old, but he had been in the woods most of his life. He had seen many women, of course, but had never met them on these terms. Awkward and embarrassed but trying to be polite, he tried to come up with some sort of answer. But before George could finish his sentence, he was sharply cut off by the voice of a large woman bearing down on him.

"Hey there, you leave my girls alone!" she shouted. It was Mrs. Perkins, the wife of the Club manager and the lady in charge of the dining room and the waitresses.

George stood flabbergasted while she scolded him. After he had a chance to state his business, however, she became very helpful and showed him the way to the Guide House, a long log bunk house built parallel to a broad, beautiful river, which he soon learned was Pine River.

To George's utter astonishment and delight, one of the first men he met in the bunkhouse at Huron Mountain was none other than his good friend, Jack the Ripper. Somehow, as was the case with a lot of good men in the north woods, fate seemed to have directed him to Huron Mountain. One can only imagine the amazement of George Baker when he learned that Jack Cassidy, the other fellow who had befriended him in the lumber camp some twelve years earlier, was also working there. George felt the world was on his side now. He was home, and glad to be working for Mrs. Bentley at Huron Mountain.

Top: Elizabeth King Bentley, Richard Bentley and Margaret Bentley having lunch on the porch of the Sands Plains cabin (August 11, 1916).
Bottom: Christ Andersen and F. C. Farwell at the Sands Plains cabin and Arbutus Pond – October 21, 1916.

Book Two

The Golden Years

On October 21, 1916, Cyrus Bentley recorded by camera a trip with Mr. Frank Farwell to the Sand Plains Camp. There had been a heavy wet snowfall of some fourteen inches the day before. It was a kind of out–of–season inspection tour, and a–crew of men was taken along for various jobs. In the crew were Charles Morrow, Ernest Gagnon, and the foreman Christ Andersen.

Reuben Swanson, Mr. Bentley's personal secretary, also made the trip. He kept an accurate account of everything either Mr. Bentley or Mr. Farwell mentioned that the cabin would need for the following season. Dry firewood was split and piled near each stove, oil lamps filled, and shutters put in place for the winter.

Later, the outside of the cabin was tightly enclosed in light paper covered with heavy "mulehide" tarpaper. Mr. Bentley hoped that, besides keeping the cabin warm, it would go a long way in keeping out the summer horde of ants. Originally the building was not to have been covered, but after a few summer sessions with the ants, it was decided to try the paper.

1917 was the first year that Arbutus Lodge on the Sand Plains was complete. A new era had started at White Deer Lake. The New Bentley Trail was now complete in every respect and the summer vacation parties, both from the south and from Huron Mountain, were numerous. Over the next ten years the whole area got its greatest use, and these were the golden years of the White Deer Lake country. There were some minor problems, but they were solved over the next few years.

One problem that arose at the Arbutus Lodge was first noticed in the summer of 1917. The water in Arbutus Lake began to rise in early May, and by mid–June was threatening the brand–new cabin. By the time Mr. Bentley arrived in June he could not get to the front steps without going over his ankles in water. The cabin had been built thirty feet from the water's edge.

Evidently, Mr. Bentley did not understand "water table," as he left orders to dig a trench around the lake at the water's edge in hopes that the water would spill into it and lower the lake level. At least some of the men working on the project either already knew or soon found out how ridiculous this was, but nevertheless the trench was dug, and a hewn log walkway put in to the second step so that the screened porch door could still be used that summer. By late July the water had begun to recede, and no permanent harm was done. Mr. Bentley never saw the water in Arbutus Lake that high again, and the matter was dropped.

At Bulldog Lake that same summer, Christ Andersen and his crew put in a rather crude hewn log walkway that was almost like his floating bridge. It was the last shortcut on the Bentley Trail. The walkway floated on muck on the northwest side of the lake, following a direct route across a huge marshy area of the drainage from Island Lake. It occurred to Christ at the time that if the water was raised enough in Bulldog Lake, a channel might be made to Island Lake, but for one reason or another the idea was never followed up.

Mrs. "Libby" Moyer, daughter of Mr. Bentley's close friend Frank Farwell, tells about another grand project that was tried in 1917 or '18. It was someone's idea to build a large cedar raft with a board deck on it for a tennis court in the middle of the lake. As there was no large flat area near the camp, this seemed like the answer, and no trees would have to be cleared. Mrs. Moyer said it was terrible – it could not be anchored, the balls constantly blew into the water, and from any standpoint the whole thing was a failure. The float had to be blown up before the end of the season, and no one talked about it again.

Besides the regular hiking, boating, swimming, and socializing, there were other recreational pursuits. Mrs. Bentley usually seemed to make the trip on the trail only out of obligation, and Mrs. McCormick, a rather large woman, only walked it once or twice. Christ Andersen told of seven men trying to fit her into a sleeping bag in the middle of Section 21. It was the last time she slept in the woods. The Halfway Cabin did not add much to the trip as far as she was concerned, and she only went there once.

In 1917 or '18 she brought a new Model T Ford up to White Deer Lake Camp, a task in itself. It was said that the Huron Bay Grade road was so bad that you didn't have to steer the car – there was no way it could get out of the ruts. And getting the vehicle up to the camp was such an arduous task that for the most part she was content to leave it there. She would occasionally make short trips on the mile or two of road that had been improved from the camp out toward the Huron Bay Grade, but most of the time she enjoyed keeping the car spotless inside and out. She would sweep it out, polish it regularly, and wipe the dust from the windshield with a clean soft cloth.

It was also in 1917 and '18 that America was drawn into World War I, and most of the younger men had to go. Due to their education and station in life, many of the Huron Mountain Club guests became officers, and for the same reason and lack of education most of the crew who passed the physical exam became enlisted men.

At first call to arms, Jim Andersen and some others were given a roaring send–off from Huron Mountain. George Baker and Roy Lawrence

Top: The Huron Bay Grade road was just two ruts for sixteen miles in 1916 – when cars began to travel on it, it became much worse.
Lower left: Cyrus McCormick III (1918).
Lower right: Jim Andersen at Camp Custer, December 21, 1918.

soon followed under the same conditions. Christ Andersen didn't have to go because of his injured foot and poor eyesight, so he would be around as at least a part–time foreman at White Deer Lake.

Mr. McCormick and Mr. Bentley had become concerned about the beaver felling trees, especially the birches along the shores of White Deer Lake. When Christ Andersen offered to "trap them out of there," Mr. Bentley was horrified. He had let it be known that he was against trapping of any kind. His suggestion was to put galvanized chicken wire around the base of the trees to discourage the beaver. They would try it with some birches in a specific area as an experiment.

Unknown to the McCormicks and Bentleys, Christ Andersen tried his method too, and between the two, not much damage occurred for the next ten years or more. Each felt that his own idea had worked. Christ, of course, had done the trapping when no one was around. Besides beaver, he trapped wolf, muskrat, otter, fisher, fox, and martin. Christ knew Mr. Bentley didn't want any animals trapped at all, and figured the less said about it the better.

Mr. McCormick also worried about several tall white pines that were left in the area around camp, especially those he had purchased on the island in among the cabins. There were indeed some eyebrows raised among guests and help alike when, during 1918, a time when because of the War nobody could get any copper even for essential projects, Mr. McCormick had a great amount of heavy copper cable and copper rod sent up to the camp for lightning rods to be put on every white pine on the island.

George in Another Plains Drama

Cyrus McCormick had headed the McCormick business since his father's death in 1884. Now 62, and having been president of the International Harvester Company since its inception, he was tired and wanted to step down. It would allow him to spend more time at White Deer Lake.

Since a huge amount of McCormick money was directly connected to the International Harvester Company, it seemed imperative that another McCormick should take over the reins, and the job went to Cyrus' younger brother Harold. He did not ask for the job and really did not want it, but he had no choice. Their other brother, Stanley, had insurmountable psychological problems and, though married, had to be under almost constant care. Their sister, Anita Blaine, probably could have run the

George Baker in France (1919).

company well but, having lived her life as a famous millionairess, society figure, and philanthropist in Chicago, she would not be able to take on this kind of responsibility.

Harold, the president–to–be, had led a rather carefree life. He liked women, flying, and fine clothes. Though he was looked on by many as a fashion plate and a playboy, he had graduated from Princeton, the same as his brothers Cyrus and Stanley, and had worked for the company. His first marriage tied together two of the world's greatest fortunes when he married his childhood sweetheart Edith Rockefeller, daughter of John D. Rockefeller, but the marriage did not turn out well. Harold and Edith had five children, two of whom died in infancy. While visiting in Switzerland, Edith met Carl Jung and eventually lived in that country, separated from Harold, for over eight years.

Because of this situation and the fact that Harold had been seeing a Polish singer named Ganna Walska, there was some very poor publicity in the papers at the time. In spite of this, Harold did take over the presidency of the International Harvester Company, and Cyrus moved up to the less demanding job of Chairman of the Board of Directors.

Since the Cyrus McCormicks now planned to be at White Deer Lake more often, they worked out a better agreement with the Bentleys as to the use of the property. On alternating years one family would have the months of May, July, and September, and the other would have June, August and October. Of course, one family might invite certain members of the other family as their guests. Then, too, the Bentleys had their cabin at Huron Mountain which they could use any time, and either family could use the Trail and Arbutus Lodge, though arrangements for their use were usually cleared through the people at White Deer Lake.

They continued to purchase land as it became available, but always in the names of third parties with whom the McCormicks and Bentleys had previous agreements. These were usually people working in the McCormick offices in Chicago. McCormick and Bentley planned to put the land into their own names later.

Margaret Bentley, the daughter of Cyrus for whom Lake Margaret was named, was going with young David Hamilton, whose family were close friends and next–door neighbors to the Bentleys at Huron Mountain Club. She later married David. Both Margaret and David had a great love for the woods and waters of the Lake Superior region. They had often walked the Bentley Trail together and, unlike some, Margaret had not had to be pushed. It was during the years of David and Margaret's courtship that an incident occurred concerning the Bentley Trail. We have George Baker to thank for this story.

Upper left: Stanley McCormick, brother of Cyrus and Harold, February 22, 1891.
Upper right: Harold F. McCormick.
Bottom: George Baker (right) working with the wood splitter at Huron Mounatin Club. 1920.

It was 1919, and George had returned to Huron Mountain from a tour of duty in France. He was now working for the Club, but continued to be Mr. Bentley's main contact when something needed to be done on the north end of the trail. If George did a specific job for Mr. Bentley, Mr. Bentley was billed for George's time through the Club. This day, George and Dutch John had been out grubbing on the north end of the trail. They had put in a long day.

David Hamilton, a student at Yale at the time, had crossed the trail to see Margaret when his father arrived at Huron Mountain with news of an impending railroad strike. Mr. Hamilton wanted to get the message to David as soon as possible so he could get back to school before the strike. If the railroad workers went on strike, there was no other way to get out east in 1919, and the only way Mr. Hamilton could get the message to David was by messenger via the trail.

Mr. Hamilton approached Mr. Perkins, the Club manager, with his problem. There were only three people among the workmen at Huron Mountain who knew all 25 miles of the Trail well enough to cross it at night: the two Andersen brothers and George Baker. Christ and Jim were not at the Club at the time, or one of them would surely have made the trip, so George was the only possibility left.

Mr. Perkins and Mr. Hamilton found him on the main Club bridge which crossed Pine River. It was a common gathering spot in the evenings. The two men quickly explained the situation to him.

George was a little taken aback. He didn't know quite what to do. He was very tired, having worked all day on the trail, and more than a little dejected over missing his supper.

After some discussion, Mr. Hamilton pulled a shiny twenty–dollar gold piece from his vest pocket and said, "George, this gold piece is yours if you'll make the trip right now."

George felt a little strength come to his tired body – this was two weeks' pay!–"All right," he said. "If you'll see that I get my supper and a lunch to take with me, I'll leave tonight. Keep the gold piece until I return – then we'll see if I've earned it."

Mr. Perkins gave the word, and George had a meal served to him in the Club kitchen. The cooks then packed a nice lunch for him to carry in a small backpack.

When George was ready, he set out for Pine Lake, carrying the backpack and a lantern. Hooked on the outside of his pack was a small empty pail for water.

He climbed into one of Oscar's new double–ended rowboats in the Club boathouse on Pine Lake, and rowed to the landing on the south side of the lake. The trip was just short of a mile, and George made it in about twelve minutes.

From the landing he took a short trail to the wagon road around Pine lake. Following the road which ended at the Iliad, George quickly climbed the hills to the Mountain Stream Bridge. On the south side of the bridge was a clearing where an old set of pine camps had been built ten or twelve years before. George had heard that the camps were never used. The camps were crumbled now, the roofs had caved in, and the clearing was growing up in brush.

George did not cross the bridge, however, as the road he was walking continued on along the north side of the river, then swung away from it toward a beach on Mountain lake. On the sand beach on the extreme northeast shore of the lake was a boathouse where George would pick up his second boat.

He decided to use the Bentley longboat with the three sets of oarlocks. It was the Rushton, light and fast, but he decided not to fool with the 1916 Evinrude motor that went with it. George thought that with darkness coming on he might never get it started. Besides, he knew from experience that by sitting in the center seat and putting his light pack in the rear, the boat would be perfectly balanced. With such a light load, each pull on the oars would send the boat gliding a long distance toward its destination.

As he pulled away from the boathouse, Fortress Mountain arose from the forest to its full glory in the setting sun. George set his bow on the far point and lined up his stern with the boathouse.

Rounding the first point on the east shore of the lake, George headed for Whiskey Point, also called Hebard Point, a mile or so down the lake.

Just west of due north was Huron Mountain, now in George's full view in the waning light, its south face rocky with scattered stunted pine.

As George rowed up Mountain Lake, darkness began to overtake him. The boat glided easily through the quiet water. At Hebard Point, he changed his course, heading toward the first point across from Dudley. This was known as the Narrows, beyond which another main body of the lake extended off to the west. George crossed this on his way to the Canyon Lake landing. You had to know this spot in the dark, though there was a white marker there that could be seen for some distance in daylight.

Pulling the longboat alongside the hewn log landing in a small cove, George clambered out of the boat, hung the oars on some wire rings provided there so that the porcupines wouldn't chew the handles, tied the boat to a tree, and lit his lantern. Though there was still a little light on the lake, it was pitch black in the woods.

He was now on the Bentley Trail headed for Canyon Lake, only a short distance away. There wasn't much to see. George's vision was limited to the small piece of the trail lighted by his lantern.

At Canyon Lake, George climbed into the flat–bottomed skiff waiting there. Placing his lighted lantern in the bow seat of the boat and his oars in the oarlocks, he let the boat drift silently between the high rock walls of the narrow lake. The faint light of the lantern danced hauntingly on the canyon walls while George paused a moment to ponder the silence and observe the weird effect. The high granite walls seemed to close in on him, and each muffled sound of the oars was magnified.

At the opposite end of the lake, about a quarter mile away, was another wooden landing with a hewn log dock, steps, and walkway. Again George tied the boat, shouldered his pack and started out on the hewn log walkway, holding his lantern high so that its faint light could further penetrate the darkness. About a hundred yards into the black forest of huge cedar trees he stopped, removed the little pail from his pack and, searching just a moment, sunk it into a hole in the dark wet moss.

This was George's spring. He had discovered it himself a few years earlier. It was really a small underground river flowing from a spring down a nearby hill to the lake. But here water could be obtained just a step or two from the trail. The water was good and cold, and in the dark he could not see the fine dark sediment that would have had to settle if it had been daylight. George drank deeply, then filled the pail again to take with him, as the next good water – other than Elm Creek, which was brown – was halfway to the Bowl, miles away.

George fairly flew up the trail. The night air was cool and damp, just right for walking, and the trail was good. He went across the Elm Creek swamp, between the twin pines, then up along the creek. Crossing the swamp in almost no time, he covered the two or three miles of side hills to the Bowl stopping twice for fresh water. He climbed up the escarpment and was soon on the Sand Plains, headed for the Halfway Cabin.

It was just about midnight when he arrived at Arbutus Lodge. He planned to sleep on a cot in the kitchen tent. He put his lantern on the table in the tent, and lit another that hung from the ridgepole. The two lights in the confined area of the tent made a bright, warm glow. It was nice to be inside, even if only in a tent. To George, it might as well have been a solid log cabin.

George ate his sandwiches and lay down to rest, but he could not get to sleep. He had looked forward to a nap at this stopover, but now that he

Top: Arbutus Lodge on the Sands Plains with the cook tent behind it and to the right.
Bottom: Constructing the men's camp on the west pond at the Sands Plains. Mike Jarvis and helper. September 1920.

was here he just didn't feel like resting. Every sense was alert, every muscle tingling, thoughts churning through his brain.

George did not know how long he lay there, just too restless to sleep. He had no choice but to go on. Leaving the pack, but taking his lantern and the little pail of water, George started out again. Rounding the west pond, he started south through the big jackpine. Gradually the country changed to spruce and tamarack and then tag alder, and soon he was on the boardwalk crossing the Yellowdog Swamp.

George hurried along from island to island until they were all behind him, and now he was on the longest stretch of corduroy through the swamp, over a quarter of a mile. The mangled trees and bushes were thick on either side of him.

Suddenly from behind him came a series of huge clumping sounds. The whole boardwalk shook. George wheeled around and held his light high. The noise behind him stopped. George stood stock–still, too terrified to make a sound. Finally the words came to him:

"Who are you?–Speak up – are you man or beast?"

Again silence, but just for a fleeting moment. Then the air was shattered by the worst scream any man ever heard. A chill shot up George Baker's spine and his hair stood right up on end – he swore it right to his dying day. His mouth moved but no sound came. His feet were rooted to the boardwalk. As he stood there, whatever it was went crashing off through the thick swamp. It was no ghost. It sounded like it was breaking huge trees in its headlong dash. For a moment there was silence, then the stillness was broken by another indescribable shriek in the distance. George turned and fled. He says no one ever covered the rest of that trail so fast.

Panting, and wringing wet with sweat, George arrived at the White Deer Lake Camp just as the cook was beginning breakfast. George told the story several times that day, and again and again at both ends of the trail over the years, but no one could come up with an animal that behaved like the thing George had run into.

David Hamilton returned via the trail that day and was off to school in plenty of time to avoid the railroad strike. And George – yes, he certainly earned his twenty–dollar piece.

Stormy Years for Cyrus McCormick

By 1919, it was obvious to Mr. Bentley that the Arbutus Lodge was not large enough. Originally it had had a sitting room, bedroom, and porch.

Upper left: Emil Christianson beside much lumber that had been carried from White Deer Lake to the Sands Plains.
Right: Elizabeth McCormick just before her untimely death.
Lower left: Gordon McCormick and his father parting at the Sands Plains cabin – September 1920.

More and more, the sitting room was being used for sleeping and the rooms were changed to the men's room and the ladies' room. Sometimes the guide would even sleep in the attic. There was a ladder–type stairway leading to it from the screen porch. Plans were made to build another small building near the Arbutus Lodge.

Emil Christiansen of Chicago had replaced Reuben Swanson as Mr. Bentley's personal secretary, and Joseph Lucius replaced Christ Andersen as the foreman. Christ had a tendency to be off in the woods too much. Emil Christiansen really enjoyed the place and the outings, seemingly even more so than his predecessor had.

The new trail was a complete success, and was used a great deal. Dr. and Mrs. Hibbs were great walkers and pioneers on both trails. They had been among the first to use both the old and new trail, and among the few who stayed more than a night or two at the Fish Camp on the Big Huron River. They were also among the regular trail users, along with the Farwells, H. B. Platt, Preston Kumber, Perry Smith, the W. N. Duanes, and the Christy family – Ethel, Abbey, and their brother Bayard.

The second generation of the McCormick and Bentley families often brought groups of friends across the trail to stay for several days at either camp. If there was a large group at the Arbutus Lodge, the young people usually stayed in tents.

The Lodge, though comparatively small, was now in full operation. Trail crews were kept busy from both ends of the trail, clearing, straightening, building bridges, and putting in hewn logs over wet spots, and in some places rerouting the trail completely if Mr. Bentley thought it best. The Lodge was completely outfitted. Tablecloths, mirrors, dishes, glasses, silverware, brooms, fly swatters, candles, and cooking utensils had all been carried the seven or so miles from the base camp at White Deer Lake.

In the fall of 1920, Mike Jarvis and a helper were sent out to build the second cabin. It was to be eight by twelve, and built out of upright logs provided by Christ Andersen. The new cabin was to be used as a guide camp, so that a guide or two who went along on a trip wouldn't have to return or sleep in the attic or the cook tent. The cabin was located on the east side of the west pond, away from the lodge. It was the Christy girls, Mrs. Hibbs, Mrs. Hasler and Miss Jones who first volunteered to carry some of the flat lumber needed for the cabin as far as the Yellowdog Swamp. There were many others who enjoyed being in on the "haul" – even Emil Christensen did his share – but they soon realized what a tremendous task they had taken on, and it fell to the crew to complete the job.

That fall (1920), Gordon McCormick and his father, along with Cyrus Bentley, walked out to the Sand Plains to see how the construction was going and to decide what else, if anything, ought to be built there. They stayed the night at Arbutus Lodge and the next day Gordon went on to Huron Mountain alone, while the two Cyruses returned to White Deer Lake.

Cyrus McCormick was spending more and more time at White Deer Lake and it seemed as though he would have many happy years of retirement there. But, as it turned out, they became some of the most trying years of his life.

Cyrus had gotten married to Harriet Bradley Hammond in 1889, just a few years before Harold married Edith Rockefeller. Before these marriages Harold and Stanley had been very close, almost inseparable. But Stanley, even before he developed his psychological problems, chose an artistic career and drifted away somewhat from Cyrus and Harold. It was Cyrus and Harold, then, with the guidance of their mother, who became the industrialists, and grew even closer. Both Cyrus and Harold had lost children – Cyrus his daughter Elizabeth, and Harold, by 1921, had lost three of his own.

Cyrus' daughter Elizabeth had died after an operation when she was only twelve. It was a great blow to Cyrus, as he was extremely fond and proud of his talented daughter. In her short life she had written both music and poetry. Of course everyone who had known her was deeply saddened, and sometimes the household servants had come on Cyrus sobbing uncontrollably in his great house on Rush Street.

Now, in January of 1921, Cyrus lost his wife of 30 years. Her death changed not only his life, but also the entire atmosphere at White Deer Lake.

At about the same time, there were other goings–on in the McCormick family that had a very sobering effect on Cyrus. They mostly had to do with Harold, who had taken over as president of the International Harvester Company and, to the chagrin of Cyrus, was receiving very bad publicity concerning his marital problems.

It was common knowledge that Edith had taken their three children and gone off to Switzerland for eight years, but now the gossip columns had picked up the fact that Harold was seeking a divorce so that he could marry Ganna Walska. He had been seeing several women over the years without much fanfare, but the fact that the Polish singer at thirty had lost one husband, divorced two others, and refused the marriage proposal of Harold McCormick, made big news. Despite the bad publicity, Harold did not give up. In 1921, Ganna finally said yes to his proposal and he brought her to Paris, where she remained while he went to Switzerland to get a divorce from Edith. When he returned to Paris with the divorce, he found that Ganna had

Nettie McCormick in her elderly years. Courtesy Jenny Lawerence.

married an American millionaire named Alexander Smith Cochran. Apparently poor Harold had taken a bit too long getting his divorce.

Harold practically camped on the doorstep of the honeymooning couple, begging Ganna to reconsider. She said she would think about it. By now, the public was as impatient as Harold to hear her answer.

About this time, to add fuel to the flames, Harold's oldest daughter Mathilde announced that she was about to marry Max Oser, her Swiss riding master. Mathilde was 16, Max in his 40s. Her family persuaded her to put off the wedding plans until she was 18.

Within a year or two, Madame Walska did get a divorce from Cochran and was free to marry Harold. She was now wealthy in her own right, having come out of the Cochran marriage with a sizable settlement.

Since Harold had, at least in a small way, been a part of the White Deer Lake family, the interest and talk there was at a high pitch, though these things were not discussed openly. The information was passed on in an undertone so as not to show disrespect, but it was passed on in great detail.

In Chicago, Cyrus naturally was humiliated by it all, and the offices of the International Harvester Company fairly shook with Harold as its president. Cyrus, always the picture of quiet dignity, felt this type of notoriety could only be very bad for business, and they finally asked Harold to step down. Harold resigned readily, as he had other things on his mind. He had not wanted the job in the first place, and was only too glad to pass it on to the capable Alexander Legge who was chosen to take his place. For the first time in nearly a century, the presidency of the McCormick business was not in the family. Legge's long years of experience with the company, working his way up through the ranks, brought the stability that was needed, and Harold was free to attend to his personal problems.

Even after divesting himself of the Harvester presidency, Harold was still in the news, but this time in an even more embarrassing way to the proud McCormick family. The story that broke into the papers this time was that he had had a transplantation of monkey glands to revive his sexual powers for the wedding. The doctor who performed the operation was identified as a prominent Chicago surgeon, Dr. V. P. Lespinasse, who was known for his experimental work in spermatogenesis and sterility. Of course Harold denied the accusations, and threatened to sue the newspapers.

At the peak of the scandal in 1922, the Mining Journal in Marquette carried a picture of a Dr. A. F. Christian and a statement by this gentleman. The article was headed "McCormick 'youth' bought, paid for, to be short–lived."–It stated that Dr. Christian, a noted Boston surgeon and authority on the transplanting of glands, "asserts that millionaire Harold F.

McCormick, Chicago, who underwent an operation to regain 'youth,' is doomed to a 'love life' of but six months.'

After the alleged operation, Harold went to Europe and married Ganna Walska. Then he brought her home to Chicago and married her again, in his mother's house in February of 1923. Sixty detectives were hired to guard the premises. Harold never returned to White Deer Lake.

On top of it all, not long after the wedding in 1923, Nettie McCormick, Cyrus and Harold's 88–year–old mother, died. And, as it turned out, Harold's marriage to Ganna Walska was a complete disaster. After several years of humiliation, during which she scorned him in public and finally left him, it finally ended with a divorce in 1931.

All of this – the shocking scandals in Harold's life and the death of his own wife and mother – took its toll on Cyrus McCormick. He was humbled, saddened, and lonely, and seemed glad to return to the soothing atmosphere of White Deer Lake. He took his daily walks, had more use than ever for a butler and valet, and enjoyed short swims in the lake. The men would chuckle among themselves when he would leave orders to be met at the Spring Landing on Bulldog Lake with clean underwear, so that he could swim, change, and ride the boat back through the channel in time for dinner. One of his favorite walks was north on the new Bentley Trail to the North Falls, then up along the east branch of the Yellowdog to the East Falls, at the top of which he would build a small fire and have tea, then go back to Bulldog Lake, an overall distance of about six miles.

The McCormick Boulder

To go back a few years in the history of the White Deer Lake country before 1921, there are several projects and events that are noteworthy.

The crew accomplished a sizable engineering feat when they built a cement dam in a rock gorge about a quarter mile below the log–and–earth dam and sluiceway built by loggers 45 years earlier.

An adjustable board spillway now made it possible to carefully regulate the levels of both White Deer and Bulldog lakes, as well as the hand–dug channel between them. Motorboats and even the scow could easily be maneuvered between the lakes, although the motors had to be run at half–speed. In late summer, however, the shallow parts of the channel would fill with grass and weeds which had to be cut.

The raising of the water also presented two other problems. Many trees, especially on Bulldog Lake, had water flooded over their roots and were

Upper left: Cyrus McCormick heading back to Bulldog Lake from the Arbutus Lodge –
September 1920.
Upper right: Cyrus McCormick standing by the East Falls.
Bottom: The dam on Bulldog Lake. It is also the beginning of the Yellowdog river.

killed. The task of cutting and removing them went on over several years. The second problem was that the old walkway built on the muskeg was no longer usable, and would eventually have to be replaced. At the time, it seemed as though the trail would have to be rerouted or abandoned in favor of the longer south side of the lakes, but nothing at all was done for a while.

There was another project that Cyrus McCormick had been mulling over for years. He had talked to Christ Andersen about it earlier, but now, with the death of Harriet, he decided to go through with it.

Apparently he and Christ had discussed moving a glacial boulder from the White Deer Lake country to the McCormick plot in Chicago's Graceland Cemetery. The plot contained the grave of their young daughter, Elizabeth.

Bill Dorais ran the International Harvester Company branch in Marquette, and was an acquaintance of Mr. McCormick's. McCormick and Dorais contracted to have a flatcar brought to Champion to carry the stone to Chicago. They agreed for Dorais to have the huge boulder brought down the Huron Bay Grade to Champion.

They chose a rock that Mrs. McCormick had enjoyed in her lifetime. Mr. McCormick could remember Harriet sitting on this particular rock. It weighed 24 tons, and had little clusters of oak fern, spleenwort, and several types of lichen growing on it.

Mike Jarvis, the Finnish carpenter who had been working around the camp for a few years, was assigned the task of crating the stone and mounting it on a skid. It was hoped that he could do so without disturbing much of the lichen, ferns, and little flowers so typical of the White Deer Lake country, in the desire to bring to Chicago a little piece of the north country they all loved so well.

This was a new type of work for Mike. He was used to working alone and would rather have done so, as the Frenchmen at the camp tended to treat him as a second–class citizen. He had worked on the guide cabin out on the Sand Plains, and for most of his stay had built rustic furniture to be used both on the docks and indoors.

Using jacks, blocks, and timbers, he slowly raised the boulder from its resting place, the exact spot where it had gently settled with the melting of the glacier ice some ten thousand years before. It was padded with damp burlap to preserve the growth, then crated. Mike saw to it that the rock was well supported inside the crate. The crated boulder was mounted on a log skid that had been made especially for this purpose.

The job of skidding the rock from its original site to Champion turned out to be tremendous; it took weeks. Using an International Harvester

Top: Mike Jarvis raising the twenty four ton McCormick boulder from its resting place near Bulldog Lake.
Bottom: The White Deer Lake stone crated and raised up on timbers ready to be placed on a skid. Mike Jarvis is standing alongside it.

Upper left: Richard Bentley Jr., grandson of Cyrus, standing on the stone in Graceland Cemetery.

Upper right: The White Deer Lake stone in the McCormick plot at Graceland Cemetery, Chicago. Elaborate stone next to it is for Marshall Field.

Bottom: Halls, in white coat, at the door of the Sands Plains kitchen tent.

tractor, a road was built to the stone. Only a few small trees were cut, but the skid road had to be built up fairly level in many places, or the crate would have slid off the skid. It soon became obvious that the old railroad bridges on the Huron Bay Grade were in no condition to take the weight, so all seven of them had to be shored up with timbers, and their foundations trussed. In one spot, they had to ford the river.

At Champion, the crated rock was loaded onto the waiting flatcar, then shipped to Chicago and placed on the McCormick plot in the Graceland Cemetery. Not one of the delicate plants survived even the first few weeks in Chicago. The hotter sun and caustic air of the city had little in common with the cool, pure air of the northwoods. Today the stone sits half sunken in the earth – bare, lifeless, and insignificant in its new surroundings, except to those very few who know its story.

Events on the Trail – Good and Bad

One particular crossing of the Bentley Trail in 1921 had special significance: on this trip, made by a group of young people, one of the newcomers to the north country was named Phoebe Norcross. Miss Norcross was thrilled with the thought of meeting the handsome Richard Bentley, Cyrus' son. She says it was during this trip on the trail that she and Richard became attracted to one another. They were married the following year.

Despite the death of Harriet McCormick and the other goings–on in the McCormick family, things at White Deer Lake were going smoothly with Cyrus Bentley as overseer to the whole operation. The butlers on the property gave the place an air of grandeur. It could no longer be called a "rough camp."–From Halls, the first butler and those succeeding him, butlers were brought out to the Arbutus Lodge, where they served the drinks and meals, hors d'oeuvres and all. There was the kitchen tent to do the cooking in, and the dining tent to eat in.

Whenever George Baker came along on a trail crossing, he was always the official trail cook. George was very particular about his outdoor cooking. He had a special large frying pan that no one else was to touch. No utensils at White Deer Lake, or at Huron Mountain for that matter, were quite right for him, so he bought his own long wooden–handled fork and spoon. He went so far as to have his name stamped on them.

When it came time to cook, George became a gourmet chef. He knew that nothing was quite good enough for the fastidious Mr. Bentley, but since George was actually working for Huron Mountain and was only "on loan" to

Mr. Bentley, he found a little extra courage and there were many times when tempers flared and cross words were exchanged. Still, they seemed to need, and even grudgingly respect, each other.

George tells about a morning when he was cooking breakfast on an open fire just behind Arbutus Lodge. He had gotten up early to gather wood, build the fire, and do all the advance preparations he could. He waited until everyone was ready to eat before he scrambled the eggs, so they would be fresh and hot. This meant, though, that Cyrus Bentley was looking over his shoulder while he scrambled the eggs, so some criticism was unavoidable. As George started to stir the eggs, Mr. Bentley shouted, "You stirred them the wrong way!–Throw them out!"

Simmering with rage, George held his tongue. He didn't always keep quiet at times like this, though, and one trail crosser quotes him as exclaiming, "Is there no pleasing you!" – a thing you simply didn't say to Cyrus Bentley.

Ted Tonkin Comes to White Deer Lake

It was in the days of the butlers at White Deer Lake that a new man was introduced to the camp who would set the tone of the place for many years to come. Mr. and Mrs. Halls, both very British, had brought to the place a certain charm which guests never failed to comment on. So when another Englishman was introduced to McCormick and Bentley, they accepted him with open arms. This English gentleman was Mr. Charles Edward Tonkin.

"Ted," as he was called, had been a shipwright in England. At the end of World War I, thousands of shipwrights had been laid off, and he had come to America on the promise of a good job by an English friend in Chicago.

On arriving in America, Tonkin found no job waiting for him, nor any to be found at all. With soldiers returning in vast numbers, jobs were extremely hard to come by, especially to a foreigner. Tonkin was very discouraged, but was willing to try any angle to get work.

He read in the paper that Lady Astor was visiting in Chicago. Tonkin had met Lady Astor in England and now, with typical British pluck, he wrote to her asking if she might intercede for him among her wealthy American friends. His letter was given to Cyrus McCormick, who passed it on to Mr. F. A. Steuert at the McCormick offices. After several interviews, Ted Tonkin was introduced to Cyrus Bentley. Bentley hired Tonkin on the spot, and arranged for them to go together to camp. The two of them arrived at White Deer Lake on Decoration Day of 1922.

The train trip from Chicago to Champion was a real test for Ted Tonkin. It was the first chance he and Bentley had to get to know one another. Tonkin learned right away that if you were going to work for Cyrus Bentley you didn't sit or eat with him. Ted understood his social place, and took it well. Mr. Bentley was pleased with his attitude, and they got along famously. They talked over so many things in detail, though, that there was no way one man could absorb them all.

In an interview years later, Ted's wife tells about one part of their conversation.

"Getting down to fine points," said Mr. Bentley, "Do you know how to make coffee?"

Mrs. Tonkin explains that in England at the time, they had what was called "coffee essence," a gooey black substance that came bottled like our ketchup. You stirred a teaspoonful of that in hot water, and called it coffee. It was a little like today's freeze–dried coffee. This stuff was pre–sweetened, though, and was intolerable to most Americans. But naturally Ted started to tell Mr. Bentley how he made coffee.

"Certainly; all you do is stir in a teaspoonful of essence and–"

"Oh, no, no, no! That's not the way we do it at all! This is how I want my coffee made..." He proceeded to give the overwhelmed Ted Tonkin explicit instructions in the true Bentley manner.

"You put the ground coffee beans in cold water, and put it on the big old cookstove and bring it to a boil. As soon as it boils, you put it on the back of the stove until the boiling subsides, then you put it on the heat again. You do this three times, and then serve it piping hot."

By this time, Ted was so chock–full of all kinds of instructions that it was a wonder he could remember any of them.

The first morning at camp, Ted was very nervous. He was trying to do everything just right to impress Mr. Bentley. He took great pains having everything just so and constantly trying to think of all his instructions. Mr. Bentley, for instance, had to have a little of every kind of fruit that was in season – and some seasons that was six or eight kinds.

Mrs. Berry, the cook, said, "Hey Teddy, how 'bout your coffee?"

"Good heavens," cried Ted, "I've forgotten all about it!"

The coffee had been boiling merrily away for some time. Mrs. Tonkin says he had boiled the everlasting daylights out of it. Ted snatched the coffee off the stove and stood there a moment, wondering what to do. He had no choice but to serve the coffee as it was, for Bentley was sitting there waiting for it. With great apprehension he poured a cupful for his new boss, fully expecting to be fired the next moment.

As Mr. Bentley was picking up his cup to try the first sip, he asked, "Did you follow my instructions, Teddy?"

"To the letter, sir, to the letter," he replied. The coffee passed muster, and Ted Tonkin stayed at White Deer Lake.

This was Ted's introduction to the place. From the first sight of it, he was thrilled. He had had a dreamlike mental picture of it from Mr. Bentley's description, but the reality was even better.

Ted Tonkin was no butler, but with his clipped British accent he talked like the ones they were used to at camp. It took some time for everyone to get over the idea, for he did act much like a butler – helpful, respectful, and dignified. It didn't take long for Ted to fit perfectly into camp life. From the first day he detected Mr. Bentley's passion for exactness, punctuality and perfection, and went along with it completely, even doing him one better when he could. He understood Mr. Bentley. If he wanted breakfast at seven, it was to be precisely seven, not a minute before or after. If Bentley arrived at the dining room door a minute or two early, he would wait on the porch and open the door exactly at the stroke of seven.

There was one terrible morning that fall when a blustering wind was blowing sheets of heavy rain from the north. Mr. Bentley, in his haste to get from the Chimney Cabin on the Island to the dining room on the mainland, had arrived a few minutes early. There was no shelter of any kind on the open porch outside the dining room, and Mr. Bentley stood there, getting drenched to the skin by the cold rain.

Finally, he spotted Tonkin coming into the room and said in a defeated voice, "Teddy, excuse me, would you mind if I came in the dining room to wait? I'm a little early."

"Certainly not; come right in," said Tonkin, and opened the door. Mr. Bentley was grateful to get warm and dry, but his punctuality had taken a beating.

Then, the Opposite of Tonkin

Another character who gave many accounts of life at White Deer Lake in those years was Willard Brunette. Willard was the son of the carpenter's helper who had worked with Ed LaBlanc so patiently after he went blind. Willard told stories of the logging days in the Peshekee country before he worked for Bentley and McCormick. He had loaded sleighs at Otter Lake and just south of the Haypress Dam. Willard nearly froze his feet, loading two sleighs a day with horses and a "Y" chain.

Upper left: Lunching at Arbutus Lodge Margaret Bentley, Preston Kumber, David Hamilton.
Upper right: Ted Tonkin and friend – White Deer Lake.
Bottom: Willard Brunette (front center) and friends in his lumberjack days. Courtesy of Willard Brunette.

He said the icer, used to ice the roads, got full of baby trout on that job. To fill the icer, a barrel was lowered into the river, then slid up the trough by horse power. When they pulled the plug, the fish went out into the ice ruts in the road. He said the Dishno Creek was just full of trout until the roads were put in.

Joe Lucius was the foreman when Willard Brunette first went to work for McCormick and Bentley. He was the foreman both before and after Christ Andersen.

There was a big rock knob in the middle of the new road into camp, at the top of a long hill. Oscar Bennett had a Chevrolet truck, the first one in Champion. The truck came all the way up the grade in the deep ruts from Champion, but got stuck ten feet from the top of the hill. Mr. Bentley thought the rock should be removed if at all possible, so Joe Lucius had Jim Hinton scrape away all the dirt from around the rock, using his team and a slusher, in preparation to dynamite the rock. He asked Willard if he had ever worked with dynamite, and Willard said, "Sure, lots of times." He said it wouldn't take much dynamite if they drilled a hole in the rock, but a lot if they didn't. They didn't want to bother drilling the hole, so Willard used a whole box of dynamite, placing it on top of the rock. Mr. Bentley wanted to watch the operation, and asked Willard which way the rock was going to blow. Willard said, "You stand over there, right behind that big maple; it'll blow the other way."

When the blast went off, a huge piece of the rock crashed into Mr. Bentley's tree. When the dust had settled, he stepped out from behind the tree, shaking, his face white.

"Willard!" He shouted. "You made a mistake!"

Willard thought it was pretty funny, but Mr. Bentley was not amused. Willard was a rather rough, happy fellow. He broke the law readily and thought nothing of it, sometimes acting like it was the thing to do. But he liked Mr. Bentley well enough, and said he was easy to work for. Willard said that when Mr. Bentley came around and you had a little sweat on your brow, he would tell you to take it easy, to sit down and rest a while. Bentley always demanded a full day's work, but if it was hard manual labor he wanted the men to work slow and steady. From all accounts he liked Willard too.

The rest of Willard's friends who worked off and on at the camp didn't feel that way. They were a rather rough bunch. They would laughingly tell all the different ways of getting trout illegally in those days.

One method they used was to put some carbide and a little water in a tin can and cover it tightly. This made acetylene gas, which they would ignite through a small hole in the can. The resulting explosion would stun fish for a great distance around, and they could be easily gathered up.

Another method was to cut the bottom out of a burlap bag and sew it to a second bag to make one very long sack. They would sew a wire hoop around the top of their giant gunny sack to keep its top open. They would mount this device in a narrow spot in a creek and then, by slapping the water with tag alders three or four hundred feet above the bag and working toward it, they would drive the fish into their trap. Willard and his friends would pick out the trout they wanted and release the rest.

While all these fellows worked at White Deer Lake over the years, they never stayed long – only when there was some extra work to do.

The First Snowmobiles

The winters, even the mild ones, were rough in the White Deer Lake country. Ted Tonkin, having seen little snow or cold in England, was amazed by both. He was soon to be initiated into the hard life of a northwoods winter during one of the reporting trips to Champion. Even as a neophyte, he had to take his turn at this job, or bear the ridicule of the other men.

Ted had never even seen a pair of snowshoes before coming to White Deer Lake, let alone used them, and it was his lot to be broken in on them on a 16–mile trip to Champion, alone. On this particular trek it was snowing, windy, and bitter cold. The trip down was tiring but uneventful. On the return trip upgrade, however, the going got a little too rough for the young Englishman. He began to doubt whether he was going to make it back to camp.

Always having believed that discretion was the better part of valor, Ted decided to turn around and go back to an upright log garage that had recently been built alongside the road, about halfway down the grade. It would afford him protection from the weather while he rested there through the night. Ted Tonkin spent a long, miserable, bitter cold night by a small fire in the garage, melting snow to drink and burning everything he could lay his hands on to keep warm. Spending the night alone in the woods is an experience every northwoodsman has to endure sometime in his life, before he can be called a woodsman. Tonkin never forgot that night he became a part of the north country. He had passed the test, and was now a woodsman.

Several interesting innovations and improvements were made in this north country between 1920 and '22. One of these was another step in the development of the snowmobile. Along in 1918, some inventive fellow in Upper Michigan made a snow machine out of a Model T Ford truck. It did pretty well in sleigh ruts in winter snow, or even new snow if it wasn't too

Top: Winter scene near the Beaver cabin.
Middle: One of the Ford snowmobiles – not the kind used at White Deer Lake or Four Island Lake. Courtesy of Ford archives/Henry Ford Museum, Deaborn, Mich.
Bottom: Typical of the snowmobiles at Woodwards and McCormicks, this was used at Grand Island. Courtesy Milo Underhill.

deep. The front wheels of the vehicle were removed, and wide wooden or metal skis attached to the front axles. The front wheels were then mounted behind the rear wheels and two endless tracks were mounted on each of the back sets of tandem wheels, over the tires and all. These strange machines showed up throughout Michgan's Upper Peninsula. The Ford Motor Company did not make them, and there was no patent on them.

The White Deer Lake camp and the Woodwards at Lake Richard each acquired one of these machines in 1921. According to George Sharon of Champion, who drove both the machines in the early 20's, they were good on packed or hard snow, but in new, deep snow or big drifts they were useless. When a good road had been broken by horse and sleigh, caretakers at the Woodward camp to the west used theirs often, but the White Deer Lake machine had such a steep hill to climb on the road into camp that it could rarely make it. For the crew, it proved to be more trouble than it was worth, and was soon abandoned as unreliable. The Woodward machine was used for six or seven winters before it was abandoned, as snowplowing came in. The machines elsewhere in the woods of the Upper Peninsula were in use on a very limited basis for about ten years, and then apparently were given up as impractical. It wasn't until 1927 that it became common practice to plow main roads with the huge, slow–moving diesel Holt tractors equipped with both "V" and double–wing plows, and it wasn't until 1931 that Mr. McCormick started having the Huron Bay Grade and the road into camp plowed all winter.

The Cache

In the years between 1923 and 1926, the new Bentley Trail reached a special degree of elegance. A third cabin had been added to the halfway group as a summer kitchen. It could also be used as an additional guide's cabin if necessary. It was built right to the east of Arbutus Lodge. The old guide's cabin on the west pond was used when there was a cook or butler along with a guide or two, but it was left fully equipped and unlocked at all times. It was known as the "Intruder's Cabin." Cyrus Bentley hoped that a cabin available to the strangers that were now beginning to make their way into this back country might deter them from breaking into the main lodge.

The older generations of the McCormick and Bentley families were now, for the most part, semi–retired, and could stay for longer periods. Mr. Bentley came often even when he was working hard. He never did fully retire. The second generation of the two families were all married except

Gordon McCormick, Cyrus' youngest son. Gordon's older brother, Cyrus III, had married Dorothy Linn. Both boys were graduates of Princeton, as were their uncles and father, and it was assumed that Cyrus III would take over the presidency of the Harvester Company. Instead, he went to England to study at Oxford. He then went with the company, starting as a salesman. In 1917 both boys went in the service, Cyrus III as a lieutenant in the Army Air Corps, and Gordon, first as an artillery instructor, then as an aide to General Charles C. Martin. Gordon then took up architectural training at Princeton. His father donated a building, McCormick Hall, for the School of Architecture there.

By this time, Phoebe Norcross had married Richard Bentley and Margaret Bentley had married David Hamilton, and these young people were using the property to a greater and greater extent.

With the trail getting regular heavy use, it was thought advisable to have a supply of food and staples at the Arbutus Lodge so it wouldn't be necessary to carry so much on every trip. Besides, by now the younger folks were making trips without guides. In 1922 one hundred dollars worth of canned and bottled food was purchased from Montgomery Ward and Company. This large order was bought expressly for the Arbutus Lodge. It was packed out to the property and buried in a cache on the northeast corner of Arbutus Lodge, near the cook tent. When Halls or one of the other butlers performed their duties there, they now had some of the little extras that had been missing before. However, the cache was opened and used so seldom over the next few years that most of the supplies were never used. They were never dug up, and they could be an interesting find today if their exact location was known.

George Baker was still the trail cook and guide for the hiking parties that originated at the north end of the trail. Even though George was working for Huron Mountain Club, Mr. Bentley had an agreement with Mr. Perkins, the Club manager, that he could use George whenever necessary.

Trail Troubles

George Baker tells some trail stories occurring in those years:

Along the upper Elm Creek part of the new Bentley Trail were some abrupt hills that had to be climbed as the trail crossed and recrossed the creek. The trail would drop down one side of a gully, cross the creek on a small bridge, and then climb the other side of the gully. Mr. Bentley had sent George and Dutch John out from Huron Mountain to improve this part of the trail.

Top: Cyrus McCormick III – late 1920's.
Bottom: Gordon McCormick 1920's.

They eyed up two large hemlocks that could be dropped across the valley of the creek and hewn to form a double bridge. They decided this would be just what was needed, and went to work on it. One tree was dropped at an angle across the river, from one side of the high ridge to the other. The log was trimmed and set into place, then hewn flat with an adz. Then the second tree was cut in the same manner across the first, set, and adzed off. The task took the two men two days to accomplish, but when they were through, both men were very proud of the improvement. They completed the bridge with a hand rail for each log, and returned to Huron Mountain.

When Cyrus Bentley came to the new double bridge for the first time on his next trip, he was delighted. He stopped and examined the work, went back and forth a few times, and made a few pleased comments. There was no dropping into the gully, crossing the river twice, and climbing out again as before. The bridge was engineered well, and was both picturesque and practical. He complimented George and John on their good judgment and clever craftsmanship.

That fall, though, two timber cruisers from the Cleveland–Cliffs Iron Co. came upon their handiwork. Cleveland–Cliffs owned the land at this point and, while Mr. Bentley had their written permission to build his trail on their land, it was spelled out on the permit that he could cut no merchantable timber. Mr. Bentley received a bill of $50 for each tree.

There was a southbound trip in 1923 on which both George and Cyrus Bentley were along. Anyone could see it was going to be a wet one; the sky was black over Lake Superior. The clouds were moving in from the west, closing in on the Huron Mountains.

George Baker had no rain gear, but he had often seen guests carrying umbrellas. Now, an umbrella is just about the least practical thing you can have in the woods. It hooks on every limb and twig. But the new Bentley Trail was trimmed out high and wide enough to use one, so George brought one along. As soon as it started to rain, up went George's umbrella. Few if any of the group noticed it, as he was walking at the end of the line, carrying the pack. The others in the party had raincoats and ponchos.

It was not long before Mr. Bentley, who was at the front of the line, glanced back and saw George with his umbrella. He quickly caught George's eye and gave him the sternest of stern looks. These were all too familiar to George. He caught the signal but said nothing, and hung onto his umbrella as if nothing had happened. George received a few more glares before the trip was over, but he ignored them all.

When they reached the Arbutus Lodge, Mr. Bentley took George aside. "Baker," he said sharply, "A northwoods guide just doesn't go through the woods carrying an umbrella."

George did not hesitate to defend himself. He explained that he had seen guests do it, and besides, he didn't own any rain gear. Furthermore, he couldn't afford to get soaking wet. He could do it when he was younger, and had done so often with no problem, but now he was drawing near forty years old, and he couldn't take the cold and wet any more. He would catch–cold and get aching muscles easily.

Mr. Bentley had no recourse. He hesitated a moment and then turned and left without a word. That Christmas, though, he sent George two beautiful woolen checkered lumberjack shirts, the finest money could buy. They were perfect for the woods. They shed water for a long time, but even if they did get wet one would stay warm.

There was another trip that didn't involve Mr. Bentley. George Baker was accompanying six young ladies as far as the Arbutus Lodge. They would be met there by another guide, who would take them to the south end of the trail while George returned to Huron Mountain.

On this particular trip, George was completely in charge. The young girls were not "woodsy" in any sense of the word. They wore long dresses, and most had very poor shoes for walking in the woods and over rock. George took it slow and easy, with plenty of rest stops. The whole group was laughing, talkative, and full of questions. George would just as soon have quit the talking and gotten on with the walking so they would reach their destination at a reasonable hour, but he wanted to be polite.

They were on the hewn log walk near George's spring, just south of Canyon Lake, when they encountered a huge bear dropping, fairly fresh and right on the hewn pathway. George hesitated a moment, then gingerly stepped over it. He turned to see just what he should do about it. He could either ignore it, or find a stick and remove it from the walkway.

It was too late. The first girl stepped over it, and each of the others in turn lifted her dress and, with the daintiest of maneuvers, stepped over the dropping. As the last girl stepped up to the obstacle she paused, and with wide eyes and complete seriousness asked, "George, did some man do this right in the middle of the trail?"

George was taken aback, but immediately retorted, "If it was a man, it was a hell of a big one."

It was during the 1920's that some women began to dress a little more sensibly for the woods. Styles for the well–dressed young woman had gone to long dresses again, but older women shortened their skirts to about mid–calf length to go hiking, and some even wore breeches or knee–length knickers. Better walking shoes for women were also coming into vogue, with low heels. The height of the shoe varied from ankle to knee. The high, knee–length boots were popular with the men at the time, and women were beginning to use them more and more.

Trips that went out from the Huron Mountain end of the trail were often ill–prepared for the long walks, as many guests were in the north country for the first time. They had no idea what to expect, and often did not have the proper boots or clothing.

From the south, however, it was a different story. The McCormick and Bentley guests were given many instructions. Then, too, there was a supply of gear and clothing in all sizes and varieties. Often a person was outfitted from the skin out, then invited to just keep the clothing. Hobnailed boots were deemed by some to be good for walking, and Gordon and young Cyrus McCormick III had theirs especially made in England.

After some 20 years of walking this country back and forth, Mr. Bentley had it down to a science. He knew, but did not always tell, where time could be made up or lost. He knew that the trip north dropped over a thousand feet in altitude, and was much easier than the trip south, where the hikers climbed the same thousand feet. Much depended on the force and direction of the wind on the various lakes, especially Mountain Lake, and even on who was rowing or running the motor.

When headed north or when Mr. Bentley was in the group, the Mountain Lake trip was often leisurely, if the crossers had made good time and the weather was nice. This was near the end of the trip and was a good time to relax and reflect on the hike, and drink in the beauty of Mountain Lake itself. Going south, however, time had to be made up on Mountain Lake if possible. This was now near the beginning of the trip, and it was essential that they be ahead of time at the start. At this point, Mr. Bentley was all business. Every little thing counted, as the long climb was ahead of them. He would be furious if there was trouble getting the motor started, or if the guide took a rambling route up the lake.

George Baker tells another story which well illustrates Mr. Bentley's anguish if the guide did not keep a straight course between two points. It was on Mountain Lake, and there was a party of several people, including Bentley, headed from Huron Mountain to White Deer Lake. The year was 1924, and George Baker was the only guide. As was often the case in those later years, George would only accompany the group as far as the Arbutus Lodge where he would cook the evening meal, and breakfast the next

Top: Complex of boathouses behind a point on the north end of Mountain Lake.
Bottom: Oscar boat at the Canyon Lake landing on Mountain Lake.

morning. He would straighten things out at the cabin after the party went south, then return to Huron Mountain. The group would be met by a second guide from the south.

The boathouses on the north end of Mountain Lake had been moved by this time, away from the sand beach to a spot across the bay hidden by a point of land. They are still located there. The move was necessary because of the predominantly west wind which was just too destructive to the boats in the old boathouses, and it sometimes presented great difficulties in getting a boat under way against the wind and waves in the shallow water.

A new bridge had been built over Mountain Stream at the lumber camp clearing above the falls, and a trail was put in along the stream to the complex of boathouses hidden behind the point. The trail hikers took this trail to the boathouses. With the increased trail use, Mr. Bentley had bought a new, graceful, six–oar boat. The new one was painted white. Its transom was too low and slanted for the motor, so the Rushton was there also.

The hiking party climbed into the Bentley longboat, the Rushton with the little deck all the way around and the nickel–plated brass rail on the bow deck. Oars were always taken along in case of motor trouble. Mr. Bentley chose the bow seat as usual to direct the course, and George Baker sat in the large stern seat to run the 1916 Evinrude outboard motor. Mr. Bentley would give directions by hand signals from the bow. George knew the routine well. No one bothered talking once the motor was started, as it was so loud that they would have to scream and shout.

Luckily, this day the motor started in just ten or fifteen pulls of the starter rope. Many were the times when the motor wouldn't start at all, but each pull of the cord, after winding it on the wheel each time, would send the boat down the lake a little distance. George had gone the whole length of the lake in this manner more than once. He had also often been blown astray while trying to start the motor. On happy occasions someone would man the oars until the motor was operating.

As soon as the boat was around the point and headed up the lake, Mr. Bentley started gesturing for George to get on course. He wanted a straight course to the end of Hebard Point, a mile or so up the lake. This was a prominent rocky point, often called "Whiskey Point" which came into view beyond Mount Homer when you were far enough out in the lake.

As the boat approached Hebard Point, a second wooded point appeared on the opposite shore. It was this second point that Mr. Bentley began concentrating on. George fixed his course at about a twenty–yard distance out from the point because he knew there was a large submerged log just off the point. Obviously Mr. Bentley had no knowledge of it, as he

Top: White Deer Lake camp crew in 1920's, L Ruben Wangburg (cook), Ted Tonkin (in rear) dining room help and butler Stevens seated in front – Mr. Bentley's secretary.
Middle: Occasionally during off season or especially when work was being done on the island a walkway was put up for the benefit of workmen.
Lower left: The garden at Bulldog Lake clearing.
Lower right: Christ Andersen – early 1920's.

signaled to George to nose the boat over toward the point. George looked him straight in the eye and did not change the course one iota.

This threw Mr. Bentley into some violent gyrations which meant only one thing – "Change course!" Baker nodded calmly but did not obey. Mr. Bentley gave him a ferocious glare, accompanied by an exaggerated hand signal over the heads of the passengers – "Get over!–Head for the point!" He was mad now. He meant business, and George Baker knew it. Since there was no way to explain about the deadhead, he adjusted his course over toward the point. Mr. Bentley nodded in satisfaction.

A moment later, just off the point, the boat hit the deadhead. The boat's momentum carried it right up out of the water, bow high in the air, with loud cracking noises that sounded as if the keel were breaking. Then the boat's balance shifted and it began to roll, nearly tipping everyone overboard. As the bow plunged toward the water, the stern rose high in the air. Then there was a mighty roar from the water–free engine which added to the fright of the passengers. Coming off the log, the boat rolled crazily before finally trimming itself into a steady course once more.

The guests looked around with stunned expressions on their faces. Not at all ready for their crash, they still did not know what had happened. Mr. Bentley looked back at George in complete bewilderment. George smiled, winked, and nodded reassuringly, as if to say, "I told you so!" Throughout the whole episode, not a single word had been spoken.

Upon reaching the Canyon Lake landing, Mr. Bentley took George down the trail, out of earshot of the rest of the party. Shaking a finger under George's nose, he scolded, "Don't you ever talk back to me again!"

Improvements at Rough Camp

Ted Tonkin eventually became the superintendent of White Deer Lake and spent the rest of his life there, although his family spent the winters in Ishpeming. Ted held the position for 38 years, and undoubtedly spent more time in the White Deer Lake country than any other person.

Sometime in the mid–1930's, Mr. Tonkin wrote a camp history. While it only covered the period from his promotion to superintendent up until 1936, it is well written, and is the most authoritative existing account covering this time period. We will rely heavily on this document in telling our story. The original is in the McCormick Estate Archives in Chicago, and a copy was owned by Mrs. Ted Tonkin, who died in Durango, Colorado in 1984. This copy is now in the possession of Mrs. Tonkin's daughter.

Ted Tonkin's early experiences at White Deer Lake from 1922 to 1925 pretty well tell the story of the goings–on at camp. When he first arrived there, the superintendent of the camp was a Swiss–German named Giovanoli who, with his wife, was only there a short time.

Bill Raymond was a trapper who also worked on the crew at the camp. A lake in the southeast part of the McCormick property seems to have been named for this fellow, though no one seems to know why. It is still called Lake Raymond today, and he probably took Mr. McCormick on his first trip there.

The carpenter at that time was Mike Jarvis, with George Sharon and Alfred LaForest as helpers. Edwing Windall was the Island Man, and Bernard LaCosse the assistant cook.

One thing impressed Tonkin right away: the fact that Bentley didn't seem to trust his employees (with good reason in a few cases) and Ted was very surprised to learn that he was expected to fill out a summary worksheet accounting for every hour of the working day. Tonkin's day started at six in the morning and went through the completion of dinner in the evening, sometimes after eight. In going over the work sheets, Mr. Bentley pointed out that there should be an hour of recreation sometime during the day.

From his first meeting with Cyrus Bentley and Cyrus McCormick, Tonkin formed a lasting impression of the two men. He felt that Bentley typified the English idea of an American millionaire, while McCormick could have been just an everyday English gentleman himself. Of Mrs. Bentley, Tonkin said, "She was, in my opinion, a grand person and did much to tell me that there were real people living in this land of hurry and riches."

In August of 1922, an argument broke out between Mr. Bentley's secretary, Emil Christiansen and the superintendent, Giovanoli. Emil packed his suitcase and walked down the road all the way to Champion. This was a northwoods custom – if things didn't go right, you walked down the road, usually without a word to anyone. It was done often in the lumber camps, but Tonkin was astonished. The next day, Mr. Giovanoli also packed his bag, took his wife, climbed into his Winton Six, and drove off down the road.

Mr. Stillwell, of the McCormick estates in Chicago, sent Mr. George Lamb, a concrete contractor, to be the next superintendent at the camp. Lamb was new to the woods, and it soon became apparent that he would not be at the camp more than a year or two at best. Also, to accommodate a large group in September of 1922, Mr. Bentley hired another butler. Unlike Tonkin, he had actually been trained for the job. He was right from England too. His name was Charles Donald Benjamin Hakin Edward Stevens. He was an amusing fellow, and very efficient. He was older than Tonkin, almost fifty, and had been a drummer in the Boer War. He had been gassed in World War I and was sent to America on a War Bond Drive. He and Tonkin became very close friends.

Under the direction of George Lamb, plumbing was put in the Chimney Cabin for the first time in 1922. It came from the springs back in the hills by gravity feed. A daily afternoon tub bath was a ritual Mr. Bentley never missed, and Tonkin says that it was a disaster when work on the plumbing interfered with this routine. The main pipe to the island was on a trestle above the lake level, a rather unsightly arrangement.

When George Lamb left at the end of the summer, he was replaced by Antoine Hebert who had worked for the camp off and on for years. But things didn't go right for Antoine either, and he too packed his bag and walked down the road. And so it went, much of the help being as hard to please as Mr. Bentley.

A caretaker's cabin was started in November of 1922, and completed in the spring of 1923. This would make it much more pleasant for a superintendent, and thus easier to get one to stay.

Again that winter, the only contact with the outside world was by snowshoe, two men at a time every other weekend. Sometimes they pulled back a toboggan load of supplies.

It was a great undertaking to prepare for an early visit from Mr. McCormick in May of 1923, but Lamb had returned in the early spring to get things organized. All the cabins on the island had to be scrubbed, lamps filled and polished, wicks trimmed, water cans polished, wood boxes filled, and a thousand other jobs had to be taken care of. Usually Mr. McCormick's visits lasted only a few days, after which Mr. Bentley would arrive and use the remainder of Mr. McCormick's month.

Almost any project that far from civilization was a big undertaking. These were the very early years of the automobile in the north country, and the road up the Grade was in terrible condition – just two deep ruts all the way, some places too deep to maneuver, some places flooded over by the river, and all of the old railroad bridges in a very poor state of repair. Up to 1923, all work on the Huron Bay Grade road from Champion was done by teams or, after 1920, sometimes a truck from Champion, but all of it paid for by McCormick and Bentley. In 1923 the work on the road was taken over by the White Deer Lake crew. The whole distance had to be brushed, and Lamb's Ford truck was used to haul gravel from several pits along the way in an attempt to fill in the ruts.

In November of 1923, the camp obtained its first tractor, a 10–20 International. It had high steel wheels with spade lugs for winter and bar lugs for summer. Lamb used the tractor well into the winter months for trips into Champion. On one of these trips the oil plug came out of the oil pan, and the machine lost its oil, unnoticed by Lamb. After a few more miles, three bearings burned out, which meant extensive repairs in Champion. When Lamb started out on his return trip to camp, he heard some other strange noises. Two more bearings should have been replaced, as they were in terrible shape when he reached camp. This, of course, meant a snowshoe hike to Champion to order the parts, and several days' wait there until they arrived.

Tonkin made the trip alone. On the return trip to camp, walking conditions were so severe that he just couldn't make it back to camp that day. Again he had to spend a long night in a garage about four miles from camp. It took him four hours the next morning to snowshoe the last four miles in the deep, soft snow.

Cyrus McCormick's sons spent a lot of time at White Deer Lake that summer. Ted Tonkin mentions one trip he went on with them and Cyrus III's wife, Dorothy Linn McCormick, who went along as an assistant compass man. Bancroft Hammond was also there. They traveled cross–country from the recently named Acropolis (a high rock knob) to Island Lake. They made another trip from the Acropolis to Bulldog Lake. It was probably during these years that Birch Lake was renamed in honor of Dorothy McCormick, young Cyrus' wife. It used to be called Lake Dorothy but, as so often happens, the lake has been misspelled on recent government maps and is now known as "Lake Dortay."

There were two gardens that summer of 1923. One of them was for potatoes out at Bulldog Lake, but it turned out to be impractical. The quack grass and the deer just took over there. Christ Andersen and his wife and baby stayed there and worked that garden while it lasted.

Mr. Bentley wanted fresh vegetables if at all possible. Since everything had to be imported from beyond Champion, they tried to raise what they could at camp. A great deal of time, effort and money was spent trying to raise peas, beans, tomatoes, cabbage, lettuce, asparagus and onions in this rock–infested country against tremendous odds. The snow didn't leave until the end of May, and there were always groundhogs, deer, and rocks of all sizes. Charles Stevens was the gardener.

It was also in 1923 that George Lamb had an operation for ulcers, and had to leave the premises for six weeks. During this period Ted Tonkin was put in charge.

Some of the Frenchmen from Champion thought this was a poor choice. They made remarks like, "Imagine giving that job to an English butler when Christ Andersen knows every inch of this country and has been

Upper left: Ruben Wangburg as Island boy (1925).
Upper right: Axel making the long cut.
Middle right: Ruben holding the ice spud over Axel's head.
Bottom: Cutting ice 1926.

living in the woods for years!" The truth was that Christ had already had his chance and, for one reason or another, it hadn't worked out. Besides, his wife didn't like it there. Christ probably wished he could have kept the foreman's job but now, with his wife vowing not to stay another summer, it was out of the question.

The floating bridge that Christ had built no longer floated after the construction of the dam at Bulldog Lake a few years earlier had raised the water level. It seemed that Mr. Bentley didn't want to destroy the bridge while Christ was still around, as if he did not want him to feel bad by seeing his clever idea and hard work undone.

For a year or so, walking the north side of the lakes meant a long detour up toward Island Lake, then across a marsh at a narrow point and through the woods for over half a mile on a lumber road to the north side of Bulldog Lake. When that spot was reached by this route, it meant an about–face to get on the Bentley Trail heading north.

The trail around the south side of the lakes was picturesque, but much longer than necessary. At any rate, it was after the Andersens left in 1923 that Mr. Bentley began making serious plans to improve this last piece of the trail. He and the crew talked about it a lot in the summer of 1924, and made some preparations and gathered materials for the work to be done.

The cake of "spring ice" had improved also. it had now evolved from a square cake to a 16 ft. x 2 ft. rectangle. When completely frozen, the long piece could easily be cut into two–foot cubes to be stored separately from the lake ice. The spring ice was used in drinks, while the lake ice was used for cooling purposes in the ice boxes.

It was in the early fall of 1923 that the Andersen family at the Bulldog Lake clearing decided that they definitely would not be returning the following summer. They had no plans except that they would be leaving. They told no one until they were ready to pull out.

Some of the crew had a little inkling of what was to come when a few special friends were invited to a party at the shack where the Andersens were living. They invited Emil Christiansen, Charles Stevens, Jack Hotz, and Ted Tonkin. It was the only affair of its kind ever held at Bulldog Lake, as the Andersens were the only family ever to live there. Christ must have played his accordion, as he always did on other occasions. There probably were a lot of stories told, and a lot of food eaten. That fall the Andersens left for Racine, Wisconsin, and left the employ of White Deer Lake forever.

Tonkin wrote in his notes, "The party at Bulldog Lake was the highlight of the summer."

Richard Bentley's first son was born on May 29, 1924. The event went unheralded at White Deer Lake, as Mr. Bentley never brought children there until they were older and Mr. McCormick had no grandchildren of his own. While the living there had become quite elegant in the summers, they still thought of it as a rough camp.

A new foreman arrived in May of 1924. He was James Berry from Chicago, who had been the superintendent of the big McCormick home called "Walden" in Lake Forest, Illinois. George Lamb stayed on a few weeks to show him the ropes.

Tonkin was sent to Chicago to study the mechanics of outboard motors. When he returned, he drove up a brand new Model S International truck loaded with camp supplies and a new outboard motor to be used for trail crossings on White Deer Lake and Bulldog Lake. The truck was used a great deal for working on the road and finishing the outside work around the new caretaker's–house, and for building a new road around the south end of this house down to the lake.

With numerous guides available at Huron Mountain, Mr. McCormick felt that there should always be at least one guide available at White Deer Lake who was capable of leading guests over any of the camp trails. With Christ Andersen gone, a new person had to be found to learn the trails. There had been so many changes in personnel in the past few years that McCormick and Bentley found themselves in a situation where none of the help knew the back country, the history, or the trails. There had been a loss of continuity. At that time Henry Ford was paying $5 a day for labor, and many local people were heading for Detroit for jobs.

Again McCormick and Bentley turned to Tonkin. He seemed steady and reliable, and appeared to have no thoughts of leaving. He was sent out to learn the trails, lakes, and surrounding country. Among other things, Ted would be the trail guide when they needed one. The other personnel at camp at that time were Mr. and Mrs. Berry, Miss Burns (the cook), Jack Hotz (the Island Man), William Raymond, and Reuben Wangberg.

Reuben was from Ishpeming. He had graduated from the Ishpeming High School and gone to work at White Deer Lake right away. He tells of working on Mr. Bentley's trail with a crew using brush hooks, spring, summer and fall. They slashed back the tree branches as well as the tall weeds. It was no small job, and it had to be done perfectly.

Mr. McCormick and Mr. Bentley each had their own ideas about how a trail should be built across a wet spot. Bentley liked long planked corduroy, while McCormick preferred rotted wood over corduroy that had been sunk into these muddy places. Bentley wanted the trail cut back wide enough to walk with an umbrella, while McCormick wanted the trail cut back very little, but insisted on a nice smooth trail to walk on. He did not like built–in steps or stumbling on debris. It worked out all right for each, as McCormick confined his interests to the trails to and around the various nearby lakes and the Castle Rock area, while Bentley kept to the two falls on the Yellowdog River and the Yellowdog Plains area to the north.

Trail crews coming off Mr. Bentley's portion of the trails had a greater distance to travel. Often they could not get back to camp in time for dinner, and ended up staying in the cabin at Bulldog Lake where Christ Andersen had lived with his family the year before.

Reuben Wangberg describes the camp at the head of Bulldog Lake, five miles from White Deer Lake camp and the camp bunkhouse. "The beds had a thick straw mattress to sleep on. No blankets, but there was a thin straw tick to cover us. Sometimes the stuff would get you itchy. Thank goodness no bedbugs – but we had them at the bunkhouse on the hill, where you came down into camp. I remember my first night in my bunk. I woke up scratching all over. Turned on my flashlight. The sheet looked all bloody, but that was crushed bedbugs. I turned my light on the logs back of the bed and saw the live bugs crawling into cracks and crannies."

Reuben also said you could be sure Mr. Bentley was going to check your work on the trail. He told of one time Mr. Bentley was walking with guests to check out the trail: "He had a bad habit of blowing wind, which was quite amusing to us because at the moment he did it he would produce a giant sized handkerchief, well perfumed, to temper the offending odor."

Toward the end of the summer of 1924, Cyrus McCormick and Cyrus Bentley asked Ted Tonkin if he would like to take over the management of White Deer Lake Camp. It seems that Mr. Berry was semi–retired and did not intend to work much longer.

Tonkin liked the northwoods and enjoyed the varied routine of camp life. He had stood up well under the rigors of the winters, and apparently had done a satisfactory job of running things during the six weeks he had taken over for George Lamb. He was also enjoying the confidence of the men. Ted Tonkin gladly accepted the offer. The change was to become effective on December 1, 1924.

Mildred Halls had been coming to White Deer Lake Camp with her parents off and on for a period of years. She eventually became a part–time cook there in 1923.

Ted Tonkin had been engaged to a girl in England, but in 1923 he received word that she had died. Soon Ted and Mildred took up together. They were a good match – both were English, both enjoyed working at the camp, and both looked forward to staying there for a long time. The culminating factor seemed to be that Ted was now about to become the superintendent.

On Thanksgiving Day, 1924, Ted Tonkin and Mildred Halls were married in Chicago. The couple returned to White Deer Lake two days later.

While the Tonkins were in Chicago, Mr. and Mrs. Cyrus McCormick III were at camp for a snowy Thanksgiving vacation. Nelson Currier from Champion was doing the cooking for them.

The same car that brought the Tonkins up the Huron Bay Grade took the McCormicks out. The only thing that marred the Tonkins' return to camp was the fact that the water was left on in the island buildings and the whole system froze solid, breaking the pipes and requiring extensive repairs.

The first two winter projects under Tonkin's direction—were to replumb the island and replace the last section of the New Bentley Trail. Both extremely important duties were completed before spring. These jobs were a test of Tonkin's abilities to get things done, and he came through with flying colors.

The plumbing took about a month. The trail took much longer, but the men got to it in January of 1925. The crewmen at the time were Gus Carlson, John Beck, Alec Sands, Andrew Mattson and John Maki. Nelson Currier was the cook, but he did not like it at White Deer Lake. It was too isolated, and he felt they were expecting too much of him. On the 24th of March he left, and Mildred Tonkin took over the cooking.

Completing the Bentley Trail

As to the completion of the Bentley Trail, Ted Tonkin had been around long enough to know what Mr. Bentley wanted. They had discussed the project many times, and had even done some preparation for the job the previous year.

Ted Tonkin tells the story:

Quite a large percentage of the material was gathered from the surrounding swampland and there was a fair amount of material which had been gathered previously with a view to doing this work. In January of 1925 the job was started, and the crew snowshoed or walked, depending on lake conditions, up to Bulldog each day, taking their noonday meal with them. A platform was built about eight feet high which could be moved from one set of posts to another. The scheme was to cut through the ice, measure with a steel rod the depth to the hardpan, cut the post to the required length, then after setting it in place, to mount to the top of the platform and hammer the post down with a huge hardwood sledge hammer. One set of posts consisted of two piles completed with a cross piece to carry the planked corduroy. The average depth of each post driven into the lake bed was seven feet. The length of the completed bridge was 1,400 feet. The weather hit a low of 40 below zero on two occasions. Fire destroyed a tent in which we had our midday meal one day, but luckily the food piled around the stove remained intact. We used a single horse from Champion with a large hand sleigh to pull the corduroy logs into position. An amazing feature is that this horse walked over the ice all the way, including the channel, and on no occasion was in danger of 'going through.'–The job was completed in early March of 1925, about the 11th.

Now, for the first time, the trail was in the shape that Mr. Bentley wanted it to be. Many crossings were made that summer, and both boats on Mountain Lake were in use.

Though the superintendent's house was completed and had been used the previous winter by the Berrys, Mr. Berry took the heating system with him when he left. So, when the Tonkins took over, they were obliged to live in two rooms below the dining room. There was a lavatory and a tub, but no hot water. Water had to be heated on the stove. The rooms were poorly heated and had cracks in the chinking right through to the outdoors. However, to the Tonkins it was ideal. They could make things more pleasant as time went on, and they had no complaints.

While they were living in these basement rooms, the superintendent's house was being remodeled to suit their needs. A bathroom was installed, the fireplace taken down, and a morning room was made into a bedroom. There were to be two apartments in the building, one for the Tonkins, one for a cook or island man, so a partition was installed in the large living room.

Mr. Bentley had the idea that the partition between the two apartments should be filled with sawdust for soundproofing. Tonkin says he sent Alex Sand and Andrew Mattson to get three or four bags of sawdust. They were both Finnish–speaking Finns and apparently there was a lack of communication. They came back with several bags of tin cans!

In April of 1925 Halls, the first butler at White Deer Lake and Mildred Tonkin's father, died at his home in Wisconsin. He had worked off

Top: The 1400 foot Bulldog Lake Causeway – Last piece of the Bentley Trail.
Bottom: Willard Brunette with wife and daughter in Champion. Courtesy of Willard Brunette.

and on at the camp when McCormick and Bentley were there, right up until a year or so before his death.

While Mildred Tonkin filled in as a cook now and then, other cooks came and went. For Mr. Bentley's visit in May of 1925, Stevens returned to cook. Later, Mildred Tonkin found Lydia and John Stimke from Iowa. Lydia did the cooking and John was a laborer at the camp.

John was a big German fellow. Reuben Wangberg tells some stories about him:

John was Reuben's saw partner when they were cutting firewood one day. Reuben says he completely wore him out, and he told Tonkin never to put him with Stimke again. It took Reuben several days to straighten out his shoulders. A sawyer on the end of a crosscut is supposed to pull a straight stroke, but John, like so many newcomers to the woods, would pull the saw to one side at the end of the stroke, causing it to bind. No one can put in an eight–hour day, or even a half–day, with a saw partner like that.

One day in the winter when they were putting up ice, Reuben and Axel Axelson were sawing the ice strips and preparing to cut a strip into cakes. John Stimke stepped on one of the strips. It broke off and he went into the lake for an ice bath. They fished him out and got him up to the bunk house to thaw out. That same afternoon John came out on the ice again in dry clothes. You guessed it – he stepped on the strip again, and had to be hauled out a second time.

Mrs. Stimke had her trials at camp too. Reuben tells a story about her:

"She always fed the squirrels outside the kitchen door. One day...one squirrel near her foot took the wrong exit and scampered up inside her skirts. He was trying every way he could to get out, without success. She was like a wild lady, the poor soul, and we couldn't help."

The trail projects that year were all aimed to put the Bentley Trail into tiptop condition. No stone must be left unturned to perfect the trail, although Mr. Bentley did admit to Tonkin that it was getting expensive and maybe Mr. McCormick's idea of rotten wood in the soft spots would be better than hewn logs in the future.

Despite the financial pinch, they did go ahead with a summer kitchen to the east of Arbutus Lodge. All material other than the logs and rafters had to be hauled to the plains on the backs of men.

Wheelbarrows and packstraps were the order of the day, and two trips per man per day was deemed a good day's work. The summer kitchen cabin turned out beautifully. It was made of upright logs like the first Guide's Cabin, complete with a Coleman stove, and for the first time there was no open–fire cooking at Arbutus Lodge. Mr. Bentley was delighted with the new summer kitchen. He felt that the trail had reached perfection that year, though the trail through the Yellowdog swamp had deteriorated somewhat and the corduroy needed replacing, as it had been there for ten or 12 years.

Reuben Wangberg says the winter of 1925–26 was a severe one, with lots of snow and the temperature dipping as low as 45 below zero several times. He wore a beard to protect his face, but his eyes suffered from the diamond–like snow. He nearly went snow blind. He says he squinted the rest of his life as a result.

Reuben was also a cook in the winter. He slept in the storeroom over the kitchen. Since all the staple foods were kept there, the mice had a good time in the prunes, currants and raisins. Reuben had to go over them, especially the currants, with a fine–toothed comb to be sure there weren't any mouse droppings in them. He says the currants were great for cooking, but he was sure he missed some of the mouse droppings. Reuben adopted a little kitten to take care of the mouse problem. It slept on his bed, and they became close friends. It soon got to the mouse situation, and caught a lot of them.

In the late spring, Mr. Bentley spotted the cat with a bird in its mouth. He ordered it destroyed. With a heavy heart, Reuben put his pal in a sack with a big rock, rowed to the middle of the lake, and dropped it in. That really hurt.

When Mr. Bentley learned that Reuben cooked for the crew in the winter, he offered to send him to cooking school in Chicago, all expenses paid. When he was through, he could come and work at White Deer Lake and cook for the guests only. Reuben thought it was very tempting, but he wasn't ready for the big city life. It scared him a little. His mother had recently been widowed, and he felt he should stay home and help her out financially. As it turned out, Reuben worked at White Deer Lake for three years and then went to work for a wealthy family in Bloomfield Hills, Michigan. He did gardening and landscaping for three different families for eighteen years. Other than farm for seven years near Boyne City, Michigan, Reuben Wangberg worked for private families for 42 years in all. The highlight of his life was a first prize from the Michigan Horticultural Society for the best–kept gardens, a great honor. In 1976 Reuben's wife died of cancer, and he spent his time between summers in Charlevoix and winters in Largo, Florida. He has a daughter and two grandchildren there today (1983).

Speaking of grandchildren, Alice Bentley was born to Richard and Phoebe Bentley on May 3, 1926. She was their second child, and the fourth grandchild of Cyrus Bentley.

Book Two

Back at camp in 1926, there was a Model S International truck, a 10–20 tractor, a Model T Ford truck, the Bentleys' Dodge touring car, and the Tonkins' modest Model T coupe. Automobiles had really taken over now, and it became necessary to have a good garage and a good road. Axel Axelson built a new and larger garage, which stood until 1984. It was the least–repaired building in camp for more than 50 years.

The road up the Huron Bay Grade needed a lot of work in that summer of 1926. The 16 miles of mud and gravel had two deep ruts all the way. Mr. Bentley had a solution. He had two boards taken out of the bed of the truck box, one just behind each rear tire. As they drove slowly down the road, a man in the back of the truck would shovel gravel into these slots. Then, Mr. Bentley suggested gathering dead leaves from the woods and doing the same thing with them, over the gravel. Reuben Wangberg says they did this for the whole 16 miles of road, working all fall. Mr. Bentley thought the leaves would stabilize the road and eliminate the bumps. They did, too, but it was a lot of work.

There were a lot of situations where things had to be accomplished by untried means. That's a part of living in the woods. Both Mr. Bentley and Ted Tonkin were good at coming up with ideas. They didn't always work, but how can you tell if you don't try?

Reuben Wangberg tells another story. One time they came to a gully like the one that Dutch John and George Baker had bridged. This time, Tonkin decided to fell a large white pine across it. This was in the heat of the summer.

Wangberg: "That day we forgot the bottles of kerosene. The bottles had notched corks in them to oil the saw. Two men couldn't put their arms around this tree. The saw stuck in the pitch. Tonkin opened a food sack and took out a half pound of butter and smeared it all over the saw on both sides. It went through easy then. We held the log with cant hooks while Axel, the Finn, went down the log, notching with a big broad axe. Then he started back taking the slab off and the surface was as smooth and flat as a floor. We turned it over and presto, we had a bridge. We also cut and barked cedar logs, in summer, to certain lengths and made cribbing to hold rocks to support bridges on approaches."

Reuben tells some more about Stimke, the big German. "He was always eating and always hungry. 24 loaves of bread were baked every week, twelve at a time, in the big wood stove. While we dined, John kept chiming to pass the bread. Finally the Finns threw the bread slices at him. One day in the woods, he opened his pack at 10:00 and was eating. He wanted me to join him, but I declined. Tonkin came upon us and, of course, while my partner was eating, I was idle. Tonkin issued John a stern warning to eat at 12 noon."

779

A very important conference with the Marquette County Road Commission was held that summer. Mr. McCormick invited them all up to the camp for lunch, and they discussed the remaining railroad bridges. Dr. VanRiper from Champion was the chairman of the County Board of Supervisors, and K. I. Sawyer from Ishpeming was the superintendent of the road commission. Mr. Sawyer suggested that the McCormick crew timber–brace the south bridge, put a center support in another, and tie all of them with cables to eliminate sway. If McCormick and Bentley would continue to maintain the road for a few years, the road commission would discuss replacing some of the bridges at county expense. McCormick could well have replaced the bridges, but did not want to go to such an expense when everyone else would be using the road.

In September, Ted Tonkin's cousin, Ernest Trevithick, arrived from England to work at White Deer Lake. He became a good friend of Reuben Wangberg's, and Reuben has some stories to tell about him also. Reuben says that Ernest had never seen snow 'til the day he arrived. By then, early winter, there was a good deal of snow in camp.

> Ernie's first try on skis was a riot. He went up a small grade into camp, kind of shaky, and decided to try the skis. When he got near the bottom he lost control, started laughing, his dentures flew out and he went head–first into a pile of snow. We roared, then pulled him out. We went to the carpenter shop and got rakes and started to rake snow to find the teeth.

It was at about this time that Mildred Tonkin gave birth to her first child. Mildred was very calm about the whole thing. She went to Ishpeming and stayed with Reuben Wangberg's parents for a few days before the baby was born. At the appointed time, Mrs. Tonkin walked through Wangberg's alley over to the hospital, got into bed, and gave birth. It was a boy, born September 21, 1926. He was named Cecil Halls Tonkin, but was always called "Teddy Bear." Later his nickname changed to "Bearsie." A few days after Bearsie was born, there was a tremendous rainstorm that caused several large washouts on the hills of the camp road, and the water was so deep at the Rock Dam on the Peshekee that it was 3 feet over the road. There was no traveling to or from camp for 3 or 4 days. McCormick crews had to remove a lot of wood from the dam to keep it from happening again.

During this storm, Reuben Wangberg was washing dishes in the kitchen when he heard several loud pops. He looked down under the sink and saw balls of fire as big as golf balls dancing back and forth between two water pipes. He got out of there in a hurry.

That fall, Mr. Bentley gave orders to go ahead and install electricity on the mainland. Tonkin went out and got bids, and the job was done by the Kohler dealer from Houghton. This was probably the biggest step toward modernization since the first automobile made its way up the grade.

The End of the Trail

Up to this time, life for the Bentleys and McCormicks at White Deer Lake had been improving every year. The rough work, the carving out and planning, were all completed. From now on, the job at hand was replacing, repairing, maintaining, and improving the camp. The road in, the electricity, and the hot water were all things that began as luxuries, then became necessities.

For Bentley, things had reached their peak when the trail was as he wanted it. Both the McCormick and Bentley families had enjoyed to the fullest their association with each other and with the north country.

The Bentleys spent more and more time at Huron Mountain, while the McCormicks had almost completely severed their connections with the Club. Mr. McCormick had dropped his membership there in 1920 just before the death of his wife.

There was a near–tragedy in the fall of 1926 which, though known by only a few people, probably had something to do with Mr. Bentley's losing interest in his wonderful trail. It was the last trail crossing for both Mr. and Mrs. Cyrus Bentley.

Mr. Bentley had written a letter to George Baker at Huron Mountain to meet him with a boat at the south end of Canyon Lake. This meant that George was to bring a boat across Pine Lake, Mountain Lake, and Canyon Lake and, meeting the Bentleys there, row them back across all three lakes. The letter specified, though, that they would not be coming if it rained that day. There was no phone to the outside from either place, so the letter had to suffice. They would depend on George to be at the appointed place at the appointed time.

Even the best–laid plans can go wrong. At Huron Mountain it rained and was cloudy all day, while thirty miles to the south the sun was out. The Bentleys had an early start and ate lunch at Arbutus Lodge. They had been taken down White Deer Lake, through the channel and across Bulldog Lake to the spring landing. The boat returned, and no guide went out with them across the trail. The part of the trail between the Arbutus Lodge and Canyon Lake is a long haul, though all downhill, and as they were crossing the swamp on the hewn logs, it began to rain. The rain impeded their progress, but they had no choice but to continue.

Meanwhile, down at the Club, George was debating whether or not to go. He talked to several people, showing them Mr. Bentley's letter. From everyone he spoke to, he received the same answer, "The Bentleys would never come in this weather." George decided not to go to meet them.

The Bentleys pushed on. When they reached Canyon Lake there was little daylight left but, worse, there was no George Baker. Mrs. Bentley had pushed herself to the limit of her endurance; she could not climb the high hill around Canyon Lake.

Leaving Mrs. Bentley in the growing darkness, Mr. Bentley had no choice but to hike to the north end of the lake, get the boat, and return for her. Then they walked to Mountain Lake. It was dark now, and raining. Luckily, Mr. Bentley was carrying a flashlight, but it is no easy task negotiating the trail on the east side of Mountain Lake in the dark and the rain. It took hours, as the trail there, besides being steep and tricky, is about three miles long. And again, he had to row a boat back and pick up the now thoroughly chilled Mrs. Bentley. Mr. Bentley knew better than to fool with the motor; he had to row. They walked to Pine Lake, where they repeated the process.

It was 10:30 or 11:00 at night and George Baker was warm and dry in the sitting room of the Guide House, playing cards with some of the men. There was a fire burning in the hearth, and the unmistakable sound of a steady rain coming from outside. A fellow came into the room and announced, rather nonchalantly, "George, Mr. Bentley is out at the side door. He wants to see you."

George dropped his cards on the table and rushed out the door, down the dimly–lit hallway to the outside door.

"Mr. Bentley," he said.

"Did you get my letter?" asked Bentley.

"Yes, I got it, but–"

"When I ask you to be at the south end of Canyon Lake at a certain time, I expect you to be there. I was depending on you to be there," said Bentley.

George had the letter in his pocket. He pulled it out and waved it fruitlessly at Mr. Bentley. There was not enough light to read it. "But – but you said if it rained, you wouldn't be coming," he stammered.

"There was no rain when we started out," said Mr. Bentley coldly. "You should have come."

The argument could not be settled under the conditions that night, nor did it ever get settled.

Mrs. Bentley was in bed for a week under a doctor's care as a result of this overtaxing experience. We can only guess at the conversation that must have gone on between her and her husband, but it seems logical that one of its themes might have been that they were getting too old for the trail.

A lot of things came to an end that night. It was the last time George had anything to do with Mr. Bentley, and the last time either Mr. or Mrs. Bentley crossed the trail. This last crossing was made in October of 1926. Mr. Bentley was 65 years old, Mrs. Bentley a little younger. Even Mr. Bentley was confined to his bed for several days. He apparently lost his enthusiasm for the trail on that trip.

The following year the Bentleys did not get to White Deer Lake at all. This was the year that Cyrus McCormick married his personal secretary, Alice Hoyt. He had lost his first wife, Harriet, in 1921, and to his employees seemed rather lonely in those years. Many felt that Alice Hoyt had taken advantage of his loneliness.

A rift appeared between the McCormicks and the Bentleys immediately after the marriage. Even though the two men had been lifelong friends, Bentley felt that McCormick had married beneath his station, and it would be extremely difficult for Bentley to deal with McCormick's secretary now on equal terms as Mrs. McCormick. It was a situation relatively unheard–of in that day and age, and nothing could be changed. The friendship began to fall apart. Mr. Bentley's opinion of Cyrus McCormick, now in his elderly years, was that he was "wont to follow the direction and devious paths of least resistance, which may take him one direction today and the opposite direction tomorrow."

There was also some distrust of the new Mrs. McCormick among Mr. McCormick's other employees. Some statements were made by a few before the wedding that she made a great pretense of loving the farm in Illinois where the McCormicks spent much time together, and especially the White Deer Lake country, but after the wedding Alice Hoyt McCormick didn't return to either place very often.

At White Deer Lake, little was known about the near–tragedy on the trail, or the growing rift between the Bentleys and McCormicks. To the Tonkins, Mr. Bentley had not changed. He went on running things by letter as usual and, although he did not actually visit the camp, he maintained an active interest in the goings–on there.

The electrical work at camp was completed in the winter of 1926–27. The electricity had been Mr. Bentley's idea. He also suggested to Tonkin that the water of Bulldog Lake be lifted over the dam by a large siphon pipe rather than opening the gates. This was supposed to prevent the fish from escaping down the river when the gates were opened.

Ted Tonkin did his best to carry out the experiment, but the pipes became plugged with debris, and that winter they froze solid and split from one end to the other. From then on, the gates were opened each fall.

To add to Mr. Bentley's mounting discouragements, Margaret Bentley Hamilton, his only daughter, died in April of 1927. She was just 35 years old. Margaret had married David Hamilton and left two small children, Margaret Bentley Hamilton II, born on September 6, 1919, and Elizabeth Mary Hamilton, born on December 18, 1922. Little "E. M." was only five when her mother died.

On the other side of the ledger, there were a few good things going on up in the north country that must have eased the proud old gentleman's burden at least a little. Marquette County called for bids to replace the two worst railroad bridges on the Huron Bay Grade. They were not to be built on the same sites as the old bridges. Walter Lindberg and Sons, contractors from Ishpeming, were the successful bidders and the work was done that summer entirely at the County's expense.

As if spurred on by the fast action of the County, Mr. Bentley sent word to go ahead with the replacement of the long corduroy through the Yellowdog Swamp. Tonkin had been anticipating this, as it had been talked about in previous years. This would put the trail, except for general maintenance, in the condition that Bentley had striven for over the years.

Tonkin worked along with Axelson, Trevithick, Wangberg, and Stevens. Their mistake was doing the job in June. Christ and Jim Andersen had done the original work of clearing and cutting out that swamp in March. Working there in June was sheer torture. Many lesser men wouldn't have done it, but Tonkin had assembled a faithful crew and worked with them. He was sure Mr. Bentley would show up in July or August to inspect the work, and he wanted it completed. The men poured creosote on themselves, but it didn't check the ever–present swarms of mosquitoes and blackflies. In desperation, they covered their bodies with birchbark to keep the bugs from biting through their clothes. They finished the job, but no inspection was made.

Tonkin informed Mr. Bentley that the Kohler light plant on the mainland had been a complete success that past winter, and Bentley proposed that they purchase one for the Island buildings. Before this work could be done, another calamity struck the camp. It was a theft of a proportion never before known at White Deer Lake, and there were some unusual circumstances since the theft was of a substantial amount of liquor. This was right in the middle of Prohibition, which had gone into effect in Michigan in 1919. In 1920, the 18th Amendment to the Constitution decreed that it was illegal to buy, sell or transport alcoholic beverages. It was not illegal to own such beverages, and McCormick and Bentley had a good supply stored in a liquor closet between the pool room and the Victor Room in the cabin at the northeast end of the Island.

To tell the whole story, we must return to some previous years when the group of rough Frenchmen from Champion were hired to work at camp on a part–time basis. Willard Brunette was one of them. Willard asked to go to town for the 4th of July, and was granted permission to do so. Later, George and Teddy Sharon and Eddie Arsenault asked if they could go too. The word came back that Willard could go, but the rest should wait until they were notified. The whole crew started complaining. Willard was assigned some work on the Island, while the other men were sent into the woods to work on the trails. They were all in a rebellious mood.

Left alone on the Island, Brunette began snooping around in the Victor Room. One cupboard was locked. He worked his fingers in enough to spring the door, and his eyes grew big as saucers when he realized the whole cupboard was full of imported whiskey and fancy wine. Willard's thoughts must have raced at the time, but he said nothing.

The group in the woods tried all kinds of mosquito dope. When nothing worked, they decided to quit. It was July 3rd that they all went down the road together – Willard, too. Of course the chances of their ever getting work at White Deer Lake again were slim, so in a few years' time the rebellious seed germinated into a plan of action.

It was nearly the same group, with a few exceptions, that planned and executed the big whiskey heist. Tom Maiger had an old Dort five–passenger touring car. He drove Willard, the Arsenault brothers, and Bill Boulie up the Huron Bay Grade during the night. While Tom, Earl Arsenault, and Bill built a small fire on the Baraga Plains and slept in the grass there, Willard and Eddie, each with an empty packsack, walked the three miles into camp.

Though it was dark when they started out, it was broad daylight when they arrived in camp, but early in the morning. They knew no one was on the Island but, to avoid being heard by people on the mainland, they poured water on the squeaky pulley as they pulled their way to the Island on the barge. Once on the Island, they easily made their way to the Living Room cabin and into the billiard room where the whiskey was stored.

They packed bottle after bottle of the precious liquors tightly into their packsacks. The sacks were stretched into awkward shapes with their great weight. They took all they could carry in the sacks, and two bottles in each hand. If there was a choice, it was by the size of the bottle, not by its contents – they took all the biggest bottles. There were green bottles, brown bottles, bottles with recessed bottoms, fancy bottles with stars in the cork – the men were jubilant in their larceny.

In telling me the story years later, Willard said with a twinkle in his eye, "There was a lot of Three Star Hennessy – that was good stuff." His voice was full of mischief.

Back to their friends they went, a long hard hike with such heavy loot. They had never worked this hard for Mr. Bentley. As they rode the Dort down the grade, they counted and sampled their plunder. There were 72 fifths in all, and it was "Try this – try that" all the way to Champion. They didn't run off the road, but only because the ruts were so deep that nobody had to steer. Sometime early in the trip, they had a flat tire, but nobody noticed it. When they reached the last bridge, the tire was completely gone, and the rim was worn smooth.

They went to where the Boulies lived to divide the loot, but Mrs. Boulie threw them out. They drank for several days, but tried to keep the bottles out of sight. Everyone who saw the bottles knew where they came from. One fellow sold three quarts for $45, and found out later that he could have gotten more.

The discovery of the theft at camp was a great shock. It had gone undiscovered for several days and they didn't know exactly when it had occurred. No one had seen, heard, or suspected a thing. Mr. Bentley's liquor cabinet had suddenly become almost empty,and nothing else was touched. It was as if the liquor had gone up in smoke.

Whether or not the identities of the thieves were suspected at camp is not known, but there were strong suspicions in the village of Champion. The police wouldn't have had to question many people, as everyone was talking about the theft. The guilty parties began to get very uneasy – they hadn't kept their deed very quiet. They decided to go to Detroit, where they had friends and relatives to stay with. Willard Brunette stopped off in Marquette. He made plans to be met at the depot in Detroit several days later. He fiddled away his money en route, and arrived in Detroit with ten cents in his pocket. He knew no one there, and stood around for hours wondering what to do. He had all but given up hope when his friends came to rescue him.

At White Deer Lake, the liquor theft was a touchy subject. It was not illegal to own liquor, just to sell or transport it. It would be embarrassing at best to invite the local police in to ask questions, as they would have a hard time believing that that much liquor had been there for eight years. Ted Tonkin reported the incident to Mr. Bentley by mail.

The letter he received in answer was a complete surprise to everyone. The original letter has been preserved by Mildred Tonkin. It is the only available document signed by Mr. Bentley which pinpoints the exact date of the McCormick/Bentley separation.

Here, quoted in its entirety, it reads:

Chicago, 31 October 1927

Dear Tonkin:

Replying to your letter of 25 October: I prefer to leave to Mr. McCormick the question whether any complaint should be made of the recent robbery perpetrated in the camp. You will understand my reason for this preference when I tell you that I am selling my interest in the camp (reserving the personal property which is my own) to Mr. McCormick, the sale to take effect tomorrow. Because of this it will not be necessary for you to send me any more work reports or write me again on the subject of the camp.

As this letter will close our business correspondence it is only fair that I should say to you that in the twenty–five years and more in which I have been dealing with one superintendent after another at the camp, I have found you in all essential respects much the best of them all and I hope you will continue for many years to serve Mr. McCormick as well as you have hitherto served us both. Please remember me to Mildred and to the men who are working with you, especially Axelson. Tell him that I hope I shall some day see him again. Believe me.

Very truly yours,
Cyrus Bentley
C. E. Tonkin esq'r
White Deer Lake
Champion, Michigan
Copy to C. S. Stillwell, esq'r

So it was on November 1, 1927 that the Bentley family severed connections with the land and the lakes, the forests and the rivers, and the memories of the White Deer Lake country.

Cyrus Bentley was giving up the trail he loved so well. It is obvious that there was no one reason for his decision. It was the coming–together of several reasons. Mr. Bentley's age of 66 probably had as much to do with it as anything. The fact that he would soon have to give up walking the trail, coupled with the falling–out with McCormick over his marriage, most likely carried the most weight. The expense of the whole operation and the opinion of Mrs. Bentley no doubt entered his thinking. She was never very excited about the rough camp, and always preferred Huron Mountain.

Cyrus Bentley had been the driving force at White Deer Lake. No buildings were ever built there until he joined McCormick in 1902, though McCormick had been going there since 1884. In the next 25 years it was Cyrus Bentley who provided the impetus to build them all, and certainly the several trails to Huron Mountain. McCormick would have been content to have the trails around only the nearby lakes. For 25 years it was Cyrus Bentley who kept track of every move that was made by the hired people at the camp, and gave all the directions. Above all, he made it clear that, though he was technically an equal partner, he was really subordinate to Cyrus McCormick. It was McCormick's camp first and, though Bentley willingly took charge and carried the full weight of responsibility, he was still the newcomer. McCormick had preceded him there by 17 years. There is no doubt that McCormick loved the place as much as Bentley, but in a different way. Cyrus Bentley provided the spirit of the place. Though he was strict and precise, punctual to a fault and forever keeping his distance above the help and many others with whom he associated, he was nevertheless the object of great admiration and respect by many who knew him and depended upon him.

None could forget his boundless energy, often up at 4:00 A. M. to get on the trail, his determination that others walk it and enjoy it – or else, his love of nature, the silent woods, the hidden waters, the storms, and the animals. He wanted it all to be there unmolested, and he wanted to be a part of it. The hike meant more to him than the cold, the wet, or the pains of arthritis. He thrilled to the quiet swamps, the placid lakes, and the roaring waterfalls. He enjoyed the hard work, the beautiful vistas and the quiet solitude of the Arbutus Lodge. He loved his bonfires, outdoor cooking and his Talking Machine concerts. These were Mr. Bentley's and, up to his elderly years, this was White Deer Lake. This is what his children grew up with. Mr. Bentley certainly left his mark on the land, although his name is found in only a few places. Bentley Lake is a very shallow and swampy but beautiful and wild beaver pond along the New Bentley Trail. The Bentley ponds are the two little isolated ponds without inlet or outlet which he called the

Arbutus Ponds. And then, of course, his trails, or as much as can now be found of them. He left them in perfect shape to the McCormicks and Huron Mountain Club, but they deteriorated rapidly in the ensuing years.

At the time of the breakup, Mr. Bentley had four grandchildren who were approaching an age at which they would have enjoyed being at the camp. They were Margaret's daughters – Margaret and Mary Hamilton – and Richard's children – Cyrus, who was three, and Alice, who was one. Exactly one month after the McCormick/Bentley separation, another daughter was born to Richard: Barbara, born December 1, 1927.

In contrast to Cyrus Bentley, Cyrus McCormick was more passive, very kind and had different interests from Bentley. He enjoyed White Deer Lake, but in a different way. He was neither precise nor demanding and, while he willingly took over the property, he had no grandchildren to enjoy it. Nor did he want to know every detail of running the place as Bentley had. Therefore many decisions now fell on the shoulders of the faithful, capable and experienced Charles Edward Tonkin, who by this time seemed committed to a life at White Deer Lake.

Tonkin had always liked and respected Mr. and Mrs. Bentley. It was to Mr. Bentley that Tonkin reported, and from him he took his orders. However, Mrs. Bentley confided to him one time, "When we're up here, Mr. Bentley is the boss but in Chicago I'm the boss."

Life Goes on at White Deer Lake

The Tonkins spent seven years at White Deer Lake before purchasing a home at 622 North Fourth Street in Ishpeming, where they could live at least part of the time so their children could go to school. Their first child, Bearsie, was practically raised at White Deer Lake.

One of the first things the Tonkins did after the breakup was to take a trip to England and visit friends and relatives. They left in December of 1927 and were gone three months. It was a much–needed vacation.

When they returned to the north country, Mildred and little Bearsie rode in the Woodward's snowmobile, which they were still using occasionally, as far as the fork where the camp road left the Huron Bay Grade, and from there into camp on a toboggan. On May 3, 1928, two big teams from Champion broke their way through the snow on the Grade and the camp road, and it remained open for that year. It was no small task.

Tonkin wrote: "The horses left the Baraga Plains (the camp road from the fork bridge) about 1:30 P. M. but the snow on the camp road gradually got deeper and deeper. The wagons were left behind at the Gate Hill, and progress for the horses was helped by shoveling, and by the camp crew walking through the snow. On the Corduroy Hill five feet of snow was measured. The teams arrived into camp about 8:00 that evening."

And later he wrote, "The usual high water by melting snows at the Rock Dam (always a precarious low point) there was five feet of water over the road." The small "A" type bridge at this point floated off its foundations. This high water and heavy rain of 1917 and 1928 were to have special significance to a chance discovery many years later.

For seven or eight months after the McCormick/Bentley partnership was dissolved, the sorting of personal and jointly owned things went on. There was no noticeable animosity between the two families, except possibly in the case of Richard Bentley, now the only living offspring of Cyrus.

Now a highly respected attorney in his own right, Richard had grown up with White Deer Lake. He was probably a little more like Cyrus McCormick than his father. He did not like it in the same way his father had, but certainly he had many fond recollections. He had met his wife, Phoebe, there, and was close friends with the two McCormick boys, Cyrus III and Gordon. Besides, he had three young children of his own who would soon be at an age where they would have enjoyed everything that beautiful, rugged country had to offer.

It is quite likely that Richard was not consulted in making the decision to sell out, but was simply told that it was about to occur. He had a number of reasons for feeling left out as a result of the breakup, but he probably had little to say to his father about it. The decision had already been made.

Mrs. Cyrus Bentley took the breakup calmly, almost with relief. She seemed happy to regroup her summer activities around Huron Mountain Club and her beautiful cabin at the mouth of Pine River.

As for Cyrus himself, within a year after the breakup his health began to fail rapidly. Mr. and Mrs. Tonkin, who visited him in his Chicago office, both remarked how rapidly he had aged in the few years since they had seen him. A year later he died.

One report from a close friend said he had died of cancer of the stomach. When going into the operating room, his final instructions to the surgeon were, "If it looks at all hopeless, let me go quickly."

Cyrus Bentley died August 1, 1930 in Chicago.

Over the next several years, many major repairs and improvements were accomplished by Mr. McCormick, with suggestions from his two sons and Ted Tonkin. Mr. McCormick visited the camp each year and became quite close to the Tonkin family. He often invited local people to come and visit the camp. These visits usually consisted of a meal, a ride in a boat or canoe, and little else. Some visitors did a little fishing and a few went hiking. These hikes were never long, usually to Lake Margaret or Island Lake.

One of the main improvements that took place right after McCormick's takeover was that the old workmen's camp was torn down and a new frame structure put up in its place. There were also porches replaced, fireplaces reconstructed, and foundations repaired and replaced under various docks and buildings. Mr. Walter C. Heimbeck of Chicago, the engineer from the McCormick Estate offices, was consulted on most of these projects and often came to camp to look things over and make suggestions.

There was much increased use of the property by Cyrus McCormick's sons in the early 1930s – that is, Cyrus III and his wife, and Gordon, still unmarried. Hiking, while still important, was not the main activity any more, as there were now other amusements for the younger set. Besides boating and swimming, they now had ping pong, tennis, and golf. They played golf with floating golf balls, driving them off the dock out over the lake. A place was cleared on the mainland behind the buildings for a clay tennis court. These activities took the place of the Talking Machine concerts, bonfires and jigsaw puzzles.

The first radio came into camp in 1930 and, as was the case across the nation, the McCormicks enjoyed listening in the evenings to their favorite programs, especially the news.

With the coming of Richard Bentley to claim the last of his father's belongings, stored in a garage, the change–over from McCormick–and–Bentley to just McCormick was complete. Flanigan Movers came from Marquette to take the last load of Bentley's items to Chicago.

Bill Dorais of Marquette had grubstaked Bill Bushey to an 80–acre homestead between Arbutus Lodge and Christ Andersen's homestead on the Yellowdog Plains. He now offered to buy Arbutus Lodge and 19 forties of huge jack pine that Mr. McCormick owned there. McCormick, with his sons' interests to consider, wanted to think about this for a while.

It was during this period that the McCormick family moved from the big home on Huron Street in Chicago to Burton Place on Astor Street. Since most of the furnishings were left in the Huron Street house, Cyrus asked the Tonkins to live there and act as caretakers for a while in 1928 and '29. They remained there until late spring.

On June 16, 1929, Mildred Tonkin gave birth to their second child, Kathleen, who was immediately nicknamed "Peanuts." While the Tonkins were in Chicago, John Maki, William Raymond, Axel Axelson and his wife looked after things at camp.

Tonkin wrote that 1930 was his most exciting year at White Deer Lake Camp. Before the year was out, there were so many people working there that they had to make makeshift rooms for some of them. These were the early years of the Great Depression. With a lot of people willing to do any kind of work, there was a lot more activity up in the woods.

Among the most noteworthy happenings were the bringing of electricity to the island; a new communications system from building to building and from the island to the mainland, which was installed by the Graybar Electric Company; a new workshop; and a new extra–long bathtub in the Chimney Cabin for Cyrus, Jr. That year the CCC boys, working in cooperation with the Department of Conservation, constructed a fire tower on a high hill just north of the road in from the Peshekee Grade. In addition to this activity, Walter Lindberg, the contractor from Ishpeming, built a set of camps to house a crew down on the Huron Bay Grade. He would be building a new bridge across the Peshekee for the County. Dr. VanRiper, then chairman of the County Board of Supervisors, and K. I. Sawyer, Superintendent of the County Road Commission, had several meetings with Cyrus McCormick and were in touch with him on this project. Frank B. Spear was a member of the County Board of Supervisors also, and Tonkin was instructed to give all the McCormick orders for lumber and materials to Frank as a matter of courtesy.

Cyrus III spent a lot of time at White Deer Lake working on his book, "A Century of the Reaper." It was a history of the first hundred years of the McCormick farm machinery business and the formation of the International Harvester Company. The book was published in 1931.

On November 26th of 1930, Tonkin was taken desperately ill with pneumonia. He had been working hard in the heat and then when it suddenly turned cold, he worked on in wet clothing. Dr. VanRiper was sent for, but a bridge was out and there was a bad snowstorm.

Joe Anderson, a carpenter, succeeded in driving his Model T Ford to Champion to pick up Dr. Van. On returning, the Doctor had to walk the last three miles or more from the Fork Bridge. He realized that pneumonia had set in and that he had no choice but to get Tonkin to the hospital. His temperature was over 103, and Mrs. Tonkin could not take care of him. She was caring for two small children and cooking for 14 men.

By eight o'clock, with the storm showing no sign of abating, Joe Anderson had finally got his Model T into camp. They wrapped Tonkin in several layers of blankets and laid him in the back seat with additional hot water bottles. With Dr. Van and Joe Anderson in the front seat and a man on the floor between the seats to keep Tonkin from rolling off,away they went to Ishpeming. They had to ford the river where the bridge was out and no one can describe how rough the ride was with so much snow and such poor visibility.

When they reached the main highway, they had to detour through Champion Park on account of highway construction. They reached Dr. VanRiper's house on Champion Hill at 11 o'clock, and the hospital in Ishpeming well after midnight.

Tonkin's recovery took over three weeks. He returned to White Deer Lake on December 21st.

Since 1928, when the word was out that Mr. Bentley was no longer using his trails, there had been others who did. In February of that year, a young man named Steven Jennings tried to cross the trail on snowshoes. He left White Deer Lake on a Monday morning, fully equipped to make a two or three day winter trip, but he lost the trail. He slept on the Sand Plains somewhere near the Arbutus Lodge, but was never able to find it. By Thursday a ski plane was ordered out to look for him. There was much concern at Huron Mountain, and it was a great thrill for a small crowd to see the plane land on Pine Lake. On Friday, Steven Jennings showed up at Ives Lake, quite exhausted but not in bad shape for his experience. No more winter attempts were made to cross the trail for some time. This one had been the first since the Andersens.

In the summers of 1928, '29, and '30, there was a group of young men from Ishpeming who made two or three trips each year. They were Harry Jacobson, Lawrence Pearce, Oscar Stensaas, and William Eade.

The group usually took a Model T Ford as far as the Barnhard Creek, north of Ishpeming. From there they would travel on foot north across the Dead River and up along the east side of Mulligan Swamp, then down the valley to the Pinnacle Falls on the Yellowdog River. They fished there and ate what they caught, sometimes camping there. Heading up the bank, they continued north to the old Marquette–L'Anse road. This was not much more than a wide trail, but was easy to follow. They would follow the road west to where the New Bentley Trail crossed it. Here they turned south and followed the trail without any trouble, as it was in excellent condition. Once they arrived at the Sawyer–Goodman clearing on the north side of Bulldog Lake, they would camp there and fish the lake from the rocks.

A few times, the same group drove around to Big Bay, down M–35(now County Road 510), where they caught the old Marquette–L'Anse road again. They would drive as far as they could on it and hike the rest of the way. Each time somebody drove on that road they would clear it out a little further, until in 1932 Bill Dorais and Bill Bushey made it all the way to the Andersen homestead.

Lawrence Pearce owned the Model T Ford, which had the usual flat tires all along the way. Everyone in those days carried a tire–patching kit, a few spare boots to put inside a tire, an air pump, and a couple of spare tires.

On one trip they set up a tent on a sand bar in the Yellowdog River bed. In the morning they discovered that a bear had been all around the tent while they slept. Another time a bear came out of the tall grass on the plains, right in front of them. One fellow had a folding camera and tried to get it ready to take a picture, but the bear gave a woof and was gone before he had time.

In all the trips – seven or eight – they never saw a soul anywhere in the woods or even at Bulldog Lake.

Occasionally some outside group would ask permission, usually by letter, to walk the Bentley Trail. In the years between 1932 and 1937, several Boy Scout troops and the Camp So–So boys from the mouth of the Iron River near Big Bay did this. Usually an organized group who contacted Mr. Tonkin would not be refused. Huron Mountain people were always welcome and a few of them walked the trails in those years also. Some young fellows even went over as far as Bulldog Lake and back in the same day.

Employees of the McCormick estate who visited the camp, usually from Chicago, would never walk the trails. They would usually stay a day or two, and sometimes up to a week. The new Mrs. McCormick visited camp only three or four times in the early 1930s, and never came back after her husband died. Most of the outside instructions about the running of the Camp in those years came from Mr. F. A. Stewart, who was an employee of the Estate. The offices were located at 606 South Michigan Avenue in Chicago.

In January of 1931, the first snowplow was used to clear the Huron Bay Grade and Camp road. The Camp kept the road open down as far as the lower part of the grade to the highway. The successful plowing of the road was a great convenience for the men at the Camp.

Since it looked like the County would eventually be replacing all the bridges on the Grade, Mr. McCormick began looking into the necessary task of replacing the Fork Bridge, the one large span on the Camp road across the Peshekee. Lindberg submitted a bid which Mr. Heimbeck felt was far too high, so they reached another agreement. Mr. McCormick negotiated a right–of–way agreement with Henry Ford, who owned the land there, to go ahead with the work. It was decided that the Camp crew would replace the bridge later. Even though it looked like the County would be taking care of all the bridges on the Grade, there was still a gentleman's agreement between Mr. McCormick and the road commission that the McCormick crew would be maintaining the entire road on the Grade. Besides rebuilding two bridges, they eliminated two more by building a new piece of road which stayed on one side of the river rather than crossing over and back.

Back at the Camp, the major improvements of 1931 were putting a wire fence around the spring, and pressurizing and replumbing the water system. A wing off the kitchen was completed for a barracks–type men's quarters, and the flagpole was moved from the roof of the living room cabin to the rock just southeast of the Library Cabin. A long tamarack pole was selected from the Bulldog Lake Swamp, and the Stars and Stripes were displayed during Mr. McCormick's August visit. They also purchased a strongly built 16 ft. x 5 ft. lap strake boat with a bow deck from Dan Kidney of DePere, Wisconsin for $175. This boat replaced a rather tippy Carvel boat.

The first electric refrigerator, a General Electric, was placed in the Billiard Room that year. Ice was still cut from the lake each winter, though.

The southernmost bridge on the Grade was also replaced in 1931 by contractor L. W. Brumm of Marquette.

In the late 1920s, the Agricultural Department of the Michigan Department of Conservation decided to eradicate all of the so–called "ribies" plants (five species, including gooseberries and currants) in the white pine regions of Michigan. It seems that the white pine blister rust, which was attacking and killing white pine trees, does not infect from tree to tree, but has an alternate host in the ribies plants. With the alternate host eliminated, the rust should all but disappear.

A concerted effort was made by the federal government in cooperation with the white pine states to get rid of the blister rust's host plants. In towns and cities across the state, men went from door to door asking people to tear out their currant and gooseberry bushes. At places like Huron Mountain Club and White Deer Lake, crews were sent into the woods to destroy the wild plants. In 1931, a Mr. Donald White was sent up to the McCormick Camp to take charge of a crew provided by Mr. McCormick. From the original crew of six men, there were two who remained at the camp after the job was completed – John R. Nicholls and Jack Saxwold. Saxwold remained at the camp for many years, eventually becoming Ted Tonkin's right–hand man. The Saxwolds lived near the Tonkins in Ishpeming.

Cyrus McCormick, Sr., his son Gordon, and many guests arrived in August of 1931. Gordon made numerous architectural suggestions for improvements to the camp buildings and bridges. It was at this time that the

Conservation Department asked for, and received, permission to erect a fire tower on a high spot just south of Gate Hill on the road into camp. An eighty–foot steel tower was to be set up, complete with telephone. Tonkin suggested that Mr. McCormick have a small cabin built near the base of the tower to house the tower man, and Mr. McCormick approved the idea.

It was also at this time that Mr. McCormick deeded Arbutus Lodge – also known as the Halfway Cabin or the Sand Plains Cabin – plus eighty acres of land, to the Huron Mountain Club as a clear gift.

Early in October of 1931, Mr. McCormick and Gordon, along with a friend, Forest Riley, came to camp. There was talk of leveling the Living Room Cabin, formerly known as the Victor Room – the cabin with the billiard room and the boathouse underneath. At this time it was in need of extensive repairs. It had mostly been used by Mr. Bentley; in fact, it was his favorite spot on the Island. Tonkin thought the building could, and should, be saved. A Mr. P. J. Foster of Milwaukee was consulted and the result was the hiring of two expert log workers, Andrew Juntilla and a man named Eliason, both recommended by Foster. With heavy jacks mounted on rocks in the lake bottom, the east end of the building was raised eight inches and several rotted logs were removed. New logs were cleverly fitted and bolted into place. Support logs were added in the boathouse underneath, and the Living Room Cabin – probably the most historic building in Camp because of its location and the many activities which had taken place there over the past twenty years – was saved.

Other buildings were strengthened at Foster's suggestion, and Gordon had some ideas of putting half–log veneer on the outside of the second floor of the workmen's house to camouflage its frame construction. He also wanted part of it covered with cedar bark and recommended a hip roof instead of a gable roof. This work was carried out the following winter.

In December of 1931, Mrs. Tonkin gave birth to her third and last child. She pretty much followed the pattern set by the first son, staying a few days at the Wangberg home in Ishpeming and at the appointed time walking through the alley to the Ishpeming Hospital. The baby was born December 20th. He was named Adrian Forest Tonkin but, following the nickname tradition of his brother Bearsie and sister Peanuts, he was promptly dubbed "Bunny."

In December and January, logs were cut and the fire warden's cabin was built at the base of the tower which had just been completed near Gate Hill. The telephone poles were placed along the Grade up to the tower, and the wire was strung which would connect White Deer Lake Camp with the outside world for the first time. The work was completed during the last week

Top: Making additions and repairs to the Living room cabin.
Bottom: The Living Room cabin.

of 1931. However, at this time the phone was at the tower itself and people from camp had to go over a mile to use it.

As the old railroad bridges along the Grade were torn out, Tonkin's crew was able to salvage some timbers and planks of the finest grade of western pine and fir to use at camp. At the same time an American #1 portable rip saw was hauled up the Grade by horse and sleigh so that boards could be cut from the timbers. Before this, any ripping that had to be done was accomplished by hand. Using some of these timbers, the boathouse on the mainland was moved about 30 yards south of its former position.

During the early part of the winter a little fawn, thought to have been run down by wolves, was rescued from the lake. Gordon called Dr. VanRiper and asked if he could come up and take a look at it. It was late at night when Dr. Van arrived, but the fawn lived and was given the name "John Doe." True to form, Dr. Van would accept no payment for working on the animal. The following Christmas, Gordon sent Dr. Van a check for $1,000. The doctor said it was the largest fee he had ever received.

The deer became quite a pet. The men made a comfortable straw–filled house for him. When the snow got deep, John Doe simply stayed in the house, and eventually lost the use of his legs and died. It was a sad day, and after that everyone felt that wildlife should be left wild.

Early in June of 1932, Mr. Kroeber of the Conservation Department sent the foreman, Dan White, up to camp to start the blister rust eradication program again. Mr. McCormick had to house and feed a crew of four men. They succeeded in pulling up nearly three thousand potential disease–spreading bushes from the area. There was not a lot of blister rust on the property anyway but, as a safeguard to protect the pine stands, it was recommended that the area be gone over again in ten years' time.

Mr. and Mrs. Fowler McCormick and their son Greg spent two weeks at the Camp in September. Fowler was later to take his turn as president of the International Harvester Company. Cyrus and Gordon arrived in October. They loved being there during the fall colors.

That year there was an added attraction: they would be planting 2,000 fingerling trout in Lake Margaret. The fish were obtained from the Marquette Fish Hatchery and transported by boat to Bulldog Lake, and then by hand in cans overland to Lake Margaret without a single casualty.

Now that the fire tower had been in operation for a season and Mr. McCormick had used the telephone many times, he was anxious to have the line extended into the Camp. As usual, the matter was referred to Mr. Heimbeck in Chicago, who obtained permission to make the extension into camp. The poles were cut and placed at 150–foot intervals, according to the

Top: Ted and Mildred Tonkin and their third child, Bunny.
Bottom: Peanuts Tonkin, Ted Tonkin, Bunny Tonkin, Mrs. Tonkin and a friend.

telephone company's instructions. The installation was completed in December of 1932, the phone being placed in the kitchen.

For 30 years White Deer Lake Camp had cordially fed passers–through, and at times even put them up for the night – or a few months as in the case of Jack Grove; however, now with the country in the depths of the Great Depression, Mr. McCormick had to give orders that there should be no one in camp other than those employed in maintenance work, trail work, or on the blister rust crew.

On July 20, 1932, Ted Tonkin sent a letter to Mr. Stewart in Chicago saying that he would comply with these orders and, for the record, listed the entire crew employed at the time. They were Joseph Anderson, handyman; Christian Hansen, Island man; William Raymond, John Maki, and Louis Cardinal, laborers; and John Nicholls and Jack Saxwold, blister rust crew.

The maintenance during these years consisted of the usual trail work – though reduced some from previous years – patching roofs, rechinking buildings, changing some rooms, indoor painting, plumbing and electrical work, and of course in the winter the making and storing of ice and wood. Then there was always snow removal from roads and roofs, and various and sundry other chores. They called in the Security Manufacturing and Construction Company of Burlington, Wisconsin to renovate all the lightning rods on the big trees of the island.

As with every project carried out at the camp, much planning, forethought, and correspondence went into the chinking of the cabins. Eventually the advice of P. J. Foster of Foster Construction Co., and John Wood, a stonemason from Ishpeming, was taken. First, if the cabin was not made of cedar, then at least all the base logs should be replaced with cedar. Next, the chinking should be done with pulp–plaster (today called wood–fiber plaster) inside, and four parts Portland cement to one part lime putty and clean, sharp, washed sand outside. The cement mixture should be two to one with mortar. The complete mixture was three parts sand, two parts mortar, one part cement. In preparing a log building for this outside chinking, the directions went on, "between the logs place 1/4" galvanized iron wire mesh screen, and plenty of 6 and 8 penny nails." This was to hold the chinking in place.

The Year 1933 brought many problems. The effects of the Depression were being felt heavily at White Deer Lake. Even this isolated Shangri–la was not spared. Also the death of Louis J. Cardinal, Sr., who for many years as depot agent had played an important role in the development of the camp, put a cloud over the place.

The Camp crew that spring consisted of only four men: Tonkin, Anderson, Maki and Hansen. The Camp budget was reduced to $7,000 for the entire year.

A few years earlier the White Deer Lake bank account had been transferred from the First National Bank of Marquette, Mr. Kaufman's bank, to the Miners' Bank of Ishpeming for the sake of convenience. On March 6, 1933, the Ishpeming banks closed. During this time, the Camp payroll was sent from Chicago in cash. The Marquette banks never did close during the Depression, while banks across the country did.

To add to these hardships, a terrific snowstorm hit the area from March 6th to the 12th. It closed all the roads, and access to the town could only be maintained by skis or snowshoes. As if that wasn't enough, on June 13th of that year the temperature plunged to three degrees Fahrenheit.

A Struggle to Revive the Trail

Both Cyrus, Sr. and Gordon McCormick became interested in keeping at least one of Mr. Bentley's trails in good shape for friends from Huron Mountain to use. The more they talked over the situation, the more excited they became and the greater their resolve to do so.

It was decided that the new trail, while a little shorter and better, demanded too much upkeep. It crossed three swamps, and the corduroy in these wet areas would always need repair. Then there was the Arbutus Lodge, which Cyrus had already turned over to the Club; it would always be a liability. Besides, the McCormicks had no special feeling for it. It was really Mr. Bentley's; they had seldom stayed there. However, Mr. McCormick thought it should belong to the Huron Mountain Club. His idea was that there must be some Club members who would be likely to use the facility, and that the Club, having a larger crew, would be in a better position to keep it in repair. Besides, both McCormicks thought the old trail was a more interesting and scenic route.

Their plan was to abandon the south part of the new trail, the part through the big swamp, let the Club maintain the north part of the new trail if they so desired, and maintain Arbutus Lodge. Then they would open the whole length of the old trail to the Club wire which, being mostly on high ground, would be easy to maintain; this would give the McCormicks a link with the past and a link with Huron Mountain which they both desired. Huron Mountain people would always be welcome at White Deer Lake. They spelled out this plan to Ted Tonkin and instructed him to check out the old trail with an eye toward reviving it.

In September of 1932, Mr. Tonkin wrote the following letter to Mr. Stewart in Chicago:

Dear Sir,

On Thursday the 28th, I set out on the expedition to Huron Mt. Club via the old Mountain Lake trail.

The morning was very damp after a previous night's rain, but there was promise of clearing and warmer weather. With one other man I left Camp at 7:15 A.M., reaching Bulldog at 7:35.

The walk along the "Homestead Trail" was excellent except for a little corduroy work needed in the meadow we call the "orchard." Brushing out is all that's needed to make the rest of the trail to the Andersen Homestead good. There is about one week's work in the swamp approaching the Homestead laying new corduroy. We reached the Homestead at 9:30.

After leaving the Homestead, the trail was less visible but easily discernible, and we wended our way north through beautiful country with underbrush thick and our feet and trousers as wet as they could be. There is one very bad swamp caused by beavers in Section 22, which will need plenty of corduroy, and I imagine it will take about a week to fix if two men work on it. The remainder of the trail to Cedar Creek is very good indeed, of course I mean in the sense that it would be good if it were brushed out and the windfalls cleared away. We reached Cedar Creek about 12:30 and sat down for lunch with the sun shining brilliantly.

Having dried ourselves as much as we could in an hour, we followed a good trail kept in condition by the Huron Mountain Club (Burnt Mountain Trail) to what is known as Cedar Creek Landing (Bentley Point) at which travelers from Camp to the Club or visa versa, will land and embark from boats that take them across Mountain Lake. We had no boat so we decided to walk around the lake to get to the Club. This journey was certainly the toughest of all, having to climb Burnt Mountain, Mount Homer, and other smaller hills over a trail that was far from easy walking.

This part of the journey, while being interesting, would not be in our province, but I thought it would be well to find out as much about it as I could.

A bridge will have to be built across Cedar Creek, but there being plenty of suitable trees there, I anticipate no difficulty.

We reached the Club about 5:15.

Tonkin

That fall the proposed improvements were made to the old trail. It was brushed out, and new corduroy was laid in the two spots Tonkin mentioned. During the next year or two (1933–34) several groups, mostly young people, made the trip from Huron Mountain to White Deer Lake and back. These trips were made on both trails, as the New Bentley Trail was still in surprisingly good shape for having been neglected for six or seven years.

One crossing of record was made during this period by Ernest Tappey Turner and John Elting of Huron Mountain.

Tap Turner wrote a little of this trip many years later:

Like his brother (Winston), he (John) was a flat–footed track man at high school and college, so I had to do a series of sprints to keep up. We got within site (sic) of "Rough Camp" but decided not to drop in for tea. We had neglected to bring our cutaways and dinner jackets. We did pause at the Halfway House a short time.

At Huron Mountain there was much fun poked at the elegance of life at the "Rough Camp" at White Deer Lake with its butlers and valets. There were families at Huron Mountain with maids and butlers also, but these were few and the place was never referred to as a "rough camp."

Tappey Turner recalled that his father, James Turner, did cross the trail some years earlier, carrying a trout rod and a tackle bag. At "Rough Camp" he was shown to a fine little cabin (Beaver Cabin) and was asked if the valet could press his dinner jacket for him. Since his tackle bag contained only a toothbrush and a fly–book, James thanked him but said he'd rough it.

Besides these Club crossings, there were other people who would use at least portions of the trails once in a while, mainly landlookers, fishermen and an occasional trapper. Young Axelson, who worked at White Deer Lake, and his friend Alfred Saari, also from Champion, certainly used the land for trapping. They trapped in and around the lakes and streams of the McCormick property in the early '30s.

The Conservation Department decided to move the tower south of Gate Hill to the top of Panorama Hill. This high prominence, to the northeast of the Gate Hill tower, entirely blocked the view of the Yellowdog Plains.

The Department proposed to Mr. McCormick that he give them permission to make a road, either from the Huron Bay Grade or from a point somewhere along the Camp road, to the top of Panorama Hill. Either road would have to cut across his property. There was a clash of philosophies here. The Conservation Department believed that a road always enhanced the value of the land, gave it fire protection, and made it accessible for logging. Since building roads in this rugged country was expensive, they thought they were doing someone a favor to build a road, free of charge, to or through private property. To McCormick, though, a road meant intruders, fires, debris and an end to the wilderness flavor. The idea did not set well with him, and he decided he'd have to think about the proposal for a long time.

That summer (1933) the Camp purchased a new Super Elto outboard motor, and Mr. Tonkin looked into the possibility of purchasing an underwater weedcutter manufactured by C. L. Hockney of Silver Lake, Wisconsin, at a cost of $550. By fall they had decided on a cheaper, second–hand unit. Its first trials showed it to be a worthwhile investment. It could do in one hour what ordinarily one man could do in a day, and with far better results.

Gleb Bourionoff spent the winter of 1933 and '34 in Camp as a guest of Gordon McCormick. Gleb and Gordon had met in Europe while Gordon was living in Paris. Gordon spoke French fluently and had lived in Paris off and on for ten years, except when he was at Camp between 1925 and 1933. Gleb was a White Russian from the province of Georgia. He was in exile and in some way Gordon had "saved" him and sent him over to stay at White Deer Lake for the winter. Gordon later hired him as a bodyguard. That year, Gleb became an expert on snowshoes and skis, and spent many hours roaming over the snow–covered woods around White Deer Lake.

A memorandum written in the winter of 1934 stated: "Apparently the hard usage of the 10–20 heavy wheeled industrial tractor in heavy snows is proving to be too much for it. A crack in the main frame was detected and to ensure its further use, a new main frame will be needed."

When this part was ready for installation, the tractor was hauled into Champion and a mechanic from Green Bay made the necessary repairs in a very short time, so the Camp was not without a means of keeping the road clear for very long.

Purchases in 1934 were a bottle gas range for the kitchen, a small concrete mixer, and a portable engine for power. Before this, the Camp had borrowed Mr. Woodward's mixer, which was used with the power takeoff on the Camp tractor.

In June, word was received that the County was contemplating the widening of the Grade Road. It was learned that this had been a foregone conclusion ever since the rebuilding of the bridges. Up to this time, the McCormicks, with the help of the Woodwards (owners of Lake Richard, now Four Island Lake) had been maintaining the road. With the widening of the road there would surely be increased traffic or, as Mr. Woodward was afraid, "...that the country be opened up to Mr. Ford and his logging interests," which he thought were at the bottom of the scheme. Some other arrangements as to maintenance would have to be made.

Early in June, Cecil Tonkin (Bearsie) started his school vacation with a bad case of scarlet fever, which had been prevalent all over the country that spring. Both Ted and Mildred Tonkin came down with the disease, Mrs. Tonkin's being a very serious case. Dr. Van, who would have cared for them, was out of town for a month, and Dr. Erickson had to come all the way from Ishpeming each day to look after the situation. Mrs. Saxwold came out from Ishpeming and stayed at Camp to look after the sick; her daughter, Helen, took care of the smaller children. Mrs. Halls, Mildred Tonkin's mother, was also there to help out with the cooking and with the care of the sick. Mrs. Halls and Mildred had a wonderful mother–daughter relationship; they were real pals and Mrs. Halls was wonderful just to have around camp. All the patients recovered.

Word was received that summer that the Conservation Department would be going ahead with the task of moving the fire tower. The new location on Panorama Hill would protect the Yellowdog Plains and the vicinity, but it seemed that another tower would be required to take care of the Peshekee Valley. The conclusion was that the Republic Tower and the Arvon and Three Lakes Towers would do the job efficiently, making the McCormick location unnecessary.

With this decision, Cyrus McCormick had two important questions. What would become of the telephone line, which he now deemed necessary for the Camp, and how would the Panorama Tower be serviced? The idea of a road through the property to Panorama Hill was unacceptable. As a countermeasure, he offered to provide transportation by motorboat for that purpose. Of course the tower man would still have to walk three miles to his post. This was to be considered by the Department, but the matter of the telephone was still urgent from both sides.

The matter was settled when the Department of Conservation and the CCC boys joined forces and opened the old Marquette–L'Anse Road, which in those days was sometimes called the "Old Silver Lead Trail." as it led to the Herlock Silver Mine. The road was opened from Big Bay to Panorama Hill. This meant making nearly two miles of new road from Christ Andersen's homestead to the tower, part of which went right down the Old Bentley Trail. Telephone poles and a line would be installed along this road, and the tower would be serviced from Big Bay. The telephone line on the Huron Bay Grade, which at that time serviced both Woodwards and McCormicks, was to be left intact. This was agreed between McCormick and the Conservation Department because the superintendent of the McCormick camp would act as keyman for the Department, which would provide forest fire protection for a wide area. McCormick was to assume full maintenance of this line.

With all this discussion of fire, the matter of fire protection for the Camp buildings began to be re-examined. Although fire hoses were already in place in the buildings, something more was needed in case fire broke out when no one was around.

Mr. Heimbeck in the Chicago offices had done considerable research on this matter, and suggested pint–size globes filled with carbon tetrachloride, to be placed strategically in each of the rooms. Knapp–Moore Inc., who produced the product, stated that in case of fire starting without warning or without anyone around, the heat generated by the fire would melt a filament which held the glass globe in a bracket on the wall. The globe would then drop to the floor and break, releasing all the carbon tetrachloride. This would absorb all the oxygen in the room, and the fire would be smothered. Years later this type of extinguisher was outlawed due to some deaths by suffocation. The cost was $886 to have the globes installed.

Improvements continued to be made to the buildings on the island that year, including the installation of a Kaustine Toilet System, concrete foundations for the buildings, and many closets, cupboards and – for the first time – showers were provided. All of these projects were carried out with a skeleton crew and on a limited budget under the watchful eye of Ted Tonkin.

During Mr. McCormick's visit, considerable thought was given to replacing the Industrial Tractor with a new track tractor which would have more traction for the heavy work around the Camp. A complete outfit which was on display at the World's Fair in Chicago (1933–34) was thought to have everything the camp needed, and cost less than a new one. It had a Baker plow with a wing attachment and a power take off. The tractor was sent to the Baker people for minor adjustments before arriving at Camp. When the snow got deep that winter, it was evident that the tractor's manufacturers had not seen the snow conditions that existed in Michigan's high country. Many of the major construction points were too weak, and had to be replaced. The Baker Company cooperated kindly, at no cost to the McCormicks.

The most important change that year was the use of coal–fired hot water heaters in the island cabins.

As far as the trails were concerned, a complete repair job was carried out on the Bulldog causeway. With the new tractor it was possible to drive almost to this long bridge on the old boulder road (the rock that went to Graceland Cemetery). This made it much easier to transport men and materials to the job rather than by snowshoes and sled, which would have been done otherwise.

The little log cabin that Mr. McCormick had built for the tower man was dismantled after the tower was removed.

The winter of 1935 brought lots of snow and bitter cold weather. With storm after heavy storm, it was almost impossible to keep the road open. The tractor had many costly breakdowns. Subzero temperatures were constant through the month of February, and drifting snow was a continual problem.

Repairs were made to the substructure of the island ferry dock, and preparations were made to build a shed which would house the weedcutter and all the fireplace wood for the island. Also, repairs were made to the long corduroy trail around the northwest bay of White Deer Lake. For all this work, huge amounts of snow had to be shoveled by hand.

When the plans arrived for the woodshed, provisions were made in them for a boat for the fire warden, should he need it to go to Panorama Hill. The building was placed out of sight, tucked in a remote corner of the northwest bay on the shore of White Deer Lake. A small boathouse for the fire warden's boat was also built at Bulldog Lake, in an inconspicuous little bay about a hundred yards west of the Spring Landing dock. During October, Mr. McCormick went out with the crew to supervise the work on the Old Bentley Trail. He wanted it redone to his liking through the swamp to Christ Andersen's homestead.

That fall (1935) Gordon stayed on at camp longer than he ever had before. In fact, his last visit that year lasted from October 4th to December 14th. The fireplace in the Chimney Cabin had been smoking, and the old–style lime masonry was showing signs of decay. Gordon became very interested in this repair job. The further the chimney was dismantled, the more evident was the danger that the old fireplace would cause a fire in the building. The walls of the building were cabled together with a turnbuckle, and the whole chimney and fireplace had to be taken down and rebuilt under Gordon's direction.

Fred Dunham at the guard cabin on Cedar Creek 1937.

Mr. McCormick, now 76 years old, asked that all the trails be made more level and easier to walk on, especially around the lakes. On the island, which was quite high, hills were unavoidable; he wanted all the steps made longer, with uniform 4 1/2 inch risers. He was having difficulty getting about, and he stumbled easily.

Late in his stay that fall, Mr. McCormick suffered a slight weak spell and Dr. Van was summoned. He diagnosed the spell as a symptom of old age. Many changes were made in order to make things easier for Mr. McCormick.

Meanwhile, road building and improvement were going on both north and south of the property. The P.W.A. (Public Works Administration) was widening the Huron Bay Grade road, and out on the Yellowdog Plains the CCC boys had pushed the road through to Panorama Hill and erected the tower there. More and more woodsmen and fishermen were making their way out on the recently opened Triple A road and discovering the Bentley trails.

One group from Big Bay that made several trips a year between 1935 and 1938 was Tom Kerner, Chuck Temple, Al Salkowskas, and Larry Simms. Larry and Al were from Chicago. They moved bag and baggage up to Big Bay around 1932 looking for a better life. Tommy Kerner came from southern Illinois about the same time, with a fellow named Frank Nelson. He spent his first year or so living with Dutch John, the homesteader who lived near the Salmon Trout River. Tom did a lot of coyote trapping with John, and soon became an accomplished woodsman. He made out well in the Depression with the hefty bounty they had on coyote at that time. One month he trapped thirty coyote when the bounty was $20 for a female and $15 for a male. In those days some men were supporting a family on less than a dollar a day. Chuck Temple was a native, born and raised in Big Bay, one of George Temple's sons.

These four, and sometimes Jack Abbott who was a game warden with the Conservation Department, used to go to the Andersen homestead by car and then hike the Old Bentley Trail north. The trip down the Cedar Creek and then west along the Cliff Stream proved to be too long and roundabout; besides, Larry worked for the Club, and didn't want to be accused of any wrongdoing. He was guiding for a lot of Club members those years and was a great fisherman himself. There were guards patrolling the Cedar Creek. Tom Kerner blazed a trail from the Old Bentley, south of the Club wire, directly northwest to Cliff Lake. This became the route they would use on their fishing trips. They usually had good luck in Cliff Lake. One time Tom caught a two pound trout and wanted to bring it to Dr. Hirwas in Big Bay as a gift. It was getting dark when they left and had to follow the blazed trail most of the way in the dark to get the trout delivered fresh.

The new life of the old trail was destined to be cut short. Things in the big woods could never return to the way they had been before the road was built. The road to the tower had opened up the country. Going south from the Andersen homestead to the tower, the new piece of road was right on the route of the trail for a mile or more. The plan to use this trail now seemed ridiculous. The spell of the wilderness was broken when a hiker stepped onto a road, and the country had now become accessible to many people, especially loggers, who would soon be there in great numbers.

By 1936, Gordon McCormick had taken a very active interest in the White Deer Lake country. He appeared destined to inherit the place, as his only brother, Cyrus III, seemed to have lost interest. Old Mr. McCormick was beginning to get a little feeble, and Gordon was trying to tailor all the walkways and stairways so that his father could get around with as little trouble as possible. The path around White Deer and Bulldog Lakes was a veritable boulevard, two and a half to three feet wide and very level. Where the land rose high above lake level, hewn log walks were built in the water at the lake's edge. The result was that for much of the distance around Bulldog and White Deer Lakes there was an upper and lower trail. The lower trail was the most beautiful walk imaginable. It had walkways, all on pilings, in the water along the cliffs. They were made of planking and equipped with pole railings. The distance by trail around the two lakes was a little over five miles.

Gordon designed a new circular stairway to the Dining Room Cabin with the uniform 4 1/2 inch risers. This job was finished in the winter. With the help of Mr. Heimbeck, he also redesigned part of the Living Room Cabin to make it more convenient and comfortable for his father by adding an alcove for a sofa, piano and a lavatory with a kaustine toilet.

It was while doing this job, in February, that they nearly lost the tractor. A sled had been loaded with tools and materials for the job and, with the tractor pulling it, started out across the ice to the far end of the island. This had been a common practice years before, in the days of the early loggers.

Tonkin tells the story: "The load set out bravely from the mainland dock and all went well...until just off Tamarack Point, we saw the tractor settle, hind end first, into the lake. It was a moment for quick action and quicker thinking. To leave it too long meant that its bulk would soon settle so deep in the mud bottom that it would be an even chance of not recovering it. A hardwood tripod was erected and, by a hurried trip in Ishpeming, we obtained a five ton chain hoist and attached it to the tripod set over the tractor. Carefully, and by a fraction of an inch each time, the tractor began to emerge from the icy waters. By nightfall we had been successful in getting it clear of the lake.

The temperature at this point hovered around the 15 below zero mark. Our greatest concern centered around the possibility that all our efforts would be wasted if the chain hoist would not hold or the tripod would break, but all went well and the next day with a colder thermometer (–20) the tractor was well clear of the water. Next a large platform was built over the hole and underneath the tractor, so that for a time we were able to relax knowing that all we had to do now was to get it to the mainland. Rigging up our old one–man stump–puller to a good solid tree, the cable was attached to the tractor and the slow, inch–by–inch pull of the stump puller started the tractor on its journey back to terra firma. This job took the better part of a day, but it did the work and we breathed a sigh of relief when it rested safely on the mainland dock."

Olaf Stolen, from Ishpeming, was hired especially to do the work on the Living Room Cabin. He had a reputation of being a fine carpenter.

The Death of Cyrus McCormick

In June, word was received at White Deer Lake of the death of Mr. Cyrus McCormick. It was a great shock to everyone at camp. The Tonkin family had grown especially close to him. Ted Tonkin, who had personally dealt with him for 14 years or so, wrote: "His kindness and understanding and this beautiful place will always be a reminder of his love for the finer and nobler things of life."

The transition from the father, Cyrus, to the son, Gordon, would be easy, as Tonkin had been dealing directly with Gordon for several years. There would be no noticable change except somewhere in the vaulted records of Marquette and Baraga Counties. Life at White Deer Lake would go on pretty much as it had before.

But that year of 1936 marked the passing of an era in the far north country. Besides the spell of its isolation being broken by roads that would open up the land, three of its stalwart pioneers had died – Nels Andersen of the Plains, Jim Leatherby six miles to the west, and Cyrus McCormick, lover and preserver of the untouched forests. All were long–time residents of this last real wilderness in Michigan, and each had added something to it.

Nels died in Wisconsin in relative obscurity. No report of it was made in any local paper. Jim Leatherby was found by two Ford timber cruisers, frozen solid, sitting in a rocking chair in the middle of his cabin waiting for a

Johnnycake to bake. The finding of his body was reported in the L'Anse Sentinel.

But all the world heard the news when Cyrus McCormick died. It crackled out of radios and darkened headlines all over the world. He had a heart attack on June 2, 1936 and passed away a short time later. Gordon was in Honolulu at the time.

The Chicago Herald and Examiner for June 4th carried an account of the funeral. The headlines read "Big Harvester Plants Still Form McCormick; 55,750 Workers Will Honor Ex–Head Today: Notables of Nation on Pallbearers List."

The article, in part, is as follows:

> While 55,750 employees in the vast network of International Harvester Company offices and plants pause in their labors, Cyrus Hall McCormick, 77, former head of the reaper company, will be buried today with leaders of the worlds of industry, finance and education present to pay their tribute.
>
> Funeral services will be held at 2:30 P.M. at the Fourth Presbyterian Church, with Dr. John Timothy Stone and Dr. Harrison Roy Anderson officiating. Private services for the family will be held at 4:30 P.M. in Graceland Cemetery.
>
> The body of the industrialist, one of the world's wealthiest men, who died Tuesday of coronary thrombosis after a brief illness, remained yesterday at Walden, the family estate in Lake Forest.

The list of 60 or so honorary pallbearers included John D. Rockefeller Jr., Governor Frank O. Lowden, William E. Dodd, the American Ambassador to Germany, Harold W. Dodds, President of Princeton University, and industrialists and bank presidents.

The article went on to say that no estimate had ever been made of the value of McCormick's vast holdings throughout the world. A 4" x 7" picture of Cyrus McCormick, the last for which he ever posed, accompanied the two–column story.

Realizing his father's wish to keep up the White Deer Lake property as it had been in the past and to keep a connection between Huron Mountain and the Camp, Gordon decided to explore the trail possibilities again.

The land and timber around the Halfway Cabin had been given to Huron Mountain, but even before Mr. McCormick's death it was sold to Bill Dorais (on May 23, 1935), who sold it to Victor Makela, the logger, on October 2nd of the same year. Makela had already started to cut some of the jackpine on the plains, and nearly everything that wasn't nailed down in the

Halfway Cabin had been carried off. The Cabin could not be used again, nor would anything be safe there any more. The trail through the swamp would be expensive to keep up, and when the jackpine on the plains was cut, there would be no trail on the plains at all. These factors left only one alternative – if there was a trail, it would have to be the Old Bentley in spite of the road. Gordon decided to take one last look at the New Bentley Trail while the timber was still standing on the plains.

Gordon McCormick made this crossing of the new trail in 1937 with Ernie Riopelle, a stonemason from Marquette. It was the last time any McCormick ever walked that trail. They stopped a while to look at Arbutus Lodge. It must have been a sad experience for Gordon, as the place was in a very sorry state.

Gordon now turned his attention to the old trail again. He made a second trip to Huron Mountain, with Tonkin this time, to see for himself what could be done to keep that trail open. To Gordon, as it had been to many others in former years, this trip – covering over 30 miles' distance by lake and trail through big timber, along rivers and past waterfalls in the heart of the last great rugged wilderness in Michigan – was one of the most thrilling and satisfying activities at White Deer Lake Camp. The trips always stood out as the highlight of any visit north. It was the one remaining rough part of "Rough Camp," a vestige of his father's and Mr. Bentley's first years together. Many at Huron Mountain held such views and memories as well, but the opening of the road to the tower had made a difference. The trip had lost something. There was a feeling among many people at Huron Mountain that the road now made the effort of keeping the trail open undesirable.

There were some, however, at Huron Mountain who wanted to see a trail kept open and to walk it once in a while. One of them was Richard Bentley. At the south end of the trail, Tonkin had been setting aside Bentley's belongings as he ran across them. When there was a large accumulation of such items, he packed them up and shipped them to Huron Mountain, after first sending Richard a letter that they would be arriving.

Richard used this as an opening to ask permission to walk the trail once again, and request a ride across White Deer and Bulldog Lakes in the motorboat.

The letter, dated July 9, 1937, is as follows:

Dear Teddy,

We have just been advised that the shipment from White Deer Lake has arrived at Huron Mountain Club. I want to thank you for attending to this and at the same time ask you for a statement of the expenses involved in the shipment, for Mother and I wish to take care of these.

I have a friend who has an island camp in Lake Michigamme. He is very anxious to see the country between his camp and Lake Superior and we have worked out a plan to walk across to Huron Mountain Club. The natural route would be via White Deer Lake.

I do not like to trespass and I am therefore writing to ask if there would be any objection to my taking two friends to White Deer Lake about the middle of August early in the morning so that we could get an early start to walk north along the Huron Mountain Trail.

If there would be no objection from the standpoint of the inhabitants of White Deer Lake it would enable us to make the trip across to Mountain Lake easily in a day, maybe half a day. In answering this, I should greatly appreciate it if you advise me which of the two trails it would be better for us to follow from Bulldog to Mountain, the old or the new trail; and also whether it is possible to motor from Champion through to the north end of Bulldog Lake.

Sincerely Yours,
Richard Bentley

Of course it is not possible to motor to the north end of Bulldog Lake except on a tractor, but Tonkin graciously offered to take them there in a motorboat. The friend who owned the island in Lake Michigamme was William Dow Harvey of McComb, Illinois. He manufactured chicken brooders for Sears and Roebuck and was leasing the island and camp from the former owners, the Rumseys. Mrs. Harvey had been a camper there at Camp Ketchewa for girls. Years earlier, the Harveys purchased the island and have returned to it every summer. As of 1985 Mr. Harvey has died and Mrs. Harvey is still living near Boston, Massachusetts. Their large family uses the camp regularly.

Another proponent of maintaining a trail was William P. Harris, Jr. His cabin was on the same sand spit as Richard Bentley's, with only the Hamilton Cabin between them. The Harris cabin was the one William M. LeMoyne of Chicago had built for Kimball Young. It had been sold to Henry Hooper in 1900 and to the father of William P. Harris, Jr. in 1917. Bill Harris and Richard Bentley were good friends, and saw each other often at Huron Mountain. When Gordon McCormick arrived at Huron Mountain with Ted Tonkin in 1937, it was with these two men that the trail situation was discussed, and therefore it was to these two that Gordon made his appeal.

The letter here quoted is from Gordon McCormick to William P. Harris, Jr., October 5, 1937:

Dear Bill,

In reviewing our trip to Huron Mountain the other day with Tonkin, I instructed him to clear out the Huron Mountain Trail where necessary from where the trail goes north off the road at Christ Andersen's old cabin up to the point where it meets the Huron Mountain Club wire. In particular the swamp at the north end of Long 22 Hill on the Section line between 22 and 15, and a short distance north of the swamp where the trail is blocked by windfall, – at which point "Mr." Bushey (a cruiser) has erroneously noted something about Section 12, which is nowhere near that point. Also, a clearing will be made across the line of Beaver Lake in 15. We will rip–saw down through all the necessary huge windfalls and clear out the young maple growth sufficient to see the next blaze. We figure that in three days away from camp a fairly thorough clearing can be done, or at least sufficient to preserve this trail for another five or six years. Otherwise, if we let it go, many parts of the trail will become obliterated completely except for the old blazes, which are hard enough to find as it is.

The trail needs very little attention from the road at Christ Andersen's cabin north to the bottom of Long 22 Hill, and I think it is best not to have this trail too clear where it comes out on the Sand Plains Road – reasons of incoming trappers, loggers, etc. For like reasons, we are not clearing the trail where it leaves Panorama Fire Tower Road and goes south through Section 19.

The question is, would Huron Mountain Club clear the Club's part of the trail from that delightful mossy rock crossing of Cedar Creek to the end of the wire in Section 15, or if not, would you and Dick undertake to do a little handy cutting of high young maples that considerably confuse the next blaze over this part of the trail in Section 11 and 15?

I started north from camp the other day with the understanding that the trail was clear and visible though rather rough in windfalls, but I had no idea that the blazes in some parts were so indistinct and difficult to follow unless one knew the trail beforehand. I think it would be an awfully nice thing to know that it was at least reasonably accessible north and south along this trail, for although, with Mr. Bentley gone, there is not the same traffic as before, still this old

Bentley Trail is certainly far more beautiful than the newer trail between the Halfway House, which latter is actually harder to keep up because of the lower, swampier ground. Furthermore, the Old Bentley Trail comes out on Mountain Lake in a more interesting region than that of Canyon Lake.

I would be glad to have your reaction to the above if you get a chance to drop me a line at camp. It may be you have some further ideas in the matter of reasons for not doing any clearing at all. Of course, I don't know the ins and outs of clearing this trail over somebody else's property, but I believe the long past complaints of landowners are now nonexistent, and a clearing may be worth the attempt, if only in order not to lose the existing old route.

Sincerely,
Gordon McCormick

P.S. Is the trail to the old fishing camp on the Huron River fairly well marked from its take–off on the Old Bentley Trail on the north line of Section 6? I certainly hope to get up there some day soon – as the last time was in 1912.

This letter was accompanied by another, strangely enough, maybe written in the same sitting, but as an afterthought.

Dear Bill,

I am enclosing a letter to Mr. Perkins, as possibly my suggestions more properly concern the trails committee. Of course, these suggestions occurred to us on one of our very infrequent (to date) trips from the south, but yet in view of all the other very clearly marked signs on your trails, these additional signs might be a good asset. I enclose a rough sketch.

I also suggest a sign To "H.M.C." (or some such) where the trail on the west side of Mountain Lake turns off north from the Cliff Lake Trail that starts from the lake shore at the south end of the lake. This is the trail that we were looking for and somehow missed on the Cliff Creek Trail.

It was nice meeting you and Mrs. Harris. I hope we can get together again, either here, at camp, in Mexico, or Arizona, or –

Sincerely,
Gordon McCormick

On this trip with no boat to meet them, Gordon headed west up Cliff Stream, crossed it and then headed north along the west side of Mountain Lake, a longer but much easier route than that on the east shore.

The letter to Mr. Perkins, manager of Huron Mountain Club, written the same day – October 5, 1937 – :

Dear Mr. Perkins,

Thanks so much for all your trouble and hospitality. I am enclosing $10 to cover expenses of our party overnight, as I judge the rooms were $1 each and the supper and breakfast $1.50 each. I gave $2 to the guide who came to meet us, and am also enclosing $1 for the man who cooked our very late dinner, for which we were most appreciative – in fact, the first hot biscuit was about the best thing I ever tasted.

I forgot to bring the small map of the lakes that showed the elevations and depths of water, and would appreciate your mailing this to camp.

May I offer a suggestion? Assuming that the landing up Cedar Creek (or Cliff Creek) near the spring is called Cedar Creek Landing, and that the landing where the boat was left one quarter of a mile east on the lake shore is called Burnt Mountain Landing, it might be well to have the correct name boards on these landings. Also, to do a thorough job it might help your fishing and hiking parties to have two similar signs with arrows at the point on the trail north of the Cedar Creek Fishing Camp where the new Cedar Creek Trail branches off to the left from the Old Burnt Mountain Trail that goes from the fishing camp over Burnt Mountain to Burnt Mountain Landing. This fork is not exactly clear unless one knows it or sees a sign.

Although the distance between Cedar Creek Landing (up the stream) and Burnt Mountain Landing (on the lake shore) is only one quarter mile, there is no direct trail between them.

The old Canyon Lake Landing on Mountain Lake has disappeared and seems to be in disuse.

We had a grand time and a grander experience. It was most considerate of you to meet us with a car, as the condition of our feet after 22 miles of hiking was none too good, although our spirits were certainly high.

Sincerely,
Gordon McCormick

That summer (1937), previous to Gordon's trip on the old trail, a crew from Huron Mountain had put in a hewn log walk, five eighths of a mile long, through the Cedar Creek swamp to the landing "upstream" that Gordon speaks of. The trail went from the Cliff Stream Landing to the "Fishing Camp," as Gordon calls it, on Cedar Creek and joined the Old Bentley Trail over Burnt Mountain just below the camp. It wasn't a fishing camp, but a cedar–shake guard cabin built early that summer by Fred Dunham of Marquette, who was employed that summer by Huron Mountain Club to patrol those two rivers because of the influx of poachers in the upper lakes and streams caused by the opening of the Triple A road.

One group of fishermen that came once a year when the trails were in good shape were from Ishpeming. James E. Flaa gives some information on these excursions. On August 12th and 13th of 1933, Jim and Al, Doc and Ket followed the Old Bentley Trail and fished Cliff Lake. On September 1st, 2nd and 3rd of 1934, they followed the New Bentley to Mountain Lake. Again in 1935, May 17th, 18th and 19th, they followed the New Bentley. Three days in May of 1936 they went to Cliff Lake through Huron Mountain Club, apparently with permission. The group was a little larger now, eight in all. In 1938, three days in July, six of them went through Skanee to Cliff Lake. Again they went through Huron Mountain, three days each in June of 1941 and May of 1942. They hit their peak of fishing this last year, with 35 fish for four people. Roughly this same group took trips every year from 1957 through '64. In the later years, they fished the upper Cliff Stream, Slate River, Big Huron and others, often without success. In the early years they saw no one; in the later years they ran into several other fishing parties and a few drunks. But fishing wasn't the biggest problem in the late '30s and early '40s. If people only fished, you would hardly have known they were there, but fires were springing up everywhere, due partly to negligent fishermen. Garbage began to appear along the trails, and beer cans were coming into common use with many of the woods travelers. Many who poached on Huron Mountain streams had crossed several good trout streams just to fish Club waters. They often came in the night, leaving by six in the morning. Some carried firearms and indiscriminately shot every living animal that came along, leaving it where it fell. The porcupine was their main target. It was not uncommon to find eight or ten dead ones along a mile of trail. To those who had been used to seeing these beautiful forest paths in their pristine state, every sign of man was disheartening.

In the few years that the Triple A road had been open, the Halfway Cabin and Christ Andersen's cabin had been ravaged, there had been numerous forest fires, and loggers were working everywhere in the area. Up to this time it was a different kind of person, a select few with generally good motives, who had made their way into these places, but now the country was

Top: The Ishpeming group at Cliff Lake 1936. The lake is now privately owned.

819

wide open. Even with Fred Dunham as a full–time guard on the Cedar Creek, the presence of outsiders was felt heavily there.

Sentiment seemed to be running high against the opening of the Bentley Trail so, rather than ask and run the chance of being turned down, Richard Bentley and William Harris decided to blaze the trail on their own. After all, many at Huron Mountain thought that these trails were something of the distant past, and a surprising number never knew they even existed.

Bill Harris answered Gordon's letter on October 26, 1937:

Dear Gordon,

I was glad to get your letter concerning the old trail between Mountain Lake and White Deer Lake. I am sure your work in clearing out the trail up to Section 15 will be much appreciated by the club, and I am sure we can do our part next spring in fixing the trail from Cedar Creek to the wire. This part of the trail is on land that we lease from the Cleveland Cliffs Iron Co., but I should think it entirely proper for us to at least freshen up the blazes and clear out a few windfalls. I think you are quite right in leaving the trail obscure at the Sand Plains Road. Since this road was put through we have had considerable trouble with poachers and fishing parties coming into our lakes and streams. In regard to the trail to the old fishing camp on the Big Huron, it is no boulevard and none too plainly marked, but it is not bad considering the time since it was kept up (25 years). I was over it two years ago, and the walk from the road to the old camp site was all I wanted for the day. The camp was burned long ago, and scarcely a trace is left to show where the camp was.

We all enjoyed your short visit to the club and I hope after our combined efforts to make the way plainer, you will be a more frequent visitor.

Sincerely,
William P. Harris, Jr.

William Harris and Richard Bentley went out twice the following year (1938) and re–blazed the Old Bentley Trail to the Huron Mountain wire, and a little beyond. Gordon McCormick and two other men worked the trail to where it hit the Panorama Road, walked the road a little over a mile and three quarters, and then worked the trail to Section 15, being careful to camouflage the portion around the Triple A road. This completed, the north–bound hiking parties would come onto the Panorama Fire Tower road about three hundred yards south of the section line between Sections 7 and 18. They would then walk on the road about one and 3/4 miles to a point just north of the Andersen Homestead, where they would go into the woods and easily pick up a good northbound trail through Sections 34, 27, 22 and on to Cedar Creek. The trail was completely blazed that year, but it was seldom used. There were occasions when Bill Harris and Richard Bentley went out on it a few miles south of Mountain Lake, more to observe its condition than to walk the full distance. When World War II came along, it fell completely into disuse.

Gordon Acquires an Architect

Gordon McCormick was doing what he could to revitalize everything in those years following the death of his father. It was difficult, even with his resources, for one man to do what the Bentley and McCormick families had done. It was all on his shoulders now, as all the other interested parties were gone. He was the one who had to provide the spirit and the leadership, if there was to be any. He still had Tonkin, without whom White Deer Lake would surely have passed into oblivion at that time.

Even though there had been continual repair and updating, everything was showing its age. Gordon felt that now, after nearly 40 years, a complete renovation should be made if he were going to keep the place. The thought of disposing of it never entered his mind. He himself was an architect, well trained but with little practical experience. He also had the services of faithful Mr. Heimbeck, also an architect and engineer, with the McCormick Estates offices in Chicago. Heimbeck had designed or approved of all the work at camp in recent years. He often spent time at camp, but he also had duties in Chicago.

If Gordon was going to do the kind of renovation he had in mind, he would need a full–time architect at his disposal, a man familiar with log construction. He began looking around for such a person.

At this period there was a man named Chilson D. Aldrich of Minneapolis, Minnesota, who many looked on as being the foremost log cabin architect in the world. He had written a very popular book back in 1928 called "The Real Log Cabin." Gordon had read the book, which told of many variations of log construction and gave the log cabin a very romantic appeal. Gordon had contacted Aldrich for advice on several occasions. Now he turned again to "Stuga" as he was called by close friends, and asked if he would work for him full time.

This proposal presented just too many problems for Mr. Aldrich. He was completing some important projects and his duties with Gordon were not specifically spelled out. He declined the offer. Gordon's next request was for Stuga Aldrich to locate a log cabin architect who was capable and willing to give his full time, for an undetermined number of years, to White Deer Lake Camp.

There were several architects who had worked for the National Park Service out west in the early 1930s with the CCC, designing and building log cabins for U. S. Parks. One of them, Bruce Wallace, was now working in Minneapolis. Aldrich contacted Wallace and asked if he would be interested in such an arrangement. This was in January of 1938. Jobs were hard to come by in this field, and Wallace had a good one. He wasn't about to give it up. However, he had a friend named Roy Norberg who had also been with the Park Service and was in town looking for a job. Wallace recommended Norberg for the job.

Roy Norberg was born and raised in Chicago, went to school there and was graduated from the University of Illinois in 1933 with a degree in architectural engineering. He worked for the Park Service developing Roosevelt National Park in Medora, North Dakota in 1934 and '35. In 1936 he accepted an offer for a good job with an architectural firm in Hinsdale, Illinois, headed by a fraternity brother: Harford Field, Inc. He married a 19–year–old North Dakotan, Lula Haas. Lula, who was from Hazen, was employed in Dickinson, North Dakota by the Resettlement Administration of the Federal Government, clearing title to the lands that would comprise Roosevelt National Park in Medora. The young couple moved to Chicago, and Roy went to work in Hinsdale.

Even though he was raised in the city, Roy just hated Chicago life after his experience in the rural west. With six months of it under his belt, he decided he couldn't stand another minute. In desperation Roy called an influential friend, Russell Ried of the State Historical Society of North Dakota, and asked if there was some way he could get his old job back or if Russell could find him a job in North Dakota. There was a job at Sibley Island in Bismarck, North Dakota, so in the spring of 1937, Roy and "Lu" packed up their few belongings and went out west again.

By the end of the summer, government funds were cut back, the Sibley Island project folded, and Roy was out of a job. That fall he and Lula worked their way back to Minneapolis because he felt he had to be where there was a lot of construction to land a job, and one could not be found on the prairies of North Dakota.

Top: The dining room, Gordon's drawing – the actual building.

In Minneapolis, Lula got a job as a secretary, but Roy could find nothing. While there, he made contact with his old friend Bruce Wallace, who recommended Roy to Stuga Aldrich. And so in February of 1938, Stuga, Bruce Wallace, and Roy Norberg all headed for Michigan's Upper Peninsula, to a small town with the strange name of "Ishpeming." Before this time, Roy and Lula didn't even know that Michigan had an Upper Peninsula. Roy had about 75 cents to his name at this point, and his wife had to hock a few things to get the money to send him off on the trip.

When the trio finally arrived at White Deer Lake in that winter of the big snow, Roy Norberg was simply dumbfounded. He called Lula in Minneapolis and said, "This is an absolute fairyland, there is such affluence here that you just cannot believe this is a backwoods camp. I've never heard nor seen anything like it in my life."

The result of this trip was that on the recommendation of Aldrich and Wallace, Gordon McCormick hired Roy Norberg as camp architect and engineer. He would move to Chicago and work in the main drafting office of the McCormick Estates. His immediate superior would be Mr. Walter Heimbeck.

Lula Norberg quit her job in St. Paul and went back to Hazen, North Dakota to stay with her widowed mother until Roy was settled in Chicago. In late March she went to join him. That was when she first met Gordon McCormick.

The Christmas Party

Lula was very impressed with Gordon from the first moment she saw him. He was in his early 40s, tall, handsome, heavy but not fat, and very dapper. Before Gordon ever met Lula he sent out his senior secretary, Mrs. Gyler, to look her over. When everything checked out to his satisfaction, he then invited the Norbergs out to a big dinner with a group of Gordon's associates to get everyone acquainted. From that time on, the Norbergs were very good friends with Gordon and became a part of his "family."

"He never became dismayed, annoyed, or disgusted with anything (we) ever did," said Mrs. Norberg years later. "He was not that way with his employees. He was hard on his employees, demanding perfection, but was always kind and understanding."

Vast plans for elaborate improvements began to be developed for the whole camp. Gordon would sketch up grandiose plans, Mr. Heimbeck would have to cut them back somewhat, and Roy Norberg would fill in the details and make the final drawings. Of course every finished plan was carefully scrutinized by both Gordon and Mr. Heimbeck, and everything was thoroughly discussed before any building started. Six different plans were drawn for a simple log footbridge over the old sluiceway in Jim Redy's dam on Bulldog Lake before it could be built.

While the Norbergs were living in Chicago, Roy, of course, made frequent trips to White Deer Lake. Lula was employed as a secretary to an attorney in Chicago, but a big Christmas get–together was planned for 1938.

Gleb Bourionoff, Gordon's White Russian bodyguard, had married one of Gordon's Chicago secretaries, a girl named Lillian. They were living in New York and were invited out to White Deer Lake for the Christmas holidays. Lula Norberg met them at the train in Chicago, and they all traveled overnight, via Pullman, to Ishpeming, where the three were met by Gordon, Ted Tonkin, Mrs. Gyler, Chris Hansen, Bruce Blezard, and Roy Norberg. They were taken to the Mather Inn, Ishpeming's finest hotel, for breakfast, spent the day Christmas shopping in Ishpeming, and had an elegant dinner at the Mather Inn that evening. After spending the night there, they were taken off the next day for the glorious sight of White Deer Lake in all its Christmas splendor. The group was housed in the guest rooms of the Chimney Cabin, with all the winter clothes they would need spread out on the beds in their rooms.

By coincidence, Gordon discovered that the Norbergs had been married on December 26th of 1936 and that they would be spending their second wedding anniversary at camp. This was all he needed to have a grand surprise celebration there. He learned that the second anniversary should be celebrated with cotton, and he had a ball buying cotton gifts and planning the secret celebration. He spared nothing in carrying out his elaborate preparations. To his delight the whole party was a great success, and did much to bring the group closer together.

During the five or six days there, they tobogganed down the hills to the lake – Gordon good–naturedly taking the brunt of the spills – snowshoed to many places, and learned to ski out on the hill on the old 1903 road. It was just a trail now, but it had been the first road into camp from the logging days. This was where Mr. Bentley and Gordon's father used to ski.

The Head Carpenter

In the early war years (1939–42) Gordon McCormick spent a lot of time at White Deer Lake. He hiked, usually with a companion, and made many elaborate plans for the improvement of the camp.

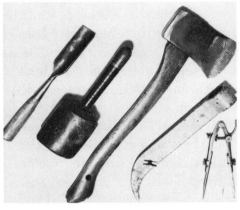

Upper left: Nestor Kallionen at Dead River 1937. Courtesy of Joe Ruesing.
Upper right: Nestor Kallionen's own tools of the trade.
Bottom: Nestor Kallionen on the job at White Deer Lake 1942.

The Panorama Tower, at the north end of the property, was being manned during the summer of 1939 by George Summers of Marquette. George lived in the log cabin a few hundred yards below the tower, with his wife and tiny baby, George, Jr. That fall or late summer, a fire broke out on the McCormick property. George located it from the tower and phoned the camp. Gordon mobilized his men. This was the first of several fires he was to fight on or near his land over the next four or five years. He really went after a fire tooth and nail; every second counted with him. There was a lot of fire–fighting equipment at camp. His family hadn't preserved a forest for two generations only to have it go up in smoke. Gordon was appalled at men standing around talking while a fire raged, some pointing nonchalantly here and there, others waiting for something or someone before they could do anything. He equipped his men with everything they needed to fight a fire, right down to a bag of sandwiches and "something for snake bite" (a north woods expression for alcohol) and they worked a fire with whatever means there was at hand – shovels, rakes, wet burlap, anything to contain the flames. The regular firefighters brought in by the state were amused by Gordon's excitement and enthusiasm. In just a few hours, the fire was under control.

A month or so later, George Summers delivered Gordon a check for 60 cents from the state of Michigan – the firefighter's wage of 30 cents an hour. Gordon laughed heartily over this, and said he would frame it.

To go along with his architect, Gordon now started to look for the best logman he could find – a technician, a carpenter with credentials and a reputation. He had already ordered some big, straight western pine to be used in the construction. It was pretty much common knowledge that the best logman in the area was an old Finnish fellow named Nestor Kallioinen. Nestor would tackle any log work there was; no job was too big or too small, and the more intricate the better. He always turned out a beautiful job. Nestor was a student of the art of log construction, studying different styles of log–fitting and devising better methods himself. He even made miniature log displays to demonstrate different methods of making corners, framing windows or doors, and grooving logs. In his early years, Nestor was in on the development of the chinkless log construction, and he was a master at it. He took his time, and the logs that he fitted looked like they were melted together. No power on earth could hurry him; he had his principles from which he could not be shaken.

Nestor Kallioinen was born in Finland in 1880. He never did learn English very well. He married in Finland and had two sons there – Frank, born in 1901, and John, born in 1904 – both on August the 25th. The family immigrated to America where two more boys were born – Niilo in 1907 and Ernest in 1908.

Nestor had always done log work, and when word was out that Louis G. Kaufman was looking for log men to build a huge lodge on Lake Superior, he joined the crew. He worked steadily on Granot Loma from 1924 through 1927. Log work was usually seasonal, but Nestor would continue to work with wood in some capacity all winter. In some respects, he was on a par with Oscar Knuusi, the head carpenter at Huron Mountain Club. They were both of the same make–up.

In 1932, '33 and '34, Nestor and a few other expert log workers built the Sam Cohodas Lodge on Lake Michigamme, and again the log work in that building is flawless. These were fitted logs with no chinking; each log fit onto the next with an airtight seal, all done by hand with no power tools. His partners on this job were Frank Mackinen, also from the Rolling Mill location south of Negaunee where the Kallioinens had settled, Charlie Wiirta, from east of Champion, and Gust Lintula from Marquette. In 1936 and '37 Nestor and his son Niilo worked together doing all kinds of repair jobs and building a small cabin or two, with Niilo acting as interpreter for his dad.

Nestor Kallioinen had been pointed out to Mr. Kaufman as one of the best log workers on the Granot Loma job, so Kaufman took special notice of Nestor. He was singled out to do intricate work in places that would show, and Mr. Kaufman would often sit by the hour and watch him work. He was a great admirer of Nestor and they became good friends. For years Mr. Kaufman kept a picture of Nestor in his apartment in New York City.

In 1938 Mr. Kaufman offered to set up Nestor with a shop in New York to make things for the lodge, but Nestor refused. He was then invited back to the lodge that year to build furniture. He and Niilo had worked there a few months when Nestor developed a hernia and went home.

Gordon McCormick contacted Nestor Kallioinen the following spring (1939). When Niilo explained his father's problem to Gordon, Gordon offered to send him to Chicago for a hernia operation, all expenses paid. But no one was going to get Nestor Kallioinen out of the U.P. that easily. Gordon would not give up on him. He begged, almost demanded, that Nestor come to White Deer Lake just to supervise the log work, if nothing else. In fact he would not be allowed to work; Gordon would hire another two or three good log men to do the work and see that Nestor didn't do any. He hired Emil Larson and Charlie Wiirta.

Emil Larson was a Finn with a Swedish name, not an uncommon thing in the area. He was born in Richmond Township in 1904. Emil's father,

Byykkonen, had defected from the Russian Army and come to the United States in the 1890s and changed his name to Larson. Emil had worked in the Isabella Mine until it closed in 1930 and then had gone to work for an old "log mechanic" (sometimes called "log butcher") named Nestor Lindfors. It was from him that Emil learned the trade.

Gordon also hired Emil's brother, John. John and Emil, with Nestor Linfors, had built the Mount Shasta Lodge in Michigamme in 1934 or so. Two Englishmen from Stillwater, Minnesota – John and Clifford Wellington – recommended by Stuga Aldrich, were also on the job. Then there was Pete Hendrickson from Republic, besides a whole crew of laborers.

Niilo was working at the prison in Marquette, and Nestor wanted to have him working as his assistant and interpreter. Dr. Hirwas of Marquette was a good friend of Nestor's and also knew Warden Busch of the prison well. They were both vacation woodsmen and fishermen. He interceded and Niilo was transferred to a different shift so that he could work with his dad at McCormick's.

Nestor Kallioinen was made the foreman of the construction gang, all expert logmen. The men respected him: a steady, quiet man who always appeared to be thinking. His philosophy was, "The only way to learn log work is to get the tools in your hands and start working." He also used to say, "Never take anything to the grave that you can teach or tell somebody else." He and Niilo usually commuted 35 or more miles each way to McCormick's, starting out before six o'clock each morning.

Niilo liked Gordon and always spoke highly of him. "He was a real polished gentleman," he said years later, "big, strong, raw–boned and healthy looking. He understood the men – a real nice man to work for. There was no liquor and no swearing among the workmen at White Deer Lake, a far cry from the mines or other places I've worked. Working there had a good influence on a man. Gordon might get upset once in a while, but you never heard him swear. And the food at the camp was always the best, you couldn't beat it. It was a healthy place to work; you went to bed at nine o'clock and were up at six A.M., and no questions asked. Ted Tonkin saw to that."

Redoing White Deer Lake Camp

In 1939, several loads of logs arrived from Covington, southeast of L'Anse. They were beautiful, straight red pine with very little taper. The next year some more loads of the same kind arrived from S. J. McCabe in Iron Mountain.

Top: Removing the porch railings.
Middle: Rebuilding the porch railings.
Bottom: Chimney cabin – the roof was raised and the whole building enclosed for rebuilding inside in winter.

Top: Ted Tonkin and Roy Norberg looking out of the roof at the Chimney cabin.
Bottom: The White Deer Lake monogram designed by Gordon, built by Nestor Kallionen for the Chimney cabin.

With the large work crew that had been assembled in 1939, they started to rebuild the Chimney Cabin. They had already soundproofed Gordon's room and winterized the whole building the year before. Now they started working in the lower rooms and replacing the porch railings, but then, as if by second thought, they decided to do a real job. With Nestor Kallioinen and Roy Norberg as chief consultants, Gordon decided to build a frame over the whole building which could then be heated inside so that they could work all winter. Then, working inside the frame, they proceeded to take apart the whole cabin right to the foundations and then rebuild it, raising it four logs higher, changing the outside appearance just a little but completely redoing the inside. The interior cabinetry and finish work was done by two German carpenters from Chicago, Emil Patzer and John Stumph.

While work was going on at the Chimney Cabin, Gordon was also busy pushing his trail crews and rough carpenters to see that every trail, bridge and stairway on the property was put in tiptop condition, as well as the rebuilding of the Crow's Nest far out on top of one of the Panorama Hills where Nels and Jim Andersen had first constructed it between two trees. A forest fire had burned the whole top of that granite knob, killing both the original trees. But Stuga Aldrich had sent in a plan for a simple tower, four long spruces anchored to heavy logs at its base with two platforms, one about 25 feet high and the other about 35 feet high. There was even a more beautiful view from this crow's nest than from the other. It had no obstructions in any direction except the south, where there were high hills. The view in every other direction was breathtaking.

The Huron Mountain end of the old Bentley Trail had not been maintained to Gordon's liking. With two dozen men working at the camp during these years, he could have easily sent a crew all the way to Mountain Lake, but was reluctant to do so. He did send his crew right to the Club wire, but all that had been done beyond that was the freshening of the blazes by Richard Bentley and Bill Harris.

The new trail was gone. Victor Makela had cut that part of the Yellowdog Plains where the Arbutus Lodge stood in 1939, and it now stood stark and naked in the hot summer sun with tree tops strewn on the ground, completely covering the trail. With the timber gone, a lot of run–off from the big snows and heavy rains of 1938 ran unchecked and Arbutus Lake had risen eight or nine feet. The water stood three feet high inside the buildings. There was no thought of ever using the lodge again. The road had ruined the pristine mood of both trails, especially the old one.

Gordon thought there was a possibility of opening the new trail when the loggers had moved out, and not use the Halfway House for anything other than a picnic spot. It hurt him to see these trails, which held such fond memories for him, slipping into the past, out of his reach.

He again wrote to Mr. Harris, expressing his worry and hoping to get some official action in restoring the weakened link between the two properties. The letter was written during the spring of 1940, to Mr. Harris at his home in Grosse Pointe Park, Michigan.

The answer revealed the new philosophy of Huron Mountain Club at that time, a philosophy that William P. Harris, Jr. had no small part in formulating:

Dear Gordon,

I received your letter of April 4th and quite understand your feeling the way you do about the trails between your camp and the club. I will try and find out if there is to be anything done on the cutover areas on the Sand Plains. I rather doubt it, but the trouble from poachers and undesirable campers is bad enough now that the road is through to the fire tower and probably will be out further through to Skanee. (Author's note: the road was already through to Skanee but neither the public nor Mr. Harris knew about it.) I hope we can get together this summer at the club to talk over what we might do from now on for our mutual protection and improvement of public relations which I feel as far as the club goes could be improved. I say "we" meaning the few large interests in the region – yourself, Longyear Estate, Cleveland–Cliffs, the club and Ford Motor Co. I think we have a unique opportunity here to do a job of cooperative conservation of the last wilderness area in the middle west. Up to now the only conservation we know anything about is government conservation and that has definite limitations that private interests do not have. We can do ourselves a lot of good and perform a public service that will make our position more secure if we cooperate to manage the resources of wildlife and forest products in such a way as to perpetuate the value we have and pass on the information to the surrounding country. To this end I have gotten research work on fish culture, forest management and wildlife under way and financed. Three years of fish research will be completed this year and a two–year program on wildlife has been started and a preliminary

Top: Work crew at White Deer Lake during the building years.
Bottom: A now famous log fitted for ten logs and other pieces.

forest survey management plan is nearing completion by the U. S. Forest Service. I would like to see this work expanded to include more territory in the future. All the information we get will be available to you, of course. Come on over this summer.

Sincerely yours,
William P. Harris, Jr.

The fish research was done by a Dr. Lloydsmith of the University of Minnesota. The wildlife study was done by Richard Manville, assisted by Wallace Tabor. Manville later became the head of the Mammology Department at the University of Michigan, and Tabor became a wildlife photographer. The Club had already carried out a vast tree–planting program years before, done a lot of fish planting over the years and, in the 1930s, in an attempt to divert poachers, had planted trout in the Yellowdog and both Garlic Rivers. Actually the members of the Huron Mountain Fish Committee did not look at this project as "warding off poachers" as some of the public did; they looked at this project as bringing all rivers in the area up to the same standards. They had discovered that the economics of putting fish in a river to be taken out the same season has never paid off. It was determined that the four sensible methods of managing a stream so as to keep it productive, full of fish and yet not detract from its primitive and peaceful qualities are (1) limit the number of fishermen, (2) control the number of fish each fisherman may take in a day, (3) restrict the kind of bait which may be used, and (4) change the river bottom, currents and eddies so as to provide the maximum protection and breeding potential for the greatest possible number of fish. On a private stream all of these methods are possible, and Huron Mountain Club has done them all. It would not be possible to do all of these in public waters.

For many years the club has worked on stream improvement, allowed only half as many fish per day as the state did, and allowed fly–fishing only – no live bait. They also carried out many programs aimed at increasing fish and game populations on their property. Pressure on the streams was also reduced by the fact that most members and guests were from the old school, where it was the unwritten law never to fish in sight of another fisherman.

Gordon McCormick could read between the lines. The shift of emphasis from the trails to conservation practices appeared to mean: drop the trails, they present problems. His answer, written in Chicago at 20 E. Burton Place, has a tone of sarcasm and discouragement. He knew he had been

Top: Nestor on the good ship "Piffle."
Bottom: L–R Elsie Guyler, Bruce Blizzard, Marguerite (Peg) Valmer and Gordon McCormick.

politely put off. In addition to this was his own knowledge of what Mr. Harris was referring to, as he and his crews came across more and more trespassers who exhibited such qualities of woodsmanship as fear, hatred and disrespect for their surroundings. Of course some good woodsmen had passed through also, but they had left no trace. From the others, fires sprang up, garbage and cans appeared along the lakes, streams and trails, and trees were wantonly and indiscriminately blazed. Messy campsites appeared at the most beautiful spots, with toilet paper and the rest nearby.

Gordon's letter to Mr. Harris, dated April 19, 1940:

Dear Bill,

Your April 8 letter about your research work on fish culture, forest management and wildlife sounds very interesting, and I shall be glad to hear more about it. Does your work extend as far as being able to tell me how to keep irresponsibles from starting thoughtless fires on one's private property? I suppose not.

I have no present idea of the exact future rights of a private landowner or private enterprise in this country and in particular in the rugged,delightful region south of Lake Superior which we both like so well.

Sometimes it is most discouraging to realize that one's thoughts and acts which are known to be right are only wrong or impossible in the light of present day events and circumstances. On planning to put up signs requesting care and respect for the woods, I am told they will be shot up or taken down.

As present events have developed we have chosen a most unholy region for our vacationing – a region infested with those who have no backyards or property to respect themselves and who therefore see no reason in respecting other people's property. But most probably ours is not the only neck of the woods where such brands of humanity live rampant.

The state and county slogan "We can't discriminate" will ricochet back on the neck of the taxpayer in the end who, of course, will do nothing about the situation. Since, for the safety of all, we will probably never enforce all automobile owners to run only up–to–date cars in good condition on the road, likewise, we will never enforce a certain standard of logging operation, nor a toll for using Conservation Department roads.

Because of a conversation at the recent New York Sportsmen's Show, I have been corresponding with the Conservation Department of Maine and New Hampshire regarding their methods of clearing a lake of perch (poisoning it) in preparation for planting trout. I am also writing the C. D. (Conservation Department) in Marquette. Do you know something or everything about this subject, and if so, could you let me know the procedure in detail when you get a moment? Or who is the best one to write to in the Marquette region? The main precaution, I understand, is preventing the poisonous chemicals from escaping into the other waters where good fishing

exists.

Here's hoping to see you next summer.

Sincerely yours,
Gordon McCormick

This seems to have been the end of the correspondence about the trails – in fact Mr. Harris had cleverly shifted from trail talk to conservation programs. And indeed he did know or soon found out about the poisoning of lakes to upgrade the fish population. Huron Mountain carried out such a program in Anne Lake in 1942.

Gordon had been wondering what to do about unwanted visitors for a long time. In an effort to keep White Deer Lake unknown to the public, he had the camp road removed from the state highway maps in 1939. The road then appeared on a filling station map, and he wrote to that oil company (Phillips 66) explaining that "This is a private camp road of four miles that is dead–end. Please remove it from your maps – it is no longer shown on state maps."

A year later, in 1940, a letter went out to Mr. George Bishop, the secretary–manager of the Upper Peninsula Development Bureau, about a picture that appeared in the Lure Book. Gordon asked that they stress the beautiful Keweenaw Peninsula for tourists but "please omit the scene taken from our private road." In this case, to soften the harshness of the request, Gordon asked Dr. VanRiper to talk to Mr. Bishop about it.

With the Chimney Cabin completed in 1941, they moved on to a new boathouse that year. Gordon made sketches and Roy Norberg drew up the plans, while constantly conferring with Nestor Kallioinen and Mr. Heimbeck. Jack Saxwold was the foreman, and Ted Tonkin still the camp superintendent.

Gordon wanted the boathouse to be built in the water at the edge of the lake, but there was an undetermined number of feet of soft muck along the shoreline there. Walter Lindbergh, the contractor from Ishpeming, was hired to sink 130 eighteen–foot wooden pilings into the mud. There was still a danger of buildings built on pilings heaving under severe ice conditions. It was decided to overcome this by making it Tonkin's responsibility to see that the Bulldog Lake dam was opened every fall and the lake level of the two lakes lowered for the winter season. Throughout his tenure at White Deer Lake, Ted Tonkin faithfully put an instrument on the boathouse foundations each spring. Only the southwest corner had risen, by less than one inch by the time of his death many years later.

The same crew who did the log work on the Chimney Cabin went to work on the boathouse. It was a work of art. The logs had been cut and peeled at just the right time and under proper conditions so that they would age and color properly. The wood under the cambium layer would turn a uniform reddish–brown. Logs that weren't to be used had their ends painted and were stored in huge sheds so that they would be out of the weather. Everything had to be done exactly according to that plan. Gordon made it clear to the workmen that there was no excuse for shoddy workmanship. They were to take all the time that was necessary to do the job right. He said it might take 30 years to have the camp redone properly, but that it was his plan to do so.

Perfection and Accuracy, Bentley Byline

John Knudsen, a young fellow who lived near the Tonkins in Ishpeming, was hired at White Deer Lake about this time. John had been hoping to get a job at the mine, where good paying jobs were much sought after by local young men. He worked at the McCormick property exactly one year and a day before his opportunity opened up with the mining company.

In recalling his stay at White Deer Lake, John spoke of a custom–built, four–door International Station Wagon that was used for trips into Ishpeming by camp personnel. He stayed in the barracks–style annex that had been built onto the Guide House to house the extra men. There had been about 12 men preparing the logs used for the various projects, and each carpenter had a laborer assigned to him as an assistant.

It was also in this period that the Fork Bridge was replaced, an item that had been pending for some time, but now the condition of the bridge made it imperative that something be done at once. They built a temporary bridge and camp road from above the next bridge up the grade. It crossed Baraga Creek and joined the old camp road a few hundred yards above the bridge to be replaced.

The new bridge was, indeed, a unique structure. It appeared to be made of wood, but in reality all the support came from cement and steel. The cement part was carefully faced with stone by John Wood, the mason from Ishpeming, and the huge "I" beams that span the river were covered with split logs. Roy Norberg knew he would soon be going off to the war, and an architect named Ralph Priestly, hired to take over when Roy left, was doing the details on the bridge as far as engineering and design. Every piece of steel was covered. Holes for metal bolts were drilled in the logs and plugged with wooden plugs to hide the nuts and bolts. The precision and thoroughness, a carry–over from the Bentley days and now stressed by Gordon and Tonkin, was one of the things that impressed Knudsen. The bridge was an example of the tremendous expense and care that were taken to camouflage any modern materials which could not be considered in keeping with the natural surroundings. The bridge still stands today, a half century later, in all appearances a rotting wooden bridge, yet strong enough to carry any piece of equipment anyone would need to drive over it.

The same type of precision was driven home to young John Knudsen on a lesser scale when John piled his first woodpile at camp. Ted Tonkin told him it was unacceptable. John was amazed; it was just a woodpile but it had to be taken down and redone. He still hadn't quite learned what perfection was, and it had to be done again. In fact he had to repile the woodpile six times before it was acceptable, but every job at camp was like that. You didn't use old lumber for bracing; you used new lumber. The aged look was hard to come by, so aged lumber was saved for special places.

Besides getting in on the end of the Chimney Cabin construction and the beginning of the new boathouse work, John had many other jobs. He cleared trails and worked on the new woodshed, another building to marvel at. It was built with the same care as the Chimney Cabin and the boathouse, with the fancy doors crafted by Nestor Kallioinen. Who but Gordon McCormick would build a $50,000 woodshed? John also helped clear the side of a hill for skiing, cut firewood and helped build a warehouse to store things that Gordon needed to stockpile, as they would soon be hard to obtain because of the war. Also they were still putting chicken wire around the birch trees to keep the beavers from chewing them, and there was constant trouble with the telephone line along the Huron Bay Grade to work on.

Jack Saxwold's son, Bob, and Bob Tall, who married Jack's daughter, were employed at the camp, as were Roy Viol, Warren Farley, John Maki, and

Top: Woodshed – designed by Gordon, built by Nester.
Bottom: Anne Maki, close friend of Lula Norberg.

Joe Arsenault. Alden Ostlund took Chris Hansen's place as Island Man about this time. While the Chimney Cabin was being rebuilt Gordon stayed in either the little Beaver Cabin or Birch Cabin, both of them on the Island. He was pretty much a steady resident at the camp during those war years.

War Years

Roy Norberg originally was supposed to spend six weeks at camp and six weeks in Chicago. However, by 1940 he was spending most of his time between Marquette and camp. He had brought in Ralph Priestly to work in the Chicago office. Lu, Roy's wife, quit her job in Chicago and moved to Marquette, where she joined Roy in an apartment he was renting upstairs in the Vierling house on Hewitt Avenue. Lu and Roy became close friends with the Phillip Spears and were asked to join the Marquette Club, which they did. Although the Norbergs spent much time at the Spear camp at Lakewood and the Spear home on East Michigan Street, Gordon was never included in these get–togethers. He was invited but chose not to mingle this closely with his supplier. During this time, Gordon would stay at the Northland Hotel, taking over nearly a whole floor with his guests. They would go dancing at the Brookton Ballroom, which they called "Ma Sambrooks," built in the early 1930's by Clare Harrington and George Sambrook. It was the largest dance floor in the U. P., purposely built just a few feet longer than the "Nightingale" in Iron Mountain. The name "Brookton" came from combining the last syllables of the two names. Later it became Ramseth's Furniture Store; (they are now out of business). Gordon just loved to dance; he was a very good dancer and could keep it up the whole evening long. They often associated with Johnny Voelker, a well–known figure around the county, and he and Roy Norberg became great friends.

John Voelker was a writer and later a supreme court judge of Michigan, but had not yet become nationally famous as the author of "Anatomy of a Murder," a best seller. There were weekend excursions to Marquette and Ishpeming and even as far as Duluth and Minneapolis. Weekends in Ishpeming were sometimes spent seeing a movie.

One such trip nearly ended in disaster. They were all going into Ishpeming to see "The Wizard of Oz." The plan was to have a meal at the Mather Inn, see the movie, stay the night and return to camp the next day.

The Tonkins left early and the rest had a drink in "Children's Corner," a room in the Chimney Cabin. Gordon, being a big man, held his liquor well. He took a crowd in his Buick, another group left in the grocery

Top: Bill Gray on White Deer Lake. (1940's)
Bottom: John Voelker of Ishpeming, author and later justice of the Michigan Supreme Court.

truck, and the Norbergs were the last to leave. Roy was driving a pickup truck. On the camp road he hit a fresh–cut stump in the road and turned the truck over. Lu was hurt so badly that she couldn't walk. Actually, as it turned out, it was mainly two fingers but she was badly shaken up and had the breath knocked out of her. Roy thought she was going to die. He carried her back to camp and sent for Dr. VanRiper.

In the meantime Gordon was at the Mather Inn pacing the floor and madder than hops; he thought they had run off on him. When they finally reached him by phone, all was settled and they saw the show the next day.

Roy Norberg was given a great send–off as he left to become a chief petty officer in the Seabees (the engineering branch of the Navy). At the time, his wife was working for Munising Wood Products, the old Piqua Handle Company in Marquette. As the country became fully mobilized, men were harder and harder to find. Tonkin's son Bearsie and some of his high school friends, including Bill Gray and Kenny Nowell, helped out. They were 17 years old and would be seniors in Ishpeming High School that fall. Ken Nowell was to return about ten years later and eventually became the superintendent after Tonkin's death. No major construction could be accomplished, as materials and supplies had dried up also.

Bearsie, Bill Gray and Ken Nowell were kept busy by Jack Saxwold. There was another fellow working there also, and the boys got a good chuckle out of him. He had a front tooth missing and he carved one out of a toothbrush handle and stuck it in the hole. Things went on pretty much as usual with the small crew.

Saxwold would wake the crew at six o'clock sharp. They would wash and eat and be at work at seven. At 9:15 there would be a break for coffee, and at twelve they would wash and eat lunch. Work started again at one o'clock, with a coffee break at 3:15. They would quit at five and swim, fish or play horseshoes. Every Saturday morning they would fill the big walk–in cooler with ice. They had the run of the property and could use the motorboats or canoes. When Gordon was there, no motor was to be used on White Deer Lake by order of Mr. Tonkin. This was so the solitude would not be broken.

Gordon had decided that there should be exposed beams in some rooms of the Chimney Cabin. Jack Saxwold took the boys into the swamp to get the long straight cedars. No holes could be put in the wood so it was pretty much hand work, wet and buggy. Jack would stand and measure each piece of firewood as the boys sawed it with a crosscut saw.

In August of 1943, when the men were working on the island, they heard Mildred Tonkin screaming at the top of her voice. She was running down the path to the dock waving a paper. It was a telegram for Bill Gray from Congressman John Bennett. Bill had just been appointed to West Point. Later in the war years of 1944 and '45, nearly everybody was gone and Tonkin was left with just a couple of men and the cook.

Ted Tonkin was a religious and patriotic man. He had a gnawing feeling that he was not doing his part for his country by being a caretaker for a rich man's camp in the wilderness. He wrote several letters of application to shipbuilding yards around the country seeking employment, justifying his requests with his experience as a shipwright in England. Though he finally succeeded in getting some war–related employment, they were not positions where his abilities would be recognized, and for this and other reasons he remained to look after the White Deer Lake property. He did, however, do his part for the war effort. Ted Tonkin wrote and received many letters from young men who went to the service of their country. He was a home root to cling to and always had plenty of news, a kind word or a spiritual message to pass on. He became an active lay preacher in the Methodist Churches throughout the county. Before the war was over, he saw his eldest son, Bearsie, go off to the service.

During these late war years Gordon McCormick spent his time between Chicago and New York, where he lived in hotels. He had always been a fancier of fine foods, and he never wanted to take chances in poor eating establishments. It was only natural, then, that he should make contact with Duncan Hines and become deeply involved in his famous book, "Adventures in Good Eating." Gordon was not only a financial backer of the book but he personally evaluated and recommended many of the places listed in the book and sampled all foods or recipes mentioned in it. In his travels, great preparations for fine food were made. Picnic baskets of fried chicken, gourmet delicacies and rich desserts always went with him when he traveled, always by train.

During this same period, Roy Norberg had been given a "mustang" promotion to Ensign and was sent to Fort Schuyler, the Maritime Academy at Throgs Neck, north of New York City, for training. He graduated with the rank of Lieutenant J. G. and was then sent to the Norfolk, Virginia Naval Operations Base for training as a gunnery officer. While he was in New York, Lu went there to be near him. Gordon McCormick was there also, living in the Gladstone Hotel in New York City. He hired a limousine and showed Lu the town for three or four days, and the whole entourage came along. There was Rudy Gabrial, a tennis pro whom Gordon had hired as a companion or bodyguard; Peg Volmer, his New York secretary, and sometimes one or two other people. Peg Volmer at that time was a member of the Board of Regents of New York State University and good friends of the New York Swope family. She also had an apartment at the Gladstone Hotel a few floors above Gordon's.

At the end of the day before Roy's graduation as Lt. J. G., the group drove out to Throgs Neck. They picked up Roy and went out to dinner. Gordon just couldn't do enough for Roy and his wife. It was his pleasure to find someone he liked and show them around, especially someone off the North Dakota prairie, like Lu, who had never been to New York. The more she enjoyed it, the more he would do for her.

Gordon tried to do the same thing for young Bill Gray while he was at West Point. Every leave he had from West Point, Bill would go up to White Deer Lake. If Gordon was there, Bill was invited to eat with him. While Gordon was in New York he called Bill at West Point several times, hoping to take him out to dinner. Bill always had to say no. He explained to Gordon that they were only allowed six free weekends a year, and three of those were for football games. Also, if they left, they would have to be back at five o'clock on Sunday afternoon. Gordon didn't seem to understand. He wanted to talk to the man in charge there, who happened to be General Maxwell Taylor at the time. Cadet Bill Gray had all he could do to keep Gordon from calling General Taylor.

With his training completed, Roy Norberg was off for Virginia Beach for gunnery training. Then Gordon and Rudy took Lu around the town. Lu had found a good job with one of New York's largest law offices and had made other friends. Gordon had helped her find an apartment and, when he was sure she had become acclimated to the city, he left his apartment at the Gladstone and moved to Chicago.

Roy was promoted to a full lieutenant and shipped out to sea. Lu remained in New York and was deluged with friends from Marquette. They usually stayed with her and she showed them the town as Gordon had shown it to her, although of course without all his resources.

Gordon's Rebuff

After the war, the Norbergs returned to North Dakota and then to Minneapolis. There they met Mrs. Gyler and some of Gordon's other associates. They were told that Gordon still had big plans to continue work at White Deer Lake and he had no doubt that Roy would be coming back to work for him. Roy had decided that he wanted to try going into business for himself, but since he loved the Marquette area he would open his office there and Gordon could be one of his clients.

Roy rented the house at 146 West Park Street in Marquette, set up an office in it and worked out of his home. Business wasn't too bad. He designed the Gerling home at the end of Ridge St. on the corner of what was "Longyear's Field," the Paul Schneider home on Cedar, planned the landscaping and brickwork plus some remodeling for Otto Young Kaufman, who had taken over the First National Bank upon the death of his father, Louis G. Kaufman. This home was across the street from the Howard School on Ridge Street. Roy also had numerous other jobs around town.

Gordon McCormick was there with work for him too, lots of it. He would show up at Roy's office often, and Roy often had to go up to White Deer Lake. Gordon seemed to be a little possessive of Roy; he would not be shaken.

As Roy's work in Marquette slacked off in 1947, he decided to go back full time working at White Deer Lake. Gordon had seen to that with more than a little prodding. But things weren't the same any more for either Roy or Gordon. Gordon had some bitter pills to swallow. He had lost a crew for one thing. but there had been another development during the war years that affected him more personally and very deeply.

Gordon had had a very close friend and sweetheart since his boyhood days named Estelle Post. He had first met her when he was just 16, and she had been his first girlfriend. She was a very pretty red–haired girl with a pleasant personality. He had known her during his Princeton years and seen her often down through the years after that. She had been his guest at White Deer Lake a few times, and they always seemed to get along well together.

Estelle was up at camp when George and Ruth Bradley were married. George was a bodyguard for Gordon, and Ruth was working for Gordon as secretary under Mrs. Gyler. The whole group, along with Roy and Lu Norberg, all went over to "Kings Gateway Lodge" at Land o' Lakes, Wis. for a long weekend ski trip. Estelle Post was along also. It was general knowledge among the group that Gordon had invited Estelle up to camp in order to ask for her hand in marriage. Gordon was rather shy and modest about things like this. He did not come right out and ask her, as he was waiting for the right time and place. He wanted her to get used to his friends and to things there at camp. They had some good times together but without someone to encourage Gordon, he seemed to dilly–dally.

It was on this ski trip that George and Ruth fell in love and announced that they were going to be married. At the same time, Estelle had another close friend named George Carpenter who was calling intermittently from Washington, D.C. He was waiting for Estelle to come there and marry him.

There was much to do about the anticipated Bradley wedding while the party was at Kings Gateway. The whole group got in on the planning. They returned to Marquette and within a short time George and Ruth were married in St. Paul's Episcopal Church in Marquette with Gordon, Estelle, the Norbergs, the Tonkins and the usual Gordon McCormick entourage as wedding guests. Gordon sponsored a wedding dinner at the Northland Hotel for the Bradleys as a climax to the wedding ceremony. After the honeymoon, the couple left White Deer Lake for good. They returned to Providence, Rhode Island, George's home, where they both got jobs.

With all of this, Estelle Post had just about had her fill. She decided that maybe this life was not for her. Gordon hadn't been pushing for the marriage, but George Carpenter had been calling regularly, saying that if Estelle didn't come to Washington he was going to look for someone else. These were still war years, and marriages of this kind were common. Estelle left for Washington and married George.

This was a great rebuff for Gordon. In retrospect it seemed as though a good part of the reason for the many improvements at the camp was for him and Estelle to spend a lot of time there in the future. Gordon had had still more plans for improvements. Two or three sheds of prepared logs were already on the property. It was likely that the Living Room Cabin, or maybe the little Beaver Cabin, was the next to be rebuilt. There were probably other reasons, but the war and Estelle Post's marrying George Carpenter appeared to be the main factors that put a damper on all of Gordon's wonderful dreams.

At White Deer Lake, things appeared to be going along as usual. It looked as though there were still plans to rebuild every old building over the next ten years or so. Gordon never gave any indication that anything had changed. But then other things began to happen. First Tonkin developed some kind of throat problem that was thought to be cancer and it appeared that it was going to develop into a serious condition. To add to this, Roy Norberg had developed a severe drinking problem.

Roy had gone back to work for Gordon on the same basis as he had been hired in the first place some ten years earlier. He and Lu stayed in their home at 146 West Park St. in Marquette, but Roy commuted back and forth to the Chicago McCormick Estates office and White Deer Lake. Lu worked for Eldridge and Eldridge, attorneys in Marquette, and later at the Michigan Corrections Department office for Wallace Kemp, Supervisor of Probation. She also went to Northern Michigan College on a part–time basis.

Gordon had assigned a lot of work to Roy during 1947, but it was during this period that Roy was doing some heavy drinking. He simply could not be depended upon, and soon dropped from Gordon's favor.

Whatever the reasons, Gordon McCormick never returned to White Deer Lake after he left in 1947. He planned to return at various times. Tonkin, who had fully recovered from his illness, would receive word from Gordon advising him of dates when he would be arriving at camp. Supplies would come into camp in great quantities for his next stay. Gordon would be in constant touch with Tonkin by phone and would even start out from his suite in the Gladstone Hotel, once or twice getting as far as Chicago, but he never got to White Deer Lake.

Gordon did stay in Chicago on occasions. The Tonkins and the Norbergs were his guests when he was in residence at a hotel there, one time at Thanksgiving and another time at Christmas. At that time his bodyguard was Olaf Thorvald, a well–known ski instructor from Norway. Mrs. Gyler and Caroline Manderfeld were the Chicago secretaries at this time.

In the years that followed, a small crew of men was kept year–round at White Deer Lake Camp and everything was kept in readiness for visitors. Gordon remained in touch with Tonkin and was kept appraised of camp affairs. Once in a while someone from the McCormick offices would arrive and use the place for a short stay, but never Gordon.

For the most part the camp stood as a beautiful museum of northwoods craftsmanship and culture, year after year, its forests untouched, its pristine lakes and wild rivers as nature had meant them to be. It was the home of the moose and the wolf, the fisher and the marten, the lynx and the cougar long after they had been run out of the rest of the peninsula. The paths and trails, bridges and walkways were kept in perfect shape, gone over each year or two for the man who never used them.

However, there was another man connected to this land, these woods and these trails – perhaps even more closely than Gordon McCormick. Let's look into the life of Christen Andersen of the Yellowdog Plains.

If you were to go to the Skandia Lutheran Church on US 41 south of Marquette and find the northwest corner of that building, there is a door there that goes into the kitchen. Walking from that door toward the graveyard, the first grave you would come to is that of Christ Andersen. His funeral was April 1st, 1971. South of Christ in that first row is Axel Anderson and Hilda Andersen. Hilda was married to Axel first and after his death she married Christ.

BARAGA COUNTY

NOVE
AUX LAKE
LAKE ANN
LITTLE HURON
MOUNTAIN LAKE
CLIFF LAKE
TROUT LAKE
CANYON LAKE
PINE LAKE
CRIPPANT LAKE
IVES LAKE
BIG BAY PT
SQUAW BEACH
BIG BAY
LAKE INDEPENDENCE
OMB ANER
TROUT RIVER
LOWER FALLS
LOWER DAM
SALMON RIVER
OLD BENTLEY TRAIL RIDGE
NEW BENTLEY TRAIL RIDGE
HURON RIVER
MT TRAIL
PANORAMA CREEK
EAST BRANCH HURON RIVER
CO. 510
CO. 550
TRIPLE A
ANT
MELE ANDERSON
CHRIST ANDERSON
ANDERSON POND
HALFWAY CABIN
BENTLEY PONDS
BENTLEY LAKE
TRIPLE A
YELLOW DOG PLAINS
CO. 510
PANORAMA TOWER
W. BRANCH
YELLOW DOG RIVER
PINNACLE FALLS
DOR RIVER ROAD
LAKE PHILLIPS
MULLIGAN SWAMP
MULLIGAN
MULLIGAN CREEK
DAM
BULL DOG LAKE
UPPER BARAGA LAKES
LAKE MARGARET
SILVER LAKE BASIN
MULLIGAN PLAINS
BARAGA LAKES
WHITE DEER LAKE
DEAD
DEAD RIVER HEADWATER
HURON HRE RIVER
CO 550
W BRANCH
LAKE RAYMOND
DEAD RIVER
DEAD RIVER
LAKE ARFELIN
DISHNO LAKE

JIM SMITH

LEGEND
IMPROVED AND PAVED ROADS
LOCAL AND UNIMPROVED ROADS

N

SCALE
0   5/8   1.25   2.5   3.75   MI

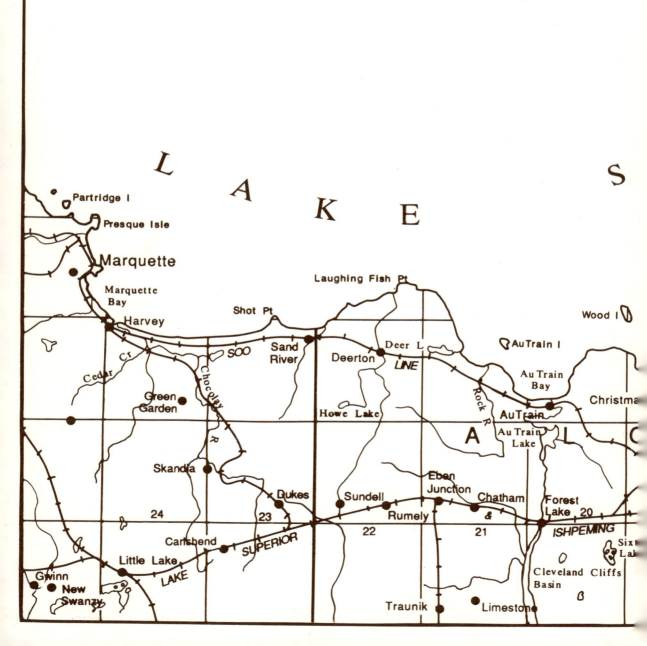

L A K E S

Partridge I

Presque Isle

Marquette

Marquette Bay

Harvey

Laughing Fish Pt

Shot Pt

Wood I

Sand River

Deer L

Au Train I

Cedar

Cr

SOO

Deerton

LINE

Au Train Bay

Christma

Chocolay R

Green Garden

Howe Lake

Rock R

Au Train

Christma

A

Au Train Lake

Skandia

Eben Junction

Dukes

Sundell

Chatham

Forest Lake 20

24

23

Rumely

&

21

ISHPEMING

22

Carlshend

SUPERIOR

Six Lak

Little Lake

LAKE

Cleveland Cliffs Basin

Gwinn

New Swanzy

Traunik

Limestone

ß